WEBSTER'S
FRENCH
dictionary

WEBSTER'S
FRENCH
dictionary

Published 2006 by Geddes & Grosset,
David Dale House, New Lanark, ML11 9DJ, Scotland
First published in this edition 2005, reprinted 2006

© 2005 Geddes & Grosset

ISBN 10: 1 84205 499 6
ISBN 13: 978 1 84205 499 4

Printed and bound in China

Abbreviations/Abréviations

abrev	abbreviation	abréviation
adj	adjective	adjectif
adv	adverb	adverbe
art	article	articule
auto	automobile	automobile
aux	auxiliary	auxiliaire
bot	botany	botanique
chem, chim	chemistry	chimie
col	colloquial term	expression familière
com	commerce	commerce
compd	compound	mot composé
comput	computers	informatique
conj	conjunction	conjonction
excl	exclamation	exclamation
f	feminine noun	substantif fémenin
fam	colloquial term	expression familière
fig	figurative	figuré
geol	geology	géologie
gr	grammar	grammaire
imp	impersonal	impersonnel
inform	computers	informatique
interj	interjection	interjection
invar	invariable	invariable
irr	irregular	irrégulier
jur	law term	jurisprudence
law	law term	jurisprudence
ling	linguistics	linguistique
m	masculine noun	substantif masculin
mar	marine term	vocabulaire marin
mat, math	mathematics	matématiques
med	medicine	médicine
mil	military term	vocabulaire militaire
mus	music	musique
n	noun	substantif
orn	ornithology	ornithologie
pej	pejorative	péjoratif
pl	plural	pluriel

pn	pronoun	pronom
poet	poetical term	vocabulaire poétique
prep	preposition	préposition
rad	radio	radio
rail	railway	chemin de fer
sl	slang	argot
teat	theatre	théâtre
tec	technology	technologie
TV	television	télévision
vi	intransitive verb	verbe intransitif
vr	reflexive verb	verbo réfléchi
vt	transitive verb	verbo transitif
zool	zoology	zoologie

French-English
Dictionary

A

à *prép* (in)to; at; on; by, per; **aller ~ l'école** to go to school; **~ neuf heures** at nine o'clock; **c'est ~ toi** it's yours; it's your turn.

abaissement *m* fall, drop.

abaisser *vt* to lower; **s'~ à faire** to stoop to doing.

abandon *m* abandonment, desertion.

abandonné *adj* relaxed.

abandonner *vt* to abandon, leave.

abasourdi *adj* stunned.

abasourdir *vt* to stun.

abats *m pl* giblets.

abat-jour *m* lampshade.

abattement *m* despondency; exhaustion.

abattoir *m* abattoir, slaughterhouse.

abattre *vt* to shoot; to slaughter.

abattu *adj* despondent; exhausted.

abbaye *f* abbey.

abbé *m* abbot.

abbesse *f* abbess.

abcès *m* abscess.

abdiquer *vt, vi* to abdicate.

abdomen *m* abdomen.

abdominal *adj* abdominal.

abeille *f* bee.

aberrant *adj* aberrant; absurd.

aberration *f* aberration.

abêtissant *adj* mindless.

abêtissement *m* mindlessness.

abîme *m* chasm.

abîmer *vt* spoil, damage; **s'~** *vr* to get spoiled *ou* damaged.

abject *adj* abject.

abjection *f* abjectness.

abjurer *vt* to abjure.

ablatif *m* ablative.

ablation *f* (*med*) removal.

abnégation *f* abnegation.

aboiement *m* bark.

abolir *vt* to abolish.

abolition *f* abolition.

abominable *adj* abominable; **~ment** *adv* abominably.

abondamment *adv* abundantly.

abondance *f* abundance.

abondant *adj* abundant, plentiful.

abonder *vi* to be abundant *ou* plentiful.

abonné *m*, **-ée** *f*, * *adj* subscriber.

abonnement *m* subscription.

abonner *vt* **~ à qn** to subscribe, take out a subscription (à to); * **s'~** *vr* to subscribe, take out a subscription (à to).

abord *m*: **d'~** first (of all).

abordable *adj* affordable.

aborder *vt* to approach.

aborigène *m* aborigine; * *adj* aboriginal.

aboutir *vi* to succeed.

aboutissement *m* outcome; success.

abrasif *adj* abrasive.

abrégé *m* summary; **en ~** briefly

abréger *vt* to shorten; to abridge.

abreuver *vt* to water.

abreuvoir *m* drinking trough.

abréviation *f* abbreviation.

abri *m* shelter.

abricot *m* apricot.

abriter *vt* to shelter; * **s'~** *vr* to shelter

abroger *vt* to repeal.

abrupt *adj* abrupt; **~ement** *adv* abruptly.

abruti *m*, **-ie** *f*; * *adj* idiotic.

abrutir *vt* to make stupid.

abrutissant *adj* stunning; mind-numbing.

abscisse *f* (*med*) abscissa.

absence *f* absence.

absent *adj* absent.

absenter(s') *vr* to leave, go out.

abside *f* apse.

absolu *adj* absolute; **~ment** *adv* absolutely; * *m* absolute.

absolution *f* absolution.

absolutisme *m* absolutism.

absorbant *adj* absorbent.

absorber *vt* to absorb.

absorption *f* absorption.

absoudre *vt* to absolve.

abstenir(s') *vr* to abstain.

abstention *f* abstention.

abstentionniste *mf* abstainer.

abstinence *f* abstinence.

abstraction *f* abstraction.

abstrait *adj* abstract; **~ement** *adv* in the abstract; * *m* abstract; abstract art.

absurde *adj* absurd; **~ment** *adv* absurdly.

absurdité *f* absurdity.

abus *m* abuse.

abuser *vt* **de** to exploit; to abuse.

abusif *adj* improper.

académicien *m*, **-ienne** *f* academician.

académie *f* academy; learned society.

académique *adj* academic.

acajou *m* mahogany.

acariâtre *adj* quarrelsome.

accablant *adj* overwhelming.

accabler *vt* to overwhelm.

accalmie *f* lull, calm.

accéder *vi*: **~ à** to reach.

accélérateur *m* accelerator.

accélération *f* acceleration.

accélérer *vi* to speed up, accelerate.

accent *m* accent.

accentuation *f* accentuation.

accentué *adj* pronounced.

accentuer *vt* to accentuate.

acceptable *adj* acceptable.

accepter *vt* to accept.

accès *m* access.

accessible *adj* accessible.

accessoire *adj* secondary; **~ment** *adv* secondarily; if need be; * *m* accessory.

accident *m* accident.

accidentel *adj* accidental; **~lement** *adv* accidentally.

acclamations *fpl* cheers; acclamation.

acclamer *vt* to acclaim, cheer.

acclimater *vt* to acclimatize; **s'~** *vr* to become acclimatized.

accolade *f* embrace.

accommodant *adj* accommodating.

accommoder *vt* to prepare; to adapt.

accompagnateur *m*, **-trice** *f* (*mus*) accompanist; guide.

accompagnement *m* accompaniment.

accompagner *vt* to accompany.

accomplir *vt* to do, accomplish.

accomplissement *m* accomplishment.

accord m agreement; **d'~!** okay!, all right!; **être d'~** to agree.

accordéon m accordion.

accorder vt to give; **s'~** vr to agree.

accoster vt to accost.

accouchement m (med) delivery.

accoucher vi to give birth.

accoudoir m armrest.

accouplement m coupling; joining.

accourir vi to run up (à, vers to).

accoutrement m outfit, dress.

accréditer vt to substantiate.

accroc m tear; to breach.

accrocher vt to hang up (à on).

accroissement m increase.

accroître vt to increase.

accroupir(s') vr to crouch.

accueil m welcome, reception.

accueillant adj welcoming.

accueillir vt to welcome.

accumulateur m battery.

accumulation f accumulation.

accumuler vt to accumulate.

accusateur adj, f **-trice** accusing.

accusatif m accusative (case).

accusation f accusation.

accusé m, **-ée** f accused, defendant.

accuser vt to accuse.

acerbe adj acerbic, acid.

acétate m acetate.

acétone f acetone.

acharné adj bitter, fierce; unrelenting.

acharnement m fierceness; determination.

acharner(s') vr **~ a faire qch** to try desperately to do something; **~ contre qn** to hound somebody.

achat m purchase.

acheminer vt to send, forward.

acheter vt to buy.

acheteur m, **-euse** f buyer.

achèvement m completion.

achever vt to finish; to complete.

acide adj acidic; * m acid.

acidité f acidity.

acidulé adj rather acid.

acier m steel.

aciérie f steelworks.

acné f acne.

acompte m deposit, down payment.

à-côté m side issue.

à-coup m jolt.

acoustique adj acoustic; * f acoustics.

acquéreur m buyer.

acquérir vt to buy, purchase.

acquiescer vi to agree; to acquiesce.

acquis adj acquired; * m experience.

acquisition f acquisition; purchase.

acquittement m acquittal; payment.

acquitter vt to acquit; to pay.

acre f acre.

âcre adj acrid.

acrobate mf acrobat.

acrobatie f acrobatics.

acrobatique adj acrobatic.

acrylique m, adj acrylic.

acte m act; deed.

acteur m, **actrice** f actor.

actif adj active; * m (ling) active (voice).

action f act, action; share.

actionnaire *mf* shareholder.

actionner *vt* to activate; to drive.

activement *adv* actively.

activer *vt* to speed up; **s'~** *vr* to bustle about.

activité *f* activity; hustle and bustle.

actualité *f* * **l'actualité** current events.

actuel *adj* current, present; **~lement** *adv* currently, at present.

acuité *f* acuteness; shrillness.

acuponcture *f* acupuncture.

adaptable *adj* adaptable.

adaptateur *m* adaptor.

adaptation *f* adaptation.

adapter *vt* to adapt (*à to*); **s'~** *vr* to adapt (*à to*).

additif *m* additive.

addition *f* addition; bill.

additionnel *adj* additional.

additionner *vt* to add up.

adepte *mf* follower; enthusiast.

adéquat *adj* suitable, appropriate.

adhérence *f* adhesion.

adhérent *m*, **-e** *f* member, adherent; * *adj* : **~ à** which adheres *ou* sticks to.

adhérer *vi* to adhere, stick.

adhésif *adj* adhesive.

adhésion *f* adherence; membership.

adjacent *adj* adjacent (*à to*).

adjectif *m* adjective.

adjoint *m* **-e** *f* assistant.

adjudant *m* warrant officer.

adjudication *f* sale by auction.

adjuger *vt* to auction.

admettre *vt* to admit; to accept; to assume.

administrateur *m*, **-trice** *f* administrator.

administratif *adj* administrative.

administration *f* management; administration.

administrer *vt* to run; to administer.

admirable *adj* admirable; **-ment** *adv* admirably, brilliantly.

admiratif *adj* admiring.

admiration *f* admiration.

admirativement *adv* admiringly.

admirer *vt* to admire.

admissible *adj* acceptable.

admission *f* admission.

adolescence *f* adolescence.

adolescent *m*, **-e** *f* adolescent.

adopter *vt* to adopt; to pass.

adoption *f* adoption; passing.

adorable *adj* adorable; **~ment** *adv* delightfully.

adorer *vt* to adore, worship.

adoucir *vt* to soften.

adrénaline *f* adrenalin.

adresse *f* address; skill.

adresser *vt* to address; to send; **s'~** *vr* **s'~ à** to address; to go and see.

adroit *adj* deft, skilful; **~ement** *adv* deftly, skilfully.

aduler *vt* to flatter.

adulte *mf* adult, grown-up; *adj* adult, full-grown.

adultère *m* adultery.

adverbe *m* adverb.

adverbial *adj* adverbial; **~ement** *adv* adverbially.

adversaire *mf* adversary, opponent.

adversité *f* adversity.

aération *f* ventilation.

aérer *vt* to air.

aérien adj air; aerial.

aérodrome m aerodrome, airfield.

aérodynamique adj aerodynamic; * f aerodynamics.

aérogare f airport; (air) terminal.

aéroglisseur m hovercraft.

aéronautique adj aeronautic; * f aeronautics.

aéronaval adj, pl **aéronavals** air and sea.

aéroport m airport.

aérospatial adj aerospace.

affable adj affable.

affaiblir vt to weaken; **s'~** vr to weaken, grow weaker.

affaiblissement m weakening.

affaire f matter.

affaissement m subsidence.

affaisser vt subside; to cave in; **s'~** vr to cause to subside ou cave in.

affamé adj starving.

affamer vt to starve.

affectation f allocation (à to); affectation.

affecté adj affected.

affecter vt to affect.

affectif adj emotional.

affection f affection.

affectueux adj affectionate.

affectueusement adv affectionately.

affermir vt to strengthen;firm.

affermissement m strengthening.

affichage m posting (up).

affiche f poster.

afficher vt to post ou put up.

affiner vt to refine.

affinité f affinity.

affirmatif adj affirmative.

affirmation f assertion.

affirmativement adv in the affirmative.

affirmer vt to assert.

affluent m tributary.

affluer vi to rush (à to).

afflux m influx.

affolant adj alarming.

affolement m panic.

affoler vt to throw into a panic; **s'~** vr to get into a panic.

affranchir vt to frank, stamp; to free.

affranchissement m stamping, franking; freeing.

affréter vt to charter.

affreux adj horrible; awful.

affreusement adv horribly, dreadfully.

affrontement m confrontation.

affronter vt to confront; **s'~** vr to confront one another.

afin prép: **~ de** (in order) to; **~ qu'il le sache** in order that, so that.

africain adj, mf African.

Afrique f Africa.

agaçant adj annoying.

agacer vt to annoy, irritate.

âge m age; **quel ~ as-tu?** how old are you?

âgé adj old; **~ de 10 ans** 10 years old.

agence f agency; branch; offices.

agencement m organization, arrangement; equipment.

agencer vt to arrange; to equip.

agenda m diary.

agenouiller(s') vr to kneel (down).

agent m agent; policeman.

agglomération f town, urban area.

aggravant *adj* aggravating.

aggravation *f* worsening, aggravation; increase.

aggraver *vt* to make worse; to increase; **s'~** *vr* to get worse, worsen; to increase.

agile *adj* agile, nimble; **~ment** *adv* nimbly.

agilité *f* agility.

agir *vi* to act.

agitateur *m*, **-trice** *f* agitator.

agitation *f* agitation.

agiter *vt* to shake; to wave; **s'~** *vr* to move about; to fidget.

agneau *m* lamb.

agonie *f* death throes.

agrafe *f* staple; hook.

agrafer *vt* to staple (together); to fasten up.

agrafeuse *f* stapler.

agraire *adj* agrarian; land.

agrandir *vt* to make bigger; to widen; to expand; **s'~** *vr* to get bigger; to widen; to expand.

agrandissement *m* enlargement.

agréable *adj* agreeable, pleasant; **~ment** *adv* agreeably, pleasantly.

agresser *vt* to attack.

agresseur *m* attacker.

agressif *adj* aggressive.

agression *f* attack.

agressivement *adv* aggressively.

agressivité *f* aggressiveness.

agricole *adj* agricultural.

agriculteur *m* farmer.

agriculture *f* agriculture, farming.

agripper *vt* to grab (hold of); **s'~ à** *vr* to grab on to.

agronome *m* agronomist.

agronomie *f* agronomy.

agrumes *m pl* citrus fruits.

ahuri *adj* stunned; stupefied.

ahurissant *adj* staggering.

aide *f* help; aid.

aider *vt* to help.

aigle *m* eagle.

aigre *adj* sour, bitter; **~ment** *adv* sourly.

aigreur *f* sourness; sharpness.

aigri *adj* bitter, embittered.

aigu *adj*, **f aiguë** shrill; acute.

aiguillage *m* shunting.

aiguille *f* needle.

aiguiller *vt* to direct; to shunt.

aiguiser *vt* to sharpen.

ail *m* garlic.

ailé *adj* winged.

aileron *m* fin; aileron.

ailleurs *adv* elsewhere; **partout ~** everywhere else; **nulle part ~** nowhere else; **d'~** moreover; by the way.

aimable *adj* kind; **~ment** *adv* kindly

aimant *m* magnet.

aimanter *vt* to magnetize.

aimer *vt* to love.

aîné *m*, **aînée** *f* eldest *ou* oldest child; * adj elder, older; eldest, oldest

ainsi *adv* so, thus; **puisque c'est ~** since this is the way it is *ou* things are.

air *m* air; **avoir l'~ content** to look happy; **d'un ~ moqueur** in a mocking fashion.

aire *f* area.

aise *f* pleasure.

aisé *adj* easy; well-off; **~ment** *adv* easily.

aisselle *f* armpit.

ajournement *m* adjournment; postponement.

ajourner *vt* to adjourn; to defer, postpone.

ajout *m* addition.

ajouter *vt* to add.

ajuster *vt* to adjust.

alarmant *adj* alarming.

alarme *f* alarm.

alarmer *vt* to alarm; **s'~** *vr* to get alarmed (*de* at, about).

albâtre *m* alabaster.

album *m* album.

albumine *f* albumin.

alcalin *adj* alkaline.

alcaloïde *m* alkaloid.

alchimie *f* alchemy.

alchimiste *m* alchemist.

alcool *m* alcohol.

alcoolique *adj* alcoholic; * *mf* alcoholic.

alcoolisme *m* alcoholism.

aléatoire *adj* uncertain; risky.

alentours *mpl* surroundings, neighbourhood.

alerte *adj* alert; agile; * *f* alarm, alert.

alerter *vt* to alert; to notify; to warn.

algèbre *f* algebra.

algébrique *adj* algebraic; **~ment** *adv* algebraically.

algorithme *m* algorithm.

algue *f* seaweed.

alibi *m* alibi.

aliénation *f* alienation.

aliéner *vt* to alienate.

alignement *m* alignment; aligning.

aligner *vt* to align, line up.

aliment *m* food.

alimentaire *adj* alimentary, food.

alimentation *f* feeding; diet; food industry.

alimenter *vt* to feed; **s'~** *vr* to eat.

alinéa *m* paragraph.

allée *f* avenue; path.

alléger *vt* to make lighter; to alleviate.

allégorie *f* allegory.

allégresse *f* exhilaration.

alléguer *vt* to give, put forward.

aller *vi* to go; **comment allez-vous?** how are you?; **allons-y** let's go; **s'en aller** to go away, leave; * *m* outward journey; single ticket.

allergie *f* allergy.

allergique *adj* allergic (*à* to).

alliage *m* alloy.

alliance *f* alliance; marriage; wedding ring.

allié *m*, **-ée** *f* ally; * *adj* allied.

allier *vt* to combine.

allô *excl* hello!

allocation *f* allocation; allowance.

allongé *adj* **être allongé** to be lying (down).

allonger *vt* to lengthen; **s'~** *vr* to lengthen; to lie down.

allouer *vt* to allocate.

allumage *m* ignition.

allumer *vt* to light; to turn *ou* switch on.

allumette *f* match.

allure *f* speed; look.

allusion *f* allusion (*à* to).

alluvions *fpl* alluvium; alluvial deposits.

alors adv then; ~ **que** while; whereas.

alouette f lark.

alourdir vt to make heavy; to increase.

alphabet m alphabet.

alphabétique adj alphabetical; ~**ment** adv alphabetically.

alpinisme m mountaineering.

alpiniste mf mountaineer.

altération f alteration, change.

altercation f altercation.

altérer vt to change, alter.

alternance f alternation.

alternatif adj alternate.

alternative f alternative.

alternativement adv in turn, alternately.

alterner vt, vi to alternate (avec with).

altitude f altitude, height.

altruisme m altruism.

aluminium m aluminium.

alvéole f cell.

amabilité f kindness.

amaigrir vt to make thin(ner).

amaigrissant adj slimming.

amalgame m combination, amalgam.

amalgamer vt to combine.

amande f almond.

amant m lover.

amarrer vt to moor.

amas m pile, heap.

amasser vt to amass, pile up.

amateur m amateur; connaisseur.

ambassade f embassy.

ambassadeur m, -**drice** f ambassador.

ambiance f atmosphere.

ambigu adj, f **ambiguë** ambiguous.

ambiguïté f ambiguity.

ambitieux adj ambitious.

ambition f ambition.

ambivalence f ambivalence.

ambre m amber.

ambulance f ambulance.

ambulant adj travelling.

âme f soul.

amélioration f improvement.

améliorer vt to improve; **s'**~ vr to improve.

aménagement m fitting out; adjustment; development.

aménager vt to fit out; to adjust; to develop.

amende f fine.

amendement m amendment.

amener vt to bring.

amer adj bitter.

amèrement adv bitterly.

Américain m, -**e** f American.

américain adj American.

Amérique f America.

amertume f bitterness.

ameublement m furniture.

ami m, -**ie** f friend.

amiante m asbestos.

amibe f amoeba.

amical adj friendly; ~**ement** adv in a friendly manner.

amincir vt to thin (down).

amiral m admiral.

amitié f friendship.

ammoniac m ammonia.

amnésie f amnesia.

amnistie f amnesty.

amnistier vt to grant an amnesty to.

amoindrir vt to weaken; to reduce.

amoindrissement m weakening; reduction.

amoncellement m pile; accumulation.

amorcer vt to bait; to begin.

amorphe adj passive.

amortir vt to soften; to deaden.

amortissement m paying off.

amour m love.

amoureux adj in love (de with).

amovible adj detachable.

ampère m ampere, amp.

amphibie adj amphibious.

amphithéâtre m amphitheatre.

ample adj roomy; wide; **~ment** adv amply, fully.

ampleur f fullness; range.

amplifier vt to increase; to amplify.

amplitude f amplitude; magnitude.

ampoule f bulb; phial; blister.

amputation f amputation.

amputer vt to amputate.

amusant adj amusing.

amuser vt to amuse.

an m year; **avoir vingt ~s** to be 20 (years old).

anabolisant m anabolic steroid.

anachronisme m anachronism.

anagramme f anagram.

analgésique adj analgesic.

analogie f analogy.

analogique adj analogical.

analogue adj analogous (à to).

analphabète adj illiterate.

analyse f analysis; test.

analyser vt to analyse.

analyste mf analyst; psychoanalyst.

analytique adj analytical; **~ment** adv analytically.

ananas m pineapple.

anarchie f anarchy.

anarchiste mf anarchist.

anathème m anathema.

anatomie f anatomy.

anatomique adj anatomical; **~ment** adv anatomically.

ancestral adj ancestral.

ancêtre m ancestor.

anchois m anchovy.

ancien adj old; former; **~nement** adv formerly.

ancienneté f (years of) service; seniority; age.

ancrage m anchorage.

ancre f anchor.

ancrer vt to anchor.

âne m ass, donkey.

anéantir vt to destroy.

anéantissement m destruction.

anecdote f anecdote.

anémie f anemia.

anémone f anemone.

anesthésie f anaesthetic; anaesthesia.

anesthésique m anaesthetic.

ange m angel.

angélique adj angelic; * f angelica.

angine f tonsillitis.

Anglais m, **-e** f Englishman; Englishwoman.

anglais adj English; * m (ling) English.

angle m angle; corner.

Angleterre f England.

anglophone adj English-speaking; mf English speaker.

angoissant *adj* agonizing.
angoisse *f* anguish.
angoisser *vt* to make anxious.
animal *m* animal.
animateur *m*, **-trice** *f* host, compère; leader.
animation *f* animation; hustle and bustle.
animé *adj* busy; lively.
animer *vt* to lead; to host; to liven up; **s'~** *vr* to liven up.
animisme *m* animism.
animosité *f* animosity.
annales *fpl* annals.
anneau *m* ring.
année *f* year; day; **les ~s soixante** the Sixties.
annexe *f* annexe; * *adj* subsidiary.
annexer *vt* to annex; to append.
annihiler *vt* to annihilate.
anniversaire *m* birthday; **joyeux ~!** happy birthday!
annonce *f* advertisement; announcement.
annoncer *vt* to announce (à to).
annoter *vt* to annotate.
annuaire *m* telephone · directory, phone book. ·
annuel *adj* annual; **~lement** *adv* annually.
annulation *f* cancellation; nullification.
annuler *vt* to cancel; to nullify.
anode *f* anode.
anodin *adj* insignificant.
anomalie *f* anomaly.
anonyme *adj* anonymous; impersonal; **~ment** *adv* anonymously.
anorexie *f* anorexia.
anorexique *adj*, *mf* anorexic.

anormal *adj* abnormal; **~ement** *adv* abnormally.
anse *f* handle.
antagonisme *m* antagonism.
antagoniste *adj* antagonistic.
antécédent *m* antecedent.
antenne *f* (*rad*, *tv*) aerial; (*zool*) feeler.
antérieur *adj* earlier, previous; **~ement** *adv* earlier, previously.
anthologie *f* anthology.
anthracite *m* anthracite.
anthropologie *f* anthropology.
anthropologue *m* anthropologist.
antiaérien *adj* anti-aircraft; air-raid.
anticancéreux *adj* cancer.
antichambre *f* antechamber.
anticipation *f* anticipation.
anticonceptionnel *adj* contraceptive.
anticonformiste *adj*, *mf* nonconformist.
anticorps *m* antibody.
anticyclone *m* anticyclone.
antidater *vt* to backdate.
antidépresseur *adj*, *m* antidepressant.
antidote *m* antidote.
antigel *m* antifreeze.
antimilitariste *adj*, *mf* antimilitarist.
antinucléaire *adj*, *mf* antinuclear.
antipathie *f* antipathy.
antipathique *adj* unpleasant.
antipode *m* antipodes; **aux ~s de** the polar opposite of.
antiquaire *mf* antique dealer.
antique *adj* ancient.
antiquité *f* antiquity; antique.

antirouille adj invar rustproof.

antisémite mf anti-semite; adj anti-semitic.

antisepsie f antisepsis.

antiseptique adj antiseptic.

antisocial adj antisocial.

antitétanique adj (anti-)tetanus.

antithèse f antithesis.

antitoxine f antitoxin.

antivol m invar anti-theft ou security device; lock; * adj invar anti-theft.

antonyme m antonym.

antre m den.

anus m anus.

anxiété f anxiety.

anxieux adj anxious.

aorte f aorta.

août m August.

apaisant adj soothing.

apaisement m calm(ing down); relief.

apaiser vt to calm (down); to relieve.

apathie f apathy.

apathique adj apathetic.

apercevoir vt to see; to catch a glimpse of.

aperçu m (overall ou general) idea.

apéritif m aperitif.

apesanteur f weightlessness.

apeuré adj frightened.

aphone adj voiceless, hoarse.

aphrodisiaque adj, m aphrodisiac.

apiculteur m beekeeper.

apitoyer vt to rouse one's pity; **s'~** vr to feel pity (sur for).

aplanir vt to level (out); to smooth away.

aplati adj flat.

aplatir vt to flatten (out).

apocalypse f apocalypse.

apocalyptique adj apocalyptic.

apogée m apogee, peak.

apolitique adj apolitical; non-political.

apologie f apology.

apoplexie f apoplexy.

apostrophe f apostrophe.

apothéose f apotheosis.

apôtre m apostle.

apparaître vi to appear.

appareil m device; appliance; (tele-)phone;**~-photo** camera.

appareillage m casting off; equipment.

appareiller vi to cast off.

apparemment adv apparently.

apparence f appearance.

apparent adj apparent.

apparition f appearance; apparition.

appartement m flat, apartment.

appartenance f membership.

appartenir vi: **~ à** to belong to.

appât m bait.

appâter vt to lure; to bait.

appauvrir vt to impoverish; **s'~** vr to grow poorer.

appauvrissement m impoverishment.

appel m call; appeal.

appeler vt to call; to call out; **s'~** vr je m'appelle Léon my name is Leon.

appellation f appellation; name.

appendicite f appendicitis.

appesantir vt to weigh down; to strengthen; **s'~** vr to grow heavier; to grow stronger.

appétissant *adj* appetizing.

appétit *m* appetite (*de* for).

applaudir *vt, vi* to applaud.

applaudissements *mpl* applause.

applicable *adj* applicable (*à* to).

application *f* application; use.

appliqué *adj* thorough, industrious.

appliquer *vt* to apply (*à* to); **s'~** *vr* to apply oneself.

apport *m* supply.

apporter *vt* to bring.

apposer *vt* to append; to affix.

appréciable *adj* appreciable.

appréciatif *adj* evaluative; appreciative.

appréciation *f* estimation, assessment

apprécier *vt* to assess; to appreciate.

appréhender *vt* to apprehend; to dread.

appréhension *f* apprehension.

apprendre *vt* to learn; **~ à lire** to learn to read; **~ à lire à un enfant** to teach a child to read.

apprenti *m*, **-ie** *f* apprentice.

apprentissage *m* apprenticeship.

apprêter *vt* to get ready; **s'~** *vr* to get ready.

apprivoiser *vt* to tame.

approbateur *adj*, *f* **-trice** approving.

approbation *f* approval.

approche *f* approach.

approcher *vt* to move near; to approach; **s'~** *vr* to approach.

approfondir *vt* to deepen.

approfondissement *m* deepening.

approprier(s') *vr* to appropriate.

approuver *vt* to approve of.

approvisionnement *m* supplying.

approvisionner *vt* to supply; **s'~** *vr* to stock up (*de, en* with).

approximatif *adj* approximate.

approximation *f* approximation.

approximativement *adv* approximately.

appui *m* support.

appuie-tête *m invar* headrest.

appuyer *vt* to press; to lean; to support *vi* to press; **s'~** to put up with; to take on; *vr* **s'~ sur** to lean on; to rely on.

âpre *adj* bitter; **~ment** *adv* bitterly.

après *prép* after; **après tout** after all; **d'~ elle** according to her; **collé ~ la vitre** stuck on the window; * *adv* after(wards); **tout de suite ~** immediately after *ou* afterwards.

après-demain *adv* the day after tomorrow.

après-midi *m/f invar* afternoon.

âpreté *f* bitterness.

a priori *m* apriorism; * *adv* a priori.

apte *adj* capable (*à* of).

aptitude *f* aptitude; ability.

aquarium *m* aquarium.

aquatique *adj* aquatic.

aqueduc *m* aqueduct.

aqueux *adj* aqueous.

arabesque *f* arabesque.

arable *adj* arable.

arachide *f* peanut, groundnut.

araignée *f* spider.

arbalète *f* crossbow.

arbitrage *m* arbitration.

arbitraire *adj* arbitrary; **~ment** *adv* arbitrarily.

arbitre *m* arbiter; referee.

arbitrer *vt* to arbitrate; to referee.

arborer *vt* to wear; to bear.

arborescence *f* arborescence.

arboriculture *f* arboriculture, tree cultivation.

arbre *m* tree.

arbrisseau *m* shrub.

arbuste *m* bush.

arc *m* bow; arc; arch.

arcade *f* arch.

arc-bouter(s') *vr* to lean.

arc-en-ciel *m*, *pl* **arcs-en-ciel** rainbow.

archaïque *adj* archaic.

archange *m* archangel.

arche *f* arche.

archéologie *f* archaeology.

archéologue *mf* archaeologist.

archétype *m* archetype.

archevêque *m* archbishop.

archipel *m* archipelago.

architecte *mf* architect.

architectonique *adj* architectonic.

architectural *adj* architectural.

architecture *f* architecture.

archiver *vt* to file, archive.

archives *fpl* archives, records.

archiviste *mf* archiviste.

ardemment *adv* ardently.

ardent *adj* ardent, burning.

ardeur *f* ardour.

ardoise *f* slate.

ardu *adj* difficult.

are *f* are (= a hundred square metres).

arène *f* arena.

arête *f* (fish)bone.

argent *m* silver; money.

argenté *adj* silver; silver-plated.

argenterie *f* silverware.

argile *f* clay.

argot *m* slang.

argument *m* argument.

argumentation *f* argumentation.

argumenter *vi* to argue (*sur* about).

aride *adj* arid.

aridité *f* aridity.

aristocrate *mf* aristocrat.

aristocratie *f* aristocracy.

aristocratique *adj* aristocratic.

arithmétique *f* arithmetic; * *adj* arithmetical; **~ment** *adv* arithmetically.

armature *f* (frame)work.

arme *f* arm, weapon.

armée *f* army.

armement *m* arms, weapons; armaments.

armer *vt* to arm; **s'~** *vr* to arm oneself.

armistice *m* armistice.

armoire *f* cupboard; wardrobe.

armure *f* armour.

aromate *m* herb; spice.

aromatique *adj* aromatic.

aromatiser *vt* to flavour.

arôme *m* aroma; flavour.

arpenteur *m* (land) surveyor.

arqué *adj* curved, arced.

arquebuse *f* arquebus.

arrachement *m* wrench; pulling *ou* tearing off.

arracher *vt* to pull (out); to tear off.

arrangeant *adj* obliging.

arrangement *m* arrangement.

arranger *vt* to arrange; to fix; **cela m'arrangerait** that would suit me; **s'~** *vr* to come to an arrangement; to manage; to get better.

arrestation f arrest.

arrêt m stopping; stop (button).

arrêté m order.

arrêter vt to stop; **s'~** vr to stop.

arrhes f pl deposit.

arrière m invar back; **en ~** back-(wards); **à l'~** at the back; * adj invar back, rear.

arriéré adj backward.

arrière-goût m aftertaste.

arrière-grand-mère f great-grand-mother.

arrière-grand-père m great-grand-father.

arrière-pays m hinterland.

arrière-pensée f ulterior motive; mental reservation.

arrière-petits-enfants m pl great-grandchildren.

arrière-plan m background.

arrimer vt to stow.

arrivage m delivery.

arrivant m, **-e** f newcomer.

arrivée f arrival, coming.

arriver vi to arrive, come.

arriviste mf careerist; social climber.

arrogance f arrogance.

arrogant adj arrogant.

arroger(s') vr to assume (without rights to).

arrondi adj round(ed).

arrondir vt to make round; to round off.

arrondissement m district.

arrosage m watering.

arroser vt to water.

arsenal m arsenal.

arsenic m arsenic.

art m art.

artère f artery; road.

artériel adj arterial.

arthrite f arthritis.

artichaut m artichoke.

article m article.

articulation f joint; knuckle.

articuler vt to articulate.

artifice m trick.

artificiel adj artificial; **~lement** adv artificially.

artillerie f artillery.

artisan m artisan, craftsman.

artisanal adj craft.

artisanat m craft industry.

artiste mf artist.

artistique adj artistic; **~ment** adv artistically.

as m ace.

ascendance f ancestry.

ascendant adj upward, rising; * m (strong) influence, ascendancy (sur over).

ascenseur m lift, elevator.

ascension f ascent.

ascète mf ascetic.

ascétique adj ascetic.

aseptiser vt to sterilize; to disinfect.

asexué adj asexual.

asiatique adj Asian.

asile m refuge; asylum.

aspect m appearance, look.

asperge f asparagus.

asperger vt to splash (de with).

aspérité f bump.

asphalte m asphalt.

asphyxie f asphyxiation, suffocation.

asphyxier vt to asphyxiate, suffocate.

aspirateur *m* vacuum cleaner.

aspiration *f* inhalation.

aspirer *vt* to inhale.

aspirine *f* aspirin.

assagir *vt* to quieten (down); **s'~** *vr* to quieten (down).

assaillant *m* assailant.

assaillir *vt* to assail.

assainir *vt* to clean up; to purify.

assainissement *m* cleaning up.

assaisonnement *m* seasoning.

assaisonner *vt* to season.

assassin *m* murderer; assassin.

assassinat *m* murder; assassination.

assassiner *vt* to assassinate.

assaut *m* assault, attack (*de* on).

assécher *vt* to drain; **s'~** *vr* to dry (up *ou* out).

assemblage *m* assembly; assembling.

assemblée *f* meeting.

assembler *vt* to assemble; **s'~** *vr* to assemble.

assentiment *m* assent.

asseoir(s') *vr* to sit down.

assermenté *adj* on oath.

assertion *f* assertion.

asservissement *m* enslavement; slavery.

assez *adv* enough; quite, rather; **avoir ~ d'argent** to have enough money; **~ bien** quite well; **j'en ai assez!** I've had enough!; I'm fed up.

assidu *adj* assiduous; regular.

assiduité *f* assiduity; regularity.

assiéger *vt* to besiege.

assiette *f* plate.

assigner *vt* to assign.

assimilation *f* assimilation; comparison; classification.

assimiler *vt* to assimilate.

assis *adj* seated, sitting (down).

assistance *f* audience; assistance.

assistant *m*, **-e** *f* assistant.

assister *vt* to attend; to assist.

association *f* association.

associé *m*, **-ée** *f* associate, partner.

associer *vt* to associate (*à* with); **s'~** *vr* to join together.

assombrir *vt* to darken; **s'~** to darken.

assommer *vt* to stun.

Assomption *f* : **l'~** the Assumption.

assortiment *m* assortment.

assortir *vt* to match; **s'~** *vr* to go well together.

assoupir(s') *vr* to doze off.

assoupissement *m* doze.

assouplir *vt* to make supple; to relax.

assouplissement *m* softening; relaxing.

assourdir *vt* to deafen; to muffle.

assourdissant *adj* deafening.

assouvir *vt* to satisfy.

assouvissement *m* satisfying, satisfaction.

assujettir *vt* to subjugate.

assumer *vt* to assume.

assurance *f* (self-)assurance; assurance; insurance (policy).

assuré *m*, **-e** *f* assured; * *adj* assured.

assurer *vt* to assure; **s'~** *vr* to insure oneself.

assureur *m* (insurance) agent; insurer(s), insurance company.

astérisque *m* asterisk.

asthmatique *adj, mf* asthmatic.

asthme *m* asthma.

asticot *m* maggot.

astigmate *adj* astigmatic.

astiquer *vt* to polish.

astre *m* star.

astreignant *adj* demanding.

astreindre *vt* to force, compel; **s'~ vr s'~ à faire** to force *ou* compel to do.

astrologie *f* astrology.

astrologique *adj* astrological.

astrologue *m* astrologer.

astronaute *mf* astronaut.

astronome *f* astronomer.

astronomie *f* astronomy.

astronomique *adj* astronomical.

astuce *f* shrewdness; (clever) trick; pun.

astucieux *adj* astute.

asymétrique *adj* asymmetric(al).

atelier *m* workshop; studio.

atermoyer *vi* to procrastinate.

athée *mf* atheist; *adj* atheistic.

athéisme *m* atheism.

athlète *mf* athlete.

athlétique *adj* athletic.

athlétisme *m* athletics.

atlas *m* atlas.

atmosphère *f* atmosphere.

atmosphérique *adj* atmospheric.

atome *m* atom.

atomique *adj* atomic.

atomiseur *m* spray; atomizer.

atout *m* trump; advantage, asset.

âtre *m* hearth.

atroce *adj* atrocious; dreadful;

~ment *adv* atrociously; dreadfully.

atrocité *f* atrocity.

atrophié *adj* atrophied.

attachant *adj* endearing.

attache *f* fastener.

attaché *m*, **-e** *f* attaché; assistant.

attachement *m* attachment (*à* to).

attacher *vt* to tie together; to tie up; to fasten; to attach (*à* to).

attaque *f* attack.

attaquer *vt* to attack; to tackle.

attarder(s') *vr* to linger.

atteindre *vt* to reach; to affect; to contact.

atteinte *f* attack (*à* on); **hors d'~** beyond *ou* out of reach.

attenant *adj* adjoining.

attendre *vt* to wait; **en attendant** meanwhile, in the meantime; **s'~ vr** : **s'~ à qch** to expect something.

attendrir *vt* to fill with pity; to move; to tenderize; **s'~ vr** to be moved (*sur* by).

attendrissant *adj* touching, moving.

attendrissement *m* emotion.

attendu *adj* expected; long-awaited.

attentat *m* attack (*contre* on); murder attempt.

attente *f* wait; expectation.

attentif *adj* attentive; careful.

attention *f* attention; care.

attentionné *adj* considerate, thoughtful (*pour* towards).

attentivement *adv* attentively; carefully.

atténuation *f* alleviation; easing.

atténuer vt to alleviate; to ease.

atterrir vi to land, touch down.

atterrissage m landing, touch-down.

attester vt to testify to.

attirail m gear.

attirant adj attractive.

attirer vt to attract; **s'~ des ennuis à qn** to cause somebody trouble.

attiser vt to stir up.

attitude f attitude; bearing.

attraction f attraction.

attrait m attraction, appeal.

attraper vt to catch.

attrayant adj attractive.

attribuer vt to attribute; to award.

attribut m attribute.

attribution f attribution.

attrister vt to sadden.

attroupement m crowd.

au = à le.

aube f dawn, daybreak.

auberge f inn; **~ de jeunesse** youth hostel.

aubergine f aubergine.

aucun adj no; not any; any; **sans ~ doute** without (any) doubt; **~ement** adv in no way; not in the least; * pron none; not any; any (one); **~ d'entre eux** none of them.

audace f audacity; daring.

audacieux adj audacious, bold; daring.

audience f audience; hearing.

audiovisuel adj audio-visual.

auditeur m, **-trice** f listener; auditor.

auditoire m audience.

augmentation f increase, rise (de in); increasing, raising (de of).

augmenter vt to increase, raise.

augure f omen; oracle.

aujourd'hui adv today.

aumône f alms; **demander/faire l'~** to beg for/give alms.

auparavant adv before, previously; before, first.

auprès prép :**~ de** next to; (compared) with.

auquel = à lequel.

auréole f halo, aureole; ring (mark).

auriculaire adj auricular; * m little finger.

aurore f dawn, first light.

ausculter vt to auscultate.

aussi adv too, also; so; **nous ~** us too; **une ~ belle journée** such a beautiful day; **il est ~ petit qu'elle** he is as small as she is.

aussitôt adv immediately; **~ dit, ~ fait** no sooner said than done; **~ que** as soon as.

austère adj austere; **~ment** adv austerely.

austérité f austerity.

autant adv as much; as many; so much; such; so many; such a lot of; the same; **~ que je sache** as far as I know; **~ que possible** as much as possible; **elle n'est pas plus heureuse pour ~** she's not any happier for it ou for all that.

autel m altar.

auteur m author.

authenticité f authenticity.

authentifier vt to authenticate.

authentique adj authentic; **~ment** adv authentically.

autobiographie f autobiography.

autobiographique *adj* autobiographical.

autocar *m* coach.

autocollant *adj* self-adhesive.

autocuiseur *m* pressure cooker.

autodéfense *f* self-defence.

autodestruction *f* self-destruction.

autodidacte *mf* self-taught.

auto-école *f* driving school.

automate *m* automaton.

automatique *adj* automatic; **~ment** *adv* automatically.

automatiser *vt* to automate.

automatisme *m* automatism.

automne *m* autumn.

automobile *f* (motor) car.

automobiliste *mf* motorist.

autonome *adj* autonomous; self-governing.

autonomie *f* autonomy; self-government.

autoportrait *m* self-portrait.

autopsie *f* autopsy, post-mortem (examination).

autoradio *m* car radio.

autorisation *f* authorization, permission; permit.

autoriser *vt* to authorize, give permission for; to allow.

autoritaire *adj* authoritarian.

autorité *f* authority.

autoroute *f* motorway.

autosatisfaction *f* self-satisfaction.

auto-stop *m* hitch-hiking; **faire de l'~** to hitch-hike.

auto-stoppeur *m*, **-euse** *f* hitch-hiker.

autour *prép* **~ de** (a)round; * *adv* (a)round; **il y en a tout ~** there is/are some all around.

autre *adj* other; **~ chose** something else *ou* different; **~ part** somewhere else; **d'~ part** on the other hand; moreover; * *pron* another (one); **j'en veux un ~** I'd like another (one); **encore deux ~s** another two; **les cinq ~s** the five others; the other five.

autrefois *adv* in the past, in days gone by.

autrement *adv* differently; otherwise; **je n'ai pas pu faire ~** I couldn't do differently *ou* otherwise.

autruche *f* ostrich.

autrui *pron* others.

aux = à les.

auxiliaire *adj* auxiliary; * *m* auxiliary; * *mf* assistant.

avachir(s') *vr* to become *ou* grow limp.

avalanche *f* avalanche.

avaler *vt* to swallow.

avance *f* advance; lead; **arriver en ~** to arrive early; **payer d'~** to pay in advance; **réserver à l'~** to book in advance; **avoir de l'~ sur** to have the lead over.

avancement *m* promotion; progress; forward movement.

avancer *vt* to move forward; to bring forward; to put forward; **s'~** *vr* to advance, move forward; * *vi* to move forward, advance; to make progress; to project, stick out.

avant *prép* before; **~ peu** shortly; **~ tout** above all; * *adv* before; **en ~** in front, ahead; * *m* front; bow; forward.

avantage *m* advantage.

avantager *vt* to favour; to flatter.

avantageux *adj* profitable, worthwhile; attractive; flattering.

avant-bras *m invar* forearm.

avant-coureur *adj* precursory.

avant-dernier *m*, **-ière** *f*, *adj* next to last, second last, last but one.

avant-garde *f* avant-garde; vanguard.

avant-goût *m* foretaste.

avant-hier *adv* the day before yesterday.

avant-première *f* preview.

avare *mf* miser; *adj* miserly.

avarice *f* avarice, miserliness.

avarie *f* damage.

avarié *adj* rotting; damaged.

avec *prép* with; to.

avènement *m* accession (*à* to); advent.

avenir *m* future.

aventure *f* adventure; venture; experience; affair.

aventurer(s') *vr* to venture.

aventurier *m*, **-ière** *f* adventurer.

avenue *f* avenue.

avérer(s') *vr* to turn out, prove to be.

averse *f* shower (of rain).

aversion *f* aversion (*pour* to); loathing (*pour* for).

avertir *vt* to warn; to inform (*de* of).

avertissement *m* warning.

aveu *m* admission, confession.

aveuglant *adj* blinding.

aveugle *adj* blind; *mf blind person (*ou* man *ou* woman).

aveuglement *m* blindness.

aveugler *vt* to blind.

aviateur *m*, **-trice** *f* pilot, aviator.

aviation *f* flying; aviation.

avide *adj* greedy; eager; **~ment** *adv* greedily; eagerly.

avidité *f* greed; eagerness.

avilir *vt* to degrade.

avilissant *adj* degrading.

avion *m* (air)plane, aircraft.

aviron *m* oar; rowing.

avis *m* opinion.

avisé *adj* wise, sensible.

aviser *vt* to advise, inform; to notice; **s'~ de** **s'aviser de** to realize suddenly.

aviver *vt* to sharpen; to deepen; to arouse.

avocat *m*, **-e** *f* barrister; * *m* avocado (pear).

avoine *f* oats.

avoir *vt* to have; **il y a** there is/are; **il y a deux mois** two months ago; **qu'as-tu?** what's wrong (with you)?; **il n'avait qu'à le dire** he only had to say (the word); * *m* resources; credit.

avortement *m* abortion.

avorter *vi* to abort; to fail.

avoué *m* solicitor.

avouer *vt* to admit (to); to confess (to).

avril *m* April.

axe *m* axis; axle; main road.

axial *adj* axial.

azote *m* nitrogen.

B

babines *fpl* chops.

babiole *f* trinket, trifle.

bâbord *m* (*naut*) port.

babouin *m* baboon.

bac *m* ferry.

bâche *f* tarpaulin, cover.

bâcler *vt* to botch; to obstruct.

bactérie *f* bacterium.

badaud *m* (*pej*) idle onlooker.

badge *m* badge.

bafouer *vt* to scorn.

bafouiller *vi* to stammer; to babble.

bagage *m* luggage; stock of knowledge.

bagarre *f* fight, brawl.

bagarrer (se) *vr* to fight; to riot.

bagatelle *f* trinket; trifling sum.

bagne *m* penal servitude; (*fig*) grind.

bague *f* ring.

baguette *f* stick; loaf of French bread.

baie *f* (*geog*) bay.

baigner *vt vi* to bathe; * **se ~** *vr* to have a bathe, swim.

baignoire *f* bathtub.

bâiller *vi* to yawn.

bâillon *m* gag.

bâillonner *vt* to gag.

bain *m* bath; bathe, swim.

baiser *m* kiss; * *vt* to kiss.

baisse *f* fall, drop.

baisser *vi* to fall, drop *vt* to lower.

bal *m* dance.

balade *f* (*fam*) walk; drive.

balader(se) *vr* (*fam*) to go for a walk; to go for a drive.

balai *m* broom, brush.

balance *f* balance; scales.

balancement *m* sway; rocking.

balancer *vt* to balance; to swing.

balançoire *f* swing; seesaw.

balayer *vt* to sweep, brush.

balbutiement *m* stammering, mumbling.

balbutier *vt* to stammer, mumble.

balbuzard *m* osprey.

balcon *m* balcony.

baleine *f* whale.

balistique *f* ballistics.

ballast *m* ballast.

balle *f* bullet; ball.

ballet *m* ballet.

ballon *m* ball; balloon.

ballotter *vt* jolt, shake about.

balourd *adj* stupid; clumsy.

balustrade *f* balustrade; handrail.

bambou *m* bamboo.

banal *adj* banal, trite; **~ement** *adv* tritely.

banalisation *f* vulgarizing; standardization.

banalité *f* banality, triteness.

banane *f* banana.

bancaire *adj* banking, bank.

bancal, pl bancals *adj* lame; rickety.

bandage *m* bandage.

bande *f* band; tape; **~ dessinée** strip cartoon.

bandeau *m* headband; blindfold.

bander *vt* to bandage; to stretch.

banderole *f* banderole, streamer.

bandit *m* bandit.

banlieue f suburbs.

bannière f banner.

bannir vt to banish; to prohibit.

bannissement m banishment.

banque f bank; banking.

banqueroute f bankruptcy.

banquet m banquet.

banquette f seat, stool.

banquier m banker.

banquise f ice field.

baptême m baptism.

baptiser vt to baptise.

bar m bar.

barbare adj barbarian; barbaric.

barbarie f barbarism; barbarity.

barbarisme m (Gram) barbarism.

barbe f beard.

barbelé adj barbed.

barbiturique adj barbituric; * m barbiturate.

barboter vi to bubble; to splash.

barbouillage m scribble; daub.

barbouiller vt to smear; to scrawl.

barbu adj bearded; * m bearded man.

barème m list, schedule.

baril m barrel, cask.

bariolé adj multicoloured, motley.

baromètre m barometer.

baron m, **-ne** f baron.

baroque adj baroque; * m baroque.

barque f small boat.

barrage m barrage, barrier.

barre f bar, rod.

barré adj barred, blocked.

barreau m rung; bar (cage).

barrer vt to bar, block.

barrette f brooch.

barricader vt to barricade; **se ~** vr to barricade oneself.

barrière f barrier; fence.

baryton m baritone.

bas adj low, base; **~sement** adv basely, meanly; * n stocking; sock.

basalte m basalt.

bas-côté m verge; aisle.

bascule f weighing machine, scales.

basculer vi to overbalance.

base f base; basis.

baser vt to base; **se baser sur** vr to depend on, rely on.

bas-fond m (naut) shallow, shoal.

basilic m (bot) basil.

basilique f basilica.

basket m basketball.

basketteur m, **-euse** f basketball player.

bas-relief m bas relief.

basse f (mus) bass; shoal, reef.

basse-cour f poultry-yard.

bassesse f meanness; vulgarity.

bassin m pond, pool; dock.

bassine f bowl.

basson m bassoon.

bastion m bastion.

bas-ventre m belly, guts.

bataille f battle.

batailler vi to battle.

batailleur adj combative, aggressive.

bataillon m (mil) battalion.

bâtard adj bastard, illegitimate.

bateau m boat, ship.

batelier m boatman.

bâtiment m building.

bâtir vt to build.

bâtisse f building; masonry.

bâton m stick, staff.

batracien *m* batrachian.

battant *m* clapper (bell); shutter.

batte *f* bat; beating.

battement *m* banging; beating.

batterie *f* battery.

batteur *m* drummer; batsman.

battre *vt* to beat, defeat.

battu *adj* beaten; frequented.

baudet *m* donkey.

baume *m* balm, balsam.

bauxite *f* bauxite.

bavard *m*, -**e** *f* chatterbox; * *adj* talkative, loquacious.

bavardage *m* chatting; chattering; gossiping.

bavarder *vi* to chat, gossip.

bave *f* dribble, slobber.

baver *vi* to dribble, drool.

bavure *f* smudge, flaw.

bazar *m* bazaar; general store.

B.D. *f* (**bande dessinée**) strip cartoon.

béant *adj* gaping, wide open.

béat *adj* blessed; complacent; ~**ement** *adv* complacently; blissfully.

béatitude *f* beatitude; bliss.

beau, *f* **belle** *adj* beautiful, lovely.

beaucoup *adv* a lot, a great deal; ~ **de monde** a lot of people; ~ **de temps** a great deal of time.

beau-fils *m* son-in-law.

beau-frère *m* brother-in-law.

beau-père *m* father-in-law.

beauté *f* beauty, loveliness.

beaux-arts *m pl* fine art.

beaux-parents *m pl* spouse's parents, in-laws.

bébé *m* baby.

bec *m* beak, bill.

béchamel *f* béchamel (sauce).

bée *adj* open-mouthed, flabbergasted.

bégaiement *m* stammering, faltering.

bégayer *vi* to stammer, stutter.

bégonia *m* begonia.

beige *adj* beige; * *m* beige.

beignet *m* fritter; doughnut.

bêlement *m* bleating.

bêler *vi* to bleat.

Belge *mf* Belgian.

belge *adj* Belgian.

Belgique *f* Belgium.

belle-fille *f* daughter-in-law.

belle-mère *f* mother-in-law.

belle-sœur *f* sister-in-law.

belligérant *m*, -**ante** *f* belligerent; * *adj* belligerent.

belliqueux *adj* aggressive; warlike.

bémol *m* (*mus*) flat.

bénédictin *m*, -**ine** *f* Benedictine.

bénédiction *f* benediction, blessing.

bénéfice *m* profit; benefit.

bénéficiaire *mf* beneficiary.

bénéficier *vi* to benefit; to enjoy.

bénévole *adj* voluntary; unpaid; ~**ment** *adv* voluntarily.

bénin, *f* **bénigne** *adj* benign; minor; harmless.

bénir *vt* to bless.

bénit *adj* consecrated, holy.

benne *f* skip; tipper.

benzène *m* benzene.

béquille *f* crutch; prop.

berceau *m* cradle.

bercement *m* rocking.

bercer *vt* to rock, cradle.

berceuse *f* lullaby; rocking chair.

béret *m* beret.

berge *f* riverbank; barge.

berger *vt* shepherd, **-ère** *f* shepherdess.

bergerie *f* sheepfold.

berner *vt* to fool, hoax.

besogne *f* work; job.

besoin *m* need; want; **avoir ~ de** to need.

bestial *adj* bestial; **~ement** *adv* bestially.

bestialité *f* bestiality; brutishness.

bétail *m* livestock; cattle.

bête *adj* stupid, silly; **~ment** *adv* stupidly, foolishly; * *f* animal.

bêtifier *vt* to play the fool; to prattle stupidly.

bêtise *f* stupidity, foolishness.

béton *m* concrete.

betterave *f* beetroot, beet.

beurre *m* butter.

beurrer *vt* to butter.

bévue *f* blunder.

biais *m* slant, angle; expedient.

biathlon *m* biathlon.

bibelot *m* bibelot, curio.

biberon *m* baby's bottle.

bible *f* bible.

bibliographie *f* bibliography.

bibliothécaire *m/f* librarian.

bibliothèque *f* library; bookcase.

bicarbonate *m* bicarbonate.

bicentenaire *m* bicentenary.

biceps *m* biceps.

biche *f* doe; darling, pet.

bicolore *adj* bi-coloured, two-tone.

bicyclette *f* bicycle.

bidon *m* tin, can; flask.

bidonville *m* shanty town.

bien *adv* well; properly; very; **c'est ~ cela** that's right; * *n* property, estate.

bien-être *m* well-being.

bienfaisant *adj* beneficial, kind.

bienfaiteur *m* benefactor, **-trice** *f* benefactress.

bienheureux *adj* blessed; lucky; happy.

bientôt *adv* soon.

bienveillant *adj* benevolent, kindly.

bienvenu *adj* welcome.

bienvenue *f* welcome.

bière *f* beer; coffin.

bifteck *m* steak.

bifurcation *f* bifurcation, fork.

bifurquer *vi* to fork, branch off.

bigot *adj* bigoted.

bihebdomadaire *adj* twice-weekly.

bijou *m* jewel.

bijouterie *f* jewellery.

bijoutier *m*, **-ière** *f* jeweller.

bilan *m* balance sheet; assessment.

bilatéral *adj* bilateral.

bile *f* bile.

bilingue *adj* bilingual.

billard *m* billiards.

bille *f* marble; billiard ball.

billet *m* ticket; note.

billetterie *f* cash dispenser.

billion *m* billion.

bimensuel *adj* twice monthly.

bimestriel *adj* every two months.

binaire *adj* binary.

biochimie *f* biochemistry.

biochimiste *m/f* biochemist.

biodégradable *adj* biodegradable.

bioéthique *f* bioethics.

biographie f biography.

biologie f biology.

biologique adj biological.

biologiste mf biologist.

biopsie f biopsy.

biosphère f biosphere.

bioxyde m dioxide.

bipède m biped.

bipolaire adj bipolar.

bisannuel adj biennial.

biscornu adj crooked, misshapen; odd, outlandish.

biscuit m cake; biscuit.

bisexuel adj bisexual.

bissextile adj bissextile, leap (year).

bistouri m bistoury.

bitume m bitumen.

bitumer vt to asphalt, tarmac.

bizarre adj bizarre, strange; **~ment** adv strangely, oddly.

bizarrerie f strangeness, singularity.

blafard adj pale, pallid.

blague f joke, trick.

blaguer vi to joke.

blagueur m, **-euse** f joker, wag; * adj jokey, teasing.

blaireau m badger.

blâme m blame, rebuke.

blâmer vt to blame, rebuke.

blanc adj, f **blanche** white; * m white; blank; *mf white person; * f minim.

blancheur f whiteness.

blanchir vi to turn white; to become lighter; * vt to whiten; to lighten.

blanchissage m laundering; refining.

blanchisserie f laundry.

blasé adj blasé.

blason m blazon, coat of arms.

blasphème m blasphemy.

blasphémer vi to blaspheme.

blé m wheat.

blême adj pale, wan.

blêmir vi to turn pale.

blessant adj cutting, hurtful.

blessé adj injured, wounded.

blesser vt to injure, wound.

blessure f injury, wound.

bleu adj blue; * n blue; bruise.

bleuet m cornflower.

bleuir vi to turn blue; * vt to make blue.

bleuté adj bluish.

blindage m armour plating.

blindé adj armoured, reinforced.

bloc m block, group, unit.

blocage m blocking, freezing.

blocus m blockade.

blond adj blond, fair.

blondir vi to turn blond, turn golden; * vt to bleach.

bloquer vt to block, blockade.

blottir (se) vr to curl up, snuggle up.

blouse f blouse; overall.

blouson m windcheater, bomber jacket.

bobine f reel, bobbin.

bocal m jar; bowl.

bœuf m ox, bullock.

bohémien m, **-ienne** f Bohemian; nonconformist.

boire vt to drink; * vi to drink, tipple.

bois m wood.

boisé adj wooded.

boisson f drink.

boîte f box.

boiter vi to limp.

boiteux adj lame.

boîtier m case, body.

boitillant adj somewhat lame.

boitiller vi to hobble slightly.

bol m bowl.

bolet m wild mushroom.

bombardement m bombardment, bombing.

bombarder vt to bombard, bomb.

bombe f bomb.

bombé adj rounded, domed.

bon adj, f **bonne** good; * m slip, coupon, bond.

bonbon m sweet, candy.

bond m leap; bounce.

bonde f stopper, plug.

bondé adj packed.

bondir vi to jump, leap; to bounce.

bonheur m happiness; luck.

bonhomme m, pl **bonshommes** chap, fellow.

bonification f improvement; bonus.

bonifier vt to improve; * **se ~** vr to improve.

bonjour m hello, good morning.

bonnet m bonnet, hat.

bonneterie f hosiery.

bonsoir m good evening.

bonté f goodness, kindness.

bon vivant m bon vivant.

bord m side, edge.

bordé adj edged, bordered.

bordée f broadside, volley.

border vt to edge, border.

bordereau m note; invoice.

bordure f frame, border.

borgne adj one-eyed.

borne f boundary; milestone.

borné adj narrow-minded.

borner vt to restrict, limit.

bosse f hump, knob.

bosseler vt to dent, emboss.

bossu m, **-ue** f hunchback; * adj hunchbacked.

botanique f botany; * adj botanical.

botaniste f botanist.

botte f boot.

bottine f ankle boot, bootee.

bouche f mouth.

bouché adj cloudy, overcast.

bouchée f mouthful.

bouche-à-bouche m kiss of life.

boucher vt to butcher; * **se ~** vr to become cloudy; m, **-ère** f butcher.

boucherie f butcher's (shop); butchery.

bouchon m cork.

boucle f curl; buckle.

boucler vt to buckle; to surround.

bouclier m shield.

bouddhisme m Buddhism.

boudeur adj sullen, sulky.

boudin m pudding.

boue f mud.

bouée f buoy.

boueur m dustman.

bouffée f whiff, puff.

bouffi adj swollen, puffed up.

bouffon m buffoon, clown.

bougeoir m candlestick.

bouger vi to move; * vt to move, shift.

bougie f candle.

bouillant adj boiling.

bouillir vi to boil.

bouilloire f kettle.

bouillon m broth, soup.

bouillonner vi to bubble; foam.

bouillotte f hot-water bottle.

boulanger m, **-ère** f baker.

boulangerie f bakery.

boule f ball, bowl.

boulet m cannonball; millstone.

boulevard m boulevard.

bouleversant adj upsetting, confusing.

bouleversement m confusion, disruption.

bouleverser vt to confuse, disrupt.

boulimie f bulimia.

boulimique adj bulimic.

boulon m bolt.

bouquet m bouquet, posy.

bouquin m fam book.

bouquiniste mf second-hand bookseller.

bourbeux adj muddy.

bourbier m quagmire.

bourdon m bumblebee.

bourdonnement m buzz, buzzing.

bourdonner vi to buzz, hum.

bourg m market-town.

bourgeois m, **-e** f bourgeois, middle-class person; * adj bourgeois, middle-class.

bourgeoisie f bourgeoisie, middle classes.

bourgeon m bud.

bourgeonner vi to bud.

bourrasque f squall, gust.

bourreau m torturer, executioner.

bourrelet m pad, cushion.

bourrer vt to stuff, cram.

bourse f purse; stock exchange.

boursier m, **-ière** f broker; speculator.

boursouflé adj bloated, swollen.

bousculade f hustle, scramble.

bousculer vt to jostle, hustle.

boussole f compass.

bout m end; piece, scrap.

boutade f whim, caprice; jest.

bouteille f bottle.

boutique f shop, store.

bouton m button.

boutonner vt to button.

boutonnière f buttonhole.

bouture f cutting.

bovin adj bovine.

boxe f boxing.

boxer vi to box.

boxeur m boxer.

boyau m guts, insides.

boycottage m boycotting.

boycotter vt to boycott.

bracelet m bracelet.

braconnier m poacher.

brader vt to sell at a discount.

braderie f discount sale.

braguette f fly (trousers).

braise f embers.

brancard m shaft, pole.

branche f branch.

branchement m branching; connection.

brancher vt to connect, link.

branchies fpl gills.

brandir vt to flourish, brandish.

branlant adj loose; shaky.

bras m arm.

brasier m brazier, furnace.

brasse f breaststroke.

brassée f armful.

brasser vt to brew; to mix.

brasserie f bar; brewery.

bravade f bravado.

brave adj brave, courageous; **~ment** adv bravely, courageously.

braver vt to brave, defy.

bravoure f bravery, courage.

brebis f ewe.

brèche f breach, gap.

bredouillant adj stammering, mumbling.

bredouille adj empty-handed.

bredouiller vi to stammer, mumble.

bref adj, f **brève** brief, concise; **en ~** adv in short.

bretelle f strap, sling.

brevet m licence, patent.

breveté adj patented.

bribe f bit, scrap.

bric-à-brac m bric-a-brac.

bricolage m DIY, odd jobs.

bricole f small job.

bricoler vi to do odd jobs.

bricoleur m handyman, **-euse** f handywoman.

bride f bridle.

bridé adj restrained, restricted.

brider vt to restrain, restrict.

brièvement adv briefly, concisely.

brièveté f brevity.

brigade f brigade.

brigadier m corporal, sergeant.

brillamment adv brilliantly.

brillant adj brilliant, shining.

briller vi to shine.

brin m stalk, strand.

brindille f twig.

brique f brick, slab.

briquet m lighter.

brise f breeze.

briser vt to smash, shatter.

brocante f second-hand dealing.

brocanteur m, **-euse** f second-hand dealer.

broche f brooch.

brochure f brochure, pamphlet.

broder vt to embroider, vi to embellish, elaborate.

broderie f embroidery.

bronche f bronchus.

bronchite f bronchitis.

bronzage m tan.

bronze m bronze.

bronzer vi to get a tan.

brosse f brush.

brosser vt to brush.

brouette f wheelbarrow.

brouillard m fog, mist.

brouiller vt to embroil, confuse.

brouillon m rough copy, draft; * adj untidy.

broussaille f brushwood, undergrowth.

broussailleux adj bushy, overgrown.

brousse f undergrowth, bush.

brouter vt, vi to graze.

broyer vt to grind, pulverize.

broyeur adj crushing, grinding.

bruine f drizzle.

bruissement m rustle.

bruit m noise, sound.

bruitage m sound-effects.

brûlant adj burning, scorching.

brûler vt, vi to burn.

brûlure f burn.

brume f haze, mist.

brumeux adj hazy, misty.

brun m dark-haired man, **brune** f brunette; * adj brown.

brusque *adj* brusque, abrupt;
 ~ment *adv* brusquely, abruptly.
brusquer *vt* to offend; to hasten.
brut *adj* crude, raw.
brutal *adj* brutal, rough; **~ement**
 adv brutally, roughly.
brutaliser *vt* to brutalize; to bully.
brutalité *f* brutality.
brute *f* brute; animal.
bruyamment *adv* noisily.
bruyant *adj* noisy.
bruyère *f* heather.
bûche *f* log.
bûcheron *m*, **-onne** *f* woodcutter,
 lumberjack.
budget *m* budget.
budgétaire *adj* budgetary.
buée *f* condensation; steam.
buffet *m* sideboard, buffet.
buisson *m* bush.

bulbe *m* bulb.
bulle *f* bubble; blister.
bulletin *m* bulletin.
buraliste *mf* tobacconist.
bureau *m* office; desk.
bureaucrate *mf* bureaucrat.
bureaucratie *f* bureaucracy.
bureaucratique *adj* bureaucratic.
burin *m* graver, chisel.
bus *m* bus.
buste *m* bust, chest.
but *m* objective, goal.
butane *m* butane.
buté *adj* stubborn.
butin *m* booty, loot.
butte *f* knoll, mound.
buvable *adj* drinkable.
buvard *m* blotting paper.
buvette *f* refreshment-room.
buveur *m*, **-euse** *f* drinker.

C

ça *pron* that; it; **~ va**? How goes it?; **~ y
 est** that's it; **qui ~** who? (do you
 mean?); **comment ~** how? (do you
 mean?); **~ alors!** you don't say!
cabale *f* cabal, intrigue.
cabane *f* cabin, shed.
cabanon *m* cottage; chalet.
cabaret *m* cabaret; tavern.
cabine *f* cabin, cab; cockpit.
cabinet *m* surgery; office, study.
câble *m* cable.
câbler *vt* to cable.
cabosser *vt* to dent.
cabotage *m* coastal navigation.
cabriolet *m* convertible.
cacahouète *f* peanut.
cacao *m* cocoa.

cache *m* cache; mask; hiding
 place.
caché *adj* hidden, secluded.
cache-col *m invar* scarf.
cache-nez *m invar* scarf.
cacher *vt* to hide, conceal; **se ~** *vr*
 to hide oneself.
cacheter *vt* to seal.
cachette *f* hideout, hiding place.
cachot *m* dungeon.
cachottier, -ière *adj* mysterious,
 secretive.
cactus *m* cactus.
cadavre *m* corpse.
cadeau *m* present.
cadenas *m* padlock.
cadenasser *vt* to padlock.

cadence f rhythm, time, cadence.

cadet m, **-ette** f youngest child.

cadrage m centring.

cadran m dial, face.

cadre m frame; context; scope.

cadrer vt to centre; to set the parameters of.

caduc adj, f **caduque** null and void; obsolete.

cafard m hypocrite; cockroach.

café m coffee.

cafétéria f cafeteria.

cafetière f coffeepot.

cage f cage.

cageot m crate.

cagoule f cowl; balaclava.

cahier m notebook.

cahot m jerk, jolt.

caillot m clot.

caillou m stone; pebble.

caisse f box; till; fund.

caissier m, **-ière** f cashier.

cajoler vt to cajole, coax; to pet.

cajou m cashew.

calamité f calamity.

calcaire m calcareous, chalky.

calcination f calcination.

calciner vt to calcine; to scorch.

calcium m calcium.

calcul m sum, calculation.

calculateur adj, f **-trice** calculating.

calculatrice, calculette f calculator.

calculer vt to calculate, reckon; vi to budget carefully.

cale f hold; dock.

caleçon m shorts, pants.

calembour m pun.

calendrier m calendar.

calepin m notebook.

caler vi to stall; to give up.

calfeutrer vt to make airtight, draughtproof.

calibre m calibre, bore.

calibrer vt to calibrate.

calice m chalice.

câlin m cuddle; * adj cuddly.

câliner vt to cuddle.

calligraphie f calligraphy.

callosité f callosity.

calmant m tranquillizer, sedative; * adj tranquillizing.

calmar m squid.

calme m calm, stillness; * adj calm, still; **~ment** adv calmly, quietly.

calmer vt to calm, soothe, pacify.

calomnie f calumny, slander.

calomnier vt to slander; to libel.

calomnieux adj calumnious, slanderous.

calorie f calorie.

calorifique adj calorific.

calque m tracing; copy.

calquer vt to trace; to copy.

calvaire m calvary, crucifix.

calvitie f baldness.

camarade m companion, friend.

camaraderie f camaraderie, friendship.

cambouis m grease.

cambré adj arched.

cambriolage m burglary.

cambrioler vt to burgle.

cambrioleur m, **-euse** f burglar.

caméléon m chameleon.

camélia m camelia.

caméra f camera.

camion m lorry.

camionneur *m* lorry driver, trucker.

camomille *f* camomile.

camouflage *m* camouflage.

camoufler *vt* to camouflage.

camp *m* camp.

campagnard *m* countryman, **-e** *f* countrywoman; * *adj* country, rustic.

campagne *f* country, countryside.

campement *m* camp, encampment.

camper *vi* to camp.

campeur *m*, **-euse** *f* camper.

canal *m* canal, channel.

canalisation *f* canalization; mains.

canaliser *vt* to channel; to funnel.

canapé *m* sofa, settee.

canard *m* duck.

cancer *m* cancer.

cancéreux *adj* cancerous.

candeur *f* candour; naïvety.

candidat *m*, **-e** *f* candidate.

candidature *f* candidature, candidacy.

candide *adj* frank, ingenuous; **~ment** *adv* openly, ingenuously.

canevas *m* canvas; framework.

canicule *m* heatwave.

canif *m* penknife.

canine *f* eye tooth.

caniveau *m* gutter.

canne *f* cane, rod.

cannelle *f* cinnamon.

canoë *m* canoe.

canon *m* cannon, gun.

canot *m* boat, dinghy.

cantate *f* cantata.

cantatrice *f* singer.

cantine *f* canteen.

cantique *m* canticle, hymn.

canton *m* canton.

cantonner(se) *vr* to take up position in.

caoutchouc *m* rubber.

cap *f* cape; course.

capable *adj* capable, competent.

capacité *f* capacity.

cape *f* cloak.

capillaire *adj* capillary.

capitaine *m* captain.

capital *adj* capital, cardinal, major; * *m* capital, stock.

capitale *f* capital (letter, city).

capitalisme *m* capitalism.

capitaliste *mf* capitalist.

capiteux *adj* heady, strong.

capitonner *vt* to pad.

capitulation *f* capitulation.

capituler *vt* to capitulate.

caporal *m* corporal.

capot *m* bonnet, hood.

capote *f* greatcoat, hood.

capoter *vt* to capsize, overturn.

câpre *m* caper.

caprice *m* caprice, whim.

capricieusement *adv* capriciously.

capricieux *adj* capricious.

capricorne *m* capricorn.

capsule *f* capsule.

capter *vt* to win; to pick up; to tap.

capteur *m* captor; pick-up.

captif *m*, **-ive** *f* captive; * *adj* captive.

captivant *adj* enthralling, captivating.

captiver *vt* to captivate, enthrall.

captivité *f* captivity.

capture *f* capture.

capturer *vt* to capture.

capuche *f* hood.

car conj for; because; * m bus; van.

carabine f carbine, rifle.

caractère m character, disposition.

caractérisé adj marked, blatant.

caractériser vt to characterize.

caractérisque f characteristic, feature; * adj characteristic.

carafe f carafe.

carambolage m affray; pile-up (car).

caramel m caramel.

caraméliser vt to caramelize.

carapace f carapace, shell.

carat m carat.

caravane f caravan.

caravelle f caravel.

carbonate m carbonate.

carbone m carbon.

carbonique adj carbonic.

carboniser vt to carbonize.

carburant m motor fuel.

carburateur m carburettor.

carburation f carburation.

carbure m carbide.

carcasse f carcass.

carcéral adj prison.

cardiaque adj cardiac.

cardigan m cardigan.

cardinal m cardinal; * adj cardinal.

cardiologie f cardiology.

cardiologue m cardiologist.

cardio-vasculaire adj cardiovascular.

carême m fast, fasting.

carence f deficiency; insolvency.

caressant adj affectionate.

caresse f caress.

caresser vt to caress, fondle.

cargaison f cargo, freight.

cargo m cargo boat.

caricatural adj caricatural; grotesque.

caricature f caricature.

caricaturer vt to caricature.

caricaturiste m caricaturist.

carie f caries.

carié adj decayed.

carillon m carillon, chime, peal.

caritatif adj charitable.

carnage m carnage.

carnassier m carnivore, **-ière** f gamebag; adj carnivorous.

carnaval m carnival.

carnet m notebook; logbook.

carnivore mf carnivore; adj carnivorous.

carotide f carotid.

carotte f carrot.

carpe f carp.

carpette f rug, doormat.

carré m square; * adj square; straightforward.

carreau m tile; pane.

carrefour m crossroads.

carrelage m tiling.

carrément adv bluntly, directly.

carrière f career.

carrosse m coach.

carrosserie f bodywork, coachwork.

carrossier m coachbuilder.

carrure f build, stature.

cartable m satchel.

carte f card; map.

cartel m cartel.

cartésien adj Cartesian.

cartilage m cartilage.

cartilagineux adj cartilaginous.

cartomancien m, **-ienne** f fortuneteller.

carton m cardboard.

cartonner vt to bind (book).

cartouche f cartridge.

cas m case; circumstance.

casanier m, **-ière** f homebody.

cascade f waterfall.

cascadeur m, **-euse** f acrobat, stuntman.

case f square; box.

caser vt (Fam) to set up (job, marriage).

caserne f barracks.

casier m compartment; filing cabinet.

casino m casino.

casque m helmet.

casquette f peaked cap.

cassant adj brittle.

casse-croûte m invar snack.

casser vt to break; **se ~** vr to break.

casserole f saucepan.

casse-tête m invar puzzle, conundrum.

cassette f cassette; cash-box.

cassis m blackcurrant.

cassure f break, crack.

caste f caste.

castor m beaver.

castration f castration.

castrer vt to castrate.

cataclysme m cataclysm.

catacombe f catacomb.

catalogue m catalogue.

cataloguer vt to catalogue.

catalyseur m catalyst.

catalytique adj catalytic.

cataplasme m cataplasm.

catapulte f catapult.

cataracte f cataract.

catastrophe f catastrophe.

catastrophique adj catastrophic.

catéchisme m catechism.

catégorie f category.

catégorique adj categorical; **~ment** adv categorically.

cathédrale f cathedral.

cathode f cathode.

cathodique adj cathodic.

catholicisme m Catholicism.

catholique adj Catholic.

cauchemar m nightmare.

cause f cause, reason.

causer vt to cause; to chat; * vi to talk, chat.

caustique adj caustic.

caution f security, guarantee.

cautionner vt to guarantee.

cavalerie f cavalry.

cavalier m, **-ière** f rider.

cave f cellar.

caveau m tomb; small cellar.

caverne f cave, cavern.

caverneux adj cavernous.

caviar m caviar.

cavité f cavity.

ce adj **cet** (before vowel and mute h), f **cette**, pl **ces** this; these; that; those; **cet homme-là** that man; * pron; **c'est le facteur** it's the postman; **~ sont mes lunettes** these are my glasses; **~ que tu veux** what you want; **c'est ~ dont je vous parle** that's what I am speaking to you about.

ceci pron this.

cécité f blindness.

céder vi to give in; * vt to give up; to transfer.

ceindre vt to put round; to encircle.

ceinture f belt, girdle.

ceinturer vt to surround.

ceinturon m belt.

cela *pron* that; *emphasis* **qui ~?** who? (do you mean)?; **comment ~?** how? (do you mean?).

célébration *f* celebration.

célèbre *adj* famous.

célébrer *vt* to celebrate.

célébrité *f* fame, celebrity.

célérité *f* celerity, speed.

céleste *adj* celestial.

célibat *m* celibacy.

célibataire *mf* single person; * *adj* single, unmarried.

cellulaire *adj* cellular.

cellule *f* cell, unit.

cellulite *f* cellulite.

celluloïde *m* celluloid.

cellulose *f* cellulose.

celui *pron*, *f* **celle** this one, *pl* **ceux** these ones.

cendre *f* ash.

cendrier *m* ashtray.

censé *adj* supposed; deemed.

censure *f* censorship.

censurer *vt* to censor.

cent *adj* a hundred; **tu as ~ fois raison** you are absolutely right; **faire les ~ pas** to walk up and down; * *m* a hundred; **~ pour ~** per cent.

centaine *f* around a hundred, a hundred or so.

centenaire *m* centenarian; * *adj* a hundred years old.

centésimal *adj* centesimal.

centième *mf* hundredth; * *adj* hundredth.

centigrade *m* centigrade.

centigramme *m* centigramme.

centime *m* centime.

centimètre *m* centimetre.

central *adj* central.

centraliser *vt* to centralize.

centre *m* centre.

centrer *vt* to centre; to focus.

centrifuge *adj* centrifugal.

centuple *adj* centuple, hundred-fold; * *mf* centuple.

cependant *conj* however.

céramique *f* ceramic.

cerceau *m* hoop.

cercle *m* circle, ring.

cercueil *m* coffin.

céréale *f* cereal.

cérébral *adj* cerebral.

cérémonial *adj* ceremonial.

cérémonie *f* ceremony.

cérémonieux *adj* ceremonious.

cerf-volant *m* kite.

cerise *f* cherry.

cerisier *m* cherry tree.

cerne *f* ring.

cerner *vt* to circle, encompass.

certain *adj* certain, sure; **~ment** *adv* certainly, most probably; **~s** *pron* some, certain.

certificat *m* certificate.

certifier *vt* to certify; to guarantee.

certitude *f* certainty, certitude.

cerveau *m* brain.

cervelle *f* brain.

cervical *adj* cervical.

césarienne *f* Caesarean.

cesser *f* to cease, stop.

cessez-le-feu *m* cease-fire.

cet *adj*, *f* **cette** *see* **ce**.

cétacé *m* cetacean.

ceux *see* **ce**.

chacun *pron* each one; **~e d'entre elles** each of them; **~ son tour** each in turn.

chagrin *m* sorrow, chagrin.

chahut *m* row, uproar.

chahuter *vi* to make a row.

chaîne *f* chain.

chaînon *m* link.

chair *f* flesh.

chaise *f* chair.

châle *m* shawl.

châlet *m* chalet.

chaleur *f* heat.

chaleureusement *adv* warmly.

chaleureux *adj* warm, cordial.

chalumeau *m* blowlamp.

chalutier *m* trawler.

chambre *f* room.

chameau *m* camel.

champ *m* field.

champêtre *adj* rural, country.

champignon *m* mushroom.

champion *m*, **-onne** *f* champion.

championnat *m* championship.

chance *f* luck.

chancelant *adj* staggering, tottering.

chanceler *vi* to stagger; to totter.

chancelier *m* chancellor.

chanceux *adj* lucky, fortunate.

chandail *m* sweater.

chandeleur *f* Candlemas.

chandelier *m* candlestick.

chandelle *f* candle.

changeant *adj* changeable, variable.

changement *m* change, changing.

changer *vi* to change; * *vt* to change.

chanson *f* song.

chant *m* song; singing.

chantage *m* blackmail.

chanter *vi, vt* to sing.

chanteur *m*, **-euse** *f* singer.

chantier *m* building site.

chantonner *vi, vt* to hum.

chanvre *m* hemp.

chaos *m* chaos.

chaotique *adj* chaotic.

chapeau *m* hat.

chapelet *m* rosary; string.

chapelle *f* chapel.

chapiteau *m* capital (column).

chapitre *m* chapter.

chaque *adj* each.

char *m* (*mil*) tank; chariot.

charabia *m* gibberish.

charbon *m* coal.

charcuterie *f* pork-meat trade.

charcutier *m*, **-ière** *f* pork butcher.

chardon *m* thistle.

charge *f* load; responsibility.

chargé *adj* loaded.

chargement *m* loading; freight.

charger *vt* to load; **se ~ de** to take responsibility for; to attend to.

chariot *m* waggon; freight car.

charisme *m* charisma.

charitable *adj* charitable, kind; **~ment** *adv* charitably.

charité *f* charity.

charlatan *m* charlatan.

charmant *adj* charming, delightful.

charme *m* charm.

charmer *vt* to charm, beguile.

charmeur *m*, **-euse** *f* charmer; * *adj* winning, enchanting.

charnel *adj* carnal.

charnière *f* hinge, pivot.

charnu *adj* fleshy.

charogne *f* carrion.

charpente *f* structure, framework.

charpentier m carpenter.

charrette f cart.

charrier vt to cart; to carry.

charrue f plough.

chartre f prison.

chasse f hunting; chase.

chasse-neige m invar snowplough.

chasser vt to hunt; to chase.

chasseur m, **-euse** f hunter.

châssis m chassis.

chaste adj chaste; **~ment** adv chastely.

chasteté f chastity.

chat m, **chatte** f cat.

châtaigne f chestnut.

châtain adj chestnut brown.

château m castle, château.

châtiment m chastisement, punishment.

chaton m kitten.

chatouiller vt to tickle.

chatoyant adj glistening.

châtrer vt to castrate.

chaud adj warm, hot; **~ement** adv warmly, hotly.

chaudière f boiler.

chaudron m cauldron.

chauffage m heating.

chauffard m road-hog.

chauffe-eau m invar water-heater.

chauffer vi to heat; * vt to heat up.

chauffeur m driver.

chaumière f cottage.

chaussée f road, street.

chausse-pied m shoehorn.

chaussette f sock.

chausson m slipper.

chaussure f shoe.

chauve adj bald.

chauve-souris f bat.

chauvin adj, f **chauvine** chauvinistic.

chauvinisme m chauvinism.

chaux f lime.

chavirer vi to capsize, overturn.

chef m head, boss; chef.

chef-d'œuvre m masterpiece.

chemin m way, road; **~ de fer** railway.

cheminée f chimney.

cheminement m progress; course.

chemise f shirt.

chemisier m shirtmaker.

chêne m oak.

chenil m kennel.

chenille f caterpillar.

chèque m cheque.

chéquier m chequebook.

cher adj, f **chère** dear, expensive.

chercher vt to look for.

chercheur m, **-euse** f researcher; seeker.

chéri m, **-ie** f darling, dearest; * adj beloved, cherished.

chétif adj puny, paltry.

cheval m horse.

chevalet m easel.

chevalier m knight.

chevelu adj long-haired.

chevelure f hair, head of hair.

chevet m chevet; pillow.

cheveu m hair.

cheville f ankle.

chèvre f goat.

chèvrefeuille m honeysuckle.

chevreuil m roe deer.

chez prép at home: **je rentre ~ moi** I'm going home; **~ ta tante** at my aunt's.

chic *m* style, stylishness; **avoir le ~ pour** to have the knack for.

chicorée *f* chicory.

chien *m*, **chienne** *f* dog.

chiffon *m* rag, cloth.

chiffonné *adj* crumpled, rumpled.

chiffre *m* figure.

chignon *m* chignon, bun.

chimère *f* chimera.

chimérique *adj* chimerical, fanciful.

chimie *f* chemistry.

chimique *adj* chemical; **~ment** *adv* chemically.

chimiste *mf* chemist.

chimpanzé *m* chimpanzee.

chiot *m* puppy.

chipoteur *m*, **-euse** *f* haggler.

chirurgical *adj* surgical.

chirurgie *f* surgery.

chirurgien *m* surgeon.

chlore *m* chlorine.

chloroforme *m* chloroform.

chlorophyle *f* chlorophyll.

chlorure *m* chloride.

choc *m* shock, crash.

chocolat *m* chocolate.

chœur *m* choir, chorus.

choir *vi* to fall.

choisir *vt* to choose.

choix *m* choice.

choléra *m* cholera.

chômage *m* unemployment.

chômeur *m*, **-euse** *f* unemployed person.

choquant *adj* shocking, appalling.

choquer *vt* to shock.

chorale *f* choral.

chorégraphe *mf* choreographer.

choréraphie *f* choreography.

choriste *mf* chorister.

chose *f* thing, matter, object.

chou *m* cabbage.

chouette *f* owl.

chou-fleur *m* cauliflower.

choyer *vt* to cherish.

chrétien *m*, **-ienne** *f* Christian, *adj* christian.

christianisme *m* Christianity.

chrome *m* chromium.

chromosome *m* chromosome.

chronique *adj* chronic; * *f* chronicle, column, page.

chroniqueur *m* chronicler; columnist

chronologie *f* chronology.

chronologique *adj* chronological; **~ment** *adv* chronologically.

chronomètre *m* chronometer.

chronométrer *vt* to time.

chrysanthème *m* chrysanthemum.

chuchotement *m* whisper, rustling.

chuchoter *vi* to whisper.

chuintement *m* hissing.

chuinter *vi* to hiss.

chute *f* fall, drop.

chuter *vi* to fall.

ci *adv*: **ces fleurs-ci** these flowers; **ci-joint** enclosed; **ci-dessous** below; **ci-contre** opposite; in the margin; annexed.

cible *f* target.

cibler *vt* to target.

cicatrice *f* scar.

cicatrisation *f* cicatrization, healing.

cicatriser *vt* to heal; **se ~** *vr* to heal; to form a scar.

cidre *m* cider.

ciel *m*, *pl* **cieux, ciels** sky.

cierge *m* candle.

cigale f cicada.

cigare m cigar.

cigarette f cigarette.

cil m eyelash.

ciller vi to blink.

cime f summit.

ciment m cement.

cimenter vt to cement.

cimetière m cemetery.

cinéaste mf film-maker.

cinéma m cinema.

cinémathèque f film library.

cinématographique adj film, cinema.

cinéphile mf film enthusiast.

cinétique adj kinetic.

cinglant adj bitter, lashing, cutting.

cingler vt to lash; to sting.

cinq m five.

cinquantaine f about fifty.

cinquante m fifty.

cinquantenaire m fiftieth anniversary.

cinquantième mf fiftieth, adj fiftieth.

cinquième mf fifth, adj fifth; * ~ment adv in fifth place.

cintre m arch.

cirage m polish.

circonférence f circumference.

circonscription f division, constituency.

circonspect adj circumspect.

circonstance f circumstance.

circuit m circuit, tour.

circulaire adj circular; ~ment adv circularly.

circulation f circulation; traffic.

circuler vi to circulate; to move.

cire f wax.

cirer vt to polish.

cirque m circus.

ciseau m chisel; scissor(s).

citadelle f citadel.

citadin m, **-e** f city dweller; * adj town, urban.

citation f citation, summons.

cité f city.

citer vt to quote, cite.

citerne f water tank.

citoyen m, **-enne** f citizen.

citron m lemon.

citrouille f pumpkin.

civière f stretcher.

civil adj civil; ~ement adv civilly.

civilisation f civilization.

civilisé adj civilized.

civiliser vt to civilize.

civique adj civic.

clair adj clear, bright; ~ement adv clearly.

clairière f clearing, glade.

claisemé adj scattered.

clairvoyance f perspicacity; clairvoyance.

clairvoyant adj perceptive; clairvoyant.

clameur f clamour.

clan m clan.

clandestin adj clandestine; ~ement clandestinely.

clandestinité f secrecy.

clapoter vi to lap (water).

clapotis m lapping.

claque f slap, smack.

claquement m clapping, slamming.

claquer vi to bang; to slam.

clarifier vt to clarify; **se ~** vr to become clear.

clarinette f clarinet.

clarté *f* light, brightness.

classe *f* class, standing.

classement *m* filing; grading.

classer *vt* to file; to classify.

classeur *m* filing cabinet.

classification *f* classification.

classique *adj* classical, standard; **~ment** *adv* classically.

clause *f* clause.

claustrer *vt* to confine.

claustrophobie *f* claustrophobia.

clavecin *m* harpsichord.

clavicule *f* collarbone.

clavier *m* keyboard.

clé, clef *f* key.

clémence *f* clemency, mildness.

clergé *m* clergy.

cliché *m* cliché; negative.

client *m*, **-e** *f* client.

clientèle *f* clientèle.

cligner *vi* to blink.

clignotant *adj* blinking, flickering; ***** *m* indicator.

clignotement *m* blinking, flickering.

clignoter *vi* to blink; to flicker.

climat *m* climate.

climatique *adj* climatic.

climatisation *f* air conditioning.

climatiser *vt* to air-condition.

clin d'œil *m* wink.

clinique *f* clinic.

cliqueter *vi* to jingle; to clink.

clitoris *m* clitoris.

clochard *m*, **-e** *f* down-and-out.

cloche *f* bell.

clocher *m* steeple.

clochette *f* hand-bell.

cloison *f* partition.

cloîtrer(se) *vr* to enter the monastic life.

clore *vt* to close, conclude.

clos *adj* closed, enclosed.

clôture *f* fence, hedge.

clou *m* nail.

clouer *vt* to nail.

club *m* club.

coagulation *f* coagulation.

coaguler *vi* to coagulate.

coaliser *vt, vi* to form a coalition.

coalition *f* coalition.

cobalt *m* cobalt.

cobaye *m* guinea-pig.

cobra *m* cobra.

cocaïne *f* cocaine.

coccinelle *f* ladybird.

coccyx *m* coccyx.

cocher *vt* to notch; to tick off.

cochon *m*, **-onne** *f* pig.

code *m* code.

coder *vt* to code.

codifier *vt* to codify.

coefficient *m* coefficient.

coéquipier *m*, **-ière** *f* team mate.

cœur *m* heart.

coexister *vi* to coexist.

coffre *m* chest; **~-fort** safe.

coffret *m* casket.

cogner *vt* to hammer; to bang.

cohabitation *f* cohabitation.

cohabiter *vi* to cohabit.

cohérence *f* coherence.

cohérent *adj* coherent.

cohésion *f* cohesion.

cohue *f* crowd.

coiffer *vt* to arrange s.o.'s hair; **se ~** *vr* to do one's hair.

coiffeur *m*, **-euse** *f* hairdresser.

coiffure *f* hairstyle.

coin *m* corner.

coincer *vt* to wedge; to jam.

coïncidence f coincidence.

coït m coitus.

col m neck.

colère f anger.

colérique adj quick-tempered, irascible.

colibri m hummingbird.

colique f diarrhoea.

colis m parcel.

collaborateur m, **-trice** f collaborator, colleague.

collaboration f collaboration.

collaborer vi to collaborate.

collant adj clinging, sticky; * m leotard.

collecte f collection.

collectif adj collective.

collection f collection.

collectionner vt to collect.

collectionneur m, **-euse** f collector.

collectivement adv collectively.

collectivité f community; collective ownership.

collège m college, school.

collègue mf colleague.

coller vt to stick; to glue; * vi to stick, be sticky.

collier m necklace.

colline f hill.

collision f collision.

colloque m colloquium.

collocataire mf co-tenant.

colombe f dove.

colon m colonist.

colonel m colonel.

colonie f colony.

colonisation f colonization.

coloniser vt to colonize.

colonne f column.

colorant m colouring.

coloration f colouring, staining.

coloré adj coloured.

colorier vt to colour in.

coloris m colouring, shade.

colossal adj colossal.

colporter vt to peddle.

colza m rape seed.

coma m coma.

comateux adj comatose.

combat m combat, fight.

combatif adj combative.

combativité f combativeness.

combattant adj fighting, combatant.

combattre vt to fight; to combat; * vi to fight.

combien adv how much, how many; ~ de temps how much time; ~ sontils? how many are they.

combinaison f combination.

combiner vt to combine.

comble m height, peak.

combler vt to fill; to fulfil.

combustible m fuel.

combustion f combustion.

comédie f comedy.

comédien m; **-ienne** f actor.

comestible adj edible.

comète f comet.

comique adj comic; ~ment adv comically.

comité m committee.

commandant m commander.

commande f command, order.

commandement m command, commandment.

commander vt, vi to order, command.

commanditer vt to finance, sponsor.

commando m commando.

comme *conj* as, like; ~ **ci** ~ **ça** so-so; ~ **il faut** properly; *adv* how.

commémoration *f* commemoration.

commémorer *vt* to commemorate.

commencement *m* beginning, start.

commencer *vt* to begin; **vi* to begin; to start.

comment *adv* how; ~ **dire?** how shall we say?; ~ **cela?** what do you mean?

commentaire *m* comment; commentary.

commentateur *m*, **-trice** *f* commentator.

commenter *vt* to comment.

commérage *m* piece of gossip.

commerçant *m*, **-e** *f* merchant, trader.

commerce *m* business, commerce.

commercial *adj* commercial; ~**ement** *adv* commercially.

commercialiser *vt* to market.

commère *f* gossip.

commettre *vt* to commit.

commissaire *m* representative; commissioner.

commissariat *m* commissionership; commissariat.

commission *f* commission, committee.

commissionnaire *m* messenger; agent.

commode *adj* convenient, comfortable.

commodité *f* convenience.

commun *adj* common, joint; ~**ément** *adv* commonly.

communal *adj* council; common, communal.

communautaire *adj* community.

communauté *f* community; joint estate.

commune *f* town, district.

communication *f* communication.

communier *vi* to receive communion.

communion *f* communion.

communiqué *m* communiqué.

communiquer *vt* to communicate; to transmit; ** vi* to communicate.

communisme *m* communism.

communiste *mf* communist.

compact *adj* compact, dense.

compagne *f* companion.

compagnie *f* company.

compagnon *m* companion.

comparable *adj* comparable.

comparaison *f* comparison.

comparaître *vi* to appear.

comparativement *adv* comparatively.

comparer *vt* to compare.

compartiment *m* compartment.

compartimenter *vt* to compart, partition.

compas *m* compass.

compassion *f* compassion.

compatibilité *f* compatibility.

compatible *adj* compatible.

compatir *vi* to sympathize.

compatissant *adj* compassionate.

compatriote *mf* compatriot.

compensation *f* compensation.

compenser *vt* to compensate; to offset; **se** ~ *vr* to balance each other, to make up for.

compétence *f* competence.

compétent *adj* competent, capable.

compétitif *adj* competitive.

compétition f competition.

compétitivité f competitiveness.

complaisance f kindness; complacency.

complaisant adj kind; complacent.

complément m complement; extension.

complémentaire adj complementary, supplementary.

complet adj complete, full.

complètement adv completely, fully.

compléter vt to complete; **se ~** vr to complement one another.

complexe adj complex, complicated.

complexé adj mixed-up.

complication f complication.

complice mf accomplice.

complicité f complicity, collusion.

compliment m compliment.

complimenter vt to compliment; to congratulate.

compliqué adj complicated, intricate.

compliquer vt to complicate.

complot m plot.

comportement m behaviour; performance.

comporter vt to consist of, comprise; **se ~** vr to behave.

composant m component, constituent.

composante f component.

composer vt to compose, make up; **se ~** vr; **se ~ de** to be made up of.

compositeur m, **-trice** f composer; typesetter.

composition f composition, formation.

compréhensible adj comprehensible.

compréhensif adj comprehensive, understanding.

compréhension f comprehension, understanding.

comprendre vt to understand; to consist of.

compresse f compress.

compresseur m compressor.

compression f compression; reduction.

comprimé adj compressed; restrained; * m tablet.

comprimer vt to compress; to restrain.

compromettant adj compromising.

compromettre vt to compromise.

compromis m compromise.

comptabilité f accountancy.

comptable adj accounting; * mf accountant.

compte m account.

compter vt, vi to count.

compteur m meter.

comptoir m counter, bar.

comte m count, **comtesse** f countess.

concave adj concave.

concéder vt to grant, concede.

concentration f concentration.

concentré adj concentrated; reserved.

concentrer vt to concentrate; **se ~** vr to concentrate.

concept m concept.

conception f conception, design.

concerner vt to concern, regard.

concert *m* concert.

concertation *f* dialogue, consultation.

concession *f* concession; privilege.

concessionnaire *mf* concessionaire, grantee.

concevoir *vt* to imagine; to conceive.

concierge *mf* caretaker, concierge.

conciliant *adj* conciliatory.

conciliation *f* conciliation; reconciliation.

concilier *vt* to reconcile; to attract.

concis *adj* concise.

concision *f* conciseness, brevity.

concluant *adj* conclusive, decisive.

conclure *vt* to conclude; to decide; **se ~** *vr* to conclude, come to an end.

conclusion *f* conclusion.

concombre *m* cucumber.

concordance *f* agreement, accord.

concorder *vi* to agree; to coincide.

concours *m* competition; conjuncture.

concret *adj* concrete, solid.

concrètement *adv* concretely.

concrétiser *vt* to put in concrete form.

concubin *m*, **-e** *f* concubine; cohabitant.

concubinage *m* concubinage; cohabitation.

concurrence *f* competition.

concurrent *m*, **-e** *f* concurrent; competing.

condamnation *f* condemnation; sentencing.

condamné *m*, **-e** *f* convict; sentenced person; * *adj* sentenced.

condamner *vt* to condemn; to sentence.

condensation *f* condensation.

condensé *adj* condensed, evaporated.

condenser *vt* to condense, compress.

condescendant *adj* condescending.

condiment *m* condiment.

condition *f* condition, term.

conditionné *adj* conditioned; packaged.

conditionnement *m* conditioning; packaging.

conditionner *vt* to condition; to package.

condoléances *fpl* condolences.

conducteur *m*, **-trice** *f* driver; operator.

conduire *vt*, *vi* to lead; to drive.

conduit *m* conduit, pipe.

conduite *f* conduct; driving; running.

cône *m* cone.

confédération *f* confederation.

conférence *f* conference.

conférencier *m*, **-lère** *f* speaker; lecturer.

confesser *vt* to confess; **se ~** *vr* to go to confession.

confession *f* confession.

confiance *f* confidence, trust.

confiant *adj* confident; confiding.

confidence *f* confidence; disclosure.

confident *m*, **-e** *f* confidant.

confidentiel *adj* confidential; **~lement** *adv* confidentially.

confier *vt* to confide; to entrust; **se ~** *vr* to confide in.

confiner *vt* to confine; **se ~** to be

confined; *vr*: **se ~ à** to confine oneself to.

confirmation *f* confirmation.

confirmer *vt* to confirm; **se ~** *vr* to be confirmed.

confiserie *f* confectionery.

confisquer *vt* to confiscate, impound.

confiture *f* jam.

conflictuel *adj* conflicting.

conflit *m* conflict, contention.

confondre *vt* to confuse, mingle.

conforme *adj* consistent; true.

conformément *adv* in accordance with.

conformer *vt* to model; **se ~** *vr* to conform.

conformiste *mf* conformist.

conformité *f* conformity; likeness.

confort *m* comfort.

confortable *adj* comfortable, cosy; **~ment** *adv* comfortably.

confrère *m* colleague.

confrontation *f* confrontation; comparison.

confronter *vt* to confront.

confus *adj* confused, indistinct; **~ément** *adv* confusedly, vaguely.

confusion *f* confusion, disorder.

congé *m* leave; holiday.

congédier *vt* to dismiss.

congélateur *m* freezer.

congeler *vt* to freeze.

congestion *f* congestion; stroke.

congratulation *f* congratulation.

congratuler *vt* to congratulate.

congrégation *f* congregation.

congrès *m* congress, conference.

conifère *m* conifer.

conjoint *m*, **-e** *f* spouse; * *adj* joint; linked; **~ement** *adv* jointly.

conjonctivite *f* conjunctivitis.

conjoncture *f* conjuncture; situation.

conjugaison *f* conjugation.

conjugal *adj* conjugal.

conjuguer *vt* to conjugate; to combine.

conjuration *f* conspiracy, plot.

conjurer *vt* to conspire; to implore.

connaissance *f* knowledge; consciousness.

connaisseur *m*, **-euse** *f* connoisseur; expert.

connaître *vt* to know, be acquainted with.

connecter *vt* to connect.

connecteur *m* connective.

connexion *f* connection, link.

connivence *f* connivance.

connotation *f* connotation.

connu *adj* known; famous.

conquérant *m*, **-e** *f* conqueror; * *adj* conquering.

conquérir *vt* to conquer.

conquête *f* conquest.

conquis *adj* conquered, vanquished.

consacrer *vt* to devote, dedicate; **se ~** *vr* to dedicate oneself to.

consciemment *adv* consciously, knowingly.

conscience *f* consciousness; conscience.

consciencieusement *adv* conscientiously.

consciencieux *adv* conscientious.

conscient *adj* conscious, aware.

consécration *f* consecration.

consécutif *adj* consecutive.

consécutivement *adv* consecutively.

conseil m advice, counsel.

conseiller m, **-ère** f counsellor, adviser; * vt to advise, counsel.

consentant adj consenting, willing.

consentement m consent.

consentir vi to consent; to acquiesce.

conséquence f consequence, result.

conséquent adj consequent, logical.

conservateur m, **-trice** f conservative; curator.

conservation f conservation.

conservatoire m conservatory; school.

conserve f canned food.

conserver vt to keep, preserve; **se ~** vr to keep.

considérable adj considerable; notable; **~ment** adv considerably.

considération f consideration, respect.

considérer vt to consider, regard.

consigne f orders, instructions.

consistance f consistency; strength.

consister vi: **~ en** to consist of; **cela consiste à** that consists in doing.

consolation f consolation, solace.

console f console.

consoler vt to console, comfort.

consolidation f consolidation, reinforcement.

consolider vt to consolidate, reinforce.

consommateur m, **-trice** f consumer.

consommation f consumption; accomplishment.

consommé adj consummate, accomplished; * m consommé.

consommer vt to consume; to use.

consonne f consonant.

conspirateur m, **-trice** f conspirator.

conspiration f conspiracy, plot.

conspirer vi to conspire, plot.

constamment adv constantly, continually.

constant adj constant, continuous.

constante f constant.

constat m report; acknowledgement.

constatation f authentication, verification.

constater vt to record; to verify.

constellation f constellation, galaxy.

consternation f consternation, dismay.

consterner vt to dismay.

constipation f constipation.

constituer vt to constitute, form.

constitution f constitution, formation.

constitutionnel adj constitutional; **~lement** adv constitutionally.

constructeur m, **-trice** f builder, maker.

constructif adj constructive.

construction f building, construction.

construire vt to construct, build.

consul m consul.

consulaire adj consular.

consulat m consulate.

consultant m, **-e** f consultant; * adj consulting.

consultation f consultation, advice.

consulter vt to consult, take advice from.

consumer vt to consume; to spend; **se ~** vr to decay, waste away.

contact m contact, touch.

contacter vt to contact, approach.

contagieux adj contagious, infectious.

contamination f contamination, pollution.

contaminer vt to contaminate, pollute.

conte m story, tale.

contemplation f contemplation, meditation.

contempler vt to contemplate, meditate.

contemporain adj contemporary.

contenance f capacity, volume.

contenir vt to contain.

contentement m contentment, satisfaction.

contenter vt to please; to satisfy; **se ~** vr: **se ~ de** to content oneself with.

contenu m contents, enclosure.

contestation f dispute, controversy.

contester vt to contest, dispute.

contexte m context.

contigu adj, f **contiguë** contiguous, adjacent.

continent m continent.

continental adj continental.

contingent m quota; draft (mil).

continu adj continuous, incessant.

continuation f continuation.

continuel adj continual, continuous; **~lement** adv continuously, continually.

continuer vt to continue, proceed with; * vi to continue, go on.

contour m contour, outline.

contourner vt to bypass, skirt.

contraceptif adj contraceptive.

contraception f contraception.

contracter vt to contract; to acquire; **se ~** vr to contract, to shrink.

contraction f contraction.

contradiction f contradiction, discrepancy.

contradictoire adj contradictory, conflicting.

contraindre vt to constrain, compel.

contrainte f constraint, compulsion.

contraire m opposite, contrary; * adj opposite, contrary; **~ment** adv contrarily.

contrariant adj contrary; perverse.

contrarier vt to annoy; to oppose.

contrariété f annoyance, disappointment.

contraste m contrast.

contrat m contract, agreement.

contre prép against; **parier à 10 ~ 1** to bet at 10 to 1; **~ toute attente** contrary to all expectations; **par ~** on the other hand.

contre-attaque f counter-attack.

contre-attaquer vi to counter-attack.

contrebalancer vt to counterbalance.

contrebande f contraband, smuggling.

contrebandier m, **-ière** f smuggler.

contrebasse f double bass.

contrecarrer vt to thwart, oppose.

contrecœur: à ~ reluctantly.

contrecoup m rebound, repercussion.

contredire vt to contradict, refute.

contrefaçon f counterfeit, forgery.

contrefaire vt to counterfeit, forge.

contre-indication f contraindication.

contremaître m foreman.

contre-offensive f counter-offensive.

contrepartie f compensation; consideration.

contre-plaqué m plywood.

contrepoison m antidote, counterpoison.

contresens m nonsense; misunderstanding; mistranslation.

contretemps m mishap; contretemps; syncopation.

contribuable mf taxpayer.

contribuer vt, vi to contribute.

contribution f contribution; tax.

contrôle m control, check.

contrôler vt to control, check.

contrôleur m, **-euse** f inspector; auditor.

controverse f controversy.

controversé adj disputed.

contusion f bruise, contusion.

convaincant adj convincing.

convaincre vt to convince, persuade.

convaincu adj convinced, persuaded.

convalescence f convalescence.

convenable adj fitting, suitable; **~ment** adv suitably, fitly.

convenir vi to agree, accord.

convention f convention, agreement.

conventionnel adj conventional; contractual; **~lement** adv conventionally.

convenu adj agreed; stipulated.

convergent adj convergent.

converger vi to converge.

conversation f conversation, talk.

conversion f conversion.

convertir vt to convert; **se ~** vr to be converted.

convexe adj convex.

conviction f conviction.

convier vt to invite; to urge.

convivial adj convivial; userfriendly.

convocation f convoking, summoning.

convoi m convoy; train.

convoiter vt to covet.

convoquer vt to convoke, convene.

convulsion f convulsion.

coopératif adj cooperative.

coopération f cooperation.

coopérative f cooperative.

coopérer vi to cooperate, collaborate.

coordinateur m, **-trice** f coordinator.

coordination f coordination; committee.

coordonnées fpl coordinates.

coordonner vt to coordinate.

copain m friend, pal.

copeau m shaving, chip.

copie f copy, reproduction.

copier vt to copy, reproduce.

copieusement adv copiously, abundantly.

copieux adj copious, abundant.

copilote m co-pilot.

copine f friend, mate.

coproduction f coproduction.

copropriété f co-ownership, joint ownership.

coq m cock, rooster.

coque f hull; shell.

coquelicot m poppy.

coquet adj stylish, smart; **~tement** adv stylishly, smartly.

coquetterie f smartness, stylishness.

coquillage m shellfish.

coquille f shell, scallop.

coquin m, **-e** f naughty, mischievous.

cor m horn.

corail m coral.

coran m Koran.

corbeau m crow.

corbeille f basket.

corbillard m hearse.

cordage m rope; rigging.

corde f rope; string.

cordée f roped mountaineering party.

cordial adj cordial, warm; **~ement** adv cordially, warmly.

cordialité f cordiality, warmth.

cordon m cord, string; cordon.

cordonnerie f shoemending.

cordonnier m, **-ière** f shoemender, cobbler.

coriace adj tough; tight.

coriandre f coriander.

corne f horn, antler.

cornée f cornea.

corneille f crow.

cornemuse f bagpipes.

cornet m cornet, cone.

corniche f cornice; ledge.

cornichon m gherkin; greenhorn.

corporatif adj corporative, corporate.

corporation f corporation, guild.

corporatisme m corporatism.

corporel adj corporal, bodily.

corps m body, corpse.

corpulence f corpulence.

corpulent adj corpulent.

corpus m corpus.

correct adj correct, accurate; **~ement** adv correctly, accurately.

correcteur m, **-trice** f examiner; proofreader.

correction f correction; proofreading.

corrélation f correlation.

correspondance f correspondence, communication.

correspondant m, **-e** f correspondent; * adj corresponding.

correspondre vi to correspond, communicate.

corridor m corridor, passage.

corrigé m corrected version, fair copy.

corriger vt to correct.

corroborer vt to corroborate.

corroder vt to corrode.

corrompre vt to corrupt, debase.

corrompu adj corrupt.

corrosif adj corrosive.

corrosion f corrosion.

corruption f corruption, debasement.

corsage m blouse, bodice.

corsaire m corsair, pirate.

corsé adj rich, full-bodied.

corset m corset.

cortège m cortège, procession.

cortex m cortex.

cortical adj cortical.

cortisone f cortisone.

corvée f fatigue duty; forced labour.
cosmétique m cosmetic.
cosmique adj cosmic.
cosmonaute mf cosmonaut.
cosmopolite adj cosmopolitan.
cosmos m cosmos.
costume m costume, dress.
cotation f quotation, valuation.
côte f coast; rib; slope.
côté m side; point.
coteau m hill.
côtelé adj ribbed.
côtelette f cutlet.
coter vt to quote; to classify.
côtier adj coastal, inshore.
coton m cotton.
cotonneux adj fleecy, downy.
côtoyer vt to mix with, skirt.
cou m neck.
couchant adj setting.
couche f layer, coat.
coucher vt to put to bed; **se ~** vr to go to bed.
coucou m cuckoo.
coude m elbow.
coudé adj angled, bent.
coudoyer vt mix with, rub shoulders with.
coudre vt, vi to sew.
couette f bearing; duvet.
coulant adj flowing; smooth.
couler vi to flow, run.
couleur f colour, shade.
couleuvre f grass snake.
coulis m sauce, purée.
coulissant adj sliding.
coulisse f groove; wings (theat).
coulisser vi to slide, run.
couloir m corridor, passage.
coup m blow; shot; **~ sur ~** one

after another, incessantly; **tout à ~** suddenly; **après ~** afterwards, after the event; **~ de feu** shot; **jeter un ~ d'œil** to glance; **~ de coude** nudge; **~ de téléphone** phone call; **~ de soleil** sunstroke.
coupable mf culprit; * adj guilty.
coupant adj cutting, sharp.
coupe f cut; cutting.
coupe-papier m invar paper knife.
couper vt to cut, slice.
couple m couple, pair.
couplet m couplet, verse.
coupole f dome.
coupon m coupon, voucher, ticket.
coupure f cut; break.
cour f court, yard, courtyard.
courage m courage, daring.
courageusement adv courageously.
courageux adj courageous.
couramment adv fluently; commonly.
courant adj current; present; * m stream, current.
courbature f stiffness; ache.
courbaturé adj aching.
courbe f curve; contour.
courbé adj curved, stooped.
courber vt to curve, bend.
coureur m, **-euse** f runner.
courgette f courgette.
courir vi to run, race.
couronne f crown, wreath.
couronnement m coronation.
couronner vt to crown.
courrier m mail, post.
courroie f strap, belt.
cours m course; flow; path.
course f running; race; flight; journey.

coursier *m*, **-ière** *f* courier, messenger.

court *adj* short, brief.

court-bouillon *m* court-bouillon, wine sauce.

court-circuit *m* short-circuit.

court-circuiter *vt* to short-circuit.

courtier *m*, **-ière** *f* broker, agent.

courtiser *vt* to court.

courtois *adj* courteous; **~ement** *adv* courteously.

courtoisie *f* courtesy, courteousness.

cousin *m*, **-e** *f* cousin.

coussin *m* cushion, pillow.

coussinet *m* pad; bearing.

coût *m* cost, charge.

couteau *m* knife.

coûter *vi*, *vt* to cost.

coûteusement *adv* expensively.

coûteux *adj* costly, expensive.

coutume *f* custom, habit.

coutumier *adj* customary, usual.

couture *f* sewing, needlework.

couturier *m* couturier, fashion designer.

couturière *f* dressmaker.

couvent *m* convent.

couver *vt* to hatch, incubate; * *vi* to smoulder, lurk.

couvercle *m* lid, cap.

couvert *m* shelter; cover; pretext; * *adj* covered; secret; obscure.

couverture *f* blanket; cover; roofing.

couvre-feu *m* curfew.

couvreur *m* roofer.

couvrir *vt* to cover; **se ~** *vr* to cover up; to become overcast.

crabe *m* crab.

crachement *m* spitting.

cracher *vt* to spit.

crachin *m* drizzle.

craie *f* chalk.

craindre *vt* to fear.

crainte *f* fear, dread.

craintif *adj* timid, cowardly.

crampe *f* cramp.

crampon *m* stud, spike, crampon.

cramponner *vt* to cramp, clamp; **se ~** *vr* to cling, hang on.

cran *m* notch, cog.

crâne *m* cranium, skull.

crânien *adj* cranial.

crapaud *m* toad.

crapule *f* villain.

crapuleux *adj* villainous, vicious.

craquellement *m* cracking.

craquement *m* crack, creaking, snap.

craquer *vi* to creak, squeak, crack.

crasseux *adj* grimy, filthy.

cratère *m* crater.

cravate *f* tie.

créancier *m*, **-ière** *f* creditor.

créateur *m*, **-trice** *f* creator, author.

créatif *adj* creative.

création *f* creation.

créativité *f* creativity.

créature *f* creature.

crèche *f* creche; crib.

crédibilité *f* credibility.

crédible *adj* credible.

crédit *m* credit, trust.

crédit-bail *m* lease; leasing.

crédule *adj* credulous, gullible.

crédulité *f* credulity, gullibility.

créer *vt* to create, produce.

crémaillère *f* rack.

crème *f* cream.

crémerie *f* dairy.

crémeux *adj* creamy.

crémier *m* dairyman, **-ière** *f* dairy-woman.

créneau *m* battlement.

crêpe *f* pancake; * *m* crepe, crape.

crêperie *f* pancake restaurant.

crépitement *m* crackling; rattling.

crépiter *vi* to crackle; to rattle.

crépu *adj* frizzy, woolly.

crépuscule *m* twilight, dusk.

cresson *m* watercress.

crête *f* crest, comb.

crétin *m*, **-e** *f* cretin, idiot.

creuser *vi* to dig, burrow; * *vt* to dig, hollow.

creuset *m* crucible.

creux *adj* hollow, empty.

crevaison *f* puncture, flat.

crevé *adj* burst, punctured.

crever *vt* to burst; to gouge; *vi* to burst; to split.

crevette *f* prawn.

cri *m* cry, howl, yell.

criant *adj* crying; striking, glaring.

criard *adj* yelling; scolding.

crible *m* riddle, sieve; **passer au ~** to riddle; to examine closely.

cribler *vt* to sift, riddle.

cric *m* jack (car).

crier *vi* to cry, shout.

crime *m* crime, offence.

criminel, **elle** *f* criminal; * *adj* criminal.

crin *m* horsehair.

crinière *f* mane.

crique *f* creek.

criquet *m* locust.

crise *f* crisis, attack.

crisper *vt* to shrivel; to clench.

cristal *m* crystal, glassware.

cristallin *adj* crystalline.

cristallisation *f* crystallization.

cristalliser *vt* to crystallize.

critère *m* criterion, standard.

critiquable *adj* censurable, open to criticism.

critique *adj* critical, censorious; * *f* criticism; critique.

critiquer *vt* to criticize, censure.

croc *m* fang; hook.

croche *f* quaver.

crochet *m* hook, clip.

crochu *adj* hooked, claw-like.

crocodile *vi* crocodile.

croire *vt* to believe; to think.

croisade *f* crusade.

croisement *m* crossing, junction.

croiser *vt* to cross; to fold; **se ~** *vr* to cross, intersect.

croisière *f* cruise.

croissance *f* growth, increase.

croissant *adj* growing, increasing; * *m* croissant; crescent.

croître *vi* to grow, rise.

croix *f* cross.

croque-monsieur *m* toasted cheese and ham sandwich.

croquer *vt* to crunch, munch.

croquette *f* croquette.

croquis *m* sketch, outline.

crosse *f* crozier; butt, grip.

crotte *f* manure, dung.

croupir *vi* to stagnate, wallow.

croustillant *adj* crusty, crisp.

croustiller *vi* to be crusty, crispy.

croûte *f* crust.

croûton *m* crust, crouton.

croyance *f* belief.

croyant *adj* believing.

cru *adj* raw, uncooked; * *m* vine-yard; wine.

cruauté f cruelty, inhumanity.

cruche f pitcher.

crucial adj crucial, decisive.

crucifix m crucifix.

crucifixion f crucifixion.

crudité f crudity, coarseness.

crue f flood.

cruel adj cruel; **~lement** adv cruelly.

crustacé m crustacean, shellfish.

crypte m crypt.

crypter vt to encode, scramble.

cube m cube, block.

cubique adj cubic.

cubisme m cubism.

cueillette f picking, gathering.

cueillir vt to pick, gather.

cuiller, cuillère f spoon, spoonful.

cuir m leather, hide.

cuirasse f cuirass, breastplate.

cuirassé adj armoured; * m battleship.

cuire vi to cook.

cuisine f kitchen; cookery.

cuisiner vt, vi to cook.

cuisinier m, **-ière** f cook.

cuisinière f cooker, stove.

cuisse f thigh.

cuisson f cooking, baking.

cuit adj cooked.

cuivre m copper.

cul m bottom, ass.

culasse f cylinder-head; breech.

cul-de-jatte mf legless cripple.

cul-de-sac m blind alley, cul-de-sac.

culinaire adj culinary.

culminer vi to culminate, tower.

culot m cheek, nerve.

culotte f knickers; underpants; shorts.

culpabiliser vt to make someone feel guilty; **se ~** vr to feel guilty.

culpabilité f guilt, culpability.

culte m cult, veneration.

cultivable adj cultivable.

cultivateur m, **-trice** f farmer.

cultivé adj cultured.

cultiver vt to cultivate; **se ~** vr to improve oneself.

culture f culture; cultivation.

culturel adj cultural.

culturisme m body-building.

cumin m cumin.

cumul m pluralism; accumulation.

cumuler vt to accumulate; to hold concurrently.

cupide adj greedy; **~ment** adv greedily.

cupidité f greed, cupidity.

cure f treatment.

curé m parish priest, parson.

cure-dents m toothpick.

curieusement adv curiously.

curieux m, **-euse** f inquisitive person; onlooker; * adj curious, inquisitive.

curiosité f curiosity, inquisitiveness.

cursus m degree course.

cutané adj skin, cutaneous.

cuve f vat, tank.

cuvette f basin, bowl.

cyanure m cyanide.

cybernétique f cybernetics.

cyclable adj cycle, for cycling.

cyclamen m cyclamen.

cycle m cycle; stage.

cyclique adj cyclical.

cyclisme m cycling.

cycliste mf cyclist; * adj cycle.

cyclomoteur m moped.

cyclone m cyclone.

cyclope m Cyclops.

cygne m swan.
cylindre m cylinder.
cylindrée f capacity (engine).
cylindrique adj cylindrical.
cymbale f cymbal.

cynique adj cynical; **~ment** adv cynically.
cynisme m cynicism.
cytologie f cytology.
cytoplasme m cytoplasm.

D

dactylographe mf typist.
dactylographie f typing, typewriting.
dactylographier vt to type.
dada m (fam) hobby-horse; gee-gee.
dahlia m dahlia.
daigner vt to deign, condescend.
daim m deer.
dalle f flagstone, slab.
dalmatien m Dalmatian.
daltonien adj colour-blind.
dame f lady; dame.
damier m draughtboard.
damnation f damnation.
damné adj damned.
damner vt to damn.
danger m danger, risk.
dangereusement adv dangerously.
dangereux adj dangerous, risky.
dans prép in; into; **il a ~ les trente ans** he's thirty or so.
dansant adj dancing.
danse f dance; dancing.
danser vi to dance.
danseur m, **-euse** f dancer.
dard m dart; sting.
datation f dating.
date f date.
dater vt to date.
datif m dative.
datte f (bot) date.

dattier m date palm.
dauphin m dolphin.
daurade f sea bream.
davantage adv more.
de prép of; from; **une femme quarante ans** a forty-year-old woman; **~ bonne heure** early; **deux ~ plus** two more; * art some, any.
dé m die; thimble.
déambuler vi to stroll.
débâcle f disaster; collapse.
déballage m unpacking; display.
déballer vt to unpack; to display.
débandade f rout, stampede.
débarbouiller vt to wash quickly; **se ~ vr** to wash oneself; to extricate oneself.
débarcadère m landing; wharf.
débardeur m docker, stevedore.
débarquement m landing, disembarkment.
débarquer vt to land, unship; * vi to disembark, land.
débarrasser vt to clear, rid; **se ~ vr: se ~ de** to rid oneself of.
débat m debate; dispute, contest.
débattre vi to debate, discuss.
débauche f debauchery, dissoluteness.
débaucher vt to debauch, corrupt.
débile adj weak, feeble.

débilitant adj debilitating, weakening.

débit m debit; turnover; flow.

débiter vt to debit; to produce.

débiteur m, **-trice** f debtor.

déblayer vt to clear away, remove.

déblocage m unblocking; freeing, releasing.

débloquer vt to release, unlock.

déboisement m deforestation.

déboiser vt to deforest.

déboîtement m dislocation.

débordant adj exuberant, overflowing.

débordé adj overwhelmed.

débordement m overflowing; outflanking.

déborder vi to overflow; to outflank.

débouché m outlet; issue.

déboucher vt to open, uncork; * vi to pass out, emerge.

debout adv upright, standing; **être ~** to stand.

déboutonner vt to unbutton.

débraillé adj untidy, disordered.

débrancher vt to disconnect.

débrayer vi to declutch; to stop work.

débris m debris, waste.

débrouiller vt to disentangle, unravel; **se ~** vr to cope, manage.

début m beginning, outset.

débutant adj novice.

débuter vi to start, begin; * vt to lead, start.

décadence f decadence, decline.

décadent adj decadent.

décaféiné adj decaffeinated.

décagone m decagon.

décalage m gap, interval; discrepancy.

décalcifier vt to decalcify.

décaler vt to stagger; to shift.

décalitre m decalitre.

décamètre m decametre.

décaper vt to clean, scour.

décapotable adj convertible; * f convertible.

décapsuler vt to take the lid off.

décapsuleur m bottle-opener.

décathlon m decathlon.

décéder vi to die.

décelable adj detectable.

déceler vt to detect; to disclose.

décembre m December.

décemment adv decently.

décence f decency.

décennal adj decennial.

décennie f decade.

décent adj decent, proper.

décentralisation f decentralization.

décentraliser vt to decentralize.

déception f disappointment; deceit.

décerner vt to award, confer.

décès m death, decease.

décevant adj disappointing; deceptive.

décevoir vt to disappoint; to deceive.

déchaîné adj wild, unbridled.

déchaîner vt to unleash; **se ~** vr to break loose, run wild.

décharge f discharge; receipt.

déchargement m unloading.

décharger vt to unload, discharge.

décharné adj lean, emaciated.

déchausser vt to take off footwear; **se ~** vr to take one's shoes off.

déchéance f decay, decline.

déchet m loss, waste.

déchiffrer vt to decipher, decode.

déchiqueter vt to tear; to slash; to shred.

déchirant adj harrowing, excruciating.

déchirement m tearing, ripping.

déchirer vt to tear, rip.

déchirure f tear, rip.

déchoir vi to decline; to sink.

déchu adj fallen; declined; deposed.

décibel m decibel.

décidé adj decided; determined; **~ment** adv positively; resolutely; certainly.

décigramme m decigram.

décilitre m decilitre.

décimal adj decimal.

décimètre m decimetre.

décisif adj decisive, conclusive.

décision f decision.

déclamer vt to declaim.

déclamation f declamation.

déclaré adj professed, avowed.

déclarer vt to declare, announce; **se ~** vr to speak one's mind.

déclenchement m release, setting off.

déclencher vt to release, set off; **se ~** vr to release itself, go off.

déclic m click; trigger.

déclin m decline, deterioration.

déclinaison f declension; declination.

déclinant adj declining.

décliner vi to decline, refuse.

déclivité f declivity, slope.

décloisonner vt to decompartmentalize.

décoder vt to decode, decipher.

décodeur m decoder, decipherer.

décoiffer vt to disarrange so's hair.

décoincer vt to loose, release.

décollage m take-off, lift-off.

décoller vi to unpaste, steam off; to take off; * vt: **se ~** vr to come unstuck, become detached.

décolleté adj low-necked, low-cut; m decolletage, low neckline.

décolorant adj bleaching, decolorizing; * m bleaching substance.

décolorer vt to decolour, bleach.

décombres mpl rubble, debris.

décomposer vt to decompose; to break up; to dissect; **se ~** vr to decompose, decay.

décomposition f decomposition, breaking up.

décompression f decompression.

décomprimer vt to decompress.

décompte m discount; deduction.

déconcentrer vt to devolve; to disperse; **se ~** vr to lose concentration.

déconcertant adj disconcerting.

déconcerter vt to disconcert.

décongeler vt to thaw, defrost.

déconnecter vt to disconnect.

déconnexion f disconnection.

décontenancé adj embarrassed; disconcerted.

décontracté adj relaxed.

décontracter vt to relax; **se ~** vr to relax.

décontraction f relaxation.

décor m scenery; setting.

décorateur m, **-trice** f decorator; set designer.

décoratif adj decorative, ornamental.

décoration f decoration, embellishment.

décorer vt to decorate, adorn.

décortiquer vt to husk, shell.

découler vi to flow; to ensue.

découpage m cutting up, carving.

découper vt to carve, cut up.

décourageant adj discouraging, disheartening.

découragement m discouragement.

décourager vt discourage, dishearten; **se ~** vr to become discouraged.

décousu adj unsewn; loose; disconnected.

découvert adj uncovered; open; * m overdraft.

découverte f discovery.

découvrir vt to discover.

décret m decree, enactment.

décréter vt to decree, enact.

décrire vt to describe.

décrocher vt to take down; to unhook.

décroissant adj decreasing, lessening.

décroître vi to decrease, diminish.

déçu adj disappointed.

décupler vi to increase tenfold.

dédaigner vt to disdain, scorn.

dédaigneusement adv disdainfully.

dédaigneux adj disdainful, scornful.

dédain m disdain, scorn.

dedans adv inside, indoors; * m inside; **au ~ inside.**

dédicace f dedication.

dédier vt to consecrate, dedicate to.

dédommagement m compensation, damages.

dédommager vt to compensate, indemnify.

dédouanement m customs clearance.

dédoubler vt to divide in two; to remove lining.

déduction f deduction.

déduire vt to deduct; to deduce.

déesse f goddess.

défaillance f faintness; exhaustion; blackout.

défaillant adj faint; weakening.

défaillir vi to faint; to weaken.

défaire vt to undo, dismantle.

défaite f defeat, overthrow.

défaitiste adj, mf defeatist.

défaut m defect, fault.

défavorable adj unfavourable; **~ment** adv unfavourably.

défavoriser vt to penalize, treat unfairly.

défection f defection.

défectueux adj defective, faulty.

défendeur m, **-deresse** f defendant.

défendre vt to defend, protect; to prohibit; **se ~** vr to defend oneself.

défense f defence; prohibition.

défenseur m defender.

défensif adj defensive.

défi m defiance; challenge.

défiant *adj* mistrustful, distrustful.
déficience *f* deficiency.
déficient *adj* deficient; weak.
déficit *m* deficit, shortfall.
déficitaire *adj* deficient, in deficit.
défier *vt* to challenge, defy.
défilé *m* procession, parade.
défiler *vi* to parade, march.
défini *adj* definite, precise.
définir *vt* to define, specify.
définitif *adj* definitive, final.
définition *f* definition.
définitivement *adv* definitively, finally.
déflagration *f* deflagration, explosion.
déflation *f* deflation.
défoncer *vt* to smash in; to dig deeply.
déformation *f* deformation, distortion.
déformer *vt* to deform, distort; **se ~** *vr* to bend; to lose its shape.
défoulement *m* outlet; release.
défouler *vt* to unwind, relax; **se ~** *vr* to get rid of one's inhibitions.
défricher *vt* to clear; to reclaim.
défunt *m*, **-e** *f* deceased; * *adj* late, deceased.
dégagé *adj* clear; open.
dégagement *m* freeing, clearance.
dégager *vt* to free, clear; **se ~** *vr* to free oneself, extricate oneself.
dégarnir *vt* to empty; to clear.
dégât *m* havoc, damage.
dégel *m* thaw.
dégeler *vt vi* to thaw, melt.
dégénérer *vi* to degenerate, decline.
dégivrer *vt* to de-ice, defrost.

dégonfler *vt* to deflate, empty.
dégourdir *vt* to warm up, revive.
dégourdissement *m* reviving, return of circulation.
dégoût *m* disgust, distaste.
dégouter *vt* to disgust.
dégradant *adj* degrading.
dégradation *f* degradation, debasement.
dégradé *m* shading off; gradation.
dégrader *vt* to degrade, debase; **se ~** *vr* to become degraded, debased.
dégrafer *vt* to unfasten, unhook.
dégraisser *vt* to remove grease.
degré *m* degree; grade.
dégrèvement *m* reduction; redemption.
dégripper *vt* to unblock; to unchoke.
déguisement *m* disguise.
déguiser *vt* to disguise; **se ~** *vr* to disguise oneself.
dégustation *f* tasting, sampling.
dehors *adv* outside, outdoors; **au ~** outwardly; **en ~ de** outside; apart from; * *m* outside, exterior.
déjà *adv* already.
déjeuner *vi* to lunch; * *m* lunch.
déjouer *vt* to elude; to thwart.
delà *adv*: **au ~ de** beyond; **par ~** beyond.
délabré *adj* dilapidated, ramshackle.
délacer *vt* to unlace, undo.
délai *m* delay; respite; time limit.
délaisser *vt* to abandon, quit.
délassant *adj* relaxing, refreshing.
délasser *vt* to refresh, relax; **se ~** *vr* to rest, relax.

délateur m, **-trice** f informer.

délation f denouncement; informing.

délavé adj diluted; faded.

délayage m dragging-out, spinning-out.

délayer vt to thin; to drag out.

délectation f delectation, delight.

délecter(se) vr to delight, revel.

délégation f delegation.

délégué m, **-e** f delegate, representative; * adj delegate, delegated.

déléguer vt to delegate.

délibération f deliberation; resolution.

délibéré adj deliberate; resolute; **~ment** adv deliberately.

délicat adj delicate, dainty; **~ement** adv delicately.

délicatesse f delicacy, daintiness.

délice m delight, pleasure.

délicieux adj delicious, delightful.

délier vt to unbind, untie.

délimitation f delimitation.

délimiter vt to delimit, demarcate.

délinquance f delinquency.

délinquant m, **-e** f delinquent, offender; * adj delinquent.

délirant adj delirious, frenzied.

délire m delirium, frenzy.

délirer vi to be delirious.

délit m offence, misdemeanour.

délivrance f deliverance; release; delivery.

délivrer vt to deliver; to release; **se ~** vr to free oneself.

déloger vt to evict, dislodge.

déloyal adj disloyal, unfaithful; **~ement** adv disloyally.

déloyauté f disloyalty, treachery.

delta m delta.

deltaplane m hang-glider.

démagogie f demagogy.

démagogique adj demagogic.

démagogue m demagogue.

demain adv tomorrow.

demande f request, petition; question.

demander vt to ask, request; **se ~** vr to wonder.

démangeaison f itch; longing.

démaquillant m make-up remover; * adj make-up removing.

démaquiller vt to remove make-up; **se ~** vr to take one's make-up off.

démarche f bearing; gait, walk.

démarrage m moving off, casting off.

démarrer vi to start up, move off; * vt to start, get started.

démarreur m starter.

démasquer vt to unmask, uncover.

démêlage m disentangling; combing.

démêler vt to disentangle, unravel; comb.

déménagement m removal; moving (house).

déménager vi to move house.

déménageur m removal man.

démener(se) vr to struggle, strive.

dément adj mad, insane, crazy.

démenti m denial, refutation.

démentir vt to deny, refute.

démesuré adj excessive, inordinate; **~ment** adv excessively, inordinately.

démettre *vt* to dislocate; to dismiss.

demeure *f* residence, dwelling place.

demeurer *vi* to live at, reside, stay.

demi *adj* half; **à ~** halfway; *** à ~** half.

demi-cercle *m* semicircle.

demi-douzaine *f* half-dozen.

demi-droite *f* half-line.

demi-finale *f* semi-final.

demi-frère *m* half-brother.

demi-heure *f* half hour.

demi-jour *m* half-light, twilight.

démilitariser *vt* to demilitarize.

demi-litre *m* half-litre.

demi-lune *f* half-moon.

demi-mesure *f* half-measure.

demi-mot *m*: **à ~** without spelling out.

demi-pension *f* half-board.

demi-sœur *f* half-sister.

démission *f* resignation.

démissionner *vi* to resign.

demi-tarif *m* half-fare.

demi-tour *m* half-turn.

démocrate *mf* democrat.

démocratie *f* democracy.

démocratique *adj* democratic; **~ment** *adv* democratically.

démocratiser *vt* to democratize.

démodé *adj* old-fashioned, out-of-date.

démographie *f* demography.

démographique *adj* demographic.

demoiselle *f* young lady; spinster; damsel.

démolir *vt* to demolish, knock down.

démolition *f* demolition.

démon *m* demon, fiend.

démoniaque *adj* demoniac, fiendish.

démonstrateur *m*, **-trice** *f* demonstrator.

démonstratif *adj* demonstrative.

démonstration *f* demonstration; proof.

démontable *adj* collapsible, that can be dismantled.

démonte-pneu *m* tyre lever.

démonter *vt* to dismantle, take down, dismount; **se ~** *vr* to come apart, be nonplussed.

démontrer *vt* demonstrate; to prove.

démoralisant *adj* demoralizing.

démoraliser *vt* to demoralize; **se ~** *vr* to become demoralized.

démouler *vt* to take out of a mould.

démunir *vt* to deprive; to divest.

démystifier *vt* to demystify, disabuse.

dénaturé *adj* denatured, disfigured.

dénégation *f* denial.

déneiger *vt* to clear snow from.

déni *m* denial, refusal.

dénicher *vt* to dislodge; to unearth.

dénier *vt* to deny, disclaim.

dénigrer *vt* to denigrate, disparage.

dénivellation *f* difference in level, unevenness.

dénombrer *vt* to number, enumerate.

dénomination *f* denomination, designation.

dénoncer *vt* to denounce; to inform against.

dénonciation *f* denunciation.

dénouement *m* dénouement; unravelling; outcome.

dénouer *vt* to unravel, untie, undo.

dénoyauter *vt* to stone (fruit).

denrée *f* commodity, provisions, foodstuff.

dense *adj* dense, thick.

densité *f* density, denseness.

dent *f* tooth.

dentaire *adj* dental.

dentelé *adj* jagged, perforated.

dentelle *f* lace.

dentier *m* denture, dental plate.

dentifrice *m* toothpaste.

dentiste *mf* dentist.

dentition *f* dentition, teething.

dénuder *vt* to bare, denude; **se ~** *vr* to strip off.

dénué *adj* devoid, bereft.

dénuement *m* destitution; deprivation.

déodorant *m* deodorant.

déontologie *f* deontology.

dépannage *m* repairing, fixing.

dépanner *vt* to repair, fix.

dépanneur *m*, **-euse** *f* breakdown mechanic.

dépanneuse *f* breakdown lorry.

dépareillé *adj* unmatched; odd.

déparer *vt* to spoil; to disfigure.

départ *m* departure; start.

département *m* department.

dépasser *vt* to exceed; to go past.

dépaysé *adj* disoriented, out of one's element.

dépaysement *m* disorientation.

dépêcher *vt* to dispatch, send; **se ~** *vr* to hurry, rush.

dépendance *f* dependence; dependency.

dépendant *adj* dependent.

dépendre *vi* to depend on, be dependent on.

dépens *mpl*: **aux ~ de** at the expense of.

dépense *f* expenditure, outlay.

dépenser *vt* to expend, spend; **se ~** *vr* to exert oneself.

dépérir *vi* to decline, waste away.

dépeupler *vt* to depopulate; to clear.

dépistage *m* tracking; detection.

dépister *vt* to track.

dépit *m* spite; grudge; **en ~ de** in spite of.

dépité *adj* vexed; frustrated.

déplacé *adj* misplaced; ill-timed.

déplacement *m* displacement; removal.

déplacer *vt* to displace; to move; **se ~** *vr* to change residence.

déplaire *vi* to displease; to offend.

déplaisant *adj* disagreeable, unpleasant.

dépliant *m* prospectus, leaflet; * *adj* extendible; folding.

déplier *vt* to unfold; to open out.

déploiement *m* deployment; display.

déplorable *adj* deplorable, disgraceful.

déplorer *vt* to deplore, bewail.

déployer *vt* to deploy; to display.

dépopulation *f* depopulation.

déportation *f* deportation, transportation.

déporté *m*, **-e** *f* deportee.

déporter *vt* to deport, transport.

déposer *vt* to lodge, deposit.

dépositaire *mf* depository; trustee.

déposition *f* deposition; evidence.

dépôt *m* deposit; warehouse.

dépouillement *m* scrutiny, perusal; despoiling.

dépouiller *vt* to strip; to despoil; to peruse.

dépourvu *adj* lacking, wanting; **au ~** off guard.

dépoussiérer *vt* to dust.

dépravation *f* depravity, corruption.

dépravé *adj* depraved, corrupt.

dépréciation *f* depreciation.

déprécier *vt* to depreciate; to disparage; **se ~** *vr* to depreciate, fall in value.

dépressif *adj* depressive.

dépression *f* depression, slump; dejection.

déprimant *adj* depressing.

déprimer *vt* to depress; to discourage.

depuis *prép* since, from; after.

député *m* deputy, delegate.

déracinement *m* uprooting, eradication.

déraciner *vt* to uproot, eradicate.

déraillement *m* derailment.

dérailler *vi* to be derailed, run off the rails.

dérailleur *m* derailleur, derailer (*rail*).

déraisonner *vi* to talk irrationally, rave.

dérangement *m* derangement; inconvenience.

déranger *vt* to upset, unsettle; **se ~** *vr* to move; to put oneself out.

dérapage *m* skid.

déraper *vi* to skid, slip.

déréglé *adj* out order; irregular; unruly.

déréglement *m* disturbance; irregularity; dissoluteness.

dérégler *vt* to disturb; to put out of order; to upset.

dérision *f* derision, mockery.

dérisoire *adj* derisory; pathetic.

dérivation *f* derivation; diversion.

dérive *f* drift; **aller à la ~** to go downhill.

dériver *vi* to drift.

dermatologie *f* dermatology.

dermatologue *mf* dermatologist.

derme *m* dermis.

dernier *adj* last; latest; back; * *m*, -**ière** *f* last one; latter.

dernièrement *adv* recently; lately.

dérobade *f* sidestepping; evasion.

dérober *vt* to steal; to hide; **se ~** *vr* to steal away, escape.

dérogation *f* derogation; dispensation.

déroger *vi* to derogate; to detract.

déroulement *m* unfolding; progress, development.

dérouler *vt* to unwind, uncoil; **se ~** *vr* to develop; to unfold.

déroutant *adj* disconcerting.

déroute *f* rout, overthrow.

dérouter *vt* to rout, overthrow.

derrière *prép* behind; * *adv*; **par ~** by the back; * *m* bottom; back; **de ~** back, rear.

des *art* = de les; *see* **un, une**.

dès *prép* from, since; **~ que** when; as soon as.

désabusé *adj* disenchanted; disabused.

désaccord *m* disagreement, discord.

désaffecté *adj* disused.

désagréable adj disagreeable, unpleasant; **~ment** adv disagreeably, unpleasantly.

désagréger vt to break up, separate; **se ~** vr to break up, become separated.

désagrément m displeasure, annoyance.

désaltérant adj thirst-quenching.

désaltérer vt to refresh; **se ~** vi to quench one's thirst.

désamorcer vt to unprime, defuse.

désapprobateur adj disapproving.

désapprobation f disapproval.

désapprouver vt to disapprove, object.

désarçonner vt to unsaddle; to nonplus, baffle.

désarmant adj disarming.

désarmement m disarmament.

désarmer vt to disarm; to unload.

désarroi m disarray, confusion.

désarticuler vt to dislocate; to upset.

désastre m disaster.

désastreux adj disastrous, unfortunate.

désavantage m disadvantage; prejudice.

désavantager vt to disadvantage, handicap.

désaveu m disavowal, retraction.

désavouer vt to disavow, retract.

descendance f descent, lineage.

descendant m, **-e** f descendant; * adj falling, descending.

descendre vi to descend, go down; * vt to take down, bring down.

descente f descent, way down.

descriptif adj descriptive, explanatory.

description f description.

désemparé adj helpless; distraught.

désenchantement m disenchantment; disillusion.

désenfler vi to become less swollen.

désensibiliser vt to desensitize.

déséquilibre m imbalance, unbalance.

déséquilibré adj unbalanced, unhinged.

déséquilibrer vt to unbalance, throw off balance.

désert m desert, wilderness; * adj deserted.

déserter vt to desert.

déserteur m deserter.

désertification f desertification.

désertion f desertion.

désertique adj desert; barren.

désespérant adj desperate, hopeless; discouraging.

désespéré adj desperate, hopeless; **~ment** adv desperately.

désespérer vi to despair, give up hope.

désespoir m despair, despondency.

déshabiller vt to undress; **se ~** vr to undress.

désherbage m weeding.

désherbant m weed killer.

désherber vt to weed.

déshériter vt to disinherit.

déshonorant adj dishonourable, disgraceful.

déshonorer vt to dishonour, disgrace.

déshydraté *adj* dehydrated.

déshydrater *vt* to dehydrate; **se ~ vr** to become dehydrated.

désignation *f* designation, nomination; name.

désigner *vt* to designate, indicate.

désillusion *f* disillusion; disappointment.

désillusionner *vt* to disillusion; to disappoint.

désincarné *adj* disincarnate, disembodied.

désinfectant *m* disinfectant; * *adj* disinfectant.

désinfecter *vt* to disinfect.

désinfection *f* disinfection.

désinformation *f* disinformation.

désintégration *f* disintegration.

désintégrer *vt* to split, break up; **se ~ vr** to disintegrate.

désintéressé *adj* disinterested, unselfish.

désintéressement *m* disinterestedness, unselfishness.

désintéresser(se) *vr* to lose interest in.

désintoxiquer *vt* to detoxify; to dry out; **se ~ vr** to dry out.

désinvolte *adj* easy, offhand, casual.

désinvolture *f* casualness, offhandedness.

désir *m* desire, wish, longing.

désirable *adj* desirable.

désirer *vt* to desire, wish, long.

désobéir *vi* to disobey.

désobéissance *f* disobedience.

désobéissant *adj* disobedient.

désobligeant *adj* disobliging; uncivil.

désodorisant *m* deodorant; * *adj* deodorizing, deodorant.

désodoriser *vt* to deodorize.

désœuvré *adj* unoccupied, idle.

désœuvrement *m* idleness.

désolation *f* desolation; ruin; grief.

désolé *adj* desolate; disconsolate, grieved.

désordonné *adj* untidy; inordinate; reckless.

désordre *m* disorder, confusion, disturbance.

désorganisation *f* disorganization.

désorienté *adj* disorientated.

désormais *adv* from now on, henceforth.

désossé *adj* boned.

despote *m* despot.

despotique *adj* despotic; ~**ment** *adv* despotically.

dessèchement *m* dryness, drying up, withering.

dessécher *vt* to dry, parch, wither; **se ~ vr** to dry out, become parched.

dessein *m* design, plan, scheme; **à ~** intentionally.

desserrer *vt* to loosen; to unscrew; to slacken; **se ~ vr** to work loose, come undone.

dessert *m* dessert, sweet.

desservir *vt* to clear (table); to do a disservice to.

dessin *m* drawing, sketch; draft.

dessinateur *m*, **-trice** *f* drawer, draughtsman.

dessiner *vt* to draw, sketch; to design.

dessous *adv* under, beneath; * *m* underside, bottom.

dessus *adv* over, above; * *m*; **prendre le ~** to gain the upper hand; **le ~ du panier** the upper crust, the pick of the bunch.

déstabiliser *vt* to destabilize.

destin *m* destiny, fate, doom.

destinataire *mf* addressee, consignee.

destination *f* destination; purpose.

destinée *f* destiny, fate.

destiner *vt* to determine; to intend, destine, aim.

destituer *vt* to dismiss, depose.

destructeur *adj* destructive, ruinous.

destruction *f* destruction.

désuétude *f* disuse **tomber en ~** to fall into disuse.

détachable *adj* detachable.

détachant *m* cleaner, stain remover.

détaché *m* staccato.

détachement *m* detachment, indifference.

détacher *vt* to detach, unfasten; **se ~** *vr* to become detached.

détail *m* detail, particular.

détaillant *m*, **-e** *f* retailer.

détailler *vt* to detail; to sell retail.

détartrage *m* descaling.

détartrant *m* descaling substance; * *adj* descaling.

détartrer *vt* to descale.

détaxe *f* reduction in tax.

détecter *vt* to detect.

détecteur *m* detector.

détection *f* detection.

détective *m* detective.

déteindre *vi* to lose colour, fade.

détendre *vt* to release, loosen; **se ~** *vr* to relax, calm down.

détendu *adj* slack; relaxed.

détenir *vt* to detain; to hold.

détente *f* relaxation, easing.

détenteur *m*, **-trice** *f* holder, possessor.

détergent *m* detergent.

détérioration *f* deterioration.

détériorer *vt* to damage; to impair; **se ~ vr** to deteriorate; to worsen.

déterminant *adj* determining, deciding.

détermination *f* determination; resolution.

déterminé *adj* determined, resolute.

déterminer *vt* to determine, decide.

déterrer *vt* to dig up, disinter.

détestable *adj* detestable, odious; **~ment** *adv* detestably.

détester *vt* to detest, hate.

détonateur *m* detonator.

détonation *f* detonation, explosion.

détonner *vi* to clash (colour); to go out of tune.

détour *m* detour; curve; evasion.

détourné *adj* indirect, oblique.

détournement *m* diversion, rerouting.

détourner *vt* to divert, reroute.

détracteur *m*, **-trice** *f* detractor, disparager.

détraquer *vt* to upset; to disorder; **se ~** *vr* to become upset; to go wrong.

détresse *f* distress, trouble.

détriment *m*: au ~ de to the detriment of.

détritus *m* refuse, rubbish.

détroit *m* strait.

détrôner *vt* to dethrone, depose.

détruire *vt* to destroy, demolish.

dette *f* debt.

deuil *m* mourning, bereavement, grief.

deux *adj* two; * *m* two; entre les ~ so-so, fair to middling; en moins de ~ in a jiffy.

deuxième *adj* second; ~ment *adv* secondly; * *mf* second.

deux-points *m* colon.

deux-roues *m* two-wheeled vehicle.

dévaler *vt vi* to hurry down, tear down.

dévaliser *vt* to burgle; to rifle.

dévalorisation *f* depreciation.

dévaloriser *vt* to depreciate, reduce the value of.

dévaluation *f* devaluation.

devancer *vt* to outstrip, outrun; to precede.

devant *prép* in front of, before; * *adv* in front; * *m* front; prendre les ~s to make the first move, pre-empt; aller au~~ de to anticipate.

devanture *f* display; shop-front.

dévaster *vt* to devastate, lay waste.

développement *m* development; growth; progress.

développer *vt* to develop, expand; se ~ *vr* to develop, grow.

devenir *vi* to become, grow.

déverrouiller *vt* to unbolt, unlock.

déverser *vt* to pour; to dump.

dévêtir *vt* to undress; se ~ *vr* to get undressed.

déviation *f* deviation; diversion.

dévier *vi* to deviate; to turn aside; to swerve.

devin *m*, -eresse *f* seer, soothsayer.

deviner *vt* to guess; to solve; to foretell.

devinette *f* riddle, poser.

devis *m* estimate, quotation.

dévisager *vt* to stare at.

devise *f* currency.

dévisser *vt* to unscrew, undo.

dévoiler *vt* to unveil, disclose.

devoir *m* duty; homework; *vt* to owe; to have to.

dévorer *vt* to devour, consume.

dévot *adj* devout, pious.

dévotion *f* devotion, piety.

dévoué *adj* devoted, dedicated.

dévouement *m* devotion, dedication.

dévouer(se) *vr* to devote oneself, sacrifice oneself.

dextérité *f* dexterity, adroitness.

diabète *m* diabetes.

diabétique *adj* diabetic.

diable *m* devil.

diablotin *m* imp; cracker (Christmas).

diabolique *adj* diabolical, devilish; ~ment *adv* diabolically.

diagnostic *m* diagnosis.

diagnostiquer *vt* to diagnose.

diagonale *f* diagonal.

diagramme *m* diagram; graph.

dialecte *m* dialect.

dialectique *f* dialectic; * *adj* dialectic.

dialogue *m* dialogue, conversation.

dialoguer *vt* to write in dialogue form.

dialyse *f* dialysis.

diamant *m* diamond.

diamètre *m* diameter.

diaphragme *m* diaphragm.

diarrhée *f* diarrhoea.

dictaphone *m* dictaphone.

dictateur *m*, **-trice** *f* dictator.

dictatorial *adj* dictatorial.

dictature *f* dictatorship.

dictée *f* dictating; dictation.

dicter *vt* to dictate, impose.

dictionnaire *m* dictionary.

dicton *m* saying, dictum.

didactique *adj* didactic.

dièse *f* sharp (*mus*).

diesel *m* diesel.

diète *f* diet.

diététicien *m*, **-ienne** *f* dietician.

diététique *adj* dietary.

dieu *m* god.

diffamation *f* defamation, slandering.

diffamer *vt* to defame, slander.

différé *adj* pre-recorded.

différemment *adv* differently.

différence *f* difference.

différenciation *f* differentiation.

différencier *vt* to differentiate.

différend *m* disagreement, difference of opinion.

différent *adj* different; various.

différer *vt* to differ; to vary.

difficile *adj* difficult; awkward, tricky; **~ment** *adv* with difficulty.

difficulté *f* difficulty; problem.

difforme *adj* deformed, misshapen.

difformité *f* deformity.

diffuser *vt* to diffuse, circulate, broadcast.

diffusion *f* diffusion, circulation, broadcasting.

digérer *vt* to digest.

digeste *adj* easily digestible.

digestif *adj* digestive.

digestion *f* digestion.

digital *adj* digital.

digne *adj* worthy; dignified; **~ment** *adv* worthily, deservedly.

dignité *f* dignity.

digression *f* digression.

digue *f* dyke; sea wall.

dilapider *vt* to squander; to embezzle.

dilatation *f* dilation, distension.

dilater *vt* to dilate, distend; **se ~** *vr* to dilate, distend.

dilemme *m* dilemma.

dilettante *mf* dilettante.

diluer *vt* to dilute.

dilution *f* dilution.

dimanche *m* Sunday.

dimension *f* dimension, size.

diminuer *vt* to diminish, reduce; * *vi* to diminish, lessen.

diminutif *m* diminutive.

diminution *f* reduction, lessening.

dinde *f* turkey hen.

dindon *m* turkey cock.

dindonneau *m* young turkey.

dîner *vi* to dine; * *m* dinner.

dinosaure *m* dinosaur.

diocèse *m* diocese.

diode *f* diode.

dioxyde *m* dioxide.

diphtérie *f* diphtheria.

diphtongue *f* diphthong.

diplomate *m* diplomat.

diplomatie *f* diplomacy.

diplomatique *adj* diplomatic; **~ment** *adv* diplomatically.

diplôme *m* diploma, certificate.

diplômé *m*, **-e** *f* holder of a diploma, *adj* qualified.

dire *vt* to say; to tell; **se ~** to say to oneself; to call oneself. *vr:* **se ~ que** to be said that.

direct *adj* direct; **~ement** *adv* directly; * *m* express.

directeur *m*, **-trice** *f* director.

direction *f* direction, management.

directive *f* directive, order.

dirigeant *m*, **-e** *f* leader, ruler; * *adj* ruling, executive.

diriger *vt* to run, direct; **se ~** *vr:* **se ~ vers** to head for, make for.

discernement *m* discernment, judgment.

discerner *vt* to discern, distinguish.

disciple *m* disciple.

disciplinaire *adj* disciplinary.

discipline *f* discipline.

discipliné *adj* disciplined.

discontinu *adj* discontinuous.

discordant *adj* discordant, conflicting.

discorde *f* discord, dissension.

discothèque *f* discotheque.

discours *m* speech, talking.

discourtois *adj* discourteous.

discréditer *vt* to discredit.

discret *adj* discreet.

discrétion *f* discretion, prudence.

discrétionnaire *adj* discretionary.

discrimination *f* discrimination.

discriminer *vt* to distinguish; to discriminate.

disculper *vt* to excuse, exonerate; **se ~** *vr* to justify oneself, excuse oneself.

discussion *f* discussion, debate.

discutable *adj* debatable, questionable.

discuter *vi*, *vt* to discuss, debate.

disgrâce *f* disgrace.

disgracieux *adj* awkward, ungraceful.

disjoncter *vi* to cut off, disconnect.

disjoncteur *m* cutout, circuit breaker.

disparaître *vi* to disappear, vanish.

disparate *adj* disparate, incongruous.

disparité *f* disparity, incongruity.

disparition *f* disappearance; death; extinction.

disparu *adj* vanished; bygone; missing.

dispensaire *m* dispensary.

dispense *f* dispensation, exemption.

dispenser *vt* to dispense, exempt; **se ~** *vr:* **se ~ de** to dispense with; to avoid.

disperser *vt* to spread, scatter; **se ~** *vr* to disperse, scatter.

dispersion *f* dispersal, scattering.

disponibilité *f* availability.

disponible *adj* available; transferable.

dispos *adj* refreshed; alert; in form.

disposer *vt* to arrange, dispose;

se ~ vr: se ~ à to prepare to do; * *vi* to leave.

dispositif *m* device, mechanism.

disposition *f* arrangement, layout.

disproportionné *adj* disproportionate.

dispute *f* dispute, argument.

disputer *vt* to dispute, rival; **se ~** *vr* to quarrel, argue.

disquaire *mf* record-dealer.

disqualifier *vt* to disqualify.

disque *m* disk; record.

disquette *f* diskette.

dissection *f* dissection.

dissemblable *adj* dissimilar; different.

disséminer *vt* to disseminate, scatter.

dissentiment *m* disagreement, dissent.

disséquer *vt* to dissect.

dissertation *f* dissertation.

dissidence *f* dissidence, dissent.

dissident *adj* dissident.

dissimulation *f* dissimulation, double-dealing.

dissimulé *adj* double-faced, dissembling.

dissimuler *vt* to dissemble, conceal; **se ~** *vr* to conceal oneself.

dissipation *f* dissipation, waste.

dissipé *adj* dissipated, undisciplined.

dissiper *vt* to dispel; to dissipate; **se ~** *vr* to disperse, become undisciplined.

dissociation *f* dissociation.

dissocier *vt* to dissociate.

dissolution *f* dissolution.

dissolvant *m* solvent, dissolvent.

dissonant *adj* dissonant; discordant.

dissoudre *vt* to dissolve.

dissuader *vt* to dissuade.

dissuasif *adj* dissuasive, deterrent.

dissuasion *f* dissuasion.

distance *f* distance, interval.

distancier(se) *vr* to distance oneself from.

distant *adj* distant.

distendre *vt* to distend, strain; **se ~** *vr* to become distended.

distillation *f* distillation.

distiller *vt* to distil.

distillerie *f* distillery.

distinct *adj* distinct, different; **~ement** *adv* distinctly.

distinctif *adj* distinctive.

distinction *f* distinction.

distingué *adj* distinguished.

distinguer *vt* to distinguish; to discern; **se ~** *vr* to distinguish oneself.

distorsion *f* distortion.

distraction *f* inattention; absent-mindedness; abstraction.

distraire *vt* to distract; to amuse; **se ~** *vr* to enjoy oneself.

distrait *adj* inattentive, absent-minded; **~ement** *adv* absent-mindedly.

distrayant *adj* entertaining, diverting.

distribuer *vt* to distribute.

distributeur *m* distributor.

distribution *f* distribution.

district *m* district.

diurétique *adj* diuretic; * *m* diuretic.

divagation f wandering, rambling.

divaguer vi to ramble, rave.

divan m divan.

divergence f divergence.

divergent adj divergent.

diverger vi to diverge, differ.

divers adj diverse, varied; ~ement adv diversely.

diversification f diversification.

diversifier vt to vary, diversify; se ~ vr to diversify.

diversion f diversion.

diversité f diversity, variety.

divertir vt to amuse, entertain; se ~ vr to amuse oneself.

divertissant adj amusing, entertaining.

divertissement m diversion, recreation.

dividende m dividend.

divin adj divine, exquisite; ~ement adv divinely.

divination f divination.

divinité f divinity.

diviser vt to divide, split; se ~ vr to split up, divide into.

division f division.

divorce m divorce.

divorcé m, -e f divorcee; * adj divorced.

divorcer vi to get divorced.

divulgation f disclosure, divulgence.

divulguer vt to divulge, disclose.

dix adj, m ten.

dix-huit adj, m eighteen.

dix-huitième adj, mf eighteenth.

dixième adj tenth; ~ment adv tenthly; * mf tenth.

dix-neuf adj, m nineteen.

dix-neuvième adj, mf nineteenth.

dix-sept adj, m seventeen.

dix-septième adj, mf seventeenth.

dizaine f ten, ten or so.

docile adj docile, submissive; ~ment adv docilely.

docilité f docility, submissiveness.

dock m dock, dockyard.

docteur m doctor.

doctorat m doctorate.

doctrine f doctrine.

document m document.

documentaire adj documentary.

documentaliste mf researcher.

documentation f documentation; information.

documenter vt to document; se ~ vr to gather information on.

dogmatique adj dogmatic.

dogme m dogma.

doigt m finger; être à deux ~s de to come very close to doing; obéir au ~ et à l'œil to toe the line.

doigté m touch; fingering technique.

domaine m domain, estate; sphere.

domanial adj domainal, belonging to an estate.

dôme m dome, vault.

domestique adj domestic, household.

domestiquer vt to domesticate, tame.

domicile m domicile, address.

domicilié adj domiciled.

dominant adj dominant, prevailing.

dominante f dominant characteristic.

dominateur adj governing; domineering.

domination f domination; to dominion.

dominer vt to dominate; to prevail; **se ~** to control oneself.

dominical adj Sunday.

dommage m damage; harm; **c'est ~** it's a pity.

dompter vt to tame, train.

dompteur m, **-euse** f trainer, tamer.

don m gift; talent.

donateur m, **-trice** f donor.

donation f donation.

donc conj so, therefore, thus; **pourquoi ~?** why was that?

donné adj given; fixed; **étant ~** seeing that, in view of.

donnée f datum.

donner vt to give; * vi to knock, beat.

donneur m, **-euse** f giver, donor; dealer.

dont pron whose, of which.

dopage m doping.

doper vt to dope; **se ~** vr to take drugs, dope oneself.

doré adj gilded; tanned.

dorénavant adv from now on, henceforth.

dorer vt to gild; to tan.

dorloter vt to pamper, pet.

dormir vi to sleep, be asleep; to be still.

dortoir m dormitory.

dos m back; top; ridge.

dosage m mixture; balance; proportioning.

dose f dose; amount; quantity.

doser vt to measure out, proportion; to strike a balance.

dossier m dossier, file; case.

dot f dowry.

doter vt to provide with a dowry; to endow.

douane f customs.

douanier m custom (s).

double adj double, duplicate, dual; **~ment** adv doubly; * m copy, double, replica; twice as much.

doubler vt vi to double, duplicate.

doublure f lining; understudy.

doucement adv softly, gently.

doucereux adj sugary; mawkish; suave.

douceur f softness, gentleness.

douche f shower.

doucher vt to give a shower to; **se ~** vr to take a shower.

doué adj gifted, endowed with.

douille f case; cartridge.

douillet adj delicate, tender; soft.

douleur f pain, ache; anguish.

douloureusement adv painfully, grievously.

douloureux adj painful, grievous.

doute m doubt, misgiving; **sans ~** without doubt.

douter vi to doubt, question; **se ~** vr **se ~ de** to suspect someone; **se ~ que** to suspect that, expect that.

douteux adj doubtful, dubious.

doux adj, f **douce** soft; sweet; mild.

douzaine f dozen.

douze adj, m twelve.

douzième adj twelfth; **~ment** twelfthly adv; * mf twelfth.

doyen m, **-enne** f dean; doyen.

draconien *adj* draconian, drastic.

dragée *f* bonbon, sugar-almond.

dragon *m* dragon.

dramatique *adj* dramatic, tragic; ~**ment** *adv* dramatically.

dramatiser *vt* to dramatize.

dramaturge *mf* playwright.

drame *m* drama.

drap *m* sheet; ~**housse** fitted sheet; **être dans de beaux ~s** to be in a fine mess.

drapeau *m* flag.

draper *vt* to drape.

dressage *m* taming; pitching.

dresser *vt* to draw up; to put up; **se ~** *vr* to stand up; to rear up.

dresseur *m*, **-euse** *f* trainer, tamer.

dribbler *vi* to dribble.

drogue *f* drug.

drogué *m*, **-e** *f* drug addict; * *adj* drugged.

droguer *vt* to drug, administer drugs; **se ~** *vr* to dose up; to take drugs.

droguerie *f* hardware trade.

droguiste *mf* hardware storekeeper.

droit *adj* right; straight; sound; honest; ~**ement** *adv* uprightly, honestly; * *adv* straight, straight ahead; * *m* right; law; tax.

droite *f* right side; right (wing); straight line.

droitier *adj* right-handed.

droiture *f* uprightness, honesty.

drôle *adj* funny, amusing; peculiar; ~**ment** *adv* funnily, peculiarly.

dromadaire *m* dromedary.

dru *adj* thick, dense; sturdy.

du *art* of the.

dû *adj* owed; due; ~**ment** *adv* duly.

dualité *f* duality.

dubitatif *adj* doubtful, dubious.

dubitativement *adv* doubtfully, dubiously.

duc *m* duke, **duchesse** *f* duchess.

duché *m* duchy.

duel *m* duel; dual.

duettiste *mf* duettist.

dune *f* dune.

duo *m* duo; duet.

duodénum *m* duodenum.

dupe *adj* easily duped; * *f* dupe.

duper *vt* to dupe, take in.

duplex *m* duplex, two-way.

dupliquer *vt* to duplicate.

dur *adj* hard, tough; difficult. ~**ement** *adv* harshly, severely.

durable *adj* durable, lasting; ~**ment** *adv* durably.

duralumin *m* duralumin.

durant *prép* during, for.

durcir *vt vi* to harden; **se ~** *vr* to become hardened.

durcissement *m* hardening.

durée *f* duration, length.

durer *vi* to last.

dureté *f* hardness; austerity, harshness.

durillon *m* callus, corn.

duvet *m* down.

duveté *adj* downy.

dynamique *f* dynamic; dynamics; * *adj* dynamic; ~**ment** *adv* dynamically.

dynamiser *vt* to energize; to potentiate.

dynamisme *m* dynamism.

dynamitage *m* dynamiting.

dynamite *f* dynamite.

dynamiter *vt* to dynamite.

dynamo *f* dynamo.
dynastie *f* dynasty.
dynastique *adj* dynastic.

dysenterie *f* dysentery.
dyslexie *f* dyslexia.
dyslexique *adj* dyslexic.

E

eau *f* water; rain.
eau-de-vie *f* brandy.
ébahir *vt* to astonish, stupefy, dumbfound.
ébahissement *m* astonishment, amazement.
ébauche *f* rough draft, rough outline.
ébaucher *vt* to sketch; to roughcast.
ébène *f* ebony.
ébéniste *m* cabinetmaker.
éblouir *vt* to dazzle; to fascinate.
éblouissant *adj* dazzling; amazing.
éblouissement *m* dazzle; bedazzlement.
ébouillanter *vt* to scald; to blanch; **s'~** *vr* to scald oneself.
éboulement *m* collapse, caving in; fall.
ébouriffé *adj* tousled, ruffled.
ébranler *vt* to shake; to unsettle, disturb.
ébrécher *vt* to chip, indent; to break into (fortune).
ébriété *f* intoxication.
ébrouer(s') *vr* to shake oneself.
ébruiter *vt* to disclose, divulge; **s'~** *vr* to spread, be noised abroad.
écaille *f* scale; shell.

écailler *vt* to scale; to chip; **s'~** *vr* to flake off, peel off.
écarlate *adj* scarlet.
écart *m* distance; interval; discrepancy; **rester à l'~** to steer clear of.
écarteler *vt* to tear apart; to quarter.
écarter *vt* to separate; to avert; to dismiss; **s'~** *vr* to make way; to swerve.
ecchymose *f* bruise, ecchymosis.
ecclésiastique *adj* ecclesiastical; * *m* ecclesiastic, clergyman.
échafaud *m* scaffold.
échafaudage *m* scaffolding.
échange *m* exchange, barter, trade.
échanger *vt* to exchange.
échantillon *m* sample.
échappée *f* breakaway; glimpse.
échappement *m* exhaust; release.
échapper *vi* to escape, avoid, elude; **s'~** *vr* to escape from; to leak.
écharde *f* splinter, sliver.
écharpe *f* scarf; arm-sling.
échassier *m* wader.
échauffement *m* heating; warm-up; constipation.
échauffer *vt* to heat, overheat; to excite; **s'~** *vr* to warm up; to get worked up.
échéance *f* expiry; maturity date.

échec m failure, defeat; chess.

échelle f ladder; scale.

échelon m rung; grade.

échelonner vt to grade; to stagger, set at intervals; **s'~** vr to be graduated, staggered.

échine f backbone, spine; **courber l'~** to submit.

échiquier m chessboard.

écho m echo; rumour.

échographie f ultrasound.

échoir vi to fall due; to befall, fall to someone's lot.

échouer vi to fail; to end up; to run aground.

éclabousser vt to splash, spatter.

éclair m flash; lightning flash; spark.

éclairage m lighting, light.

éclairagiste m electrician; lighting engineer.

éclaicie f clear interval, bright spot; glade.

éclaircir vt to lighten; to down; to brighten up; **s'~** vr to clear; to clear up.

éclaircissement m clearing up, explanation, elucidation.

éclairer vt to light, illuminate; clarify, explain.

éclat m brightness, glare; splinter; splendour.

éclatant adj bright, blazing; resounding; blatant.

éclatement m explosion, bursting, rupture.

éclater vi to explode; to break out; to exclaim.

éclectique adj eclectic.

éclipse f eclipse.

éclipser vt to eclipse, overshadow; **s'~** vr to disappear, vanish.

éclore vi to hatch out; to blossom.

éclosion f hatching; blooming; birth.

écluse f lock.

écœurant adj disgusting, nauseating.

écœurement m nausea, disgust; discouragement.

écœurer vt to nauseate, disgust.

école f school, schooling; sect, doctrine.

écolier m schoolboy, **-ière** f schoolgirl.

écologie f ecology.

écologique adj ecological.

écologiste mf ecologist.

économe adj thrifty; * mf steward, treasurer.

économie f economy, thrift; economics.

économique adj economic; **~ment** adv economically.

économiser vt to economize; to save.

écorce f bark, peel, skin.

écorchure f scratch; graze.

Ecossais m Scotsman, **-e** f Scotswoman.

écossais adj Scottish.

Ecosse f Scotland.

écoulement m flow, discharge, outlet; disposal, selling.

écouler vt to flow, discharge; to sell; **s'~** vr to leak, flow out; to pass by; to sell.

écoute f listening, audience.

écouter vt to listen to, hear.

écran m screen.

écrasant adj crushing; overwhelming.

écraser vt to crush; to overwhelm; to run over; **s'~** vr to crash; to get crushed.

écrémer vt to skim, cream.

écrevisse f crayfish.

écrin m box, casket.

écrire vt to write; to spell.

écrit adj written; * m document; piece of writing.

écriteau m notice, sign.

écriture f writing; handwriting; script.

écrivain m writer.

écrou m nut.

écroulement m collapse, caving in.

écrouler(s') vr to collapse; to crumble.

écru adj raw; unbleached; untreated.

ectoplasme m ectoplasm.

écueil m reef, shelf; peril.

écume f foam, froth; scum.

écureuil m squirrel.

écurie f stable.

écusson m badge, shield.

eczéma m eczema.

édification f erection, construction.

édifice m edifice, building.

édifier vt to build, construct; to edify.

éditer vt to publish, produce; to edit.

éditeur m, **-trice** f publisher; editor.

édition f publishing; edition; editing.

éditorial m leading article, editorial.

éducatif adj educational.

éducation f education; upbringing.

édulcorant m sweetener; * adj sweetening.

éduquer vt to educate; to bring up, raise.

effacer vt to efface, erase, wipe off; **s'~** vr to wear away, become obliterated.

effaré adj alarmed, bewildered.

effaroucher vt to frighten; to shock.

effectif m staff; size, complement; * adj effective, positive.

effectivement adv effectively, positively.

effectuer vt to effect, execute, carry out.

effervescence f effervescence; excitement, ferment.

effervescent adj effervescent; excited.

effet m effect, impression; spin; bill, note.

efficace adj effective; efficient; **~ment** adv effectively, efficiently.

efficacité f effectiveness, efficiency.

effleurer vt to touch lightly, skim across.

effondrement m collapse, caving in.

effondrer(s') vr to collapse, cave in.

efforcer(s') vr to endeavour, do one's best.

effort m effort, exertion; stress, strain.

effraction f breaking and entering.

effrayant *adj* frightening, fearsome.

effrayer *vt* to frighten, scare.

effriter *vt* to crumble; to exhaust (land); **s'~** *vr* to crumble away, disintegrate.

effroi *m* terror, dismay.

effronté *adj* shameless, impudent, cheeky; **~ment** *adv* shamelessly, impudently.

effroyable *adj* horrifying, appalling; **~ment** *adv* horrifyingly, appallingly.

égal *adj* equal; even, level; equable; **~ement** *adv* evenly; equally; also, as well.

égaler *vt* to equal, match.

égalisation *f* equalization; levelling.

égaliser *vt* to equalize; to level out.

égalitaire *adj* egalitarian.

égalité *f* equality; equableness; evenness.

égard *m* consideration, respect; **à l'~ de** concerning, regarding; **à tous ~s** in all respects.

égarer *vt* to mislead, lead astray; **s'~** *vr* to get lost; to wander from the point.

égayer *vt* to enliven, cheer up.

églantine *f* eglantine, wild rose.

église *f* church.

égocentrique *adj* egocentric, self-centred.

égoïsme *m* selfishness, egoism.

égoïste *mf* egotist; * *adj* egotistic; **~ment** *adv* egotistically.

égout *m* sewer.

égoutter *vt* to strain; to wring out.

égratignure *f* scratch, scrape.

éjecter *vt* to eject, throw out.

élaboration *f* elaboration, development.

élaborer *vt* to elaborate, develop.

élan *m* surge, momentum, speed; spirit, elan.

élancer(s') *vr* to rush, spring, hurl oneself.

élargir *vt* to widen, stretch; **s'~** *vr* to get wider.

élargissement *m* widening, stretching, enlarging.

élastique *adj* elastic; flexible; * *m* elastic, elastic band.

électeur *m*, **-trice** *f* voter, elector.

élection *f* election; choice.

électoral *adj* electoral.

électorat *m* electorate; constituency; franchise.

électricien *m* electrician.

électricité *f* electricity.

électrique *adj* electric.

électrocardiogramme *m* electrocardiogram.

électrode *f* electrode.

électrolyse *f* electrolysis.

électroménager *m* household appliance; * *adj* electrical (household).

électron *m* electron.

électronicien *m* electronics engineer.

électronique *f* electronics; * *adj* electronic.

élégance *f* elegance, stylishness.

élégant *adj* elegant, stylish.

élément *m* element, component; cell; fact.

élémentaire *adj* elementary; basic.

éléphant *m* elephant.

élevage *m* rearing, breeding.

élève *mf* pupil, student.

élevé *adj* high; heavy; lofty, exalted.

élever *vt* to bring up, raise; to put up, lift up.; **s'~** *vr* to rise, go up.

éleveur *m*, **-euse** *f* stockbreeder.

éligible *adj* eligible.

élimination *f* elimination.

éliminatoire *adj* eliminatory; * *f* preliminary heat.

éliminer *vt* to eliminate, discard.

élire *vt* to elect.

élite *f* elite.

élitisme *m* elitism.

elle *pron* she; it; her; **c'est à ~** it's up to her; it's her's; **~~même** herself.

elliptique *adj* elliptic; **~ment** *adv* elliptically.

élocution *f* elocution, diction.

éloge *m* praise; eulogy.

élogieux *adj* laudatory, eulogistic.

éloigné *adj* distant, remote.

éloigner *vt* to move away, take away; **s'~** *vr* to go away; to grow distant.

éloquence *f* eloquence.

éloquent *adj* eloquent.

élu *adj* chosen, elected.

élucider *vt* to elucidate, clear up.

émacié *adj* emaciated, wasted.

émail *m* enamel.

émailler *vt* to enamel.

émancipation *f* emancipation, liberation.

émanciper *vt* to emancipate, liberate; **s'~** *vr* to become emancipated, liberated.

émaner *vi* to emanate, issue.

emballage *m* packing paper, wrapping paper.

emballer *vt* to pack up, wrap up.

embarcadère *m* landing stage, pier.

embarcation *f* boat, craft.

embargo *m* embargo.

embarquement *m* loading; embarkation.

embarquer *vt* to embark; to load; * *vi* to embark, go aboard.

embarras *m* embarrassment, confusion; trouble.

embarrassant *adj* embarrassing, uncomfortable.

embarrassé *adj* embarrassed, self-conscious.

embarrasser *vt* to embarrass; to hinder, hamper; **s'~** *vr* to burden oneself with; to be troubled with.

embaucher *vt* to take on, hire.

embellir *vt* to beautify, make more attractive.

embellissement *m* embellishment, improvement.

embêter *vt* (*fam*) to bore; to get on one's nerves; **s'~** *vr* to be bored, fed up.

emblème *m* symbol, emblem.

emboîter *vt* to fit together; to follow closely; **s'~** *vr* to fit together; to fit into each other.

embonpoint *m* stoutness, plumpness.

embouchure *f* mouth (river); mouthpiece.

embouteillage *m* traffic jam; bottling.

embranchement *m* junction; side road.

embrasser *vt* to kiss, embrace.

embrayage *m* clutch.

embrayer *vi* to engage the clutch.

embrouiller vt to tangle up, mix up; **s'~** vr to become muddled, confused.

embryon m embryo.

embryonnaire adj embryonic.

embuscade f ambush.

émeraude f emerald.

émerger vi to emerge; to stand out.

émeri m emery.

émerveiller vt to astonish, amaze; **s'~** vr to marvel at.

émetteur adj transmitting.

émettre vt to send out, emit, transmit.

émeute f riot.

émietter vt to crumble; to disperse, break up; **s'~** vr to crumble; to disperse, break up.

émigration f emigration.

émigré m, **-e** f émigré, expatriate.

émigrer vi to emigrate.

éminence f hill, elevation; eminence, distinction.

éminent adj eminent, distinguished.

émir m emir.

émission f sending out; transmission; broadcast; emission.

emmêler vt to entangle; confuse; **s'~** vr to tangle.

emménager vi to move in.

emmener vt to take away; to lead.

émoi m agitation, emotion.

émotif adj emotional; emotive.

émotion f emotion; commotion.

émotivité f emotionalism.

émouvant adj moving, touching.

émouvoir vt to move, disturb, upset; **s'~** vr to be moved; to get worried, upset.

empailler vt to stuff.

empaqueter vt to parcel up, pack.

emparer(s') vr to seize, grab; to take possession of.

empêchement m obstacle, hitch; impediment.

empêcher vt to prevent, stop; **s'~** vr: **s'~ de** to refrain from doing something.

empereur m emperor.

empester vt to stink of; to poison, infect.

empêtrer vt to entangle,; **s'~** vr to get involved in, get mixed up in.

emphase f pomposity; emphasis, stress.

empiéter vi to encroach, overlap.

empiler vt to pile up, stack.

empire m empire; influence, ascendancy.

empirer vi to get worse, deteriorate.

empirique adj empirical; **~ment** adv empirically.

emplacement m site, location.

emploi m use; job, employment.

employé m, **-e** f employee.

employer vt to use; to spend; to employ.

employeur m, **euse** f employer.

empoisonner vt to poison; to annoy.

emporter vt to take; to carry off; to involve; **s'~** vr to lose one's temper.

empreinte f imprint, impression, stamp.

empresser(s') vi to rush to; to press around, fuss around.

emprise f hold, ascendancy.

emprisonner vt to imprison; to trap.

emprunt m borrowing, loan.

emprunter vt to borrow; to assume; to derive.

ému adj moved; filled with emotion; touched; excited.

émulsion f emulsion.

en prép in; to; by; on; ~ **tant que** as; pron from there; of it, of them; **je n'~ veux plus** I don't want any more of them; **s'~ faire** to worry; **il ~ va de même pour** the same goes for.

encadré m box; framed text.

encadrement m framing; training; managerial staff.

encadrer vt to frame; to train; to surround.

encaissement m collection; receipt; cashing.

encaisser vt to collect, receive; to cash.

encastrer vt to embed, fit in, encase.

enceinte f pregnant.

encens m incense.

encenser vt to cense; to shower praise on.

encercler vt to encircle, surround.

enchaînement m linking; link; sequence.

enchaîner vt to chain.

enchanté adj enchanted, delighted.

enchantement m enchantment, delight.

enchanter vt to enchant, delight.

enchâsser vt to set, imbed.

enchère f bid, offer.

enchevêtrement m entanglement, confusion.

enclave f enclave.

enclencher vt to engage; to set in motion.

enclin adj inclined, prone.

enclore vt to enclose, shut in.

enclume f anvil; engine block.

encoder vt to encode.

encolure f neck; collar size.

encombrant adj unwieldy, cumbersome.

encombrement m congestion; jumble; obstruction.

encombrer vt to clutter, obstruct; **s'~** vr to burden oneself.

encore adv still; only; again; more; ~ **que** even though.

encourageant adj encouraging, heartening.

encouragement m encouragement.

encourager vt to encourage; to incite.

encre f ink.

encyclopédie f encyclop(a)edia.

endettement m indebtedness; debt.

endetter vt to get so into debt; **s'~** vr to get into debt.

endive f chicory.

endoctrinement m indoctrination.

endoctriner vt to indoctrinate.

endommager vt to damage.

endormir vt to put to sleep; **s'~** vr to fall asleep.

endossement m endorsement.

endosser vt to put on; to shoulder; to endorse.

endroit m place; side part; **à l'~** regarding.

enduire vt to coat, smear.

enduit m coating.

endurance f endurance, stamina.

endurci adj hardened; hard-hearted.

endurcir vt to harden; **s'~** vr to become hardened.

endurer vt to endure, bear.

énergétique adj energy; energizing.

énergie f energy; spirit, vigour.

énergique adj energetic, vigorous; **~ment** adv energetically.

énervant adj enervating; irritating.

énervement m irritation; nervousness.

énerver vt to irritate, annoy; to get on one's nerves; **s'~** vr to get excited, worked up.

enfance f childhood; infancy.

enfant mf child; native.

enfanter vt to give birth to.

enfantillage m childishness.

enfantin adj childish, infantile.

enfer m hell.

enfermer vt to lock up; to confine; to box in.

enfiévrer vt to stir up, inflame.

enfiler vt to string, thread; to put on.

enfin adv at last; in short; after all.

enflammer vt to set on fire; to inflame, kindle; **s'~** vr to catch fire, ignite.

enflé adj swollen; bombastic, turgid.

enfler vi to swell up, inflate.

enfoncer vt to stick in, thrust; to break open; **s'~** vr to sink into, disappear into.

enfouir vt to bury.

enfuir(s') vr to run away, flee.

engagement m agreement, commitment, undertaking; engaging; opening.

engager vt to bind; to involve; to

insert; to open; **s'~** vr to undertake to; to take a job.

engelure f chilblain.

engendrer vt to create, engender; to father.

engin m machine; instrument; contraption.

englober vt to include, encompass.

engloutir vt to wolf down; to engulf.

engorgement m obstruction, clogging; glut.

engouement m infatuation; fad, craze.

engouffrer vt to devour, swallow up, engulf; **s'~** vr to sweep, surge.

engourdi adj numb; dull.

engourdir vt to numb; to dull, blunt; **s'~** vr to become numb, to grow sluggish.

engourdissement m numbness; sleepiness.

engrais m fertilizer; manure.

engraisser vi to get fatter; * vt to fatten; to fertilize.

engrenage m gears, gearing.

énigmatique adj enigmatic; **~ment** adv enigmatically.

énigme f enigma, riddle.

enivrer vt to intoxicate, make drunk; **s'~** vr to get drunk.

enjeu m stake.

enjoliver vt to ornament; to embroider (truth).

enlacer vt to embrace, intertwine.

enlaidir vt to make ugly; **s'~** vr to become ugly.

enlèvement m abduction, kidnapping; removal.

enlever *vt* to remove; to take off; to deprive; to abduct.

enliser *vt* to get stuck (car); **s'~** *vr* to get bogged down, get sucked into.

enneigé *adj* snowy, snowbound.

enneigement *m* snow coverage.

ennemi *m*, **-e** *f* enemy.

ennui *m* boredom, tedium, weariness.

ennuyer *vt* to bore, bother; **s'~** *vr* to get bored.

ennuyeux *adj* boring, tedious.

énorme *adj* enormous, huge.

énormément *adv* enormously.

énormité *f* enormity, hugeness; howler.

enquête *f* inquiry, investigation; survey.

enquêter *vi* to hold an inquiry; to investigate.

enraciner *vt* to implant, root; **s'~** *vr* to take root; to settle down somewhere.

enragé *adj* furious; keen.

enregistrement *m* recording; registration.

enregistrer *vt* to record; to register.

enrichi *adj* improved, enriched; nouveau riche.

enrichir *vt* to enrich, expand; **s'~** *vr* to get rich.

enrichissant *adj* enriching.

enrichissement *m* enrichment.

enrober *vt* to wrap, cover, coat.

enrôler *vt* to enlist, enrol.

enrouement *m* hoarseness.

enrouer *vt* to make hoarse.

enrouler *vt* to roll up, wind up.

enseignant *m*, **-e** *f* teacher.

enseigne *f* sign; ensign.

enseignement *m* education, training, instruction.

enseigner *vt* to teach.

ensemble *adv* together, at the same time; * *m* unity; whole.

ensoleillé *adj* sunny.

ensorceler *vt* to bewitch, enchant.

ensuite *adv* then, next, afterwards.

entaille *f* cut, gash.

entamer *vt* to start, open, make a hole in.

entassement *m* piling up, heaping up.

entasser *vt* to pile up, heap up.

entendement *m* understanding, comprehension.

entendre *vt* to hear; to intend, mean; to understand; **s'~** *vr* to agree; to know how to.

entendu *adj* agreed; **bien ~** of course.

entente *f* harmony, understanding; accord.

enterrement *m* burial; funeral.

enterrer *vt* to bury, inter.

en-tête *m* heading, header.

entêté *adj* stubborn, obstinate.

entêtement *m* stubbornness, obstinacy.

entêter *vt* to go to the head of; **s'~** *vr* to persist in.

enthousiasme *m* enthusiasm.

enthousiasmer *vt* to fill with enthusiasm; **s'~** *vr* to be enthusiastic about.

enthousiaste *adj* enthusiastic; * *mf* enthusiast.

entier *adj* entire, whole; intact.

entièrement *adv* entirely, wholly, completely.

entité *f* entity.

entonnoir *m* funnel; swallow hole; shell-hole.

entorse *f* sprain.

entortiller *vt* to twist, twine; to hoodwink, wheedle.

entourage *m* set, circle; entourage.

entourer *vt* to surround, frame, encircle; **s'~ de:** **s'~ de** to surround oneself with.

entracte *m* interval, intermission.

entraide *f* mutual aid.

entraider(s') *vr* to help one another.

entrailles *fpl* entrails, guts; womb.

entrain *m* spirit, liveliness.

entraînement *m* training, coaching; force, impetus.

entraîner *vt* to drag; to lead; to train; **s'~** *vr* to train oneself.

entraîneur *m* trainer, coach.

entrave *f* hindrance, obstacle; shackle.

entraver *vt* to hold up; to shackle.

entre *prép* between, among, into.

entrebâiller *vt* to half-open; **s'~** to be half-open.

entrecôte *f* rib steak.

entrecouper *vt* to intersperse, interrupt with.

entrée *f* entry, entrance; admission; insertion; **~ en matière** introduction; **d'~ de jeu** from the outset.

entrejambes *m* crotch.

entrelacer *vt* to intertwine, interlace.

entremêler *vt* to intermingle, intermix.

entremets *m* sweet, dessert.

entreposer *vt* to store, put into storage.

entrepôt *m* warehouse, bonded warehouse.

entreprenant *adj* enterprising.

entreprendre *vt* to embark upon, undertake.

entrepreneur *m*, **-euse** *f* contractor; entrepreneur.

entreprise *f* company; venture, business.

entrer *vi* to enter, go in.

entresol *m* entresol, mezzanine.

entretemps *adv* meanwhile.

entretenir *vt* to maintain, look after; to speak with.

entretien *m* upkeep, maintenance; conversation.

entrevoir *vt* to make out; to glimpse; to anticipate.

entrevue *f* meeting, interview.

entrouvert *adj* half-open.

entrouvrir *vt* to half-open; **s'~** *vr* to half-open; to gape.

énumération *f* enumeration, listing.

énumérer *vt* to enumerate, list.

envahir *vt* to invade, overrun.

envahissant *adj* invasive; intrusive; pervasive.

enveloppe *f* envelope; covering; exterior.

envelopper *vt* to envelop; to wrap up; to veil.

envergure *f* breadth, scope, scale.

envers *prép* towards, to; * *m*; **à l'~** inside out, upside down.

envie *f* desire, longing, inclination; envy.

envier *vt* to envy.

envieux *adj* envious.

environ *adv* about, around; **~s** *mpl* vicinity, neighbourhood.

environnant *adj* surrounding.

environnement *m* environment.

environnemental *adj* environmental.

environner *vt* to surround, encircle.

envisager *vt* to view, envisage.

envoi *m* dispatch, remittance; kick-off.

envol *m* takeoff, flight.

envoler(s') *vr* to fly away; to disappear.

envoûtant *adj* bewitching, entrancing.

envoûter *vt* to bewitch.

envoyé *m*, **-e** *f* messenger, envoy.

envoyer *vt* to send, dispatch; hurl, fire.

enzyme *m* enzyme.

épais *adj* thick; deep.

épaisseur *f* thickness; depth.

épaissir *vi* to thicken; to deepen; * *vt*; **s'~** *vr* to thicken, get thicker.

épanoui *adj* radiant, beaming.

épanouir *vt* to brighten, light up; open out; **s'~** *vr* to bloom.

épanouissement *m* blooming; lighting up; opening out.

épargne *f* saving, savings.

épargner *vt* to save; to spare.

éparpiller *vt* to scatter, distribute; **s'~** *vr* to scatter.

épaule *f* shoulder.

épauler *vt* to support, back up.

épave *f* wreck; derelict; ruin.

épée *f* sword.

épeler *vt* to spell.

éperdu *adj* distraught, overcome;

~ment *adv* frantically, desperately.

éperon *m* spur; cutwater.

épervier *m* sparrowhawk.

éphémère *adj* ephemeral, fleeting.

épi *m* ear; tuft.

épice *m* spice.

épicé *adj* spicy; juicy.

épicerie *f* grocery trade; grocer's shop.

épicier *m*, **-ière** *f* grocer; greengrocer.

épidémie *f* epidemic.

épidémique *adj* epidemic; contagious.

épiderme *m* epidermis; skin.

épier *vt* to spy on.

épiglotte *f* epiglottis.

épilation *f* removal of hair.

épilepsie *f* epilepsy.

épileptique *adj* epileptic.

épiler *vt* to remove hair, pluck.

épilogue *m* epilogue; conclusion.

épinard *m* spinach.

épine *f* spine; thorn; quill.

épineux *adj* thorny, prickly; tricky.

épingle *f* pin.

épiphanie *f* Epiphany.

épique *adj* epic.

épiscopal *adj* episcopal.

épiscopat *m* episcopate.

épisode *m* episode.

épisodique *adj* occasional; transitory; **~ment** *adv* occasionally.

épitaphe *f* epitaph.

épithète *f* epithet.

éplucher *vt* to clean; to peel; to sift.

épluchure *f* peeling, paring.

éponge *f* sponge.

éponger *vt* to sponge, mop.

épopée f epic.

époque f time, epoch, age, period.

épouser vt to marry, wed; espouse.

épousseter vt to dust.

épouvantable adj terrible, appalling; **~ment** adv terribly, appallingly.

épouvantail m scarecrow.

épouvante f terror, dread.

épouvanter vt to terrify, appall.

époux m, **épouse** f spouse.

éprendre(s') vr to fall in love with.

épreuve f test; ordeal, trial; proof.

éprouvant adj trying, testing.

éprouver vt to feel, experience.

éprouvette f test tube.

épuisé adj exhausted; sold out.

épuisement m exhaustion.

épuiser vt to exhaust, wear out; **s'~** vr to run out; to exhaust oneself.

épuisette f landing net.

épurer vt to purify, refine.

équateur m equator.

équation f equation.

équatorial adj equatorial.

équerre f square; brace.

équestre adj equestrian.

équilibre m balance, equilibrium; harmony.

équilibrer vt to balance; **s'~** vr to balance each other.

équipage m crew; gear, equipment.

équipe f team, crew, gang, staff.

équipement m equipment; fitting out, fittings.

équiper vt to equip, fit out.

équipier m, **-ière** f team member.

équitable adj equitable, fair; **~ment** adv equitably, fairly.

équitation f equitation, riding.

équivalence f equivalence.

équivalent adj equivalent, same; ***** m equivalent.

équivoque adj equivocal, questionable.

érable m maple.

érafler vt to scratch, scrape.

ère f era.

érection f erection; establishment.

éreintant adj exhausting, backbreaking.

ergot m spur; lug.

ériger vt to erect; to establish.

ermite m hermit.

éroder vt to erode.

érosion f erosion.

érotique adj erotic.

érotisme m eroticism.

errant adj wandering, stray.

errer vi to wander, roam.

erreur f error, mistake, fault.

erroné adj erroneous.

éructation f eructation.

érudit adj erudite, learned.

érudition f erudition, learning.

éruptif adj eruptive.

éruption f eruption.

escabeau m stool; stepladder.

escadron m squadron, platoon.

escalade f climbing; escalation.

escalader vt to climb, scale.

escale f port of call, touchdown.

escalier m stairs, steps.

escalope f escalope.

escamoter vt to dodge, evade; to pilfer.

escapade f escapade; prank, jaunt.

escargot m snail.

escarpement m escarpment; steepness.

esclavage m slavery, bondage.

esclavagisme m proslavery.

esclave mf slave.

escompte m discount.

escompter vt to discount.

escorte f escort; retinue.

escorter vt to escort.

escrime f fencing.

escrimeur m, **-euse** f fencer.

escroc m crook, con man.

escroquer vt to swindle, con.

ésotérique adj esoteric.

espace m space, interval.

espacement m spacing, interval.

espacer vt to space out.

espadon m swordfish.

espadrille f espadrille, rope-soled sandal.

espèce f sort, kind; species.

espérance f hope, expectation.

espérer vt to hope.

espion m, **-onne** f spy.

espionnage m espionage, spying.

espionner vt to spy.

esplanade f esplanade.

espoir m hope.

esprit m mind, intellect; spirit; wit.

esquimau m, **-aude** f Eskimo.

esquisse f sketch, outline.

esquisser vt to sketch, outline.

esquiver vt to dodge; to shirk.

essai m test, trial; attempt; essay.

essaim m swarm.

essayage m fitting, trying on.

essayer vt to test, try, try on.

essence f petrol; essential oil.

essentiel adj essential, basic; **-lement** adv essentially, basically.

essieu m axle.

essorage m wringing, mangling.

essorer vt to wring, mangle.

essouffler vt to wind; **s'~** vr to get out of breath.

essuyer vt to wipe, mop; **s'~** vr to wipe oneself.

est m east.

esthète mf aesthete.

esthéticien m, **-ienne** f beautician.

esthétique adj aesthetic; attractive; **~ment** adv aesthetically; * f aesthetics.

estimation f valuation; estimation, reckoning.

estime f esteem, respect, regard.

estimer vt to value, assess, estimate.

estival adj summer.

estivant m, **-e** f holidaymaker, summer visitor.

estomac m stomach.

estomper vt to blur, dim **s'~** vr to become blurred.

estrade f platform, rostrum.

estragon m tarragon.

et conj and.

étable f cowshed.

établi adj established; * m workbench.

établir vt to establish, set up; **s'~** vr to settle; to set oneself up as; to become established.

établissement m establishing, building; establishment.

étage m floor, storey; stage, level.

étagère f shelf.

étalage m display, display window; stall.

étalagiste mf window dresser; stallholder.

étaler vt to spread, strew; to stagger; to display.

étalon m stallion.

étanche *adj* waterproof.

étanchéité *f* waterproofness.

étang *m* pond.

étape *f* stage, leg; staging point.

état *m* state, condition; statement.

étatique *adj* under state control.

étatiser *vt* to bring under state control, nationalize.

état-major *m* (*mil*) staff; staff headquarters.

étau *m* vice.

étayer *vt* to prop up, support.

été *m* summer.

éteindre *vt* to put out, extinguish; **s'~** *vr* to go out; to die; to evaporate.

éteint *adj* faded; extinct.

étendard *m* standard.

étendre *vt* to spread, extend; to floor; **s'~** *vr* to spread; to stretch out; to increase.

étendu *adj* extensive, sprawling, wide.

étendue *f* expanse, area; duration.

éternel *adj* eternal, everlasting; **~lement** *adv* eternally.

éterniser *vt* to draw out; to immortalize; **s'~** *vr* to drag on, linger on.

éternité *f* eternity; ages.

éternuer *vi* to sneeze.

éthane *m* ethane.

éther *m* ether.

ethnie *f* ethnic unit.

ethnique *adj* ethnic.

ethnologie *f* ethnology.

ethnologue *mf* ethnologist.

étincelant *adj* sparkling; gleaming.

étinceler *vi* to sparkle, gleam.

étincelle *f* spark; gleam, glimmer.

étiqueter *vt* to label, mark.

étiquette *f* label, ticket; etiquette.

étirement *m* stretching.

étirer *vt* to stretch, draw out; **s'~** *vr* to stretch out.

étoffe *f* material, fabric; stuff.

étoile *f* star.

étoilé *adj* starry.

étonnant *adj* astonishing, surprising.

étonné *adj* astonished, surprised.

étonnement *m* surprise, astonishment.

étonner *vt* to astonish, surprise; **s'~** *vr* to be astonished.

étouffant *adj* stifling.

étouffer *vt* to suffocate; to muffle; **s'~** *vr* to be suffocated, to swelter.

étourderie *f* absentmindedness.

étourdi *adj* absentminded; **~ment** *adv* absentmindedly.

étourdir *vt* to stun, daze; to deafen.

étourdissant *adj* deafening; stunning.

étourdissement *m* blackout, dizzy spell; surprise.

étourneau *m* starling.

étrange *adj* strange, funny; **~ment** *adv* strangely, oddly.

étranger *m*, **-ère** *f* foreigner, stranger, alien; * *adj* foreign, strange, unknown.

étrangeté *f* strangeness, oddness.

étranglement *m* strangulation; bottleneck.

étrangler *vt* to strangle, stifle; **s'~** *vr* to strangle oneself, choke.

être *vi* to be; **c'est-à-dire** namely, that is to say; * *m* being, person, soul.

étreindre vt to embrace, hug; to seize.

étreinte f embrace; stranglehold.

étrier m stirrup.

étroit adj narrow; strict; **~ement** adv closely; strictly.

étude f study; survey; office.

étudier vt to study, examine.

étui m case; holster.

étymologie f etymology.

étymologique adj etymological.

eu = p.p. avoir had.

eucalyptus m eucalyptus.

eucharistie f eucharist.

euphémisme m euphemism.

euphorie f euphoria.

euphorique adj euphoric.

européen m, **-enne** f European; * adj European.

euthanasie f euthanasia.

eux pron they, them; **c'est à ~** it's up to them; it's theirs; **~-mêmes** themselves.

évacuation f evacuation; emptying.

évacuer vt to evacuate, clear.

évader(s') vr to escape.

évaluation f evaluation, appraisal.

évaluer vt to evaluate, appraise.

évangélique adj evangelical.

évangéliser vt to evangelize.

évangile m gospel.

évanouir(s') vr to faint, pass out.

évanouissement m faint, blackout.

évaporation f evaporation.

évaporer(s') vr to evaporate.

évasif adj evasive.

évasion f escape; escapism.

évasivement adv evasively.

évêché m bishopric.

éveil m awakening; dawning.

éveiller vt to waken, arouse; **s'~** vr to wake up.

événement m event, incident.

éventail m fan; range.

éventaire m tray; stall.

éventualité f eventuality, possibility.

éventuel adj possible; **~lement** adv possibly.

évêque m bishop.

évertuer(s') vr to strive to.

évidemment adv obviously, evidently.

évidence f evidence, proof.

évident adj obvious, evident.

évier m sink.

évincer vt to oust; to evict.

éviter vt to avoid; to spare.

évocation f evocation, recall.

évolué adj developed, advanced; enlightened.

évoluer vi to evolve, develop.

évolution f evolution, development.

évoquer vt to evoke, recall.

exacerber vt to exacerbate, aggravate.

exact adj exact, accurate; **~ement** adv exactly.

exactitude f exactness, accuracy.

exagération f exaggeration.

exagéré adj exaggerated, excessive; **~ment** adv exaggeratedly.

exagérer vt to exaggerate.

exaltation f elation; extolling, praising.

exalter vt to exalt, glorify; to elate.

examen m examination, survey, investigation.

examinateur m, **-trice** f examiner.

examiner vt to examine, survey.
exaspération f exasperation.
exaspérer vt to exasperate.
exaucer vt to fulfil, grant.
excédent m surplus, excess.
excédentaire adj surplus, excess.
excellent adj excellent.
exceller vi to excel.
excentricité f eccentricity.
excentrique adj eccentric; ~ment adv eccentrically.
excepté adj apart, aside; * prép except, but for.
exception f exception, derogation.
exceptionnel adj exceptional; ~lement adv exceptionally.
excès m excess, surplus.
excessivement adv excessively.
excitant m stimulant; * adj exciting, stimulating.
excitation f excitation, stimulation; incitement.
exciter vt to excite, stimulate; s'~ vr to get excited.
exclamation f exclamation.
exclamer(s') vr to exclaim.
exclu adj excluded, outcast.
exclure vt to exclude, oust, expel.
exclusif adj exclusive.
exclusion f exclusion, suspension.
exclusivement adv exclusively.
exclusivité f exclusive rights.
excrément m excrement.
excroissance f excrescence, outgrowth.
excursion f excursion, trip.
excursionniste mf tripper; walker.
excuse f excuse, pretext.
excuser vt to excuse, forgive; s'~ vr to apologize for.

exécrable adj execrable, atrocious; ~ment adv atrociously, execrably.
exécration f execration, loathing.
exécrer vt to execrate, loathe.
exécuter vt to execute, carry out, perform; to produce.
exécution f execution, carrying out, performance.
exemplaire m copy, archetype; * adj model, exemplary; ~ment adv exemplarily.
exemple m example, model, instance.
exempt adj exempt, free from.
exercer vt to exercise, perform, fulfil; s'~ vr to practise.
exercice m exercise, practice, use; financial year.
exhaustif adj exhaustive.
exhaustivement adv exhaustively.
exhiber vt to exhibit, show; to produce; s'~ vr to show off; to expose oneself.
exhibition f exhibition, show; display.
exhibitionniste mf exhibitionist.
exhortation f exhortation.
exhorter vt to exhort, urge.
exigeant adj demanding, exacting.
exigence f demand, requirement; exigency.
exiger vt to demand, require.
exigu, exiguë adj scanty, exiguous.
exiguïté f exiguity, scantiness.
exil m exile.
exilé adj, m, -e exile; * adj exiled.
exiler vt to exile, banish; s'~ vr to go into exile.
existant adj existing.
existence f existence, life.

exister *vi* to exist; to be.

exode *m* exodus; drift, loss.

exonération *f* exemption.

exonérer *vt* to exempt.

exorbitant *adj* exorbitant, outrageous.

exorciser *vt* to exorcise.

exotique *adj* exotic.

exotisme *m* exoticism.

expansif *adj* expansive; outgoing, forthcoming.

expansion *f* expansion, development.

expatrié *m*, **-e** *f* expatriate; * *adj* expatriate.

expatrier *vt* to expatriate; **s'~** *vr* to expatriate oneself.

expectative *f* expectation, hope; **être dans l'~** to be still waiting (to see, to hear).

expédier *vt* to send, dispatch; to dispose of.

expéditeur *m*, **-trice** *f* sender; shipper, consignor.

expéditif *adj* quick, expeditious.

expédition *f* dispatch; consignment.

expérience *f* experience; experiment.

expérimental *adj* experimental; **~ement** *adv* experimentally.

expérimentateur *m*, **-trice** *f* experimenter.

expérimentation *f* experimentation.

expérimenté *adj* experienced.

expérimenter *vt* to test; to experiment with.

expert *adj* expert, skilled in; * *m* expert; connoisseur; assessor.

expertise *f* expertise; expert appraisal.

expiation *f* expiation, atonement.

expier *vi* to expiate, atone for.

expiration *f* expiry; expiration, exhalation.

expirer *vi* to breathe out, expire.

explicatif *adj* explanatory.

explication *f* explanation, analysis.

explicite *adj* explicit **~ment** *adv* explicitly.

expliquer *vt* to explain, account for; to analyse.

exploitant *m*, **-e** *f* farmer, smallholder.

exploitation *f* working; exploitation; operating; concern; smallholding.

exploiter *vt* to work, exploit; run, operate.

explorateur *m*, **-trice** *f* explorer.

exploration *f* exploration.

explorer *vt* to explore.

exploser *vi* to explode.

explosif *adj* explosive; * *m* explosive.

explosion *f* explosion.

exportateur *m*, **-trice** *f* exporter.

exportation *f* export, exportation.

exporter *vt* to export.

exposé *m* exposition, overview, statement.

exposer *vt* to display; to explain, state; to expose; **s'~** *vr* to expose oneself, to run the risk of.

exposition *f* display; exposition; exposure.

exprès *adj* formal, express.

express *adj* fast; * *m* fast train.

expressif *adj* expressive.

expression *f* expression.

expressionnisme *m* expressionism.

expressionniste *mf* expressionist;
* *adj* expressionist, expressionistic.

exprimer *vt* to express, voice; **s'~**
vr to express oneself.

expropriation *f* expropriation.

expulser *vt* to expel; to evict.

expulsion *f* expulsion; eviction.

exquis *adj* exquisite; **~ément** *adv*
exquisitely.

extase *f* ecstasy; rapture.

extasier(s') *vr* to go into ecstasies.

extensible *adj* extensible, extendable.

extension *f* extension; stretching;
expansion.

exténuant *adj* exhausting.

exténuer *vt* to exhaust; **s'~** *vr* to
exhaust oneself.

extérieur *m* exterior, outside; * *adj*
outer, external, exterior; **~ement**
adv externally, outwardly.

extérioriser *vt* to show, express; to
exteriorize.

extermination *f* extermination.

exterminer *vt* exterminate.

externe *adj* external, outer.

extincteur *m* extinguisher.

extinction *f* extinction, extinguishing.

extraction *f* extraction; mining.

extradition *f* extradition.

extraire *vt* to extract; to mine.

extrait *m* extract; abstract.

extraordinaire *adj* extraordinary;
~ment *adv* extraordinarily.

extraterrestre *mf* extraterrestrial;
* *adj* extraterrestrial.

extravagant *adj* extravagant, wild.

extraverti *m*, **-e** *f* extrovert; * *adj*
extrovert.

extrême *adj* extreme; **~ment** *adv*
extremely.

extrémiste *mf*, *adj* extremist.

extrémité *f* extremity, limit; straits.

exubérance *f* exuberance.

exubérant *adj* exuberant.

exulter *vi* to exult.

F

fable *f* fable, story, tale.

fabricant *m*, **-ante** *f* manufacturer,
maker.

fabrication *f* manufacture, production; counterfeiting.

fabrique *f* factory.

fabriquer *vt* to manufacture; to
forge; to fabricate.

fabuleux *adj* fabulous, mythical,
legendary.

façade *f* façade, front.

face *f* face, side, surface, aspect;
en ~ opposite, over the road; **~ à**

facing; **faire ~ à** to confront, face
up to; **de ~** fullface, frontal; **~ à ~**
face to face.

face à face *m* encounter, interview.

facette *f* facet.

fâché *adj* angry; sorry.

fâcher *vt* to anger, make angry; to
grieve; **se ~** *vr* to get angry.

fâcheux *adj* deplorable, regrettable.

facile *adj* easy; facile; **~ment** *adv*
easily.

facilité *f* easiness, ease; ability;
facility.

faciliter vt to make easier, facilitate.

façon f way, fashion; make; imitation; **de toute ~** at any rate; **non merci, sans ~** no thanks, honestly; **de ~ à** so that, so as to.

façonner vt to shape, fashion, model; to till.

fac-similé m facsimile.

facteur m postman.

factice adj artificial, imitation.

faction f faction; sentry-duty.

facturation f invoicing.

facture f bill, invoice; construction, technique.

facturer vt to invoice, charge for.

facultatif adj optional.

faculté f faculty; power, ability; right.

fade adj insipid, bland, dull.

fagot m faggot, bundle of firewood.

faible adj weak, feeble; slight, poor; **~ment** adv weakly, faintly, feebly.

faiblesse f weakness, feebleness, faintness.

faiblir vi to fail, flag, weaken; to wane.

faïence f earthenware, crockery.

faille f fault; flaw; weakness.

faillir vi to come close to; to fail **j'ai failli tomber** I almost fell.

faillite f bankruptcy; collapse.

faim f hunger; appetite; famine.

fainéant m, **-ante** f idler, loafer.

faire vt to do; to make; **rien à ~!** nothing doing!; **se ~ à** to get used to; **s'en ~** to worry.

faire-part m announcement (birth, marriage, death).

faisable adj feasible.

faisan m pheasant.

faisceau m bundle, stack; beam.

fait m event; fact; act.

faîte m summit; rooftop.

falaise f cliff.

falloir vi: to be necessary **il faut que tu partes** you must leave.

falsifier vt to falsify, alter.

famélique adj starving, scrawny.

fameux adj first-rate; downright, out-and-out.

familial adj family, domestic.

familiariser vt to familiarize; **se ~** vr to familiarize oneself.

familiarité f familiarity.

familier adj familiar; colloquial; informal.

familièrement adv familiarly, informally.

famille f family.

famine f famine.

fanatique adj fanatic; **~ment** adv fanatically; • mf fanatic; zealot.

fanatisme m fanaticism.

fané adj faded, withered.

faner vt to turn (hay); to fade; **se ~** vr to wither, fade.

fanfare f fanfare, flourish; brass band.

fantaisie f whim, extravagance; imagination.

fantasme m fantasy.

fantasmer vi to fantasize.

fantastique adj fantastic; **~ment** adv fantastically; eerily.

fantôme m ghost, phantom.

faon m fawn.

farce f joke, prank; farce.

farceur m, **-euse** f joker; clown.

farci adj crammed, packed.

farcir vt to stuff, cram.

fard m make-up.

fardeau m load, burden.

farder vt to make up; to disguise; **se ~** vr to make oneself up.

farine f flour.

farineux adj floury, powdery; * m starchy food.

farouche adj shy, timid; unsociable; fierce; **~ment** adv fiercely.

fascicule m fascicle, part, instalment.

fascinant adj fascinating.

fascination f fascination.

fasciner vt to fascinate, bewitch.

fascisme m fascism.

fasciste mf, adj fascist.

faste m pomp, ostentation.

fastidieux adj tedious, boring.

fastueux adj sumptuous, luxurious.

fatal adj fatal, deadly; fateful; **~ement** adv inevitably, unavoidably.

fataliste mf fatalist; * adj fatalistic.

fatalité f fatality; inevitability.

fatidique adj fateful; fatal.

fatigant adj tiring, fatiguing.

fatigue f fatigue, tiredness.

fatigué adj tired, weary; overworked, strained.

fatiguer vt to tire; to overwork, strain; **se ~** vr to get tired.

faubourg m suburb.

faucher vt to reap; to flatten, knock down.

faucille f sickle.

faucon m falcon, hawk.

faufiler vt to tack; to insinuate, introduce; **se ~** vr to worm one's way in.

faune f wildlife, fauna.

faussaire mf forger.

faussement adv wrongly; falsely.

fausser vt to distort, alter; to warp.

fausseté f falseness; deceitfulness.

faute f mistake, foul, fault; **~ de mieux** for lack of anything better.

fauteuil m armchair.

fautif m, **-ive** f culprit, guilty party; * adj at fault, guilty; faulty, incorrect.

fauve m wildcat; fawn.

faux adj false, forged, fake; wrong; bogus.

faux-filet m sirloin.

faux-fuyant m evasion, equivocation.

faux-semblant m sham, pretence.

faveur f favour.

favorable adj favourable, sympathetic; **~ment** adv favourably.

favori m, **-ite** f favourite; * adj favourite.

favoriser vt to favour, further.

fébrile adj feverish, febrile; **~ment** adv feverishly.

fébrilité f feverishness.

fécond adj fertile; prolific, fruitful; creative.

fécondation f impregnation, fertilization.

féconder vt to impregnate; to fertilize, pollinate.

fécondité f fertility, fecundity.

fécule f starch.

féculent adj starchy; * m starchy food.

fédéral adj federal.

fédération f federation.

fée f fairy.

féerique adj magical, fairy.

feindre vt to feign, pretend.

feinte f dummy, feint.

fêlé adj cracked, hare-brained.

félicitation f congratulation.

féliciter vt to congratulate.

félin adj feline; * m feline.

femelle f feminism.

féminin adj feminine, female.

féminisme m feminism.

féministe mf; * adj feminist.

féminité f femininity.

femme f woman; wife; ~ **de ménage** housewife; ~ **de chambre** chambermaid.

fémur m femur.

fendiller vt to chink; to crack, craze; **se** ~ vr to be covered in small cracks.

fendre vt to split, cleave; to crack, **se** ~ vr to crack.

fenêtre f window.

fenouil m fennel.

fente f crack, fissure; slot.

féodal adj feudal.

fer m iron, point, blade; ~ **à cheval** horseshoe.

férié adj holiday.

ferme adj firm, steady; definite; **~ment** adv firmly; * f farm.

fermé adj closed; exclusive; inscrutable.

ferment m ferment, leaven.

fermentation f fermentation, fermenting.

fermenter vi to ferment, work.

fermer vt to close; block; turn off; **se** ~ vr to close, shut up; to close one's mind to.

fermeté f firmness, steadiness.

fermeture f closing, shutting; latch; fastener.

fermier m, **-ière** f farmer.

féroce adj ferocious; savage; **~ment** adv ferociously, savagely.

férocité f ferocity, fierceness.

ferraille f scrap iron.

ferronnerie f ironworks; ironwork.

ferroviaire adj railway.

fertile adj fertile, productive.

fertilisation f fertilization.

fertiliser vt to fertilize.

fertilité f fertility.

fervent adj fervent, ardent.

ferveur f fervour, ardour.

fesse f buttock.

festin m feast.

festival m festival.

fête f feast, holiday.

fêter vt to celebrate, fête.

fétichisme m fetishism.

fétichiste mf; * adj fetishist.

fétide adj fetid.

feu m fire; light; hearth; **en** ~ on fire.

feuillage m foliage, greenery.

feuille f leaf.

feuillet m leaf, page, layer.

feuilleté adj foliated; laminated.

feuilleter vt to leaf through; to glance at.

feuilleton m serial, series.

feutre m felt; felt hat.

fève f broad bean.

fiabilité f accuracy; dependability.

fiable adj reliable; dependable.

fiançailles fpl engagement, betrothal.

fiancer(se) vr to become engaged.

fiasco m fiasco.

fibre f fibre.

fibreux adj fibrous, stringy.

fibrome m fibroid, fibroma.

ficeler vt to tie up.

ficelle f string; stick (bread).

fiche f card; sheet; certificate.

ficher vt to file, put on file.

fichier m catalogue;file.

fictif adj fictitious; imaginary.

fiction f imagination, fiction.

fidèle adj faithful, loyal; **~ment** adv faithfully; * mf believer.

fidélité f fidelity, loyalty.

fief m fief; stronghold, preserve.

fier(se) vr to trust, rely on.

fier adj proud, haughty; noble.

fièrement adv proudly.

fierté f pride; arrogance.

fièvre f fever, temperature; excitement.

fiévreux adj feverish.

figer vt to congeal, freeze; clot; **se ~** vr to congeal, freeze; clot.

figue f fig.

figuier m fig tree.

figurant m, **-e** f extra, walk-on; stooge.

figuratif adj figurative, representational.

figure f face; figure; illustration, diagram.

figuré adj figurative, metaphorical, diagrammatic; * m: **au ~** in the figurative sense.

figurer vt to represent; * vi to appear, feature; **se ~** vr to imagine.

figurine f figurine.

fil m thread; wire; cord; **~ de fer** wire; **~ à plomb** plumb line; **au ~ des jours** with the passing days.

filament m filament, strand, thread.

filature f spinning; mill; tailing.

file f line, queue; **à la ~** in line, in succession; **stationner en double ~** to double-park.

filer vt to spin; to tail; to draw out; * vi to run, trickle; to fly by; to make off.

filet m dribble, trickle; fillet; net.

filiation f filiation; relation.

filière f path; procedures; network.

fille f daughter, girl.

fillette f (small) girl.

filleul m, **-eule** f godson, godchild.

film m film, picture.

filmer vt to film.

filon m vein, seam.

fils m son.

filtre m filter.

filtrer vt to filter; to screen.

fin f end, finish; **prendre ~** to terminate, come to an end; * adj thin, fine; delicate; **~ement** adv finely, delicately.

final adj final; **~ement** adv finally.

finale f finale.

finance f finance.

financement m financing.

financer vt to finance.

financier m, **-ière** f financier.

financièrement adv financially.

finesse f fineness; sharpness; neatness; delicacy.

fini adj finished, over, complete.

finir vt to finish, complete; * vi to finish, end; to die.

finition f finish, finishing.

fisc m tax department.

fiscal adj fiscal, tax.

fissure f crack, fissure.

fixation f fixation; fixing; fastening.

fixe adj fixed, permanent, set; **~ment** adv fixedly, steadily.

fixer vt to fix, fasten; to arrange; **se ~ vr** to settle.

flacon m bottle, flask.

flageolant adj shaky.

flageolet m flageolet.

flagrant adj flagrant, blatant.

flair m sense of smell, nose; intuition.

flairer vt to smell, sniff; to scent.

flambeau m torch; candlestick.

flamboyant adj blazing; flamboyant.

flamboyer vi to blaze, flash, gleam.

flamme f flame; fervour; ardour.

flan m custard tart; mould.

flanc m flank, side.

flanelle f flannel.

flâner vi to stroll; to lounge about.

flasque adj flaccid; spineless.

flatter vt t flatter, gratify; to pander; to delight.

flatterie f flattery.

flatteur m, **-euse** f flatterer.

fléau m scourge; plague.

flèche f arrow.

fléchir vi to bend, yield, weaken; * vt to bend, sway.

fléchissement m bending; flexing; bowing.

flegmatique adj phlegmatic.

flegme m composure, phlegm.

flétrir vt to wither, fade; to stigmatize; **se ~ vr** to wither, wilt.

fleur f flower.

fleuri adj in bloom; flowery.

fleurir vi to blossom, flower; * vt to decorate with flowers.

fleuriste mf florist.

fleuve m river. .

flexibilité f flexibility.

flexible adj flexible, pliant.

flic m (fam) cop, policeman.

flocon m fleck, flake.

floraison f flowering, blossoming.

floral adj floral, flower.

flore f flora.

florissant adj flourishing, blooming.

flot m stream, flood; floodtide; wave.

flotte f fleet; rain.

flottement m wavering; vagueness, imprecision.

flotter vi to float; to drift; to wander; to waver.

flotteur m float.

flou adj blurred, hazy.

fluctuant adj fluctuating.

fluctuation f fluctuation.

fluide adj fluid, flowing.

fluidité f fluidity.

fluor m fluorine.

fluorescent adj fluorescent.

fluorure m fluoride.

flûte f flute; French stick.

flûtiste mf flautist.

flux m flood; flow; flux.

focaliser vt to focus; **se ~ vr** to be focused on.

fœtus m foetus.

foi f faith, trust.

foie m liver.

foin m hay.

foire f fair, trade fair.

fois f time, occasion.

folie f madness, insanity; extravagance.

folklore m folklore.

folklorique adj outlandish.

follement adv madly, wildly.

foncé adj dark, deep (colours).

foncer vi to hammer along, rush at; * vt to make darker; to sink, bore.

foncier adj land, landed, property.

foncièrement adv fundamentally, basically.

fonction f post, duty; function.

fonctionnaire mf civil servant.

fonctionnement m working, functioning, operation.

fonctionner vi to work, function, operate.

fond m bottom, back; **au ~** basically, in fact; **à ~** thoroughly, in depth; **dans le ~** in reality, basically; **~ de teint** foundation cream.

fondamental adj fundamental, basic; **~ement** adv fundamentally.

fondamentalisme m fundamentalism.

fondamentaliste mf; * adj fundamentalist.

fondant adj thawing, melting.

fondateur m, **-trice** f founder.

fondation f foundation.

fondement m foundation; ground.

fonder vt to found; to base.

fondre vi to melt; to vanish; to slim; * vt to melt; to cast; to merge.

fonds m business; fund; money; stock.

fondu adj melted; molten; cast.

fontaine f fountain, spring.

fonte f melting; casting; smelting.

football m football, soccer.

forage m drilling, boring.

forain m, **-e** f stallholder; fairground entertainer; * adj fairground.

force f strength, force, violence, energy; **à ~ de** by dint of.

forcé adj forced; emergency; **~ment** adv inevitably.

forcené adj deranged, frenzied.

forcer vt to force, compel; track down; * vi to overdo, strain; **se ~** vr to force oneself to.

forestier adj forest; forestry.

forêt f forest.

forfait m set price, package; withdrawal.

forfaitaire adj fixed, set, inclusive.

forge f forge, smithy.

forger vt to forge, form, mould.

forgeron m blacksmith, smith.

formaliser(se) vr to take offence at.

formalité f formality.

format m format, size.

formation f formation; training.

forme f form, shape; mould, fitness; **être en ~** to be on form; **en ~** de forming.

formel adj definite, positive; formal; **~lement** adv positively, definitely; formally.

former vt to form, make up; to train; **se ~** vr to form, gather; to train oneself.

formidable adj tremendous; fantastic; **~ment** adv tremendously, fantastically.

formulaire *m* form.

formule *f* formula; phrase; system.

formuler *vt* to formulate; express.

fort *adj* strong; high; loud; pronounced; **~ement** *adv* strongly; highly; very much; * *m* fort; strong point, forte.

forteresse *f* fortress.

fortifiant *m* tonic; * *adj* fortifying; invigorating.

fortification *f* fortification.

fortifier *vt* to fortify, strengthen; **se ~** *vr* to grow stronger.

fortuit *adj* fortuitous, chance; **~ement** *adv* fortuitously.

fortune *f* fortune, luck.

fortuné *adj* wealthy; fortunate.

fosse *f* pit; grave.

fossé *m* ditch; gulf.

fossette *f* dimple.

fossile *m* fossil.

fou *adj*, *f* **folle** mad, wild; tremendous; erratic.

foudre *f* lightning, thunderbolt.

foudroyant *adj* lightning; thundering; violent.

foudroyer *vt* to strike (lightning).

fouet *m* whip; whisk.

fouetter *vt* to whip, flog.

fougère *f* fern.

fougue *f* ardour, spirit.

fougueux *adj* fiery, ardent.

fouille *f* frisking; excavations.

fouiller *vt* to search, scour.

foulard *m* scarf.

foule *f* crowd; masses, heaps.

four *m* oven; furnace; fiasco.

fourbe *adj* deceitful, two-faced.

fourbu *adj* exhausted.

fourche *f* pitchfork; crotch.

fourchette *f* fork .

fourchu *adj* forked; cloven.

fourgon *m* coach, wagon, van.

fourmi *f* ant.

fourmilière *f* anthill.

fourmillement *m* swarming, milling.

fourmiller *vi* to swarm, teem.

fourneau *m* stove.

fournir *vt* to supply, provide.

fournisseur *m*, **-euse** *f* purveyor, supplier.

fourniture *f* supplying, provision.

fourrage *m* fodder, forage.

fourré *adj* filled; fur-lined; * *m* thicket.

fourrer *vt* to stuff; to line.

fourrière *f* pound (car).

fourrure *f* coat, fur.

foutu *adj* bloody, damned; lousy.

foyer *m* home; fireplace; club; focus.

fracas *m* crash; roar, din.

fraction *f* fraction, part.

fractionnement *m* splitting up, division.

fracture *f* fracture.

fracturer *vt* to fracture, break open.

fragile *adj* fragile, delicate.

fragilité *f* fragility, flimsiness.

fragment *m* fragment.

fragmentation *f* fragmentation; splitting up.

fragmenter *vt* to break up, fragment; **se ~** *vr* to fragment, break up.

fraîcheur *f* freshness, coolness.

frais *mpl* expenses; * *adj*, *f* **fraîche** fresh, cool.

fraise *f* strawberry.

framboise *f* raspberry.

franc *adj*, *f* **franche** frank, open; clear; absolute.

Français *m* Frenchman, **-e** *f* Frenchwoman.

français *adj* French; * *m* French.

France *f* France.

franchement *adv* frankly, openly; boldly; clearly.

franchir *vt* to clear, get over, cross.

franchise *f* frankness, openness; exemption; franchise.

francophone *mf* French-speaker, *adj* French-speaking.

francophonie *f* French-speaking communities.

frange *f* fringe; threshold.

frappant *adj* striking.

frapper *vt* to hit; to strike down; to infringe; * *vi* to strike, knock.

fraternel *adj* fraternal; **~lement**; * *adv* fraternally.

fraterniser *vi* to fraternize.

fraternité *f* fraternity.

fraude *f* fraud, cheating.

frauduleux *adj* fraudulent.

trayeur *f* fright.

frein *m* brake; check.

freinage *m* braking; slowing down.

freiner *vi* (*auto*) to brake; to slow down; * *vt* (*auto*) to slow down; to curb, check.

frêle *adj* flimsy, fragile.

frémir *vi* to quiver, tremble.

frémissant *adj* quivering, trembling.

frémissement *m* shudder, quiver.

frénétique *adj* frenetic; **~ment** *adv* frenetically.

fréquemment *adv* frequently.

fréquence *f* frequency.

fréquent *adj* frequent.

frère *m* brother.

fresque *f* fresco.

friand *adj* partial to, fond of.

friandise *f* delicacy, sweetmeat.

fric *m* (*fam*) cash, lolly.

friction *f* friction.

frigidaire *m* refrigerator.

frigide *adj* frigid.

frileux *adj* susceptible to cold; chilly.

frire *vt* to fry.

frisé *adj* curly, curly-haired.

friser *vi* to curl, be curly; * *vt* to curl; to graze, skim.

frisson *m* shiver, shudder.

frissonnant *adj* shivering, shuddering.

frissonnement *m* shuddering, shivering.

frissonner *vi* to shudder, tremble, shiver.

frite *f* chip.

friteuse *f* chip pan.

friture *f* frying; frying fat.

frivole *adj* frivolous, shallow.

frivolité *f* frivolity.

froid *adj* cold, cool; **~ement** *adv* coldly, coolly; * *m* cold; coolness; refrigeration.

froideur *f* coldness, chilliness.

froissement *m* creasing; rustling; rustle.

froisser *vt* to crease; to offend; **se ~** *vr* to crease; to take offence.

frôler *vt* to brush against; to verge on.

fromage *m* cheese.

front *m* forehead; face; front.

frontal *adj* frontal.

frontalier *adj* border, frontier.

frontière *f* border, frontier.

frottement *m* rubbing, scraping.

frotter *vt* to rub, scrape.

fructifier *vi* to bear fruit.

fructueux *adj* fruitful, profitable.

frugal *adj* frugal; **~ement** *adv* frugally.

frugalité *f* frugality.

fruit *m* fruit, result.

fruité *adj* fruity.

frustration *f* frustration.

frustrer *vt* to frustrate, deprive.

fugace *adj* fleeting, transient.

fugitif *m*, **-ive** *f* fugitive; * *adj* fugitive, runaway.

fugue *f* running away.

fuir *vi* to avoid; to flee; to leak.

fuite *f* flight, escape; leak.

fulgurant *adj* lightning; dazzling.

fumant *adj* smoking, fuming.

fumé *adj* smoked.

fumée *f* smoke; vapour.

fumer *vi* to smoke, steam, give off smoke; * *vt* to smoke.

fumet *m* aroma.

fumeur *m*, **-euse** *f* smoker.

fumier *m* dung, manure.

funèbre *adj* funeral; funerary.

funérailles *fpl* funeral.

funéraire *adj* funeral, funerary.

funeste *adj* disastrous; harmful.

fureur *f* fury; violence.

furie *f* shrew; fury, rage.

furieusement *adv* furiously.

furieux *adj* furious, violent.

furtif *adj* furtive; stealthy.

furtivement *adv* furtively.

fusée *f* rocket, missile.

fusible *m* fuse.

fusil *m* rifle, gun.

fusillade *f* fusillade; gunfire; shoot-out.

fusiller *vt* to shoot.

fusion *f* fusion; melting; merger; blending.

fusionner *vt* to merge, combine.

fût *m* trunk; shaft; barrel.

futé *adj* crafty, cunning.

futile *adj* futile; **~ment** *adv* futilely.

futilité *f* futility.

futur *adj* future; * *m* intended, fiancé; future.

fuyant *adj* fleeting; evasive.

fuyard *m*, **-e** *f*; * *adj* runaway.

G

gabarit *m* size, build; calibre.

gâcher *vt* to mix; to waste.

gachette *f* trigger.

gâchis *m* mess.

gadget *m* gadget; gimmick.

gaffe *f* blunder; boat hook.

gage *m* security; pledge; proof.

gagnant *m*, **-e** *f* winner; * *adj* winning.

gagner *vt* to earn, to win, beat; to gain; * *vi* to win; to spread.

gai *adj* cheerful, happy, gay; **~ement** *adv* cheerfully, happily.

gaieté *f* cheerfulness, gaiety.

gain *m* earnings; gain, profit, benefit; saving.

gaine *f* girdle; sheath.

gala *m* official reception; gala.

galamment *adv* courteously, gallantly.

galant *adj* gallant, courteous.

galanterie *f* gallantry.

galaxie *f* galaxy.

galère *f* galley.

galerie *f* gallery; tunnel.

galet *m* pebble.

galette *f* pancake.

Gallois *m* Welshman, **-e** *f* Welshwoman.

gallois *adj* Welsh; * *m* Welsh (language).

galon *m* braid; stripe.

galop *m* gallop; canter.

galoper *vi* to gallop; to run wild.

galvaniser *vt* to galvanize.

gambas *fpl* prawns.

gamin *m*, **-e** *f* kid, street urchin.

gaminerie *f* playfulness; childishness.

gamme *f* range; scale.

ganglion *m* ganglion.

gangrène *f* gangrene.

gant *m* glove.

gap *m* gap; difference, discrepancy.

garage *m* garage.

garagiste *mf* garage owner.

garant *m*, **-e** *f* guarantor.

garantie *f* guarantee, surety.

garantir *vt* to guarantee, secure.

garçon *m* boy; assistant; waiter.

garde *f* custody; guard; surveillance; * *m* guard, warder.

garde-à-vous *m* standing to attention.

garde-boue *m* mudguard.

garde-chasse *m* gamekeeper.

garde-fou *m* railing; parapet; safeguard.

garder *vt* to look after; to stay in; to keep on.

garderie *f* day nursery.

garde-robe *f* wardrobe.

gardien *m*, **-ienne** *f* guard, guardian, warden; protector; **~ de but** *m* goalkeeper.

gare *f* rail station; basin; depot.

garer *vt* to park; to dock; **se ~** *vr* to avoid, steer clear of.

gargariser(se) *vr* to gargle; to crow about.

gargarisme *m* gargle.

gargouillement *m* gurgling; rumbling.

gargouiller *vi* to gurgle; to rumble.

garnir *vt* to fit with; to trim, decorate.

garnison *f* (*mil*) garrison.

garniture *f* trimming, lining; garnish.

garrot *m* garrotte; tourniquet.

gars *m* (*fam*) lad; bloke.

gaspillage *m* waste; squandering.

gaspiller *vt* to waste, squander.

gastrique *adj* gastric.

gastronome *m* gourmet, gastronome.

gastronomie *f* gastronomy.

gâté *adj* ruined; spoiled.

gâteau *m* cake.

gâter *vt* to ruin; to spoil; **se ~** *vr* to go bad, go off.

gâteux *adj* senile; doddering.

gauche *adj* left; awkward, clumsy; **~ment** *adv* awkwardly; * *f* left; left wing.

gaucher *adj* left-handed.

gauchisant *m*, **-e** *f* leftist; * *adj* of leftist tendencies.

gauchiste *mf*; * *adj* leftist.

gaufre f waffle.

gaver vt to force-feed; to fill up; **se ~** vr to stuff oneself; to devour.

gaz m invar gas; fizz; wind.

gaze f gauze.

gazelle f gazelle.

gazeux adj gaseous; fizzy.

gazon m lawn; turf.

gazouiller vi to chirp, warble.

géant m giant, **-e** f giantess.

geindre vi to groan; to whine.

gel m frost; gel.

gélatine f gelatine.

gelé adj cold, unresponsive.

gelée f frost; jelly.

geler vi to freeze, be frozen; * vt to freeze, turn to ice; to suspend.

gélule f capsule.

gémeaux mpl Gemini.

gémir vi to groan, moan.

gémissement m groan, moan; groaning.

gênant adj annoying; awkward.

gencive f gum.

gendarme m policeman; gendarme.

gendarmerie f police force, constabulary.

gendre m son-in-law.

gêne f discomfort; trouble; embarrassment; **être sans ~** to be inconsiderate.

généalogie f genealogy.

généalogique adj genealogist.

gêner vt to bother; to hinder; to make uneasy; **se ~** vr to put oneself out.

général adj general, broad; common; **~ement** adv generally; * m

general, **-e** f general's wife; call to arms.

généralisation f generalization.

généraliser vt to generalize; **se ~** vr to become widespread.

généraliste m general practitioner; * adj general-interest; non-specialized.

généralité f majority; general points.

générateur m generator.

génération f generation.

générer vt to generate.

généreusement adv generously; nobly.

généreux adj generous; noble; magnanimous.

générosité f generosity; nobility; magnanimity.

génétique adj genetic; **~ment** adv genetically.

génial adj inspired, of genius.

génie m genius; spirit; genie.

génital adj genital.

génocide m genocide.

genou m knee.

genre m kind, type; gender; genre.

gens mpl people, folk.

gentil, adj f **gentille** kind; good; pleasant.

gentillesse f kindness; favour.

gentiment adv kindly; nicely.

géographe mf geographer.

géographie f geography.

géographique adj geographic.

géologie f geology.

géologue mf geologist.

géomètre m surveyor.

géométrie f geometry.

géométrique adj geometric; **~ment** adv geometrically.

géranium *m* geranium.

gérant *m*, **-e** *f* manager.

gerbe *f* sheaf, bundle; collection.

gercer *vt* to chap, crack; **se ~** *vr* to chap, crack.

gerçure *f* (small) crack.

gérer *vt* to manage, administer.

germe *m* germ; seed.

germer *vi* to sprout, germinate.

gérondif *m* gerundive; gerund.

gésier *m* gizzard.

gestation *f* gestation.

geste *m* gesture; act, deed.

gesticuler *vi* to gesticulate.

gestion *f* management, administration.

gestionnaire *adj* administrative, management.

ghetto *m* ghetto.

gibier *m* game; prey.

gicler *vi* to spurt, squirt.

gicleur *m* jet.

gifle *f* slap, smack.

gifler *vt* to slap, smack.

gigantesque *adj* gigantic, immense.

gigot *m* leg (mutton/lamb), haunch.

gilet *m* waistcoat.

gingembre *m* ginger.

girafe *f* giraffe.

giratoire *adj* gyrating, gyratory.

girouette *f* weather vane.

gisement *m* deposit; mine; pool.

gitan *m*, **-e** *f* gipsy.

gîte *m* shelter; home; gîte.

givre *m* frost, rime.

givré *adj* covered in frost.

glace *f* ice; ice cream; mirror.

glacé *adj* icy; frozen; glazed; chilly.

glacer *vt* to freeze; to chill; to glaze.

glacial *adj* icy; freezing.

glacier *m* glacier; ice cream maker.

glacière *f* icebox.

glaçon *m* icicle; ice cube.

glaïeul *m* gladiola.

glaise *f* clay.

gland *m* acorn.

glande *f* gland.

glaner *vt* to glean.

glauque *adj* blue-green; shabby, run-down.

glissade *f* slide, skid.

glissant *adj* slippery.

glissement *m* sliding; gliding; downturn, downswing.

glisser *vi* to slide, slip, skid.

glissière *f* slide; runner.

global *adj* global, overall; **~ement** *adv* globally.

globe *m* globe, sphere; earth.

globulaire *adj* global; corpuscular.

globule *m* globule; corpuscle.

globuleux *adj* globular; protruding.

gloire *f* glory; distinction; celebrity.

glorieux *adj* glorious.

glorifier *vt* to glory, honour; **se ~** *vr* to glory in; to boast.

glossaire *m* glossary.

glouton *m*, **-onne** *f* glutton; * *adj* gluttonous, ravenous; **~nement** *adv* gluttonously.

gluant *adj* sticky, gummy.

glucide *m* glucide.

glucose *m* glucose.

glycérine *f* glycerine.

gobelet *m* beaker, tumbler.

gober vt to swallow.

goéland m seagull, gull.

goinfre m pig, adj piggish.

golf m golf.

golfeur m, **-euse** f golfer.

gomme f gum; rubber, eraser.

gommer vt to rub out; to gum.

gond m hinge.

gondole f gondola.

gondoler vi to crinkle, warp, buckle; **se ~** vr to crinkle; to split one's sides laughing.

gonflable adj inflatable.

gonflement m inflation, swelling.

gonfler vt to pump up, inflate; **se ~** vr to swell; to be puffed up.

gong m gong; bell.

gorge f throat.

gorgée f mouthful.

gorille m gorilla.

gosier m throat, gullet.

gosse mf (fam) kid.

gothique m, adj Gothic.

goudron m tar.

goudronner vt to tar.

gouffre m gulf, chasm, abyss.

goulu adj greedy, gluttonous.

goulûment adv greedily, gluttonously.

goupille f pin.

gourd adj numb (with cold).

gourde f gourd; flask.

gourdin m club, cudgel.

gourmand adj greedy.

gourmandise f greed, greediness.

gourmet m gourmet.

gourmette f chain bracelet.

gousse f pod.

goût m taste; liking; style.

goûter vt to taste; to appreciate; * vi to have a snack; to taste good; * m snack.

goutte f drop; dram; gout.

gouttière f gutter; drainpipe.

gouvernail m rudder; helm.

gouvernement m government.

gouvernemental adj government, governmental.

gouverner vt to govern, rule; to control; to steer.

gouverneur m governor.

goyave f guava.

grâce f grace; favour; mercy; pardon; ~ à thanks to.

gracier vt to pardon.

gracieusement adv gracefully; kindly.

gracieux adj gracious.

grade m rank; grade; degree.

gradé m officer; * adj promoted.

gradin m tier; step; terrace.

graduel adj gradual; progressive; **~lement** adv gradually.

graduer vt to step up; to graduate.

graffiti mpl graffiti.

grain m grain, seed; bead.

graine f seed.

graissage m greasing, lubricating.

graisse f grease, fat.

graisser vt to grease, lubricate.

grammaire f grammar.

grammairien m, **-ienne** f grammarian.

grammatical adj grammatical; **~ement** adv grammatically.

gramme m gramme.

grand adj big; tall; great; leading; **pas ~chose** not a lot, not up to much; **~ement** adv greatly; a great deal; nobly.

grandeur f size; greatness; magnitude.

grandiose adj imposing, grandiose.

grandir vi to grow bigger, increase; * vt to magnify; exaggerate.

grand-mère f grandmother.

grand-père m grandfather.

grand-parents mpl grandparents

granit(e) m granite.

granulé m granule; * adj granular.

granuleux adj granular; grainy.

graphique m graph; * adj graphic; ~ment adv graphically.

graphite m graphite.

grappe f cluster, bunch.

gras adj, f **grasse** fatty; fat; greasy; crude.

gratification f gratuity; bonus.

gratin m cheese dish, gratin.

gratis adv free, gratis.

gratitude f gratitude, gratefulness.

gratter vt to scratch, scrape.

gratuit adj free, gratuitous; disinterested; ~ement adv free; gratuitously.

grave adj grave, solemn; ~ment adv gravely, solemnly.

graver vt to engrave, imprint.

graveur m engraver, woodcutter.

gravier m stone, gravel.

gravir vt to climb.

gravitation f gravitation.

gravité f gravity.

gravure f engraving, carving.

gré m: liking, taste; **au ~ de** depending on, at the mercy of; **bon ~ mal** ~ like it or not, willy-nilly; **savoir ~** to be grateful.

greffe f transplant, graft.

greffer vt to transplant, graft.

grégaire adj gregarious.

grêle f hail.

grêlon m hailstone.

grelotter vi to shiver.

grenade f pomegranate; grenade.

grenat m garnet.

grenier m attic, garret.

grenouille f frog.

grès m sandstone; stoneware.

grésiller vi to sizzle; splutter.

grève f strike; shore.

gribouillage m scrawl, scribble.

gribouiller vi to doodle; * vt to scribble, scrawl.

grièvement adv seriously.

griffe f claw.

griffer vt to scratch.

griffonner vt to scribble, jot down.

grignoter vi to nibble at, pick at; * vt to nibble at; to eat away.

gril m grill pan; rack.

grillade f grill.

grillage m toasting; grilling.

grille f railings; gate; grill.

grille-pain m invar toaster.

griller vt to toast, scorch; to put bars on; * vi to toast, grill.

grillon m cricket.

grimace f grimace

grimper vi to climb up.

grincement m grating, creaking.

grincer vi to grate, creak.

grincheux adj grumpy.

griotte f Morello cherry; marble.

grippe f flu, influenza.

grippé adj suffering from flu.

gris adj grey.

grisant *adj* exhilarating; intoxicating.

griser *vt* to intoxicate; **se ~** *vr* to get drunk.

grisonnant *adj* greying.

grive *f* thrush.

grog *m* grog.

grognement *m* grunt, grunting.

grogner *vi* to grumble, moan.

grognon *m* grumbler, moaner, *adj* grumpy, surly.

grommeler *vi* to mutter; to grumble; * *vt* to mutter.

grondement *m* rumbling, growling.

gronder *vt* to scold; * *vi* to rumble, growl.

gros *adj, f* **grosse** big; fat; thick; serious; heavy; coarse; **en ~** in bulk; * *m* bulk; wholesale; fat man.

groseille *f* currant.

grossesse *f* pregnancy.

grosseur *f* thickness; weight; fatness.

grossier *adj* coarse; unrefined; base.

grossièrement *adv* roughly; coarsely.

grossièreté *f* rudeness; coarseness.

grossir *vi* to get fatter; to swell, grow; * *vt* to magnify; to exaggerate.

grossiste *mf* wholesaler.

grotesque *adj* grotesque, ludicrous; **~ment** *adv* grotesquely.

grotte *f* cave; grotto.

grouiller *vi* to mill about; to swarm; **se ~** *vr* (*fam*) to get a move on.

groupe *m* group; party; cluster.

groupement *m* grouping; group.

grouper *vt* to group together; to bulk; **se ~** *vr* to gather.

grue *f* crane.

grumeau *m* lump.

gruyère *m* gruyère (cheese).

guenon *f* female monkey; hag.

guépard *m* cheetah.

guêpe *f* wasp.

guêpier *m* trap; wasp's nest.

guère *adv* hardly, scarcely.

guéri *adj* cured.

guéridon *m* pedestal table.

guérir *vi* to get better; to heal; * *vt* to cure, heal; **se ~** *vr* to get better; to recover from.

guérison *f* recovery; curing.

guérisseur *m*, **-euse** *f* healer.

guerre *f* war; warfare.

guerrier *m*, **-ière** *f* warrior.

guet *m* watch; **faire le ~** to be on the watch.

guetter *vt* to watch; to lie in wait for.

gueule *f* mouth; face; muzzle.

gueuler *vi* (*fam*) to bawl; bellow.

guichet *m* counter; ticket office, booking office.

guichetier *m*, **-ière** *f* counter clerk.

guidage *m* guides; guidance.

guide *m* guide.

guider *vt* to guide; **se ~** *vr* to be guided by.

guidon *m* handlebars.

guignol *m* puppet; puppet show.

guillemet *m* inverted comma; quotation mark.

guillotine *f* guillotine.

guimauve *f* marshmallow.

guindé *adj* stiff, uptight.

guirlande *f* garland.

guise *f* manner, way. **en ~ de** by way of; **à ta ~** as you please.

guitare *f* guitar.

guitariste *mf* guitarist.

guttural *adj* guttural

H

habile *adj* skilful, skilled; clever; **~ment** *adv* skilfully.

habileté *f* skill, skilfulness; clever move.

habiliter *vt* to qualify; to authorize.

habillement *m* clothing, dress, outfit.

habiller *vt* to dress, clothe; **s'~** *vr* to get dressed.

habit *m* clothes; apparel; dress–coat; outfit

habitable *adj* inhabitable.

habitant *m*, **-e** *f* inhabitant; occupant; dweller.

habitat *m* habitat; housing conditions.

habitation *f* dwelling; residence; house.

habité *adj* manned.

habiter *vi* to live; * *vt* to live in; occupy.

habitude *f* habit, custom, routine.

habituel *adj* usual, customary; **~lement** *adv* usually, generally.

habituer *vt* to accustom; to teach; **s'~** *vr* to get used to.

hache *f* axe, hatchet.

hacher *vt* to chop, mince.

hachoir *m* chopper, cleaver.

hachure *f* hatching, hachure.

gymnase *m* gymnasium; secondary school.

gymnastique *f* gymnastic.

gynécologie *f* gynaecology.

gynécologue, gynécologiste *mf* gynaecologist.

gyrophare *m* revolving light.

hagard *adj* wild; haggard; distraught.

haie *f* hedge.

haine *f* hatred.

haineux *adj* full of hatred; malevolent.

haïr *vt* to hate, detest.

hâle *m* tan, sunburn.

hâlé *adj* tanned, sunburnt.

haleine *f* breath, breathing.

haletant *adj* panting, gasping.

haleter *vi* to pant, gasp for breath.

hall *m* hall, foyer.

halle *f* covered market; hall.

hallucination *f* hallucination.

halo *m* halo.

halte *f* stop, break; stopping place.

haltère *m* dumbbell.

hamac *m* hammock.

hameçon *m* fish-hook.

hamster *m* hamster.

hanche *f* hip; haunch.

handball *m* handball.

handballeur *m*, **-euse** *f* handball player.

handicap *m* handicap.

handicaper *vt* to handicap

hangar *m* shed, barn; hangar.

hanneton *m* maybug.

hanter *vt* to haunt.

happer *vt* to snap up, snatch.

harassant *adj* exhausting, wearing.

harcèlement *m* harassing; pestering.

harceler *vt* to harass; to pester; to plague.

hardi *adj* bold, daring; brazen; **~ment** *adv* boldly, daringly; brazenly.

hareng *m* herring.

hargne *f* spite.

hargneux *adj* aggressive, belligerent.

haricot *m* bean.

harmonica *m* harmonica.

harmonie *f* harmony; wind section.

harmonieusement *adv* harmoniously.

harmonieux *adj* harmonious; well-matched.

harmoniser *vt* to harmonize; **s'~** *vr* to be in harmony.

harnacher *m* to harness.

harnais *m* harness; equipment.

harpe *f* harp.

harpiste *mf* harpist.

harpon *m* harpoon.

hasard *m* chance; accident; hazard; risk.

hasardeux *adj* hazardous, risky.

hâte *f* haste; impatience.

hâter *vt* to hasten; to quicken; **se ~** *vr* to hurry.

hâtif *adj* precocious; early; hasty.

hâtivement *adv* hastily.

hausse *f* rise, increase.

hausser *vt* to raise; to heighten.

haut *adj* high, tall; upper; superior; **~ement** *adv* highly.

hautain *adj* haughty, lofty.

hautbois *m* oboe.

hauteur *f* height; elevation; haughtiness; bearing.

haut-parleur *m* loudspeaker.

hebdomadaire *adj*; * *m* weekly.

hébergement *m* accommodation; lodging.

héberger *vt* to accommodate, lodge.

hectare *m* hectare.

hectogramme *m* hectogram.

hectolitre *m* hectolitre.

hectomètre *m* hectometre.

hélice *f* propeller; helix.

hélicoptère *m* helicopter.

hélium *m* helium.

hématome *m* severe bruise, haematoma.

hémicycle *m* semicircle, hemicycle; amphitheatre.

hémiplégique *mf* person paralysed on one side, hemiplegic; * *adj* hemiplegic.

hémisphère *m* hemisphere.

hémoglobine *f* haemoglobin.

hémophile *adj* haemophiliac.

hémophilie *f* haemophilia.

hémorragie *f* bleeding, haemorrhage.

hémorroïde *f* haemorrhoid, pile.

henné *m* henna.

hépatique *adj* hepatic.

hépatite *f* hepatitis.

herbe *f* grass; **en ~** under grass.

herbivore *m* herbivore; *adj* herbivorous.

herboriste *mf* herbalist.

héréditaire *adj* hereditary.

hérédité *f* heredity; heritage; right of inheritance.

hérésie f heresy.

hérétique adj heretical.

hérissé adj bristling; spiked.

hérisser vt to bristle; to spike; * **se ~** vr to stand on end; to bristle.

hérisson m hedgehog.

héritage m inheritance; heritage, legacy.

hériter vi to inherit.

héritier m heir, **-ière** f heiress.

hermaphrodite m hermaphrodite; * adj hermaphrodite.

hermétique adj airtight, watertight, hermetic; **~ment** adv hermetically.

hermine f ermine.

hernie f hernia, rupture.

héroïne f heroine; heroin.

héroïque adj heroic; **~ment** adv heroically.

héroïsme m heroism.

héron m heron.

héros m hero.

herpès m herpes; cold sore.

hésitant adj hesitant.

hésitation f hesitation.

hésiter vi to hesitate.

hétéroclite adj heterogeneous; sundry; eccentric.

hétérogène adj heterogeneous.

hétérosexuel adj heterosexual.

hêtre m beech.

heure f hour; time of day; **de bonne ~** early; **tout à l'~** a short time ago, just now.

heureusement adv luckily; happily.

heureux adv lucky; happy.

heurter vt to strike, hit; to jostle.

hexagone m hexagon.

hibernation f hibernation.

hibou m owl.

hideux adj hideous.

hier adv yesterday.

hiérarchie f hierarchy.

hiérarchique adj hierarchical; **~ment** adv hierarchically

hilarant adj hilarious, side-splitting.

hilarité f hilarity, laughter.

hindouisme m Hinduism.

hippisme m riding, equestrianism.

hippocampe m sea horse.

hippodrome m racecourse.

hippopotame m hippopotamus.

hirondelle f swallow.

hirsute adj hirsute, hairy.

hisser vt to hoist, haul up.

histoire f history; story; business; **~ de dire** just to say.

historien m, **-ienne** f historian.

historique adj historic; historical; **~ment** adv historically.

hiver m winter.

hivernal adj winter; wintry.

H.L.M. (habitation à loyer modéré) f/m public sector housing.

hocher vt to nod; to shake one's head.

hochet m rattle; toy.

holocauste m holocaust.

homard m lobster.

homéopathe mf homeopath.

homéopathie f homeopathy.

homicide m homicide.

hommage m homage, tribute; **rendre ~ à** to pay homage to.

homme m man.

homme-grenouille m frogman.

homogène adj homogeneous.

homogénéiser *vt* to homogenize.
homogénéité *f* homogeneity.
homologue *adj* homologous; equivalent.
homologuer *vt* to ratify; to approve.
homonyme *m* homonym; * *adj* homonymous.
homosexualité *f* homosexuality.
homosexuel *m*, **-elle** *f* homosexual.
honnête *adj* honest; decent; honourable; **~ment** *adv* honestly, decently.
honnêteté *f* honesty, decency.
honneur *m* honour; integrity; credit; **en l'~ de** in honour of.
honorable *adj* honourable; reputable; **~ment** *adv* honourably.
honoraire *adj* honorary.
honoraires *mpl* fees.
honorer *vt* to honour; to esteem; to do credit; **s'~** *vr*: **s'~ de** to pride oneself on.
honte *f* shame, disgrace.
honteusement *adv* shamefully; disgracefully.
honteux *adj* shameful; disgraceful.
hôpital *m* hospital.
hoquet *m* hiccough.
horaire *m* timetable; * *adj* hourly.
horizon *m* horizon.
horizontal *adj* horizontal; **~ement** *adv* horizontally.
horloge *f* clock.
horloger *m*, **-ère** *f* watchmaker, clockmaker.
hormone *f* hormone.
horoscope *m* horoscope.
horreur *f* horror.

horrible *adj* horrible; dreadful; **~ment** *adv* horribly
horrifier *vt* to horrify.
hors *prép* outside; beyond; save; except; **~ série** incomparable, outstanding.
hors-bord *m invar* speedboat.
hors-d'œuvre *m invar* hors' oeuvre, starter.
hors-jeu *m invar* offside.
hors-piste *m invar* off-piste.
hortensia *m* hydrangea.
horticulteur *m* horticulturist.
horticulture *f* horticulture.
hospice *m* home, asylum; hospice.
hospitalier *adj* hospital; hospitable.
hospitalisation *f* hospitalization.
hospitaliser *vt* to hospitalize.
hospitalité *f* hospitality.
hostie *f* host.
hostile *adj* hostile; **~ment** *adv* hostilely.
hostilité *f* hostility.
hôte *m*, **hôtesse** *f* host; landlord.
hôtel *m* hotel.
hôtelier *m*, **-ière** *f* hotelier; * *adj* hotel.
hôtellerie *f* inn; hotel business.
hotte *f* basket.
houblon *m* hop.
houille *f* coal.
houle *f* swell.
houleux *adj* stormy; turbulent.
houppe *f* tuft; tassel.
housse *f* cover, dust-sheet.
houx *m* holly.
hublot *m* porthole.
huer *vt* to boo.

huile f oil; petroleum.

huissier m bailiff; usher.

huit adj, m eight.

huitaine f eight or so.

huitième adj eighth; **~ment** adv eighthly; * mf eighth.

huître f oyster.

humain adj human; humane; **~ement** adv humanly; humanely; * m human.

humanisme m humanism.

humaniste m humanist; * adj humanist.

humanitaire adj humanitarian.

humanité f humanity.

humble adj humble; modest; **~ment** adv humbly.

humecter vt to dampen, moisten.

humeur f mood, humour; temper.

humide adj humid.

humidité f humidity.

humiliant adj humiliating.

humiliation f humiliation.

humilier vt to humiliate.

humilité f humility.

humoristique adj humorous.

humour m humour.

hurlement m roar, yell; howl.

hurler vi; * vt to roar, yell.

hutte f hut.

hybride adj ; * m hybrid.

hydratant adj moisturizing.

hydratation f hydration; moisturizing.

hydrater vt to hydrate; to moisturize.

hydraulique adj hydraulic.

hydravion m seaplane.

hydrocarbure m hydrocarbon.

hydrogène m hydrogen.

hydrolyse f hydrolysis.

hydrophile adj hydrophilic.

hydroxyde m hydroxide.

hyène f hyena.

hygiène f hygienics; hygiene.

hygiénique adj hygienic; **~ment** adv hygienically.

hymne m hymn.

hyperbole f hyperbole; hyperbola.

hypermarché m hypermarket.

hypermétrope adj long-sighted; * mf long-sighted person.

hypertension f hypertension.

hypertrophié adj hypertrophied.

hypnose f hypnosis.

hypnotique adj hypnotic.

hypnotiser vt to hypnotize.

hypocondriaque mf ; * adj hypochondriac.

hypocrisie f hypocrisy.

hypocrite mf hypocritical; * adj hypocrite; **~ment** adv hypocritically.

hypophyse f pituitary gland, hypophysis.

hypothalamus m hypothalamus.

hypothèque f mortgage.

hypothéquer vt to mortgage.

hypothèse f hypothesis; assumption.

hypothétique adj hypothetical; **~ment** adv hypothetically.

hystérie f hysteria.

hystérique mf hysterical; * adj hysteric.

I

ibis *m* ibis.

iceberg *m* iceberg.

idéal *adj;* * *m* ideal.

idéaliser *vt* to idealize.

idéaliste *mf* idealistic; * *adj* idealist.

idée *f* idea.

identifier *vt* to identify; **s'~** *vr* to identify with.

identique *adj* identical; **~ment** *adv* identically.

identité *f* identity; similarity.

idéologie *f* ideology.

idiot *m*, **-e** *f* idiot, fool; * *adj* idiotic, stupid; **~ement** *adv* idiotically.

idole *f* idol.

igloo, iglou *m* igloo.

ignoble *adj* ignoble, mean, base.

ignorance *f* ignorance.

ignorant *adj* ignorant; unacquainted; uninformed.

ignorer *vt* to be ignorant of; to be unaware of; to ignore.

iguane *m* iguana.

il *pron* he, it.

île *f* island, isle.

illégal *adj* illegal; unlawful; **~ement** *adv* illegally.

illégalité *f* illegality.

illégitime *adj* illegitimate; unwarranted.

illettré *adj* illiterate.

illicite *adj* illicit; **~ment** *adv* illicitly.

illimité *adj* unlimited; limitless.

illisible *adj* illegible, unreadable.

illogique *adj* illogical.

illumination *f* illumination, lighting.

illuminer *vt* to light up, illuminate; to enlighten.

illusion *f* illusion

illusoire *adj* illusory; illusive; **~ment** *adv* illusorily.

illustration *f* illustration.

illustre *adj* illustrious, renowned.

illustrer *vt* to illustrate.

îlot *m* islet; block (flats).

image *f* image, picture; reflection.

imagé *adj* colourful; full of imagery.

imaginaire *adj* imaginary.

imagination *f* imaginative.

imaginer *vt* to imagine; to suppose; to devise; **s'~** *vr* to imagine oneself; to think.

imbattable *adj* unbeatable.

imbécile *mf* idiot, imbecile; * *adj* stupid, idiotic.

imbiber *vt* to soak, moisten.

imbriquer *vt* to fit into; to overlap; **s'~** *vr* to be linked.

imbuvable *adj* undrinkable; unbearable.

imitation *f* imitation; mimicry; forgery.

imiter *vt* to imitate.

immaculé *adj* spotless, immaculate.

immangeable *adj* inedible.

immatriculation *f* registration.

immatriculer *vt* to register.

immédiat *adj* immediate; instant; **~ement** *adv* immediately, instantly.

immense *adj* immense, boundless.

immensément *adv* immensely; hugely.

immensité *f* immensity; immenseness.

immergé *adj* submerged.

immersion *f* immersion; submersion.

immeuble *m* building; block of flats; real estate.

immigrant *m*, **-e** *f* immigrant.

immigration *f* immigration.

immigré *m*, **-e** *f* immigrant.

imminent *adj* imminent, impending.

immobile *adj* motionless, still.

immobilier *adj* property; * *m* property business.

immobiliser *vt* to immobilize; to bring to a standstill; **s'~** *vr* to stop, stand still.

immobilité *f* stillness; immobility; permanence.

immonde *adj* squalid; base, vile.

immoral *adj* immoral.

immoralité *f* immorality.

immortaliser *vt* to immortalize.

immortel *adj* immortal.

immuable *adj* unchanging, immutable; **~ment** *adv* immutably.

immuniser *vt* to immunize.

immunité *f* immunity.

impact *m* impact.

impair *adj* odd, uneven.

impalpable *adj* impalpable.

impardonnable *adj* unforgivable, unpardonable.

imparfait *adj* imperfect; **~ement** *adv* imperfectly.

impartial *adj* impartial; **~ement** *adv* impartially.

impartialité *f* impartiality.

impasse *f* dead end, cul-de-sac; impasse.

impassible *adj* impassive.

impatiemment *adv* impatiently.

impatience *f* impatience.

impatient *adj* impatient.

impatienter *vt* to irritate, annoy; **s'~** *vr* to grow, get impatient.

impeccable *adj* perfect; faultless, impeccable; **~ment** *adv* perfectly, impeccably.

impénétrable *adj* impenetrable; inscrutable.

impensable *adj* unthinkable.

impératif *adj* imperative; mandatory; * *m* requirement; demand; constraint.

impératrice *f* empress.

imperceptible *adj* imperceptible; **~ment** *adv* imperceptibly.

imperfection *f* imperfection.

impérial *adj* imperial.

impérialisme *m* imperialism.

imperméable *adj* impermeable, waterproof; impervious to.

impersonnel *adj* impersonal.

impertinence *f* impertinence.

impertinent *adj* impertinent.

imperturbable *adj* unshakeable; imperturbable; **~ment** *adv* imperturbably.

impétueux *adj* impetuous.

impitoyable *adj* merciless, pitiless; **~ment** *adv* mercilessly, pitilessly.

implacable *adj* implacable; **~ment** *adv* implacably.

implantation *f* implantation; establishment; introduction.

implanter *vt* to introduce; to establish; to implant; **s'~** *vr* to be established; to become implanted.

implication *f* implication; involvement.

implicite *adj* implicit; **~ment** *adv* implicitly.

impliquer *vt* to imply; to necessitate; to implicate; **s'~** *vr* to get involved in one's work.

impoli *adj* impolite, rude.

impolitesse *f* impoliteness, rudeness.

impopulaire *adj* unpopular.

importance *f* importance, significance; size.

important *adj* important, significant; sizeable.

importateur *m*, **-trice** *f* importer; ***** *adj* importing.

importation *f* import, importation.

importer *vt* to import; ***** *vi* to matter; **que m'importe que** what does it matter to me that; **peu importe** whatever; **n'importe qui** anybody; **n'importe quoi** anything; **n'importe comment** anyhow; **n'importe quel** any.

importuner *vt* to importune, bother.

imposant *adj* imposing; stately.

imposer *vt* to impose, lay down; to fix (prices); **s'~** *vr* to be essential; to assert oneself.

impossibilité *f* impossibility.

impossible *adj* impossible.

imposteur *m* impostor.

impôt *m* tax, duty.

impotent *adj* disabled, crippled.

imprégner *vt* impregnate; to permeate; to imbue; **s'~** *vr* to become

impregnated with; to become imbued with.

impresario *m* manager, impresario.

impression *f* feeling, impression.

impressionnant *adj* impressive; upsetting.

impressionner *vt* to impress; to upset.

impressionisme *m* impressionism.

impressioniste *mf*; ***** *adj* impressionist.

imprévisible *adj* unforeseeable; unpredictable.

imprévoyant *adj* improvident.

imprévu *adj* unforeseen, unexpected.

imprimante *f* printer.

imprimé *adj* printed; ***** *m* printed form; printed material.

imprimer *vt* to print.

imprimerie *f* printing works; printing house.

imprimeur *m* printer.

improbable *adj* improbable, unlikely.

improductif *adj* unproductive.

improvisation *f* improvisation.

improviser *vt* to improvise.

improviste(à l') *adv* unexpectedly.

imprudence *f* carelessness, imprudence.

imprudent *adj* careless, imprudent.

impudence *f* impudence; shamelessness.

impudique *adj* immodest, shameless.

impuissance f powerlessness, helplessness.

impuissant adj powerless, helpless.

impulsif adj impulsive.

impulsion f impulse; impetus.

impulsivement adv impulsively.

impunément adv with impunity.

impur adj impure; mixed.

impureté f impurity.

inacceptable adj unacceptable.

inaccessible adj inaccessible; obscure; incomprehensible.

inaccoutumé adj unusual.

inachevé adj unfinished, uncompleted.

inactif adj inactive, idle.

inaction f inactivity, idleness.

inactivité f inactivity.

inadapté adj unsuitable; maladjusted.

inadéquat adj inadequate.

inadmissible adj inadmissible.

inaltérable adj stable; unchanging, permanent.

inamovible adj irremovable; fixed.

inanimé adj inanimate; unconscious.

inaperçu adj: unnoticed **passer ~** to go unnoticed.

inappréciable adj invaluable, inestimable.

inapte adj incapable.

inattaquable adj unassailable; irrefutable.

inattendu adj unexpected, unforeseen.

inattention f inattention, lack of attention.

inauguration f inauguration, opening.

inaugurer vt to inaugurate, open.

inavouable adj shameful; undisclosable.

incapable adj incapable; incompetent.

incapacité f incompetence; disability; **être dans l'~ de** to be unable to do.

incarcérer vt to incarcerate.

incarnation f incarnation.

incarner vt to incarnate, embody.

incendiaire adj incendiary; inflammatory; * mf arsonist.

incendie m fire, blaze.

incendier vt to set alight; to kindle.

incertain adj uncertain, unsure.

incertitude f uncertainty; **être dans l'~** to feel uncertain.

incessant adj incessant, ceaseless.

inceste m incest.

incident m incident, point of law.

incinération f incineration; cremation.

inciser vt to incise; to lance.

incisive f incisive; piercing.

incitation f incitement; incentive.

inciter vt to incite, urge.

inclinaison f incline; gradient.

incliner vt to bend; to slope; to bow.

inclure vt to include; to insert.

inclus adj enclosed; included; **ci-~** herein enclosed.

incohérence f incoherence; inconsistency.

incohérent adj incoherent; inconsistent.

incolore adj colourless; clear.

incommode adj inconvenient; awkward.

incommoder *vt* to disturb, bother.

incomparable *adj* incomparable; **~ment** *adv* incomparably.

incompatibilité *f* incompatibility.

incompatible *adj* incompatible.

incompétence *f* incompetence.

incompétent *adj* incompetent; inexpert.

incomplet *adj* incomplete.

incompréhensible *adj* incomprehensible.

incompréhension *f* lack of understanding.

inconcevable *adj* inconceivable.

inconciliable *adj* irreconcilable.

inconditionnel *adj* unconditional; unreserved; unquestioning.

inconfortable *adj* uncomfortable; awkward; **~ment** *adv* uncomfortably.

incongru *adj* unseemly; incongruous.

inconnu *m*, **-e** *f* stranger, unknown person; * *m* unknown?; * *adj* unknown.

inconsciemment *adv* unconsciously; thoughtlessly.

inconscience *f* unconsciousness; thoughtlessness.

inconscient *adj* unconscious; thoughtless, reckless; * *m* subconscious, unconscious.

inconsidéré *adj* inconsiderate; thoughtless; **~ment** *adv* inconsiderately.

inconsistant *adj* flimsy; colourless; watery.

inconsolable *adj* disconsolate; inconsolable.

inconstant *adj* fickle; variable, inconstant.

incontestable *adj* incontestable, unquestionable; **~ment** *adv* incontestably, unquestionably.

inconvénient *m* drawback, inconvenience.

incorporation *f* incorporation; integration; blending.

incorporer *vt* to incorporate, integrate.

incorrect *adj* faulty, incorrect; **~ement** *adv* incorrectly.

incorrigible *adj* incorrigible.

incorruptible *adj* incorruptible.

incrédule *adj* incredulous; * *mf* unbeliever, non-believer.

incrédulité *f* incredulity, lack of belief.

incroyable *adj* incredible; unbelievable; **~ment** *adv* incredibly, unbelievably.

incruster *vt* to inlay; to superimpose; **s'~** *vr* to become imbedded in; to become rooted in.

inculpation *f* inculcation, instilling.

inculpé *m*, **-e** *f* accused; * *adj* accused.

incurable *adj* incurable.

indécent *adj* incurably, hopelessly.

indéchiffrable *adj* indecipherable; incomprehensible.

indécis *adj* indecisive; unsettled; undefined.

indéfini *adj* undefined; indefinite; **~ment** *adv* indefinitely.

indéfinissable *adj* indefinable.

indemne *adj* unharmed, unhurt.

indemniser *vt* to indemnify; to compensate.

indemnité *f* compensation; indemnity.

indéniable *adj* undeniable, indisputable; **~ment** *adv* undeniably.

indépendance *f* independence.

indépendant *adj* independent.

indestructible *adj* indestructible.

indéterminé *adj* undetermined; unspecified; undecided.

index *m* index; index finger.

indexer *vt* to index.

indicatif *m* signature tune; dialling code; * *adj* indicative.

indication *f* indication; piece of information; instruction.

indice *m* indication; clue; sign.

indifféremment *adv* indiscriminately, equally.

indifférence *f* indifference.

indifférent *adj* indifferent; immaterial.

indigène *mf* native; local; * *adj* indigenous, native.

indigeste *adj* indigestible.

indigestion *f* indigestion.

indigne *adj* unworthy; undeserving.

indigner *vt* to annoy, make indignant; **s'~** *vr* to be indignant.

indiquer *vt* to indicate, point out; to tell.

indirect *adj* indirect; circumstantial; collateral; **~ement** *adv* indirectly.

indiscipliné *adj* undisciplined.

indiscret *adj* indiscreet; inquisitive.

indiscrétion *f* indiscretion; inquisitiveness.

indiscutable *adj* indisputable; unquestionable; **~ment** *adv* indisputably.

indispensable *adj* indispensable; essential.

indisponible *adj* unavailable.

indistinct *adj* indistinct, vague; **~ement** *adv* indistinctly.

individu *m* individual.

individuel *adj* individual; **~le-ment** *adv* individually.

indolore *adj* painless.

indubitable *adj* indubitable; certain; **~ment** *adv* indubitably.

indulgence *f* indulgence; leniency.

indulgent *adj* indulgent; lenient.

industrialisation *f* industrialization.

industrie *f* industry; dexterity, ingenuity.

industriel *m*, **-elle** *f* industrialist, manufacturer; * *adj* industrial.

inébranlable *adj* steadfast, unwavering.

inédit *adj* unpublished; original.

inefficace *adj* ineffective; inefficient.

inefficacité *f* ineffectiveness; inefficiency.

inégal *adj* unequal; uneven; irregular; **~ement** *adv* unequally; unevenly.

inégalité *f* inequality; difference; disparity.

inéluctable *adj* ineluctable, unavoidable; **~ment** *adv* ineluctably.

inépuisable *adj* inexhaustible.

inerte *adj* inert; lifeless.

inertie f inertia, apathy.

inespéré adj unexpected.

inestimable adj inestimable, invaluable.

inévitable adj inevitable, unavoidable.

inexact adj inexact, inaccurate.

inexactitude f inaccuracy.

inexistant adj nonexistent.

inexorable adj inexorable; ~ment adv inexorably.

inexpérimenté adj inexperienced; inexpert.

inexplicable adj inexplicable; ~ment adv inexplicably.

inexprimable adj inexpressible.

infaillible adj infallible.

infâme adj infamous; base, vile.

infantile adj infantile, childish.

infatigable adj indefatigable, tireless; ~ment adv indefatigably.

infect adj vile; revolting; filthy.

infecter vt to infect; to contaminate; s'~ vr to become infected.

infection f infection.

inférieur adj inferior; lower.

infériorité f inferiority.

infernal adj infernal, diabolical.

infester vt to infest;overrun.

infidèle adj unfaithful, disloyal.

infidélité f infidelity.

infiltration f infiltration.

infini adj infinite; interminable; ~ment adv infinitely.

infinitif m infinitive.

infirme adj feeble; crippled, disabled.

infirmerie f infirmary; sick bay.

infirmier m, -ière f nurse.

infirmité f disability; infirmity.

inflammation f inflammation.

inflation f inflation.

inflexible adj inflexible, rigid.

infliger vt to inflict; to impose.

influence f influence.

influencer vt to influence, sway.

informaticien m, -ienne f computer scientist.

information f piece of information; information; inquiry.

informatique f computing; data processing; * adj computer.

informer vt to inform, tell; s'~ vr to find out, inquire.

infraction f infraction, infringement; offence.

infranchissable adj impassable; insuperable.

infrarouge adj infrared.

infrastructure f infrastructure; substructure.

infructueux adj fruitless, unsuccessful.

infusion f infusion, herb tea.

ingénieur m engineer.

ingénieux adj ingenious, clever.

ingénu adj ingenuous, naive.

ingrat adj ungrateful; unprofitable.

ingratitude f ingratitude.

ingrédient m ingredient; component.

inhabité adj uninhabited, unoccupied.

inhabituel adj unusual, unaccustomed.

inhumain adj inhuman.

inimaginable adj unimaginable.

inimitable adj inimitable.

ininterrompu adj uninterrupted; unbroken.

initial *adj* initial; **~ement** *adv* initially.

initiation *f* initiation.

initiative *f* initiative; enterprise.

initier *vt* to initiate.

injecter *vt* to inject.

injection *f* injection.

injure *f* injury; insult.

injurier *vt* to abuse; insult.

injuste *adj* unjust, unfair; **~ment** *adv* unjustly.

injustice *f* injustice.

injustifié *adj* unjustified.

inné *adj* innate, inborn.

innocence *f* innocence.

innocent *m*, **-e** *f* innocent person; simpleton; * *adj* innocent.

innocenter *vt* to clear, prove innocent.

innovation *f* innovation.

innover *vi* to innovate, make innovations.

inodore *adj* odourless, scentless.

inoffensif *adj* inoffensive, harmless.

inondation *f* inundation.

inonder *vt* to flood, inundate.

inopportun *adj* ill-timed, inopportune.

inoubliable *adj* unforgettable.

inouï *adj* unprecedented, unheard of.

inox *m* stainless steel.

inqualifiable *adj* unspeakable.

inquiet *adj* worried, anxious, uneasy.

inquiéter *vt* to worry, disturb **s'~** *vr* to get worried.

inquiétude *f* restlessness, uneasiness.

insaisissable *adj* elusive; imperceptible.

insalubre *adj* insalubrious; unhealthy.

insatiable *adj* insatiable; **~ment** *adv* insatiably.

insatisfaction *f* dissatisfaction.

inscription *f* inscription; registration; matriculation.

inscrire *vt* to inscribe; to enter; to set down; to register; **s'~** *vr* to join; to register, enrol.

insecte *m* insect.

insecticide *m* insecticide.

insémination *f* insemination.

insensé *adj* insane, demented.

insensible *adj* insensible, unfeeling, insensitive; imperceptible; **~ment** *adv* imperceptibly; insensibly.

inséparable *adj* inseparable.

insérer *vt* to insert.

insertion *f* insertion, inserting.

insidieux *adj* insidious.

insignifiant *adj* insignificant, trifling.

insinuation *f* insinuation.

insinuer *vt* to insinuate, imply; **s'~** *vr* to insinuate oneself into; to creep into.

insipide *adj* insipid, tasteless.

insister *vi* to insist, be insistent; to stress.

insolence *f* insolence.

insolent *adj* insolent; brazen.

insolite *adj* unusual; strange.

insomnie *f* insomnia.

insouciance *f* unconcern; carelessness.

insouciant *adj* carefree; careless.

insoutenable *adj* unbearable; untenable.

inspectez *vt* to inspect, examine.

inspecteur *m*, **-trice** *f* inspector

inspection *f* inspection.

inspiration *f* inspiration; suggestion.

inspirer *vt* to inspire; to breathe in; **s'~** *vr*: **s'~ de** to be inspired by.

instable *adj* unstable; unsettled.

installation *f* installation; installing.

installer *vt* to install; to fit out; **s'~** *vr* to set oneself up as; to settle down.

instant *m* moment, instant.

instantané *adj* instant, instantaneous; **~ment** *adv* instantly.

instaurer *vt* to institute; to impose.

instinct *m* instinct.

instinctif *adj* instinctive.

instinctivement *adv* instinctively.

institut *m* institute; school.

instituteur *m*, **-trice** *f* teacher.

institution *f* institution; establishment.

instructif *adj* instructive.

instruction *f* instruction; education; inquiry.

instruire *vt* to instruct; to teach; to conduct an inquiry; **s'~** *vr* to educate oneself; to obtain information about.

instrument *m* instrument, implement.

insuffisance *f* insufficiency, inadequacy.

insuffisant *adj* insufficient, inadequate.

insuline *f* insulin.

insulte *f* insult.

insulter *vt* to insult, affront.

insupportable *adj* unbearable, intolerable; **~ment** *adv* unbearably, intolerably.

insurrection *f* insurrection, revolt.

intact *adj* intact.

intégral *adj* integral; uncut; complete; **~ement** *adv* integrally; in full.

intégralité *f* whole; entirety.

intégrer *vt* to integrate; **s'~** *vr* to become integrated; to fit in.

intégrité *f* integrity.

intellectuel *m*, **-uelle** *f* intellectual; * *adj* intellectual, mental.

intelligence *f* intelligence; understanding.

intelligent *adj* intelligent, shrewd, bright.

intelligible *adj* intelligible.

intempéries *fpl* bad weather.

intendant *m*, **-e** *f* bursar; steward, stewardess.

intense *adj* intense; severe.

intensément *adv* intensely.

intensifier *vt* to intensify; **s'~** *vr* to intensify.

intensité *f* intensity; severity.

intention *f* intention; purpose, intent.

interaction *f* interaction.

intercaler *vt* to intercalate; to interpolate.

intercepter *vt* to intercept.

interchangeable *adj* interchangeable.

interdiction *f* interdiction, prohibition, ban.

interdire vt to forbid, ban, prohibit.

interdit adj forbidden, prohibited; dumbfounded.

intéressant adj interesting; attractive, worthwhile.

intéresser vt to interest; to affect; **s'~** vr: **s'~ à** to be interested in, take an interest in.

intérêt m interest; significance, importance.

interférence f interference; conjunction.

intérieur adj interior, internal, inland; **à l'~** inside; within; **~ement** adv inwardly.

intérimaire adj acting; interim; temporary.

interligne m line space; interlining; lead.

interlocuteur m, **-trice** f interlocutor, speaker.

intermède m interlude.

intermédiaire adj intermediate; intermediary.

interminable adj interminable; endless; **~ment** adv interminably, endlessly.

intermittent adj intermittent, sporadic.

international adj international.

interne adj internal; * mf boarder; house doctor.

interpeller vt to call out to; to interpellate.

interphone m intercom, interphone.

interposer vt to interpose; **s'~** vr to intervene.

interprétation f interpretation, rendering.

interprète mf interpreter.

interpréter vt to interpret; to perform.

interrogation f interrogation, questioning; question.

interrogatoire m questioning; cross-examination.

interroger vt to question; to interrogate; **s'~** vr to wonder.

interrompre vt to interrupt, break; **s'~** vr to break off, interrupt oneself.

interrupteur m switch.

interruption f interruption, break.

intervalle m interval; space, distance.

intervenir vi to intervene; to take part in.

intervention f intervention; operation.

intestinal adj intestinal.

intestin m intestine.

intime adj intimate; private; **~ment** adv intimately; * mf close friend.

intimider vt to intimidate.

intimité f intimacy; privacy.

intituler vt to call, entitle; **s'~** vr to be called; to call oneself.

intolérable adj intolerable.

intolérance f intolerance.

intolérant adj intolerant.

intonation f intonation.

intoxication f poisoning; indoctrination.

intransigeant adj intransigent, uncompromising.

intransitif adj intransitive.

intrépide adj intrepid, fearless; **~ment** adv intrepidly.

intrigant *adj* scheming.
introduction *f* introduction; launching; institution.
introduire *vt* to introduce, insert; to present; **s'~** *vr* to find one's way in; to be introduced.
introuvable *adj* undiscoverable; not to be found.
introverti *m*, **-e** *f* introvert; * *adj* introverted.
intrus *m*, **-e** *f* intruder; * *adj* intruding, intrusive.
intuitif *adj* intuitive.
intuition *f* intuition.
inutile *adj* useless; unavailing; pointless; **~ment** *adv* uselessly, needlessly.
inutilisable *adj* unusable.
invalide *adj* disabled; invalid.
invariable *adj* invariable; unvarying; **~ment** *adv* invariably.
invasion *f* invasion.
inventaire *m* inventory; stock list.
inventer *vt* to invent; to devise; to make up.
inventeur *m*, **-trice** *f* inventor.
invention *f* invention; inventiveness.
inverse *adj* opposite; * *m* opposite, reverse.
inverser *vt* to reverse, invert.
inversion *f* inversion; reversal.
investir *vt* to invest; to surround.
investissement *m* investment; investing.
invincible *adj* invincible, indomitable.
invisible *adj* invisible; unseen.

invitation *f* invitation.
invité *m*, **-e** *f* guest.
inviter *vt* to invite, ask.
involontaire *adj* involuntary; unintentional; **~ment** *adv* involuntarily.
invoquer *vt* to invoke; to call up; to plead.
invraisemblable *adj* unlikely, improbable; **~ment** *adv* improbably.
invulnérable *adj* invulnerable.
iode *m* iodine.
ion *m* ion.
iris *m* iris.
Irlandais *m* Irishman, **-e** *f* Irishwoman
irlandais *adj* Irish.
Irlande *f* Ireland.
ironie *f* irony.
ironique *adj* ironic; **~ment** *adv* ironically.
irradiation *f* irradiation; radiation.
irrationnel *adj* irrational.
irrécupérable *adj* irretrievable.
irréel *adj* unreal.
irréfléchi *adj* unconsidered; hasty.
irrégularité *f* irregularity; variation; unevenness.
irrégulier *adj* irregular; varying; uneven.
irrégulièrement *adv* irregularly; unevenly.
irrémédiable *adj* irreparable; incurable; **~ment** *adv* irreparably.
irremplaçable *adj* irreplaceable.
irréparable *adj* irreparable; irretrievable; **~ment** *adv* irreparably.
irrésistible *adj* irresistible; **~ment** *adv* irresistibly.
irresponsable *adj* irresponsible

irréversible *adj* irreversible; **~ment**
adv irreversibly.
irrigation *f* irrigation.
irriguer *vt* to irrigate.
irriter *vt* to irritate; to provoke.
irruption *f* irruption.
Islam *m* Islam.
isolement *m* loneliness; isolation;
insulation.

isoler *vt* to isolate; to insulate; **s'~**
vr to cut oneself off.
issu *adj* descended from; stem-
ming from.
issue *f* outlet; solution; outcome.
ivoire *m* ivory.
ivre *adj* drunk, inebriated.
ivresse *f* drunkenness.
ivrogne *mf* drunkard.

J

jachère *f* fallow; leaving land fallow.
jade *m* jade.
jadis *adv* formerly, long ago.
jaguar *m* jaguar.
jaillir *vi* to spout, gush; to spring.
jalon *m* staff; landmark, milestone.
jalonner *vt* to mark out.
jalousie *f* jealousy, envy.
jaloux *m*, **-ouse** *f* jealous person;
* *adj* jealous, envious.
jamais *adv* never, not ever; **à ~** for
ever.
jambe *f* leg.
jambon *m* ham.
janvier *m* January.
jardin *m* garden.
jardinage *m* gardening.
jardiner *vi* to garden.
jardinier *m*, **-ière** *f* gardener.
jargon *m* jargon, slang; gibberish.
jarret *m* hock; shin.
jaser *vi* to chatter; to twitter; to
babble.
jasmin *m* jasmine.
jauge *f* gauge; capacity; tonnage.
jauger *vt* to gauge the capacity of;
to size up.

jaunâtre *adj* yellowish.
jaune *adj* yellow; * *m* yellow.
jaunir *vi* to yellow, turn yellow;
* *vt* to make yellow.
jaunisse *f* jaundice.
jazz *m* jazz.
je, j' *pron* I.
jésuite *m* Jesuit.
jet *m* jet, spurt; throwing.
jetable *adj* disposable.
jetée *f* pier.
jeter *vt* to throw; to discard; to give
out; **se ~** *vr* to throw oneself; to
rush at.
jeton *m* token; counter.
jeu *m* play; game; gambling; **~ de
jambes** footwork; **~ de mots**
pun, play on words; **cacher son
~** to conceal one's intentions.
jeudi *m* Thursday.
jeun(à) *adv* on an empty stomach.
jeune *adj* young; junior; new;
youthful; * *m* youth, young man;
f young girl.
jeûne *m* fast.
jeûner *vi* to fast.
jeunesse *f* youth, youthfulness.
joaillerie *f* jewelling; jewellery.

joaillier *m*, **-ière** *f* jeweller.

joie *f* joy, happiness; pleasure.

joindre *vt* to join, link; to attach; **se ~** *vr* to join, join in.

joint *m* joint; join.

jointure *f* joint (*anat*).

joli *adj* pretty; good, handsome; **~ment** *adv* nicely, attractively.

jonc *m* rush; cane.

joncher *vt* to strew with.

jonction *f* junction.

jongler *vi* to juggle.

jongleur *m*, **-euse** *f* juggler.

jonquille *f* daffodil, jonquil.

joue *f* cheek.

jouer *vi* to play; to gamble; to act.

jouet *m* toy.

joueur *m*, **-euse** *f* player; gambler.

joufflu *adj* chubby; round-faced.

joug *m* yoke.

jouir *vi* to enjoy; to delight in.

jouissance *f* enjoyment; use.

jour *m* day; daylight; **tous les ~s** every day; **à ~** up to date; **vivre au ~ le ~** to live from day to day; **~ férié** public holiday; **mise à ~** updating; update; **du ~ au lendemain** overnight.

journal *m* newspaper; bulletin, journal; **~ de bord** logbook; **~ télévisé** television news.

journalisme *m* journalism.

journaliste *mf* journalist.

journée *f* day; day's work.

jovial *adj* jovial, jolly.

jovialité *f* joviality.

joyau *m* jewel, gem.

joyeusement *adv* joyfully, cheerfully.

joyeux *adj* joyful, cheerful.

jubiler *vi* to be jubilant, exult.

judaïsme *m* Judaism.

judiciaire *adj* judicial, legal.

judicieusement *adv* judiciousy

judicieux *adj* judicious.

judo *m* judo.

judoka *mf* judoka.

juge *m* judge.

jugement *m* judgment; sentence; opinion.

juger *vt* to judge; to decide; to consider.

juif *m* Jew; Jewish; **juive** *f* Jewess; Jewish.

juillet *m* July.

juin *m* June.

jumeau *m*, **-elle** *f* twin; * *adj* twin; double.

jumelage *m* twinning.

jumelé *adj* twinned, twin.

jumelle(s) *f(pl)* binoculars.

jument *f* mare.

jungle *f* jungle.

jupe *f* skirt.

jurer *vt* to swear, pledge.

juridiction *f* jurisdiction; court of law.

juridique *adj* legal, juridical; **~ment** *adv* juridically, legally.

jurisprudence *f* case law, jurisprudence.

juriste *m* lawyer; jurist.

juron *m* oath, curse.

jury *m* jury; board of examiners.

jus *m* juice.

jusque, jusqu' *prép* to, as far as; until.

justaucorps *m* jerkin; leotard.

juste *adj* just, fair; exact; sound; **~ment** *adv* exactly, precisely

justesse *f* accuracy; aptness; soundness.

justice *f* justice, fairness.

justicier *m*, **-ière** *f* justiciary; dispenser of justice.

justificatif *adj* supporting, justificatory.

justification *f* justification; proof.

justifier *vt* to justify, prove; **se ~** *vr* to justify oneself.

jute *m* jute.

juteux *adj* juicy; lucrative.

juvénile *adj* young, youthful.

juxtaposer *vt* to juxtapose.

juxtaposition *f* juxtaposition.

K

kaki *adj* khaki.

kaléidoscope *m* kaleidoscope.

kangourou *m* kangaroo.

karaté *m* karate.

kayac, kayak *m* kayak.

képi *m* kepi.

kermesse *f* fair; bazaar.

kérosène *m* kerosene, aviation fuel.

kidnapper *vt* to kidnap, abduct.

kidnappeur *m*, **-euse** *f* kidnapper.

kilogramme *m* kilogramme.

kilohertz *m* kilohertz.

kilométrage *m* total kilometres travelled (mileage).

kilomètre *m* kilometre.

kimono *m* kimono.

kinésithérapeute *mf* physiotherapist.

kiosque *m* kiosk, stall.

kiwi *m* kiwi, Chinese gooseberry.

klaxon *m* horn.

klaxonner *vi* to sound one's horn.

kleptomane *mf* kleptomaniac.

kleptomanie *f* kleptomania.

koala *m* koala. **la** *art*, *pron*: *see* **le**.

kyste *m* cyst.

L

là *adv* there; over there; then; **par ~** that way; **~-dedans** inside, in there; **~ -dessous** underneath, under there; **~ -dessus** on that; thereupon; **~ -haut** up there, up on top; **celui-~** that one.

label *m* label; seal.

labeur *m* labour, toil.

laboratoire *m* laboratory.

laborieux *adj* laborious, toilsome.

labourer *vt* to plough; to dig over; to rip open.

labyrinthe *m* labyrinth.

lac *m* lake.

lacer *vt* to lace up; to tie up.

lacérer *vt* to lacerate; to tear.

lacet *m* lace.

lâche *adj* slack; loose; lax; cowardly; **~ment** *adv* loosely; in a cowardly manner.

lâcher *vt* to loosen; to release.

lâcheté *f* cowardice; meanness.

laconique *adj* laconic; **~ment** *adv* laconically.

lacté *adj* milky, lacteal.

lactique *adj* lactic.

lacune *f* lacuna; gap.

lagon m lagoon.

lagune f lagoon.

laïc m layman, **laïque** f laywoman;
* **laïque** adj lay, civil.

laid adj ugly, unsightly.

laideur f ugliness, unsightliness.

lainage m woollen article.

laine f wool.

laisse f leash, string, lead.

laisser vt to leave; to let; **~ tomber**
to drop; **se ~ aller** to let oneself
go.

laisser-passer m invar pass, permit.

lait m milk.

laitage m milk; milk products.

laiton m brass.

laitue f lettuce.

lama m llama; lama.

lambeau m shred; tatter.

lambris m plastering; panelling.

lame f blade; strip; metal plate.

lamelle f slide, lamella.

lamentable adj lamentable, distressing; **~ment** adv lamenta-
bly.

lamentation f lamentation; wailing.

lamenter(se) vr to lament, bewail.

laminer vt to laminate.

lampadaire m standard-lamp; street
lamp.

lampe f lamp, light; bulb.

lance f lance, spear.

lance-flammes m invar flame-
thrower.

lancement m launching; starting
up; throwing.

lance-pierres m invar catapult.

lancer vt to throw; to launch; **se ~**
vr to leap, jump; to embark on.

lancinant adj piercing; haunting.

lande f moor.

langage m language, speech.

langoureux adj languid, languor-
ous.

langouste f spiny lobster.

langoustine f Dublin bay prawn.

langue f tongue; language.

languette f tongue; tongue-like
strip.

langueur f languor.

languir vi to languish; to linger.

lanière f thong; lash.

lanoline f lanolin.

lanterne f lantern; lamp.

lapin m, **-e** f rabbit.

lapsus m slip, mistake.

laque f shellac, lacquer; * m lacquer article.

lard m fat; bacon.

lardon m lardon.

large adj wide; generous; lax;
great; **~ment** adv widely; greatly.

largeur f width, breadth.

larguer vt to loose, release; cast
off.

larme f tear.

larmoyant adj tearful, weeping.

larve f larva, grub.

laryngite f laryngitis.

larynx m larynx.

las adj, **lasse** f weary, tired.

lasagne f lasagne.

laser m laser.

lasser vt to tire; **se ~** vr to grow
tired of.

lassitude f tiredness, weariness.

latent adj latent.

latéral adj lateral, side; **~ement**
adv laterally.

latex *m* latex.

latin *adj* Latin; * *m* Latin.

latitude *f* latitude; margin.

latte *f* lath.

lauréat *m*, **-e** *f* prize winner.

laurier *m* bay-tree, laurel.

lavabo *m* washbasin.

lavage *m* washing; bathing.

lavande *f* lavender.

lave *f* lava.

lavement *m* enema.

laver *vt* to wash; to cleanse; **se ~** *vr* to wash oneself.

laverie *f* laundry.

lave-vaisselle *m invar* dishwasher.

laxatif *adj* laxative; * *m* laxative.

laxisme *m* laxness.

layette *f* baby clothes.

le *art*, *f* **la**, *devant voyelle* **l'**, *pl* **les** the; * *pron* him, her, them.

lécher *vt* to lick.

leçon *f* lesson; reading; class.

lecteur *m*, **-trice** *f* reader.

lecture *f* reading; perusal.

légal *adj* legal, lawful; **~ement** *adv* legally.

légaliser *vt* to legalize.

légalité *f* legality, lawfulness.

légendaire *adj* legendary.

légende *f* legend; inscription.

léger *adj* light; slight; faint; inconsiderate.

légèrement *adv* lightly; thoughtlessly

légèreté *f* lightness; nimbleness; thoughtlessness.

légion *f* legion.

législatif *adj* legislative; * *m* legislature.

législation *f* legislation, laws.

légitime *adj* legitimate, lawful; **~ment** *adv* legitimately.

légitimité *f* legitimacy.

legs *m* legacy, bequest.

léguer *vt* to bequeath; to devise.

légume *m* vegetable.

lendemain *m* next day, day after.

lent *adj* slow; tardy; sluggish; **~ement** *adv* slowly.

lente *f* nit.

lenteur *f* slowness.

lentille *f* lentil; lens.

léopard *m* leopard.

lèpre *f* leprosy.

lépreux *m*, **-euse** *f* leper; * *adj* leprous.

lequel *pron*, *f* **laquelle**, *pl* **lesquels**, **lesquelles** who, whom, which.

lesbienne *f* lesbian.

léser *vt* to wrong; to damage.

lésion *f* wrong; lesion, wound.

lessive *f* washing powder.

leste *adj* nimble, agile; **~ment** *adv* nimbly.

lester *vt* to fill; to ballast.

léthargie *f* lethargy.

léthargique *adj* lethargic.

lettre *f* letter, note; literature; **en toutes ~s** in black and white; **suivre à la ~** to carry out to the letter; **avant la ~** in advance, premature.

leucémie *f* leukaemia.

leucocyte *m* leucocyte.

leur *pron* them; **le ~**, **la ~**, **les ~s** theirs.

leurrer *vt* to deceive; to lure; **se ~** *vr* to delude oneself.

levain *m* leaven.

lever vt to lift, raise; to levy; **se ~** to get up; * m rising; getting up.

levier m lever.

lèvre f lip.

lévrier m greyhound.

levure f yeast.

lexique m vocabulary, lexis.

lézard m lizard.

lézarde f crack.

liaison f affair; connection; liaison, link.

liasse f bundle.

libellule f dragonfly.

libéral adj liberal; **~ement** adv liberally; * m liberal.

libéraliser vt to liberalize.

libéralisme m liberalism.

libéralité f liberality, generosity.

libération f release, liberation.

libérer vt to release; to liberate; **se ~** vr to free oneself.

liberté f liberty, freedom.

libido f libido.

libraire mf bookseller.

librairie f bookshop; bookselling.

libre adj free; independent; **~ment** adv freely.

licence f degree; permit; licentiousness.

licenciement m redundancy; dismissal.

licencier vt to make redundant; to dismiss.

lichen m lichen.

licorne f unicorn.

lie f dregs, sediment.

liège m cork.

lien m bond; link, connection; tie.

lier vt to bind; to link; **se ~** vr: **se ~ avec** to make friends.

lierre m ivy.

lieu m place, position; cause; occasion; **avoir ~** to take place; **en premier ~** in the first place; **au ~ de** instead of.

lieutenant m (mil) lieutenant.

lièvre m hare.

ligament m ligament.

ligature f ligature; tying up.

ligne f line; row; range.

lignée f lineage; offspring.

lignite m lignite.

ligoter vt to bind hand and foot.

ligue f league.

lilas m lilac; * adj lilac.

limace f slug.

limande f sole.

lime f file.

limer vt to file down.

limitation f limitation, restriction.

limite f boundary, limit; **à la ~** ultimately.

limiter vt to limit, restrict; **se ~** vr to limit oneself to.

limitrophe adj border.

limon m silt, mud.

limonade f lemonade.

limpide adj limpid, clear.

limpidité f limpidity, clearness.

lin m flax; linen.

linceul m shroud.

linéaire adj linear.

linge m linen; washing.

lingerie f linen room; underwear, lingerie.

lingot m ingot.

linguiste mf linguist.

linguistique f linguistics; * adj linguistic.

lion m lion, **lionne** f lioness.

lionceau m lion cub.

lipide m lipid.

liquéfier vt to liquefy; **se ~** vr to liquefy.

liqueur f liqueur; liquid.

liquidation f liquidation; winding up; elimination.

liquide m liquid.

liquider vt to settle; to wind up; to eliminate

lire vt to read.

lis m lily.

lisible adj legible; readable; **~ment** adv legibly.

lisière f edge; border; selvage; outskirts.

lisse adj smooth, glossy.

lisser vt to smooth, gloss.

liste f list; schedule.

lit m bed; layer.

litanie f litany.

literie f bedding.

lithographie f lithography.

litière f litter.

litige m lawsuit; dispute.

litigieux adj litigious.

litre m litre.

littéraire adj literary.

littéral adj literal; **~ement** adv literally.

littérature f literature; writing.

littoral m coast; * adj coastal, littoral.

liturgie f liturgy.

livide adj livid, pale.

livraison f delivery; number, issue.

livre m book; * f pound (weight, currency).

livrer vt to deliver, hand over; to give away; **se ~** vr to abandon oneself; to practise.

livret m libretto; booklet.

livreur m delivery man, **-euse** f delivery woman.

lobe m lobe.

lobotomie f lobotomy.

local adj local; **~ement** adv locally.

localisation f localization.

localiser vt to localize.

localité f locality; town.

locataire mf tenant; lodger.

location f renting; lease, leasing.

locomotion f locomotion.

locomotive f locomotive, engine; dynamo.

locution f locution, idiom.

logarithme m logarithm.

loge f lodge; dressing room; box.

logement m housing; accommodation.

loger vt to accommodate; to billet; * vi to live in.

logiciel m software.

logique f logic; * adj logical; **~ment** adv logically.

logistique f logistics.

logo m logo.

loi f law; act, statute; rule.

loin adv far, a long way; * m distance; background; **au ~** in the distance; **de ~** from a distance; **moins ~** not so far; **plus ~** further, farther.

lointain adj distant, remote; * m distance; background

loir m dormouse.

loisir m leisure, spare time.

lombaire adj lumbar; * f lumbar vertebra.

lombric m earthworm.

long *adj*, *f* **longue** long, lengthy; **~uement** *adv* at length.

longer *vt* to border; to walk along.

longévité *f* longevity.

longitude *f* longitude.

longtemps *adv* for a long time.

longueur *f* length.

longue-vue *f* telescope.

loquace *adj* loquacious, talkative.

loque *f* rag.

loquet *m* latch; clasp.

lorgner *vt* to leer, ogle.

lors *adv*: then ~ **de** at the time of; **dès** ~ from that time.

lorsque *conj* when.

losange *m* lozenge, diamond.

lot *m* prize; lot; portion.

loterie *f* lottery; raffle.

lotion *f* lotion.

lotissement *m* allotment; site; housing development.

lotus *m* lotus.

louange *f* praise, commendation.

louche *adj* dubious; suspicious, shady.

loucher *vi* to squint; to ogle.

louer *vt* to rent, lease; to book.

loup *m* wolf.

loupe *f* magnifying glass.

louper *vt* (*fam*) to botch, bungle; to flunk.

lourd *adj* heavy; sultry; unwieldy; **~ement** *adv* heavily.

lourdeur *f* heaviness.

loutre *f* otter.

louve *f* she-wolf; sling.

louveteau *m* wolf-cub.

loyal *adj* loyal, faithful; **~ement** *adv* loyally.

loyauté *f* loyalty

loyer *m* rent.

lubrifiant *m* lubricant; * *adj* lubricating.

lubrifier *vt* to lubricate.

lubrique *adj* lustful, lecherous; **~ment** *adv* lustfully.

lucarne *f* skylight

lucide *adj* lucid, clear; **~ment** *adv* lucidly.

lucidité *f* lucidity, clearness.

lucratif *adj* lucrative.

ludique *adj* play.

lueur *f* glimmer, gleam; glimpse.

luge *f* sledge, toboggan.

lugubre *adj* lugubrious, gloomy; **~ment** *adv* lugubriously.

lui *pron* him, her, it; **c'est à ~** it is his; **~-même** himself, herself, itself.

luire *vt* to shine, gleam.

luisant *adj* gleaming, shining.

lumbago *m* lumbago.

lumière *f* light; daylight; lamp; insight.

lumineux *adj* luminous; illuminated.

lunaire *adj* lunar, moon.

lunatique *adj* fantastical, whimsical, quirky.

lundi *m* Monday.

lune *f* moon.

lunette *f* telescope; sight; **~s** glasses.

lustré *adj* glossy; shiny.

luth *m* lute.

luthérien *adj* Lutheran.

luthiste *mf* lutanist.

lutin *adj* mischievous, impish.

lutte *f* struggle; contest; strife.

lutter *vi* to struggle, fight.

lutteur m, **-euse** f wrestler, fighter.

luxation f dislocation, luxation.

luxe m luxury, excess.

luxeusement adv luxuriously.

luxueux adj luxurious.

luxure f lust.

luxuriance f luxuriance.

luxuriant adj luxuriant.

luzerne f lucerne.

lycée m secondary school.

lycéen m secondary schoolboy, **-éenne** f secondary schoolgirl.

lymphatique adj lymphatic.

lymphe f lymph.

lymphocyte m lymphocyte.

lyncher vt to lynch.

lynx m lynx.

lyre f lyre.

lyrique adj lyric; **~ment** adv lyrically.

lyrisme m lyricism.

M

macabre adj macabre, deathly.

macadam m tarmac.

macaque m macaque.

macédoine f medley, hotchpotch; macedoine.

macérer vt to macerate; to mortify oneself; * vi to macerate, steep.

mâche f corn-salad.

mâcher vt to chew.

machiavélique adj Machiavellian.

machin m (fam) gadget; thingamajig.

machinal adj mechanical, automatic; **~ement** adv mechanically.

machination f machination, plot.

machine f machine; engine; apparatus.

machinerie f machinery, plant.

machiniste m machinist; driver; stagehand.

mâchoire f jaw.

maçon m builder, mason.

maçonnerie f masonry; building.

macrobiotique adj macrobiotic; * f macrobiotics

madame f Madam; Mrs; lady.

madeleine f madeleine.

mademoiselle f Miss; young lady.

magasin m shop, store; warehouse.

magazine m magazine.

mage m magus; seer.

magicien m, **-ienne** f magician.

magie f magic

magique adj magic; magical; **~ment** adv magically.

magistral adj masterly; authoritative; **~ement** adv in a masterly fashion.

magistrat m magistrate.

magistrature f magistracy; magistrature.

magnanime adj magnanimous; **~ment** adv magnanimously.

magnanimité f magnanimity.

magnat m magnate.

magnésium m magnesium.

magnétique adj magnetic.

magnétiser vt to magnetize; to hypnotize.

magnétisme m magnetism; hypnotism.

magnétophone *m* tape recorder.

magnétoscope *m* video recorder; videotape.

magnifique *adj* magnificent; sumptuous; **~ment** *adv* magnificently.

magnolia *m* magnolia.

magot *m* (*fam*) savings, hoard, nest egg.

magouille *f* (*fam*) fiddle; scam; scheming.

mai *m* May.

maigre *adj* thin; meagre, scarce; **~ment** *adv* meagrely.

maigreur *f* thinness; meagreness; sparseness.

maigrir *vi* to get thinner; to waste away.

maille *f* stitch; mesh; link.

maillet *m* mallet.

maillon *m* link; shackle.

maillot *m* jersey; leotard.

main *f* hand; **avoir la ~** to have the lead; **passer la ~** to make way for so.

main-d'œuvre *f* workforce.

maintenance *f* maintenance, servicing.

maintenant *adv* now; **à partir de ~** from now on.

maintenir *vt* to keep, maintain; preserve; **se ~ vr** to persist; to hold one's own.

maintien *m* maintenance; preservation; keeping up.

maire *m* mayor, **-esse** *f* mayoress.

mairie *f* mayoralty; town hall.

mais *conj* but.

maïs *m* maize.

maison *f* house; home; building; premises.

maître *m* **-esse** *f* master; ruler; lord; proprietor.

maîtresse *f* mistress; teacher.

maîtrise *f* mastery; control; expertise.

maîtriser *vt* to control; to master; **se ~ vr** to control oneself.

majesté *f* majesty, grandeur.

majestueusement *adv* majestically.

majestueux *adj* majestic.

majeur *adj* major; main; chief; superior; * *m* major *mf* adult.

majoration *f* increased charge; overestimation.

majordome *m* major-domo.

majorer *vt* to increase, raise.

majorette *f* majorette.

majoritaire *adj* majority.

majorité *f* majority.

majuscule *f* capital letter.

mal *adv* wrong, badly; * *m* evil, wrong; harm; pain.

malachite *f* malachite.

malade *adj* sick, ill; diseased; * *mf* invalid, sick person.

maladie *f* illness; malady, complaint; disorder.

maladresse *f* clumsiness; awkwardness.

maladroit *adj* clumsy, awkward; **~ement** *adv* clumsily.

malaise *m* uneasiness, discomfort; indisposition.

malchance *f* ill luck; misfortune; mishap.

malchanceux *adj* unlucky, unfortunate.

mâle *m* male; * *adj* male; manly, virile.

malédiction *f* malediction, curse.

maléfique *adj* hurtful; malignant; baleful.

malencontreux *adj* unfortunate, untoward.

malentendu *m* misunderstanding.

malfaisant *adj* malevolent; harmful; wicked.

malfaiteur *m* criminal; malefactor.

malgré *prép* in spite of; despite.

malheur *m* misfortune; calamity.

malheureusement *adv* unfortunately.

malheureux *adj* unfortunate; unlucky; unhappy.

malhonnête *adj* dishonest, crooked; uncivil; ~**ment** *adv* dishonestly.

malhonnêteté *f* dishonesty; incivility.

malice *f* malice, spite; mischievousness.

malicieux *adj* malicious, spiteful; mischievous.

malin *adj* shrewd, cunning, crafty; malignant.

malintentionné *adj* ill-disposed, spiteful.

malle *f* trunk.

malléable *adj* malleable.

malmener *vt* to ill-treat, maltreat.

malnutrition *f* malnutrition.

malsain *adj* unhealthy, unwholesome; immoral.

malt *m* malt.

maltraiter *vt* to abuse; to handle roughly.

malveillance *f* malevolence, spite.

malveillant *adj* malevolent, spiteful.

maman *f* mother, mummy, mum.

mamelle *f* breast; udder.

mamelon *m* nipple, teat.

mammifère *m* mammal.

manche *f* sleeve; game, round; * *m* handle, shaft.

manchot *m*, **-e** *f* one-armed person; * *adj* one-armed; * *m* penguin.

mandarin *m* mandarin, Mandarin.

mandarine *f* tangerine.

mandat *m* mandate; money order; proxy.

mandataire *mf* proxy; representative.

mandibule *f* mandible, jaw.

mandoline *f* mandolin.

manège *m* roundabout, merry-go-round.

manette *f* lever, tap.

manganèse *m* manganese.

mangeable *adj* edible.

manger *vt* to eat; to consume, squander

mangeur *m*, **-euse** *f* eater.

mangouste *f* mongoose.

mangue *f* mango.

maniable *adj* handy, workable, tractable; amenable.

maniaque *adj* eccentric; fussy; * *mf* maniac; fusspot; fanatic.

manie *f* mania.

maniement *m* handling; management, use.

manier *vt* to handle; to manipulate.

manière *f* manner, way, style.

maniéré *adj* affected.

manifestation f demonstration; expression, manifestation.

manifeste adj manifest, evident, obvious; **~ment** adv manifestly, obviously; * m manifesto.

manifester vt to display, make known; to demonstrate; **se ~** vr to make oneself known; to appear; to express itself.

manigancer vt to contrive; to scheme.

manipulation f handling; manipulation.

manipuler vt to handle; to manipulate

manivelle f crank.

mannequin m model; dummy.

manœuvre f manoeuvre, operation; scheme; * m labourer.

manœuvrer vt to manoeuvre; to operate; * vi to manoeuvre, move.

manoir m manor.

manomètre m manometer.

manquant adj missing.

manque m lack, shortage; shortcoming, deficiency.

manquer vt to miss; to fail; to be absent.

mansarde f attic, garret.

manteau m coat; mantle, blanket; cloak.

manuel m manual, handbook; * adj manual; **~lement** adv manually.

manufacture f factory; manufacture.

manufacturier m, **-ière** f factory owner; manufacturer; * adj manufacturing.

manuscrit m manuscript; typescript; * adj handwritten.

manutention f handling.

mappemonde f map of the world.

maquereau m mackerel.

maquette f model; mock-up; dummy; sketch.

maquillage m make-up.

maquiller vt to make up; to fake; to fiddle; **se ~** vr to put on one's make-up.

marais m marsh, swamp.

marasme m stagnation; depression, slump.

marathon m marathon.

marbre m marble; marble statue.

marbré adj marbled; mottled, blotchy.

marbrier m marble-cutter; monumental mason.

marchand, -e f shopkeeper; dealer; merchant; * adj market, trade.

marchandage m bargaining, haggling.

marchander vi to bargain over, haggle.

marchandise f merchandise, commodity; goods.

marche f walk; journey; progress; movement; **mettre en ~** to start up; to turn on.

marché m market; transaction, contract.

marcher vi to walk, march; to progress; to work.

marcheur m, **-euse** f walker, pedestrian.

mardi m Tuesday.

mare f pool, pond.

marécage *m* marsh, swamp.

maréchal *m* marshal.

marée *f* tide/

margarine *f* margarine.

marge *f* margin; latitude, freedom; mark-up.

marginal *adj* marginal.

marginaliser *vt* to marginalize.

marguerite *f* daisy.

mari *m* husband.

mariage *m* marriage.

marié *m* bridegroom; * *adj* married.

marier *vt* to marry; blend, harmonize; **se ~** *vr* to get married.

marin *m* sailor.

marine *f* navy; seascape; marine.

mariner *vi* to marinate; to hang about; * *vt* to marinate

marionnette *f* puppet; puppet show.

maritime *adj* maritime; seaboard.

marjolaine *f* marjoram.

marmelade *f* compote; marmalade.

marmite *f* pot.

marmonner *vt* to mumble, mutter.

marmotte *f* marmot.

maroquinerie *f* tannery; fine leather craft.

maroquinier *m* leather craftsman; dealer in fine leather.

marquant *adj* outstanding, vivid.

marque *f* mark, sign; brand; make.

marquer *vt* to mark; to note down; to score.

marquis *m* marquis, **-e** *f* marchioness.

marraine *f* godmother; sponsor.

marron *m* chestnut; brown; * *adj* brown.

marronnier *m* chestnut tree.

mars *m* March.

marsouin *m* porpoise.

marteau *m* hammer; knocker.

marteler *vt* to hammer; to beat.

martial *adj* martial, warlike.

martin-pêcheur *m* kingfisher.

martyr *m* , **-e** *f* martyr; * *adj* martyred.

martyre *m* martyrdom.

martyriser *vt* to torture, martyr.

mascarade *f* farce, mascarade.

masculin *adj* masculine.

masochisme *m* masochism.

masochiste *mf* masochist; * *adj* masochistic.

masque *m* mask; facade, front.

masquer *vt* to mask, conceal; to disguise.

massacre *m* massacre; slaughter.

massacrer *vt* to massacre, slaughter.

massage *m* massage.

masse *f* mass, heap; bulk; mob.

masser *vt* to mass, assemble; to massage.

masseur *m* masseur, **-euse** *f* masseuse.

massif *adj* massive, solid, heavy; * *m* massif; clump.

massivement *adv* en masse, massively, heavily.

massue *f* club.

mastic *m* mastic; cement; putty.

mastiquer *vt* to chew, masticate.

masturbation *f* masturbation.

masturber *vt*; **se ~** *vr* to masturbate.

mat *adj* matt, dull; dead, dull-sounding.

mât *m* mast; pole.

match *m* match; game.

matelas *m* mattress.

matelassé *adj* stuffed; padded, cushioned.

matelot *m* sailor; seaman.

mater *vt* to subdue; to control, curb; to spy on; to ogle.

matérialiser *vt* to make materialize, embody; **se** ~ *vr* to materialize.

matériaux *mpl* material, materials.

matériel *adj* material, physical; practical; **~lement** *adv* materially, practically.

maternel *adj* maternal, motherly; **~lement** *adv* maternally.

maternité *f* motherhood; pregnancy; maternity hospital.

mathématicien *m*, **-ienne** *f* mathematician.

mathématique *adj* mathematical; **~ment** *adv* mathematically; * *f* mathematics.

matière *f* material, matter; subject; ~ **première** raw material.

matin *m* morning; dawn.

matinal *adj* morning.

matinée *f* morning; matinée.

matraque *f* truncheon; cosh.

matrice *f* womb; mould; matrix.

matricule *m* reference number; * *f* roll, register.

matrimonial *adj* matrimonial, marriage.

maturation *f* maturing; maturation.

maturité *f* maturity; prime.

maudire *vt* to curse.

maudit *adj* cursed; blasted, damned.

maussade *adj* sulky, sullen; **~ment** *adv* sulkily, sullenly.

mauvais *adj* bad; wicked; faulty; hurtful; poor.

mauve *adj* mauve; * *f* mallow.

maximal *adj* maximal.

maxime *f* maxim.

maximum *m* maximum.

mayonnaise *f* mayonnaise.

me, m' *pron* me; myself.

mécanicien *m*, **-ienne** *f* mechanic; engineer.

mécanique *f* mechanics; mechanical engineering; * *adj* mechanical; **~ment** *adv* mechanically.

mécanisme *m* mechanism, working.

mécène *m* patron.

méchamment *adv* spitefully; wickedly.

méchanceté *f* spitefulness; wickedness; mischievousness.

méchant *adj* spiteful; wicked; mischievous.

mèche *f* wick, fuse; tuft.

méconnaissable *adj* unrecognizable.

méconnu *adj* unrecognized; misunderstood.

mécontent *adj* discontent, displeased.

mécontentement *m* discontent; displeasure.

médaille *f* medal; stain, mark.

médaillon *m* medallion; locket.

médecin *m* doctor, physician.

médecine *f* medicine.

médiateur *m*, **-trice** *f* mediator; arbitrator.

médiatique *adj* media.

médical *adj* medical; **~ement** *adv* medically.

médicament *m* medicine, drug.

médicinal *adj* medicinal.

médiéval *adj* medieval.

médiocre *adj* mediocre; passable; indifferent; **~ment** *adv* indifferently; poorly.

médisant *adj* slanderous.

méditation *f* meditation.

méditer *vi* to meditate; * *vt* to contemplate, have in mind.

médium *m* medium.

méduse *f* jellyfish.

méfiance *f* distrust, mistrust.

méfiant *adj* distrustful, mistrustful.

méfier(se) *vr* to mistrust, distrust; to be suspicious.

mégalomane *adj* megalomaniac; * *mf* megalomaniac.

mégaphone *m* megaphone.

mégot *m* cigarette-end, stub.

meilleur *adj* better, preferable; **le ~, la ~e** the best.

mélancolie *f* melancholy, gloom.

mélancolique *adj* melancholy; melancholic; **~ment** *adv* melancholically.

mélange *m* mixing, blending; mixture.

mélanger *vt* to mix, blend; to muddle.

mêlée *f* melée, fray; scrum.

mêler *vt* to mix; to combine; **se ~** *vr* to mix, mingle; **se ~ à** to join; **se ~ de** to get mixed up in.

mélisse *f* balm.

mélodie *f* melody, tune.

mélodieusement *adv* melodiously, tunefully.

mélodieux *adj* melodious, tuneful.

mélomane *mf* music lover.

melon *m* melon.

membrane *f* membrane.

membre *m* member; limb.

même *adv* even; **tout de ~** nevertheless, all the same; * *adj* same, identical; * *pron*: **le ~, la ~, les ~s** the same, the same one.

mémoire *f* memory; * *m* memorandum, report.

mémorable *adj* memorable.

mémoriser *vt* to memorize.

menaçant *adj* menacing, threatening.

menace *f* threat; intimidation; danger.

menacer *vt* to threaten, menace; to impend.

ménage *m* housework, housekeeping; household.

ménager *vt* to treat with caution; to manage; to arrange.; **se ~** *vr* to take care of oneself; * *adj* household, domestic.

ménagère *f* housewife.

ménagerie *f* menagerie.

mendiant *m*, **-e** *f* beggar, mendicant.

mendier *vt* to beg; to implore.

mener *vt* to lead, guide; to steer; to manage.

meneur *m*, **-euse** *f* leader; agitator.

menhir *m* menhir, standing stone.

méningite *f* meningitis.

ménopause *f* menopause.

menottes *fpl* handcuffs.

mensonge *m* lie, falsehood; error, illusion.

menstruation *f* menstruation.

mensuel *adj* monthly.

mental *adj* mental; **~ement** *adv* mentally.

mentalité *f* mentality.

menteur *m*, **-euse** *f* liar; * *adj* lying, deceitful.

menthe *f* mint.

menthol *m* menthol.

mention *f* mention; comment; grade.

mentionner *vt* to mention.

mentir *vi* to lie; to be deceptive.

menton *m* chin.

menu *m* menu; meal; * *adj* slender, thin; petty; minor.

menuiserie *f* joinery, carpentry.

menuisier *m* joiner, carpenter.

mépris *m* contempt, scorn.

méprisant *adj* contemptuous, scornful.

mépriser *vt* to scorn, despise.

mer *f* sea; tide.

mercenaire *m* mercenary.

mercerie *f* haberdashery.

merci *m* thank you; * *f* mercy; **sans ~** merciless; **être à la ~ de** to be at the mercy of.

mercredi *m* Wednesday.

mercure *m* mercury.

mère *f* mother.

méridien *m* meridian; midday.

méridional *adj* southern.

meringue *f* meringue.

merisier *m* wild cherry.

mérite *m* merit, worth; quality.

mériter *vt* to deserve, merit.

merlan *m* whiting.

merle *m* blackbird.

mezveille *f* marvel, wonder.

merveilleusement *adv* marvellously, wonderfully.

merveilleux *adj* marvellous, wonderful.

mésange *f* tit (*orn*).

mésentente *f* misunderstanding.

mesquin *adj* mean, niggardly; petty; **~ement** *adv* meanly, pettily.

message *m* message.

messager *m*, **-ère** *f* messenger.

messagerie *f* parcels office, parcels service.

messe *f* mass.

messie *m* messiah.

mesure *f* measure; gauge; measurement; moderation; step; **au fur et à ~** as; one by one; **sans commune ~ avec** there is no possible comparison with; **dans la mesure où** insofar as; **en ~** in time.

mesurer *vt* to measure; to assess; to limit; **se ~** *vr* to try one's strength; **se ~ à** to pit oneself against, measure one's strength against.

métabolisme *m* metabolism.

métal *m* metal.

métallique *adj* metallic.

métallisé *adj* metallic, metallized.

métallurgie *f* metallurgy.

métallurgiste *m* steelworker, metalworker.

métamorphose *f* metamorphosis.

métamorphoser *vt* to transform, metamorphose; **se ~** *vr* to be metamorphosed.

métaphore f metaphor.

métaphorique adj metaphorical; **~ment** adv metaphorically.

métaphysique adj metaphysical; * f metaphysics.

météore m meteor.

météorite m/f meteorite.

météorologue, météorologiste mf meteorologist.

méthane m methane.

méthode f method, way.

méthodique adj methodical; **~ment** adv methodically.

méthylène m methyl alcohol; methylene.

méticuleusement adv meticulously.

méticuleux adj meticulous.

métier m job; occupation; **~ à tricoter** knitting machine; **~ à tisser** weaving loom.

métis m, **-isse** f half-caste; hybrid; mongrel; * adj half-caste; hybrid, mongrel.

mètre m metre.

métro m underground, metro.

métronome m metronome.

métropole f metropolis.

métropolitain adj metropolitan; underground.

mets m dish.

metteur en scène m director (cin)

mettre vt to put, place; to put on; **~ en marche** to start up; **se ~** vr to place oneself; to sit down; **se à** to begin to; **se ~ en route** to start off.

meuble m piece of furniture.

meubler vt to furnish.

meule f millstone; grindstone.

meurtre m murder.

meurtrier m murderer, **-ière** f murderess.

meurtrir vt to bruise.

meute f pack.

mezzanine f mezzanine.

mi- adj half; **à ~chemin** halfway; **~clos** half-closed; **à ~jambe** up to the knees; **à ~voix** in a low voice.

miauler vi to mew.

miche f round loaf.

microbe m germ, microbe.

microbien adj microbial, microbic.

microclimat m microclimate.

microfilm m microfilm.

micro-informatique f microcomputing.

micro-onde f microwave; * m **micro-ondes** microwave oven.

micro-ordinateur m microcomputer.

microphone m microphone.

microprocesseur m microprocessor.

microscope m microscope.

microscopique adj microscopic.

midi m midday, noon.

mie f crumb, soft part of a loaf.

miel m honey.

mien pron, f **mienne**: **le ~, la mienne, les ~s, les miennes** mine, my own.

miette f crumb; remnant; morsel.

mieux m improvement; **le ~** the best; **de ~ en ~** better and better.

mignon adj sweet, pretty.

migraine f headache; migraine.

migrateur m migrant.

migration f migration.

mijoter vi to simmer, be brewing; * vt to simmer; to scheme, plot.

milice f militia.

milieu m middle, centre; medium; environment.

militaire m serviceman; * adj military, army.

militant m, **-e** f militant; * adj militant.

militer vi to militate; to be a militant.

mille m one thousand; * adj one thousand.

millénaire m millennium, a thousand years; thousandth anniversary * adj thousand-year-old; millennial.

mille-pattes m millipede.

millésime m year, date; vintage.

millet m millet.

milliard m thousand million; milliard.

milliardaire adj worth (many) millions; * mf multimillionaire.

milliardième adj thousand millionth; * m thousand millionth.

millième adj thousandth; * m thousandth.

millier m thousand.

milligramme m milligramme.

millilitre m millilitre.

millimètre m millimetre.

million m million.

millionième adj millionth; * m millionth.

millionnaire adj millionaire; worth millions; * mf millionaire.

mime m mime ; * mf mimic.

mimer vt to mime; to mimic, imitate.

mimétisme m mimicry; mimetism.

mimosa m mimosa.

minable adj seedy, shabby; **~ment** adv shabbily.

mince adj thin, slender; meagre, trivial.

mincir vi to get slimmer, get thinner.

mine f expression; appearance; mine; **avoir bonne ~** to look good.

mineral m ore.

minéral adj mineral; inorganic; * m mineral.

minéralogique adj mineralogical.

mineur m, **-e** f minor; * adj minor; * m miner.

miniature f miniature.

mini-jupe f miniskirt.

minimal adj minimal, minimum.

minime adj minor, minimal.

minimum m minimum.

ministère m ministry; agency.

ministériel adj ministerial.

ministre m minister; clergyman.

minoritaire adj minority.

minorité f minority.

minuit f midnight.

minuscule adj minuscule, tiny, minute.

minute f minute, moment.

minuterie f time switch; regulator.

minutieux adj meticulous; minute.

mirabelle f plum.

miracle m miracle, wonder.

miraculeux adj miraculous.

mirage m mirage.

miroir m mirror, reflection.

misanthrope mf misanthrope; misanthropist; * adj misanthropic.

mise *f* putting, placing; stake; deposit; investment; **~ en scène** production, staging; **~ en liberté** release; **~ en ordre** ordering, arrangement; **~ en œuvre** implementation.

miser *vt* to stake, to bet.

misérable *adj* miserable; destitute; pitiable; **~ment** *adv* miserably.

misère *f* misery; poverty; destitution.

miséricorde *f* mercy, forgiveness.

misogyne *mf* misogynist; * *adj* misogynous.

missile *m* missile.

mission *f* mission, assignment.

missionnaire *m* missionary.

mi-temps *f* half-time; half.

miteux *adj* dingy, shabby, poverty-stricken.

mitigé *adj* mitigated; lukewarm.

mitoyen *adj* common; semi-detached.

mitrailler *vt* to machine-gun.

mitraillette *f* submachine gun.

mitrailleuse *f* machine gun.

mixer *vt* to mix; to blend.

mixte *adj* mixed; joint; combined.

mixture *f* mixture, concoction.

mobile *adj* moving, movable; mobile; nimble; * *m* motive; moving body.

mobilier *m* furniture; * *adj* movable; personal; transferable.

mobilisation *f* mobilization, calling up.

mobilité *f* mobility.

mobylette *f* moped.

moche *adj* (*fam*) ugly, lousy.

mode *f* fashion; custom; * *m* form, mode; way.

modèle *m* model; pattern; design; example.

modeler *vt* to model; to shape; **se ~** *vr:* **se ~ sur** to model oneself on.

modem *m* modem.

modération *f* moderation; diminution.

modéré *adj* ; **~ment** *adv*

modérer *vt* moderate, restrained; **se ~** *vr* to control oneself, keep one's temper.

moderne *adj* modern, up-to-date.

moderniser *vt* to modernize.

modeste *adj* modest, simple; unassuming; **~ment** *adv* modestly.

modestie *f* modesty.

modification *f* modification, alteration.

modifier *vt* to modify, alter; **se ~** *vr* to be modified.

modulation *f* modulation; adjustment.

moelle *f* marrow; core.

moelleux *adj* mellow; soft; smooth.

mœurs *fpl* morals; customs.

moi *pron* me, I; **c'est à ~ it** is mine, it is my turn; **~-même** myself.

mois *m* month.

moisi *adj* mouldy, mildewed; * *m* mould.

moisir *vi* to go mouldy.

moisissure *f* mould, mildew.

moisson *f* harvest.

moissonner *vt* to reap, mow.

moite *adj* moist, damp.

moitié *f* half.

molaire *f* molar.

molécule *f* molecule.

mollement adv softly; gently.

mollusque m mollusc.

moment m moment, instant, while; time; opportunity.

momentané adj momentary; brief; **~ment** adv momentarily.

momie f mummy.

mon pron, f **ma**, pl **mes** my, my own.

monarchie f monarchy.

monastère m monastery.

mondain adj worldly, mundane; society, fashionable.

monde m world, earth; society, company; **il y a du ~** there are some people there.

mondial adj world, world-wide; **~ement** adv the world over.

monétaire adj monetary.

moniteur m, **-trice** f instructor, coach; supervisor.

monnaie f currency; coin; change.

monoculture f single-crop farming, monoculture.

monologue m monologue.

monopole m monopoly.

monopoliser vt to monopolize.

monotone adj monotonous.

monotonie f monotony, sameness.

monseigneur m my lord, your grace.

monsieur m sir, gentleman, Mr, pl **messieurs** gentlemen, Messrs.

monstre m monster.

monstrueux adj monstrous.

mont m mountain; mount.

montage m assembly; setting up; editing.

montagnard m, **-e** f mountain dweller.

montagne f mountain.

montagneux adj mountainous.

montant m upright; total, total sum; * adj upward, rising; upstream.

montée f climb, climbing; ascent; rise.

monter vi to go up, ascend; get into (vehicle); * vt to go up; to carry/bring up.

monteur m, **-euse** f fitter; editor.

montre f watch.

montrer vt to show, point to; to prove; **se ~** vr to appear; to prove oneself.

monture f mount; setting; frame.

monument m monument, memorial.

monumental adj monumental, colossal.

moquer(se) vr to make fun, jeer, laugh at.

moqueur m, **-euse** f mocker, scoffer; * adj mocking.

moral adj moral, ethical; intellectual; **~ement** adv morally.

moralité f morals, morality.

morbide adj morbid, unhealthy.

morceau m piece, morsel, fragment; extract.

mordant adj cutting, mordant; * m mordant.

mordre vt to bite, gnaw; to grip.

morgue f morgue; mortuary.

morille f morel.

morne adj gloomy, dismal.

morose adj sullen, morose.

morphine f morphine.

morphologie f morphology.

morse m Morse (code); (zool) walrus.

morsure f bite.

mort m dead man, **-e** f dead woman; * adj dead; * f death.

mortalité f mortality; death rate.

mortel adj mortal; fatal; **~lement** adv mortally.

mortier m mortar.

mortuaire adj mortuary; funeral.

morue f cod.

mosaïque f mosaic.

mosquée f mosque.

mot m word; saying; **~s croisés** crossword.

moteur m engine, motor; * adj motor, driving.

motif m motive, grounds; motif, design.

motion f motion; **~ de censure** censure motion.

motivation f motivation.

motiver vt to justify; to motivate.

moto f motorbike.

moto-cross m motocross, scrambling.

motte f clod, lump; slab.

mou adj, f **molle** soft; gentle; muffled.

mouche f fly.

moucher vt to wipe so's nose; **se ~** vr to blow one's nose.

moucheron m midge, gnat.

moucheté adj speckled; flecked.

mouchoir m handkerchief.

moudre vt to mill, grind.

moue f pout; **faire la ~** to pout.

mouette f gull.

moufle f mitten.

mouillé adj wet, soaked.

mouiller vt to wet; to water down; **se ~** vr to get wet.

moulage m moulding, casting.

moule m mould; * f mussel.

mouler vt to mould; to model.

moulin m mill.

moulu adj ground; bruised.

mourant m dying man, **-e** f dying woman; * adj dying.

mourir vi to die.

mousse f moss; foam, froth.

mousser vi to froth, foam

mousseux adj sparkling; frothy; * m sparkling wine.

moustache f moustache; whiskers.

moustachu adj moustached; * m moustached man.

moustiquaire f mosquito net.

moustique m mosquito.

moutarde f mustard.

mouton m sheep; mutton.

mouvement m movement, motion; animation.

mouvementé adj eventful; turbulent.

mouvoir vt to drive, power; **se ~** vr to move.

moyen m means; way; * adj average, medium, moderate; **~nement** adv fairly, moderately; **~ âge** Middle Ages.

moyenne f average.

moyeu m hub; boss.

mue f moulting; shedding.

muer vi to moult; to slough.

muet m mute (man), **muette** f mute (woman); * adj dumb; silent, mute.

mufle m muffle; muzzle.

muguet m thrush.

mule f she-mule.

mulet m mule.

multicolore *adj* multicoloured.

multinationale *f* multinational.

multiple *adj* numerous, multiple; * *m* multiple.

multiplication *f* multiplication.

multiplier *vt* ; **se ~** *vr* to multiply, increase.

multitude *f* multitude, crowd.

municipal *adj* municipal; local.

municipalité *f* town, municipality.

munir *vt* to provide, equip with; **se ~** *vr* to equip oneself.

munition *f* munition, ammunition.

mur *m* wall.

mûr *adj* ripe, mature; worn out.

muraille *f* city wall, rampart.

mûre *f* blackberry.

mûrir *vi* to ripen, mature.

murmure *m* murmur; muttering; grumbling.

murmurer *vi* to murmur; to whisper; grumble; to babble * *vt* to murmur.

muscle *m* muscle.

musclé *adj* muscular, brawny.

musculaire *adj* muscular.

muse *f* muse.

museau *m* muzzle, snout.

musée *m* art gallery, museum.

musicien *m*, **-ienne** *f* musician; * *adj* musical.

musique *f* music.

musulman *m*, **-e** *f* Moslem; * *adj* Moslem.

mutant *m*, **-e** *f* mutant; * *adj* mutant.

mutation *f* transfer; transformation; mutation.

muter *vt* to transfer, move.

mutilation *f* mutilation, maiming.

mutiler *vt* to mutilate; **se ~** *vr* to injure oneself.

mutisme *m*

mutuel *adj* ; **~lement** *adv*

mutuelle *f* mutual insurance company

mycose *f* mycosis.

mygale *f* mygale, trap-door spider.

myope *mf* short-sighted person; * *adj* short-sighted.

myopie *f* short-sightedness.

myosotis *m* forget-me-not.

myrtille *f* bilberry.

mystère *m* mystery.

mystérieusement *adv* mysteriously.

mystérieux *adj* mysterious.

mystifier *vt* to mystify; to hoax.

mystique *adj* mystical; * *mf* mystic.

mythe *m* myth.

mythique *adj* mythical.

mythologie *f* mythology.

N

nacre *f* mother-of-pearl.

nacré *adj* nacreous, pearly, iridescent.

nageoire *f* fin, flipper.

nager *vi* to swim.

nageur *m*, **-euse** *f* swimmer; rower.

naïf *adj* naïve, artless, ingenuous.

nain *m*, **-e** *f* dwarf; * *adj* dwarfish, dwarf.

naissance f birth, extraction; dawn, beginning.

naître vi to be born; to arise, spring up.

naïvement adj naïvely.

naïveté f naïvety, artlessness, gullibility.

nanti m rich man, adj rich, well-to-do.

nappe f tablecloth; layer; sheet, expanse.

napper vt to top with.

napperon m tablemat.

narcisse m narcissus.

narcotique mdrug, narcotic; * adj narcotic.

narguer vt to flout, defy; to cheek.

narine f nostril.

narrateur m, **-trice** f narrator.

narration f narration, narrative.

nasal adj nasal.

naseau m nostril.

natalité f birth rate.

natation f swimming.

nation f nation.

national adj national; domestic.

nationaliser vt to nationalize.

nationaliste mf nationalist; * adj nationalist.

nationalité f nationality.

natte f plait, braid.

naturalisation f naturalization.

naturaliser vt to naturalize; to stuff.

naturaliste mf naturalist; taxidermist; * adj naturalist.

nature f nature; kind, sort; temperament.

naturel adj natural; bodily; native; unsophisticated; **~lement** adv naturally; of course.

naufrage m shipwreck; ruin, foundering.

nausée f nausea.

nautique adj nautical, water.

naval adj naval, shipbuilding.

navet m turnip.

navette f shuttle; **faire la ~** to shuttle between.

navigateur m navigator, sailor.

navigation f sailing, navigation.

navire m ship, vessel.

navrant adj distressing, upsetting.

ne adv no, not.

né adj born.

néanmoins adv nevertheless.

néant m nothing, nothingness, emptiness.

nécessaire adj necessary; requisite; indispensable; **~ment** adv necessarily.

nécessité f necessity; need; inevitability.

nécessiter vt to require, necessitate.

nécropole f necropolis.

nectar m nectar.

nectarine f nectarine.

néfaste adj harmful; unlucky; ill-fated.

négatif adj negative.

négation f negation; negative.

négativement adv negatively.

négligemment adv negligently; carelessly; nonchalantly.

négligence f negligence, carelessness.

négligent adj negligent, careless; nonchalant.

négliger vt to neglect; to be negligent about.

négociant m, **-e** f merchant.

négociation f negotiation.

négocier vi to negotiate; to trade; * vt to negotiate.

neige f snow.

neiger vi to snow, be snowing.

nénuphar m water lily.

néophyte mf neophyte; novice * adj newly converted.

nerf m nerve.

nerveusement adv nervously; irritably.

nerveux adj nervous; vigorous; excitable.

nervosité f nervousness; excitability.

nervure f nervure, vein; rib.

net adj, f **nette** clean; clear; plain; sharp; net; **~tement** adv cleanly; clearly; plainly.

netteté f neatness; clearness; sharpness.

nettoyage m cleaning; clearing up.

nettoyer vt to clean; to ruin, clean out.

neuf adj nine; * m nine.

neurologie f neurology.

neurone m neuron.

neutraliser vt to neutralize.

neutralité f neutrality.

neutre adj neutral; neuter.

neutron m neutron.

neuvième adj ninth; **~ment** adv ninthly; * mf ninth.

neveu m nephew.

névralgie f neuralgia.

névrose f neurotic.

nez m nose; flair; **avoir du ~ to** have flair.

niais adj silly, simple, inane; **~ement** adv inanely.

niche f niche, nook; kennel; trick.

nickel m nickel.

nicotine f nicotine.

nid m nest; den; berth.

nièce f niece.

nier vt to deny; to repudiate.

nigaud m, **-e** f simpleton.

nitrate m nitrate.

nitroglycérine f nitroglycerine.

niveau m level; standard; par; gauge.

niveler vt to level; to even out, equalize.

noble adj noble, dignified; **~ment** adv nobly.

noblesse f nobleness, nobility.

noce f wedding, wedding feast; marriage ceremony.

nocif adj noxious, harmful.

noctambule m night reveller, night owl; sleepwalker; * adj enjoying night life; noctambulant.

nocturne adj nocturnal, night; * f evening fixture; late night opening.

nodule m nodule.

Noël m Christmas.

nœud m knot, bow; crux.

noir adj black; dark; * m black; darkness; black man

noircir vt to blacken; to dirty; vi to tan; to ripen; **se ~** vr to darken, grow black.

noire f black woman.

noisetier m hazel tree.

noisette f hazel.

noix f walnut

nom m name; fame; noun.

nomade *mf* nomad.

nombre *m* number, quantity.

nombreux *adj* numerous, frequent.

nombril *m* navel.

nomenclature *f* list, catalogue; nomenclature.

nominal *adj* nominal; noun; **~ement** *adv* nominally.

nominatif *m* nominative.

nomination *f* appointment; nomination.

nommer *vt* to appoint; nominate.

non *adv* no; not.

nonchalance *f* nonchalance.

nonchalant *adj* nonchalant.

non-conformiste *mf* nonconformist; * *adj* nonconformist.

non-lieu *m* insufficient ground to prosecute.

non-sens *m* nonsense.

non-violence *f* non-violence.

nord *m* north, northerly (wind).

nordique *adj* Nordic; Scandinavian.

normal *adj* normal, usual; standard-sized; **~ement** *adv* normally, usually.

norme *f* norm; standard.

nostalgie *f* nostalgia.

nostalgique *adj* nostalgic.

notable *adj* notable; noteworthy; **~ment** *adv* notably.

notaire *m* notary; solicitor.

notamment *adv* notably; in particular.

note *f* note; minute; mark; bill.

noter *vt* to note down; to notice; to mark.

notice *f* note; directions; instructions.

notion *f* notion, idea.

notoire *adj* notorious; well-known, acknowledged; **~ment** *adv* notoriously.

notoriété *f* notoriety; fame.

notre *adj, pl* **nos** ours, our own.

nôtre *pron:* **le ~, la ~, les ~s** ours, our own.

nouer *vt* to tie, knot; **se ~** *vr* to join together.

nouille *f* piece of pasta.

nourrice *f* child-minder, nanny.

nourrir *vt* to feed, provide for; to stoke; **se ~** *vr* to feed oneself.

nourrissant *adj* nourishing, nutritious.

nourrisson *m* infant, nursling.

nourriture *f* food; sustenance.

nous *pron* we; us; **c'est à ~** it's ours; it's our turn; **~-mêmes** ourselves.

nouveau *adj* new; recent; additional.

nouveau-né *m*, **-e** *f* new-born child.

nouveauté *f* novelty; newness.

nouvelle *f* piece of news; short story.

novembre *m* November.

novice *mf* novice, beginner; * *adj* novice, unpractised, inexperienced.

noyade *f* drowning, drowning incident.

noyau *m* stone, pit; core; nucleus.

noyer *vt* to drown; to flood; **se ~** *vr* to drown, drown oneself; * *m* walnut (tree).

nu *adj* naked, nude; plain, unadorned.

nuage *m* cloud.

nuageux *adj* cloudy, overcast.

nuance *f* shade, hue; faint difference, nuance.

nucléaire *adj* nuclear; * *m* nuclear energy.

nudiste *mf* nudist; * *adj* nudist.

nudité *f* nakedness, nudity.

nuée *f* thick cloud; horde, swarm.

nuire *vi* to harm, injure; to prejudice.

nuisible *adj* harmful; noxious; **~ment** *adv* harmfully.

nuit *f* night, darkness.

nul *adj* no; nil; null and void; non-existent; **~lement** *adv* not at all, not in the least.

nullité *f* nullity; uselessness.

numéral *adj* numeral; * *m* numeral.

numérique *adj* numerical; digital.

numéro *m* number; issue.

numérotation *f* numbering, numeration.

numéroter *vt* to number.

nuptial *adj* nuptial, wedding.

nuque *f* nape (of the neck).

nutritif *adj* nutritious, nourishing.

nutrition *f* nutrition.

nylon *m* nylon.

nymphe *f* nymph.

O

oasis *m* oasis.

obéir *vt* to obey, be obedient; to comply.

obéissance *f* obedience; compliance.

obéissant *adj* obedient.

obèse *adj* obese.

obésité *f* obesity.

objecter *vt* to object.

objectif *adj* objective, unbiased; * *m* objective, target.

objection *f* objection.

objectivement *adv* objectively.

objet *m* object, thing; purpose; matter.

obligation *f* obligation, duty; bond.

obligatoire *adj* obligatory, compulsory; **~ment** *adv* obligatorily.

obligé *adj* obliged, compelled; inevitable; necessary.

obliger *vt* to oblige, require; to bind.

oblique *adj* oblique, sidelong.

oblitérer *vt* to obliterate; to cancel (stamp).

obscène *adj* obscene.

obscénité *f* obscenity.

obscur *adj* obscure, dark, gloomy; **~ément** *adv* obscurely.

obscurcir *vt* to darken; to obscure; **s'~** *vr* to get dark.

obscurité *f* obscurity; darkness.

obséder *vt* to obsess, haunt.

obsèques *fpl* funeral.

observateur *m*, **-trice** *f* observer; * *adj* observant.

observation *f* observation; remark.

observatoire *m* observatory.

observer *vt* to observe, watch; to notice; to comply with.

obsession *f* obsession.

obstacle *m* obstacle, hindrance.

obstétrique *f* obstetrics.

obstination f obstinacy, stubbornness.

obstiné adj obstinate, stubborn; **~ment** adv obstinately.

obstiner(s') vr to insist, persist.

obtenir vt to obtain, procure, get; to achieve.

obturation f stopping, closing up, obturation.

obus m shell.

occasion f occasion, opportunity; cause; bargain; **d'~** casual.

occident m west.

occidental adj western; Occidental.

occulte adj occult.

occupant m, **-e** f occupant, occupier.

occupation f occupation, pursuit; work, job; occupancy.

occuper vt to occupy; to employ; to inhabit; **s'~** vr to keep busy.

océan m ocean.

ocre m ochre; * adj ochre.

octane m octane.

octave f octave.

octet m byte.

octobre m October.

octroyer vt to grant, bestow; **s'~** vr to allow oneself.

oculaire adj ocular.

odeur f smell, odour.

odieux adj hateful, obnoxious.

odorat m smell (sense).

œdème m oedema.

œil m, pl **yeux** eye; look; bud.

œillet m carnation.

œsophage m oesophagus.

œuf m egg.

œuvre f work; action, deed; production.

offense f offence; injury, wrong.

offenser vt to offend; to injure, shock; **s'~** vr to take offence.

offensif adj offensive; forceful, aggressive.

offensive f offensive, attack.

office m office, bureau; duty; function.

officiel adj official; **~lement** adv officially.

officier m officer.

officieusement adv officiously; unofficially.

officieux adj officious, over-obliging; unofficial.

offrande f offering.

offre f offer, tender, bid.

offrir vt to offer.

offusquer vt to offend; **s'~** vr to take offence.

ogive f ogive, pointed arch.

ogre m ogre, **-esse** f ogress.

ohm m ohm.

oie f goose.

oignon m onion; bulb.

oiseau m bird.

oisif adj idle.

oisiveté f idleness.

oléagineux adj oleaginous, oily.

oléoduc m oil pipeline.

olfactif adj olfactory.

oligarchie f oligarchy.

oligo-élément m trace element.

olive f olive.

olivier m olive tree.

olympique adj Olympic.

ombilical adj umbilical.

ombragé adj shaded, shady.

ombre *f* shade, shadow.

omelette *f* omelette.

omettre *vt* to leave out, miss out.

omission *f* omission.

omnibus *m* local train; omnibus.

omnipotent *adj* omnipotent.

omniprésent *adj* omnipresent.

omoplate *f* shoulder blade.

on *pron* one; someone, anyone.

once *f* ounce.

oncle *m* uncle.

onctueux *adj* smooth, creamy.

onde *f* wave.

ondoyant *adj* undulating, flowing; changeable.

ondulation *f* undulation; wave.

onduler *vi* to undulate; to ripple.

onéreux *adj* onerous; expensive, costly.

ongle *m* nail; claw, talon; hoof.

onomatopée *f* onomatopoeia.

onyx *m* onyx.

onze *adj* eleven; * *m* eleven.

onzième *adj* eleventh; ~**ment** *adv* in eleventh place; * *mf* eleventh.

opale *f* opal.

opaque *adj* opaque; impenetrable.

opéra *m* opera.

opération *f* operation, performance; transaction, deal.

opérationnel *adj* operational.

opératoire *adj* operating; operative, surgical.

opérer *vt* to operate; to carry out, implement.

opérette *f* operetta, light opera.

ophtalmie *f* ophthalmia.

opiniâtre *adj* stubborn; persistent; ~**ment** *adv* stubbornly; persistently.

opinion *f* opinion, view.

opium *m* opium.

opportun *adj* timely, opportune; ~**ément** *adv* opportunely.

opportuniste *mf* opportunist; * *adj* opportunist.

opportunité *f* opportuneness, expediency, timeliness.

opposant *m*, **-e** *f* opponent; * *adj* opposing.

opposé *adj* opposite, contrary; facing; * *m*; **à l'~** contrary to; conversely.

opposer *vt* to oppose; to contrast; to object; **s'~** *vr* to be opposed to; to clash, conflict.

opposition *f* opposition; conflict.

oppresser *vt* to oppress, weigh down.

oppressif *adj* oppressive.

oppression *f* oppression.

opprimer *vt* to oppress, crush.

opticien *m*, **-ienne** *f* optician.

optimisme *m* optimism.

optimiste *mf* optimist; * *adj* optimistic.

option *f* option, choice.

optionnel *adj* optional.

optique *adj* optical; * *f* optics.

opulence *f* opulence, wealth.

opulent *adj* opulent, wealthy.

or *m* gold; * *conj* now.

oracle *m* oracle.

orage *m* storm, tempest, thunderstorm.

orageux *adj* stormy.

oral *adj* oral, verbal; ~**ement** *adv* orally

orange *f* orange; * *adj invar* orange.

oranger *m* orange tree.

orang-outan(g) *m* orang-utan.

orateur *m*, **-trice** *f* orator.

orbite *f* orbit; socket; sphere.

orchestral *adj* orchestral.

orchestre *m* orchestra.

orchestrer *vt* to orchestrate, score.

orchidée *f* orchid.

ordinaire *adj* ordinary, common, usual; **~ment** *adv* ordinarily, usually; * *m* custom, usual routine; **d'~, à l'~** ordinarily, usually.

ordinateur *m* computer.

ordonnance *f* prescription, order, edict.

ordonner *vt* to arrange; to order; to prescribe

ordre *m* order, command; class.

ordure *f* filth, dirt; excrement; rubbish.

oreille *f* ear; hearing; wing; handle.

oreiller *m* pillow.

oreillons *mpl* mumps.

orfèvre *m* silversmith, goldsmith

orfèvrerie *f* silversmith's (goldsmith's) craft.

organe *m* organ; instrument; medium.

organigramme *m* organizational chart.

organique *adj* organic.

organisateur *m*, **-trice** *f* organizer.

organisation *f* organization.

organiser *vt* to organize, arrange; **s'~** *vr* to organize o.s.

organisme *m* organism.

organiste *mf* organist.

orgasme *m* orgasm.

orge *f* barley.

orgie *f* orgy.

orgue *m* (*mus*) organ

orgueil *m* pride, arrogance.

orgueilleux *adj* proud, arrogant.

orient *m* orient, east.

oriental *adj* eastern, oriental.

orientation *f* orientation; positioning; directing; trend.

orienter *vt* to orientate; to position; to direct; **s'~** *vr* to ascertain one's position; to turn towards.

orifice *m* orifice; aperture, opening.

originaire *adj* originally from, native to; **~ment** *adv* originally, primitively.

original *adj* original, novel; peculiar, bizarre; * *m* original; top copy.

originalité *f* originality; oddness.

origine *f* origin, source, derivation; **à l'~** originally.

originel *adj* original, primitive.

orme *m* elm.

ornement *m* ornament, embellishment.

ornemental *adj* ornamental.

orner *vt* to adorn, decorate.

ornière *f* rut.

ornithologie *f* ornithology.

ornithologiste, ornithologue *mf* ornithologist.

orphelin *m*, **-e** *f* orphan.

orphelinat *m* orphanage.

orteil *m* toe.

orthodoxe *adj* orthodox; * *mf* orthodox.

orthogonal *adj* orthogonal.

orthographe *f* orthography.

orthopédie *f* orthopaedics.

orthopédique *adj* orthopaedic.

ortie *f* nettle.

orvet *m* slow worm.

os *m* bone

oscillation *f* oscillation, swinging.

osciller *vi* to oscillate, swing.

oseille *f* sorrel.

oser *vt* to dare.

osier *m* osier, willow.

osmose *f* osmosis.

ossature *f* skeleton; framework.

ossements *mpl* bones.

ostensible *adj* open, conspicuous; **~ment** *adv* openly; conspicuously.

ostentation *f* ostentation.

ostéopathe *mf* osteopath.

ostracisme *m* ostracism.

otage *m* hostage.

otarie *f* sea-lion.

ôter *vt* to take away, remove; to deprive, deduct.

otite *f* ear infection.

oto-rhino-laryngologie *f* otorhinolaryngology.

oto-rhino(-laryngologiste) *mf* ear, nose and throat specialist.

ou *conj* or

où *adv* where, in which; *pron* where.

ouate *f* cotton wool.

oubli *m* forgetfulness; oblivion; oversight, omission.

oublier *vt* to forget;to omit, neglect.

oubliette *f* oubliette.

ouest *m* west; *adj* west.

oui *adv* yes.

ouïe *f* hearing.

ouragan *m* hurricane, whirlwind.

ourlet *m* hem.

ours *m*, **-e** *f* bear.

oursin *m* sea urchin.

ourson *m* bear cub.

outil *m* tool, implement.

outillage *m* (set of) tools; equipment.

outiller *vt* to equip; to provide with tools.

outrage *m* outrage, insult, wrong.

outrageant *adj* outrageous, insulting.

outre *prép* as well as, besides; **en ~** moreover; **~ mesure** to excess, inordinately; **passer ~** to go on, to take no notice; **~** *f* goatskin, leather bottle.

outré *adj* excessive, exaggerated.

outremer *m* lapis lazuli; ultramarine.

outrepasser *vt* to exceed; to transgress.

ouvert *adj* open; exposed; frank; **~ment** *adv* openly, overtly.

ouverture *f* opening; mouth; overture; means, way.

ouvrable *adj* working, business.

ouvrage *m* work; piece of work.

ouvre-boîte *m* tin-opener.

ouvre-bouteille *m* bottle-opener.

ouvrier *m*, **-ière** *f* worker; * *adj* working-class; industrial; labour.

ouvrir *vt* to open; to unlock; to broach; **s'~** *vr* to open; to open one's mind; to cut o.s.

ovaire *m* ovary.

ovale *adj* oval; * *m* oval.

ovation *f* ovation.

ovni *m* UFO.

ovulation *f* ovulation.

ovule *m* ovum; ovule.
oxydation *f* oxidization, oxidation.
oxyde *m* oxide.

oxyder *vt* to oxidize; **s'~** *vr* to become oxidized.
oxygène *m* oxygen.
ozone *f* ozone.

P

pacifier *vt* to pacify.
pacifique *adj* peaceful, pacific; **~ment** *adv* peacefully, pacifically.
pacifiste *mf* pacifist; * *adj* pacifist.
pacte *m* pact, treaty.
pactiser *vi* to covenant; to come to terms with.
pagaie *f* paddle.
pagayer *vi* to paddle.
page *f* page; passage.
pagne *m* loincloth.
paiement *m* payment
païen *m*, -ienne *f* pagan; * *adj* pagan.
paillasse *f* straw mattress.
paillasson *m* doormat.
paille *f* straw.
paillette *f* sequin; spangle.
pain *m* bread; loaf; bar.
pair *adj* even; * *m* peer; par; **hors ~** peerless, matchless.
paire *f* pair; yoke; brace.
paisible *adj* peaceful; calm; **~ment** *adv* peacefully; calmly.
paître *vi* to graze.
paix *f* peace; quiet; stillness; tranquillity.
palais *m* palace; law courts; palate.
palan *m* hoist.
pâle *adj* pale, pallid.
palette *f* palette; pallet; paddle.
pâleur *f* paleness, pallor.

palier *m* landing; level; degree.
pâlir *vi* to turn pale; to dim; to fade.
palissade *f* fence; boarding; stockade.
palliatif *m* palliative; * *adj* palliative.
pallier *vt* to palliate; to offset.
palmarès *m* prize list; medal record.
palme *f* palm leaf; palm.
palmé *adj* palmate; webbed.
palmeraie *f* palm grove.
palmier *m* palm tree.
palmipède *m* palmiped.
palpable *adj* palpable.
palper *vt* to feel, touch; to palpate.
palpitation *f* palpitation; throbbing; quivering.
palpiter *vi* to palpitate; to beat; to race.
paludisme *m* malaria.
pamplemousse *m* grapefruit.
panache *m* panache; gallantry.
panaché *adj* variegated; motley.
pancarte *f* sign, notice; placard.
pancréas *m* pancreas.
panda *m* panda.
pané *adj* covered in breadcrumbs.
panier *m* basket; pannier.
panique *f* panic.
paniquer *vi* to panic, get panicky.

panne f breakdown; fault, problem.

panneau m panel; sign, notice.

panoplie f outfit; display.

panorama m panorama.

panoramique adj panoramic.

pansement m dressing, bandage.

panser vt to dress, bandage.

pantalon m trousers; pants; knickers.

panthéon m pantheon.

panthère f panther.

pantin m jumping-jack; puppet.

pantomime f pantomime; mime.

pantoufle f slipper.

paon m peacock.

papa m dad; daddy.

papauté f papacy.

papaye f papaya.

pape m pope.

papeterie f stationery; stationer's shop; paper mill.

papetier m, **-ière** f stationer; papermaker.

papier m paper; article; wrapper.

papillon m butterfly.

papillote f sweet wrapper.

papoter vi to chatter.

Pâques fpl Easter.

paquebot m liner, steamer.

pâquerette f daisy.

paquet m packet, pack; bag; parcel.

par prép by, with, through; from; along; **~ci**, **~là** here and there, now and then; **~derrière** round the back; **~dessous** underneath; **~dessus** over, above.

parabole f parabola; parable.

parachever vt to perfect; to complete.

parachute m parachute.

parachuter vt to parachute.

parachutiste m parachutist.

parade f parade, show; parry.

paradis m paradise; gallery.

paradoxal adj paradoxical; **~ement** adv paradoxically.

paradoxe m paradox.

paraffine f paraffin.

parages mpl: vicinity; waters. **dans les ~** in the area.

paragraphe m paragraph; section.

paraître vi to appear; to be published; to look, seem; **il paraît que** apparently.

parallèle adj parallel; **~ment** adv parallel; at the same time.

paralyser vt to paralyse.

paralysie f paralysis.

paralytique mf paralytic; * adj paralytic.

paramètre m parameter.

paranoïa f paranoia.

paranoïaque adj paranoiac, paranoid; * mf paranoiac, paranoid.

paraphraser vt to paraphrase.

parapluie m umbrella.

parasite m parasite, sponger.

parasol m parasol; sunshade.

paratonnerre m lightning conductor.

paravent m folding screen, partition.

parc m park; grounds; depot.

parcelle f fragment, particle; parcel.

parce que conj because.

parchemin m parchment.

parcimonie f parsimony.

parcmètre m meter (parking).

parcourir vt to travel through; to scour; to traverse.

pardon m pardon, forgiveness.

pardonner vt to pardon;to excuse, overlook.

pare-brise m invar windscreen.

pare-chocs m invar bumper.

pareil m, -**eille** f equal; match **sans ~** unparalleled, unequalled; * adj like, equal, similar; identical; **~lement** adv likewise, equally.

parent m, -**e** f relative, relation; (pl) parents.

parental adj parental.

parenté f relationship, kinship.

parenthèse f parenthesis, digression.

parer vt to adorn, deck out; to ward off; to parry; **~ à** to deal with, overcome.

paresse f laziness; sluggishness.

paresseux m, -**euse** f lazy person, loafer; * adj lazy.

parfaire vt to perfect, bring to perfection.

parfait adj perfect, flawless; **~ement** adv perfectly; completely, absolutely.

parfois adv sometimes, occasionally.

parfumer vt to perfume, scent; **se ~** vr to use perfume.

parfumerie f perfumery.

parfumeur m, -**euse** f perfumer.

pari m bet, wager.

parier vt to bet, wager.

parking m car park; parking.

parlement m Parliament.

parlementaire adj parliamentary; * mf member of parliament.

parler vi to talk, speak; * vt to speak.

parmesan m parmesan (cheese).

parmi prép among.

parodie f parody.

paroi f wall; surface.

paroisse f parish.

parole f word; speech; voice; lyrics.

paroxysme m paroxysm; crisis.

parquer vt to park; to enclose, pen.

parquet m floor, floorboards.

parrain m godfather; patron; promoter.

parrainage m sponsorship; promoting; sponsorship.

parrainer vt to sponsor, propose.

parsemer vt to sprinkle, strew.

part f part; share; portion; **prendre ~ à** to participate in; **faire ~ de** to announce; **de sa part** for his part; **autre ~** elsewhere; **nulle ~** nowhere; **d'autre ~** moreover.

partage m sharing, distribution; portion.

partager vt to divide up, share out.

partenaire mf partner.

parti m party; option; match.

partial adj partial, biased; **~ement** adv in a biased way.

participant m, -**e** f participant, member; * adj participant, participating.

participation f participation; involvement.

participe m participle.

participer vi to take part in, participate.

particularité f particularity, characteristic.

particule f particle.

particulier adj particular, specific; peculiar, characteristic; * m person, private individual; character.

particulièrement adv particularly, especially.

partie f part; subject; game; party; **faire ~ de** to be a part of.

partiel adj part, partial; **~lement** adv partially, in part.

partir vi to leave, set off; to start up; **à ~ de** from.

partisan m, **-e** f partisan, supporter, proponent.

partition f partition; score.

partout adv everywhere.

parvenir vi: **~ à** to reach; to achieve.

pas m step; pace; footprint; gait; * adv no, not.

passable adj passable, tolerable; **~ment** adv tolerably; reasonably.

passage m passage, passing by; transit.

passager m, **-ère** f passenger; * adj passing, transitory.

passant m, **-e** f passer-by, wayfarer; * adj much frequented, busy.

passe f pass; permit; channel.

passé m past.

passeport m passport.

passer vi to pass; to elapse; to disappear, fade; **se ~** vr to pass; to take place; **se ~ de** to do without.

passerelle f footbridge; bridge; gangway.

passe-temps m invar pastime.

passif adj passive; * m passive.

passion f passion; suffering; fondness.

passionnant adj fascinating; exciting.

passionné adj passionate, impassioned; **~ment** adv passionately.

passionner vt to fascinate; to interest deeply, impassion; **se ~** vr to be fascinated by, have a passion for.

passivement adv passively.

passivité f passivity, passiveness.

pastel m pastel.

pastèque f watermelon.

pasteur m minister, pastor.

pasteuriser vt to pasteurize.

pastiche m pastiche.

pastille f pastille, lozenge.

patate f (fam) spud; sweet potato.

patauger vi to wade about, splash about.

pâte f pastry, pasta, dough, batter.

pâté m pâté.

paternel adj paternal, fatherly; **~lement** adv paternally.

paternité f paternity; fatherhood.

pathétique adj pathetic.

patiemment adv patiently.

patience f patience, endurance.

patient adj patient, enduring.

patienter vi to wait.

patin m skate; **~ à glace** iceskate; **~ à roulettes** roller skate.

patinage m skating; slipping; spinning.

patiner vi to skate; to slip; to spin.

patineur m, **-euse** f skater.

patinoire f ice rink.

pâtisserie f cake shop, confectioner's.

pâtissier *m*, **-ière** *f* pastry cook, confectioner.

patois *m* patois, provincial dialect.

patrie *f* homeland, country.

patrimoine *m* inheritance, patrimony.

patriote *mf* patriot; * *adj* patriotic.

patriotisme *m* patriotism.

patron *m* owner, boss, proprietor. **-onne** *f* owner, boss, proprietress.

patronat *m* employers.

patronner *vt* to patronize, sponsor.

patrouille *f* patrol.

patte *f* leg, paw, foot.

pâturage *m* pasture, pasturage, grazing.

pâture *f* pasture; food.

paume *f* palm.

paumer *vt* (*fam*) to lose; **se ~** *vr* to get lost.

paupière *f* eyelid.

paupiette *f* stuffed slice of meat.

pause *f* pause; half-time.

pauvre *adj* poor; indigent; scanty; weak; **~ment** *adv* poorly; * *mf* poor person, pauper.

pavé *m* cobblestone, paving stone.

pavillon *m* house; pavilion; flag.

pavot *m* poppy.

paye *f* pay, wages.

payer *vt* to pay, settle; to reward.

pays *m* country; region; village; land.

paysage *m* landscape; scenery.

paysan *m* countryman, farmer, **-anne** *f* countrywoman.

P.D.G. (**président-directeur général**) *m* chairman and managing director.

péage *m* toll; tollgate.

peau *f* skin; hide, pelt.

pêche *f* peach; fishing.

pécher *vi* to sin.

pêcher *vt* to fish; to catch; * *m* peach tree.

pécheur *m*, **-eresse** *f* sinner

pêcheur *m* fisherman, **-euse** *f* fisherwoman.

pectoral *adj* pectoral; throat, cough.

pectoraux *mpl* pectorals.

pédagogie *f* education; educational methods.

pédagogue *mf* teacher; educationalist; * *adj* pedagogic.

pédale *f* pedal; treadle.

pédaler *vi* to pedal.

pédalier *m* pedal-board, crank-gear.

pédestre *adj* pedestrian.

pédiatre *mf* paediatrician.

pédicure *mf* chiropodist.

peigne *m* comb.

peigner *vt* to comb; to card; **se ~** *vr* to comb one's hair.

peignoir *m* dressing gown.

peindre *vt* to paint; to depict, portray.

peine *f* effort; sadness; pain; punishment; difficulty.

peiner *vi* to toil; to struggle.

peintre *m* painter; portrayer.

peinture *f* painting, picture; paintwork.

péjoratif *adj* pejorative.

pelage *m* coat, fur.

peler *vi* to peel.

pèlerin *m* pilgrim; peregrine falcon.

pèlerinage *m* pilgrimage.

pélican m pelican.

pelle f shovel; spade.

pellicule f film; thin layer.

pelote f ball; pelota.

peloton m pack; squad; platoon.

pelouse f lawn, field; ground.

pelure f peeling, piece of peel.

pénal adj penal; criminal.

pénaliser vt to penalize.

pénalité f penalty.

penalty m penalty (kick).

pencher vi to lean; to tilt; to list; * vt to tip up; tilt; **se ~** vr to bend down; to study, look at.

pendant prép during; for; **~ que** while, whilst; * adj hanging, drooping; pending.

pendentif m pendant; (archit) pendentive.

pendre vi to hang, dangle; * vt to hang; **se ~** vr to hang oneself.

pendule f clock; * m pendulum.

pénétrant adj penetrating, piercing; searching; acute.

pénétration f penetration; perception.

pénétrer vi to enter, penetrate; * vt to penetrate, pierce; to pervade.

pénible adj hard, tiresome; difficult; laborious; **~ment** adv painfully; with difficult.

péniche f barge.

péniciline f penicillin.

péninsule f peninsula.

pénis m penis.

pénitence f penitence, penance; punishment.

pénitent m, **-e** f penitent; * adj penitent.

pénitencier m prison, penitentiary.

pénombre f half-light; penumbra.

pensée f thought; thinking; mind.

penser vt to think, suppose, believe; * vi to think.

pensif adj pensive, thoughtful.

pension f pension; boarding house.

pensionnaire mf boarder; lodger.

pensionnat m boarding school.

pensivement adv pensively, thoughtfully.

pentagone m pentagon.

pentathlon m pentathlon.

pente f slope; gradient.

Pentecôte f Pentecost.

pénurie f shortage, scarcity; penury.

pépère m granddad, grandpa.

pépin m pip; snag, hitch.

pépinière f tree nursery; breeding-ground.

pépite f nugget.

perçant adj piercing, shrill.

percée f opening, clearing; breach; breakthrough.

perce-oreille m earwig.

perception f perception; collection.

percer vt to pierce; to drill; to see through.

percevoir vt to perceive, detect; to collect.

percher vt to stick; to place on; **se ~** vr to perch.

percussion f percussion.

percussionniste mf percussionist.

percuter vt to strike; to crash into.

perdant m, **-e** f loser; * adj losing.

perdre vt to lose; to waste; to miss;

* *vi* to lose; **se ~** *vr* to lose one's way.

perdrix *f* partridge.

perdu *adj* lost; wasted; missed.

père *m* father; sire.

péremptoire *adj* peremptory.

perfection *f* perfection.

perfectionnement *m* perfection, perfecting; improvement.

perfectionner *vt* to improve, perfect; **se ~** *vr* to improve, improve oneself.

perfectionniste *mf* perfectionist; * *adj* perfectionist.

perfide *adj* perfidious, treacherous; **~ment** *adv* perfidiously.

perforation *f* perforation.

perforer *vt* to perforate; to pierce.

performance *f* result, performance.

performant *adj* outstanding; high-performance, high-return.

péricliter *vi* to collapse; to be in jeopardy.

péril *m* peril, danger.

périlleux *adj* perilous.

périmé *adj* out-of-date; expired.

périmètre *m* perimeter.

période *f* period; epoch, era; wave, spell.

périodique *adj* periodic; **~ment** *adv* periodically.

péripétie *f* event, episode.

périphérie *f* periphery.

périphérique *adj* peripheral, outlying; * *m* ring road; peripheral.

périple *m* voyage; journey.

périr *vi* to perish, die.

périscope *m* periscope.

périssable *adj* perishable.

perle *f* pearl; bead; gem.

permanence *f* permanence; permanency.

permanent *adj* permanent, continuous.

permanente *f* perm.

permanenter *vt* to perm.

perméable *adj* permeable; pervious.

permettre *vt* to allow, permit; **se ~** *vr* to allow oneself.

permis *adj* permitted; * *m* permit, licence.

permission *f* permission; leave.

permutation *f* permutation.

permuter *vt* to change, switch round; to permutate.

pernicieux *adj* pernicious.

perpendiculaire *adj* perpendicular; **~ment** *adv* perpendicularly.

perpétuel *adj* perpetual; permanent; **~lement** *adv* perpetually.

perpétuer *vt* to perpetuate, carry on; **se ~** *vr* to be perpetuated; to survive.

perpétuité *f* perpetuity.

perplexe *adj* perplexed, confused.

perplexité *f* perplexity, confusion.

perquisition *f* search.

perquisitionner *vt* to make a search.

perron *m* steps, perron.

perroquet *m* parrot.

perruche *f* budgerigar; chatterbox.

perruque *f* wig.

persécuter *vt* to persecute; to harass.

persécution *f* persecution.

persévérance *f* perseverance.

persévérant *adj* persevering.

persévérer vi to persevere; to persist in.

persil m parsley.

persistance f persistence.

persistant adj persistent; evergreen.

persister vi to persist, keep up.

personnage m character, individual.

personnaliser vt to personalize.

personnalité f personality.

personne f person; self; appearance; **en ~** in person; * pron anyone, anybody; nobody.

personnel adj personal; selfish; **~lement** adv personally.

personnifier vt to personify.

perspective f perspective; view; angle.

perspicace adj shrewd, perspicacious.

perspicacité f insight, perspicacity.

persuader vt to persuade; to convince.

persuasif adj persuasive; convincing.

persuasion f persuasion; conviction.

perte f loss, losing; ruin.

pertinent adj pertinent.

perturbation f disruption; perturbation.

perturber vt to disrupt, disturb.

pervenche f periwinkle.

pervers adj perverse; perverted.

perversité f perversity.

pesant adj heavy, weighty; deep.

pesanteur f gravity; heaviness.

pèse-personne m scales.

peser vt to weigh; to press; to evaluate; * vi to weigh, weigh down; to hang over; **se** ~ to weigh in.

pessimisme m pessimism.

pessimiste mf pessimist; * adj pessimistic.

peste f pest, nuisance; plague.

pesticide m pesticide.

pétale f petal.

pétanque f petanque.

pétard m firecracker; detonator; charge; racket, row.

pétillant adj bubbly, fizzy.

pétiller vi to crackle; to bubble; to sparkle.

petit adj small, tiny; slim; young.

petitesse f smallness, modesty; meanness.

petit-fils m grandson.

petite-fille f granddaughter.

pétition f petition.

petits-enfants mpl grandchildren.

pétrifié adj petrified; transfixed; fossilized.

pétrin m kneading trough; scrape, mess, tight spot.

pétrir vt to knead; to mould, shape.

pétrole m oil, petroleum.

pétrolier m oil tanker; * adj petroleum, oil, oil-producing.

pétrolifère adj oil-bearing.

pétunia m petunia.

peu adv little, not much, few; **un petit ~** a little bit; **quelque ~** a little; **pour ~ que** however little; **~ de** little, few.

peuplade f tribe, people.

peuple m people, nation; crowd.

peuplement m populating; stocking.

peupler vt to populate, stock; to plant.

peuplier m poplar.

peur f fear, terror, apprehension; **avoir ~** to be afraid.

peureux adj fearful, timorous.

peut-être adv perhaps.

phalange f phalanx.

phallocrate m male chauvinist.

pharaon m pharaoh.

phare m lighthouse; headlight.

pharmaceutique adj pharmaceutical.

pharmacie f pharmacy; pharmacology.

pharmacien m, **-ienne** f pharmacist; chemist.

pharynx m pharynx.

phase f phase, stage.

phénoménal adj phenomenal.

phénomène m phenomenon; freak; character.

philanthrope m philanthropist.

philatélie f philately, stamp collecting.

philologie f philology.

philosophe mf philosopher; * adj philosophical.

philosopher vi to philosophize.

philosophie f philosophy.

philosophique adj philosophical; **~ment** adv philosophically.

phobie f phobia.

phonétique f phonetics; * adj phonetic; **~ment** adv phonetically.

phoque m seal; sealskin.

phosphate m phosphate.

phosphore m phosphorus.

phosphorescent adj luminous, phosphorescent.

photo f photo.

photocopie f photocopy.

photocopier vt to photocopy.

photocopieur m, **photocopieuse** f photocopier.

photogénique adj photogenic.

photographe mf photograph.

photographie f photography.

photographier vt to photograph.

photographique adj photographic.

phrase f sentence; phrase.

physicien m, **-ienne** f physicist.

physiologie f physiology.

physiologique adj physiological.

physionomie f countenance, physiognomy.

physionomiste adj good at remembering faces.

physiothérapie f physiotherapy.

physique f physics; * adj physical; **~ment** adv physically.

pianiste mf pianist.

piano m piano.

pic m peak; **à ~** vertically, sheer.

pichet m pitcher, jug.

picorer vt to peck; to nibble.

picot m picot, burr.

picotement m tickle; prickling.

picoter vt to tickle; to prickle; to smart, sting.

pictural adj pictorial.

pie f magpie; chatterbox.

pièce f piece; object; component; room; paper, document.

pied m foot; track; hoof; bottom; **à ~ on foot**; **être sur ~** to be underway.

pied-à-terre m invar pied-à-terre.

piédestal m pedestal.

piège m trap; pit; snare.

piéger vt to trap, set a trap.

pierre f stone.

piété f piety.

piétiner vi to stamp (one's foot); * vt to trample on.

piéton m pedestrian; * adj pedestrian.

pieu m post, stake, pile.

pieusement adv piously, devoutly.

pieux adj pious, devout.

pigeon m pigeon; dupe, mug.

pigment m pigment.

pigmentation f pigmentation.

pignon m gable; cogwheel.

pile f pile; pier; battery; * adv dead; just, right, exactly.

piler vt to crush, pound.

pilier m pillar.

pillage m pillaging, looting.

piller vt to pillage, loot.

pilon m pestle; wooden leg.

pilote m pilot; driver.

piloter vt to pilot, fly; to drive.

pilotis m pile, pilotis.

pilule f pill.

piment m pepper, capsicum.

pimenter vt to add spice.

pin m pine.

pince f crowbar; pincer; dart.

pinceau m brush, paintbrush.

pincée f pinch.

pincer vt to pinch, nip; to grip.

pinède f pine forest.

pingouin m penguin.

ping-pong m table tennis.

pintade f guinea-fowl.

pinte f pint.

pioche f pick, pickaxe.

piocher vt to use a pick; to swot.

piolet m ice axe.

pion m pawn; draught.

pionnier m pioneer.

pipe f pipe.

pipette f pipette.

piquant adj prickly; pungent; piquant; * m quill, spine; prickle.

pique f pike, lance.

pique-nique m picnic.

pique-niquer vi to picnic.

piquer vt to sting, bite; to goad; to puncture.

piquet m post, picket.

piqûre f prick; sting; bite.

pirate m pirate.

pire adj worse; **le ~, la ~, les ~s** the worst.

pirogue f pirogue, dugout canoe.

pirouette f pirouette; about-turn.

pis m udder.

pis-aller m invar last resort, stop-gap.

piscine f swimming pool.

pissenlit m dandelion.

pistache f pistachio.

piste f track, trail; course; runway; lead, clue.

pistolet m pistol, gun.

piston m piston.

pistonner vt to pull strings for; recommend.

piteux adj pitiful, pathetic.

pitié f pity, mercy.

pitoyable adj pitiful, pitiable.

pittoresque adj picturesque.

pivoine f peony.

pivot m pivot; mainspring.

pivoter vi to revolve, pivot.

placard m cupboard; poster, notice.

place f place; square; seat; space; position; **à la ~ de** instead of.

placebo *m* placebo.
placement *m* placing; investment.
placenta *m* placenta; afterbirth.
placer *vt* to place, put; to fit; to seat; to sell; to invest; **se ~** *vr* to take up position; to stand; to find a job.
placide *adj* placid, calm.
placidité *f* placidity, calmness.
plafond *m* ceiling; roof.
plafonner *vi* to reach a ceiling/maximum.
plage *f* beach.
plagiat *m* plagiarism, plagiary.
plagier *vt* to plagiarize.
plaider *vt* to plead; to defend; * *vi* to plead for, go to court.
plaidoirie *f* defence speech; plea.
plaidoyer *m* defence speech; plea.
plaie *f* wound, cut; scourge.
plaignant *m*, **-e** *f* plaintiff.
plaindre *vt* to pity; to begrudge; **se ~** *vr* to complain.
plaine *f* plain.
plainte *f* complaint; moan, groan.
plaintif *adj* plaintive, complaining.
plaire *vi* to please, be pleasant; **se ~** *vr* to enjoy, take pleasure in.
plaisant *adj* pleasant, agreeable.
plaisanter *vi* to joke, jest.
plaisanterie *f* joking; pleasantry; humour.
plaisir *m* pleasure; delight; entertainment; **faire ~** to please.
plan *m* plan, scheme, project; plane, level.
planche *f* plank, board; plate; shelf.
plancher *m* floor.

planchette *f* small board, small shelf.
plancton *m* plankton.
planer *vi* to glide, soar; to hover over.
planétaire *adj* planetary.
planète *f* planet.
planeur *m* glider.
planifier *vt* to plan.
planisphère *m* planisphere.
planning *m* programme, schedule.
plantation *f* plantation; planting.
plante *f* plant.
planter *vt* to plant; to hammer in; to stick, dump.
plantureux *adj* copious, ample.
plaque *f* sheet, plate; plaque; slab.
plaqué *m* plated.
plaquer *vt* to plate, veneer; to jilt; to tackle.
plaquette *f* plaque; tablet; slab.
plasma *m* plasma.
plastifier *vt* to coat with plastic.
plastique *m* plastic; * *adj* plastic.
plat *adj* flat; straight; dull, insipid; **~ement** *adv* dully, insipidly; * *m* plate, dish; course.
platane *m* plane tree.
plateau *m* tray; turntable; plateau; stage.
plate-bande *f* border, flower-bed.
plate-forme *f* platform.
platine *m* platinum; * *f* deck; turntable; stage.
platitude *f* platitude; flatness, dullness.
platonique *adj* platonic.
plâtre *m* plaster.
plâtrer *vt* to plaster; to set in plaster.

plâtrier *m* plasterer.

plausible *adj* plausible.

plébiscite *m* plebiscite.

plébisciter *vt* to elect by plebiscite.

plein *adj* full; entire, whole; busy;
~**ement** *adv* fully, in full; wholly;
* *m* filling up; full house; height,
middle.

plénitude *f* plenitude, fullness.

pléonasme *m* pleonasm.

pleur *m* tear, sob; **en ~s** in tears.

pleurer *vi* to cry, weep; * *vt* to
mourn for, lament.

pleurésie *f* pleurisy.

pleuvoir *vi* to rain; to shower
down, rain down.

plexus *m* plexus.

pli *m* fold; crease; wrinkle; envelope.

pliant *adj* collapsible, folding.

plier *vt* to fold; to bend; * *vi* to
bend; to yield; **se ~** *vr* to fold up;
to submit.

plinthe *f* plinth; skirting board.

plissement *m* creasing, folding;
puckering.

plisser *vt* to pleat, fold;to pucker;
* *vi* to become creased.

pliure *f* fold; bend.

plomb *m* lead; sinker; fuse.

plombage *m* weighting; leading;
filling.

plomber *vt* to weight; to fill.

plomberie *f* plumbing.

plombier *m* plumber.

plongée *f* diving, dive.

plongeoir *m* diving board.

plongeon *m* dive.

plonger *vi* to dive; to plunge, dip
sharply.

plongeur *m*, **-euse** *f* diver; washer-
up.

ployer *vi* to bend, to sag.

pluie *f* rain; shower.

plumage *m* plumage, feathers.

plume *f* feather.

plumeau *m* feather duster.

plumer *vt* to pluck.

plupart *f* most, most part, majority
la ~ de most of.

pluriel *m* plural; * *adj* plural.

plus *adv* more, most; **~ grand que**
bigger than; **de ~ en ~** more and
more; **de ~** besides, moreover;
non ~ neither, not either.

plusieurs *adj* several.

plus-que-parfait *m* pluperfect.

plus-value *f* appreciation; increase
in value.

plutonium *m* plutonium.

plutôt *adv* rather, quite, fairly;
sooner.

pluvieux *adj* rainy, wet.

pneu *m* tyre.

pneumatique *adj* pneumatic; * *m*
tyre.

pneumonie *f* pneumonia.

poche *f* pocket; pouch; bag.

pocher *vt* to poach.

pochette *f* pocket handkerchief;
wallet; envelope.

pochoir *m* stencil.

podium *m* podium.

poêle *m* stove; * *f* frying pan.

poème *m* poem.

poésie *f* poetry.

poète *m* poet.

poétique *adj* poetic; ~**ment** *adv*
poetically.

poids *m* weight, influence; **~ lourd**

heavyweight; ~ **plume** feather weight.

poignant adj poignant.

poignard m dagger.

poignarder vt to stab.

poigne f grip; hand.

poignée f handful; ~ **de mains** handshake.

poignet m wrist; cuff.

poil m hair; coat; bristle.

poilu adj hairy.

poinçon m hallmark, style; awl.

poinçonner vt to stamp;to hallmark.

poindre vi to break, dawn; to afflict.

poing m fist; **coup de** ~ punch.

point m point, spot; stage; full stop; **mettre au** ~ to finalize; to perfect; **faire le** ~ to take a bearing; **être sur le** ~ **de** to be about to; **à**~ medium, just right, when due; ~**virgule** semicolon; ~ **de vue** point of view.

pointage m checking off; sighting; scrutiny.

pointe f point, head; spike, tack; **tailler en** ~ to cut to a point; **sur la** ~ **des pieds** on tiptoe.

pointer vi to clock in; to soar up; to peep out; * vt to check off; to clock in; to stick into.

pointillé m stipple engraving; dotted line.

pointilleux adj particular, fastidious.

pointu adj pointed, sharp; subtle.

pointure f size, number.

poire f pear.

poireau m leek.

poirier m pear tree.

pois m pea; ~ **chiche** chickpea; **petits** ~ garden peas.

poison m poison.

poisseux adj sticky.

poisson m fish.

poissonnerie f fishmonger's, fish shop.

poissonnier m, **-ière** f fishmonger.

poitrail m breast, chest.

poitrine f chest, breast; bosom.

poivre m pepper.

poivrer vt to pepper, put pepper in.

poivrière f pepperpot.

poivron m green pepper, capsicum.

polaire adj polar.

polariser vt to polarize; to attract.

polarité f polarity.

polaroïd m polaroid; * adj polaroid.

pôle m pole; centre.

polémique f controversy, polemic; * adj controversial, polemic.

poli adj polite; polished, smooth; ~**ment** adv politely.

police f police; policing; regulations.

polichinelle m buffoon.

policier m policeman, **-ière** f policewoman.

poliomyélite f poliomyelitis.

polir vt to polish; to refine.

politesse f politeness, courtesy.

politicien m, **-ienne** f politician; * adj politicking.

politique f politics; policy; * adj political; ~**ment** adv politically.

politiser vt to politicize; to make a political issue of.

pollen m pollen.

polluant *adj* polluting; * *m* pollutant.

polluer *vt* to pollute.

pollution *f* pollution.

polo *m* polo.

poltron *m*, **-onne** *f* coward; * *adj* cowardly, craven.

polyamide *m* polyamide.

polycopier *vt* to duplicate, stencil.

polyester *m* polyester.

polygame *m* polygamist.

polygamie *f* polygamy.

polyglotte *adj* polyglot; * *mf* polyglot.

polygone *m* polygon.

polymère *m* polymer; * *adj* polymeric.

polyvalent *adj* polyvalent; varied; versatile.

pommade *f* pomade; ointment.

pomme *f* apple.

pomme de terre *f* potato.

pommette *f* cheekbone.

pommier *m* apple tree.

pompe *f* pump.

pomper *vt* to pump.

pompeux *adj* pompous; pretentious.

pompier *m* fireman.

pompiste *mf* pump attendant.

poncer *vt* to sand down, rub down.

ponction *f* puncture.

ponctualité *f* punctuality.

ponctuation *f* punctuation.

ponctuel *adj* punctual; **~lement** *adv* punctually.

ponctuer *vt* to punctuate; to phrase.

pondéré *adj* weighted.

pondre *vt* to lay; to produce.

poney *m* pony.

pont *m* bridge; deck; axle.

ponte *f* laying; clutch.

pontifical *adj* pontifical.

ponton *m* pontoon; landing stage.

populaire *adj* popular; working-class; vernacular.

populariser *vt* to popularize.

popularité *f* popularity.

population *f* population.

porc *m* pig; pork.

porcelaine *f* porcelain.

porc-épic *m* porcupine.

porche *m* porch.

porcherie *f* pigsty.

pore *m* pore.

poreux *adj* porous.

pornographique *adj* pornographic.

port *m* port, harbour; pass; carrying, wearing.

portail *m* portal.

portatif *adj* portable.

porte *f* door; gate; threshold.

porte-avions *m invar* aircraft carrier.

porte-bagages *m invar* luggage rack.

porte-bonheur *m invar* lucky charm.

porte-clefs, porte-clés *m invar* key ring.

porte-documents *m invar* briefcase.

portée *f* reach, range; capacity; impact, significance; **à ~ de** within reach; **hors de ~** out of reach.

portefeuille *m* wallet; portfolio.

porte-jarretelles *m invar* suspender belt.

portemanteau *m* coat hanger; hat stand.

porte-parole *m invar* spokesperson.

porte-plume *m invar* penholder.

porter *vt* to carry; to take; to wear; to hold, keep; **se ~** *vr* to put oneself forward; to go

porteur *m*, **-euse** *f* porter; carrier; * *adj* booster; strong, buoyant.

portier *m* commissionaire.

portière *f* door.

portillon *m* gate, barrier.

portion *f* portion, share.

portique *m* portico.

portrait *m* portrait.

portraitiste *mf* portraitist.

pose *f* pose, posture; laying, fitting, setting.

poser *vt* to put; to install; to set out; to ask; **se ~** *vr* to land, settle; to come up, arise.

positif *adj* positive, definite.

position *f* position; situation; state; stance.

positionner *vt* to position, locate.

positivement *adv* positively.

posologie *f* posology.

posséder *vt* to possess, have; to know inside out.

possesseur *m* possessor, owner.

possessif *adj* possessive.

possession *f* possession, ownership.

possibilité *f* possibility; potential.

possible *adj* possible, feasible; potential; * *m*; **faire son ~** to do one's best.

postal *adj* postal, mail.

poste *f* post office, post; * *m* post, position; station; job.

poster *vt* to post, mail; to station; **se ~** *vr* to take up a position.

postérieur *adj* later, subsequent; back, posterior.

postérité *f* posterity; descendants.

posthume *adj* posthumous.

postiche *adj* false; postiche; pretended; * *m* hairpiece; toupee.

postier *m*, **-ière** *f* post office worker.

postillon *m* postilion.

postulant *m*, **-e** *f* applicant.

postuler *vt* to apply for; to postulate.

posture *f* posture, position.

pot *m* jar; pot; can.

potable *adj* drinkable; passable.

potage *m* soup.

potager *m* kitchen garden; * *adj* vegetable, edible.

potassium *m* potassium.

pot-au-feu *m invar* stew.

pot-de-vin *m* bribe.

potée *f* hotpot.

poteau *m* post, stake.

potelé *adj* plump, chubby.

potence *f* gallows; bracket.

potentiel *adj* potential; * *m* potential.

poterie *f* pottery, piece of pottery.

potiche *f* figurehead.

potier *m* potter.

potion *f* potion.

potiron *m* pumpkin.

pou *m* louse.

poubelle *f* dustbin.

pouce *m* thumb; big toe; inch.

poudre *f* powder, dust.

poudrer vt to powder.

poudrière f powder magazine.

poulailler m henhouse.

poulain m foal; protégé.

poule f hen, fowl.

poulet m chicken.

poulie f pulley.

poulpe m octopus.

pouls m pulse.

poumon m lung.

poupe f stern.

poupée f doll.

poupon m baby.

pouponnière f day nursery, crèche.

pour prép for; to; in favour of; on account of; in order; ~ que so that, in order that; être ~ to be in favour of.

pourboire m tip.

pourceau m pig, swine.

pourcentage m percentage.

pourchasser vt to pursue; to harry.

pourparlers mpl talks, negotiations.

pourpre adj crimson; * m crimson

pourquoi adv why; ~ pas? why not?; * m reason, question.

pourri adj rotten, decayed; corrupt; * m rotten part, rottenness.

pourrir vi to rot, go rotten; to deteriorate.

pourriture f rot, rottenness.

poursuite f pursuit; prosecution.

poursuivant m, -e f pursuer; plaintiff.

poursuivre vt to pursue; to seek; to prosecute.

pourtant adv however, yet, nevertheless.

pourtour m circumference, perimeter.

pourvoir vt to provide, equip.

pourvu conj ~ que provided that.

pousse f shoot; sprouting.

poussée f pressure, pushing; thrust; upsurge.

pousser vt to push; to drive; to incite; * vi to push; to grow, expand; se ~ vr to move, shift.

poussette f push chair.

poussière f dust.

poussiéreux adj dusty.

poussin m chick; junior.

poutre f beam.

pouvoir vi can, be able; may, be allowed; * m power, ability; authority; proxy.

pragmatique adj pragmatic.

prairie f meadow, prairie.

pralin m praline.

praline f praline, sugared almond.

praticable adj practicable; passable.

pratiquant m, -e f churchgoer; * adj practising.

pratique f practice; exercise; observance; * adj practical; ~ment adv practically.

pratiquer vt to practise, exercise; to carry out.

pré m meadow.

préalable adj preliminary; previous; ~ment adv previously, first.

préambule m preamble, prelude.

préau m covered playground; inner yard.

préavis m notice, advance warning.

précaire adj precarious.

précarité f precariousness.

précaution f precaution; care.

précautionneux adj cautious, careful.

précédent adj previous, preceding; * m precedent.

précéder vt to precede, go before.

précepte m precept.

prêcher vt to preach; * vi to preach, sermonize.

prêcheur m, -euse f preacher.

précieux adj precious; invaluable.

précipice m precipice; abyss.

précipitamment adv hurriedly, hastily.

précipitation f haste, violent hurry.

précipiter vt to throw, push down; to hasten, precipitate; **se ~** vr to rush forward; to speed up.

précis adj precise, exact; ~**ément** adv precisely.

préciser vt to specify; to clarify; **se ~** vr to become clear.

précision f precision, preciseness.

précoce adj precocious, premature.

préconçu adj preconceived.

préconiser vt to recommend; to advocate.

précurseur m forerunner, precursor; * adj precursory, preceding.

prédateur m predator.

prédécesseur m predecessor.

prédestiné adj predestined, fated.

prédiction f prediction.

prédire vt to predict, foretell.

prédisposition f predisposition.

prédominance f predominance.

prédominant adj predominant.

prédominer vi to predominate.

préfabriqué adj prefabricated.

préface f preface, prelude.

préfecture f prefecture.

préférable adj preferable; better; ~**ment** adv preferably.

préféré m, -e f favourite; adj favourite, preferred.

préférence f preference.

préférer vt to prefer.

préfet m prefect.

préfigurer vt to prefigure.

préhistoire f prehistory.

préhistorique adj prehistoric.

préjudice m loss; harm; wrong; damage.

préjudiciable adj prejudicial, detrimental.

préjudicier vt to be prejudicial.

préjugé m prejudice.

prélasser(se) vr to sprawl, lounge.

prélèvement m taking; levying; imposition.

prélever vt to take; to levy; to deduct.

préliminaire m preliminary; * adj preliminary.

prélude m prelude; warm-up.

prématuré adj premature; untimely; ~**ment** adv prematurely.

préméditation f premeditation.

prémédité adj premeditated.

premier m first, first floor, -ière f first, first gear; * adj first; former; chief; early; primary.

première f première.

premièrement adv firstly, in first place.

prémonition f premonition.

prémonitoire adj premonitory.

prénatal adj prenatal.

prendre vt to take; to pick up; to catch; * vi to take root; to harden; to start; **se ~** vr to consider oneself; **s'y ~ mal** to set about the wrong way; **s'en ~ à** to set upon, take it out on.

prénom m first name, forename.

préoccuper vt to worry; to preoccupy; **se ~** vr to concern oneself.

préparatif m preparation.

préparation f preparation; making up; training.

préparatoire adj preparatory.

préparer vt to prepare, get ready; to train **se ~** vr to prepare oneself.

prépondérant adj preponderant, dominating.

préposition f preposition.

prérogative f prerogative.

près adv near, close; nearly, almost; **de ~** closely; **à peu ~** just about, near enough; **à peu de choses ~** more or less.

présage m omen, sign, presage.

presbytère m presbytery.

presbytie f long-sightedness, presbyopia.

prescrire vt to prescribe; to stipulate.

présélection f preselection.

présence f presence.

présent m present, gift **-e** f this letter, the present letter; * adj present; * m present; **à ~** just now.

présentable adj presentable.

présentateur m, **-trice** f host, compere; presenter.

présentation f presentation; introduction; **faire les ~s** to make the introductions.

présenter vt to introduce; to present; to explain; **se ~** vr to appear; to come forward; to introduce oneself.

présentoir m display shelf.

préservatif m condom.

préserver vt to preserve; to protect; **se ~** vr to protect oneself.

présidence f presidency; chairmanship.

président m, **-e** f president.

présidentiel adj presidential.

présider vt to preside, chair; to direct.

présomption f presumption, assumption.

présomptueux adj presumptuous.

presque adv almost, nearly; hardly, scarcely.

presqu'île f peninsula.

pressant adj urgent, pressing.

presse f press, newspapers; throng.

pressé adj hurried, urgent.

presse-citron m invar lemon squeezer.

pressentiment m presentiment, foreboding.

pressentir vt to have a presentiment of.

presse-papiers m invar paperweight.

presser vt to press; to squeeze; to hurry up; **se ~** vr to hurry; to crowd around.

pression f pressure.

pressoir m press (wine, cider)

prestation f benefit; service; payment; allowance.

prestidigitateur m, **-trice** f conjurer; magician.

prestige m prestige.

prestigieux adj prestigious.

présumer vt to presume; to assume.

prêt adj ready; prepared, willing; * m loan, lending.

prêt-à-porter m ready-to-wear.

prétendant m, **-e** f candidate.

prétendre vt to claim, maintain; to want; to intend, mean.

prétendu adj so-called, supposed; ~**ment** supposedly, allegedly.

prétentieux adj pretentious.

prétention f pretension, claim; pretentiousness.

prêter vt to lend; to attribute; to give.

prétérit m preterite tense.

prétexte m pretext, excuse.

prêtre m priest.

preuve f proof, evidence.

prévaloir vi to prevail.

prévenant adj considerate, thoughtful.

prévenir vt to prevent; to warn, inform; to anticipate.

préventif adj preventive.

prévention f prevention.

prévisible adj foreseeable.

prévision f prediction; forecast.

prévoir vt to anticipate; to plan; to provide for.

prévoyance f foresight, forethought.

prévoyant adj provident.

prévu adj provided for.

prier vi to pray; * vt to pray to; to beg; to invite.

prière f prayer; entreaty.

primaire adj primary; elementary.

primate m primate.

primauté f primacy.

prime f premium, subsidy; free gift.

primer vi to dominate; to take first place; * vt to outdo; to prevail.

primeurs fpl early fruit and vegetable.

primevère f primrose.

primitif adj primitive.

primordial adj primordial, essential.

prince m prince.

princesse f princess.

principal m principal; headmaster; * adj main, principal; ~**ment** adv principally.

principe m principle; origin; element; **en** ~ in principle.

printanier adj spring.

printemps m spring.

prioritaire adj having priority, priority.

priorité f priority.

pris adj taken; busy, engaged.

prise f hold, grip; catch; plug; dose; **lâcher** ~ to let go one's hold; ~ **de sang** blood sample; ~ **de courant** plug, power point; ~ **de conscience** awareness, realization.

prisme m prism.

prison f prison; jail.

prisonnier m, **-ière** f prisoner; * adj captive.

privation f deprivation; forfeiture.

privatiser vt to privatize.

privé adj private; unofficial; independent.

priver vt to deprive; **se** ~ vr to go without.

privilège m privilege.
privilégié m, **-e** f privileged person; * adj privileged, favoured.
privilégier vt to favour.
prix m price, cost; prize.
probabilité f probability, likelihood.
probable adj probable, likely; **~ment** adv probably.
problématique adj problematical; * f problem; problematics.
problème m problem, issue.
procédé m process; behaviour.
procéder vi to proceed.
procédure f procedure; proceedings.
procès m proceedings; lawsuit, trial.
procession f procession.
processus m process; progress.
procès-verbal m minutes; report.
prochain adj next; imminent; **~ement** adv soon, shortly; * m neighbour.
proche adj nearby; close, imminent.
proclamation f proclamation.
proclamer vt to proclaim, declare.
procuration f proxy, power of attorney.
procurer vt to procure, provide; **se ~** vr to procure, obtain for oneself.
procureur m prosecutor.
prodige m marvel, wonder.
prodigieusement adv prodigiously, incredibly.
prodigieux adj prodigious.
prodiguer vt to be lavish, be unsparing; to squander.

producteur m, **-trice** f producer; * adj producing, growing.
productif adj productive.
production f production; generation; output.
productivité f productivity.
produire vt to produce; to grow; to generate; **se ~** vr to happen, take place.
produit m product; goods; yield, profit.
proéminent adj prominent.
profane adj secular, profane; * mf layman, lay person.
profaner vt to profane; to defile.
proférer vt to utter, pronounce.
professeur m teacher, professor.
profession f profession; occupation, trade.
professionnel m, **-elle** f professional; skilled worker; * adj professional; occupational; technical; **~lement** adv professionally.
profil m profile, outline.
profiler vt to profile; to streamline; **se ~** vr to stand out, be profiled.
profit m profit; advantage, benefit.
profitable adj profitable; **~ment** adv profitably.
profiter vi to profit; to thrive.
profiteur m, **-euse** f profiteer.
profond adj deep, profound; heavy; **~ément** adv deeply, profoundly.
profondeur f depth; profundity.
profusion f profusion, wealth; **à ~** plenty, in profusion.
programme m programme; syllabus; schedule.

programmer *vt* to programme; to schedule.

progrès *m* progress; improvement; advance.

progresser *vi* to progress; to advance.

progression *f* progress; progression, spread.

progressivement *adv* progressively.

prohiber *vt* to prohibit, ban.

proie *f* prey, victim.

projecteur *m* projector; spotlight, floodlight.

projectile *m* projectile; missile.

projection *f* projection, casting; showing.

projet *m* plan; draft.

projeter *vt* to plan; to throw out; to cast, project.

prolétaire *mf* proletarian.

prolétariat *m* proletariat.

prolifération *f* proliferation.

proliférer *vi* to proliferate.

prologue *m* prologue.

prolongation *f* prolongation, extension.

prolongement *m* continuation, extension.

prolonger *vt* to prolong, extend; **se ~** *vr* to go on, persist.

promenade *f* walk, stroll; drive, spin.

promener *vt* to take out for a walk; **se ~** *vr* to go for a walk.

promeneur *m*, **-euse** *f* walker.

promesse *f* promise.

prometteur *adj* promising.

promettre *vt* to promise.

promontoire *m* promontory, headland.

promoteur *m*, **-trice** *f* promoter, instigator.

promotion *f* promotion; advancement.

promouvoir *vt* to promote, upgrade.

prompt *adj* prompt; swift; ready; **~ement** *adv* promptly; swiftly.

promptitude *f* promptness; swiftness.

promulgation *f* promulgation.

promulguer *vt* to promulgate.

prôner *vt* to laud; to advocate.

pronom *m* pronoun.

prononcer *vt* to pronounce, utter; **se ~** *vr* to reach a verdict.

prononciation *f* pronunciation.

pronostic *m* forecast; prognosis; tip.

pronostiquer *vt* to forecast, prognosticate.

propagande *f* propaganda.

propagation *f* propagation; spreading.

propager *vt* to propagate, spread; **se ~** *vr* to spread, be propagated.

propane *m* propane.

prophète *m* prophet.

prophétie *f* prophecy.

prophétique *adj* prophetic.

prophétiser *vt* to prophesy.

propice *adj* propitious, favourable.

proportion *f* proportion, ratio.

proportionné *adj* proportional; proportionate.

proportionnel *adj* proportional; **~lement** *adv* proportionally.

propos *m* talk, remarks; intention; **à ~ de** about, on the subject of; **hors de ~** irrelevant.

proposer *vt* to propose, suggest; **se ~** *vr* to offer one's services; to intend to.
proposition *f* proposition, suggestion
propre *adj* clean, neat; honest; own; peculiar; suitable; **~ment** *adv* cleanly; exactly; specifically.
propreté *f* cleanliness; tidiness.
propriétaire *mf* owner; landlord.
propriété *f* ownership, property; appropriateness, suitability.
propulser *vt* to propel, power.
propulsion *f* propulsion.
prorogation *f* prorogation; deferment; extension.
proroger *vt* to prorogue; to defer; to extend.
prosaïque *adj* mundane, prosaic.
proscrire *vt* to proscribe; to prohibit.
prose *f* prose.
prospecter *vt* to prospect; to canvass.
prospecteur *m*, **-trice** *f* prospector.
prospection *f* prospecting; canvassing.
prospectus *m* leaflet; prospectus.
prospère *adj* prosperous, flourishing.
prospérer *vi* to prosper, flourish.
prospérité *f* prosperity.
prostate *f* prostate.
prosterner(se) *vr* to prostrate oneself.
prostituée *f* prostitute.
prostitution *f* prostitution.
prostré *adj* prostrate, prostrated.
protagoniste *m* protagonist
protecteur *m*, **-trice** *f* protector; patron; * *adj* protective; patronizing.

protection *f* protection; patronage.
protectionnisme *m* protectionism.
protégé *m*, **-e** *f* favourite, protégé; * *adj* protected, sheltered.
protéger *vt* to protect; to patronize; **se ~** *vr* to protect oneself.
protéine *f* protein.
protestant *m*, **-e** *f* Protestant; * *adj* Protestant.
protestantisme *m* Protestantism.
protestation *f* protest, protestation.
protester *vi* to protest; to affirm.
prothèse *f* prosthesis; prosthetics.
protocole *m* protocol; etiquette.
prototype *m* prototype.
protubérance *f* protuberance, bulge.
proue *f* prow; bows.
prouesse *f* prowess.
prouver *vt* to prove; to demonstrate.
provenir *vi* to come from; to be due to.
proverbe *m* proverb.
proverbial *adj* proverbial.
providence *f* providence.
providentiel *adj* providential.
province *f* province.
provincial *m*, **-e** *f* provincial; * *adj* provincial
provision *f* provision; supply, stock.
provisoire *adj* provisional, temporary; **~ment** *adv* provisionally.
provocant *adj* provocative.
provocation *f* provocation.
provoquer *vt* to provoke; to cause.
proximité *f* proximity, closeness; imminence.

prudemment *adv* prudently, carefully.

prudence *f* prudence, care.

prudent *adj* prudent, careful.

prune *f* plum.

pruneau *m* prune.

prunelle *f* sloe; pupil, eye.

prunier *m* plum tree.

psaume *m* psalm.

pseudonyme *m* pseudonym; pen name; alias.

psoriasis *m* psoriasis.

psychanalyse *f* psychoanalysis.

psychanalyser *vt* to psychoanalyse.

psychanalyste *mf* psychoanalyst.

psychédélique *adj* psychedelic.

psychiatre *mf* psychiatrist

psychiatrie *f* psychiatry.

psychiatrique *adj* psychiatric.

psychique *adj* psychic, psychological.

psychisme *m* psyche, mind.

psychologie *f* psychology.

psychologique *adj* psychological; ~ment *adv* psychologically.

psychologue *mf* psychologist; * *adj* psychological.

psychopathe *mf* psychopath; mentally ill person.

psychose *f* psychosis; obsessive fear.

psychosomatique *adj* psychosomatic.

psychothérapie *f* psychotherapy.

puberté *f* puberty.

pubis *m* pubis.

public *adj*, *f* **publique** public, state; * *m* public, audience; public sector.

publication *f* publication, publishing.

publicité *f* publicity.

publier *vt* to publish; to make public.

publiquement *adv* publicly.

puce *f* flea.

puceron *m* aphid, greenfly.

pudeur *f* modesty, decency.

pudique *adj* modest; chaste; ~ment *adv* modestly.

puer *vi* to stink; * *vt* to stink.

puéricultrice *f* paediatric nursing.

puéril *adj* puerile, childish; ~ement *adv* puerilely, childishly.

puérilité *f* puerility, childishness.

puis *adv* then, next.

puiser *vt* to draw from, extract.

puisque *conj* since; as; seeing that.

puissance *f* power, strength; output; force.

puissant *adj* powerful; potent.

puits *m* well; shaft.

pull-over *m* pullover, sweater.

pulluler *vi* to swarm, pullulate.

pulmonaire *adj* pulmonary, lung.

pulpe *f* pulp.

pulsation *f* beat; beating; pulsation.

pulsion *f* drive, urge.

pulvériser *vt* to pulverize; to powder.

puma *m* puma.

punaise *f* bug.

punir *vt* to punish.

punition *f* punishment.

pupille *f* pupil; ward.

pupitre *m* desk; console; lectern.

pur *adj* pure; neat; clear; ~ement *adv* purely.

purée f mashed potatoes; purée.
pureté f purity, pureness.
purge f purge; purgative; draining.
purger vt to purge; to drain.
purifier vt to purify, cleanse.
purin m liquid manure.
puritain m, -e f puritan; * adj puritan.
puritanisme m puritanism.
pur-sang m invar thoroughbred.
purulent adj purulent.

pus m pus.
putois m polecat.
putréfaction f putrefaction.
putréfier vt to putrefy, rot.
pyjama m pyjamas.
pylône m pylon.
pyramide f pyramid.
pyrex m Pyrex.
pyromane mf pyromaniac; arsonist.
python m python.

Q

quadragénaire adj mf forty-year-old.
quadrangle m quadrangle.
quadrature f quadrature.
quadriceps m quadriceps.
quadrilatère m quadrilateral.
quadrillage m covering, control; check pattern.
quadriller vt to mark out in squares; to cover, control.
quadrupède adj m quadruped.
quadruple adj m quadruple.
quai m quay, wharf; platform.
qualificatif adj qualifying.
qualification f qualification.
qualifier vt to describe; to qualify; **se ~** vr to qualify for; to call oneself.
qualitatif adj qualitative.
qualitativement adv qualitatively.
qualité f quality; skill; position.
quand conj when, whenever, while.
quant prep: **~ à lui** as for him, it.
quantifier vt to quantify.
quantitatif adj quantitative.

quantitativement adv quantitatively.
quantité f quantity, amount.
quarantaine f about forty; **avoir la ~** to be in one's forties.
quarante adj, minv forty.
quarantième adj, mf fortieth.
quart m quarter; beaker; watch.
quartette m quartet.
quartier m district, neighbourhood; quarters; quarter.
quartz m quartz.
quasi adv almost, nearly.
quasiment adv almost, nearly.
quaternaire adj quaternary, m Quaternary.
quatorze adj, m fourteen.
quatorzième adj, mf fourteenth; **~ment** adv in fourteenth place.
quatre adj, m four.
quatre-vingt(s) adj, m eighty.
quatre-vingt-dix adj, m ninety.
quatre-vingtième adj, mf eightieth.
quatrième adj, mf fourth; **~ment** adv in fourth place.

quatuor *m* quartet.

que *conj* that; than; * *pron* that; whom; what; which.

quel, *f* **quelle** *adj* who, what, which.

quelconque *adj* some, any; least, slight; poor, indifferent.

quelque *adj* some; ~ **part** somewhere.

quelque chose *pron* something.

quelquefois *adv* sometimes

quelqu'un, *f* **-une** someone, somebody, *pl* **quelques-uns, -unes** *pron* some, a few; il y a ~? is there someone there?

quémander *vt* to beg for.

querelle *f* quarrel; row; debate.

quereller (se) *vp* to quarrel, squabble.

question *f* question; matter, issue.

questionnaire *m* questionnaire.

questionner *vt* to question.

quête *f* quest, search; collection; en ~ **de** in search of.

quêter *vi* to seek; to collect money.

queue *f* tail; stalk; queue; **faire la ~** to queue.

qui *pron* who; whom; which.

quiche *f* quiche.

quiconque *pron* whoever, whosoever.

quiétude *f* quiet; peace; tranquillity.

quille *f* skittle; keel.

quincaillerie *f* hardware, ironmongery.

quinine *f* quinine.

quinquagénaire *adj mf* fifty-year-old.

quinquennal *adj* five-year, quinquennial.

quinquina *m* cinchona.

quinte *f* fifth (*mus*); coughing fit.

quintette *m* quintet.

quintuple *adj* quintuple; * *m* quintuple.

quintupler *vt* to multiply by five; * *vi* to quintuple, increase fivefold.

quintuplés *m pl*, **-ées** *f pl* quintuplets.

quinzaine *f* about fifteen; fortnight.

quinze *adj*, *m* fifteen.

quinzième *adj*, *mf* fifteenth; ~**ment** *adv* in fifteenth place.

quiproquo *m* mistake; misunderstanding.

quittance *f* receipt; bill.

quitte *adj* even, quits; **être ~ envers** to be quits, all square with; ~ **à** even if it means, although it may mean; ~ **ou double** double or quits.

quitter *vt* to leave; to give up; **se ~** *vr* to part company, separate.

quoi *pron* what; ~ **que** whatever.

quoique *conj* although, though.

quolibet *m* gibe, jeer.

quote-part *f* share.

quotidien *adj* daily, everyday; ~**nement** *adv* daily, every day; * *m* everyday life.

quotient *m* quotient.

R

rabâcher *vi* to harp on, keep on; * *vt* to rehearse, harp on.

rabais *m* reduction, discount; **au ~** at a reduced price.

rabaisser *vt* to humble, disparage; to reduce; **se ~** *vr* to belittle oneself.

rabattre *vt* to close; to pull down; to reduce; **se ~** *vr* to cut across, pull in front of; **se ~ sur** to fall back on.

rabbin *m* rabbi.

rabot *m* plane.

raboter *vt* to plane; to scrape.

rabougri *adj* stunted, puny.

racaille *f* rabble, scum.

raccommodage *m* mending, repairing.

raccommoder *vt* to mend, repair.

raccompagner *vt* to see back to; to accompany home.

raccord *m* join; link; pointing.

raccordement *m* linking; joining; connecting.

raccorder *vt* to link up, join up; **se ~** *vr* to link, join up.

raccourci *m* shortcut; **en ~** in miniature.

raccourcir *vt* to shorten, curtail; * *vi* to shrink; to grow shorter.

raccrocher *vt* to ring off; to hang up; to grab; **se ~** *vr* to catch; to cling to.

race *f* race; stock; breed.

rachat *m* repurchase, purchase.

racheter *vt* to repurchase; to redeem; to ransom.

rachitique *adj* rachitic; scrawny.

racial *adj* racial.

racine *f* root; **~ carrée** square root.

racisme *m* racism.

raciste *mf* racist; * *adj* racist.

racler *vt* to scrape; to rake.

racoler *vt* to accost; to solicit.

raconter *vt* to tell, recount.

radar *m* radar.

rade *f* harbour, roads.

radeau *m* raft.

radiateur *m* radiator; heater.

radiation *f* radiation.

radical *adj* radical; **~ement** *adv* radically.

radieux *adj* radiant, dazzling.

radin *m*, **-e** *f* skinflint; * *adj* mean, stingy.

radio *f* radio; X-ray.

radioactif *adj* radioactive.

radioactivité *f* radioactivity.

radiodiffuser *vt* to broadcast (radio).

radiodiffusion *f* broadcasting (radio).

radiographie *f* radiography; X-ray photography.

radiologie *f* radiology.

radiologue *mf* radiologist.

radiophonique *adj* radiotelephony.

radioscopie *f* radioscopy.

radio-taxi *m* radio taxi.

radis *m* radish.

radium *m* radium.

radoter *vi* to ramble; to dote.

radoucir vt to soften; **se ~** vr to calm down; to mellow.

rafale f gust, blast; flurry.

raffermir vt to harden; to strengthen; **se ~** vr to become strengthened.

raffinage m refining.

raffiné adj refined, sophisticated.

raffinement m refinement, sophistication.

raffiner vt to refine.

raffoler vi: **~ de** to be crazy about.

rafle f raid, round-up.

rafraîchir vt to cool, freshen, chill; **se ~** vr to freshen up; to get colder.

rafraîchissant adj refreshing, cooling.

rafraîchissement m cooling; cold drink.

rage f rage, fury; mania; rabies.

rageur adj quick-tempered; bad-tempered.

ragot m (fam) malicious gossip.

ragoût m ragout; stew.

raid m raid; trek.

raide adj stiff; steep; rough; broke.

raideur f stiffness; steepness; roughness.

raidir vt to stiffen; to tighten; to harden.

raie f line; furrow; scratch.

raifort m horseradish.

rail m rail; railway.

railler vt to scoff at, mock.

raillerie f mockery, scoffing.

railleur adj mocking, scoffing.

rainette f tree frog.

raisin m grape.

raison f reason; motive; sense;

ground; ratio; **avoir ~** to be right; **en ~ de** because of.

raisonnable adj reasonable, sensible; **~ment** adv reasonably.

raisonnement m reasoning; argument.

raisonner vi to reason; to argue.

rajeunir vi to feel younger; to be modernized; * vt to rejuvenate.

rajouter vt to put in; to add; **en ~** to exaggerate.

rajuster vt to readjust, rearrange; to tidy up.

râle m groan; death rattle.

ralenti adj slow; slackened; * m slow motion; **au ~** ticking over, idling.

ralentir vi to slow down, let up; * vt to slow down, check.

ralentissement m slowing down; slowing up.

râler vi to groan, moan.

ralliement m rallying, winning over; uniting.

rallier vt to rally; to win over; **se ~** vr to join; to side with.

rallonge f extension, lengthening; extension lead.

rallumer vt to relight; to switch on again; to revive.

ramadan m Ramadan.

ramage m song; foliage.

ramassage m collection; gathering.

ramasser vt to pick up; to collect, gather.

rambarde f guardrail.

rame f oar; underground train; stake.

rameau m branch; ramification.

ramener vt to bring back, restore.

ramer vi to row.

rameur m, **euse** f rower.

ramification f ramification.

ramifier(se) vr to ramify; to branch out.

ramollir vt to soften; to weaken; **se ~** vr to go soft.

ramoner vt to sweep.

ramoneur m chimney sweep.

rampant adj crawling, creeping.

rampe f ramp, slope; gradient.

ramper vi to crawl, slither.

rance adj rancid, rank.

rancœur f rancour, resentment.

rançon f ransom.

rancune f grudge, rancour.

rancunier adj rancorous, spiteful.

randonnée f drive; ride; ramble.

randonneur m, **-euse** f hiker, rambler.

rang m row, line; rank; class.

rangée f row, range, tier.

rangement m arranging, putting in order.

ranger vt to arrange, array; to put in order; **se ~** vr to line up; to make room; to park.

ranimer vt to reanimate, revive; to rekindle.

rapace m bird of prey.

rapatrié m, **-e** f repatriate; * adj repatriated.

rapatriement m repatriation.

rapatrier vt to repatriate.

râpe f rasp, rough file.

râper vt to grate; to rasp.

râpeux adj rough.

rapide adj rapid, quick; steep; **~ment** adv rapidly, quickly.

rapidité f rapidity, quickness.

rapiécer vt to patch up.

rappel m recall; reminder

rappeler vt to recall; to remind; **se ~** vr to remember.

rapport m report; relation; reference; profit; **en ~ avec** in touch with.

rapporter vt to report; to bring back; to yield; **se ~ vr: se ~ à** to relate to.

rapporteur m, **-euse** f reporter; tell-tale; * adj tell-tale; * m protractor.

rapprochement m drawing closer; reconciliation.

rapprocher vt to bring nearer; to reconcile; **se ~** vr to approach; to come together, to be reconciled.

rapt m abduction.

raquette f racket.

rare adj rare; few, odd; exceptional; **~ment** adv rarely, seldom.

raréfier(se) vr to rarefy; become scarce.

rareté f rarity; scarcity; infrequency.

rarissime adj extremely rare.

ras adj close-shaven, shorn; **à ~** short; level with; **à ~ bords** to the brim; **en avoir ~ le bol** (fam) to be fed up.

rasage m shaving; shearing.

raser vt to shave off; to scrape; to raze; **se ~** vr to have a shave.

rasoir m razor.

rassasier vt to satisfy.

rassemblement m assembling, mustering; crowd; political group.

rassembler vt to rally, gather together; **se ~** vr to gather, assemble.

rasseoir(se) vr to sit down again.

rasséréner vt to clear up, restore serenity to.

rassis adj settled; calm; stale.

rassurant adj reassuring, comforting.

rassurer vt to reassure; to comfort; **se ~** vr to be reassured.

rat m rat.

ratatiner vt to shrivel; to wrinkle; **se ~** vr to become wrinkled.

ratatouille f ratatouille.

rate f spleen.

raté m, **-e** f failure; * m misfire.

râteau m rake.

râtelier m rack; denture.

rater vt to miss; to spoil; to fail; * vi to misfire; to miss.

ratification f ratification.

ratifier vt to ratify, confirm.

ration f ration, allowance.

rationnel adj rational.

rationnement m rationing.

rationner vt to ration, put on rations; **se ~** vr to ration oneself.

ratisser vt to rake; to comb.

rattacher vt to refasten; to attach; to link.

rattraper vt to catch again, retake; to recover; **se ~** vr to catch hold of; to make up for.

rature f deletion, erasure.

raturer vt to delete, erase.

rauque adj hoarse, raucous.

ravage m havoc; ravaging, laying waste.

ravager vt to ravage; devastate.

ravaler vt to swallow again; to restore.

ravi adj delighted.

ravin m ravine, gully.

ravir vt to delight.

raviser (se) vr to think better of it, change one s mind.

ravissant adj ravishing, delightful; ravenous.

ravitaillement m revictualling; refuelling.

ravitailler vt to revictual; to resupply; **se ~** vr to be resupplied; to refuel.

raviver vt to revive, reanimate; **se ~** vr to be revived.

rayer vt to scratch; to rule; to cross out.

rayon m ray, beam; spoke; shelf.

rayonnant adj radiant, beaming.

rayonnement m radiance, effulgence; influence.

rayonner vi to radiate, shine; to be influential.

rayure f stripe; streak; groove.

réaccoutumer vt to reaccustom; **se ~** vr to become reaccustomed.

réacteur m reactor; jet-engine.

réaction f reaction.

réactionnaire adj reactionary; * mf reactionary.

réactiver vt to reactivate.

réadaptation f rehabilitation; readjustment.

réadapter vt to readjust; to rehabilitate.

réagir vi to react.

réalisateur m, **-trice** f director, film-maker.

réalisation f realization; carrying out; achievement.

réaliser vt to realize; to carry out; to achieve; **se ~** vr to be realized, come true.

réalisme m realism.

réaliste adj realistic; * mf realist.

réalité f reality; **en ~** in fact, in reality.

réanimation f resuscitation.

réanimer vt to reanimate; to resuscitate.

réapparaître vi to reappear.

rébarbatif adj stern, grim, forbidding.

rebattu adj hackneyed.

rebelle mf rebel; * adj rebel, rebellious.

rebeller(se) vr to rebel.

rébellion f rebellion.

reboisement m reafforestation.

reboiser vt to reafforest.

rebondir vi to bounce; to rebound.

rebondissement m rebound, bouncing.

rebord m rim, edge; hem.

rebrousser vt to brush back; **~ chemin** to turn back.

rébus m rebus, puzzle.

rebut m scrap; repulse, rebuff.

récalcitrant adj recalcitrant, stubborn.

récapituler vt to recapitulate, sum up.

receler vt to receive; to harbour.

récemment adv recently.

recensement m census, inventory.

recenser vt to make a census of; to record.

récent adj recent; new.

récépissé m receipt.

récepteur m receiver.

réceptif adj receptive.

réception f reception, welcome; receipt.

réceptionniste mf receptionist.

récession f recession.

recette f recipe; formula; receipt.

receveur m, **-euse** f recipient; collector.

recevoir vt to receive, welcome; to take, collect.

rechange m: change; spare; **de ~** spare.

recharge f recharging; reloading.

rechargeable adj rechargeable; reloadable.

recharger vt to recharge; to reload.

réchaud m stove; dish-warmer.

réchauffer vt to reheat; to warm up; **se ~** vr to get warmer.

rêche adj rough, harsh.

recherche f search; inquiry; investigation; research; **être à la ~ de** to be in search of.

recherché adj sought after, in demand; choice, exquisite.

rechercher vt to seek; to investigate.

rechigner vi to look sulky; to balk.

rechute f relapse; lapse.

récidive f second offence, relapse into crime; recidivism.

récidiver vi to offend again; (med) to recur.

récidiviste mf recidivist, habitual criminal.

récif m reef.

récipient m container, receptacle.

réciproque adj reciprocal, mutual; **~ment** adv reciprocally.

récit m account, story.

récital m, pl **-als** recital.

récitation f recitation; recital.

réciter vt to recite.

réclamation f complaint; demand; claim.

réclame f advertisement; publicity; **en ~** on offer.

réclamer vt to claim, demand, ask for; * vi to complain.

reclus adj shut up, secluded.

réclusion f reclusion; confinement.

recoiffer vt to do somebody's hair; **se ~** vr to do one s hair.

recoin m corner, nook.

recoller vt to restick.

récolte f harvest; collection; result.

récolter vt to harvest; to collect.

recommandation f recommendation, reference.

recommander vt to recommend; to commend; to register (letter).

recommencement m renewal; fresh beginning.

recommencer vi to begin again; * vt to begin again, resume.

récompense f reward; award.

réconciliation f reconciliation.

réconcilier vt to reconcile; **se ~** vr to become reconciled.

reconduire vt to bring back; to see home, escort.

réconfort m comfort.

réconfortant adj comforting; tonic.

réconforter vt to comfort; to fortify; **se ~** vr to take some refreshment.

reconnaissance f recognition; acknowledgement; gratitude.

reconnaissant adj grateful.

reconnaître vt to recognize; to acknowledge; to be grateful.

reconnu adj recognized, accepted.

reconquérir vt to reconquer; to recover.

reconsidérer vt to reconsider.

reconstituer vt to reconstitute; rebuild, restore.

reconstitution f reconstitution; rebuilding, restoration.

reconstruire vt to reconstruct, rebuild.

reconversion f reconversion, redeployment.

recopier vt to copy again.

record m record.

recoudre vt to sew up again.

recoupement m crosscheck.

recourbé adj curved, hooked.

recourir vi to run again **~ à** to appeal.

recours m recourse; redress; appeal.

recouvrir vt to cover again; to cover up.

récréatif adj recreative; entertaining.

récréation f recreation; break.

récrimination f recrimination, remonstration.

récriminer vi to recriminate, remonstrate.

recroqueviller(se) vr to shrivel up.

recrudescence f recrudescence; upsurge; further outbreak.

recrue f recruit.

recrutement m recruiting, recruitment.

recruter vt to recruit.

rectal adj rectal.

rectangle m rectangle.

rectangulaire adj rectangular.

recteur m priest, rector.

rectificatif m correction; * adj corrected, rectified.

rectification f rectification; correction.

rectifier vt to rectify, correct; to adjust.

rectiligne adj straight; rectilinear.

recto m recto, first side; front.

rectum m rectum.

reçu p.p. recevoir accepted, successful; * m receipt.

recueil m collection, miscellany.

recueillement m meditation.

recueillir vt to gather, collect; to record; **se ~** vr to collect one's thoughts.

recul m retreat; recession; decline.

reculer vi to fall back, retreat; * vt to move back; to defer.

récupération f recovery; retrieval.

récupérer vt to recover, retrieve; to recuperate; * vi to recover.

récurer vt to scour.

recycler vt to recycle.

rédacteur m, **-trice** f editor, compiler; drafter; writer; sub-editor.

rédaction f drafting, drawing up.

rédemption f redemption.

redescendre vi to go down again; * vt to bring down again, go down again.

redevable adj indebted, owing; liable.

redevance f rent; tax; fees.

rediffusion f repeat, reshowing.

rédiger vt to write; to compile; to draft.

redire vt to repeat, say again; **trouver à ~ à** to find fault with.

redoubler vt to increase, intensify; * vi to increase, intensify; **~ de** to redouble.

redoutable adj redoubtable, formidable.

redouter vt to dread, fear.

redresser vt to rectify; to true; to set up again; **se ~** vr to stand up; to right itself.

réduction f reduction; discount; mitigation.

réduire vt to reduce, diminish; **se ~** vr: **se ~ à** to boil down to.

réduit adj reduced, limited; miniature; * m retreat; recess; small room.

rééducation f re-education; rehabilitation.

rééduquer vt to re-educate; to rehabilitate.

réel adj real, genuine; **~lement** adv really.

réélire vt to re-elect.

rééquilibrer vt to restabilize.

réévaluer vr to revalue.

refaire vt to redo; to remake; to renew.

réfectoire m canteen, refectory.

référence f reference.

référendum m referendum.

refermer vt to close again.

réfléchi adj well-considered; reflective, thoughtful.

réfléchir vi to think, reflect; * vt to realize; to mirror.

reflet m reflection; reflex.

refléter vt to reflect, mirror.

réflexe m reflex.

réflexion f thought, reflection; remark; **à la ~** on reflection; **~ faite** all things considered.

reflux m reflux, ebb.

réforme f reform, amendment; discharge.

réformer vt to reform, correct; to invalid out; to scrap.

refouler vt to drive back, repel.

réfraction f refraction.

refrain m refrain, chorus.

réfréner vt to curb, hold in check.

réfrigérateur m refrigerator.

réfrigérer vt to refrigerate.

refroidir vt to cool; * vi to cool down, get cold.

refroidissement m cooling; chill.

refuge m refuge, shelter; lay-by.

réfugié m, **-e** f refugee; * adj refugee.

réfugier(se) vr to take refuge.

refus m refusal.

refuser vt to refuse; to reject; to deny; **se ~** vr to deny oneself; **se ~ à** to reject.

réfuter vt to refute.

regagner vt to regain, win back.

regain m renewal; revival.

régal m delight, treat.

régaler vt to regale; to treat; **se ~** vr to treat oneself.

regard m look; glance; expression; peephole.

regardant adj particular, meticulous; stingy.

regarder vt to look at; to glance; to be opposite; to concern; **~ à** to think about.

régates fpl regattas.

régénération f regeneration.

régénérer vt to regenerate, revive.

régent m, **-e** f regent.

régenter vt to rule over, domineer.

régie f administration; state control.

régime m system, régime; scheme; diet; rate, speed.

régiment m regiment.

région f region, area.

régional adj regional.

régir vt to govern, rule.

régisseur m manager; steward; bailiff.

registre m register, record; style; compass.

réglable adj adjustable.

réglage m regulation, adjustment; tuning.

règle f rule; order; regularity; period.

règlement m regulation, rules; settlement.

réglementaire adj regulation; statutory.

réglementation f regulations; control.

réglementer vt to regulate, control.

régler vt to settle, pay; to regulate.

réglisse f liquorice.

règne m reign.

régner vi to reign; to prevail.

regorger vi: **~ de** to overflow with; abound in.

régresser vi to regress; to recede.

régression f regression.

regret m regret, yearning; **à ~** regretfully.

regrettable adj regrettable.

regretter vt to regret, be sorry; to miss.

regroupement m gathering together; reassembly

regrouper vt to group together; to reassemble; **se ~** vr to assemble.

régulariser vt to regularize; straighten out.

régularité f regularity; consistency.

régulier adj regular; consistent; steady; even; legitimate.

régulièrement adv regularly; consistently; lawfully.

réhabilitation f rehabilitation; discharge; reinstatement.

réhabiliter vt to rehabilitate; to discharge; to reinstate.

réhabituer vt to reaccustom somebody to; **se ~** vr to reaccustom oneself to.

rehausser vt to heighten, raise.

rein m kidney.

réincarnation f reincarnation.

reine f queen.

reine-claude f greengage.

réinsertion f reinsertion, reintegration.

réintégrer vt to reinstate; to return to.

réitérer vt to reiterate, repeat.

rejaillir vi to gush out; to rebound on.

rejet m rejection, dismissal; throwing up.

rejeter vt to reject, dismiss; throw up.

rejoindre vt to rejoin; to catch up with.

rejouer vt to replay; to perform again; * vi to play again.

réjouir vt to delight; to entertain; **se ~** vr to rejoice, be delighted.

réjouissance f rejoicing, merrymaking.

relâche f intermission, respite; **faire ~** to be closed; **sans ~** without intermission.

relâchement m relaxation, loosening; laxity.

relâcher vt to relax, slacken; **se ~** vr to relax; to become lax.

relais m relay; shift; staging post.

relatif adj relative; relating to.

relation f relation, relationship; reference; acquaintance; account; **être en ~ avec** to be in contact with.

relativement adv relatively.

relativisme m relativism.

relativité f relativity.

relaxant adj relaxing.

relaxation f relaxation.

relaxer vt to relax; to acquit; to release; **se ~** vr to relax.

relayer vt to relieve, take the place of; **se ~** vr to take turns.

relecture f rereading.

reléguer vt to relegate; to banish.

relève f relief; relief party.

relevé m statement; list; bill; * adj turned up, rolled up; elevated.

relever vt to set up again, raise again, right; to rebuild; to relieve;

se ~ vr to stand up again; to get up.

relief m relief; contours; depth.

relier vt to link up, connect; to bind.

religieux m monk, **-euse** f nun; * adj religious.

religion f religion.

relique f relic.

relire vt to reread.

reliure f binding; bookbinding.

reluire vi to gleam, shine.

remaniement m recasting; altering; revision; amendment.

remanier vt to recast, revise; to amend.

remarquable adj remarkable, notable; **~ment** adv remarkably.

remarque f remark, comment.

remarquer vt to remark; to notice.

rembourrer vt to stuff; to pad.

remboursement m reimbursement, repayment.

rembourser vt to reimburse, pay back.

remède m remedy, cure.

remédier vi: **~ à** to remedy, cure.

remerciement m thanks; thanking.

remercier vt to thank.

remettre vt to put back; to replace; to restart; to revive; **se ~** vr to recover, get better; **se ~ à** to start doing something again; **se ~ de** to get over something.

réminiscence f reminiscence.

remise f delivery; remittance; discount; deferment; **~ à neuf** restoration; **~ en état** repairing; **~ en jeu** throw-in; **~ en question**

calling into question; **~ en cause** calling into question; **~ de peine** reduction in sentence.

remmener vt to take back.

remontant m tonic; * adj invigorating, fortifying.

remonte-pente m ski tow.

remonter vi to go up again; to rise, increase; to return; * vt to go up; to take up.

remontrance f remonstrance.

remords m remorse.

remorque f trailer; towrope.

remorquer vt to tow.

remorqueur m tug.

rémouleur m knife-grinder.

remous m back-wash; eddy, swirl.

rempailler vt to reseat (chair).

rempart m rampart; defence.

remplaçant m, **-e** f replacement.

remplacement m replacing; substitution.

remplacer vt to replace; stand in for.

remplir vt to fill; to fill in; to fulfil; **se ~** vr to fill up.

remplissage m filling up; padding.

remporter vt to take away.

remuant adj restless, fidgety.

remue-ménage m invar commotion; hullabaloo.

remuer vi to move; to fidget; * vt to move, shift; to stir; **se ~** vr to move; to shift oneself.

rémunération f remuneration, payment.

rémunérer vt to remunerate, pay.

renaissance f rebirth, Renaissance.

renaître vi to be reborn; to be revived; to reappear.

renard *m* fox.

renchérir *vi* to go further, go one better; to bid higher.

renchérissement *m* increase in price.

rencontre *f* meeting, encounter; conjuncture; collision.

rencontrer *vt* to meet; to find; to strike; **se ~** *vr* to meet each other.

rendement *m* yield; output.

rendez-vous *m* appointment; date; meeting place.

rendormir *vt* to put to sleep again; **se ~** *vr* to go back to sleep.

rendre *vt* to render; to give back, return; to yield; **se ~** *vr* to surrender; to give way.

rêne *f* rein.

renfermé *adj* withdrawn, close; * *m* fusty/close smell.

renfermer *vt* to contain, hold.

renflement *m* bulge.

renflouer *vt* to refloat; to bail out.

renfoncement *m* recess.

renfoncer *vt* to drive further in; to recess.

renforcer *vt* to strengthen, reinforce.

renfort *m* reinforcement; help.

renfrogné *adj* frowning, glum.

renier *vt* to repudiate, disown.

renifler *vi* to sniff, snuffle.

renne *m* reindeer.

renom *m* renown, fame.

renommée *f* renowned, famed.

renoncement *m* renouncement; renunciation.

renoncer *vi* to renounce, give up.

renonciation *f* renunciation; waiver.

renouer *vt* to tie again; to renew.

renouveau *m* spring; renewal.

renouveler *vt* to renew; to revive; **se ~** *vr* to be renewed.

renouvellement *m* renewal; revival.

rénovation *f* renovation; renewal.

rénover *vt* to renovate.

renseignement *m* information; intelligence.

renseigner *vt* to inform, give information to; **se ~** *vr* to ask for information.

rentabiliser *vt* to make profitable.

rentable *adj* profitable.

rente *f* rent; profit; annuity.

rentier *m*, **-ière** *f* stockholder, fundholder; rentier.

rentrée *f* reopening; reassembly; reappearance.

rentrer *vi* to re-enter; to return home; to begin again; * *vt* to bring in.

renversement *m* inversion; reversal; overturning.

renverser *vt* to turn upside down; to reverse; to overturn.

renvoi *m* sending back; returning; dismissal.

renvoyer *vt* to send back; to return; to dismiss.

réorganisation *f* reorganization.

réorganiser *vt* to reorganize.

réouverture *f* reopening.

repaire *m* den, lair.

répandre *vt* to pour out; to scatter, spread; **se ~** *vr* to spread; to be spilled.

répandu *adj* widespread.

réparateur *m*, **-trice** *f* repairer.

réparation *f* repairing; restoration.

réparer *vt* to repair; to restore; to make up for.

repartie *f* retort **avoir de la ~** to be quick at repartee.

repartir *vi* to set off again; to start up again.

répartir *vt* to share out; to distribute; **se ~** *vr* to be divided.

répartition *f* sharing out; allocation.

repas *m* meal.

repassage *m* ironing; grinding; sharpening.

repasser *vt* to cross again; to resit; * *vi* to go past again.

repêcher *vt* to fish out, retrieve.

repeindre *vt* to repaint.

repenti *adj* repentant.

repentir *m* repentance, contrition.

repentir(se) *vr* to repent, rue.

répercussion *f* repercussion.

répercuter *vt* to reverberate; to echo; **se ~** *vr* to reverberate; to echo.

repère *m* line, mark; **point de ~** indication, reference mark.

repérer *vt* to spot, pick out; to mark out.

répertoire *m* index, catalogue; repertory.

répertorier *vt* to itemize; to index.

répéter *vt* to repeat; to rehearse; **se ~** *vr* to repeat oneself; to reoccur.

répétitif *adj* repetitive.

répétition *f* repetition; rehearsal.

repiquer *vt* to plant out; transplant.

répit *m* respite, rest.

repli *m* fold, coil, meander; withdrawal; downturn.

replier *vt* to fold up; to withdraw; **se ~** *vr* to coil up, curl up.

réplique *f* reply, retort; counterattack.

répliquer *vt* to reply; to retaliate.

répondant *m*, **-e** *f* guarantor; bail, surety.

répondeur *m* answering machine.

répondre *vt* to answer, reply.

réponse *f* response, reply.

report *m* postponement, deferment; carrying forward.

reportage *m* report; commentary; reporting.

reporter *vt* to take back; to carry forward; to transfer; * *m* reporter.

repos *m* rest; tranquillity; landing.

reposant *adj* restful, refreshing.

reposer *vt* to put back; to rest; to ask again; **se ~** *vr* to rest oneself.

repoussant *adj* repulsive; repellent.

repousser *vt* to push again; to repel.

reprendre *vt* to retake, recapture; to resume; **se ~** *vr* to correct oneself; to pull oneself together.

représailles *fpl* reprisals; retaliation.

représentant *m* representative.

représentatif *adj* representative.

représentation *f* representation; performance.

représenter *vt* to represent, depict; to perform; to symbolize.

répressif *adj* repressive.

répression *f* repression.

réprimande *f* reprimand, rebuke.

réprimander *vt* to reprimand, rebuke.

réprimer *vt* to repress; to quell.

reprise f resumption; recapture, taking back; **à plusieurs ~s** several times.

repriser vt to darn.

réprobation f reprobation.

reproche m reproach; objection.

reprocher vt to reproach, blame.

reproduction f reproduction; copy; duplicate.

reproduire vt to reproduce, copy; to repeat; **se ~ vr** to reproduce, breed.

reptile m reptile.

repu adj full, satiated.

républicain m, **-e** f republican; * adj republican.

république f republic.

répudier vt to repudiate; to renounce.

répugnance f repugnance, disgust.

répugnant adj repugnant, disgusting.

répulsion f repulsion, repugnance.

réputation f reputation; character; fame.

réputé adj reputable, renowned; supposed, reputed.

requérir vt to call for, request.

requête f petition, request.

requin m shark.

requis adj required, requisite.

réquisition f requisition; conscription.

réquisitionner vt to requisition; to conscript.

rescapé m, **-e** f survivor.

réseau m network, net.

réservation f reservation, booking.

réserve f reserve; reservation, caution.

réservé f reserved.

réserver vt to reserve, save; to book; to lay by.

réservoir m tank; reservoir.

résidence f residence; apartment block.

résidentiel adj residential

résider vi to reside, dwell.

résidu m residue.

résignation f resignation.

résigner(se) vr to resign oneself.

résilier vt to terminate; to annul.

résine f resin.

résistance f resistance.

résistant adj resistant; tough, unyielding.

résister vi to resist, withstand.

résolu adj resolved, determined; **~ment** adv resolutely.

résolution f resolution, determination; solution.

résonner vi to resound, resonate.

résorber vt to reduce; to absorb; **se ~ vr** to be reduced.

résoudre vt to solve; to resolve; to annul; **se ~ vr: se ~ à** to decide to do.

respect m respect, regard, deference.

respectable adj respectable; sizeable.

respecter vt to respect; to comply with.

respectif adj respective.

respectivement adv respectively.

respectueusement adv respectfully.

respectueux adj respectful.

respirable adj breathable.

respiration f breathing, respiration.

respiratoire adj respiratory.

respirer vi to breathe, respire; to rest; * vt to breathe in.

resplendissant adj shining, radiant.

responsabilité f responsibility; liability.

responsable adj responsible; liable; * mf official, manager.

resquiller vi to sneak in; to take a free ride.

ressaisir(se) vr to regain one's self-control.

ressemblance f resemblance, likeness; similarity.

ressemblant adj lifelike.

ressembler vi to resemble, be like; **se ~** vr to be alike.

ressemelage m soling, resoling.

ressentiment m resentment.

ressentir vt to feel, experience; **se ~** vr: **se ~ de** to feel the effects of.

resserrement m contraction, tightening; narrowing.

resserrer vt to tighten; to strengthen; **se ~** vr to grow tighter.

ressort m spring; motivation.

ressortir vi to go out again; to stand out.

ressortissant m, -e f national.

ressource f resource, resort, expedient.

ressusciter vt to revive, reawaken; to come back to life; * vt to resuscitate; to revive.

restant adj remaining; * m rest, remainder.

restaurant m restaurant.

restaurateur m, -**trice** f restaurateur; restorer.

restauration f restoration, rehabilitation; catering.

restaurer vt to restore; to feed; **se ~** vr to take refreshment.

reste m rest, left-over, remainder; **du ~** besides; **être en ~** to be outdone.

rester vi to remain, stay; to be left; to continue; to pause.

restituer vt to return, restore; to refund.

restitution f restoration; restitution.

restreindre vt to restrict, curtail; **se ~** vr to restrain oneself.

restreint adj restricted, limited.

restrictif adj restrictive.

restriction f restriction, limitation; reserve.

restructurer vt to restructure.

résultat m result, outcome; profit.

résulter vi: **~ de** to result, follow from, ensue.

résumé m summary, recapitulation; **en ~** in brief.

résumer vt to sum up; **se ~** vr: **se ~ à** to amount to.

résurrection f resurrection.

rétablir vt to re-establish, restore; **se ~** vr to recover, get well again.

rétablissement m re-establishment, restoring.

retard m lateness; delay; **être en ~** to be behind; to be backward.

retardataire mf latecomer; * adj obsolete.

retardé adj backward, slow.

retarder vt to delay; to hinder; to put back; * vi to be out of touch.

retenir vt to hold back, retain; to remember; **se ~** vr to control oneself.

rétention f retention; withholding.

retentir vi to resound; to ring.

retentissant adj resounding; ringing.

retenue f discretion; deduction; stoppage; reservoir.

réticence f reticence.

réticent adj reticent.

rétine f retina.

retiré adj remote, isolated.

retirer vt to take off; to take out, withdraw; to redeem; **se ~** vr to retire, withdraw; to stand down.

retombée f fallout; repercussions.

retomber vi to fall again; to have a relapse; **~ sur** to come across.

rétorquer vt to retort.

retouche f touching up; alteration.

retoucher vt to touch up; to alter.

retour m return; recurrence; vicissitude, reversal, **être de ~** to be back.

retournement m reversal; turnaround.

retourner vt to reverse, turn over; to return; **~ à** to return, go back; **se ~** vr to turn over; to overturn.

rétracter vt to retract, take back; **se ~** vr to retract, withdraw one's evidence.

retrait m ebb; retreat; withdrawal; **être en ~** to be set back.

retraite f retreat; retirement; refuge; **à la ~** retired.

retraité m, **-e** f pensioner; * adj retired.

retranchement m curtailment; entrenchment.

retrancher vt to curtail; to entrench.

retransmettre vt to retransmit.

retransmission f retransmission.

rétrécir vt to narrow; to shrink; * vt to take in, make narrower; **se ~** vr to narrow; to shrink.

rétrécissement m narrowing; shrinking.

rétribuer vt to remunerate.

rétribution f retribution.

rétroactif adj retrospective; retroactive.

rétroaction f retroaction; retrospective action.

rétrograde adj reactionary, backward.

rétrograder vi to go backward, regress.

rétroprojecteur m overhead projector.

rétrospectif adj retrospective.

rétrospective f retrospective.

rétrospectivement adv retrospectively.

retrousser vt to roll up, hitch up.

retrouvailles fpl reunion.

retrouver vt to find again, to regain; to recover; to recognize; **se ~** vr to meet up; to end up in.

rétroviseur m rear-view mirror.

réunifier vt to reunify.

réunion f collection; gathering.

réunir vt to unite; to collect,

gather; to combine; **se ~** *vr* to meet; to assemble.

réussir *vi* to succeed, be a success; * *vt* to make a success of.

réussite *f* success, successful outcome.

revanche *f* revenge; **en ~** on the other hand.

rêvasser *vi* to daydream.

rêve *m* dream, dreaming; illusion.

réveil *m* waking, awaking; alarm clock.

réveiller *vt* to wake; **se ~** *vr* to awaken.

réveillon *m* midnight feast.

révélation *f* revelation, disclosure; developing.

révéler *vt* to reveal, disclose; **se ~** *vr* to be revealed; to prove to be

revenant *m*, **-e** *f* ghost.

revendeur *m*, **-euse** *f* retailer; dealer.

revendication *f* claiming; claim; demand.

revendiquer *vt* to claim; to demand.

revendre *vt* to resell

revenir *vi* to come back, reappear; to happen again; **ne pas en ~** to not recover from, not pull through; **~ à soi** to come round.

revenu *m* income, revenue.

rêver *vi* to dream; to muse; * *vt* to dream of.

réverbération *f* reverberation.

réverbère *m* street lamp.

révérence *f* bow, curtsey.

révérend *adj* reverend.

révérer *vt* to revere.

rêverie *f* reverie, musing.

revers *m* back, reverse; counterpart.

réversible *adj* reversible.

revêtement *m* coating, surface.

revêtir *vt* to don; to assume.

rêveur *m*, **-euse** *f* dreamer; * *adj* dreamy

revigorer *vt* to invigorate; to revive.

revirement *m* change of mind; reversal; turnaround.

réviser *vt* to review; to revise.

révision *f* review; auditing; revision.

revivre *vt* to relive; * *vi* to live again, come alive again.

révocation *f* removal; dismissal; revocation.

revoir *vt* to see again; **se ~** *vr* to meet each other again.

révoltant *adj* revolting, appalling.

révolte *f* revolt, rebellion.

révolter *vt* to revolt, outrage; **se ~** *vr* to rebel, revolt.

révolu *adj* past, bygone.

révolution *f* revolution.

révolutionnaire *mf* revolutionary; * *adj* revolutionary.

révolutionner *vt* to revolutionize; to upset.

revolver *m* revolver.

révoquer *vt* to revoke; to dismiss.

revue *f* review; inspection.

rez-de-chaussée *m invar* ground floor.

rhabiller *vt* to dress somebody again; to fit somebody out again; **se ~** *vr* to dress oneself again.

rhésus *m* rhesus.

rhétorique *f* rhetoric; * *adj* rhetorical.

rhinocéros *m* rhinoceros.

rhododendron *m* rhododendron.

rhubarbe *f* rhubarb.

rhum *m* rum.

rhumatisme *m* rheumatism.

rhume *m* cold.

riant *adj* smiling; cheerful.

ribambelle *f* swarm, herd.

ricanement *m* snigger, sniggering.

ricaner *vi* to snigger, giggle

riche *adj* rich, wealthy; abundant; **~ment**; * *mf* rich person.

richesse *f* richness; wealth; abundance.

ricochet *m* ricochet; rebound.

rictus *m* grin, grimace.

ride *f* wrinkle; ripple; ridge.

ridé *adj* wrinkled

rideau *m* curtain.

ridicule *adj* ridiculous; * *m* ridiculousness; absurdity; ridicule.

ridiculiser *vt* to ridicule.

rien *pron* nothing; **de ~** don't mention it; **il n en est ~** he's nothing of the sort; * *m* nothingness; mere nothing; pinch, shade; **en un ~ de temps** in no time **pour un ~** at the slightest little thing.

rieur *adj* cheerful; laughing.

rigide *adj* rigid; **~ment** *adv* rigidly.

rigidité *f* rigidity, stiffness.

rigole *f* channel; rivulet.

rigoler *vi* (*fam*) to have a good laugh.

rigoureusement *adv* harshly, rigorously.

rigoureux *adj* rigorous, harsh.

rigueur *f* rigour; harshness, severity.

rime *f* rhyme.

rimer *vi* to rhyme (with).

rince-doigts *m invar* finger-bowl.

rincer *vt* to rinse out; to rinse.

ring *m* boxing ring.

riposte *f* riposte, retort.

riposter *vi* to answer back, retaliate.

rire *vi* to laugh; to smile; to joke; * *m* laughter, laugh.

risée *f* laugh; ridicule; mockery, derision.

risible *adj* laughable, ridiculous.

risque *m* risk, hazard.

risqué *adj* risky, hazardous; risqué.

risquer *vt* to risk; to venture; **se ~** *vr* to venture, dare.

ristourne *f* discount, rebate.

rite *m* rite.

rituel *adj* ritual.

rivage *m* shore.

rival *m*, **-e** *f* rival; **sans ~** unrivalled; * *adj* rival.

rivaliser *vi* to rival, compete with; **~ de** to vie with.

rivalité *f* rivalry.

rive *f* shore, bank.

river *vt* to clinch; to rivet.

riverain *m*, **-e** *f* lakeside resident; riverside resident; * *adj* lakeside, riverside.

rivière *f* river.

riz *m* rice.

robe *f* dress; gown; **~ de chambre** dressing gown.

robinet *m* tap.

robot *m* robot.

robotique *f* robotics.

robuste *adj* robust.

robustesse f robustness.

roc m rock.

rocaille f loose stones; rocky ground.

rocailleux adj rocky.

roche f rock.

rocher m rock, boulder.

rodage m grinding, polishing; running in, breaking in.

roder vt to grind, polish; to run in

rôder vi to roam; to prowl about.

rôdeur m, **-euse** f prowler.

rogner vt to pare, prune, clip.

rognon m kidney.

roi m king

rôle m role, character; roll, catalogue.

roman m novel; romance.

romancier m, **-ière** f novelist.

romanesque adj fabulous; storybook; novelistic.

romantique adj romantic.

romantisme m romanticism.

rompre vt to break; to snap; to dissolve; * vi to break; to burst.

ronce f bramble.

rond m circle, ring; slice; round; * adj round; chubby, plump; frank; **~ement** adv briskly, frankly.

ronde f patrol; round; beat.

rondelle f slice, round; disc.

rondeur f plumpness; roundness.

rondin m log.

rond-point m roundabout.

ronflement m snore, snoring; humming; roaring.

ronfler vi to snore; to hum; to roar.

ronger vt to gnaw.

ronronner vi to purr; to hum.

rosbif m roast beef.

rose f rose; * adj pink; * m pink.

roseau m reed.

rosée f dew.

rosier m rosebush.

rossignol m nightingale.

rot m belch, burp.

roter vi to belch, burp.

rotation f rotation; turnover.

rôti m joint, roast.

rotin m rattan.

rôtir vt to roast.

rôtisserie f rotisserie, steakhouse.

rotonde f rotunda; roundhouse.

rotule f kneecap, patella.

rouage m cog; gearwheel.

roucouler vi to coo; to bill.

roue f wheel.

rouge adj red; * m red; ~ à lèvres lipstick.

rouge-gorge m robin.

rougeole f measles.

rougeur f redness, blushing.

rougir vi to blush, go red; * vt to make red, redden.

rouille f rust.

rouiller vi to rust; * vt to make rusty.

roulant adj on wheels; moving.

rouleau m roll; roller.

roulement m rotation; movement; rumble, rumbling.

rouler vi to wheel, roll along; * vi to go, run (train); to drive.

roulette f castor; trundle; roulette.

roulis m rolling.

roulotte f caravan.

rouquin m, **-e** f redhead; * adj redhaired.

route f road; way; course, direction.

routier adj road; * m lorry driver; transport cafe.

routine f routine.

routinier adj humdrum, routine.

roux m, **rousse** f redhead; * adj red, auburn.

royal adj royal, regal; **~ement** adv royally.

royaliste mf royalist; * adj royalist.

royaume m kingdom.

royauté f monarchy.

ruade f kick (horse).

ruban m ribbon; tape, band.

rubéole f rubella.

rubis m ruby.

rubrique f column; heading, rubric.

ruche f hive.

rude adj rough; hard; unrefined; **~ment** adv roughly, harshly.

rudesse f roughness; harshness.

rudiment m rudiment; principle.

rudimentaire adj rudimentary.

rudoyer vt to treat harshly.

rue f street.

ruée f rush, stampede.

ruelle f alley.

ruer vi to kick (horse); **se ~** vr to pounce on.

rugby m rugby.

rugbyman m rugby player.

rugir vi to roar.

rugissement m roar, roaring.

rugueux adj rough; coarse.

ruine f ruin; wreck.

ruiner vt to ruin.

ruineux adj ruinous; extravagant.

ruisseau m stream, brook.

ruisseler vi to stream, flow.

ruissellement m streaming; cascading.

rumeur f rumour; murmur; hum.

ruminer vt to ruminate; to brood over.

rupture f break, rupture; breach; split.

rural adj rural, country.

ruse f cunning, slyness.

rusé adj cunning, crafty.

rustine ® f rubber repair patch.

rustique adj rustic.

rutilant adj gleaming, rutilant.

rythme m rhythm; rate, speed.

rythmique adj rhythmic.

S

sabbatique adj sabbatical.

sable m sand.

sablé m shortbread biscuit; * adj sandy, sanded.

sablier m hourglass, sandglass.

sabot m clog; hoof.

sabotage m sabotage.

saboter vt to sabotage; to mess up.

saboteur m, **-euse** f saboteur; bungler.

sabre m sabre.

sac m bag, sack; **~ à main** handbag; **~ de voyage** travelling bag.

saccade f jerk, jolt.

saccadé adj jerky, broken, staccato.

saccager vt to sack; to wreck, devastate.

saccharine f saccharin.

sacerdoce m priesthood.

sacerdotal adj priestly, sacerdotal.

sachet m bag; sachet; packet.

sacoche f saddlebag, satchel.

sacre m coronation; consecration.

sacré adj sacred, holy; damned, confounded.

sacré-cœur m Sacred Heart.

sacrer vt to crown; to consecrate.

sacrifice m sacrifice.

sacrifier vt to sacrifice; to give up; **se ~** vr to sacrifice oneself.

sacrilège m sacrilege.

sacristie f sacristy.

sacrum m sacrum.

sadique adj sadistic; * mf sadist.

sadisme m sadism.

sadomasochiste adj sadomasochistic; * mf sadomasochistic.

safari m safari.

safran m saffron.

saga f saga.

sagace adj sagacious, shrewd.

sagacité f sagacity, shrewdness.

sage adj wise, sensible; well-behaved; **~ment** adv wisely, sensibly; * m sage, wise man.

sage-femme f midwife.

sagesse f wisdom, sense; good behaviour.

sagittaire m archer; Sagittarius.

saignant adj bleeding; underdone.

saignement m bleeding.

saigner vi to bleed; * vt to bleed; to stick.

saillant adj prominent, protruding.

saillie f projection; sally; flash of wit.

saillir vi to gush out; to project, jut.

sain adj healthy; sound; sane; **~ement** adv healthily; soundly.

saindoux m lard.

saint m, -e f saint; * adj holy, saintly; **Saint-Sylvestre** New Year's Eve; **Saint-Esprit** Holy Spirit.

saint-bernard m St Bernard.

sainteté f saintliness; holiness.

saisie f seizure, distraint; capture.

saisir vt to take hold of; to seize, distrain; to capture.

saisissant adj gripping, startling, striking.

saison f season.

saisonnier adj seasonal.

salade f salad; jumble, miscellany.

saladier m salad bowl.

salaire m salary, pay; reward.

salamandre f salamander.

salarié m, -e f salaried employee; * adj salaried.

sale adj dirty, filthy; obscene; nasty; **~ment** adv dirtily.

salé adj salty, salted; savoury.

saler vt to salt, add salt.

saleté f dirtiness, dirt; rubbish; obscenity.

salière f saltcellar.

salin adj saline.

salir vt to make dirty, soil; **se ~** vr to get dirty.

salissant adj dirty; that gets dirty easily.

salive f saliva.

saliver vi to salivate; to drool

salle f room; hall; theatre; audience; **~ de séjour** living room;

~ à manger dining room; **~ de bain** bathroom; **~ de cinéma** cinema.

salon m lounge, sitting room; exhibition.

salopette f overalls.

salpêtre m saltpetre.

salsifis m salsify, oyster-plant.

salubre adj healthy, salubrious.

saluer vt to greet; to salute.

salut m safety, salvation; welfare; wave (hand); salute.

salutaire adj salutary; profitable; healthy.

salutation f salutation, greeting.

samedi m Saturday.

sanatorium m sanatorium.

sanctifier vt to sanctify, bless.

sanction f sanction, penalty; approval.

sanctionner vt to punish; to sanction, approve.

sanctuaire m sanctuary.

sandale f sandal.

sandwich m sandwich.

sang m blood; race; kindred.

sang-froid m sangfroid, cool, calm.

sanglant adj bloody, gory; blood-shot; blood-red.

sangle f strap; girth.

sanglier m wild boar.

sanglot m sob.

sangloter vi to sob.

sangsue f leech.

sanguinaire adj sanguinary, blood-thirsty.

sanitaire adj health, sanitary.

sans-abris mf invar homeless person.

sans-gêne adj inconsiderate; * m invar inconsiderate type.

santal m sandalwood.

santé f health, healthiness.

saper vt to undermine, sap.

sapeur-pompier m fireman.

saphir m sapphire.

sapin m fir tree, fir.

sarcasme m sarcasm.

sarcastique adj sarcastic.

sarcler vt to weed; to hoe.

sarcophage m sarcophagus.

sardine f sardine.

sardonique adj sardonic.

S.A.R.L. (société à responsabilité limitée) f limited liability company.

sarrasin m buckwheat.

sas m airlock; sieve.

satanique adj satanic, diabolical.

satellite m satellite.

satiété f satiety, satiation; **à ~** ad nauseam.

satin m satin.

satiné adj satiny, satin-smooth; glazed.

satire f satire, lampoon.

satirique adj satirical.

satisfaction f satisfaction; gratification; appeasement.

satisfaire vt to satisfy; to gratify; to appease.

satisfaisant adj satisfactory; satisfying.

satisfait adj satisfied.

saturation f saturation.

saturé adj saturated; overloaded, jammed.

saturer vt to saturate; to surfeit; to congest.

satyre m satyr.

sauce f sauce, dressing.

saucière *f* sauceboat.

saucisse *f* sausage.

saucisson *m* large sausage; salami.

sauf *prép* save, except; unless; * *adj* safe, unhurt.

sauge *f* sage.

saugrenu *adj* preposterous, absurd.

saule *m* willow.

saumon *m* salmon.

sauna *m* sauna.

saupoudrer *vt* to sprinkle; to dust.

saut *m* jump, bound; waterfall.

sauté *adj* sauté.

sauter *vi* to jump, leap; to blow up; to get sacked.

sauterelle *f* grasshopper.

sautiller *vi* to hop, skip.

sauvage *adj* savage, wild; unsociable; ~**ment** *adv* savagely.

sauvegarde *f* safeguard; backup.

sauvegarder *vt* to safeguard.

sauver *vt* to save, rescue; to preserve; **se ~** *vr* to save oneself; to escape.

sauvetage *m* rescue; salvage.

sauveteur *m* rescuer.

savant *adj* learned; expert; skilled; * *m* scientist, scholar.

savate *f* old shoe.

saveur *f* flavour; savour.

savoir *vt* to know; to be aware; to understand; to be able; * *m* learning, knowledge.

savoir-faire *m* know-how.

savoir-vivre *m* good manners, good breeding.

savon *m* soap.

savonner *vt* to soap, lather.

savonnette *f* bar of soap.

savoureux *adj* tasty, savoury.

saxophone *m* saxophone.

saxophoniste *mf* saxophonist.

scabreux *adj* scabrous; dangerous; improper.

scalpel *m* scalpel.

scandale *m* scandal.

scandaleux *adj* scandalous.

scandaliser *vt* to scandalize, shock deeply; **se ~** *vr* to be scandalized.

scanner *m* scanner; * *vt* to digitize.

scaphandre *m* diving suit.

scarabée *m* beetle, scarab.

scarlatine *f* scarlet fever.

sceau *m* seal.

scélérat *m*, **-e** *f* villain, rascal; * *adj* villainous, wicked.

sceller *vt* to seal.

scénario *m* scenario; screenplay.

scénariste *mf* scriptwriter.

scène *f* stage; scenery, scene.

scepticisme *m* scepticism.

sceptique *adj* sceptical; * *mf* sceptic.

sceptre *m* sceptre.

schéma *m* diagram, sketch; outline.

schématique *adj* diagrammatic, schematic; ~**ment** *adv* diagrammatically.

schématiser *vt* to schematize.

schisme *m* schism; split.

schiste *m* schist, shale.

schizophrène *mf* schizophrenic; * *adj* schizophrenic.

schizophrénie *f* schizophrenia.

sciatique *f* sciatica.

scie *f* saw; bore.

sciemment *adv* knowingly, on purpose.

science *f* science; skill; knowledge.

science-fiction *f* science fiction.

scientifique *adj* scientific; ~**ment** *adv* scientifically.

scierie *f* sawmill.

scinder *vt* to split, divide up.

scintillant *adj* sparkling, glistening.

scintillement *m* sparkling, glistening.

scintiller *vi* to sparkle, glisten.

scission *f* split, scission.

sciure *f* sawdust.

sclérose *f* sclerosis.

scléroser(se) *vr* to become sclerotic.

scolaire *adj* school; academic.

scolariser *vt* to send to school; to provide schools.

scolarité *f* schooling.

scoliose *f* scoliosis, curvature of the spine.

scooter *m* scooter.

score *m* score.

scorie *f* slag, scoria.

scorpion *m* scorpion.

scout *m* scout, boy scout.

script *m* printing; script.

scrupule *m* scruple, qualm, doubt.

scrupuleusement *adv* scrupulously.

scrupuleux *adj* scrupulous.

scruter *vt* to scrutinize, scan.

scrutin *m* ballot, poll.

sculpter *vt* to sculpt; to carve.

sculpteur *m* sculptor.

sculpture *f* sculpture.

se *pron* oneself, himself, herself, itself, themselves.

séance *f* meeting, sitting, session; seat.

seau *m* bucket, pail.

sec *adj*, *f* **sèche** dry, arid; barren; unfeeling; curt; neat.

sécateur *m* secateurs.

séchage *m* drying; seasoning.

sèche-cheveux *m invar* hairdrier.

sèchement *adv* dryly; curtly.

sécher *vi* to dry, dry out; * *vt* to dry, wipe.

sécheresse *f* drought; dryness.

séchoir *m* drying room; ~ **à linge** clothes horse

second *adj* second, in second place; * *m* second; second floor; second in command.

secondaire *adj* secondary.

seconde *f* second.

seconder *vt* to assist, help.

secouer *vt* to shake, toss; **se ~** *vr* to shake oneself.

secourir *vt* to help, assist.

secouriste *mf* first-aid worker.

secours *m* help, assistance; relief; rescue.

secousse *f* jolt, bump.

secret *m* secret; privacy; mystery; * *adj* secret; private; discreet.

secrétaire *mf* secretary; * *m* writing desk.

secrétariat *m* office of secretary; secretariat.

secrètement *adv* secretly.

secréter *vt* to secrete, exude.

sécrétion *f* secretion.

secte *f* sect.

secteur *m* sector, section, district.

section *f* section, division; branch.

sectionner *vt* to sever; to divide into sections.

séculaire *adj* secular, century-old, once a century.

sécurisant *adj* reassuring, lending security.

sécuriser *vt* to make somebody feel secure.

sécuritaire *adj* security.

sécurité *f* security; safety.

sédatif *adj* sedative; * *m* sedative.

sédentaire *adj* sedentary; * *m* sedentary.

sédiment *m* sediment.

sédimentation *f* sedimentation.

séducteur *m* seducer, **-trice** *f* seductress.

séduction *f* seduction; captivation

séduire *vt* to seduce; to charm, captivate.

séduisant *adj* seductive; enticing, attractive.

segment *m* segment.

segmenter *vt* to segment.

ségrégation *f* segregation.

seigle *m* rye.

seigneur *m* lord, nobleman; master.

sein *m* breast, bosom; womb; **au ~ de** within.

séisme *m* earthquake, seism.

seize *adj*, *m* sixteen.

seizième *adj*, *mf* sixteenth; **~ment** *adv* in sixteenth place.

séjour *m* stay, sojourn; abode; **salle de ~** living room.

séjourner *vi* to stay, sojourn.

sel *m* salt; wit.

sélecteur *m* selector; gear lever.

sélectif *adj* selective.

sélection *f* choosing, selection.

sélectionner *vt* to select, pick.

sélectivement *adv* selectively.

self-service *m* self-service restaurant.

selle *f* saddle.

selon *prép* according to; pursuant to.

semaine *f* week.

semblable *adj* like, similar, alike; such.

semblant *m* appearance, look; pretence; **faire ~ (de)** to pretend to.

sembler *vi* to seem, appear.

semelle *f* sole.

semence *f* seed; semen.

semer *vt* to sow; to scatter, strew.

semestre *m* half-year; semester.

semestriel *adj* half-yearly; semestral.

semi-conducteur *m* semiconductor.

séminaire *m* seminary; seminar.

semi-remorque *f* trailer, semi-trailer.

semis *m* seedling; sowing; seedbed.

semoule *f* semolina.

sénat *m* senate.

sénateur *m* senator.

sénile *adj* senile.

sénilité *f* senility.

sens *m* sense; judgement; consciousness; meaning; direction; **bon ~** good sense.

sensation *f* sensation, feeling.

sensationnel *adj* fantastic, sensational.

sensé *adj* sensible.

sensibiliser *vt* to make sensitive to, heighten awareness of.

sensibilité *f* sensitivity, sensitiveness.

sensible *adj* sensitive; perceptive; appreciable; **~ment** *adv* approximately; noticeably.

sensoriel *adj* sensory.

sensualité *f* sensuality.

sensuel *adj* sensual.

sentence *f* sentence.

sentencieux *adj* sententious.

sentier *m* path, track.

sentiment *m* feeling, sentiment; emotion.

sentimental *adj* sentimental.

sentimentalisme *m* sentimentalism.

sentinelle *f* sentry, sentinel.

sentir *vt* to feel; to perceive, guess; to smell.

séparation *f* separation; division; pulling apart.

séparatiste *mf* separatist.

séparément *adv* separately.

séparer *vt* to separate, divide; to pull off; to split; **se ~** *vr* to separate, divide; to part with.

sept *adj*, *m* seven.

septembre *m* September

septième *adj*, *mf* seventh; **~ment** *adv* in seventh place.

sépulture *f* sepulture, burial.

séquelle *f* gang, crew; after-effects.

séquence *f* sequence.

séquestre *m* sequestration, confiscation.

séquestrer *vt* to sequester, impound.

serein *adj* serene, calm; **~ement** *adv* serenely.

sérénade *f* serenade.

sérénité *f* serenity, calmness.

sergent *m* sergeant; police constable.

série *f* series, string; class; rank.

sérieusement *adv* seriously, responsibly.

sérieux *adj* serious; responsible; * *m* seriousness, reliability.

seringue *f* syringe.

serment *m* oath; pledge.

sermon *m* sermon.

sermonner *vt* to lecture, reprimand.

séropositif *adj* HIV positive, seropositive.

serpe *f* billhook, bill.

serpent *m* serpent, snake.

serpenter *vi* to meander, wind.

serpentin *m* coil, worm (still).

serre *f* greenhouse; claw.

serré *adj* tight; close, compact.

serrer *vt* to tighten, fasten; to clench; **se ~** *vr* to crowd, huddle.

serrure *f* lock.

serrurerie *f* locksmithing.

serrurier *m* locksmith.

sérum *m* serum.

servante *f* servant, maidservant.

serveur *m* waiter, **-euse** *f* waitress.

serviable *adj* obliging, helpful.

service *m* service; function; department; operation; **rendre ~** to do a favour; **~ militaire** national service.

serviette *f* towel; serviette, napkin.

servile *adj* servile, slavish; **~ment** *adv* servilely, slavishly.

servilité *f* servility.

servir *vi* to be of use, be useful; * *vt* to serve, attend to; **se ~ de** to help oneself; **se ~ de** to use, make use of.

servitude *f* servitude; easement.

sésame *m* sesame.

session *f* session, sitting.

seuil *m* threshold.

seul *adj* alone; single; sole; **~ement** *adv* only; but; solely.

sève *f* sap; pith, vigour.

sévère *adj* severe, austere; **~ment** *adv* severely; strictly.

sévérité *f* severity; strictness

sévir *vi* to deal severely; to rage, hold sway.

sevrer *vt* to wean; to deprive.

sexe *m* sex; genitals.

sexiste *mf* sexist; * *adj* sexist.

sexualité *f* sexuality.

sexuel *adj* sexual, sex; **~lement** *adv* sexually.

sexy *adj* sexy.

seyant *adj* becoming.

shampooing *m* shampoo.

shooter *vt* to shoot, make a shot.

shopping *m* shopping.

short *m* shorts.

si *adv* so, so much, however much; yes; * *conj* if; whether.

siamois *adj* Siamese.

sida *m* Aids.

sidéral *adj* sidereal.

sidérer *vt* to flabbergast, stagger.

sidérurgie *f* steel metallurgy

sidérurgique *adj* steel-making.

sidérurgiste *mf* steel maker.

siècle *m* century; period.

siège *m* seat, bench; head office.

siéger *vi* to sit; to be located.

sien *pron*, *pl* **sien**: **le ~ his**, its, his own, its own, **la sienne** her, its, her own, its own, **les ~s**, **les siennes** their, their own.

sieste *f* nap, snooze; siesta.

sifflement *m* whistling; hissing.

siffler *vi* to whistle; to hiss; * *vt* to whistle for; to hiss, boo.

sifflet *m* whistle; catcall.

sigle *m* abbreviation; acronym.

signal *m* signal, sign.

signalement *m* description, particulars.

signaler *vt* to signal, indicate; to point out.

signalisation *f* signalling system; installing signs.

signature *f* signature; signing.

signe *m* sign; mark; indication; symptom.

signer *vt* to sign; to hallmark.

signet *m* bookmark.

significatif *adj* significant, revealing.

signification *f* significance; meaning.

signifier *vt* to mean, signify; to make known; to serve notice.

silence *m* silence; stillness.

silencieusement *adv* silently.

silencieux *adj* silent; still.

silhouette *f* silhouette, outline.

silice *f* silica.

silicone *f* silicone.

sillage *m* wake; slipstream; trail.

sillon *m* furrow; fissure.

sillonner *vt* to plough, furrow; to criss-cross.

silo *m* silo.

similaire adj similar.

similarité f similarity.

similitude f similitude.

simple adj simple; mere; single; common; ~**ment** adv simply, merely.

simplicité f simplicity; simpleness.

simplification f simplification.

simplifier vt to simplify.

simpliste adj simplistic.

simulation f simulation, simulation.

simuler vt to simulate, feign.

simultané adj simultaneous; ~**ment** adv simultaneously.

sincère adj sincere, honest; ~**ment** adv sincerely.

sincérité f sincerity, honesty.

singe m monkey.

singulariser vt to singularize; make conspicuous; **se** ~ vr to make oneself conspicuous.

singularité f singularity; peculiarity.

singulier adj singular, peculiar; remarkable.

singulièrement adv singularly; remarkably.

sinistre m disaster; accident; * adj sinister; ~**ment** adv in a sinister way.

sinistré m, -e f disaster victim; * adj disaster-stricken.

sinon conj otherwise, if not; except.

sinueux adj sinuous, winding.

sinus m sinus; sine.

sinusite f sinusitis.

siphon m siphon.

sirène f mermaid; siren, hooter.

sirop m syrup.

sirupeux adj syrupy.

sismique adj seismic.

site m setting, beauty spot.

sitôt adv so soon, as soon; **pas de** ~ not for a while; ~ **que** as soon as.

situation f situation, position; state of affairs.

situer vt to site, situate; **se** ~ vr to place oneself; to be situated.

six adj, m six.

sixième adj, mf sixth; ~**ment** adv in sixth place.

sketch m sketch.

ski m ski, skiing.

skier vi to ski.

skieur m, -**euse** f skier.

slalom m slalom.

slip m briefs, panties, swimming trunks.

slogan m slogan.

snack(-bar) m snack bar.

snob adj snobbish.

snobisme m snobbery, snobbishness.

sobre adj sober, temperate; ~**ment** adv soberly, temperately.

sobriété f sobriety, temperance.

sobriquet m nickname.

sociable adj sociable; social.

social adj social; ~**ement** adv socially.

social-démocrate mf social democrat; * adj social democrat.

socialisme m socialism.

socialiste mf socialist; * adj socialist.

sociétaire mf associate; member.

société f society; company; partnership.

socio-économique *adj* socio-economic.

sociologie *f* sociology.

sociologique *adj* sociological; **~ment** *adv* sociologically.

sociologue *m* sociologist.

socle *m* socle, plinth; base.

socquette *f* ankle sock.

sodium *m* sodium.

sodomie *f* sodomy.

sœur *f* sister; nun.

sofa *m* sofa.

soi *pron* one(self); self; **~même** oneself, himself, herself, itself; **~disant** so called.

soie *f* silk.

soif *f* thirst.

soigné *adj* neat, well-kept.

soigner *vt* to look after, care for; **se ~** *vr* to take care of oneself.

soigneusement *adv* neatly; carefully.

soigneux *adj* neat; careful.

soin *m* care; attention; trouble.

soir *m* evening; night; afternoon.

soirée *f* evening; evening party.

soit *conj* either; or; whether; * *adv* granted; that is to say.

soixantaine *f* about sixty.

soixante *adj, m* sixty.

soixantième *adj, mf* sixtieth.

soja *m* soya.

sol *m* ground; floor; soil.

solaire *adj* solar.

soldat *m* soldier.

solde *f* pay; * *m* balance; clearance sale.

solder *vt* to pay; to settle, discharge; **se ~** *vr*: **se ~ par** to show (profit, loss).

sole *f* sole; hearth.

soleil *m* sun, sunshine; sunflower.

solennel *adj* solemn; **~lement** *adv* solemnly.

solfège *m* musical theory; sol-fa.

solidaire *adj* jointly and separately liable; interdependent; **~ment** *adv* jointly and severally.

solidarité *f* solidarity.

solide *adj* solid; stable; sound; **~ment** *adv* solidly; soundly.

solidifier *vt* to solidify; **se ~** *vr* to solidify.

solidité *f* solidity; soundness.

soliste *mf* soloist.

solitaire *mf* recluse, hermit; * *adj* solitary, lone; **~ment** *adv* alone.

solitude *f* solitude; loneliness.

sollicitation *f* entreaty, appeal.

solliciter *vt* to seek, solicit; to appeal to.

sollicitude *f* solicitude, concern.

solo *m* solo.

solstice *m* solstice.

soluble *adj* soluble, solvable.

solution *f* solution; solving; answer.

solvable *adj* solvent; creditworthy.

solvant *m* solvent.

somatique *adj* somatic.

sombre *f* dark; gloomy; dismal.

sombrer *vi* to sink, founder.

sommaire *m* summary, argument; * *adj* basic, brief, summary; **~ment** *adv* basically, summarily.

sommation *f* summons; demand.

somme *m* nap, snooze.

sommeil *m* sleep; sleepiness, drowsiness.

sommeiller *vi* to slumber, doze.

sommelier m wine waiter.

sommet m summit; top; crest; apex.

sommier m springs, divan base; ledger.

sommité f leading light, eminent person.

somnambule mf sleepwalker; * adj sleepwalking.

somnifère m sleeping pill, soporific.

somnolent adj sleepy, drowsy.

somnoler vi to doze, drowse.

somptueux adj sumptuous, lavish.

son m sound; * adj, f **sa**; pl **ses** his, her, its.

sonate f sonata.

sondage m drilling; probing; sounding.

sonde f sounding line; probe; drill.

sonder vt to sound; to probe; to drill.

songe m dream.

songer vt to dream; to imagine; to consider.

songeur adj pensive.

sonner vi to ring; to go off; * vt to ring, sound.

sonnerie f ringing, bells; chimes.

sonnette f small bell; house-bell.

sonore adj resonant, deep-toned.

sonorisation f sound recording; sound system.

sonorité f sonority, tone; resonance.

sophistiqué adj sophisticated.

soporifique m sleeping drug; soporific; * adj soporific.

soprano mf soprano.

sorbet m sorbet, water ice.

sorcellerie f witchcraft, sorcery.

sorcier m sorcerer.

sorcière f witch, sorceress.

sordide adj sordid, squalid; **~ment** adv sordidly, squalidly.

sort m fate, destiny, lot.

sortant adj outgoing, retiring.

sorte f sort, kind, manner.

sortie f exit, way out; trip; sortie; outburst; export.

sortilège m spell (magical).

sortir vi to go out, emerge; to result; to escape; **se ~** vr to get out of; to extricate oneself; **s'en ~** to get over, pull through.

sosie m double, second self.

sot adj, f **sotte** silly, foolish; **~tement** adv foolishly, stupidly.

sottise f stupidity; stupid remark, action.

sou m five centimes; cent.

soubresaut m jolt; start.

souche f stump; stock.

souci m worry; concern.

soucier(se) vr: **se ~ de** to care about.

soucieux adj concerned, worried.

soucoupe f saucer.

soudain adj sudden, unexpected; **~ement** adv suddenly.

soude f soda.

souder vt to solder; to weld.

soudeur m, **-euse** f solderer; welder.

soudoyer vt to bribe, buy over.

soudure f soldering, welding.

souffle m blow, puff; breath.

soufflé m soufflé; flabbergasted.

souffler vi to blow; to breathe; to puff.

soufflerie *f* bellows.

soufflet *m* slap in the face; affront.

souffrance *f* suffering; pain; suspense.

souffrant *adj* suffering; in pain.

souffrir *vi* to suffer, be in pain.

souhait *m* wish.

souhaitable *adj* desirable.

souhaiter *vt* to wish for, desire.

souiller *vt* to soil, dirty; to tarnish.

soulagement *m* relief.

soulager *vt* to relieve, soothe.

soulèvement *m* relief.

soulever *vt* to lift, raise; to excite, stir up; **se ~** *vr* to rise; to revolt.

soulier *m* shoe.

souligner *vt* to underline.

soumettre *vt* to subdue, subjugate; to submit, deliver; **se ~** *vr* to subject oneself to.

soumis *adj* submissive.

soumission *f* submission.

soupape *f* valve; safety valve.

soupçon *m* suspicion, conjecture; hint.

soupçonner *vt* to suspect, surmise.

soupçonneux *adj* suspicious.

soupe *f* soup.

soupeser *vt* to feel the weight of; to weigh up.

soupière *f* soup tureen.

soupir *m* sigh; gasp.

soupirail *m* ventilator; basement window.

soupirer *vi* to sigh; to gasp.

souple *adj* supple; pliable; **~ment** *adv* supply, flexibly.

souplesse *f* suppleness; flexibility.

source *f* source; origin; spring.

sourcil *m* eyebrow.

sourd *m*, **-e** *f* deaf person; * *adj* deaf; muted; veiled; **~ement** *adv* dully; silently.

sourdine *f* mute.

sourd(e)-muet(te) *m(f)* deaf-mute; * *adj* deaf and dumb.

souriant *adj* smiling, cheerful.

sourire *vi* to smile, grin.

souris *f* mouse.

sournois *adj* deceitful; sly; **~ement** *adv* deceitfully.

sous *prép* under, beneath, below.

sous-alimenté *adj* undernourished.

sous-bois *m* undergrowth.

sous-chef *m* second-in-command.

souscrire *vi* to subscribe.

sous-développé *adj* underdeveloped.

sous-directeur *m*, **-trice** *f* submanager.

sous-entendre *vt* to imply, infer.

sous-entendu *adj* implied, understood.

sous-estimer *vt* to underestimate.

sous-jacent *adj* subjacent, underlying.

sous-louer *vt* to sublet.

sous-marin *m* submarine; * *adj* underwater.

sous-multiple *adj* submultiple.

sous-officier *m* non-commissioned officer.

sous-préfecture *f* sub-prefecture.

sous-préfet *m* sub-prefect.

soussigné *adj* undersigned.

sous-sol *m* subsoil; basement.

sous-titre *m* subtitle.

sous-titrer *vt* to subtitle.

soustraction *f* subtraction.

soustraire *vt* to subtract; to remove; **se ~ vr: se ~ à** to escape, elude.

sous-traitance *f* subcontracting.

sous-traitant *m* subcontractor.

sous-traiter *vi* to be subcontracted.

sous-vêtement *m* undergarment.

soutane *f* cassock, soutane.

soute *f* hold; baggage hold.

soutenir *vt* to hold up; to sustain; to endure.

souterrain *m* underground passage; * *adj* underground.

soutien *m* support.

soutien-gorge *m* bra.

soutirer *vt* to extract from.

souvenir *m* memory; recollection; reminder.

souvenir(se) *vr* to remember, recollect.

souvent *adv* often, frequently.

souverain *m*, **-e** *f* sovereign; * *adj* sovereign; supreme; **~ement** *adv* supremely.

soyeux *adj* silky.

spacieux *adj* spacious, roomy.

spaghettis *mpl* spaghetti.

sparadrap *m* sticking plaster.

spasme *m* spasm.

spasmophilie *f* spasmophilia.

spatial *adj* spatial; space.

spatule *f* spatula.

spécial *adj* special, particular; **~ement** *adv* specially.

spécialisation *f* specialization.

spécialiser *vt* to specialize; **se ~ vr** to be a specialist.

spécialiste *mf* specialist.

spécialité *f* speciality; specialism.

spécieux *adj* specious.

spécification *f* specification.

spécifier *vt* to specify, determine.

spécifique *adj* specific; **~ment** *adv* specifically.

spécimen *m* specimen; sample.

spectacle *m* spectacle, scene.

spectaculaire *adj* spectacular.

spectateur *m*, **-trice** *f* spectator.

spectre *m* ghost.

spéculateur *m*, **-trice** *f* speculator.

spéculation *f* speculation.

spéculer *vi* to speculate.

spéléologie *f* speleology; caving.

spermatozoïde *m* sperm; spermatozoon.

sperme *m* sperm, semen.

sphère *f* sphere.

sphérique *adj* spherical.

sphinx *m* sphinx.

spirale *f* spiral.

spiritisme *m* spiritualism.

spiritualité *f* spirituality.

spirituel *adj* witty; spiritual; **~lement** *adv* wittily; spiritually.

splendeur *f* splendour, brilliance.

splendide *adj* splendid, magnificent **~ment** *adv* splendidly.

spongieux *adj* spongy.

sponsor *m* sponsor.

sponsoriser *vt* to sponsor.

spontané *adj* spontaneous; **~ment** *adv* spontaneously.

sporadique *adj* sporadic.

sport *m* sport.

sportif *m* sportsman, **-ive** *f* sportswoman; * *adj* sports *compd*; competitive; athletic.

square m square.

squatter vi to squat in.

squelette m skeleton.

squelettique adj skeleton-like, scrawny.

stabiliser vt to stabilize, consolidate; **se ~** vr to stabilize, become stabilized.

stabilité f stability.

stable adj stable, steady.

stade m stadium; stage.

stage m training course; articles; probation.

stagiaire mf trainee.

stagnation f stagnation.

stagner vi to stagnate.

standard m standard; switchboard; * adj standard.

standardiser vt to standardize.

standardiste mf switchboard operator.

star f star.

starter m choke.

station f station; stage, stop; resort; posture.

stationnaire adj stationary.

stationnement m parking.

stationner vi to park.

station-service f service station.

statique adj static.

statistique f statistics; * adj statistical.

statue f statue.

statuer vt to rule, give a verdict.

statu quo m status quo.

statut m statute, ordinance; status.

statutaire adj statutory; **~ment** adv statutorily.

stencil m stencil.

sténodactylo mf shorthand typist.

sténographie f shorthand.

stentor m **une voix de ~** stentorian voice.

steppe f steppe.

stère m stere.

stéréo(phonique) adj stereophonic.

stéréotype m stereotype.

stérile adj sterile, infertile.

stérilet m coil, I.U.D.

stériliser vt to sterilize.

stérilité f sterility.

sternum m breastbone, sternum.

stéroïde adj steroidal; * m steroid.

stigmate m mark, scar; stigmata.

stimulant adj stimulating; * m stimulant, stimulus.

stimulation f stimulation.

stimuler vt to stimulate, spur on.

stipuler vt to stipulate, specify.

stock m stock, supply.

stockage m stocking; stockpiling.

stocker vt to stock, stockpile.

stoïcisme m stoicism.

stoïque adj stoical; **~ment** adv stoically; * mf stoic.

stop m stop; stop sign; brakelight.

stopper vt to stop, halt; * vi to stop, halt.

store m blind, shade.

strabisme m squinting; strabismus.

strapontin m foldaway seat; minor role.

stratégie f strategy.

stratégique adj strategic; **~ment** adv strategically.

stratifié adj strategy.

stress m stress.

stressant adj stressful.

stresser vt to cause stress to.

strict adj strict, severe; **~ement** adv strictly.

strident adj strident, shrill.

strié adj streaked, striped, ridged.

stroboscope m stroboscope.

strophe f verse, stanza.

structural adj structural.

structure f structure.

structurel adj structural.

structurer vt to structure; **se ~** vr to develop a structure.

stuc m stucco.

studieux adj studious.

studio m studio; film theatre.

stupéfaction f stupefaction, amazement.

stupéfait adj astounded, dumbfounded.

stupéfiant adj astounding, amazing; drug, stupefacient.

stupéfier vt to stupefy; to astound.

stupeur f amazement; stupor.

stupide adj stupid, foolish; **~ment** adv stupidly.

stupidité f stupidity.

style m style; stylus.

stylet m stiletto.

styliste mf designer; stylist.

stylo m pen.

su m knowledge.

suave adj suave, smooth.

subalterne mf subordinate; * adj subordinate.

subconscient m subconscious; * adj subconscious.

subdiviser vt to subdivide.

subdivision f subdivision.

subir vt to sustain, support; to undergo, suffer.

subit adj sudden; **~ement** adv suddenly.

subjectif adj subjective.

subjectivement adv subjectively.

subjectivité f subjectivity.

subjonctif m subjunctive; * adj subjunctive.

subjuguer vt to subjugate; to captivate.

sublime adj sublime; * m sublime.

sublimer vt to sublimate.

subliminal adj subliminal.

submerger vt to submerge, flood; to engulf.

submersible m submarine; * adj submarine.

subordination f subordination.

subordonné m, **-e** f subordinate; * adj subordinate.

subordonner vt to subordinate.

subreptice adj surreptitious; **~ment** adv surreptitiously.

subséquent adj subsequent.

subside m grant.

subsidiaire adj subsidiary.

subsistance f subsistence, maintenance, sustenance.

subsister vi to subsist; to live on.

substance f substance.

substantiel adj substantial; **~lement** adv substantially.

substantif m noun, substantive; * adj substantival, nominal.

substituer vt to substitute, replace.

substitut m substitute.

substitution f substitution.

subterfuge m subterfuge.

subtil adj subtle; **~ement** adv subtly.

subtiliser vt to steal, spirit away.

subtilité f subtlety.
subvenir vi: ~ **à** to provide for.
subvention f grant, subsidy.
subventionner vt to subsidize.
subversif adj subversive.
suc m sap; juice.
succéder vi: ~ **à** to succeed, follow; * **se** ~ vr to succeed one another.
succès m success; hit.
successeur m successor.
successif adj successive.
succession f succession; inheritance, estate.
successivement adv successively.
succinct adj succinct; ~**ement** adv succinctly.
succomber vi to succumb, give way.
succulent adj succulent, delicious.
sucursale f branch.
sucer vt to suck.
sucette f lollipop; dummy.
suçon m love bite.
sucre m sugar.
sucrer vt to sugar, sweeten.
sucrerie f sugar refinery.
sucrier m sugar bowl; * adj sugar; sugar-producing.
sud m south.
suer vi to sweat, perspire.
sueur f sweat.
suffire vi to suffice, be sufficient; **il suffit de** it is enough to, it only takes.
suffisamment adv sufficiently, enough.
suffisant adj sufficient, adequate.
suffoquer vi to choke, suffocate; * vt to choke, stifle.

suffrage m suffrage; vote; commendation, approval.
suggérer vt to suggest, put forward.
suggestion f suggestion.
suicidaire adj suicidal; * mf person with suicidal tendencies.
suicide m suicide.
suicider(se) vr to commit suicide.
suie f soot.
suif m tallow.
suintement m oozing; sweating.
suinter vi to ooze; to sweat.
suite f rest; sequel; continuation; series; connection; progress; **tout de** ~ at once; **deux fois de** ~ two times in a row; **et ainsi de** ~ and so on; **à la suite de** after, behind; **par la** ~ afterwards; **donner** ~ **à** to follow up.
suivant, -**e** f next one; attendant; * adj following, next; * prép according to; ~ **que** according to whether.
suivi adj steady, regular; widely adopted; * m follow-up.
suivre vt to follow; to attend, accompany; to exercise; ~ **son cours** to take its course; **à suivre** to be continued; **se** ~ vr to follow each other; to be continuous.
sujet m subject, topic; ground; reason; * adj:**être** ~ **à** to be subject to, liable to.
sujétion f subjection; constraint.
sulfate m sulphate.
sulfater vt to apply copper sulphate.
sulfure m sulphur.
sulfureux adj sulphurous.

sulfurique adj sulphuric.

sultan m sultan, **-e** f sultana.

summum m climax, height.

super m super, four-star petrol; * adj (fam) ultra, super.

superbe adj superb, splendid; **~ment** adv superbly.

supercarburant m high-octane petrol.

supercherie f trick, trickery.

superficie f area, surface.

superficiel adj superficial; **~lement** adv superficially.

superflu adj superfluous.

supérieur adj upper; superior; higher, greater; **~ement** adv exceptionally well.

supériorité f superiority.

superlatif m superlative; * adj superlative.

superposer vt to superpose, stack; to superimpose; **se ~** vr to be superimposed.

superposition f superposing; superimposition.

supersonique adj supersonic.

superstitieux adj superstitious.

superstition f superstition.

superviser vt to supervise.

supplanter vt to supplant, oust.

suppléant m, **-e** f substitute, understudy; * adj substitute.

supplément m supplement; extra charge.

supplémentaire adj supplementary, additional.

suppliant adj beseeching, entreating.

supplication f supplication; entreaty.

supplice m corporal punishment; torture.

supplier vt to beseech, entreat.

support m support, prop; stand.

supporter vt to support; to endure, bear.

supporter m supporter.

supposer vt to suppose; to assume; to imply.

supposition f supposition, surmise.

suppositoire m suppository.

suppression f suppression; deletion; cancellation.

supprimer vt to suppress; to cancel.

suppurer vi to suppurate.

suprématie f supremacy.

suprême adj supreme.

sur prép on; over, above; into; out of, from.

sûr adj sure, certain; secure; **~ de soi** self-assured; **bien ~** of course; **à coup ~** for sure; **~ement** adv surely, certainly.

surabondance f overabundance.

suranné adj outmoded, outdated.

surcharge f overloading; excess; surcharge.

surcharger vt to overload.

surchauffe f overheating.

surcroît m: surplus, excess **de ~** in addition.

surdité f deafness.

sureau m elder tree.

surélever vt to raise, heighten.

surenchérir vi to outbid.

surestimer vt to overestimate; to overvalue.

sûreté f safety; guarantee, surety; **être en ~** to be safe.

surexcité adj overexcited.

surface *f* surface.

surgeler *vt* to deep-freeze.

surgir *vi* to rise, appear; to arise, crop up.

surhomme *m* superman.

surintendant *m* superintendent.

surlendemain *m* day after tomorrow.

surmenage *m* overwork; overtaxing.

surmener *vt* to overwork; **se ~** *vr* to overwork.

surmonter *vt* to surmount, overcome.

surnager *vi* to float.

surnaturel *adj* supernatural.

surnom *m* nickname.

surnommer *vt* to nickname.

surpasser *vt* to surpass, outdo.

surplomb overhang m: **en ~** overhanging.

surplomber *vt* to overhang.

surplus *m* surplus, remainder, excess.

surpopulation *f* overpopulation.

surprenant *adj* surprising, amazing.

surprendre *vt* to surprise, amaze.

surprise *f* surprise.

surproduction *f* overproduction.

surréalisme *m* surrealism.

surréaliste *mf* surrealist; * *adj* surrealistic.

sursaut *m* start, jump.

sursauter *vi* to start, jump.

sursis *m* reprieve; deferment.

sursitaire *adj* deferred; suspended.

surtaxe *f* surcharge.

surtout *adv* especially; above all.

surveillance *f* surveillance; supervision; inspection.

surveillant *m*, **-e** *f* warder, guard.

surveiller *vt* to watch; to supervise; to inspect.

survenir *vi* to take place, occur.

survêtement *m* tracksuit.

survie *f* survival.

survivant *m*, **-e** *f* survivor; * *adj* surviving.

survivre *vi* to survive.

survoler *vt* to fly over.

susceptible *adj* sensitive; susceptible; capable; likely; **être ~ de** to be liable to.

susciter *vt* to arouse, incite.

suspect *m*, **-e** *f* suspect; * *adj* suspicious, suspect.

suspecter *vt* to suspect.

suspendre *vt* to hang up; to suspend, defer.

suspendu *adj* hanging; suspended.

suspens *m*: **en ~** in abeyance; shelved.

suspense *m* suspense.

suspension *f* suspension; deferment; adjournment.

suspicieux *adj* suspicious.

suspicion *f* suspicion.

susurrer *vt* to whisper.

suture *f* suture; **points de ~** stitches.

svelte *adj* svelte, slim.

S.V.P. *abrév* de s'il vous plaît. please.

syllabe *f* syllable.

sylvestre *adj* forest.

symbole *m* symbol

symbolique *adj* symbolic; token; nominal; **~ment** *adv* symbolically.

symboliser vt to symbolize.
symbolisme m symbolism.
symétrie f symmetry.
symétrique adj symmetrical; **~ment** adv symmetrically.
sympa adj invar (fam) nice, friendly.
sympathie f liking; fellow feeling; sympathy.
sympathique adj likeable, nice; friendly.
sympathisant m, -e f sympathizer; * adj sympathizing.
sympathiser vi to get on well with.
symphonie f symphony.
symphonique adj symphonic.
symptomatique adj symptomatic.
symptôme m symptom.
synagogue f synagogue.
synchronisation f synchronization.
synchroniser vt to synchronize.

syncope f blackout, syncope.
syncopé adj syncopated.
syndical adj trade-union.
syndicalisme m trade unionism.
syndicaliste mf trade unionist; * adj trade union.
syndicat m trade union; association.
syndiquer vt to unionize; **se ~** vr to form a trade union.
syndrome m syndrome.
synonyme m synonym; * adj synonymous.
syntaxe f syntax.
synthèse f synthesis.
synthétique adj synthetic.
synthétiser vt to synthesize.
synthétiseur m synthesizer.
syphilis f syphilis.
systématique adj systematic; **~ment** adv systematically.
système m system.

T

tabac m tobacco.
tabagisme m nicotine addiction.
tabatière f snuffbox; skylight.
table f table; **~ de nuit** bedside table; **~ ronde** round-table conference.
tableau m table; chart; timetable; scene; **~ de bord** dashboard.
tablette f bar; tablet; block.
tablier m apron; pinafore; overall.
tabou m taboo.
tabouret m stool.
tache f mark; stain; spot.
tâche f task, assignment; work.
taché adj stained, blemished.

tâcher vi to endeavour.
tacheté adj spotted; freckled.
tachycardie f tachycardia.
tacite adj tacit; **~ment** adv tacitly.
taciturne adj taciturn, silent.
tact m tact; **avoir du ~** to have tact, be tactful.
tactile adj tactile.
tactique f tactics; * adj tactical.
taffetas m taffeta.
tagliatelles fpl tagliatelli.
taillader vt to slash, gash.
taille f height, stature, seize; **de ~** considerable, sizeable; **être de ~ à** to be up to it.

taille-crayons *m* pencil sharpener.

tailler *vt* to cut; to carve; to sharpen; **se ~** *vr* (*fam*) to clear off, split.

tailleur *m* tailor; cutter, hewer.

taillis *m* copse, coppice.

taire *vt* to hush up; to conceal; **se ~** *vr* to be quiet; to fall silent.

talc *m* talc, talcum powder.

talent *m* talent, ability.

talentueux *adj* talented.

talisman *m* talisman.

talon *m* heel; crust; spur.

talonner *vt* to follow closely; to hound.

talquer *vt* to put talcum powder on.

talus *m* embankment.

tambour *m* drum; barrel.

tambourin *m* tambourine.

tambouriner *vi* to drum; to beat, hammer.

tamis *m* sieve; riddle.

tamiser *vt* to sieve; to sift.

tampon *m* stopper, plug; tampon; buffer.

tamponner *vt* to mop up; to stamp.

tam-tam *m* tom-tom; row.

tandem *m* tandem; duo.

tandis *conj*: **~ que** while; whereas.

tangent *adj* tangent, tangential.

tangible *adj* tangible.

tango *m* tango.

tanguer *vi* to pitch (ship).

tanière *f* den, lair.

tank *m* tank.

tanné *adj* tanned; weathered.

tanner *vt* to tan, weather.

tanneur *m* tanner.

tant *adv* so much; **~ que** as long as; **~ soit peu** ever so slightly; **~**

mieux so much the better; that's a good job; **~ pis** too bad; **~ bien que mal** as well as can be expected.

tante *f* aunt.

tantôt *adv* sometimes; this afternoon; shortly.

taon *m* horsefly, gadfly.

tapage *m* din, uproar, racket.

tapageur *adj* noisy, rowdy; showy.

tape *f* slap.

taper *vi* to hit, tap, stamp; to beat down; * *vt* to beat; to slap; to type.

tapioca *m* tapioca.

tapir(se) *vr* to crouch; to hide away.

tapir *m* tapir.

tapis *m* carpet; rug; cloth.

tapisser *vt* to wallpaper; to cover; to carpet.

tapisserie *f* tapestry; tapestry-making; **faire ~** to stand on the sidelines.

tapoter *vt* to pat; to tap; to strum.

taquin *adj* teasing.

taquiner *vt* to tease; to plague.

tarauder *vt* to tap; to thread.

tard *adv* late.

tarder *vi* to delay, put off; to dally.

tardif *adj* late; tardy; slow; backward.

tardivement *adv* late; tardily.

tare *f* tare; defect, flaw.

taré *adj* tainted, corrupt; sickly.

tari *adj* dried up.

tarif *m* tariff; price-list.

tarir *vt* to dry up; to exhaust; **se ~** *vr* to dry up.

tarot *m* tarot.

tartare *adj* Tartar.

tarte *f* tart, flan.

tartelette *f* tartlet, tart.

tartine *f* slice of buttered bread.

tartiner *vt* to spread with butter, jam, etc.

tartre *m* tartar; fur, scale.

tas *m* heap, pile; lot, set.

tasse *f* cup; coffee cup.

tassement *m* settling, sinking.

tasser *vt* to heap up; **se ~** *vr* to sink; subside.

tata *f* auntie.

tâter *vt* to feel, try; **se ~** *vr* to feel oneself.

tâtonnement *m* trial and error; experimentation.

tâtonner *vi* to feel one's way, grope along.

tatouage *m* tattooing; tattoo.

tatouer *vt* to tattoo.

taudis *m* hovel, slum.

taupe *f* mole.

taureau *m* bull.

tauromachie *f* bullfighting.

taux *m* rate; ratio; **~ de change** exchange rate.

taverne *f* tavern.

taxation *f* taxation, taxing.

taxe *f* tax; duty; rate.

taxer *vt* to tax; to fix the price of.

taxi *m* taxi.

tchin-tchin! *interj* cheers!

te *pron* you, yourself.

technicien *m*, **-ienne** *f* technician.

technique *f* technique; * *adj* technical; **-ment** *adv* technically.

technocrate *m* technocrat.

technocratie *f* technocracy.

technologie *f* technology.

technologique *adj* technological.

téflon *m* teflon.

teigne *f* moth.

teindre *vt* to dye.

teint *m* complexion, colouring.

teinte *f* tint, colour, shade.

teinter *vt* to tint; to stain.

teinture *f* dye; dyeing.

teinturerie *f* dyeing; dye-works; dry cleaner's.

teinturier *m*, **-ère** *f* dyer; dry cleaner.

tel *adj* such; like, similar; **~ quel** such as it is; **en tant que ~** as such, in such a capacity; **il n'y a rien de ~** there's nothing like....

télé *f* TV, telly.

télécarte *f* phonecard.

télécommande *f* remote control.

télécommunication *f* telecommunication.

télécopie *f* facsimile transmission; fax.

télécopieur *m* fax machine.

télédiffusion *f* television broadcasting.

téléphérique *m* cableway; cable-car.

télégramme *m* telegram; cable.

télégraphier *vt* to telegraph, cable.

téléguider *vt* to radio-control.

télématique *f* telematics.

téléobjectif *m* telephoto lens.

télépathie *f* telepathy.

téléphone *m* telephone.

téléphoner *vi* to telephone.

téléphonique *adj* telephone; telephonic.

télescope *m* telescope.

télescopique *adj* telescopic.

télésiège *m* chairlift.

téléski m lift, tow.

téléspectateur m, **-trice** f television viewer.

téléviseur m television set.

télévision f television.

télex m telex.

tellement adj so, so much; ~ **de** so many, so much.

téméraire adj rash, reckless; **~ment** adv rashly; recklessly.

témérité f rashness; recklessness.

témoignage m testimony; evidence; certainty.

témoigner vi to testify.

témoin m witness; evidence; proof.

tempérament m constitution; temperament; character.

tempérance f temperance.

température f temperature.

tempéré adj temperate; tempered.

tempérer vt to temper; to assuage, soothe.

tempête f tempest.

temple m temple.

tempo m tempo, pace.

temporaire adj temporary; **~ment** adv temporarily.

temporel adj worldly, temporal.

temporiser vi to temporize, delay.

temps m time; while; tense; beat; weather; **de ~ en ~** from time to time; **entre ~** meanwhile.

tenace adj tenacious, stubborn, persistent; **~ment** adv tenaciously.

ténacité f tenacity; stubbornness.

tenaille f pincers; tongs.

tenailler vt to torture; to rack.

tendance f tendency; leaning; trend.

tendancieux adj tendentious.

tendinite f tendinitis.

tendon m tendon, sinew.

tendre adj tender, soft; delicate; **~ment** adv tenderly, affectionately.

tendresse f tenderness; fondness.

tendu adj tight; stretched; concentrated; delicate, fraught.

ténèbres fpl darkness, gloom.

ténébreux adj dark, gloomy.

teneur f terms; content; grade.

tenir vt to hold, keep; to stock; to run; * vi to hold, stay in place; **à** to value, care about; **~ de** to take after; **se ~** vr to hold on to; to behave; **s'en ~ à** to limit oneself to, stick to.

tennis m tennis; **~ de table** table tennis.

ténor m tenor; leading light.

tentacule m tentacle.

tentant adj tempting, inviting.

tentation f temptation.

tentative f attempt, bid.

tente f tent.

tenter vt to tempt.

tenture f hanging; curtain.

tenue f holding; session; deportment, good behaviour; dress; appearance.

tergal m terylene.

tergiverser vi to procrastinate, beat about the bush.

terme m term; termination, end; word, expression; **au ~ de** the end of.

terminaison f ending.

terminal adj terminal; * m terminal.

terminer *vt* to terminate; to finish off; **se ~** *vr* to terminate; to come to an end.

terminologie *f* terminology.

termite *m* termite.

terne *adj* colourless; lustreless, drab; spiritless.

ternir *vt* to tarnish; to dull.

terrain *m* ground, soil, earth; plot; position; site; field.

terrasse *f* terrace.

terrasser *vt* to floor, knock down; to strike down, overcome.

terre *f* earth; world; ground, land; **mettre pied à ~** to land, alight.

terre à terre *adj* down to earth, commonplace.

terreau *m* compost.

terre-plein *m* terreplein; platform; central reservation.

terrer(se) *vr* to crouch down; to lie low, go to ground.

terrestre *adj* land; terrestrial.

terreur *f* terror, dread.

terreux *adj* earthy; dirty; ashen.

terrible *adj* terrible, dreadful; terrific, great; **~ment** *adv* terribly.

terrien *m* countryman; earthling. **-ienne** *f* countrywoman; earthling.

terrier *m* burrow; earth; terrier.

terrifiant *adj* terrifying, fearsome.

terrifier *vt* to terrify.

terrine *f* earthenware dish, terrine.

territoire *m* territory, area.

territorial *adj* land, territorial.

terroir *m* soil.

terroriser *vt* to terrorize.

terrorisme *m* terrorism.

terroriste *mf* terrorist; * *adj* terrorist.

tertiaire *adj* tertiary.

test *m* test.

testament *m* will, testament.

tester *vt* to test; to make out one's will.

testicule *m* testicle, testis.

tétanos *m* tetanus; lockjaw.

têtard *m* tadpole.

tête *f* head; face; front; top; sense, judgment; **tenir ~** to cope; **faire la ~** to pout, sulk; **~ de turc** whipping boy; **~ de mort** skull and crossbones; **être en ~** to head.

tête à tête *m* private conversation; **en ~** in the lead.

tétée *f* sucking; nursing.

téter *vt* to suck.

tétine *f* teat; udder; dummy.

téton *m* breast.

têtu *adj* headstrong, stubborn.

texte *m* text; theme; passage.

textile *adj* textile.

textuel *adj* textual, literal, exact; **~lement** *adv* literally; word for word.

texture *f* texture.

thé *m* tea.

théâtral *adj* theatrical, dramatic.

théâtre *m* theatre; drama.

théière *f* teapot.

thématique *adj* thematic.

thème *m* theme.

théologie *f* theology.

théorème *m* theorem.

théoricien *m*, **-ienne** *f* theoretician, theorist.

théorie *f* theory.

théorique *adj* theoretical; **~ment** *adv* theoretically.

thérapeute *mf* therapist.

thérapie *f* therapy.

thermal *adj* thermal; hydropathic.

thermique *adj* thermal; thermic.

thermomètre *m* thermometer.

thermos *f/m* thermos.

thermostat *m* thermostat.

thésaurus *m* thesaurus.

thèse *f* thesis.

thon *m* tuna.

thoracique *adj* thoracic; **cage ~** ribcage.

thorax *m* thorax.

thrombose *f* thrombosis.

thym *m* thyme.

thyroïde *f* thyroid.

tibia *m* tibia.

tic *m* twitch, tic; mannerism.

ticket *m* ticket.

tiède *adj* lukewarm, tepid.

tien *pron*, *f* **tienne**: **le ~, la tienne, les ~s, les tiennes** yours, your own.

tiercé *m* tierce.

tiers *adj* third; **~~monde** Third World; * *m* third; third party.

tige *f* stem, stalk.

tigre *m* tiger.

tigresse *f* tigress.

tilleul *m* lime, linden.

timbale *f* kettledrum.

timbre *m* stamp; postmark; bell; tone, timbre.

timbré *adj* stamped; resonant.

timbrer *vt* to stamp; to postmark.

timide *adj* timid, shy; **~ment** *adv* timidly.

timidité *f* timidity, shyness.

timonier *m* (*mar*) helmsman.

tintamarre *m* hubbub, uproar.

tintement *m* ringing; chiming; toll.

tinter *vi* to ring, toll; to chime.

tique *f* tick.

tiquer *vi* to make a face; to wink.

tir *m* shooting, firing, fire; shot; **~ à l'arc** archery.

tirade *f* tirade; monologue.

tirage *m* drawing, drawing off; printing; circulation; friction.

tiraillement *m* tugging; pulling.

tirailler *vt* to tug; to plague; to pester.

tire-bouchon *m* corkscrew.

tire-fesses *m* ski tow.

tirelire *f* moneybox.

tirer *vt* to pull; to draw; to extract; **se ~ vr** (*fam*) to clear off; **bien s'en ~** to make a good job of it.

tiret *m* dash; hyphen.

tireur, -euse *f* gunner, sharpshooter; printer; drawer (of cheque).

tiroir *m* drawer.

tison *m* brand.

tisonnier *m* poker.

tissage *m* weaving.

tisser *vt* to weave.

tissu *m* texture, fabric; tissue.

titan *m* titan.

titane *m* titanium.

titanesque *adj* titanic.

titre *m* title; heading; denomination; claim, right; deed; **à ~ de** by right of; **à juste ~** deservedly, justly; **en ~** titular, acknowledged.

tituber *vi* to stagger.

titulaire *mf* incumbent, holder; * *adj* titular; entitled.

toast m slice of toast; toast; **porter un ~** to drink a toast.

toboggan m toboggan.

toc m tap, knock; imitation jewellery, etc; **en ~** imitation, fake.

toi pron you; **~-même** yourself; **c'est à ~** it's your's; it's your turn.

toile f cloth; canvas; sheet.

toilette f cleaning, grooming; washstand; **faire sa ~** to wash oneself; **cabinet de ~** bathroom.

toiser vt to survey; to evaluate.

toison f fleece.

toit m roof; home.

toiture f roof, roofing.

tôle f sheet metal.

tolérable adj tolerable, bearable.

tolérance f tolerance.

tolérant adj tolerant.

tolérer vt to tolerate; to put up with.

tomate f tomato.

tombe f tomb; grave.

tombeau m tomb.

tomber vi to fall; to sink; to decay; **laisser ~** to drop; **~ malade** to fall sick; **~ amoureux** to fall in love; **~ sur** to come across; **bien/mal ~** to be lucky/unlucky.

tombola f tombola.

tome m book; volume.

ton adj, f **ta**, pl **tes** your; * m tone; pitch; shade.

tonalité f tonality; key.

tondeuse f clippers, shears; mower.

tondre vt to shear, clip; mow.

tonifiant m tonic; * adj bracing; invigorating.

tonifier vt to tone up; to invigorate.

tonique adj tonic; fortifying; invigorating m tonic.

tonitruant adj thundering.

tonnage m tonnage; displacement.

tonne f ton, tonne.

tonneau m barrel, cask.

tonnelle f bower, arbour.

tonnerre m thunder.

tonton m (fam) uncle.

tonus m tone; energy.

top m pip, stroke.

topaze f topaz.

topographie f topography.

toquade f infatuation; fad, craze.

toque f fur hat; cap.

toquer vi to tap, rap.

torche f torch.

torcher vt to wipe, mop up; **se ~** vr to wipe oneself.

torchon m cloth; duster.

tordre vt to twist, contort; **se ~** vr to bend, twist; to sprain.

tordu adj twisted, crooked, bent.

tornade f tornado.

torpeur f torpor.

torpille f torpedo.

torpiller vt to torpedo.

torréfaction f roasting; toasting.

torrent m torrent.

torrentiel adj torrential.

torride adj torrid; scorching.

torsade f twist; cable moulding.

torse m chest; torso.

torsion f twisting; torsion.

tort m fault; wrong; prejudice; **avoir ~** to be wrong; **en ~** in the wrong; **à ~ ou à raison** wrongly or rightly; **faire du ~** to harm;

à ~ et à travers wildly, here there and everywhere.

torticolis m torticollis; stiff neck.

tortiller vt to twist; **se ~** vr to wriggle; to squirm.

tortionnaire mf torturer; * adj pertaining to torture.

tortue f tortoise.

tortueux adj tortuous, winding, meandering.

torture f torture.

torturer vt to torture.

tôt adv early; soon, quickly; **au plus ~** as soon as possible; **plus ~** sooner.

total adj total; absolute; **~ement** adv totally.

totaliser vt to totalize, add up.

totalitaire adj totalitarian.

totalitarisme m totalitarianism.

totalité f totality; whole.

totem m totem.

touchant adj touching, moving.

touche f touch; trial; stroke; key.

toucher vt to touch; to feel; * m touch, feeling.

touffe f tuft, clump.

touffu adj bushy, thick.

toujours adv always; still; all the same; **pour ~** for ever; **~ est-il que** the fact remains that.

toupet m quiff, tuft; cheek.

toupie f spinning top.

tour f tower; * m turn, round; circuit; tour; trick; trick play; **faire un ~** to take a stroll; **faire le tour de** to go around; **fermer à double ~** to double-lock; **jouer un ~** to play a trick; **~ à ~** by turns.

tourbe f peat.

tourbillon m whirlwind, whirlpool.

tourbillonner vi to whirl, eddy.

tourisme m tourism.

touriste mf tourist.

touristique adj tourist.

tourment m torment, agony.

tourmente f storm, tempest.

tourmenter vt to rack, torment; **se ~** vr to fret; to worry.

tournage m turning; (cin) shooting.

tournant m bend; turning point; * adj revolving, swivel; winding.

tournedos m fillet steak.

tournée f tour; round.

tourner vt to turn; to round; * vi to turn; to work; to change; **se ~** vr to turn round; to change.

tournesol m sunflower.

tourneur m turner.

tournevis m screwdriver.

tourniquet m tourniquet; turnstile.

tournis m: sturdy, staggers **avoir le ~** to feel giddy.

tournoi m tournament.

tournoyer vi to whirl, swirl.

tournure f turn; turn of phrase.

tourte f pie.

tourerelle f turtledove.

tourtière f pie tin.

Toussaint f All Saints' Day.

tousser vi to cough.

tout adj, pl **tous, toutes** all; whole; every; **~ le monde** everybody; * pron everything; all; **c'est ~** that is all; * m whole, only thing; **pas du ~** not at all; **du ~ au ~** completely; * adv entirely, quite; **~ droit** straight on; **~ à fait** completely, quite; **~ de suite** immediately.

toutefois adv however.

tout-puissant adj all-powerful.

toux f cough.

toxicomane mf drug addict; * adj drug addicted.

toxicomanie f drug addiction.

toxine f toxin.

toxique adj toxic.

trac m nerves, stage fright.

tracas m bustle, turmoil; worry.

tracasser vt to worry; to harass.

trace f track, impression; outline, sketch; vestige, trace.

tracé m layout, plan.

tracer vt to draw, trace; to open up.

trachée f trachea, windpipe.

tract m leaflet, tract.

tractation f transaction; bargaining.

tracteur m tractor.

traction f traction; pulling.

tradition f tradition.

traditionaliste mf traditionalist; * adj traditionalist.

traditionnel adj traditional; usual; **~lement** adv traditionally.

traducteur m, **-trice** f translator.

traduction f translation.

traduire vt to translate.

trafic m traffic; trading; dealings.

trafiquant m, **-ante** f trafficker.

trafiquer vi to traffic, trade.

tragédie f tragedy.

tragédien m, **-ienne** f tragedian, tragic actor.

tragique adj tragic; **~ment** adv tragically.

trahir vt to betray.

trahison f betrayal, treason.

train m train; pace, rate; **être en ~ de** to be in the act of doing st.

traînasser vi to dawdle; to loiter.

traîne f dragging; train; **être à la ~** to be in tow.

traîneau m sleigh, sledge.

traînée f trail, track; drag.

traîner vi to lag, dawdle; to drag on; * vt to drag, pull; to protract; **se ~** vr to drag oneself; to crawl along.

train-train m humdrum routine.

traire vt to milk.

trait m trait, feature; deed; relation; **avoir ~ à** to have reference; **~ d'union** hyphen, connecting link.

traite f trade; draft, bill; milking.

traité m treaty; treatise, tract.

traitement m treatment; salary, processing.

traiter vt to treat; to process; * vi to treat, negotiate.

traiteur m caterer; trader.

traître m traitor, **-esse** f traitress.

traîtrise f treachery, treacherousness.

trajectoire f trajectory.

trajet m distance; journey; course, path.

trame f framework; web.

tramer vt to plot; to weave.

trampoline m trampoline.

tramway m tram, tramway.

tranchant adj sharp, cutting.

tranche f slice; edge; section.

tranchée f trench; cutting.

trancher vt to cut, sever; to conclude; to settle; * vi to cut; to resolve; to stand out.

tranquille *adj* quiet, tranquil;
~**ment** *adv* quietly, tranquilly.

tranquillisant *m* tranquillizer; * *adj*
soothing, tranquillizing.

tranquilliser *vt* to reassure.

tranquillité *f* tranquillity.

transaction *f* transaction, arrangement.

transatlantique *m* transatlantic
liner; * *adj* transatlantic.

transcendant *adj* transcendent;
transcendental.

transcender *vt* to transcend.

transcription *f* transcription; copy.

transcrire *vt* to transcribe; copy out.

transe *f* trance.

transept *m* transept.

tranférer *vt* to transfer.

transfert *m* transfer; conveyance.

transfiguration *f* transfiguration.

transfigurer *vt* to transfigure.

transformateur *m* transformer.

transformation *f* transformation.

transformer *vt* to transform,
change; **se ~** *vr* to be transformed; to change.

transfuge *mf* renegade.

transfuser *vt* to transfuse.

transfusion *f* transfusion.

transgresser *vt* to transgress, infringe.

transgression *f* transgression,
infringement.

transi *adj* numb, paralysed.

transiger *vi* to compromise, come
to terms.

transistor *m* transistor.

transit *m* transit.

transiter *vi* to pass in transit.

transitif *adj* transitive.

transition *f* transition.

transitoire *adj* transitory.

translucide *adj* translucent.

transmettre *vt* to transmit; to pass
on, hand down.

transmissible *adj* transmissible.

transmission *f* transmission; passing on; handing down.

transmuter *vt* to transmute.

transparaître *vi* to show through.

transparence *f* transparency.

transparent *adj* transparent.

transpercer *vt* to pierce; to penetrate.

transpiration *f* transpiration; perspiration.

transpirer *vi* to perspire; to come
to light.

transplanter *vt* to transplant.

transport *m* carrying; transport;
conveyance; transfer.

transportable *adj* transportable.

transporter *vt* to carry; to transport

transporteur *m* haulier; carrier.

transposer *vt* to transpose.

transposition *f* transposition.

transsexuel *adj* transsexual.

transvaser *vt* to decant.

transversal *adj* transverse; ~**ement**
adv crosswise; transversely.

transvider *vt* to pour into another
container.

trapèze *m* trapeze.

trapéziste *mf* trapeze artist.

trappe *f* trap door.

trappeur *m* trapper.

trapu *adj* squat; thickset.

traquer *vt* to track; to hunt down.

traumatisant *adj* traumatizing.

traumatiser *vt* to traumatize.

traumatisme m traumatism.

travail m work; job, occupation; labour pl **travaux** work, labour.

travailler vi to work; to endeavour; * vt to work, shape; to cultivate; to fatigue.

travailleur m, **-euse** f worker; * adj diligent; hard-working.

travers m breadth; irregularity; fault; à ~ through, across; de ~ obliquely, askew; en ~ across, crosswise.

traversée f crossing, going through; traverse.

traverser vt to cross, traverse.

traversin m bolster.

travesti m drag artist; transvestite; * adj disguised.

trébucher vi to stumble, trip up.

trèfle m clover.

tréfonds m subsoil, bottom.

treille f climbing vine.

treillis m trellis; wire mesh.

treize adj, m thirteen.

treizième adj, mf thirteenth; **~ment** adv in thirteenth place.

tréma m dieresis.

tremblant adj trembling, shaking.

tremblement m trembling; shiver; vibration; ~ **de terre** earthquake.

trembler vi to tremble, shake.

trembloter vi to tremble slightly, flicker.

trémousser(se) vr to wriggle.

tremper vt to soak; to dip; * vi to soak; to take part in.

tremplin m springboard; ski-jump.

trentaine f about thirty.

trente adj, m thirty.

trentième adj, mf thirtieth.

trépasser vi to pass away.

trépidant adj pulsating, quivering.

trépied m tripod.

trépigner vi to stamp one's feet.

très adv very; most; very much.

trésor m treasure.

trésorerie f treasury.

trésorier m, **-ière** f treasurer.

tressaillir vi to thrill; to shudder; to wince.

tressauter vi to start, jump.

tresse f plait, braid.

tresser vt to plait, braid.

tréteau m trestle.

treuil m winch.

trêve f truce; respite, rest.

tri m sorting out; selection; grading.

triage m sorting out.

triangle m triangle.

triangulaire adj triangular.

triathlon m triathlon.

tribal adj tribal.

tribord m starboard.

tribu f tribe.

tribunal m court, tribunal.

tribune f gallery, stand; rostrum.

tribut m tribute.

tributaire adj dependent, tributary.

tricher vi to cheat.

tricheur m, **-euse** f cheater.

trichloréthylène m trichlorethylene.

tricolore adj three-coloured, tricolour.

tricot m jumper; knitting.

tricoter vt to knit.

tridimensionnel *adj* three-dimensional.

triennal *adj* triennial; three-yearly.

trier *vt* to sort out; to pick over.

trifouiller *vi (fam)* to rummage about; * *vt* to rummage about in.

trigonométrie *f* trigonometry.

trilingue *adj* trilingual.

trilogie *f* trilogy.

trimer *vi* to slave away.

trimestre *m* quarter; term.

trimestriel *adj* quarterly; three-monthly.

tringle *f* rod.

trinité *f* trinity.

trinquer *vi* to toast; to booze.

trio *m* trio.

triomphal *adj* triumphal; **~ement** *adv* triumphantly.

triomphant *adj* triumphant.

triomphe *m* triumph, victory.

triompher *vi* to triumph.

triparti, tripartite *adj* tripartite.

tripe *f* tripe; guts.

triple *adj* triple, treble.

tripler *vi* to triple, increase threefold; * *vt* to triple, treble.

tripoter *vt* to play with, speculate with.

trique *f* cudgel.

triste *adj* sad, melancholy; **~ment** *adv* sadly.

tristesse *f* sadness; melancholy.

triton *m* triton; tritone.

triturer *vt* to grind up, triturate.

trivial *adj* mundane, trivial; coarse, crude.

trivialité *f* triviality; crudeness.

troc *m* exchange; barter.

troglodyte *m* cave dweller, troglodyte.

trognon *m* core; stalk.

trois *adj*, *m* three.

troisième *adj*, *mf* third; **~ment** *adv* thirdly.

trombe *f*: **~ d'eau** cloudburst, downpour; **entrer/sortir en ~** to dash in/out.

trombone *m* trombone.

trompe *f* trumpet; trunk, snout.

trompe-l'œil *m invar* trompe-l'œil.

tromper *vt* to deceive, trick; **se ~** *vr* to be mistaken.

tromperie *f* deception, deceit.

trompette *f* trumpet.

trompettiste *mf* trumpet player.

trompeur *adj* deceitful; deceptive.

tronc *m* trunk, shaft.

tronçon *m* section, part.

tronçonner *vt* to cut up, cut into sections.

tronçonneuse *f* chain saw.

trône *m* throne.

trôner *vi* to sit on the throne.

tronquer *vt* to truncate, curtail.

trop *adv* too; too much, unduly; *m* **~** too much, too many.

trophée *m* trophy.

tropical *adj* tropical.

tropique *m* tropic.

trop-plein *m* overflow; excess.

troquer *vt* to barter, swap.

trot *m* trot.

trotter *vi* to trot; to run about; to toddle.

trottiner *vi* to jog along; to trot along.

trottinette f scooter.

trottoir m pavement.

trou m hole; gap; cavity.

troublant adj disturbing, disquieting.

trouble adj unclear; murky, suspicious; * m disturbance, confusion; disorder.

trouble-fête mf spoilsport, killjoy.

troubler vt to disturb, disconcert; to cloud, darken; **se ~** vr to become cloudy; to become flustered.

trouer vt to make a hole in; to pierce.

trouille f: **avoir la ~** to have the wind up.

troupe f troupe; troop, band.

troupeau m herd, drove.

trousse f case, kit; wallet.

trousseau m trousseau; outfit.

trouvaille f windfall; inspired idea.

trouver vt to find, detect; to think; **se ~** vr to find oneself; to be located; **il se trouve que** it happens that.

truand m (fam) gangster; tramp.

truc m (fam) trick; gadget, thingummy.

truculent adj truculent; colourful, vivid.

truelle f trowel.

truffe f truffle.

truie f sow.

truite f trout.

truquage m rigging, fixing; fiddling.

truquer vt to rig, fix; to fiddle.

tsar m tsar.

tu pron you.

tuant adj exhausting; exasperating.

tuba m tuba, snorkel.

tube m tube, pipe; duct.

tuberculose f tuberculosis.

tuer vt to kill; **se ~** vr to be killed; to kill oneself.

tuerie f slaughter.

tueur m, **-euse** f killer.

tuile f tile.

tulipe f tulip.

tulle m tulle.

tuméfié adj puffed-up, swollen.

tumeur f tumour.

tumulte m tumult, commotion.

tumultueux adj tumultuous, stormy.

tungstène m tungsten.

tunique f tunic; smock.

tunnel m tunnel.

turban m turban.

turbine f turbine.

turbo m turbo.

turbulence f turbulence; excitement.

turbulent adj turbulent.

turpitude f turpitude, baseness.

tutelle f guardianship, supervision.

tuteur m, **-trice** f guardian; * m stake, prop.

tutoyer vt to address somebody as 'tu'.

tuyau m pipe.

tuyauterie f piping.

T.V.A. (taxe à la valeur ajoutée) f VAT.

tympan m eardrum, tympanum.

type m type; model; sample; bloke, chap.

typé adj typical.

typhoïde f typhoid; * adj typhoid.

typhon m typhoon.

typhus *m* typhus.

typique *adj* typical; **~ment** *adv*
typically.

tyran *m* tyrant.

tyrannie *f* tyranny.

tyrannique *adj* tyrannical.

tyranniser *vt* to tyrannize.

U

ulcère *m* ulcer.

ulcérer *vt* to sicken; to embitter.

ultérieur *adj* later, subsequent;
~ement *adv* later, subsequently.

ultimatum *m* ultimatum.

ultime *adj* ultimate, final.

ultra-violet *m* ultraviolet ray; * *adj*
ultraviolet.

un, une *art* a, an; (number) one;
les ~ some; **l'~ l'autre, les ~s les
autres** one another.

unanime *adj* unanimous; **~ment**
adj unanimously.

uni *adj* plain, self-coloured; close;
smooth; **~ment** *adv* plainly,
smoothly.

unification *f* unification; standardization.

unifier *vt* to unify; to standardize.

uniforme *adj* uniform, regular; * *m*
uniform.

uniformément *adv* uniformly, regularly.

uniformité *f* uniformity; regularity.

unilatéral *adj* unilateral.

union *f* union; combination, blending.

unique *adj* only, single; unique;
~ment *adv* only, solely, exclusively; only, merely.

unir *vt* to unite; to join; to combine; **s'~** *vt* to unite; to be joined
in marriage.

unisson *m* unison; **à l'~** in unison.

unitaire *adj* unitary, unit.

unité *f* unity; unit.

univers *m* universe; world.

universalité *f* universality.

universel *adj* universal; all-pur-
pose; **~lement** *adv* univer-
sally.

universitaire *adj* university; * *mf*
academic.

université *f* university.

uranium *m* uranium.

urbain *adj* urban, city.

urbanisation *f* urbanization.

urbaniser *vt* to urbanize.

urbanisme *m* town planning.

urbaniste *mf* town planner.

urée *f* urea.

urgence *f* urgency; emergency.

urgent *adj* urgent.

urinaire *adj* urinary.

urine *f* urine.

uriner *vi* to urinate.

urne *f* ballot box; urn.

urticaire *f* hives, urticaria.

usage *m* use; custom; usage; practice; wear; **faire ~ de** to exercise;
to make use of.

usagé *adj* worn, old; second-hand.

usager *m* ère *f* user.

usé *adj* worn; threadbare; banal,
trite.

user *vt* to make use of, enjoy; to

wear out; **~ de** to exercise; to employ; **s'~** *vr* to wear out.
usine *f* factory.
usiner *vt* to machine; to manufacture.
usité *adj* in common use, common.
ustensile *m* implement; utensil.
usuel *adj* ordinary; everyday; **~lement** *adv* ordinarily.
usufruit *m* usufruct.
usure *f* usury.
usurier *m*, **-ière** *f* usurer.

usurper *vt* to usurp.
utérus *m* womb, uterus.
utile *adj* useful; **~ment** *adv* usefully.
utilisateur *m*, **-trice** *f* user.
utilisation *f* use, utilization.
utiliser *vt* to use, utilize; to make use of.
utilitaire *adj* utilitarian.
utilité *f* usefulness; use; profit.
utopie *f* utopia.
utopique *adj* utopian.

V

vacance *f* vacancy; **~s** holiday, vacation.
vacancier *m*, **-ière** *f* holidaymaker.
vacant *adj* vacant, unoccupied.
vacarme *m* racket, row.
vaccin *m* vaccine.
vaccination *f* vaccination.
vacciner *vt* to vaccinate.
vache *f* cow; cowhide.
vachement *adv* (*fam*) damned, bloody.
vacher *m*, **-ère** *f* cowherd.
vacherie *f* (*fam*) rottenness, meanness; nasty remark/trick.
vaciller *vi* to sway, totter; to falter.
va-et-vient *m invar* comings and goings; to and fro.
vagabond *m*, **-e** *f* tramp, vagabond.
vagabondage *m* wandering, roaming; vagrancy.
vagabonder *vi* to wander, roam.
vagin *f* vagina.
vaginal *adj* vaginal.

vague *adj* vague, hazy, indistinct; **~ment** *adv* vaguely; * *m* vagueness; * *f* wave.
vaguer *vi* to wander, roam.
vaillamment *adv* bravely, courageously.
vaillant *adj* brave, courageous.
vain *adj* vain; empty; hollow; shallow; **en ~** in vain; **~ement** *adv* vainly.
vaincre *vt* to defeat, overcome.
vaincu *adj* defeated, beaten.
vainqueur *m* conqueror, victor.
vaisseau *m* vessel; ship.
vaisselle *f* crockery; dishes; **faire la ~** to do the washing up.
valable *adj* valid, legitimate; worthwhile.
valet *m* valet; servant.
valeur *f* value, worth; security; share; meaning.
valide *adj* able, able-bodied; **~ment** *adv* validly.
valider *vt* to validate.

validité f validity.

valise f suitcase.

vallée f valley.

vallon m vale, dale.

vallonné adj undulating.

valoir vt to be worth; to be valid; **il vaut mieux** it is better to; **~ la peine** to be worth the trouble.

valoriser vt to develop; to enhance; to actualize.

valse f waltz.

valser vi to waltz.

valve f valve.

vampire m vampire.

vandale mf vandal.

vandalisme m vandalism.

vanille f vanilla.

vanité f vanity, conceit.

vaniteux adj vain, conceited.

vanne f gate, sluice.

vannerie f basketry; wickerwork.

vantard adj boastful, bragging.

vantardise f boastfulness; boast.

vanter vt to praise, vaunt; **se ~** vr to boast, brag.

vapeur f haze, vapour.

vaporeux adj filmy, vaporous.

vaporisateur m spray, atomizer.

vaporiser vt to spray; to vaporize.

varappe f rock-climbing.

variable adj variable, changeable.

variante f variant; variation.

variation f variation, change.

varice f varicose vein.

varicelle f chickenpox.

varié adj varied; variegated; various.

varier vi to vary, change; * vt to vary.

variété f variety, diversity.

variole f smallpox.

vasculaire adj vascular.

vase m vase, bowl; * f silt, mud.

vaseline f vaseline.

vaseux adj woolly, muddled; muddy, silty.

vasistas m fanlight.

vaste adj vast, huge.

vaudeville m vaudeville.

vaudou m voodoo.

vaurien m, **-ienne** f good-for-nothing.

vautour m vulture.

vautrer(se) vr to wallow in.

veau m calf; veal.

vecteur m vector.

vécu adj real, true-life; lived; * m real-life.

vedette f star; leading light.

végétal adj vegetable.

végétarien m, **-ienne** f vegetarian; * adj vegetarian.

végétatif adj vegetative.

végétation f vegetation.

végéter vi to vegetate; to stagnate.

véhémence f vehemence.

véhément adj vehement.

véhicule m vehicle.

veille f wakefulness; watch; eve.

veillée f evening; evening meeting.

veiller vi to stay up, sit up.

veilleur m watchman.

veilleuse f night light; sidelight.

veinard m, **-e** f lucky person; * adj lucky, jammy.

veine f vein, seam; inspiration; luck.

vêler vi to calve.

velléité f vague desire, vague impulse.

vélo m cycle.

vélodrome m velodrome.

vélomoteur m motorized bike.

velours m velvet.

velouté adj velvety, downy.

velu adj hairy.

vénal adj venal, mercenary.

vendange f wine harvest; vintage.

vendanger vt to harvest grapes from; * vi to harvest the grapes.

vendangeur m, **-euse** f grape-picker.

vendetta f vendetta.

vendeur m, **-euse** f seller, sales-person.

vendre vt to sell.

vendredi m Friday.

vénéneux adj poisonous.

vénérable adj venerable.

vénération f veneration.

vénérer vt to venerate.

vénérien adj venereal.

vengeance f vengeance, revenge.

venger vt to avenge; **se ~** vr to avenge oneself.

venimeux adj venomous, poisonous; vicious.

venin m venom; poison.

venir vi to come; to happen; to grow; **~ de** to come from; to derive from; **~ au monde** to be born.

vent m wind; breath; emptiness, vanity.

vente f sale; selling; auction; **en ~** for sale.

ventilateur m ventilator, fan.

ventiler vt to ventilate; to divide up.

ventouse f sucker; suction disc.

ventre m stomach, belly; womb.

ventricule m ventricle.

ventriloque mf ventriloquist; * adj ventriloquous.

venue f coming.

ver m worm; grub; **~ de terre** earthworm.

véracité f veracity; truthfulness.

véranda f veranda.

verbal adj verbal; **~ement** adv ver-bally.

verbe m verb; language, word.

verbiage m verbiage.

verdeur f vigour, vitality.

verdict m verdict.

verdir vi to go green; * vt to turn green.

verdure f greenery, verdure.

verge f stick, cane.

verger m orchard.

verglas m black ice.

véridique adj truthful, veracious; **~ment** adv truthfully.

vérification f check; verification.

vérifier vt to verify, check; to audit.

véritable adj real, genuine; **~ment** adv really, genuinely.

vérité f truth; truthfulness, sincer-ity; **en ~** really, actually.

vermeil adj vermilion, ruby, cherry; * m vermeil.

vermicelle m vermicelli.

vermillon m vermilion; scarlet.

vermine f vermin.

vermisseau m vermicule, small worm.

vermoulu adj worm-eaten.

verni adj varnished.

vernis m varnish; glaze; shine.

vernissage m varnishing; glazing.

verre m glass; lens; drink.

verrerie f glassworks; glass-making.

verrière f window; glass roof.

verrou m bolt.

verrouillage m bolting; locking.

verrouiller vt to bolt; to lock.

verrue f wart, verruca.

vers prép towards; around; about; * m line, verse.

versatile adj versatile.

verse f: pleuvoir à ~ to pour down.

verseau m Aquarius.

verser vt to pour, shed; to pay; to assign.

verset m verse.

version f version.

verso m back.

vert m green; * adj green; **langue ~e** slang; **~ement** adv sharply, brusquely.

vertébral adj vertebral.

vertèbre f vertebra.

vertical adj vertical; **~ement** adv vertically.

vertige m vertigo; dizziness.

vertigineux adj vertiginous, breath-taking.

vertu f virtue; courage; **en ~ de** in accordance with.

vertueux adj virtuous.

verve f verve, vigour.

verveine f vervain, verbena.

vésicule f vesicle.

vessie f bladder, vesica.

veste f jacket.

vestiaire m cloakroom; changing-room.

vestibule m hall, vestibule.

vestige m relic; trace, vestige.

veston m jacket.

vêtement m garment.

vétéran m veteran.

vétérinaire mf veterinary surgeon; * adj veterinary.

vêtir vt to clothe, dress; **se ~** vr to dress oneself.

veto m veto.

vêtu adj dressed; clad, wearing.

vétuste adj dilapidated, ancient.

veuf m widower; * adj widowed.

veuve f widow; * adj widowed.

veule adj spineless.

vexant adj annoying, vexing.

vexer vt to annoy; to hurt.

viable adj viable.

viaduc m viaduct.

viande f meat.

vibration f vibration.

vibrer vi to vibrate; to quiver.

vibromasseur m vibrator.

vicaire m curate, vicar.

vice m vice; fault, defect.

vice-président m vice-president; deputy chairman.

vice-versa adv vice versa.

vicieux adj licentious; dissolute; incorrect.

vicissitude f vicissitude, change; trial.

vicomte m viscount, **-esse** f viscountess.

victime f victim, casualty; **être ~ de** to be the victim of.

victoire f victory.

victorieusement adv victoriously.

victorieux adj victorious.

vidange f emptying; waste outlet.

vidanger vt to empty; to drain off.

vide adj empty, vacant, devoid; * m vacuum; gap; void.

vidéo f video; * adj invar video.

vidéocassette f videocassette.

vide-ordures m invar rubbish chute.

vider vt to empty; to drain; to vacate; to gut.

videur m bouncer.

vie f life; living; **être en ~** to be alive.

vieillard m old man.

vieillesse f old age; the elderly; oldness.

vieillir vi to get old; * vt to age; to put years on.

vieillissement m ageing; obsolescence.

vierge f virgin; * adj virgin; blank; unexposed.

vieux adj, f **vieille** old; ancient; obsolete.

vif adj alive, lively; quick; eager, passionate.

vigilance f vigilance.

vigilant adj vigilant.

vigile m vigil.

vigne f vine; vineyard.

vigneron m, **-onne** f wine grower.

vignette f vignette; illustration; seal.

vignoble m vineyard.

vigoureusement adv vigorously, energetically.

vigoureux adj vigorous.

vigueur f vigour, strength, energy.

vil adj vile; lowly.

vilain m naughty boy, **-e** f naughty girl.

villa f villa, detached house.

village m village.

villageois m, **-e** f village, rustic.

ville f town, city.

villégiature f holiday; vacation.

vin m wine.

vinaigre m vinegar.

vinaigrette f vinaigrette, oil and vinegar dressing.

vindicatif adj vindictive.

vingt adj, m twenty.

vingtaine f about twenty.

vingtième adj, mf twentieth; **~ment** adv in twentieth place.

vinicole adj wine, wine-growing.

vinyl m vinyl.

viol m rape.

violation f violation; transgression.

violemment adv violently.

violence f violence; force, duress.

violent adj violent; considerable, excessive.

violer vt to violate, desecrate; to rape.

violet adj purple, violet; * m purple, violet.

violette f (bot) violet.

violeur m rapist.

violon m violin.

violoncelle m cello, violoncello.

violoncelliste mf cello player.

violoniste mf violinist.

vipère f viper, adder.

virage m turn, bend; tacking.

viral adj viral.

virement m turning, tacking; transfer, clearance.

virer vt to transfer; * vi to turn, tack.

virevolter vi to spin round, pirouette.

virginité f virginity; purity.

virgule f comma; point.

viril *adj* virile; male, masculine;
  ~ement *adv* in a virile way.
virilité *f* virility; masculinity.
virtuel *adj* virtual; potential;
  ~lement *adv* virtually.
virtuose *mf* virtuoso, master.
virulence *f* virulence, viciousness.
virulent *adj* virulent, vicious.
virus *m* virus.
vis *f* screw.
visa *m* stamp, visa.
visage *m* face; expression.
vis-à-vis *prép*: opposite; **~ de** towards; as regards; * *m* encounter; person opposite; **en ~** opposite each other.
viscéral *adj* visceral; deep-rooted.
viscère *m* viscera; intestines.
viser *vt* to aim, target; to visa.
viseur *m* sights; viewfinder.
visibilité *f* visibility.
visible *adj* visible; evident, obvious; **~ment** *adv* visibly; obviously.
visière *f* peak; eyeshade; visor.
vision *f* eyesight; vision.
visionnaire *mf* visionary; * *adj*
  visionary.
visite *f* visit; visiting, inspection;
  visitor.
visiter *vt* to visit; to examine, inspect.
visiteur *m*, **-euse** *f* visitor; representative.
vison *m* mink.
visqueux *adj* viscous, thick.
visser *vt* to screw on.
visuel *adj* visual.
vital *adj* vital.
vitalité *f* energy, vitality.
vitamine *f* vitamin.

vite *adv* quickly, fast; soon. *adj*
  swift; quick.
vitesse *f* speed, swiftness; gear.
viticole *adj* wine, wine-growing.
viticulteur *m* wine grower.
vitrage *m* glazing; windows.
vitrail *m* stained-glass window.
vitre *f* pane, window.
vitreux *adj* glassy, glazed, vitre-
  ous.
vitrier *m* glazier.
vitrine *f* shop window; display
  cabinet.
vitriol *m* vitriol.
vitupérer *vi* to vituperate, reprimand.
vivace *adj* inveterate, steadfast;
  hardy, perennial.
vivacité *f* vivacity, liveliness; vivid-
  ness; acuteness.
vivant *adj* alive, living; lively.
vivement *adv* quickly, briskly;
  keenly, acutely.
vivier *m* fishpond.
vivifiant *adj* refreshing, invigorating.
vivifier *vt* to enliven, invigorate,
  refresh.
vivre *vi* to live, be alive; to last, endure; **vive la mariée!** three
  cheers for the bride; * *vt* to live,
  spend; to live through.
vivres *mpl* victuals, supplies.
V.O. (version originale) *f* original
  version.
vocabulaire *m* vocabulary.
vocal *adj* vocal; **~ement** *adv* voc-
  ally.
vocalise *f* singing exercise.
vocation *f* vocation, calling.

vociférer *vi* to vociferate, bawl.

vœu *m* vow; wish.

vogue *f* fashion, vogue; **en ~ in** fashion.

voici *prép* here is, here are; ago, past.

voie *f* way, road; means; process; **~ ferrée** railway; **~ d'eau** leak; **en ~ de** in the process of.

voilà *prép* there is, there are; ago; **et ~!** so there!

voile *f* sail; * *m* veil.

voilé *adj* veiled; hazy, blurred.

voiler *vt* to veil, shroud; **se ~** *vr* to wear a veil; to mist over.

voilier *m* sailing boat, yacht.

voir *vt* to see; to deal with; to understand; **avoir à ~ avec** to have to do with; **se ~** *vr* to find oneself; to show.

voisin *m*, **-e** *f* neighbour; fellow; * *adj* neighbouring, next.

voisinage *m* neighbourhood, vicinity.

voiture *f* car; carriage; cart.

voix *f* voice; vote; **parler à ~ basse/haute** to speak in a low/ high voice.

vol *m* flight; flock; **à ~ d'oiseau** as the crow flies.

volaille *f* fowl, poultry.

volant *m* steering wheel; * *adj* flying.

volatile *adj* volatile.

volatiliser *vt* to volatilize; to extinguish; **se ~** *vr* to volatilize; to vanish.

volcan *m* volcano.

volcanique *adj* volcanic.

volée *f* flight; volley; **à la ~ in** mid-

air; rashly, at random; **demi-~** half-volley.

voler *vi* to fly; **~ en éclats** to smash into pieces; * *vt* to steal; to rob.

volet *m* shutter; flap, paddle.

voleur *m*, **-euse** *f* thief; * *adj* dishonest, thieving.

volley-ball *m* volleyball.

volleyeur *m*, **-euse** *f* volleyball player.

volontaire *adj* voluntary; intentional; **~ment** *adv* voluntarily; intentionally.

volonté *f* will, wish; willingness; willpower.

volontiers *adv* willingly; gladly.

volt *m* volt.

volte-face *f invar* volte-face, about-turn **faire ~** to turn round.

voltige *f* acrobatics; trick riding.

voltiger *vi* to flutter about.

volubile *adj* voluble.

volume *m* volume.

volumineux *adj* voluminous, bulky.

volupté *f* voluptuousness, sensual pleasure.

voluptueux *adj* voluptuous.

volute *f* volute, scroll; wreath.

vomir *vi* to vomit, be sick; * *vt* to vomit, bring up.

vomissement *m* vomiting.

vorace *adj* voracious; **~ment** *adv* voraciously.

voracité *f* voracity, voraciousness.

vos = *pl* **votre**.

votant *m*, **-e** *f* voter.

vote *m* vote; voting.

voter *vi* to vote.

votre *adj*, *pl* **vos** your, your own.

vôtre *pron*: le ~, la ~, les ~s yours, your own.

vouer *vt* to vow; to devote, dedicate.

vouloir *vt* to want, wish; to require; to try; ~ **du mal à** to wish somebody harm; **en ~ à** to have something against somebody; **bien ~ to** be happy that.

voulu *adj* required; deliberate.

vous *pron* you, you yourself.

voûte *f* vault.

voûté *adj* vaulted.

vouvoyer *vt* to use the 'vous' form.

voyage *m* journey, trip; travelling.

voyager *vi* to travel, journey.

voyageur *m*, **-euse** *f* traveller, passenger.

voyant *m*, **-e** *f* visionary, seer; * *m* signal light; * *adj* gaudy, showy.

voyelle *f* vowel.

voyeur *m*, **-euse** *f* voyeur.

voyou *m* lout, loafer, hoodlum.

vrac *adv*: **en ~** in bulk.

vrai *adj* true, genuine; ~**ment** *adv* truly, really.

vraisemblable *adj* likely, probable; ~**ment** *adv* probably.

vrille *f* tendril; spiral; **descendre en ~** to come down in a spin.

vrombir *vi* to roar, hum.

vu *adj* seen; considered, regarded; **être bien/mal ~** to be well/poorly thought of; **ni ~ ni connu** you won't discover anything; * *prép* in view of.

vue *f* sight, eyesight; **en ~ de** with a view to; **avoir des ~s sur** to have designs on.

vulgaire *adj* vulgar, crude; ~**ment** *adv* vulgarly.

vulgariser *vt* to popularize; to coarsen.

vulgarité *f* vulgarity, coarseness.

vulnérable *adj* vulnerable.

vulve *f* vulva.

WXYZ

wagon *m* wagon, truck, freight car; wagonload.

wagon-citerne *m* tanker.

wagon-lit *m* sleeper.

wagon-restaurant *m* restaurant car.

water-polo *m* water polo.

watt *m* watt.

W.-C. (water-closet) *mpl* lavatory.

week-end *m* weekend.

western *m* western.

whisky *m* whisky.

xénophobe *mf* xenophobe; * *adj* xenophobic.

xénophobie *f* xenophobia.

xylophone *m* xylophone.

yacht *m* yacht.

yang *m* yang.

yaourt *m* yoghurt.

yard *m* yard.

yeux = *pl* œil

yin *m* yin.

yoga *m* yoga

yoghurt *m* = **yaourt**.

yogi *m* yogi.

yo-yo *m* yo-yo.

yucca *m* yucca.

yuppie *mf* yuppy.
zèbre *m* zebra.
zébu *m* zebu.
zèle *m* zeal.
zélé *adj* zealous.
zen *m* Zen.
zénith *m* zenith.
zéro *m* zero, nought, nothing.
zézayer *vi* to lisp.
zigzag *m* zigzag.
zigzaguer *vi* to zigzag.
zinc *m* zinc.
zizanie *f* ill-feeling.
zizi *m* (*fam*) willy.

zodiaque *m* zodiac.
zona *m* shingles.
zone *f* zone, area.
zoo *m* zoo.
zoologie *f* zoology.
zoologiste *mf* zoologist.
zoom *m* zoom; zoom lens.
zoophile *adj* zoophilic, zoophilous.
zozoter *vi* (*fam*) to lisp.
Z.U.P. (**zone à urbaniser en priorité**) *f* urban development zone.
zut *interj* damn! rubbish! shut up!

English-French
Dictionary

A

a *art* un, une.

aback *adv* to be taken ~ *vi* être décontenancé.

abacus *n* abaque, boulier *m*.

abandon *vt* abandonner, laisser.

abandonment *n* abandon *m*.

abase *vt* avilir; humilier.

abasement *n* avilissement *m*; humiliation *f*.

abash *vt* couvrir de honte.

abate *vt* baisser; * *vi* baisser; se calmer.

abatement *n* baisse, réduction *f*.

abbess *n* abbesse *f*.

abbey *n* abbaye *f*.

abbot *n* abbé *m*.

abbreviate *vt* abréger, raccourcir.

abbreviation *n* abréviation *f*.

abdicate *vt* abdiquer; renoncer à.

abdication *n* abdication *f*; renonciation *f*.

abdomen *n* abdomen *m*.

abdominal *adj* abdominal.

abduct *vt* kidnapper, enlever.

abductor *n* abducteur *m*.

abed *adv* au lit.

aberrant *adj* aberrant.

aberration *n* aberration *f*.

abet *vt*: to aid and ~ être complice de.

abeyance *n* suspension *f*.

abhor *vt* abhorrer, exécrer.

abhorrence *n* exécration, horreur *f*.

abhorrent *adj* exécrable.

abide *vt* supporter, souffrir.

ability *n* capacité, aptitude *f*; abilities *pl* talents *mpl*.

abject *adj* misérable; abject, méprisable; ~ly *adv* misérablement.

abjure *vt* abjurer; renoncer à.

ablative *n* (*gr*) ablatif *m*.

ablaze *adj* enflammé.

able *adj* capable; to be ~ pouvoir.

able-bodied *adj* robuste.

ablution *n* ablution *f*.

ably *adv* habilement.

abnegation *n* renoncement *m*.

abnormal *adj* anormal.

abnormality *n* anomalie *f*.

aboard *adv* à bord.

abode *n* domicile *m*.

abolish *vt* abolir, supprimer.

abolition *n* abolition, suppression *f*.

abominable *adj* abominable; ~bly *adv* abominablement.

abomination *n* abomination *f*.

aboriginal *adj* aborigène.

aborigines *npl* aborigènes *mpl*.

abort *vi* avorter.

abortion *n* avortement *m*.

abortive *adj* raté.

abound *vi* abonder; to ~ with abonder en.

about *prep* au sujet de; vers; I carry no money ~ me je n'ai pas d'argent sur moi; * *adv* çà et là; to be ~ to être sur le point de; to go ~ aller de- ci de- là; to go ~ a thing entreprendre quelque chose; all ~ partout.

above *prep* au-dessus de; * *adv* au-dessus; ~ all surtout, principalement; ~ mentioned mentionné cidessus.

aboveboard *adj* légitime.

abrasion *n* écorchure *f*.

abrasive *adj* abrasif.

abreast *adv* de front.

abridge *vt* abréger, raccourcir.

abridgment *n* abrégement *m*; version abrégée *f*.

abroad *adv* à l'étranger; **to go ~** se rendre à l'étranger.

abrogate *vt* abroger.

abrogation *n* abrogation *f*.

abrupt *adj* abrupt; brusque; **~ly** *adv* brusquement; rudement.

abscess *n* abcès *m*.

abscond *vi* s'enfuir.

absence *n* absence *f*.

absent *adj* absent; * *vi* s'absenter.

absentee *n* absent *m*, -e *f*.

absenteeism *n* absentéisme *m*.

absent-minded *adj* distrait.

absolute *adj* absolu; **~ly** *adv* absolument.

absolution *n* absolution *f*.

absolutism *n* absolutisme *m*.

absolve *vt* absoudre.

absorb *vt* absorber.

absorbent *adj* absorbant.

absorbent cotton *n* coton hydrophile *m*.

absorption *n* absorption *f*.

abstain *vi* s'abstenir.

abstemious *adj* sobre; **~ly** *adv* sobrement.

abstemiousness *n* sobriété *f*.

abstinence *n* abstinence *f*.

abstinent *adj* abstinent. .

abstract *adj* abstrait; * *n* abrégé *m*; **in the ~** dans l'abstrait.

abstraction *n* abstraction *f*; extraction *f*.

abstractly *adv* abstraitement.

abstruse *adj* abstrus, obscur; **~ly** *adv* obscurément.

absurd *adj* absurde; **~ly** *adv* absurdement.

absurdity *n* absurdité *f*.

abundance *n* abondance *f*.

abundant *adj* abondant; **~ly** *adv* abondamment.

abuse *vt* abuser de; insulter; maltraiter; * *n* abus *m*; injures *fpl*; mauvais traitements *mpl*.

abusive *adj* injurieux; **~ly** *adv* injurieusement.

abut *vi* confiner.

abysmal *adj* abominable.

abyss *n* abîme *m*.

acacia *n* acacia *m*.

academic *adj* universitaire; scolaire; théorique.

academician *n* universitaire *mf*.

academy *n* académie *f*.

accede *vi* accéder.

accelerate *vt* accélérer.

accelerator *n* accélérateur *m*.

acceleration *n* accélération *f*.

accent *n* accent *m*; * *vt* accentuer.

accentuate *vt* accentuer.

accentuation *n* accentuation *f*.

accept *vt* accepter.

acceptable *adj* acceptable.

acceptability *n* acceptabilité *f*.

acceptance *n* acceptation *f*.

access *n* accès *m*.

accessible *adj* accessible.

accession *n* augmentation *f*; accession *f*.

accessory *n* accessoire *m*; (*law*) complice *m*.

accident *n* accident *m*; hasard *m*.

accidental *adj* accidentel; **~ly** *adv* par hasard.

acclaim *vt* acclamer.

acclamation *n* acclamation *f*.

acclimate *vt* acclimater.

accommodate *vt* loger; accommoder.

accommodating *adj* obligeant.

accommodations *npl* logement *m*.

accompaniment *n* (*mus*) accompagnement *m*.

accompanist *n* (*mus*) accompagnateur *m*, -trice *f*.

accompany *vt* accompagner.

accomplice *n* complice *mf*.

accomplish *vt* accomplir.

accomplished *adj* accompli.

accomplishment *n* accomplissement *m*; **~s** *pl* talents *mpl*.

accord *n* accord *m*; **with one ~** d'un commun accord; **of one's own ~** de son propre chef.

accordance *n*: **in ~ with** conformément à.

according *prep* selon; **~ as** selon que; **~ly** *adv* en conséquence.

accordion *n* (*mus*) accordéon *m*.

accost *vt* accoster.

account *n* compte *m*; **on no ~** en aucun cas; **on ~ of** en raison de; **to call to ~** demander des comptes; **to turn to ~** mettre à profit; * *vt* **to ~ for** expliquer; représenter.

accountability *n* responsabilité *f*.

accountable *adj* responsable.

accountancy *n* comptabilité *f*.

accountant *n* comptable *mf*.

account book *n* livre de comptes *m*.

account number *n* numéro de compte *m*.

accrue *vi* s'accumuler; revenir.

accumulate *vt* accumuler; * *vi* s'accumuler.

accumulation *n* accumulation *f*.

accuracy *n* exactitude *f*.

accurate *adj* exact; **~ly** *adv* exactement.

accursed *adj* maudit.

accusation *n* accusation *f*.

accusative *n* (*gr*) accusatif *m*.

accusatory *adj* accusateur.

accuse *vt* accuser.

accused *n* accusé *m*, -e *f*.

accuser *n* accusateur *m*, -trice *f*.

accustom *vt* accoutumer.

accustomed *adj* accoutumé.

ace *n* as *m*; **within an ~ of** à deux doigts de.

acerbic *adj* acerbe.

acetate *n* (*chem*) acétate *m*.

ache *n* douleur *f*; * *vi* faire mal.

achieve *vt* réaliser; obtenir.

achievement *n* réalisation *f*; exploit *m*.

acid *adj* acide; aigre; * *n* acide *m*.

acidity *n* acidité *f*.

acknowledge *vt* reconnaître, admettre.

acknowledgment *n* reconnaissance *f*.

acme *n* apogée *m*.

acne *n* acné *f*.

acorn *n* gland *m*.

acoustics *n* acoustique *f*.

acquaint *vt* informer, aviser.

acquaintance *n* connaissance *f*.

acquiesce *vi* acquiescer, consentir.

acquiescence *n* consentement *m*.

acquiescent *adj* consentant.

acquire *vt* acquérir.

acquisition *n* acquisition *f*.

acquit vt acquitter.

acquittal n acquittement m.

acre n acre f.

acrid adj âcre; acerbe.

acrimonious adj acrimonieux.

acrimony n acrimonie f.

across adv en travers, d'un côté à l'autre; * prep à travers; **to come ~** tomber sur.

act vt jouer; * vi agir; jouer la comédie; * n acte m; **~s of the apostles** Actes des Apôtres mpl.

acting adj provisoire.

action n action f; combat m.

action replay n répétition f.

activate vt activer.

active adj actif; **~ly** adv activement.

activity n activité f.

actor n acteur m.

actress n actrice f.

actual adj réel; concret; **~ly** adv en fait; réellement.

actuary n actuaire mf.

acumen n perspicacité f.

acute adj aigu; perspicace; **~ accent** n accent aigu m; **~ angle** n angle aigu m; **~ly** adv vivement; avec perspicacité.

acuteness n perspicacité f.

ad n annonce f.

adage n adage m.

adamant adj inflexible.

adapt vt adapter, ajuster.

adaptability n facilité d'adaptation f.

adaptable adj adaptable.

adaptation n adaptation f.

adaptor n adaptateur m.

add vt ajouter; **to ~ up** additionner.

addendum n addendum m.

adder n vipère f.

addict n intoxiqué m, -e f.

addiction n dépendance f.

addictive adj qui crée une dépendance.

addition n addition f.

additional adj additionnel; **~ly** adv de plus.

additive n additif m.

address vt adresser; s'adresser à; * n adresse f; discours m.

adduce vt mentionner, citer.

adenoids npl végétations fpl.

adept adj adroit.

adequacy n suffisance f; capacité f.

adequate adj adéquat; suffisant; **~ly** adv convenablement; suffisamment.

adhere vi adhérer.

adherence n adhérence f.

adherent n adhérent, partisan m.

adhesion n adhérence f; adhésion f.

adhesive adj adhésif.

adhesive tape n (med) sparadrap m.

adhesiveness n adhérence f.

adieu adv adieu; * n adieux mpl.

adipose adj adipeux.

adjacent adj adjacent, contigu.

adjectival adj adjectival; **~ly** adv adjectivalement.

adjective n adjectif m.

adjoin vi être contigu.

adjoining adj contigu.

adjourn vt reporter, remettre.

adjournment n ajournement m.

adjudicate vt décider; juger.

adjunct n adjoint m, -e f.

adjust vt ajuster, adapter.

adjustable adj ajustable, adaptable.

adjustment n ajustement m; réglage m.

adjutant n (mil) adjudant m.

ad lib vt improviser.

administer vt administrer; distribuer; to ~ an oath faire prêter serment.

administration n administration f; gouvernement m.

administrative adj administratif.

administrator n administrateur m, -trice f.

admirable adj admirable; ~bly adv admirablement.

admiral n amiral m.

admiralship n amirauté f.

admiralty n ministère de la Marine m.

admiration n admiration f.

admire vt admirer.

admirer n admirateur m, -trice f.

admiringly adv avec admiration.

admissible adj admissible.

admission n admission, entrée f.

admit vt admettre; to ~ to reconnaître.

admittance n admission f.

admittedly adv il est vrai (que).

admixture n mélange m.

admonish vt admonester, réprimander.

admonition n admonestation f; conseil m.

admonitory adj d'admonestation.

ad nauseam adv à saturation.

ado n agitation f.

adolescence n adolescence f.

adopt vt adopter.

adopted adj adoptif.

adoption n adoption f.

adoptive adj adoptif.

adorable adj adorable.

adorably adv adorablement.

adoration n adoration f.

adore vt adorer.

adorn vt orner.

adornment n ornement m.

adrift adv à la dérive.

adroit adj adroit, habile.

adroitness n adresse f.

adulation n adulation f.

adulatory adj adulateur.

adult adj adulte; * n adulte mf.

adulterate vt falsifier; * adj falsifié.

adulteration n falsification f.

adulterer n adultère m.

adulteress n adultère f.

adulterous adj adultère.

adultery n adultère m.

advance vt avancer; * vi avancer; faire des progrès; * n avance f.

advanced adj avancé.

advancement n avancement m.

advantage n avantage m; to take ~ of profiter de.

advantageous adj avantageux; ~ly adv avantageusement.

advantageousness n avantage m.

advent n venue f; Advent n Avent m.

adventitious adj accidentel.

adventure n aventure f.

adventurer n aventurier m, -ière f.

adventurous adj aventureux; ~ly adv aventureusement.

adverb n adverbe m.

adverbial adj adverbial; ~ly adv adverbialement.

adversary n adversaire mf.

adverse adj défavorable, contraire.

adversity n adversité f; malheur m.

advertise vt faire de la publicité pour; mettre une annonce pour.

advertisement n publicité f; annonce f.

advertising n publicité f.

advice n conseil m; avis m.

advisability n opportunité f.

advisable adj prudent, conseillé.

advise vt conseiller; aviser.

advisedly adv de manière avisée.

advisory adj consultatif.

advocacy n défense f.

advocate n avocat m; * vt plaider pour.

advocateship n barreau m.

aerial n antenne f.

aerobics npl aérobic m.

aerometer n aéromètre m.

aeroplane n avion m.

aerosol n aérosol m.

aerostat n aérostat m.

afar adv au loin; **from ~** de loin.

affability n affabilité f.

affable adj affable; **~bly** adv affablement.

affair n affaire f.

affect vt toucher; affecter.

affectation n affectation f.

affected adj affecté; **~ly** adv avec affectation.

affectingly adv avec affection.

affection n affection f.

affectionate adj affectueux; **~ly** adv affectueusement.

affidavit n déclaration sous serment f.

affiliate vt affilier.

affiliation n affiliation f.

affinity n affinité f.

affirm vt affirmer, déclarer.

affirmation n affirmation f.

affirmative adj affirmatif; **~ly** adv affirmativement.

affix vt coller; apposer; * n (gr) affixe m.

afflict vt affliger.

affliction n affliction f.

affluence n abondance f.

affluent adj riche; abondant.

afflux n afflux m, affluence f.

afford vt fournir; **to be able to ~** avoir les moyens d'acheter.

affray n bagarre f.

affront n affront m, injure f; * vt affronter; insulter.

aflame adv en flammes.

afloat adv à flot.

afore prep avant; * adv d'abord.

afraid adj apeuré; **I am ~** j'ai peur.

afresh adv à nouveau.

aft adv (mar) en poupe.

after prep après; * adv après; **~ all** après tout.

afterbirth n placenta m.

after-crop n deuxième récolte f.

after-effects npl répercussions fpl.

afterlife n vie après la mort f.

aftermath n conséquences fpl.

afternoon n après-midi mf.

afterpains npl tranchées utérines fpl.

aftershave n après-rasage m.

aftertaste n arrière-goût m.

afterward(s) adv ensuite.

again adv à nouveau; **~ and ~** de nombreuses fois; **as much ~** la même chose.

against prep contre; **~ the grain** à contre fil; de mauvaise volonté.

agate n agate f.

age n âge m; vieillesse f; under ~ mineur; * vt vieillir.

aged adj âgé.

agency n agence f.

agenda n ordre du jour m.

agent n agent m.

agglomerate vt agglomérer.

agglomeration n agglomération f.

aggrandizement n agrandissement m.

aggravate vt aggraver; énerver.

aggravation n aggravation f; énervement m.

aggregate n agrégat m.

aggregation n agrégation f.

aggression n agression f.

aggressive adj agressif.

aggressor n agresseur m.

aggrieved adj offensé.

aghast adj horrifié.

agile adj agile; adroit.

agility n agilité f; adresse f.

agitate vt agiter.

agitation n agitation f.

agitator n agitateur m, -trice f.

ago adv: how long ~? il y a combien de temps?

agog adj ému.

agonizing adj atroce.

agony n agonie f.

agrarian adj agraire.

agree vt convenir; * vi être d'accord.

agreeable adj agréable; ~bly adv agréablement; ~ with conforme à.

agreeableness n caractère agréable m.

agreed adj convenu; ~! adv d'accord!

agreement n accord m.

agricultural adj agricole.

agriculture n agriculture f.

agriculturist n agriculteur m.

aground adv (mar) échoué.

ah! excl ah!

ahead adv en avant; à l'avance; (mar) sur l'avant.

ahoy! excl (mar) ohé!

aid vt aider, secourir; to ~ and abet être complice de; * n aide f, secours m; aide mf.

aide-de-camp n (mil) aide de camp m.

AIDS n SIDA m.

ail vt affliger.

ailing adj souffrant.

ailment n maladie f.

aim vt pointer; viser; aspirer à; * n but m; cible f.

aimless adj sans but; ~ly à la dérive, sans but.

air n air m; * vt aérer.

air balloon n ballon m.

airborne adj aéroporté.

air-conditioned adj climatisé.

air-conditioning n climatisation f.

aircraft n avion m.

air cushion n coussin d'air m.

air force n armée de l'air f.

air freshener n appareil de conditionnement d'air m.

air gun n carabine à air comprimé f.

air hole n trou d'aération m.

airiness n aération, ventilation f.

airless adj mal aéré, mal ventilé.

airlift n pont aérien m.

airline n ligne aérienne f.

airmail n: by ~ par avion.

aeroplane n avion m.

airport n aéroport m.

air pump n compresseur m.

airsick adj: to be ~ avoir le mal de l'air.

airstrip n piste d'atterrissage f.

air terminal n aérogare f.

airtight adj hermétique.

airy adj aéré; léger.

aisle n nef d'église f.

ajar adj entrouvert.

akimbo adj les poings sur les hanches.

akin adj ressemblant.

alabaster n albâtre m; * adj d'albâtre.

alacrity n vivacité f.

alarm n alarme f; * vt alarmer; inquiéter.

alarm bell n sonnette d'alarme f.

alarmist n alarmiste mf.

alas adv hélas.

albeit conj bien que.

album n album m.

alchemist n alchimiste m.

alchemy n alchimie f.

alcohol n alcool m.

alcoholic adj alcoolisé; * n alcoolique mf.

alcove n alcôve f.

alder n aulne m.

ale n bière f.

alehouse n taverne, brasserie f.

alert adj vigilant; vif; * n alerte f.

alertness n vigilance f; vivacité f.

algae npl algues fpl.

algebra n algèbre f.

algebraic adj algébrique.

alias adj alias.

alibi n (law) alibi m.

alien adj étranger; * n étranger m, -ère f; extra-terrestre mf.

alienate vt aliéner.

alienation n aliénation f.

alight vi mettre pied à terre; * adj en feu.

align vt aligner.

alike adj semblable, égal; * adv de la même façon.

alimentation n alimentation f.

alimony n aliments mpl.

alive adj en vie, vivant; actif.

alkali n alcali m.

alkaline adj alcalin.

all adj tout; * adv totalement; ~ at once, ~ of a sudden soudain; ~ the same cependant; ~ the better tant mieux; not at ~! pas du tout!; il n'y a pas de quoi!; once for ~ une fois pour toutes; * n tout m.

allay vt apaiser.

all clear n feu vert m.

allegation n allégation f.

allege vt alléguer.

allegiance n loyauté, fidélité f.

allegorical adj allégorique; ~ly adv allégoriquement.

allegory n allégorie f.

allegro n (mus) allegro m.

allergy n allergie f.

alleviate vt alléger.

alleviation n allègement m.

alley n ruelle f.

alliance n alliance f.

allied adj allié.

alligator n alligator m.

alliteration n allitération f.

all-night adj ouvert toute la nuit.

allocate vt allouer.

allocation n allocation f.

allot vt assigner.

allow vt permettre; accorder; to ~ for tenir compte de.

allowable adj admissible, permis.

allowance n allocation f; concession f.

alloy n alliage m.

all-right adv bien.

all-round adj complet.

allspice n poivre de la Jamaïque m.

allude vi faire allusion à.

allure n charme, attrait m.

alluring adj attrayant; ~ly adv avec charme.

allurement n attrait m.

allusion n allusion f.

allusive adj allusif; ~ly adv par allusion.

alluvial adj alluvial.

ally n allié m, -e f; * vt allier.

almanac n almanach m.

almighty adj omnipotent, tout-puissant.

almond n amande f.

almond-milk n lait d'amandes m.

almond tree n amandier m.

almost adv presque.

alms n aumône f.

aloft prep au-dessus.

alone adj seul; * adv seul; **to leave ~** laisser tranquille.

along adv le long (de); ~ **side** à côté.

aloof adv à l'écart.

aloud adj à voix haute.

alphabet n alphabet m.

alphabetical adj alphabétique; ~ly adv par ordre alphabétique, alphabétiquement.

alpine adj alpin.

already adv déjà.

also adv aussi.

altar n autel m.

altarpiece n retable m.

alter vt modifier.

alteration n modification f.

altercation n altercation f.

alternate adj alterné; * vt alterner; ~ly adv alternativement.

alternating adj alterné.

alternation n alternance f.

alternator n alternateur m.

alternative n alternative f; * adj alternatif; ~ly adv sinon.

although conj bien que, malgré.

altitude n altitude f.

altogether adv complètement.

alum n alun m.

aluminium n aluminium m.

aluminous adj alumineux.

always adv toujours.

a.m. adv du matin.

amalgam n amalgame m.

amalgamate vt amalgamer; vi s'amalgamer.

amalgamation n amalgamation f.

amanuensis n secrétaire mf.

amaryllis n (bot) amaryllis f.

amass vt accumuler, amasser.

amateur n amateur m.

amateurish adj d'amateur.

amatory adj amoureux; érotique.

amaze vt stupéfier.

amazement n stupéfaction f.

amazing adj stupéfiant; ~ly adv incroyablement.

amazon n amazone f.

ambassador n ambassadeur m.

ambassadress n ambassadrice f.

amber n ambre m; * adj ambré.

ambidextrous adj ambidextre.

ambient adj ambiant.

ambiguity n ambiguïté f.

ambiguous *adj* ambigu; **~ly** *adv* de manière ambiguë.

ambition *n* ambition *f*.

ambitious *adj* ambitieux; **~ly** *adv* ambitieusement.

amble *vi* marcher tranquillement.

ambulance *n* ambulance *f*.

ambush *n* embuscade *f*; **to lie in ~** être embusqué; * *vt* tendre une embuscade à.

ameliorate *vt* améliorer.

amelioration *n* amélioration *f*.

amenable *adj* responsable.

amend *vt* modifier; amender.

amendable *adj* réparable, corrigible.

amendment *n* modification *f*; amendement *m*.

amends *npl* compensation *f*.

amenities *npl* commodités *fpl*.

America *n* Amérique *f*.

American *adj* américain.

amethyst *n* améthyste *f*.

amiability *n* amabilité *f*.

amiable *adj* aimable.

amiableness *n* amabilité *f*.

amiably *adv* aimablement.

amicable *adj* amical; **~bly** *adv* amicalement.

amid(st) *prep* entre, parmi.

amiss *adv*: **something's ~** il se passe quelque chose.

ammonia *n* ammoniaque *m*.

ammunition *n* munitions *fpl*.

amnesia *n* amnésie *f*.

amnesty *n* amnistie *f*.

among(st) *prep* entre, parmi.

amoral *adj* amoral.

amorous *adj* amoureux; **~ly** *adv* amoureusement.

amorphous *adj* informe.

amount *n* montant *m*; quantité *f*; * *vi* se monter.

amp(ere) *n* ampère *m*.

amphibian *n* amphibie *m*.

amphibious *adj* amphibie.

amphitheatre *n* amphithéâtre *m*.

ample *adj* spacieux; en quantité abondante.

ampleness *n* abondance *f*.

amplification *n* amplification *f*.

amplifier *n* amplificateur *m*.

amplify *vt* amplifier.

amplitude *n* amplitude *f*.

amply *adv* amplement.

amputate *vt* amputer.

amputation *n* amputation *f*.

amulet *n* amulette *f*.

amuse *vt* distraire, divertir.

amusement *n* distraction *f*, divertissement *m*.

amusing *adj* divertissant; **~ly** *adv* de manière divertissante.

an *art* un, une.

anachronism *n* anachronisme *m*.

anaemia *n* anémie *f*.

anaemic *adj* (*med*) anémique.

anaesthetic *n* anesthésique *m*.

analog *adj* (*comput*) analogique.

analogous *adj* analogue.

analogy *n* analogie *f*.

analysis *n* analyse *f*.

analyst *n* analyste *mf*.

analytical *adj* analytique; **~ly** *adv* analytiquement.

analyse *vt* analyser.

anarchic *adj* anarchique.

anarchist *n* anarchiste *mf*.

anarchy *n* anarchie *f*.

anatomical *adj* anatomique; **~ly** *adv* anatomiquement.

anatomize *vt* disséquer.

anatomy *n* anatomie *f*.

ancestor *n* ancêtre *mf*.

ancestral *adj* ancestral.

ancestry *n* ascendance *f*.

anchor *n* ancre *f*; * *vi* jeter l'ancre.

anchorage *n* ancrage *m*.

anchovy *n* anchois *m*.

ancient *adj* ancien, antique; **~ly** *adv* anciennement.

ancientness *n* ancienneté *f*.

ancillary *adj* auxiliaire.

and *conj* et.

anecdotal *adj* anecdotique.

anecdote *n* anecdote *f*.

anemone *n* (*bot*) anémone *f*.

anew *adv* de nouveau.

angel *n* ange *m*.

angelic *adj* angélique.

anger *n* colère *f*; * *vt* mettre en colère, irriter.

angle *n* angle *m*; * *vi* pêcher à la ligne.

angled *adj* anguleux.

angler *n* pêcheur à la ligne *m*.

anglicism *n* anglicisme *m*.

angling *n* pêche à la ligne *f*.

angrily *adv* avec colère.

angry *adj* en colère, irrité.

anguish *n* angoisse *f*.

angular *adj* angulaire.

angularity *n* caractère anguleux *m*.

animal *n adj* animal *m*.

animate *vt* animer; * *adj* vivant.

animated *adj* animé.

animation *n* animation *f*.

animosity *n* animosité *f*.

animus *n* haine *f*.

anise *n* anis *m*.

aniseed *n* graine d'anis *f*.

ankle *n* cheville *f*; **~ bone** astragale *m*.

annals *n* annales *fpl*.

annex *vt* annexer; * *n* annexe *f*.

annexation *n* annexion *f*.

annihilate *vt* annihiler, anéantir.

annihilation *n* anéantissement *m*.

anniversary *n* anniversaire *m*.

annotate *vt* annoter.

annotation *n* annotation *f*.

announce *vt* annoncer.

announcement *n* annonce *f*.

announcer *n* présentateur *m*, -trice *f*.

annoy *vt* ennuyer.

annoyance *n* ennui *m*.

annoying *adj* ennuyeux.

annual *adj* annuel; **~ly** *adv* annuellement.

annuity *n* rente viagère *f*.

annul *vt* annuler.

annulment *n* annulation *f*.

annunciation *n* annonciation *f*.

anodyne *adj* calmant.

anoint *vt* oindre.

anomalous *adj* anormal.

anomaly *n* anomalie, irrégularité *f*.

anon *adv* plus tard.

anonymity *n* anonymat *m*.

anonymous *adj* anonyme; **~ly** *adv* anonymement.

anorexia *n* anorexie *f*.

another *adj* un autre; **one ~** l'un l'autre.

answer *vt* répondre à; **to ~ for** répondre de; **to ~ to** répondre à; * *n* réponse *f*.

answerable *adj* responsable.

answering machine *n* répondeur téléphonique *m*.

ant n fourmi f.
antagonism n antagonisme m; rivalité f.
antagonist n antagoniste mf.
antagonize vt provoquer.
antarctic adj antarctique.
anteater n fourmilier m.
antecedent n: ~**s** pl antécédents mpl.
antechamber n antichambre f.
antedate vt antidater.
antelope n antilope f.
antenna n antenne f.
anterior adj antérieur, précédent.
anthem n hymne m.
ant-hill n fourmilière f.
anthology n anthologie f.
anthracite n anthracite m.
anthropology n anthropologie f.
anti-aircraft adj antiaérien.
antibiotic n antibiotique m.
antibody n anticorps m.
Antichrist n Antéchrist m.
anticipate vt prévoir.
anticipation n attente f; prévision f.
anticlockwise adv dans le sens contraire des aiguilles d'une montre.
antidote n antidote m.
antifreeze n antigel m.
antimony n antimoine m.
antipathy n antipathie f.
antipodes npl antipodes fpl.
antiquarian n antiquaire mf.
antiquated adj vieux; suranné.
antique n antiquité f.
antiquity n antiquité f.
antiseptic adj antiseptique.
antisocial adj antisocial.
antithesis n antithèse f.
antler n corne f.
anvil n enclume f.

anxiety n anxiété f; désir m.
anxious adj anxieux; ~**ly** adv anxieusement.
any adj pn n'importe quel, n'importe quelle; un, une; tout; ~**body** quelqu'un; n'importe qui; personne; ~**how** de toute façon; de n'importe quelle manière; ~**more** plus; ~**place** n'importe où; nulle part; ~**thing** quelque chose; n'importe quoi; rien.
apace adv rapidement.
apart adv séparément.
apartment n appartement m.
apartment house n immeuble m.
apathetic adj apathique.
apathy n apathie f.
ape n singe m; * vt singer.
aperture n ouverture f.
apex n sommet m; apex m.
aphorism n aphorisme m.
apiary n rucher m.
apiece adv chacun, chacune.
aplomb n aplomb m.
Apocalypse n Apocalypse f.
apocrypha npl apocryphes mpl.
apocryphal adj apocryphe.
apologetic adj d'excuse.
apologist n apologiste mf.
apologize vt excuser.
apology n apologie, défense f.
apoplexy n apoplexie f.
apostle n apôtre m.
apostolic adj apostolique.
apostrophe n apostrophe f.
apotheosis n apothéose f.
appall vt horrifier, atterrer.
appalling adj horrible.
apparatus n appareil m.
apparel n vêtements mpl.

apparent *adj* évident, apparent;
~**ly** *adv* apparemment.

apparition *n* apparition, vision *f*.

appeal *vi* faire appel; * *n* (*law*)
appel *m*.

appealing *adj* attrayant.

appear *vi* paraître.

appearance *n* apparence *f*.

appease *vt* apaiser.

appellant *n* (*law*) appelant *m*.

append *vt* annexer.

appendage *n* appendice *m*.

appendicitis *n* appendicite *f*.

appendix *n* appendice *m*.

appertain *vi* appartenir (à).

appetite *n* appétit *m*.

appetizing *adj* appétissant.

applaud *vt*, *vi* applaudir.

applause *n* applaudissements *mpl*.

apple *n* pomme *f*.

apple pie *n* tourte aux pommes *f*;
in ~ order parfaitement en ordre.

apple tree *n* pommier *m*.

appliance *n* appareil *m*.

applicability *n* applicabilité *f*.

applicable *adj* applicable.

applicant *n* candidat *m*, -e *f*.

application *n* application *f*; candidature *f*.

applied *adj* appliqué.

apply *vt* appliquer; * *vi* s'adresser.

appoint *vt* nommer.

appointee *n* personne nommée *f*.

appointment *n* rendez-vous *m*;
nomination *f*.

apportion *vt* répartir.

apportionment *n* répartition *f*.

apposite *adj* adapté.

apposition *n* apposition *f*.

appraisal *n* estimation *f*.

appraise *vt* évaluer.

appreciable *adj* appréciable, sensible.

appreciably *adv* sensiblement.

appreciate *vt* apprécier; être
conscient de.

appreciation *n* appréciation *f*.

appreciative *adj* reconnaissant.

apprehend *vt* appréhender.

apprehension *n* appréhension *f*;
arrestation *f*.

apprehensive *adj* appréhensif.

apprentice *n* apprenti *m*; * *vt* mettre en apprentissage.

apprenticeship *n* apprentissage *m*.

apprise, apprize *vt* informer.

approach *vi* approcher(s'); * *vt*
(s')approcher de; * *n* approche *f*.

approachable *adj* accessible, ap-
prochable.

approbation *n* approbation *f*.

appropriate *vt* s'approprier; * *adj*
approprié, adéquat.

approval *n* approbation *f*.

approve (of) *vt* approuver.

approximate *vi* s'approcher; * *adj*
approximatif; ~**ly** *adv* approximativement.

approximation *n* approximation *f*.

apricot *n* abricot *m*.

April *n* avril *m*.

apron *n* tablier *m*.

apse *n* abside *f*.

apt *adj* idéal; susceptible; ~**ly** *adv*
opportunément.

aptitude *n* aptitude *f*.

aqualung *n* scaphandre autonome *m*.

aquarium *n* aquarium *m*.

Aquarius *n* Verseau *m* (signe du
zodiaque).

aquatic *adj* aquatique.
aqueduct *n* aqueduc *m*.
aquiline *adj* aquilin.
arabesque *n* arabesque *f*.
arable *adj* arable.
arbiter *n* arbitre *m*.
arbitrariness *n* caractère arbitraire *m*.
arbitrary *adj* arbitraire.
arbitrate *vt* arbitrer.
arbitration *n* arbitrage *m*.
arbitrator *n* arbitre *m*.
arbor *n* tonnelle *f*.
arcade *n* galerie *f*.
arch *n* arc *m*; * *adj* malicieux.
archaic *adj* archaïque.
archangel *n* archange *m*.
archbishop *n* archevêque *m*.
archbishopric *n* archevêché *m*.
archeological *adj* archéologique.
archeology *n* archéologie *f*.
archer *n* archer *m*.
archery *n* tir à l'arc *m*.
architect *n* architecte *mf*.
architectural *adj* architectural.
architecture *n* architecture *f*.
archives *npl* archives *fpl*.
archivist *n* archiviste *m*.
archly *adv* malicieusement.
archway *n* arcade, voûte *f*.
arctic *adj* arctique.
ardent *adj* ardent; ~**ly** *adv* ardemment.
ardor *n* ardeur *f*.
arduous *adj* ardu, difficile.
area *n* région *f*; domaine *m*.
arena *n* arène *f*.
arguably *adv* peut-être.
argue *vi* se disputer; * *vt* soutenir.
argument *n* argument *m*; dispute *f*.

argumentation *n* argumentation *f*.
argumentative *adj* raisonneur.
aria *n* (*mus*) aria *f*.
arid *adj* aride.
aridity *n* aridité *f*.
Aries *n* Bélier *m* (signe du zodiaque).
aright *adv* bien; **to set** ~ rectifier.
arise *vi* se lever; survenir.
aristocracy *n* aristocratie *f*.
aristocrat *n* aristocrate *mf*.
aristocratic *adj* aristocratique; ~**ally** *adv* aristocratiquement.
arithmetic *n* arithmétique *f*.
arithmetical *adj* arithmétique; ~**ly** *adv* arithmétiquement.
ark *n* arche *f*.
arm *n* bras *m*; arme *f*; * *vt* armer; * *vi* (s')armer.
armament *n* armement *m*.
armchair *n* fauteuil *m*.
armed *adj* armé.
armful *n* brassée *f*.
armhole *n* emmanchure *f*.
armistice *n* armistice *m*.
armour *n* armure *f*.
armoured car *n* voiture blindée *f*.
armoury *n* arsenal *m*.
armpit *n* aisselle *f*.
armrest *n* accoudoir *m*.
army *n* armée *f*.
aroma *n* arôme *m*.
aromatic *adj* aromatique.
around *prep* autour de; * *adv* autour.
arouse *vt* éveiller; exciter.
arraign *vt* accuser.
arraignment *n* accusation *f*; procès criminel *m*.
arrange *vt* arranger, organiser.

arrangement n arrangement m.
arrant adj absolu.
array n série f.
arrears npl arriéré m; retard m.
arrest n arrestation f; * vt arrêter.
arrival n arrivée f.
arrive vi arriver.
arrogance n arrogance f.
arrogant adj arrogant; ~ly adv avec arrogance.
arrogate vt s'arroger.
arrogation n usurpation f.
arrow n flèche f.
arsenal n (mil) arsenal m.
arsenic n arsenic m.
arson n incendie criminel m.
art n art m.
arterial adj artériel.
artesian well n puits artésien m.
artery n artère f.
artful adj malin, astucieux.
artfulness n astuce f; habileté f.
art gallery n musée d'art m.
arthritis n arthrite f.
artichoke n artichaut m.
article n article m.
articulate vt articuler.
articulated adj articulé.
articulation n articulation f.
artifice n artifice m.
artificial adj artificiel; ~ly adv artificiellement.
artificiality n caractère artificiel m.
artillery n artillerie f.
artisan n artisan m.
artist n artiste mf.
artistic adj artistique.
artistry n habileté f.
artless adj naturel, simple; ~ly adv naturellement, simplement.

artlessness n simplicité f, naturel m.
art school n école des beaux-arts f.
as conj comme; pendant que; aussi; ~ for, ~ to quant à.
asbestos n asbeste m, amiante f.
ascend vi monter.
ascendancy n ascendant m.
ascension n ascension f.
ascent n montée f.
ascertain vt établir.
ascetic adj ascétique; * n ascète mf.
ascribe vt attribuer.
ash n (bot) frêne m; cendre f.
ashcan n poubelle f.
ashamed adj honteux.
ashore adv à terre; to go ~ débarquer.
ashtray n cendrier m.
Ash Wednesday n mercredi des Cendres m.
aside adv de côté.
ask vt demander; to ~ after demander des nouvelles de; to ~ for demander; to ~ out inviter.
askance adv avec méfiance.
askew adv de côté.
asleep adj endormi; to fall ~ s'endormir.
asparagus n asperge f.
aspect n aspect m.
aspen n tremble m.
aspersion n calomnie f.
asphalt n asphalte m.
asphyxia n (med) asphyxie f.
asphyxiate vt asphyxier.
asphyxiation n asphyxie f.
aspirant n aspirant m, -e f.
aspirate vt aspirer; * n aspiration f.
aspiration n aspiration f.
aspire vi aspirer, désirer.

aspirin n aspirine f.

ass n âne m; **she ~** ânesse f.

assail vt assaillir, attaquer.

assailant n assaillant, agresseur m.

assassin n assassin m.

assassinate vt assassiner.

assassination n assassinat m.

assault n assaut m; agression f;
* vt agresser.

assemblage n assemblage m.

assemble vt assembler; * vi
s'assembler.

assembly n assemblée f.

assembly line n chaîne de montage f.

assent n assentiment m; * vi donner son assentiment.

assert vt soutenir; affirmer.

assertion n assertion f.

assertive adj péremptoire.

assess vt évaluer.

assessment n évaluation f.

assessor n assesseur m.

assets npl biens mpl.

assiduous adj assidu; ~ly adv assidûment.

assign vt assigner.

assignation n rendez-vous m;
allocation f.

assignment n allocation f; mission f.

assimilate vt assimiler.

assimilation n assimilation f.

assist vt assister, aider; secourir.

assistance n assistance, aide f;
secours m.

assistant n aide mf, assistant m,
-e f.

associate vt associer; * adj associé; * n associé m, -e f.

association n association f.

assonance n assonance f.

assorted adj assorti.

assortment n assortiment m.

assuage vt calmer, adoucir.

assume vt assumer; supposer.

assumption n supposition f; **Assumption** n Assomption f.

assurance n assurance f.

assure vt assurer.

assuredly adv assurément.

asterisk n astérisque m.

astern adv (mar) en poupe.

asthma n asthme m.

asthmatic adj asthmatique.

astonish vt surprendre, stupéfier.

astonishing adj stupéfiant; ~ly
adv incroyablement.

astonishment n surprise, stupéfaction f.

astound vt ébahir.

astraddle adv à cheval.

astray adv: **to go ~** s'égarer; **to
lead ~** détourner du droit chemin.

astride adv à cheval.

astringent adj astringent.

astrologer n astrologue mf.

astrological adj astrologique.

astrology n astrologie f.

astronaut n astronaute mf.

astronomer n astronome mf.

astronomical adj astronomique.

astronomy n astronomie f.

astute adj malin.

asylum n asile, refuge m.

at prep à; en; **~ once** tout de suite;
~ all du tout; **~ all events** en
tout cas; **~ first** au début, d'abord;
~ last enfin.

atheism n athéisme m.

atheist n athée mf.

athlete n athlète mf.

athletic adj athlétique.

atlas n atlas m.

atmosphere n atmosphère f.

atmospheric adj atmosphérique.

atom n atome m.

atom bomb n bombe atomique f.

atomic adj atomique.

atone vt expier.

atonement n expiation f.

atop adv en haut.

atrocious adj atroce; **~ly** adv atrocement.

atrocity n atrocité, énormité f.

atrophy n (med) atrophie f.

attach vt joindre.

attaché n attaché m, -e f.

attachment n attachement m.

attack vt attaquer; * n attaque f.

attacker n attaquant m, -e f.

attain vt atteindre, obtenir.

attainable adj accessible.

attempt vt essayer; * n essai m, tentative f.

attend vt servir; assister à; **to ~ to** s'occuper de; * vi faire attention.

attendance n service m; assistance f; présence f.

attendant n serviteur m.

attention n attention f; soin m.

attentive adj attentif; **~ly** adv attentivement.

attenuate vt atténuer.

attest vt attester.

attic n grenier m.

attire n atours mpl.

attitude n attitude f.

attorney n avocat m.

attract vt attirer.

attraction n attraction f; attrait m.

attractive adj attrayant.

attribute vt attribuer; * n attribut m.

attrition n frottement m; usure f.

auburn adj auburn.

auction n vente aux enchères f.

auctioneer n commissaire-priseur m.

audacious adj audacieux, téméraire; **~ly** adv audacieusement.

audacity n audace, témérité f.

audible adj audible; **~ly** adv audiblement.

audience n audience f; auditoire m.

audit n audit m; * vt vérifier.

auditor n vérificateur(-trice) de comptes m(f); auditeur m, -trice f.

auditory adj auditif.

augment vt, vi augmenter.

augmentation n augmentation f.

August n août m.

august adj auguste, majestueux.

aunt n tante f.

au pair n (jeune fille) au pair f.

aura n aura f.

auspices npl auspices mpl.

auspicious adj favorable, propice; **~ly** adv favorablement.

austere adj austère, sévère; **~ly** adv austèrement.

austerity n austérité f.

authentic adj authentique; **~ly** adv authentiquement.

authenticate vt légaliser.

authenticity n authenticité f.

author n auteur m.

authoress n femme auteur f, auteur m.

authoritarian adj autoritaire.

authoritative adj autoritaire; **~ly** adv autoritairement.

authority n autorité f.
authorization n autorisation f.
authorize vt autoriser.
authorship n paternité f.
auto n voiture f.
autocrat n autocrate mf.
autocratic adj autocratique.
autograph n autographe m.
automated adj automatisé.
automatic adj automatique.
automaton n automate m.
autonomy n autonomie f.
autopsy n autopsie f.
autumn n automne m.
autumnal adj automnal.
auxiliary adj auxiliaire.
avail vt: **to ~ oneself of** profiter de; * n: **to no ~** en vain.
available adj disponible.
avalanche n avalanche f.
avarice n avarice f.
avaricious adj avare.
avenge vt venger.
avenue n avenue f.
aver vt affirmer, déclarer.
average n atteindre la moyenne de; * n moyenne f, moyen terme m.
aversion n aversion f, dégoût m.
avert vt détourner, écarter.
aviary n volière f.
avoid vt éviter; échapper à.

avoidable adj évitable.
await vt attendre.
awake vt réveiller; * vi se réveiller; * adj éveillé.
awakening n réveil m.
award n attribuer; * n prix m; décision f.
aware adj conscient; au courant.
awareness n conscience f.
away adv absent; loin; ~! va-t-en!; allez-vous-en! **far and ~** de loin.
away game n match à l'extérieur m.
awe n peur, crainte f.
awe-inspiring, awesome adj terrifiant; imposant.
awful adj horrible, terrible; ~**ly** adv horriblement, terriblement.
awhile adv un moment.
awkward adj gauche, maladroit; délicat; ~**ly** adv maladroitement.
awkwardness n maladroitesse f; difficulté f.
awl n alène f.
awning n (mar) taude f.
awry adv de travers.
axe n hache f; * vt licencier; supprimer.
axiom n axiome m.
axis n axe m.
axle n axe m.
ay(e) excl oui.

B

baa n bêlement m; * vi bêler.
babble vi bavarder, babiller; ~, **babbling** n bavardage, babillage m.
babbler n bavard m.

babe, baby n bébé, enfant en bas-âge m; nourrisson m.
baboon n babouin m.
babyhood n petite enfance f.
babyish adj enfantin; puéril.

baby carriage n voiture d'enfant f.
baby linen n layette f.
bachelor n célibataire m; licencié m, -e f.
bachelorship n célibat m.
back n dos m; * adv en arrière, à l'arrière; **a few years ~** il y a quelques années, quelques années en arrière; * vt soutenir, appuyer, renforcer.
backbite vt médire de, sur.
backbiter n détracteur m, -trice f.
backbone n colonne vertébrale, épine dorsale f.
backdate vt antidater.
backdoor n porte de derrière f.
backer n partisan m, -e f.
backgammon n (jeu de) jacquet m.
background n fond m.
backlash n réaction violente f.
backlog n accumulation de travail en retard f.
back number n vieux numéro (magazine, journal) m.
backpack n sac à dos m.
back payment n rappel de salaire m.
backside n derrière m.
back-up lights npl (auto) feux de marche arrière mpl.
backward adj rétrograde; retardé; lent; * adv en arrière.
bacon n lard m.
bad adj mauvais, de mauvaise qualité; méchant; malade; **~ly** adv mal.
badge n plaque f, insigne m, badge m; symbole m; signe m.
badger n blaireau m; * vt harceler; importuner.

badminton n badminton m.
badness n mauvaise qualité f; méchanceté f.
baffle vt déconcerter, confondre.
bag n sac m; valise f.
baggage n bagages mpl; équipement m.
bagpipe n cornemuse f.
bail n mise en liberté sous caution, caution f; * vt mettre en liberté sous caution; caution en dépôt.
bailiff n huissier m; régisseur m.
bait vt tourmenter; appâter; * n appât m; amorce f.
baize n serge f.
bake vt faire cuire au four.
bakery n boulangerie f.
baker n boulanger m, -ère f; **~'s dozen** treize à la douzaine.
baking n cuisson f; fournée f.
baking powder n levure f.
balance n balance f; équilibre m; solde d'un compte m; **to lose one's ~** perdre l'équilibre; * vt peser; penser le pour et le contre; solder; équilibrer.
balance sheet n bilan m.
balcony n balcon m.
bald adj chauve.
baldness n calvitie f.
bale n balle f; * vt emballer; écoper.
baleful adj sinistre, funeste, maléfique; **~ly** adv sinistrement; lugubrement.
ball n balle f; boule f; ballon m.
ballad n ballade f.
ballast n lest m; * vt lester.
ballerina n ballerine f.

ballet n ballet m.

ballistic adj balistique.

balloon n montgolfière f, aérostat m.

ballot n scrutin m; vote m; * vi voter au scrutin secret.

ballpoint (pen) n stylo à bille m.

ballroom n salle de bal f.

balm, balsam n baume m; * vt enduire de baume.

balmy adj balsamique, parfumé; doux.

balustrade n balustrade f.

bamboo n bambou m.

bamboozle vt (fam) embobiner.

ban n interdiction f; * vt interdire.

banal adj banal.

banana n banane f.

band n bande f; reliure f; courroie de transmission f; orchestre m.

bandage n bande f, bandage m; * vt bander.

bandaid n pansement m.

bandit n bandit m.

bandstand n kiosque à musique m.

bandy vt échanger; discuter.

bandy-legged adj aux jambes arquées.

bang n coup violent, claquement m, détonation f; * vt frapper violemment; claquer.

bangle n bracelet m.

bangs npl frange (courte et droite) f.

banish vt bannir, exiler, chasser, expatrier.

banishment n exil, bannissement m.

banister(s) n(pl) rampe d'escalier f.

banjo n banjo m.

bank n rive f; remblai m; banque f; banc m; digue f; * vt déposer de l'argent à la banque; to ~ on compter sur.

bank account n compte en banque m.

bank card n carte bancaire f.

banker n banquier m, -ière f.

banking n opérations bancaires f pl.

banknote n billet de banque m.

bankrupt adj failli; * n banqueroute f, failli m.

bankruptcy n banqueroute, faillite f.

bank statement n relevé de compte m.

banner n bannière f; étendard m.

banquet n banquet m.

baptism n baptême m.

baptismal adj de baptême, baptismal.

baptistery n baptistère m.

baptize vt baptiser.

bar n barre f; barre f; obstacle m; (law) barreau m; * vt empêcher; interdire; exclure.

barbarian n barbare mf; * adj barbare, cruel.

barbaric adj barbare.

barbarism n (gr) barbarisme m; barbarie f.

barbarity n barbarie, atrocité f.

barbarous adj barbare, cruel.

barbecue n barbecue m.

barber n coiffeur (pour hommes) m.

bar code n code barres m.

bard n barde m; poète m.

bare adj nu, dépouillé; simple; pur; * vt dénuder, découvrir.

barefaced adj éhonté, impudent.

barefoot(ed) adj aux pieds nus.

bareheaded adj nu-tête.

barelegged adj aux jambes nues.

barely *adv* à peine, tout juste.

bareness *n* nudité *f*.

bargain *n* affaire *f*; contrat, marché *m*; occasion *f*; * *vi* conclure un marché; négocier; **to ~ for** s'attendre à.

barge *n* péniche *f*.

baritone *n* (*mus*) baryton *m*.

bark *n* écorce *f*; aboiement *m*; * *vi* aboyer.

barley *n* orge *m*.

barmaid *n* serveuse *f*.

barman *n* barman *m*.

barn *n* grange *f*; étable *f*.

barnacles *npl* anatife *m*.

barometer *n* baromètre *m*.

baron *n* baron *m*.

baroness *n* baronne *f*.

baronial *adj* de baron.

barracks *npl* caserne *f*.

barrage *n* barrage *m*; (*fig*) torrent *m*.

barrel *n* tonneau *f*, fût *m*; canon *m* de fusil *m*.

barrelled *adj* (firearms) chargé.

barrel organ *n* orgue de Barbarie *m*.

barren *adj* stérile, infertile, improductif.

barricade *n* barricade *f*; barrière *f*; * *vt* barricader, barrer.

barrier *n* barrière *f*; obstacle *m*.

barring *adv* excepté, sauf.

barrow *n* brouette *f*.

bartender *n* barman *m*.

barter *vi* faire du troc; * *vt* troquer, échanger.

base *n* base *f*; partie inférieure *f*; pied *m*; point de départ *m*; * *vt* fonder sur; * *adj* vil, abject.

baseball *n* baseball *m*.

baseless *adj* sans fondement, injustifié.

basement *n* sous-sol *m*.

baseness *n* bassesse, vilenie *f*.

bash *vt* frapper.

bashful *adj* timide, modeste; **~ly** *adv* timidement.

basic *adj* fondamental, de base; **~ally** *adv* fondamentalement.

basilisk *n* basilic *m*.

basin *n* cuvette *f*; lavabo *m*.

basis *n* base *f*; fondement *m*.

bask *vi* se faire dorer au soleil.

basket *n* panier *m*, corbeille *f*.

basketball *n* basket-ball *m*.

bass *n* (*mus*) contrebasse *f*.

bassoon *n* basson *m*.

bass viol *n* viole de gambe *f*.

bass voice *n* voix de basse *f*.

bastardy *n* bâtardise *f*.

bastard *n*, *adj* bâtard *m*.

baste *vt* arroser la viande de son jus; bâtir.

bastion *n* (*mil*) bastion *m*.

bat *n* chauve-souris *f*.

batch *n* fournée *f*.

bath *n* bain *m*.

bathe *vt* (*vi*) (se) baigner.

bathing suit *n* maillot de bain *m*.

bathos *n* platitudes (dans un texte littéraire) *fpl*.

bathroom *n* salle de bain *f*.

baths *npl* piscine *f*.

bathtub *n* baignoire *f*.

baton *n* bâton *m*.

battalion *n* (*mil*) bataillon *m*.

batter *vt* battre; frapper, martyriser; * *n* pâte à frire *f*.

battering ram n (mil) bélier m.

battery n pile, batterie f.

battle n bataille f; combat m; * vi se battre, combattre.

battle array n ordre de bataille m.

battlefield n champ de bataille m.

battlement n remparts m pl.

battleship n cuirassé m.

bawdy adj paillard.

bawl vi brailler, (fam) gueuler.

bay n baie f; laurier m; * vi aboyer, hurler; * adj bai.

bayonet n baïonnette f.

bay window n fenêtre en saillie f.

bazaar n bazar m.

be vi être.

beach n plage f.

beacon n phare, signal lumineux m.

bead n perle f; ~s npl chapelet m.

beagle n beagle m.

beak n bec m.

beaker n gobelet m.

beam n rayon m; poutre f; * vi rayonner, resplendir.

bean n haricot m; French ~ haricot vert m.

beansprouts npl germes de soja m pl.

bear vt porter, supporter, produire; * vi se diriger.

bear n ours m; **she** ~ ourse f.

bearable adj supportable.

beard n barbe f.

bearded adj barbu.

bearer n porteur m, -euse f; arbre fructifère m.

bearing n relation f; maintien, port m.

beast n bête f; brute f; ~ of burden bête de somme f.

beastliness n bestialité, brutalité f.

beastly adj bestial, brutal; abominable; * adv terriblement.

beat vt battre; * vi battre, palpiter; * n battement m; pulsation f.

beatific adj béatifique; béat.

beatify vt béatifier, sanctifier.

beating n correction, raclée f; battement m.

beatitude n béatitude f.

beautiful adj beau, belle, magnifique; ~ly adv à la perfection, merveilleusement.

beautify vt embellir; décorer.

beauty n beauté f; ~ salon n institut de beauté m; ~ spot n site touristique m.

beaver n castor m.

because conj parce que; * prép: ~ of en raison de.

beckon vi faire signe.

become vt convenir, aller à; * vi devenir, se faire.

becoming adj convenable, seyant.

bed n lit m.

bedclothes npl couvertures et draps mpl.

bedding n literie f.

bedecked adj orné.

bedlam n maison de fous f.

bed-post n colonne de lit f.

bedridden adj cloué au lit; grabataire.

bedroom n chambre f.

bedspread n dessus-de-lit m invar.

bedtime n heure d'aller au lit f.

bee n abeille f.

beech n hêtre m.

beef n bœuf (viande) m.

beefburger n hamburger m.

beefsteak n bifteck m.

beehive n ruche f.

beeline n ligne droite f.

beer n bière f.

beeswax n cire f.

beet n betterave f.

beetle n scarabée m.

befall vi arriver, survenir; * vt arriver à.

befit vt convenir à.

before adv, prep avant; devant; * conj avant de, avant que.

beforehand adv à l'avance, au préalable.

befriend vt traiter en ami; aider.

beg vt mendier; solliciter; supplier; * vi demander la charité.

beget vt engendrer.

beggar n mendiant m, -e f.

begin vt, vi commencer.

beginner n débutant m, -e f; novice mf.

beginning n commencement, début m, origine f.

begrudge vt donner à contrecœur; envier.

behalf n faveur f, intérêt m; nom m, part f.

behave vi se comporter, se conduire.

behavior n conduite f; comportement m.

behead vt décapiter.

behind prep derrière; * adv derrière, par-derrière, en arrière.

behold vt voir; contempler; observer.

behove vt incomber à.

beige adj beige.

being n existence f; être m.

belated adj tardif.

belch vi éructer; * vt vomir; * n éructation f, rot m.

belfry n beffroi, clocher m.

belie vt démentir, tromper.

belief n foi, croyance f; conviction, opinion f, credo m.

believable adj croyable.

believe vt croire; * vi penser, croire.

believer n croyant m, -e f; adepte mf, partisan m, -e f.

belittle vt rabaisser.

bell n cloche f.

bellicose adj belliqueux.

belligerent adj belligérant.

bellow vi beugler, mugir; hurler; * n beuglement, mugissement m.

bellows npl soufflet m.

belly n ventre m.

bellyful n ventrée f; ras-le-bol m.

belong vi appartenir à.

belongings npl affaires fpl.

beloved adj chéri, bien-aimé.

below adv en dessous, en bas; * prep sous, au-dessous de, en dessous.

belt n ceinture f.

beltway n périphérique m.

bemoan vt déplorer; pleurer.

bemused adj déconcerté.

bench n banc m.

bend vt courber, plier; incliner; * vi se courber, s'incliner; * n courbe f.

beneath adv au-dessous; * prep sous, au-dessous de.

benediction n bénédiction f.

benefactor n bienfaiteur m, -trice f.

benefice n bénéfice m; bénéfice ecclésiastique m.

beneficent *adj* bienfaisant.

beneficial *adj* profitable, salutaire, utile.

beneficiary *n* bénéficiaire *mf*.

benefit *n* intérêt, avantage *m*; profit *m*; bienfait *m*; * *vt* profiter à; * *vi* bénéficier.

benefit night *n* soirée de bienfaisance *f*.

benevolence *n* bienveillance *f*; générosité *f*.

benevolent *adj* bienveillant; de bienfaisance.

benign *adj* bienveillant, doux, affable; bénin.

bent *n* penchant *m*.

benzine *n* (*chem*) benzine *f*.

bequeath *vt* léguer à.

bequest *n* legs *m*.

bereave *vt* priver.

bereavement *n* perte *f*; deuil *m*.

beret *n* béret *m*.

berm *n* accotement *m*.

berry *n* baie *f*.

berserk *adj* fou furieux.

berth *n* (*mar*) couchette *f*.

beseech *vt* supplier, implorer, conjurer.

beset *vt* assaillir.

beside(s) *prep* à côté de; excepté; * *adv* de plus, en outre.

besiege *vt* assiéger, assaillir.

best *adj* le meilleur, la meilleure; * *adv* le mieux; * *n* le meilleur, le mieux *m*.

bestial *adj* bestial, brutal; **~ly** *adv* bestialement.

bestiality *n* bestialité, brutalité *f*.

bestow *vt* accorder, conférer; consacrer.

bestseller *n* best-seller *m*.

bet *n* pari *m*; * *vt* parier.

betray *vt* trahir.

betrayal *n* trahison *f*.

betroth *vt* promettre en mariage.

betrothal *n* fiançailles *f pl*.

better *adj*, *adv* meilleur, mieux; **so much the ~** tant mieux; * *vt* améliorer.

betting *n* pari *m*.

between *prep* entre;* *adv* au milieu.

bevel *n* biseau *m*.

beverage *n* boisson *f*.

bevy *n* bande *f*.

beware *vi* prendre garde.

bewilder *vt* déconcerter, dérouter.

bewilderment *n* perplexité *f*.

bewitch *vt* ensorceler, enchanter.

beyond *prep* au-delà de; audessus de; plus de; sauf; * *adv* au-delà, plus loin.

bias *n* préjugé *m*; tendance, inclination *f*.

bib *n* bavoir *m*.

Bible *n* Bible *f*.

biblical *adj* biblique.

bibliography *n* bibliographie *f*.

bicarbonate of soda *n* bicarbonate de soude *m*.

bicker *vi* se chamailler.

bicycle *n* bicyclette *f*.

bid *vt* ordonner, commander; offrir; * *n* offre, tentative *f*.

bidding *n* ordre *m*; enchère, offre *f*.

bide *vt* attendre, supporter.

biennial *adj* biennal, bisannuel.

bifocals *npl* verres à double foyer *mpl*.

bifurcated *adj* divisé en deux branches.

big *adj* grand, gros; important.

bigamist *n* bigame *mf*.

bigamy *n* bigamie *f*.

big dipper *n* Grande Ourse *f*.

bigheaded *adj* frimeur.

bigness *n* grandeur, grosseur *f*.

bigot *n* fanatique *mf*.

bigoted *adj* fanatique.

bike *n* vélo *m*.

bikini *n* bikini *m*.

bilberry *n* airelle *f*.

bile *n* bile *f*.

bilingual *adj* bilingue.

bilious *adj* bilieux.

bill *n* bec (d'oiseau) *m*; addition *f*; billet *m*.

billboard *n* panneau d'affichage *m*.

billet *n* logement *m*.

billfold *n* portefeuille *m*.

billiards *npl* billard *m*.

billiard-table *n* table de billard *f*.

billion *n* mil milliard *m*.

billy *n* matraque *f*.

bin *n* coffre *m*.

bind *vt* attacher; lier; entourer; relier.

binder *n* relieur *m*, -euse *f*.

binding *n* reliure *f*, extra-fort *m*.

binge *n* beuverie, bringue *f*.

bingo *n* loto *m*.

biochemistry *n* biochimie *f*.

binoculars *npl* jumelles *f pl*.

biographer *n* biographe *mf*.

biographical *adj* biographique.

biography *n* biographie *f*.

biological *adj* biologique.

biology *n* biologie *f*.

biped *n* bipède *m*.

birch *n* bouleau *m*.

bird *n* oiseau *m*.

bird's-eye view *n* vue d'ensemble *m*.

bird-watcher *n* ornithologue *mf*.

birth *n* naissance *f*.

birth certificate *n* extrait de naissance *m*.

birth control *n* limitation des naissances *f*.

birthday *n* anniversaire *m*.

birthplace *n* lieu de naissance *m*.

birthright *n* droit de naissance *m*.

biscuit *n* biscuit *m*.

bisect *vt* couper en deux.

bishop *n* évêque *m*.

bison *n* bison *m*.

bit *n* morceau *m*; peu *m*.

bitch *n* chienne *f*; (*fig*) plainte *f*.

bite *n* bouchée *f*; (*fam*) mordre la poussière; * *n* morsure *f*.

bitter *adj* amer, âpre; cuisant, acerbe; glacial; ~ly *adv* amèrement; avec amertume; âprement.

bitterness *n* amertume *f*; rancœur *f*.

bitumen *n* bitume *m*.

bizarre *adj* étrange, bizarre.

blab *vi* jacasser; lâcher le morceau.

black *adj* noir, obscur; * *n* noir *m*.

blackberry *n* mûre *f*.

blackbird *n* merle *m*.

blackboard *n* tableau (noir) *m*.

blacken *vt* noircir, ternir.

black ice *n* verglas *m*.

blackjack *n* vingt-et-un *m*.

blackleg *n* jaune *m*.

blacklist *n* liste noire *f*.

blackmail *n* chantage *m*; * *vt* faire chanter.

black market *n* marché noir *m*.

blackness *n* couleur noire *f*; obscurité *f*; noirceur *f*.

black pudding *n* boudin *m*.

black sheep n brebis galeuse f.

blacksmith n forgeron m.

blackthorn n épine noire f.

bladder n vessie f.

blade n lame f.

blame vt blâmer; * n faute f.

blameless adj irréprochable; **~ly** adv irréprochablement.

blanch vt blanchir.

bland adj affable, suave; doux; apaisant.

blank adj blanc; vide, déconcerté; * n blanc m.

blank check n chèque en blanc m.

blanket n couverture f.

blare vi retentir.

blasé adj blasé.

blaspheme vt blasphémer.

blasphemous adj blasphématoire.

blasphemy n blasphème m.

blast n souffle d'air m; explosion f; * vt faire sauter.

blast-off n lancement m, mise à feu f.

blatant adj flagrant.

blaze n flamme f; * vi flamber; resplendir.

bleach vt blanchir; décolorer; * vi blanchir; * n eau de Javel f.

bleached adj blanchi; décoloré.

bleachers npl gradins m pl.

bleak adj morne, lugubre, glacial, désolé.

bleakness n froid m; austérité f.

bleary(-eyed) adj larmoyant.

bleat n bêlement m; * vi bêler.

bleed vi, vt saigner.

bleeding n saignement m.

bleeper n bip m.

blemish vt gâter; ternir; * n tache f; infamie f.

blend vt mélanger.

bless vt bénir.

blessing n bénédiction f; bienfait m.

blight vt détruire.

blind adj aveugle; **~ alley** n impasse f; * vt aveugler; éblouir; * n aveugle mf; **(Venetian) ~** store vénitien m.

blinders npl œillères f pl.

blindfold vt bander les yeux de; **~ed** adj les yeux bandés.

blindly adv à l'aveuglette, aveuglément.

blindness n cécité f.

blind side n côté faible de quelqu'un m.

blind spot n angle mort m.

blink vi clignoter.

blinkers npl clignotants m pl.

bliss n bonheur extrême m; félicité f.

blissful adj heureux; béat, bienheureux; **~ly** adv heureusement.

blissfulness n bonheur extrême m, félicité f.

blister n ampoule f; * vi se couvrir de cloques.

blitz n bombardement aérien m.

blizzard n tempête de neige f.

bloated adj gonflé, boursouflé, bouffi.

blob n goutte, tache f.

bloc n bloc m.

block n bloc m; encombrement, blocage m; pâté de maisons m; **~ (up)** vt bloquer.

blockade n blocus m; * vt faire le blocus, bloquer.

blockage n obstruction f.

blockbuster n grand succès m.

blockhead n lourdaud, sot, crétin m.

blond adj blond; * n blond m, -e f.

blood n sang m.

blood donor n donneur(-euse) de sang m(f).

blood group n groupe sanguin m.

bloodhound n limier m.

bloodily adv cruellement.

bloodiness n (fig) cruauté f.

bloodless adj exsangue, anémié; sans effusion de sang.

blood poisoning n empoisonnement du sang m.

blood pressure n pression artérielle f.

bloodshed n effusion de sang f; carnage m.

bloodshot adj injecté de sang.

bloodstream n système sanguin m.

bloodsucker n sangsue f; (fig) vampire m.

blood test n analyse de sang f.

bloodthirsty adj sanguinaire.

blood transfusion n transfusion sanguine f.

blood vessel n veine f; vaisseau sanguin m.

bloody adj sanglant, ensanglanté; cruel; **~ minded** adj sanguinaire; pas commode.

bloom n fleur f; (also fig); * vi éclore, fleurir.

blossom n fleur f.

blot vt tacher; sécher; effacer; * n tache f.

blotchy adj marbré; couvert de taches.

blotting pad n buvard m.

blotting paper n papier buvard m.

blouse n chemisier m.

blow vi souffler; sonner; * vt souffler; faire voler; jouer de; **to ~ up** exploser; * n coup m.

blowout n éclatement m.

blowpipe n sarbacane f.

blubber n blanc de baleine m; * vi pleurnicher.

bludgeon n gourdin m; matraque f.

blue adj bleu.

bluebell n campanule f.

bluebottle n (bot) bleuet m; mouche bleue f.

blueness n bleu m.

blueprint n (fig) projet m.

bluff n esbroufe f; * vt faire de l'esbroufe.

bluish adj bleuâtre.

blunder n gaffe f; * vi faire une gaffe.

blunt adj émoussé, obtus; direct; * vt émousser.

bluntly adv carrément; sans ménagements.

bluntness n brusquerie, rudesse f.

blur n tache f; * vt tacher.

blurt out vt laisser échapper.

blush n rougeur f; fard à joues m; * vi rougir.

blustery adj de tempête, violent.

boa n boa m (serpent).

boar n verrat m; **wild ~** sanglier m.

board n planche f; table f; conseil m; * vt monter à bord de.

boarder n pensionnaire mf.

boarding card n carte d'embarquement f.

boarding house n internat m; pension (de famille) f.

boarding school n pensionnat m.

boast vi se vanter; * n vantardise f; rodomontade f.

boastful *adj* vantard.

boat *n* bateau *m*; canot *m*; barque *f*.

boating *n* canotage *m*; promenade en bateau *f*.

bobsleigh *n* bobsleigh *m*.

bode *vt* présager, augurer.

bodice *n* corsage *m*.

bodily *adj*, *adv* physique(ment).

body *n* corps *m*; cadavre *m*; **any ~** n'importe qui; **every ~** tout le monde.

body-building *n* culturisme *m*.

bodyguard *n* garde du corps *m*.

bodywork *n* (*auto*) carrosserie *f*.

bog *n* marécage *m*.

boggy *adj* marécageux.

bogus *adj* faux.

boil *vi* bouillir; * *vt* faire bouillir; * *n* furoncle *m*; ébullition *f*.

boiled egg *n* œuf à la coque *m*.

boiled potatoes *npl* pommes de terre à l'eau *f pl*.

boiler *n* casserole *f*; chaudière *f*.

boiling point *n* point d'ébullition *m*.

boisterous *adj* bruyant; turbulent; tumultueux; **~ly** *adv* bruyamment, tumultueusement.

bold *adj* audacieux, téméraire, osé, hardi; **~ly** *adv* audacieusement, hardiment.

boldness *n* intrépidité *f*; audace *f*; effronterie *f*.

bolster *n* traversin *m*; * *vt* soutenir.

bolt *n* verrou *m*; * *vt* verrouiller, fermer au verrou.

bomb *n* bombe *f*; **~ disposal** déminage *m*.

bombard *vt* bombarder.

bombardier *n* bombardier *m*.

bombardment *n* bombardement *m*.

bombshell *n* (*fig*) bombe *f*.

bond *n* lien *m*; attache *f*; engagement *m*; obligation *f*.

bondage *n* esclavage, asservissement *m*.

bone holder *n* obligataire *mf*.

bone *n* os *m*; * *vt* désosser.

boneless *adj* désossé, sans os.

bonfire *n* feu (de joie) *m*.

bonnet *n* bonnet *m*.

bonny *adj* joli.

bonus *n* prime *f*.

bony *adj* osseux.

boo *vt* huer.

booby trap *n* mine *f*.

book *n* livre *m*; **to bring to ~** obliger à rendre les comptes.

bookbinder *n* relieur(-euse) de livres *m(f)*.

bookcase *n* bibliothèque *f*.

bookkeeper *n* comptable *mf*.

bookkeeping *n* comptabilité *f*.

bookmaking *n* prise des paris *f*.

bookmarker *n* signet *m*.

bookseller *n* libraire *mf*.

bookstore *n* librairie *f*.

bookworm *n* rat de bibliothèque *m*.

boom *n* grondement *m*; essor *m*; * *vi* gronder.

boon *n* bienfait *m*, aubaine *f*; faveur *f*.

boor *n* rustre *m*; brute *f*.

boorish *adj* rustre, rustique.

boost *n* stimulation *f*; * *vt* stimuler.

booster *n* propulseur *m*.

boot *n* botte *f*; coffre *m*; **to ~** *adv* de plus, de surcroît.

booth *n* cabine *f*; baraque *f*.

booty *n* butin *m*.

booze vi se saôuler; * n alcool m.

border n bord m; bordure f; lisière f; frontière f; * vt border, avoisiner.

borderline n limite f.

bore vt forer, percer; ennuyer; * n perceuse f; calibre m; raseur m.

boredom n ennui m.

boring adj ennuyeux.

born adj né; originaire.

borrow vt emprunter.

borrower n emprunteur m, -euse f.

bosom n sein m, poitrine f.

bosom friend n ami(e) intime m(f).

boss n chef m; patron(ne) m(f).

botanic(al) adj botanique.

botanist n botaniste mf.

botany n botanique f.

botch vt cochonner.

both pron tou(te)s les deux, l'un(e) et l'autre; * adj les deux; * conj à la fois; autant que.

bother vt ennuyer, déranger; * n ennui, problème m.

bottle n bouteille f; * vt mettre en bouteille.

bottleneck n embouteillage m; goulot m.

bottle-opener n ouvre-bouteille m invar.

bottom n fond m; fondement m; * adj du bas; dernier.

bottomless adj sans fond, insondable; inépuisable.

bough n branche f; rameau m.

boulder n gros galet m.

bounce vi rebondir; bondir, faire des bonds; * n bond, rebond m.

bound n limite f; saut m; répercus-

sion f; * vi bondir, sauter; * adj à destination de.

boundary n limite f; frontière f.

boundless adj illimité, infini.

bounteous, bountiful adj abondant; prodigue, généreux; bienfaisant.

bounty n libéralité, générosité f.

bouquet n bouquet m.

bourgeois adj bourgeois.

bout n attaque f; accès m; combat m.

bovine adj bovin.

bow vt incliner, baisser; * vi se courber; faire une révérence; * n salut m, révérence f.

bow n arc m; archet m; nœud m.

bowels npl intestins m pl; entrailles f pl.

bowl n bol, saladier m; boule f; * vt jouer aux boules.

bowling n boules fpl.

bowling alley n bowling m.

bowling green n terrain de boules m.

bowstring n corde (d'arc) f.

bow tie n nœud papillon m.

box n boîte, caisse f; loge f; ~ **on the ear** gifle f; * vt mettre en boîte; * vi boxer.

boxer n boxeur m.

boxing n boxe f.

boxing gloves npl gants de boxe m pl.

boxing ring n ring m.

box office n guichet m.

box-seat n place à côté du siège du cocher f.

boy n garçon m.

boycott vt boycotter; * n boycottage m.

boyfriend n petit ami m.

boyish adj d'enfant, puéril; de garçon.

bra n soutien-gorge m.

brace n attache f; bretelle f; appareil dentaire m.

bracelet n bracelet m

bracing adj vivifiant, tonifiant.

bracken n (bot) fougère f.

bracket n tranche f; parenthèse f; crochet m; * **to ~ with** vt réunir par une accolade; mettre ensemble.

bracing adj vivifiant, tonifiant.

brag n fanfaronnade f; * vi se vanter, fanfaronner.

braid n tresse f; * vt tresser.

brain n cerveau m; tête f; * vt assommer, défoncer le crâne à.

brainchild n invention personnelle f.

brainwash vt faire un lavage de cerveau à.

brainwave n idée lumineuse f.

brainy adj intelligent.

brainless adj stupide.

brake n frein m; * vt freiner.

brake fluid n liquide de frein m.

brake light n feu de stop m.

bramble n ronce f.

bran n son m.

branch n branche f; ramification f; * vi se ramifier.

branch line n (rail) ligne d'embranchement f.

brand n marque f; marque au fer f; * vt marquer au fer.

brandish vt brandir.

brand-new adj flambant-neuf.

brandy n cognac m.

brash adj grossier; impertinent.

brass n cuivre m.

brassiere n soutien-gorge m.

brat n môme, gosse mf.

bravado n bravade f.

brave adj courageux, brave, vaillant; * vt braver; * n brave m; **~ly** adv bravement, courageusement.

bravery n bravoure f; courage m; magnificence f.

brawl n bagarre, rixe f; * vi se bagarrer.

brawn n muscle m; fromage de tête m.

bray vi braire; * n braiment m.

braze vt souder au laiton.

brazen adj de cuivre; impudent, effronté; * vi crâner.

brazier n brasero m.

breach n rupture f; brèche f; violation f.

bread n pain m; (also fig); **brown ~** pain bis m.

breadbox n panière f.

breadcrumbs npl miettes de pain f pl.

breadth n largeur f.

breadwinner n soutien de famille m.

break vt casser; briser; violer; interrompre; * vi se casser; **to ~ into** entrer par effraction; **to ~ out** s'échapper; * n cassure, rupture f; interruption f; **~ of day** point du jour m, aube f.

breakage n rupture f.

breakdown n panne f; dépression nerveuse f.

breakfast n petit déjeuner m; * vi déjeuner.

breaking n bris m; violation f; fracture f.

breakthrough n percée, innovation f.

breakwater n digue f.

breast n poitrine f, sein m; cœur m.

breastbone n sternum m.

breastplate n pectoral m; plastron m.

breaststroke n brasse f.

breath n haleine f; respiration f; souffle m.

breathe vt vi respirer; exhaler.

breathing n respiration f; souffle m.

breathing space n moment de répit m.

breathless adj hors d'haleine.

breathtaking adj stupéfiant.

breed n race, espèce f; * vt élever, engendrer; produire; éduquer; * vi se reproduire.

breeder n éleveur m, -euse f.

breeding n élevage m; éducation f.

breeze n brise f.

breezy adj frais.

brethren npl frères m pl.

breviary n bréviaire m.

brevity n brièveté f; concision f.

brew n faire infuser; brasser; comploter * vi infuser; se tramer; * n infusion f.

brewer n brasseur m.

brewery n brasserie f.

briar, brier n ronce f.

bribe n pot-de-vin m; * vt acheter, soudoyer.

bribery n corruption f.

bric-a-brac n bric-à-brac m.

brick n brique f; * vt bâtir en briques.

bricklayer n maçon m.

bridal adj de noces, nuptial.

bride n mariée f.

bridegroom n marié m.

bridesmaid n demoiselle d'honneur f.

bridge n pont m; arête du nez f; chevalet m; **to ~ (over)** vt relier par un pont.

bridle n bride f; frein m; * vt brider; refréner.

brief adj bref, concis, succint; * n affaire f brève.

briefcase n serviette f.

briefly adv brièvement, en peu de mots.

brier n = briar.

brigade n (mil) brigade f.

brigadier n (mil) général de brigade f.

brigand n bandit, brigand m.

bright adj clair, brillant, éclatant; **~ly** adv avec éclat.

brighten vt faire briller; * vi s'éclairer.

brightness n éclat, brillant m.

brilliance n éclat m.

brilliant adj éclatant; génial; **~ly** adv avec éclat.

brim n bord m.

brimful adj plein jusqu'au bord.

bring vt apporter; amener; persuader; **to ~ about** entraîner, provoquer; **to ~ forth** produire, provoquer; **to ~ up** élever.

brink n bord m.

brisk adj vif, rapide, frais.

brisket n poitrine de bœuf f.

briskly adj vivement; rapidement.

bristle n poil m; soie f; * vi se hérisser.

bristly adj hérissé.

brittle adj cassant, fragile.

broach vt aborder.

broad adj large.

broadbeans npl fèves fpl.

broadcast n émission f; * vt, vi diffuser, émettre.

broadcasting n radiodiffusion f; émission de télévision f.

broaden vt élargir; * vi s'élargir.

broadly adv généralement.

broad-minded adj tolérant, aux idées larges.

broadness n largeur f.

broadside n flanc (d'un navire) m; dépliant m.

broadways adv en large, dans le sens de la largeur.

brocade n brocart m.

broccoli n brocoli m.

brochure n brochure f, dépliant m.

brogue n accent m.

broil vt griller.

broken adj cassé; interrompu; ~ English mauvais anglais m.

broker n courtier m.

brokerage n courtage m.

bronchial adj des bronches.

bronchitis n bronchite f.

bronze n bronze m; * vt bronzer, brunir.

brooch n broche f.

brood vi couver; ruminer; * n couvée f; nichée f.

brood-hen n couveuse f.

brook n ruisseau m.

broom n genêt m; balai m.

broomstick n manche à balai m.

broth n bouillon de viande et de légumes m.

brothel n bordel m.

brother n frère m.

brotherhood n fraternité f.

brother-in-law n beau-frère m.

brotherly adj fraternel; adv fraternellement.

brow n sourcil m; front m; sommet m.

browbeat vt rudoyer.

brown adj marron; brun; ~ **paper** n papier d'emballage m; ~ **bread** n pain bis m; ~ **sugar** n cassonade f; * n marron m; * vt brunir.

browse vt brouter; * vi paître.

bruise vt faire un bleu à; * n bleu m, ecchymose f.

brunch n brunch m.

brunette n brune f.

brunt n choc m.

brush n brosse f; pinceau m; accrochage m; * vt brosser.

brushwood n broussailles fpl; brindilles fpl.

brusque adj brusque.

Brussels sprout n chou de Bruxelles m.

brutal adj brutal; ~**ly** adv brutalement.

brutality n brutalité f.

brutalize vt brutaliser.

brute n brute f; * adj bestial, féroce.

brutish adj brutal, bestial; féroce; ~**ly** adv brutalement.

bubble n bulle f; * vi faire des bulles, bouillonner; pétiller.

bubblegum n bubble-gum m.

bucket n seau m.

buckle n boucle f; * vt attacher, boucler; * vi se déformer.

bucolic adj bucolique.

bud n bourgeon, bouton m; * vi bourgeonner.

Buddhism n bouddhisme m.

budding adj en bouton.

buddy n copain m.

budge vi bouger, remuer; céder.

budgerigar n perruche f.

budget n budget m.

buff n mordu m.

buffalo n bison m.

buffers npl (rail) pare-chocs m invar.

buffet n buffet m; * vt gifler; frapper.

buffoon n bouffon m.

bug n punaise f.

bugbear n épouvantail, croquemitaine m.

bugle(horn) n clairon m.

build vt construire, bâtir.

builder n constructeur m; entrepreneur m.

building n bâtiment m; immeuble, édifice m.

building society n organisme de crédit immobilier m.

bulb n bulbe m; oignon m.

bulbous adj bulbeux.

bulge vi se renfler; * n gonflement, renflement m.

bulk n masse f; volume m; grosseur f; majeure partie f; **in ~** en gros.

bulky adj volumineux; encombrant.

bull n taureau m.

bulldog n bouledogue m.

bulldozer n bulldozer m.

bullet n balle f.

bulletin board n panneau d'affichage m.

bulletproof adj pare-balles, blindé.

bullfight n corrida f.

bullfighter n torero m.

bullfighting n tauromachie f.

bullion n or en barre m.

bullock n bouvillon m.

bullring n arène f.

bull's-eye n centre de la cible m.

bully n tyran m; * vt tyranniser.

bulwark n rempart m.

bum n clochard m.

bumblebee n bourdon m.

bump n heurt m; secousse f; bosse f; * vt heurter.

bumpkin n rustre m; plouc m.

bumpy adj cahoteux, bosselé.

bun n petit pain m; chignon m.

bunch n botte f; groupe m.

bundle n paquet m, liasse f; ballot m; fagot m; * vt empaqueter, mettre en liasse.

bung n bonde f; * vt boucher.

bungalow n bungalow m.

bungle vi bousiller; * vi faire mal les choses.

bunion n oignon m.

bunk n couchette f.

bunker n abri m; bunker m.

buoy n (mar) bouée f.

buoyancy n flottabilité f; optimisme m.

buoyant adj flottable; gai, enjoué.

burden n charge f; fardeau m; * vt charger.

bureau n commode f; bureau m.

bureaucracy n bureaucratie f.

bureaucrat n bureaucrate mf.

burglar n cambrioleur m, -euse f.

burglar alarm n signal d'alarme, signal antivol m.

burglary n cambriolage m.

burial n enterrement m; obsèques f pl.

burial place n lieu de sépulture m.

burlesque n caricature, parodie f; * adj burlesque, caricatural.

burly adj robuste, de forte carrure.

burn vt brûler; incendier, mettre le feu à; * vi brûler; * n brûlure f.

burner n brûleur m.

burning adj brûlant.

burrow n terrier m; * vi se terrer.

bursar n intendant(e) m(f).

burse n bourse f.

burst vi éclater; **to ~ into tears** éclater en sanglots; **to ~ out laughing** éclater de rire; * vt **to ~ into** faire irruption dans; * n éclatement m; explosion f.

bury vt enterrer, inhumer.

bus n (auto)bus m.

bush n buisson, taillis m.

bushy adj touffu, plein de buissons.

busily adv activement, avec empressement.

business n entreprise f; commerce m; affaires f pl; activité f.

businesslike adj sérieux.

businessman n homme d'affaires m.

business trip n voyage d'affaires m.

businesswoman n femme d'affaires f.

bust n buste m.

bus-stop n arrêt d'autobus m.

bustle vi s'affairer; s'activer; * n remue-ménage m; animation f.

bustling adj animé.

busy adj occupé; actif.

busybody n mouche du coche f.

but conj mais; sauf, excepté, seulement.

butcher n boucher m, -ère f; * vt abattre, massacrer.

butcher's (shop) n boucherie f.

butchery n boucherie f, carnage m.

butler n majordome m.

butt n butte f; mégot m; * vt donner un coup de tête à.

butter n beurre m; * vt beurrer.

buttercup n (bot) bouton d'or m.

butterfly n papillon m.

buttermilk n babeurre m.

buttocks npl fesses f pl.

button n bouton m; * vt boutonner.

buttonhole n boutonnière f.

buttress n contre-fort m; soutien m; * vt soutenir.

buxom adj bien en chair.

buy vt acheter.

buyer n acheteur m, -euse f.

buzz n bourdonnement, murmure m; * vi bourdonner.

buzzard n buse f.

buzzer n interphone m.

by prep à côté de, près de; par; de; **~ and ~** bientôt; **~ the ~** à propos; **~ much** de loin; **~ all means** certainement; * adv près.

bygone adj passé.

by-law n arrêté municipal m.

bypass n route de contournement f.

by-product n sous-produit m.

by-road n chemin de traverse m.

bystander n spectateur m -trice f.

byte n (comput) octet m.

byword n proverbe, dicton m.

C

cab n taxi m.

cabbage n chou m.

cabin n cabine f; cabane f.

cabinet n conseil des ministres m; meuble de rangement m; console f.

cabinet-maker n ébéniste m.

cable n (mar) câble m.

cable car n téléphérique m.

cable television n télévision par câble f.

caboose n (mar) coquerie f.

cabstand n station de taxis f.

cache n cachette f.

cackle vi caqueter, jacasser; * n caquetage m; jacasserie f.

cactus n cactus m.

cadence n (mus) cadence f.

cadet n cadet m.

cadge vt taper (fam).

cafe n café m.

cafeteria n cafétéria f.

caffein(e) n caféine f.

cage n cage f; prison f; * vt mettre en cage; emprisonner.

cagey adj circonspect.

cajole vt cajoler pour amadouer.

cake n gâteau m.

calamitous adj calamiteux, catastrophique.

calamity n calamité f, désastre m.

calculable adj calculable.

calculate vt calculer, compter.

calculation n calcul m.

calculator n calculatrice f.

calculus n calcul m.

calendar n calendrier m.

calf n veau m; vachette f; mollet m.

calibre n calibre m.

calisthenics npl gymnastique rythmique f.

call vt appeler; appeler au téléphone; convoquer; to ~ for demander, nécessiter ; aller chercher quelqu'un; to ~ on rendre visite à; to ~ attention demander l'attention; to ~ names insulter; * n appel m; cri m; visite f; nomination f; vocation f; profession f.

caller n visiteur m, -euse f.

calligraphy n calligraphie f.

calling n profession, vocation f.

callous adj dur ; insensible.

calm n calme m, tranquillité f; * adj calme, tranquille; * vt calmer; apaiser ; ~ly adv calmement.

calmness n calme m, tranquillité f.

calorie n calorie f.

calumny n calomnie f.

Calvary n Calvaire m.

calve vi vêler, mettre bas.

Calvinist n calviniste m.

camel n chameau m.

cameo n camée m.

camera n appareil photographique m; caméra f.

cameraman n cameraman, cadreur m.

camomile n camomille f.

camouflage n camouflage m.

camp n camp m; * vi camper.

campaign n campagne f; * vi faire campagne.

campaigner n militant, candidat en campagne électorale m.

camper n campeur m, -euse f.

camping n camping m.

camphor n camphre m.

campsite n camping m.

campus n campus m.

can v aux pouvoir; * n boîte de conserve f.

canal n conduit m; canal m.

cancel vt annuler.

cancellation n annulation f.

cancer n cancer m.

Cancer n Cancer m (signe du zodiaque).

cancerous adj cancéreux.

candid adj candide, simple, sincère; ~ly adv candidement, franchement.

candidate n candidat(e) m(f).

candied adj confit.

candle n bougie f; cierge m.

candlelight n lueur d'une bougie f.

candlestick n bougeoir m.

candor n candeur f; sincérité f.

candy n bonbon m.

candy floss n barbe à papaf.

cane n canne f; bâton m.

canine adj canin.

canister n boîte f.

cannabis n cannabis m.

cannibal n cannibale mf; anthropophage mf.

cannibalism n cannibalisme m.

cannon n canon m.

cannonball n boulet de canon m.

canny adj rusé; prudent.

canoe n canoë m.

canon n canon m; règle f; ~law droit canon m.

canonization n canonisation f.

canonize vt canoniser.

can opener n ouvre-boîte m.

canopy n baldaquin m, marquise f.

cantankerous adj acariâtre, atrabilaire.

canteen n cantine f.

canter n petit galop m.

canvas n toile f.

canvass vt sonder, examiner; débattre; * vi solliciter des voix; faire du démarchage.

canvasser n prospecteur m, -trice f, démarcheur m, -euse f.

canyon n canyon m.

cap n casquette f.

capability n capacité, aptitude, faculté f; potentiel m.

capable adj capable.

capacitate vt rendre capable.

capacity n capacité, aptitude f; potentiel m.

cape n cap, promontoire m.

caper n cabriole f, gambade f; * vi cabrioler; gambader.

capillary adj capillaire.

capital adj capital; principal; * n capital m; capitale f; majuscule f.

capitalism n capitalisme m.

capitalist n capitaliste mf.

capitalize vt capitaliser; **to ~ on** profiter de.

capital punishment n peine de mort, peine capitale f.

Capitol n Capitole m.

capitulate vi capituler.

capitulation n capitulation f.

caprice n caprice m.

capricious adj capricieux; ~ly adv capricieusement.

Capricorn n Capricorne m (signe du zodiaque).

capsize vt (mar) chavirer.

capsule n capsule f.
captain n capitaine m.
captaincy, captainship n grade de capitaine m; statut de capitaine m.
captivate vt captiver.
captivation n fascination f.
captive n captif m, -ive f, prisonnier m, -ière f.
captivity n captivité f.
capture n capture f; * vt prendre, capturer.
car n voiture f, automobile f; wagon m.
carafe n carafe f.
caramel n caramel m.
carat n carat m.
caravan n caravane f.
caraway n (bot) cumin m.
carbohydrates npl hydrates de carbone m pl.
carbon n carbone m.
carbon copy n copie carbone f, double carbone m.
carbonize vt carboniser.
carbon paper n papier carbone m.
carbuncle n escarboucle f; furoncle m, tumeur maligne f.
carburetor n carburateur m.
carcass n cadavre m.
card n carte f.
cardboard n carton m.
card game n jeu de cartes m.
cardiac adj cardiaque.
cardinal adj cardinal, principal; * n cardinal m.
card table n table de jeu f.
care n soin m; souci m; * vi se soucier de, être concerné par; **what do I ~?** qu'est-ce que cela peut me faire ? **to ~ for** vt soigner; aimer.

career n carrière f; cours m; * vi aller à toute vitesse.
carefree n insouciant.
careful adj soigneux, consciencieux , prudent; **~ly** adv soigneusement.
careless adj insouciant, négligent; indolent; **~ly** adv négligemment.
carelessness n négligence, indifférence f.
caress n caresse f; * vt caresser.
caretaker n gardien m, -ienne f, concierge mf.
car-ferry n ferry m.
cargo n cargaison de navire f.
car hire n location de voiture f.
caricature n caricature f; * vt caricaturer.
caries n carie f.
caring adj aimant; humanitaire.
Carmelite n carmélite f.
carnage n carnage m.
carnal adj charnel; sensuel; **~ly** adv charnellement.
carnation n œillet m.
carnival n carnaval m.
carnivorous adj carnivore.
carol n chant m.
carpenter n charpentier m; **~'s bench** banc de menuisier m.
carpentry n charpenterie f.
carpet n tapis m; * vt recouvrir d'un tapis; moquetter.
carpeting n moquette f.
carriage n port m; voiture f; wagon m.
carriage-free adj franco de port.
carrier n porteur, transporteur m.
carrier pigeon n pigeon voyageur m.
carrion n charogne f.

carrot n carotte f.

carry vt porter; transporter; conduire; * vi porter; **to ~ the day** être victorieux; **to ~ on** continuer.

cart n charrette f; chariot m; * vt charrier.

cartel n cartel m.

carthorse n cheval de trait m.

Carthusian n chartreux m.

cartilage n cartilage m.

cartload n charretée f.

carton n pot m; boîte f.

cartoon n dessin animé m.

cartridge n cartouche f.

carve vt tailler, sculpter, ciseler.

carving n sculpture f.

carving knife n couteau à découper m.

car wash n station de nettoyage pour voitures f.

case n boîte f; valise f; cas m; étui m; enveloppe f; **in ~** au cas où.

cash n espèces fpl; * vt encaisser.

cash card n carte bancaire f.

cash dispenser n distributeur automatique de billets m.

cashier n caissier m, -ière f.

cashmere n cachemire m.

casing n chambranle m; enveloppe f.

casino n casino m.

cask n tonneau, fût m.

casket n cercueil m.

casserole n cocotte f.

cassette n cassette f.

cassette player, recorder n lecteur de cassettes, magnétophone m.

cassock n soutane f.

cast vt jeter, lancer; couler; * n coup m; moule m.

castanets npl castagnettes f pl.

castaway n réprouvé, paria m.

caste n caste f.

castigate vt punir sévèrement.

casting vote n voix prépondérante f.

cast iron n fonte f.

castle n château m.

castor oil n huile de ricin f.

castrate vt castrer.

castration n castration f.

cast steel n acier fondu m.

casual adj accidentel, fortuit; **~ly** adv par hasard, fortuitement.

casualty n victime f, mort m, -e f.

cat n chat m, chatte f.

catalog n catalogue m.

catalyst n catalyseur m.

cataplasm n cataplasme m.

catapult n catapulte f.

cataract n cascade f; déluge m.

catarrh n rhume m; catarrhe m.

catastrophe n catastrophe f.

catcall n sifflet m.

catch vt attraper, saisir; prendre; surprendre; **to ~ cold** attraper froid; **to ~ fire** prendre feu; * n prise f; capture f; (mus) canon m; attrape f.

catching adj contagieux, communicatif.

catchphrase n rengaine f.

catchword n slogan m.

catchy adj qui attire l'attention; accrocheur.

catechism n catéchisme m.

catechize vt catéchiser; interroger.

categorical adj catégorique; **~ly** adv catégoriquement.

categorize vt classer par catégories.

category n catégorie f.
cater vi approvisionner en nourriture.
caterer n fournisseur, traiteur m.
catering n restauration f.
caterpillar n chenille f.
catgut n boyau de chat m.
cathedral n cathédrale f.
catholic adj n catholique mf.
Catholicism n catholicisme m.
cattle n bétail m.
cattle show n exposition bovine f.
caucus n réunion d'un comité électoral f.
cauliflower n chou-fleur m.
cause n cause f; raison f; motif m; procès m; * vt causer.
causeway n chaussée f.
caustic adj, n caustique m/f.
cauterize vt cautériser.
caution n prudence, précaution f; avertissement m; * vt avertir.
cautionary adj d'avertissement.
cautious adj prudent, circonspect.
cavalier adj arrogant.
cavalry n cavalerie f.
cave n grotte f; caverne f.
caveat n avertissement m; mise en garde f; (law) notification f.
cavern n caverne f.
cavernous adj caverneux.
caviar n caviar m.
cavity n cavité f.
cease vt cesser, arrêter; * vi cesser.
ceasefire n cessez-le-feu m.
ceaseless adj incessant, continuel; ~ly adv continuellement.
cedar n cèdre m.
cede vt céder.

ceiling n plafond m.
celebrate vt célébrer, fêter.
celebration n fête f.
celebrity n célébrité f.
celery n céleri m.
celestial adj céleste, divin.
celibacy n célibat m.
celibate adj célibataire.
cell n cellule f.
cellar n cave f; cellier m.
cello n violoncelle m.
cellophane n cellophane f.
cellular adj cellulaire.
cellulose n (chem) cellulose f.
cement n ciment m; (also fig); * vt cimenter.
cemetery n cimetière m.
cenotaph n cénotaphe m.
censor n censeur m, critique mf.
censorious adj sévère, critique.
censorship n censure f.
censure n censure, critique f; * vt censurer, condamner; critiquer.
census n recensement m.
cent n centime m.
centenarian n centenaire mf.
centenary n centenaire m; * adj centenaire.
centennial adj centenaire.
centigrade n centigrade m.
centilitre n centilitre m.
centimetre n centimètre m.
centipede n mille-pattes m invar.
central adj central; ~ly adv de façon centralisée; dans le centre.
centralize vt centraliser.
centre n centre m; * vt centrer; concentrer; * vi se concentrer.
centrifugal adj centrifuge.
century n siècle m.

ceramic adj en céramique.

cereals npl céréales f pl.

cerebral adj cérébral.

ceremonial adj, n cérémonial m; rituel m.

ceremonious adj cérémonieux; ~ly adv solennellement.

ceremony n cérémonie f; cérémonies f pl.

certain adj certain, sûr; ~ly adv certainement, sans aucun doute.

certainty, certitude n certitude, conviction f.

certificate n certificat, acte m.

certification n authentification f.

certified mail n envoi avec accusé de réception m.

certify vt certifier, assurer.

cervical adj cervical.

cesarean section, ~ operation n (med) césarienne f.

cessation n cessation f.

cesspool n cloaque m; fosse d'aisances f.

chafe vt irriter; frotter.

chaff n menue paille f.

chaffinch n pinson m.

chagrin n dépit m.

chain n chaîne f; série, suite f; * vt enchaîner; attacher avec une chaîne.

chain reaction n réaction en chaîne f.

chainstore n grand magasin à succursales m.

chair n chaise f; * vt présider.

chairman n président m.

chalice n calice m.

chalk n craie f.

challenge n défi m; * vt défier.

challenger n provocateur m, -trice f.

challenging adj provocateur.

chamber n pièce f; chambre f.

chambermaid n femme de chambre f.

chameleon n caméléon m.

chamois leather n peau de chamois f.

champagne n champagne m.

champion n champion m, -ionne f; * vt défendre.

championship n championnat m.

chance n hasard m; chance f; occasion f; **by** ~ par hasard; * vt faire par hasard.

chancellor n chancelier m.

chancery n chancellerie f.

chandelier n lustre m.

change vt changer; * vi changer, se transformer; * n changement m, modification f; variété f; change m.

changeable adj changeant, variable; inconstant.

changeless adj constant, immuable.

changing adj variable, changeant.

channel n canal m; chaîne f; * vt canaliser.

chant n chant m; * vt chanter.

chaos n chaos m.

chaotic adj chaotique.

chapel n chapelle f.

chaplain n chapelain m.

chapter n chapitre m.

char vt carboniser.

character n caractère m; personnage m.

characteristic adj caractéristique; ~ally adv typiquement.

characterize vt caractériser.

characterless adj sans caractère.

charade n charade f.

charcoal n charbon de bois m.

charge vt charger; accuser; * n fardeau m; accusation f; (mil) attaque f; prix m.

chargeable adj passible.

charge card n carte de crédit f.

charitable adj caritatif; charitable;
~**bly** adv charitablement.

charity n charité, bienfaisance f;
aumône f.

charlatan n charlatan m.

charm n charme m; attrait m; * vt charmer, enchanter.

charming adj charmant.

chart n carte de navigation f; diagramme m.

charter n charte f; privilège m; * vt affréter.

charter flight n vol charter m.

chase vt donner la chasse à; poursuivre; * n chasse f.

chasm n abîme m.

chaste adj chaste; pur; sobre.

chasten vt châtier, corriger.

chastise vt châtier, punir, corriger.

chastisement n châtiment m.

chastity n chasteté, pureté f.

chat vi causer; * n petite conversation f, bavardage m.

chatter vi bavarder; jacasser; * n bavardage m; jacasserie f.

chatterbox n moulin à paroles m, pipelette f.

chatty adj bavard.

chauffeur n chauffeur m.

chauvinist n chauvin m, -e f.

cheap adj bon marché, peu cher;
~**ly** adv bon marché.

cheapen vt baisser le prix de.

cheaper adj moins cher.

cheat vt tromper, frauder; * n fraude, tricherie f; tricheur m, -euse f.

check vt vérifier; contrôler; réprimer, enrayer; stopper; enregistrer; * n contrôle m.

checkmate n échec et mat m.

checkout n caisse f.

checkpoint n poste de contrôle m.

checkroom n consigne f.

checkup n bilan de santé m.

cheek n joue f; culot (fam) m.

cheekbone n pommette f.

cheer n gaieté f; joie f; applaudissement m; * vt réconforter, égayer.

cheerful adj gai, enjoué, joyeux;
~**ly** adv gaiement.

cheerfulness, cheeriness n gaieté f; bonne humeur f.

cheese n fromage m.

chef n chef (de cuisine) m.

chemical adj chimique.

chemist n chimiste mf; pharmacien m, -ienne f.

chemistry n chimie f.

cheque n chèque m.

cheque account n compte courant m.

chequerboard n échiquier m.

chequered adj à carreaux.

cherish vt chérir, aimer.

cheroot n petit cigare m.

cherry n cerise f; * adj vermeil.

cherrytree n cerisier m.

cherub n chérubin m.

chess n échecs mpl.

chessboard n échiquier m.

chessman n pièce de jeu d'échecs f.

chest n poitrine f; cage thoracique f; ~ **of drawers** commode f.

chestnut n châtaigne f.

chestnut tree n châtaigner m.

chew vt mâcher, mastiquer.

chewing gum n chewing-gum m.

chic adj chic.

chicanery n chicane, chicanerie f.

chick n poussin m; (fig) poulette (fam), nana (fam) f.

chicken n poulet m.

chickenpox n varicelle f.

chickpea n pois chiche m.

chicory n chicorée f.

chide vt gronder, réprimander.

chief adj principal, en chef; ~**ly** adv principalement; * n chef m.

chief executive n directeur général m.

chieftain n chef m.

chiffon n mousseline de soie f.

chilblain n engelure f.

child n enfant m; **from a** ~ tout enfant; **with** ~ enceinte.

childbirth n accouchement m.

childhood n enfance f.

childish adj enfantin, puéril; ~**ly** adv puérilement.

childishness n enfantillage m, puérilité f.

childless adj sans enfants.

childlike adj d'enfant.

children npl de **child**: enfants mpl.

chill adj froid, frais, f fraîche; * n froid m; * vt refroidir; glacer.

chilly adj froid, très frais.

chime n carillon m; harmonie f; * vi sonner; s'accorder.

chimney n cheminée f.

chimpanzee n chimpanzé m.

chin n menton m.

china(ware) n porcelaine f.

chink n fente f; tintement m; * vi tinter.

chip vt ébrécher; * vi s'ébrécher; * n fragment, éclat m; puce f; frite f.

chiropodist n pédicure mf.

chirp vi pépier, gazouiller; * n pépiement, gazouillis m.

chirping n chant des oiseaux m.

chisel n ciseau m; * vt ciseler.

chitchat n bavardage, papotage m.

chivalrous adj chevaleresque.

chivalry n chevalerie f.

chives npl ciboulette f.

chlorine n chlore m.

chloroform n chloroforme m.

chock-full adj plein à craquer, comble.

chocolate n chocolat m.

choice n choix m, préférence f; assortiment m; sélection f; * adj de choix, de qualité.

choir n chœur m.

choke vt étrangler; étouffer.

cholera n choléra m.

choose vt choisir, élire.

chop vt trancher, couper, hacher; * n côtelette f; ~**s** pl (sl) babines f pl.

chopper n hélicoptère m.

chopping block n billot m.

chopsticks npl baguettes f pl.

chore n corvée f; travail routinier m.

choral adj choral.

chord n corde f.

chorist, chorister n choriste mf.

chorus n chœur m.

Christ n Jésus-Christ.

christen vt baptiser.

Christendom n christianisme m; chrétienté f.

christening n baptême m.

Christian adj, n chrétien m, -ne f; ~ **name** prénom m.

Christianity n christianisme m; chrétienté f.

Christmas n Noël f.

Christmas card n carte de Noël f.

Christmas Eve n veille de Noël f.

chrome n chrome m.

chronic adj chronique.

chronicle n chronique f.

chronicler n chroniqueur m.

chronological adj chronologique; ~**ly** adv chronologiquement.

chronology n chronologie f.

chronometer n chronomètre m.

chubby adj potelé.

chuck vt lancer, jeter.

chuckle vi rire, glousser.

chug vi souffler, haleter.

chum n copain m, copine f.

chunk n gros morceau m.

church n église f.

churchyard n cimetière m.

churlish adj fruste, grossier; hargneux.

churn n baratte f; * vt baratter.

cider n cidre m.

cigar n cigare m.

cigarette n cigarette f.

cigarette case n étui à cigarettes m.

cigarette end n mégot m.

cigarette holder n fume-cigarette m invar.

cinder n cendre f.

cinema n cinéma m.

cinnamon n cannelle f.

cipher n chiffre m.

circle n cercle m; groupe m; * vt encercler; tourner autour de * vi décrire des cercles.

circuit n circuit m; tour m; tournée f.

circuitous adj détourné, indirect.

circular adj circulaire; * n circulaire f.

circulate vi circuler.

circulation n circulation f.

circumcise vt circoncire.

circumcision n circoncision f.

circumference n circonférence f.

circumflex n accent circonflexe m.

circumlocution n circonlocution f.

circumnavigate vt contourner.

circumnavigation n circumnavigation f.

circumscribe vt circonscrire.

circumspect adj circonspect.

circumspection n circonspection f.

circumstance n circonstance, situation f.

circumstantial adj circonstancié; accessoire.

circumstantiate vt détailler.

circumvent vt circonvenir.

circumvention n tromperie f; tricherie f.

circus n cirque m.

cistern n citerne f.

citadel n citadelle f.

citation n citation f.

cite vt citer.

citizen n citoyen m, -enne f.

citizenship n citoyenneté f.

city n ville f.

civic *adj* civique.

civil *adj* civil, courtois; **~ly** *adv* poliment.

civil defence *n* défense passive *f*.

civil engineer *n* ingénieur des travaux publics *m*.

civilian *n* civil *m*, -e *f*.

civility *n* civilité, courtoisie *f*.

civilization *n* civilisation *f*.

civilize *vt* civiliser.

civil law *n* droit civil *m*.

civil war *n* guerre civile *f*.

clad *adj* vêtu, habillé.

claim *vt* revendiquer, réclamer; * *n* demande *f*; réclamation *f*.

claimant *n* demandeur *m*.

clairvoyant *n* voyant *m*, -e *f*.

clam *n* palourde *f*.

clamber *vi* grimper (avec difficulté).

clammy *adj* moite.

clamor *n* clameur *f*, cris *m pl*; * *vi* vociférer.

clamp *n* attache *f*; * *vt* serrer; imposer; **to ~ down on** resserrer le contrôle.

clan *n* clan, groupe *m*.

clandestine *adj* clandestin.

clang *n* bruit métallique *m*; * *vi* faire un bruit métallique.

clap *vt, vi* applaudir.

clapping *n* applaudissements *mpl*.

claret *n* vin rouge de Bordeaux *m*.

clarification *n* clarification *f*, éclaircissement *m*.

clarify *vt* clarifier, éclaircir.

clarinet *n* clarinette *f*.

clarity *n* clarté *f*.

clash *vi* se heurter; s'entrechoquer; * *n* choc *m*; affrontement *m*.

clasp *n* fermoir *m*; boucle *f*; étreinte *f*; * *vt* agrafer; étreindre.

class *n* classe *f*; catégorie *f*; * *vt* classer, classifier.

classic(al) *adj* classique; * *n* auteur classique *m*.

classification *n* classification *f*.

classified advertisement *n* petite annonce *f*.

classify *vt* classifier, classer.

classmate *n* camarade de classe *mf*.

classroom *n* salle de classe *f*.

clatter *vi* résonner; cliqueter; * *n* cliquetis *m*.

clause *n (gram)* proposition *f*; clause *f*.

claw *n* griffe *f*; serre *f*; pince *f*; * *vt* griffer; agripper.

clay *n* argile *f*.

clean *adj* propre; net; * *vt* nettoyer.

cleaning *n* nettoyage *m*.

cleanliness *n* propreté, pureté *f*.

cleanly *adj* propre; * *adv* proprement, nettement.

cleanness *n* propreté *f*.

cleanse *vt* nettoyer.

clear *adj* clair; net; transparent; évident; * *adv* distinctement; * *vt* clarifier, éclaircir; dégager; disculper; * *vi* s'éclaircir.

clearance *n* déblaiement *m*; autorisation *f*.

clear-cut *adj* net.

clearly *adv* clairement; manifestement.

cleaver *n* couperet *m*.

clef *n* clé *f*.

cleft *n* fissure, crevasse *f*.

clemency n clémence f.

clement adj clément.

clenched adj serré.

clergy n clergé m.

clergyman n ecclésiastique m.

clerical adj clérical, ecclésiastique.

clerk n ecclésiastique m; employé m.

clever adj intelligent; habile; astucieux; **~ly** adv intelligemment, habilement.

click vt claquer; * vi faire un bruit sec.

client n client m, -e f.

cliff n falaise f.

climate n climat m.

climatic adj climatique.

climax n point culminant m, apogée m.

climb vt grimper, escalader; * vi grimper, escalader.

climber n alpiniste mf.

climbing n alpinisme m.

clinch vt serrer fort.

cling vi s'accrocher (à), se cramponner (à); adhérer, (se) coller.

clinic n clinique f.

clink vt faire tinter; * vi tinter, résonner; * n tintement m.

clip vt couper; * n clip m; pince f.

clipping n coupure f.

clique n clique f.

cloak n cape f; prétexte m; * vt masquer.

cloakroom n vestiaire m.

clock n horloge f.

clockwork n mécanisme d'horloge m; * adj précis.

clod n motte (de terre) f.

clog n sabot m; * vi se boucher.

cloister n cloître m.

close vt fermer; clore, conclure; terminer; * vi se fermer; * n fin f; conclusion f; * adj proche; étroit; ajusté; dense; réservé; * adv de près; **~ by** tout près.

closed adj fermé.

closely adv étroitement; de près.

closeness n proximité f; fidélité, exactitude f; intimité f; minutie f.

closet n placard m.

close-up n gros plan m.

closure n fermeture f; clôture f.

clot n caillot m; grumeau m.

cloth n tissu m; chiffon m; toile f; clergé m.

clothe vt habiller, vêtir.

clothes npl vêtements mpl; linge m; **bed ~** draps m et couvertures mpl.

clothes basket n panière à linge f.

clotheshorse n séchoir à linge m.

clothesline n corde à linge f.

clothespin n pince à linge f.

clothing n vêtements mpl.

cloud n nuage m; nuée f; * vt rendre trouble; assombrir; * vi se couvrir; s'obscurcir.

cloudiness n nébulosité f; obscurité f.

cloudy adj nuageux, nébuleux; obscur; sombre, trouble.

clout n coup de poing m.

clove n clou de girofle m.

clover n trèfle m.

clown n clown m.

club n matraque f; club m.

club car n wagon-restaurant m.

clue n indice m, indication f; idée f.

clump n massif m.

clumsily adv gauchement.

clumsiness n gaucherie f.

clumsy adj gauche, maladroit; lourd.

cluster n bouquet m; grappe f; groupe m; * vt grouper; * vi se rassembler.

clutch n prise f; embrayage m; * vt empoigner, agripper.

clutter vt encombrer.

coach n autocar m; wagon m; entraîneur m; * vt entraîner, donner des cours particuliers à.

coach trip n excursion en car f.

coagulate vt coaguler; agglutiner; * vi se coaguler; s'agglutiner.

coal n charbon m.

coalesce vi s'unir, se fondre.

coalfield n gisement charbonnier m.

coalition n coalition f.

coalman n charbonnier m.

coalmine n mine de charbon, houillère f.

coarse adj rude; grossier; **~ly** adv grossièrement.

coast n côte f.

coastal adj côtier.

coastguard n gendarmerie maritime f.

coastline n littoral m.

coat n manteau m; pelage m; couche f; * vt enduire, revêtir.

coat hanger n cintre m.

coating n revêtement m.

coax vt cajoler.

cob n épi de maïs m.

cobbler n cordonnier m.

cobbles, cobblestones npl pavés ronds mpl.

cobweb n toile d'araignée f.

cocaine n cocaïne f.

cock n coq m; macho m; * vt armer; dresser.

cock-a-doodle-doo n cocorico m.

cockcrow n chant du coq m.

cockerel n jeune coq m.

cockfight(ing) n combat de coqs m.

cockle n (mar) coque f.

cockpit n cabine de pilotage f.

cockroach n cafard m.

cocktail n cocktail m.

cocoa n cacao m.

coconut n noix de coco f.

cocoon n cocon m.

cod n morue f.

code n code m; indicatif m.

cod-liver oil n huile de foie de morue f.

coefficient n coefficient m.

coercion n coercition, contrainte f.

coexistence n coexistence f.

coffee n café m.

coffee break n pause-café f.

coffee house n café m.

coffeepot n cafetière f.

coffee table n table basse f.

coffer n coffre m; caisse f.

coffin n cercueil m.

cog n dent d'engrenage m.

cogency n puissance, force f.

cogent adj convaincant, puissant; **~ly** adv d'une manière convaincante.

cognac n cognac m.

cognate adj apparenté.

cognition n connaissance f; cognition f.

cognisance n connaissance f; compétence f.

cognisant adj instruit; (law) compétent.

cogwheel n roue dentée f.

cohabit vi cohabiter.

cohabitation n cohabitation f.

cohere vi se tenir; être cohérent.

coherence n cohérence f.

coherent adj cohérent; logique.

cohesion n cohésion f.

cohesive adj cohésif.

coil n rouleau m; bobine f; * vt enrouler.

coin n pièce de monnaie f; * vt frapper.

coincide vi coïncider.

coincidence n coïncidence f.

coincident adj coïncident.

coke n coke m.

colander n passoire f.

cold adj froid; indifférent; ~ly adv froidement; avec froideur; * n froid m; rhume m.

cold-blooded adj insensible.

coldness n froideur f.

cold sore n bouton de fièvre m.

coleslaw n salade de chou cru f.

colic n coliques fpl.

collaborate vi collaborer.

collaboration n collaboration f.

collapse vi s'écrouler; * n écroulement; (med) évanouissement m.

collapsible adj pliant.

collar n col m.

collarbone n clavicule f.

collate vt collationner, confronter.

collateral adj concomitant; parallèle; * n nantissement subsidiaire m.

collation n collation f.

colleague n collègue mf, confrère m, consœur f.

collect vt rassembler; collectionner.

collection n collection f.

collective adj collectif; ~ly collectivement.

collector n collectionneur m, -euse f.

college n collège m.

collide vi entrer en collision, se heurter.

collision n collision f, heurt m.

colloquial adj familier; parlé; ~ly adv familièrement.

colloquialism n expression familière f.

collusion n collusion f.

colon n deux-points m invar; (med) colon m.

colonel n (mil) colonel m.

colonial adj colonial.

colonist n colon m.

colonize vt coloniser.

colony n colonie f.

colossal adj colossal.

colossus n colosse m.

colour n couleur f; prétexte m; ~s pl drapeau m; * vt colorer; * vi se colorer.

colour-blind adj daltonien.

colourful adj coloré.

colouring n teint m; coloris m.

colourless adj sans couleur, incolore.

colour television n télévision en couleur f.

colt n poulain m.

column n colonne f.

columnist n chroniqueur m.

coma n coma m.

comatose adj comateux.

comb n peigne m; * vt peigner.

combat n combat m; single ~ duel m; * vt combattre.

combatant n combattant m, -e f.

combative adj combatif.

combination n combinaison, association f.

combine vt combiner; * vi s'unir.

combustion n combustion f.

come vi venir; ~ **across**, ~ **upon** vt rencontrer par hasard, tomber sur; **to** ~ **by** vt obtenir; **to** ~ **down** vi descendre; se résumer à; **to** ~ **from** vt provenir de; être originaire de; **to** ~ **in for** vt être l'objet de; **to** ~ **into** vt hériter de; **to** ~ **round**, ~ **to** vi revenir à soi; **to** ~ **up with** vt suggérer.

comedian n comédien m; comique m.

comedienne n comédienne f; comique f.

comedy n comédie f.

comet n comète f.

comfort n confort m; aises fpl; commodités fpl; consolation f; * vt réconforter; soulager; consoler.

comfortable adj confortable; réconfortant.

comfortably adv confortablement; agréablement.

comforter n personne qui réconforte f; édredon m.

comic(al) adj comique; ~**ly** adv comiquement.

coming n venue, arrivée f; * adj à venir.

comma n (gr) virgule f.

command vt ordonner, commander; * n ordre m.

commander n commandant m.

commandment n commandement m.

commando n commando m.

commemorate vt commémorer.

commemoration n commémoration f.

commence vt, vi commencer.

commencement n commencement m.

commend vt recommander, confier à; louer.

commendable adj louable.

commendably adv élogieusement.

commendation n louange f; recommandation f.

commensurate adj proportionné.

comment n commentaire m; * vt commenter.

commentary n commentaire m; observation f.

commentator n commentateur m, -trice f.

commerce n commerce m; affaires fpl; relations fpl.

commercial adj commercial.

commiserate vt compatir avec.

commiseration n commisération f, pitié f.

commissariat n intendance f, ravitaillement m.

commission n commission f; * vt commissionner; commander.

commissioner n commissionnaire, coursier m.

commit vt commettre; confier à; engager.

commitment n engagement m.

committee n comité m.

commodity n produit m, denrée f.

common adj commun; ordinaire; **in** ~ en commun; * n terrain communal m.

commoner n roturier m, -ière f.

common law n droit coutumier m.

commonly adv communément, généralement.

commonplace n lieux communs mpl; * adj banal.

common sense n bon sens m.

Commonwealth n Commonwealth m.

commotion n vacarme m; perturbation f.

commune vi discuter avec sincérité.

communicable adj communicable, transmissible.

communicate vt communiquer, transmettre; * vi communiquer.

communication n communication f.

communicative adj communicatif.

communion n communion f.

communiqué n communiqué m.

communism n communisme m.

communist n communiste mf.

community n communauté f.

community center n centre social m.

community chest n fonds commun m.

commutable adj interchangeable, permutable.

commutation ticket n carte d'abonnement f.

commute vt échanger.

compact adj compact, serré, dense; * n accord, contrat m; **~ly** adv de façon compacte; en peu de mots.

compact disc n disque compact m.

companion n compagnon m, compagne f.

companionship n camaraderie f; compagnie f.

company n compagnie, fréquentation f; société f.

comparable adj comparable.

comparative adj comparatif; **~ly** adv comparativement.

compare vt comparer.

comparison n comparaison f.

compartment n compartiment m.

compass n boussole f.

compassion n compassion f.

compassionate adj compatissant.

compatibility n compatibilité f.

compatible adj compatible.

compatriot n compatriote mf.

compel vt contraindre, obliger, forcer.

compelling adj irrésistible.

compensate vt compenser.

compensation n compensation f; dédommagement m.

compere n animateur m, -trice f.

compete vi rivaliser (avec), faire concurrence (à).

competence n compétence f; aptitude f.

competent adj compétent; suffisant; **~ly** adv avec compétence.

competition n compétition f; concurrence f.

competitive adj concurrentiel, compétitif.

competitor n concurrent m, -e f.

compilation n compilation f.

compile vt compiler.

complacency n suffisance f.

complacent adj suffisant.

complain vi se plaindre; déposer une plainte.

complaint n plainte f; réclamation f.

complement n complément m.

complementary adj complémentaire.

complete adj complet; achevé; **~ly** adv complètement; * vt achever, mener à bien, compléter.

completion n achèvement m.

complex adj complexe.

complexion n teint m; aspect m.

complexity n complexité f.

compliance n conformité f; soumission f.

compliant adj docile, soumis.

complicate vt compliquer.

complication n complication f.

complicity n complicité f.

compliment n compliment m; * vt complimenter.

complimentary adj flatteur; à titre gracieux.

comply vi se soumettre, se plier, se conformer.

component adj composant.

compose vt composer; constituer.

composed adj calme, posé.

composer n auteur m; compositeur m, -trice f.

composite adj composite, composé.

composition n composition f.

compositor n compositeur m, -trice f.

compost n compost m.

composure n maîtrise de soi f, calme m, sang-froid m.

compound vt composer, combiner; * adj, n composé m.

comprehend vt comprendre; englober.

comprehensible adj compréhensible; **~ly** adv intelligiblement.

comprehension n compréhension f; inclusion f.

comprehensive adj global; complet; compréhensif; **~ly** adv globalement.

compress vt comprimer, concentrer; * n compresse f.

comprise vt comprendre, embrasser.

compromise n compromis m; * vt compromettre; * vi adopter un compromis.

compulsion n contrainte f; compulsion f.

compulsive adj compulsif; **~ly** adv compulsivement.

compulsory adj obligatoire.

compunction n remords, scrupule m.

computable adj computable, calculable.

computation n computation f, calcul m.

compute vt calculer.

computer n ordinateur m.

computerize vt traiter par ordinateur, informatiser.

computer programing n programmation f.

computer science n informatique f.

comrade n camarade mf, compagnon m, compagne f.

comradeship n camaraderie f.

con vt duper; * n duperie f.

concave adj concave.

concavity n concavité f.

conceal vt cacher, dissimuler.

concealment n dissimulation f; recel m.

concede vt concéder, accorder.

conceit n vanité f; trait d'esprit m.

conceited adj vaniteux, prétentieux.

conceivable adj concevable.

conceive vt concevoir; * vi concevoir.

concentrate vt concentrer.

concentration n concentration f.

concentration camp n camp de concentration m.

concentric adj concentrique.

concept n concept m.

conception n conception f.

concern vt concerner, toucher; * n affaire f; souci m.

concerning prep en ce qui concerne, concernant.

concert n concert m.

concerto n concerto m.

concession n concession f.

conciliate vt concilier.

conciliation n conciliation f.

conciliatory adj conciliateur, conciliant.

concise adj concis, succinct; ~ly adv avec concision.

conclude vt conclure; décider; déduire.

conclusion n conclusion, déduction f; fin f.

conclusive adj décisif, concluant; ~ly adv de façon concluante.

concoct vt confectionner, fabriquer.

concoction n préparation f; élaboration f.

concomitant adj concomitant.

concord n entente, harmonie f.

concordance n accord m.

concordant adj concordant.

concourse n rassemblement m; carrefour m; foule f.

concrete n béton m; * vt bétonner.

concubine n concubine f.

concur vi coïncider; s'entendre.

concurrence n consentement m, coïncidence f; union f.

concurrently adv simultanément.

concussion n commotion f.

condemn vt condamner; désapprouver.

condemnation n condamnation f.

condensation n condensation f.

condense vt condenser.

condescend vi condescendre; daigner.

condescending adj condescendant.

condescension n condescendance f.

condiment n condiment m.

condition vt conditionner; * n condition, situation f; état m.

conditional adj conditionnel, hypothétique; ~ly adv conditionnellement.

conditioned adj conditionné.

conditioner n après-shampoing m.

condolences npl condoléances fpl.

condom n préservatif m.

condominium n condominium m, copropriété f.

condone vt pardonner, fermer les yeux sur.

conducive adj propice, opportun.

conduct n conduite f; comportement m; * vt conduire, mener.

conductor n receveur m; chef d'orchestre m; conducteur m.

conduit n conduit m; tuyau m.

cone n cône m.

confection n sucrerie, confiserie f; confection f.

confectioner n confiseur m, -euse f.

confectioner's (shop) n confiserie f; pâtisserie f.

confederacy n confédération f.

confederate vi se confédérer; * adj, n confédéré m.

confer vt, vi conférer.

conference n conférence f.

confess vt confesser; * vi se confesser.

confession n confession f.

confessional n confessionnal m.

confessor n confesseur m.

confetti n confetti m.

confidant n confident m, -e f.

confide vt confier; ~ **in** se confier à.

confidence n confiance f; assurance f.

confidence trick n abus de confiance m, escroquerie f.

confident adj confiant, assuré, sûr (de soi).

confidential adj confidentiel.

configuration n configuration f.

confine vt limiter; emprisonner.

confinement n détention f; alitement m.

confirm vt confirmer; ratifier.

confirmation n confirmation f; ratification f; corroboration f.

confirmed adj invétéré, endurci.

confiscate vt confisquer.

confiscation n confiscation f.

conflagration n incendie m; conflagration f.

conflict n conflit m; lutte f; dispute f.

conflicting adj contradictoire.

confluence n confluence f; rencontre f.

conform vt conformer, adapter; * vi se conformer (à), s'adapter (à).

conformity n conformité f, accord m.

confound vt confondre.

confront vt confronter; affronter.

confrontation n affrontement m, confrontation f.

confuse vt confondre; embarrasser; embrouiller.

confusing adj déroutant.

confusion n confusion f; désordre m.

congeal vt solidifier, congeler; * vi se solidifier, se congeler.

congenial adj sympathique; similaire.

congenital adj congénital.

congested adj encombré, congestionné.

congestion n encombrement m, congestion f.

conglomerate vt conglomérer, agglomérer; * adj aggloméré; * n (com) conglomérat m.

conglomeration n agglomération f.

congratulate vt complimenter, féliciter.

congratulations npl félicitations fpl.

congratulatory adj de félicitations.

congregate vt rassembler, réunir.

congregation n assemblée f, rassemblement m.

congress n congrès m; conférence f.

congressman n membre du Congrès m.

congruity n congruence f.

congruous adj congru, approprié.

conic(al) adj conique.

conifer n conifère m.

coniferous adj (bot) conifère.

conjecture n conjecture, supposition f; * vt conjecturer, supposer.

conjugal adj conjugal.

conjugate vt (gr) conjuguer.

conjugation n conjugaison f.

conjunction n conjonction f; union f.

conjuncture n conjoncture f; occasion f.

conjure vt conjurer; exorciser.

conjurer n magicien m, -ienne f, illusionniste mf.

con man n escroc m.

connect vt relier, joindre, rattacher.

connection n liaison, connexion f.

connivance n connivence f.

connive vi fermer les yeux (sur); être de connivence.

connoisseur n connaisseur m, -euse f.

conquer vt conquérir; vaincre.

conqueror n vainqueur m; conquérant m.

conquest n conquête f.

conscience n conscience f.

conscientious adj consciencieux; de conscience; **~ly** adv consciencieusement.

conscious adj conscient; intentionnel; **~ly** adv consciemment, sciemment.

consciousness n conscience f.

conscript n conscrit m.

conscription n conscription f.

consecrate vt consacrer.

consecration n consécration f.

consecutive adj consécutif; **~ly** adv consécutivement.

consensus n consensus m.

consent n consentement m; assentiment m; * vi consentir.

consequence n conséquence f; importance f.

consequent adj consécutif; **~ly** adv par conséquent.

conservation n conservation f.

conservative adj conservateur.

conservatory n conservatoire m.

conserve vt conserver; * n conserve f.

consider vt considérer, examiner; * vi penser, délibérer.

considerable adj considérable; important; **~bly** adv considérablement.

considerate adj prévenant, attentionné; prudent; **~ly** adv avec prévenance; prudemment.

consideration n considération f; réflexion f; estime f; rémunération f.

considering conj étant donné que; **~ that** vu que; étant donné que.

consign vt confier, remettre, expédier.

consignment n expédition f, envoi m.

consist vi consister (en).

consistency n consistance f; cohérence f; constance f.

consistent adj constant; cohérent; compatible; **~ly** adv régulièrement.

consolable adj consolable.

consolation n consolation f; réconfort m.

consolatory adj consolateur.

console vt consoler.

consolidate vt consolider, grouper; * vi se consolider.

consolidation n consolidation f.

consonant adj en accord; * n (gr) consonne f.

consort n consort m; associé m, -e f.

conspicuous adj voyant, manifeste; notable; ~ly adv manifestement .

conspiracy n conspiration f.

conspirator n conspirateur m, -trice f.

conspire vi conspirer.

constancy n constance, fermeté d'âme f; persévérance f.

constant adj constant; persévérant; ~ly adv constamment.

constellation n constellation f.

consternation n consternation f.

constipated adj constipé.

constituency n électorat m; circonscription f.

constituent n composant m; * adj constituant.

constitute vt constituer; établir.

constitution n constitution f.

constitutional adj constitutionnel.

constrain vt contraindre, forcer, obliger.

constraint n contrainte f.

constrict vt serrer; gêner.

construct vt construire, bâtir.

construction n construction f.

construe vt interpréter, analyser.

consul n consul m.

consular adj consulaire.

consulate, consulship n consulat m.

consult vt consulter; * vi (se) consulter.

consultation n consultation, délibération f.

consume vt consommer; dissiper; consumer, brûler; * vi se consommer.

consumer n consommateur m, -trice f.

consumer goods npl biens de consommation mpl.

consumerism n consumérisme m.

consumer society n société de consommation f.

consummate vt consommer, accomplir; perfectionner; * adj accompli, consommé.

consummation n consommation f; perfection f.

consumption n consommation f.

contact n contact m.

contact lenses npl lentilles de contact fpl.

contagious adj contagieux.

contain vt contenir, renfermer; réfréner.

container n récipient m.

contaminate vt contaminer; ~d adj contaminé.

contamination n contamination f.

contemplate vt contempler.

contemplation n contemplation f.

contemplative adj contemplatif.

contemporaneous, contemporary adj contemporain.

contempt n mépris, dédain m.

contemptible adj méprisable, vil; ~ly adv vilement.

contemptuous adj méprisant, dédaigneux; ~ly adv dédaigneusement.

contend vi combattre, lutter; * vt affirmer.

content adj content, satisfait; * vt

contenter, satisfaire; * n contentement m; **~s** pl contenu m; table des matières f.

contentedly adv avec contentement.

contention n querelle, altercation f.

contentious adj litigieux; querelleur; **~ly** adv en chicanant.

contentment n contentement m, satisfaction f.

contest vt contester, discuter, disputer; * n concours m; altercation f.

contestant n concurrent m, -e f.

context n contexte m.

contiguous adj contigu, voisin.

continent adj continent, chaste; * n continent m.

continental adj continental.

contingency n contingence f; événement imprévu m; éventualité f.

contingent n contingent m; * adj contingent, éventuel; **~ly** adv fortuitement.

continual adj continuel; **~ly** adv continuellement.

continuation n continuation, reprise, suite f.

continue vt, vi continuer.

continuity n continuité f.

continuous adj continu; **~ly** adv sans interruption.

contort vt tordre, déformer.

contortion n contorsion f.

contour n contour m.

contraband n contrebande f; * adj de contrebande.

contraception n contraception f.

contraceptive n contraceptif m; * adj contraceptif.

contract vt contracter; *vi se contracter; * n contrat m.

contraction n contraction f.

contractor n entrepreneur m.

contradict vt contredire.

contradiction n contradiction f.

contradictory adj contradictoire.

contraption n gadget, bidule (fam) m.

contrariness n esprit de contradiction m.

contrary adj contraire, opposé; * n contraire m; **on the ~** au contraire.

contrast n contraste m; * vt contraster, mettre en contraste.

contrasting adj contrasté, opposé.

contravention n infraction f.

contributary adj contributif.

contribute vt contribuer.

contribution n contribution f; cotisation f.

contributor n souscripteur(-trice), collaborateur(-trice) m(f).

contributory adj contribuant.

contrite adj contrit, repentant.

contrition n contrition f, repentir m.

contrivance n dispositif m; invention f.

contrive vt inventer, combiner; trouver le moyen de.

control n contrôle m; maîtrise f; autorité f; * vt maîtriser; régler; contrôler; gouverner.

control room n salle des commandes f.

control tower n tour de contrôle f.

controversial adj polémique.

controversy n polémique f.

contusion n contusion f.

conundrum n énigme f.

conurbation n conurbation f.

convalesce vi être en convalescence.

convalescence n convalescence f.

convalescent adj convalescent.

convene vt convoquer; réunir; * vi se réunir.

convenience n commodité, convenance f.

convenient adj commode, pratique; qui convient; **~ly** adv commodément.

convent n couvent m.

convention n convention f; contrat m; assemblée f.

conventional adj conventionnel.

converge vi converger.

convergence n convergence f.

convergent adj convergent.

conversant adj au courant; compétent.

conversation n conversation f.

converse vi converser.

conversely adv inversement, réciproquement.

conversion n conversion; transformation f.

convert vt convertir; * n converti m, -e f.

convertible adj convertible; * n décapotable f.

convex adj convexe.

convexity n convexité f.

convey vt transporter; transmettre, communiquer.

conveyance n transport m; transfert m; cession f.

conveyancer n notaire m.

convict vt déclarer coupable; * n détenu m, -e f.

conviction n condamnation f; conviction f.

convince vt convaincre, persuader.

convincing adj convaincant.

convincingly adv de façon convaincante.

convivial adj jovial.

conviviality n convivialité f.

convoke vt convoquer.

convoy n convoi m.

convulse vt ébranler.

convulsion n convulsion f; bouleversement m; forte agitation f.

convulsive adj convulsif; **~ly** adv convulsivement.

coo vt, vi roucouler.

cook n cuisinier m, -ière f; * vt cuire; falsifier; * vi faire la cuisine, cuisiner.

cookbook n livre de cuisine m.

cooker n cuisinière f.

cookery n cuisine f.

cookie n petit gâteau m.

cool adj frais; calme; * n fraîcheur f; * vt rafraîchir, refroidir.

coolly adv fraîchement; de sang-froid.

coolness n fraîcheur f; froideur f; sang-froid m.

cooperate vi coopérer.

cooperation n coopération f.

cooperative adj coopératif.

coordinate vt coordonner.

coordination n coordination f.

cop n (fam) flic m.

copartner n coassocié m, -e f.

cope vi se débrouiller.

copier n photocopieuse f.

copious adj copieux, abondant; **~ly** adv abondamment.

copper n cuivre m.

coppice, copse n taillis m.

copulate vi copuler.

copy n copie f; reproduction f; exemplaire m; * vt copier; imiter.

copybook n cahier m.

copying machine n photocopieuse f.

copyist n copiste mf.

copyright n droit d'auteur m.

coral n corail m.

coral reef n récif de corail m.

cord n corde f, cordon m.

cordial adj cordial, chaleureux; **~ly** adv cordialement.

corduroy n velours côtelé m.

core n trognon m; noyau, centre, cœur m.

cork n liège m; bouchon m; * vt boucher.

corkscrew n tire-bouchon m.

corn n maïs m; grain m; blé m.

corncob n épi de maïs m.

cornea n cornée f.

corned beef n corned-beef m.

corner n coin m; angle m.

cornerstone n pierre angulaire f.

cornet n cornet m.

cornfield n champ de maïs m.

cornflakes npl flocons de maïs, cornflakes mpl.

cornice n corniche f.

cornstarch n farine de maïs f.

corollary n corollaire m.

coronary n infarctus m.

coronation n couronnement m.

coroner n coroner m.

coronet n couronne f.

corporal n caporal m.

corporate adj en commun; d'entreprise.

corporation n corporation f; société par actions f.

corporeal adj corporel.

corps n corps m.

corpse n cadavre m.

corpulent adj corpulent.

corpuscle n corpuscule m; électron m.

corral n corral m.

correct vt corriger; rectifier; * adj correct, juste; **~ly** adv correctement.

correction n correction f; rectification f.

corrective adj correcteur, correctif; * n correcteur m.

correctness n correction f.

correlation n corrélation f.

correlative adj corrélatif.

correspond vi correspondre.

correspondence n correspondance f.

correspondent adj correspondant; * n correspondant m, -e f.

corridor n couloir, corridor m.

corroborate vt corroborer.

corroboration n corroboration f.

corroborative adj qui corrobore.

corrode vt corroder.

corrosion n corrosion f.

corrosive n corrosif m.

corrugated iron n tôle ondulée f.

corrupt vt corrompre; * vi se corrompre, se pourrir; * adj corrompu; dépravé.

corruptible adj corruptible.

corruption n corruption f; dépravation f.

corruptive adj qui corrompt.

corset n corset m, gaine f.

cortege n cortège m.

cosily adv confortablement, douillettement.

cosmetic adj, n cosmétique m.

cosmic adj cosmique.

cosmonaut n cosmonaute mf.

cosmopolitan adj cosmopolite.

cosset vt dorloter.

cost n prix, coût m; * vi coûter.

costly adj coûteux, cher.

costume n costume m.

cottage n cottage m.

cotton n coton m.

cotton candy n barbe à papa f.

cotton mill n filature de coton f.

cotton wool n coton hydrophile m.

couch n canapé, divan m.

couchette n couchette f.

cough n toux f; * vi tousser.

council n conseil m.

councillor n membre du conseil m; conseiller m, -ère f.

counsel n conseil m; avocat m.

counsellor n conseiller m, -ère f; avocat m.

count vt compter, dénombrer; calculer; **to ~ on** compter sur; * n compte m; calcul m; chef d'accusation m.

countdown n compte à rebours m.

countenance n visage m; aspect m; mine f.

counter n comptoir m; jeton m.

counteract vt contrecarrer; neutraliser; contrebalancer.

counterbalance vt contrebalancer; compenser; * n contrepoids m.

counterfeit vt contrefaire; * adj faux.

countermand vt annuler.

counterpart n contrepartie f; homologue m.

counterproductive adj qui va à l'encontre du but visé.

countersign vt contresigner.

countess n comtesse f.

countless adj innombrable.

countrified adj rustique; campagnard.

country n pays m; patrie f; campagne f; région f; * adj rustique; campagnard.

country house n maison de campagne f.

countryman n campagnard m; compatriote m.

county n comté m.

coup n coup m.

coupé n coupé m.

couple n couple m; **a ~ of** deux; * vt unir, associer.

couplet n distique m; couplet m.

coupon n coupon m.

courage n courage m.

courageous adj courageux; **~ly** adv courageusement.

courier n messager m; guide m.

course n cours m; route f; chemin m; plat m; marche à suivre f; **of ~** bien sûr, naturellement.

court n cour f; tribunal m; * vt courtiser; solliciter.

courteous adj courtois; poli; **~ly** adv courtoisement.

courtesan n courtisane f.

courtesy n courtoisie f.

courthouse n palais de justice m.

courtly adj élégant, raffiné.

court martial n conseil de guerre m.

courtroom n salle de tribunal f.

courtyard n cour f.

cousin n cousin m, -e f; **first ~** cousin(e) germain(e) m(f).

cove n (mar) crique, anse f.

covenant n contrat m; convention f; * vi convenir, stipuler par contrat.

cover n couverture f; abri m; prétexte m; * vt (re)couvrir; dissimuler; protéger.

coverage n reportage m, couverture f.

coveralls npl bleu de travail m.

covering n couverture f; couche f.

cover letter n lettre explicative f.

covert adj voilé; caché, secret; **~ly** adv secrètement.

cover-up n dissimulation f.

covet vt convoiter.

covetous adj avide, cupide.

cow n vache f.

coward n lâche mf.

cowardice n lâcheté f.

cowardly adj lâche; adv lâchement.

cowboy n cowboy m.

cower vi se tapir.

cowherd n vacher m.

coy adj timide; coquet; évasif; **~ly** adv évasivement.

coyness n timidité f; modestie f.

cozy adj douillet.

crab n crabe m.

crab apple n pomme sauvage f; **crab-apple tree** n pommier sauvage m.

crack n craquement m; fente, fissure f; * vt fêler, craquer; **to ~ down on** réprimer; * vi se fêler; craquer.

cracker n pétard m ; biscuit salé m.

crackle vi crépiter, pétiller.

crackling n crépitement m; friture f.

cradle n berceau m; * vt bercer.

craft n habileté f; métier manuel m; barque f.

craftily adv astucieusement.

craftiness n astuce, ruse f.

craftsman n artisan m.

craftsmanship n artisanat m.

crafty adj astucieux, rusé.

crag n rocher escarpé m.

cram vt bourrer; fourrer; * vi s'entasser.

crammed adj bourré.

cramp n crampe f; * vt entraver.

cramped adj à l'étroit.

crampon n crampon m.

cranberry n canneberge f.

crane n grue f.

crash vi s'écraser; * n fracas m; collision f.

crash helmet n casque m.

crash landing n atterrissage en catastrophe m.

crass adj grossier, crasse.

crate n caisse f; cageot m.

crater n cratère m.

cravat n foulard m, cravate f.

crave vt avoir extrêmement besoin de.

craving adj désespéré; insatiable; * n désir extrême m.

crawfish n écrevisse f.

crawl vi ramper; **to ~ with** grouiller de.

crayfish n écrevisse f.

crayon n crayon de couleur m.

craze n manie f, engouement m.

craziness n folie f.

crazy adj fou.

creak vi grincer, craquer.

cream n crème f; * adj crème.

creamy adj crémeux.

crease n pli m; * vt froisser.

create vt créer; causer.

creation n création f.

creative adj créatif.

creator n créateur m, -trice f.

creature n créature f.

credence n croyance, foi f; crédence f.

credentials npl lettres de créance fpl; preuves d'identité fpl.

credibility n crédibilité f.

credible adj crédible.

credit n crédit m; honneur m; reconnaissance f; * vt croire, reconnaître; créditer.

creditable adj estimable, honorable; **~bly** adv honorablement.

credit card n carte de crédit f.

creditor n créancier m, -ière f.

credulity n crédulité f.

credulous adj crédule; **~ly** adv avec crédulité.

creed n credo m.

creek n ruisseau m.

creep vi ramper; avancer lentement.

creeper n (bot) plante grimpante f.

creepy adj terrifiant, qui donne la chair de poule.

cremate vt incinérer.

cremation n incinération, crémation f.

crematorium n crématoire m.

crescent adj croissant; * n croissant de lune m.

cress n cresson m.

crest n crête f.

crested adj à crête.

crestfallen adj découragé, abattu.

crevasse n crevasse f.

crevice n fissure, lézarde f.

crew n bande, équipe f; équipage m.

crib n berceau m; mangeoire f.

cricket n grillon m.

crime n crime m; délit m.

criminal adj criminel; **~ly** adv criminellement; * n criminel m, -elle f.

criminality n criminalité f.

crimson adj, n cramoisi m.

cripple n, adj invalide mf; * vt estropier; (fig) paralyser.

crisis n crise f.

crisp adj frais; croquant.

crispness n croquant m.

criss-cross adj entrecroisé.

criterion n critère m.

critic n critique m.

critic(al) adj critique; exigeant, sévère; **~ally** adv d'un œil critique; sévèrement.

criticism n critique f.

criticize vt critiquer.

croak vi coasser, croasser.

crochet n crochet m; * vt faire au crochet; vi faire du crochet.

crockery n poterie f.

crocodile n crocodile m.

crony n copain (copine) de longue date m(f).

crook n (fam) escroc m; filou m.

crooked adj tordu; malhonnête.

crop n culture f; récolte f; * vt récolter.

cross n croix f; croisement m; * adj de mauvaise humeur, fâché; * vt traverser, croiser; **to ~ over** traverser.

crossbar n barre transversale f.

crossbreed n hybride m.

cross-country n cross-country m.

cross-examine vt soumettre à un contre-interrogatoire.

crossfire n feux croisés mpl.

crossing n traversée f; passage pour piétons m.

cross-purpose n malentendu m; quiproquo m; **to be at ~s** comprendre (quelqu'un) de travers.

cross-reference n renvoi m, référence f.

crossroad n carrefour m.

crosswalk n passage clouté m.

crotch n entre-jambes m.

crouch vi s'accroupir, se tapir.

crow n corbeau m; chant du coq m; * vi chanter victoire.

crowd n foule f; monde m; * vt entasser; * vi s'entasser.

crown n couronne f; sommet m; * vt couronner.

crown prince n prince héritier m.

crucial adj crucial.

crucible n creuset m.

crucifix n crucifix m.

crucifixion n crucifixion f.

crucify vt crucifier.

crude adj brut, grossier; **~ly** adv crûment.

cruel adj cruel; **~ly** adv cruellement.

cruelty n cruauté f.

cruet n huilier-vinaigrier m.

cruise n croisière f; * vi croiser.

cruiser n croiseur m.

crumb n miette f.

crumble vt émietter; effriter; * vi s'émietter; se désintégrer.

crumple vt froisser.

crunch vt croquer; * n (fig) crise f.

crunchy adj croquant.

crusade n croisade f.

crush vt écraser; opprimer; * n cohue f.

crust n croûte f.

crusty adj croustillant; hargneux; bourru.

crutch n béquille f.

crux n cœur m.

cry vt, vi crier; pleurer; * n cri m; sanglot m.

crypt n crypte f.

cryptic adj énigmatique.

crystal n cristal m.

crystal-clear adj clair comme de l'eau de roche.

crystalline adj cristallin; pur.

crystallize vi se cristalliser; * vt cristalliser.

cub n petit m.

cube n cube m.

cubic adj cubique.

cuckoo n coucou m.

cucumber n concombre m.

cud n: **to chew the ~** ruminer; (also fig).

cuddle vt embrasser; * vi s'enlacer; * n étreinte f.

cudgel n gourdin m, trique f.

cue n queue de billard f.

cuff n manchette f; revers de pantalon m.

culinary adj culinaire.

cull vt sélectionner; éliminer.

culminate vi culminer.

culmination n point culminant m.

culpability n culpabilité f.
culpable adj coupable; blâmable; **~bly** adv coupablement.
culprit n coupable mf.
cult n culte m.
cultivate vt cultiver; améliorer, perfectionner.
cultivation n culture f.
cultural adj culturel.
culture n culture f.
cumbersome adj encombrant; lourd, pesant.
cumulative adj cumulatif.
cunning adj astucieux, rusé; **~ly** adv astucieusement; habilement; * n astuce, finesse f.
cup n tasse, coupe f; (bot) corolle f.
cupboard n placard m.
curable adj guérissable.
curate n vicaire m.
curator n conservateur m; curateur m.
curb n frein m; bord du trottoir m; * vt freiner, juguler, modérer.
curd n lait caillé m.
curdle vt cailler, figer; vi se cailler, se figer.
cure n remède m; cure f; * vt guérir.
curfew n couvre-feu m.
curing n salaison f.
curiosity n curiosité f.
curious adj curieux; **~ly** adv avec curiosité; curieusement.
curl n boucle de cheveux f; * vt boucler; friser; * vi friser.
curling iron n, **curling tongs** npl fer à friser m.
curly adj frisé, bouclé.
currant n groseille f.
currency n monnaie f; circulation f; cours m.

current adj courant; actuel; * n cours m; tendance f; courant m.
current affairs npl actualité f; problèmes actuels mpl.
currently adv actuellement.
curriculum vitae n curriculum vitae m.
curry n curry m.
curse vt maudire; * vi jurer; * n malédiction f.
cursor n curseur m.
cursory adj superficiel; hâtif.
curt adj succinct; sec.
curtail vt réduire; écourter.
curtain n rideau m.
curtain rod n tringle à rideaux f.
curtsy n révérence f; * vi faire une révérence.
curvature n courbure f.
curve vt courber; * n courbe f.
cushion n coussin m.
custard n crème anglaise f.
custodian n gardien m, -ienne f.
custody n garde f; emprisonnement m.
custom n coutume f, usage m.
customary adj habituel, coutumier, ordinaire.
customer n client m, -e f.
customs npl douane f.
customs duty n droits de douane mpl.
customs officer n douanier m.
cut vt découper; couper; tailler; réduire; blesser; **to ~ short** écourter; interrompre; **to ~ a tooth** percer une dent; * vi couper; se couper; * n coup m; coupure f; réduction f; **~ and dried** adj arrangé.
cutback n réduction f.
cute adj mignon.

cutlery n couverts mpl.

cutlet n côtelette f.

cut-rate adj à prix réduit.

cut-throat n assassin m; * adj acharné.

cutting n coupure f; * adj coupant; tranchant.

cyanide n cyanure m.

cycle n cycle m; bicyclette f; * vi aller à bicyclette.

cycling n cyclisme m.

cyclist n cycliste mf.

cyclone n cyclone m.

cygnet n jeune cygne m.

cylinder n cylindre m; rouleau m.

cylindric(al) adj cylindrique.

cymbals n cymbale f.

cynic(al) adj cynique; sceptique; * n cynique mf.

cynicism n cynisme m.

cypress n cyprès m.

cyst n kyste m.

czar n tsar m.

D

dab n petit peu m; touche f.

dabble vi barboter.

Dacron n térylène m.

dad(dy) n papa m.

daddy-long-legs n cousin m.

daffodil n narcisse m, jonquille f.

dagger n poignard m.

daily adj quotidien; * adv quotidiennement, tous les jours; * n quotidien m.

daintily adv délicatement.

daintiness n élégance f; délicatesse f.

dainty adj délicat; élégant.

dairy n laiterie f.

dairy farm n laiterie f.

dairy produce n produits laitiers mpl.

daisy n marguerite f.

daisy wheel n marguerite f.

dale n vallée f.

dally vi traîner.

dam n barrage m; * vt endiguer.

damage n dommage m; tort m; * vt endommager; faire du tort à.

damask n damas m; * adj damassé.

dame n dame f; fille f.

damn vt condamner; * adj maudit.

damnable adj maudit; ~bly adv terriblement.

damnation n damnation f.

damning adj accablant.

damp adj humide; * n humidité f; * vt humidifier.

dampen vt humidifier.

dampness n humidité f.

damson n prune de Damas f.

dance n danse f; soirée dansante f; * vi, vt danser.

dance hall n dancing m.

dancer n danseur m, -euse f.

dandelion n pissenlit m.

dandruff n pellicules fpl.

dandy adj génial.

danger n danger m.

dangerous adj dangereux; ~ly adv dangereusement.

dangle vi pendre.

dank adj humide.

dapper adj soigné.

dappled adj tacheté.

dare vi oser; * vt défier.

daredevil n casse-cou m invar.

daring n audace f; * adj audacieux; ~ly adv audacieusement.

dark adj sombre, obscur; * n obscurité f; ignorance f.

darken vt assombrir, obscurcir; * vi s'assombrir, s'obscurcir.

dark glasses npl lunettes de soleil fpl.

darkness n obscurité f.

darkroom n chambre noire f.

darling n, adj chéri m, -e f.

darn vt repriser.

dart n dard m.

dartboard n jeu de fléchettes f.

dash vi se dépêcher; * n goutte f; tiret, trait m; **at one** ~ tout d'un coup.

dashboard n tableau de bord m.

dashing adj impétueux; élégant.

dastardly adj lâche.

data n données fpl.

database n base de données f.

data processing n traitement de données m.

date n date f; rendez-vous m; (bot) datte f; * vt dater; sortir avec.

dated adj démodé.

dative n (gr) datif m.

daub vt barbouiller.

daughter n fille f; ~ **in-law** belle-fille f.

daunting adj décourageant.

dawdle vi traîner.

dawn n aube f; * vi se lever.

day n jour m, journée f; **by** ~ de jour; ~ **by** ~ de jour en jour.

daybreak n aube f.

day laborer n journalier m.

daylight n lumière du jour, lumière

naturelle f; ~ **saving time** n heure d'été f.

daytime n journée f, jour m.

daze vt étourdir.

dazed adj étourdi.

dazzle vt éblouir.

dazzling adj éblouissant.

deacon n diacre m.

dead adj mort; ~**wood** n bois mort m; ~ **silence** n silence de mort m; **the** ~ npl les morts mpl.

dead-drunk adj ivre-mort.

deaden vt amortir.

dead heat n arrivée ex-aequo f.

deadline n date limite f.

deadlock n impasse f.

deadly adj mortel; * adv terriblement.

dead march n marche funèbre f.

deadness n inertie f.

deaf adj sourd.

deafen vt assourdir.

deaf-mute n sourd(e)-muet(te) mf.

deafness n surdité f.

deal n accord m; marché m; **a great** ~ beaucoup; **a good** ~ pas mal; * vt distribuer, donner; * vi **to** ~ **in** être dans le commerce de; **to** ~ **with** avoir affaire à.

dealer n commerçant m; trafiquant m; donneur m.

dealings npl rapports mpl; transactions fpl.

dean n doyen m.

dear adj, ~**ly** adv cher.

dearness n cherté f.

dearth n pénurie f.

death n mort f.

deathbed n lit de mort m.

deathblow n coup mortel m.

death certificate n acte de décès m.

death penalty n peine de mort f.

death throes npl agonie f.

death warrant n condamnation à mort f.

debacle n débâcle f.

debar vt exclure.

debase vt dégrader.

debasement n dégradation f.

debatable adj discutable.

debate n débat m; * vt discuter; examiner.

debauched adj débauché.

debauchery n débauche f.

debilitate vt débiliter.

debit n débit m; * vt (com) débiter.

debt n dette f; **to get into ~** s'endetter.

debtor n débiteur m, -trice f.

debunk vt démystifier.

decade n décennie f.

decadence n décadence f.

decaffeinated adj décaféiné.

decanter n carafe f.

decapitate vt décapiter.

decapitation n décapitation f.

decay vi décliner; pourrir; * n déclin m; pourrissement m; carie f.

deceased adj décédé.

deceit n tromperie f.

deceitful adj trompeur; **~ly** adv faussement.

deceive vt tromper.

December n décembre m.

decency n décence f; pudeur f.

decent adj décent; bien, bon; **~ly** adv décemment.

deception n tromperie f.

deceptive adj trompeur.

decibel n décibel m.

decide vt decider; * vi se décider.

decided adj décidé.

decidedly adv décidément.

deciduous adj (bot) à feuilles caduques.

decimal adj décimal.

decimate vt décimer.

decipher vt déchiffrer.

decision n décision, détermination f.

decisive adj décisif; **~ly** adv avec décision.

deck n pont m; * vt orner.

deckchair n chaise longue f.

declaim vt, vi déclamer.

declamation n déclamation f.

declaration n déclaration f.

declare vt déclarer.

declension n déclinaison f.

decline vt (gr) décliner; refuser; * vi décliner; * n déclin m; décadence f.

declutch vi débrayer.

decode vt décoder.

decompose vt décomposer.

decomposition n décomposition f.

decor n décor m; décoration f.

decorate vt décorer, orner.

decoration n décoration f.

decorative adj décoratif.

decorator n décorateur m, -trice f.

decorous adj correct, convenable; **~ly** adv convenablement.

decorum n décorum m.

decoy n leurre m.

decrease vt diminuer; * n diminution f.

decree n décret m; * vt décréter; ordonner.

decrepit adj décrépit.

decry vt décrier.

dedicate vt dédier; consacrer.

dedication n dédicace f; consacration f.

deduce vt déduire, conclure.

deduct vt déduire, soustraire.

deduction n déduction f.

deed n action f; exploit m.

deem vt juger.

deep adj profond.

deepen vt approfondir.

deep-freeze n congélateur m.

deeply adv profondément.

deepness n profondeur f.

deer n cerf m.

deface vt défigurer.

defacement n défiguration f.

defamation n diffamation f.

default n défaut m; manque m; * vi manquer à ses engagements.

defaulter n (law) défaillant m, -e f.

defeat n défaite f; * vt vaincre; frustrer.

defect n défaut m.

defection n désertion f.

defective adj défectueux.

defend vt défendre; protéger.

defendant n accusé m, -e f.

defense n défense f; protection f.

defenseless adj sans défense.

defensive adj défensif; ~ly adv défensivement.

defer vt déférer.

deference n déférence f.

deferential adj respectueux.

defiance n défi m.

defiant adj provocant.

deficiency n défaut m; manque m.

deficient adj insuffisant.

deficit n déficit m.

defile vt salir.

definable adj définissable.

define vt définir.

definite adj sûr; précis; ~ly adv sans aucun doute.

definition n définition f.

definitive adj définitif; ~ly adv définitivement.

deflate vt dégonfler.

deflect vt dévier.

deflower vt déflorer.

deform vt déformer.

deformity n déformité f.

defraud vt frauder.

defray vt payer.

defrost vt dégivrer; décongeler.

defroster n dégivreur m.

deft adj habile; ~ly adv habilement.

defunct adj défunt.

defuse vt désamorcer.

degenerate vi dégénérer; * adj dégénéré.

degeneration n dégénération f.

degradation n dégradation f.

degrade vt dégrader.

degree n degré m; diplôme m.

dehydrated adj déshydraté.

de-ice vt dégivrer.

deign vi daigner.

deity n divinité f.

dejected adj découragé.

dejection n découragement m.

delay vt retarder; * n retard m.

delectable adj délectable.

delegate vt déléguer; * n délégué m, -e f.

delegation n délégation f.

delete vt effacer.

deliberate vt examiner; * adj délibéré; ~ly adv délibérément, exprès.

deliberation n délibération f.

deliberative adj délibérant.

delicacy n délicatesse f.

delicate adj délicat; **~ly** adv délicatement.

delicious adj délicieux, exquis; **~ly** adv délicieusement.

delight n délice m; enchantement m; * vt enchanter; * vi adorer.

delighted adj enchanté.

delightful adj charmant; **~ly** adv merveilleusement.

delineate vt détailler; détailler.

delineation n tracé m; détail m.

delinquency n délinquance f.

delinquent adj délinquant m, -e f.

delirious adj délirant.

delirium n délire m.

deliver vt livrer; délivrer; prononcer.

deliverance n libération f.

delivery n livraison f; accouchement m.

delude vt tromper.

deluge n déluge m.

delusion n tromperie f; illusion f.

delve vi creuser; chercher.

demagog(ue) n démagogue m.

demand n demande f; * vt exiger; réclamer.

demanding adj exigeant.

demarcation n démarcation f.

demean vi s'abaisser.

demeanor n conduite f, comportement m.

demented adj dément.

demise n disparition f.

democracy n démocratie f.

democrat n démocrate mf.

democratic adj démocratique.

demolish vt démolir.

demolition n démolition f.

demon n démon, diable m.

demonstrable adj démontrable; **~bly** adv manifestement.

demonstrate vt démontrer, prouver; * vi manifester.

demonstration n démonstration f; manifestation f.

demonstrative adj démonstratif.

demonstrator n manifestant m, -e f.

demoralization n démoralisation f.

demoralize vt démoraliser.

demote vt rétrograder.

demur vi émettre une objection; hésiter.

demure adj réservé; **~ly** adv avec réserve.

den n antre m.

denatured alcohol n alcool dénaturé m.

denial n dénégation f.

denims npl jean m.

denomination n valeur f; dénomination f.

denominator n (math) dénominateur m.

denote vt dénoter, indiquer.

denounce vt dénoncer.

dense adj dense, épais.

density n densité f.

dent n bosse f; * vt cabosser.

dental adj dentaire.

dentifrice n dentifrice m.

dentist n dentiste mf.

dentistry n dentisterie f.

denture n dentier m.

denude vt dénuder, dépouiller.

denunciation n dénonciation f.

deny vt nier.

deodorant n déodorant m.

deodorize vt déodoriser.

depart vi partir.

department n département m; service m.

department store n grand magasin m.

departure n départ m.

departure lounge n salle d'embarquement f.

depend vi dépendre; ~ on/upon compter sur.

dependable adj fiable; sûr.

dependant n personne à charge f.

dependency n dépendance f.

dependent adj dépendant.

depict vt dépeindre, décrire.

depleted adj réduit.

deplorable adj déplorable, lamentable; ~bly adv déplorablement.

deplore vt déplorer, lamenter.

deploy vt (mil) déployer.

depopulated adj dépeuplé.

depopulation n dépopulation f.

deport vt déporter; expulser.

deportation n déportation f; expulsion f.

deportment n comportement m.

deposit vt déposer; * n dépôt m; caution f.

deposition n déposition f.

depositor n déposant m, -e f.

depot n dépôt m.

deprave vt dépraver, corrompre.

depraved adj dépravé.

depravity n dépravation f.

deprecate vt désapprouver.

depreciate vi se déprécier.

depreciation n dépréciation f.

depredation n pillage m.

depress vt déprimer.

depressed adj déprimé.

depression n dépression f.

deprivation n privation f.

deprive vt priver.

deprived adj défavorisé.

depth n profondeur f.

deputation n députation f.

depute vt députer, déléguer.

deputize vi remplacer.

deputy n remplaçant m, -e f; député m; délégué m, -e f.

derail vt faire dérailler.

deranged adj dérangé.

derby n chapeau melon m.

derelict adj abandonné.

deride vt se moquer de.

derision n dérision f.

derisive adj ridicule; moqueur.

derivable adj déductible.

derivation n dérivation f.

derivative n dérivé m.

derive vt, vi dériver.

derogatory adj désobligeant.

derrick n derrick m.

descant n (mus) déchant m.

descend vi descendre.

descendant n descendant m, -e f.

descent n descente f.

describe vt décrire.

description n description f.

descriptive adj descriptif.

descry vt distinguer.

desecrate vt profaner.

desecration n profanation f.

desert n désert m; * adj désert.

desert vt abandonner; déserter; * n mérite m.

deserter n déserteur m.

desertion n désertion f.

deserve vt mériter.

deservedly adv à juste titre.

deserving adj méritant.

deshabille n déshabillé m.

desideratum n desideratum m.

design vt concevoir; dessiner; * n dessein m; design m; dessin m.

designate vt désigner.

designation n désignation f.

designedly adv exprès, délibérément.

designer n créateur m, -trice f; styliste mf.

desirability n avantage m; attrait m.

desirable adj désirable.

desire n désir m; * vt désirer.

desirous adj désireux.

desist vi abandonner.

desk n bureau m.

desolate adj désert, désolé.

desolation n désolation f.

despair n désespoir m; * vi se désespérer.

despairingly adv désespérément.

despatch = dispatch.

desperado n bandit m.

desperate adj désespéré; ~ly adv désespérément; extrêmement.

desperation n désespoir m.

despicable adj méprisable.

despise vt mépriser.

despite prep malgré.

despoil vt dépouiller.

despondency n abattement m.

despondent adj abattu.

despot n despote m.

despotic adj despotique; ~ally adv despotiquement.

despotism n despotisme m.

dessert n dessert m.

destination n destination f.

destine vt destiner.

destiny n destin, sort m.

destitute adj indigent.

destitution n indigence f.

destroy vt détruire.

destruction n destruction f.

destructive adj destructeur.

desultory adj irrégulier; sans méthode.

detach vt séparer, détacher.

detachable adj détachable.

detachment n (mil) détachement m.

detail n détail m; in ~ en détail; * vt détailler.

detain vt retenir; détenir.

detect vt détecter.

detection n détection f; découverte f.

detective n détective m.

detector n détecteur m.

detention n détention f.

deter vt dissuader.

detergent n détergent m.

deteriorate vt détériorer.

deterioration n détérioration f.

determination n détermination f.

determine vt déterminer, décider.

determined adj déterminé.

deterrent n force de dissuasion f.

detest vt détester.

detestable adj détestable.

dethrone vt détrôner.

dethronement n détrônement m.

detonate vi détoner.

detonation n détonation f.

detour n déviation f.

detract vt détourner.

detriment n détriment m.

detrimental adj préjudiciable.

deuce n deux m; égalité f.

devaluation n dévaluation f.

devastate vt dévaster.

devastating adj dévastateur.

devastation n dévastation f.

develop vt développer.

development n développement m.

deviate vi dévier.

deviation n déviation f.

device n mécanisme m.

devil n diable, démon m.

devilish adj diabolique; **~ly** adv diaboliquement.

devious adj tortueux.

devise vt inventer; concevoir.

devoid adj dépourvu.

devolve vt déléguer.

devote vt consacrer.

devoted adj dévoué.

devotee n partisan m, -e f.

devotion n dévotion f.

devotional adj dévot.

devour vt dévorer.

devout adj dévot, pieux; **~ly** adv pieusement.

dew n rosée f.

dewy adj couvert de rosée; ingénu.

dexterity n dextérité f.

dexterous adj adroit, habile.

diabetes n diabète m.

diabetic n diabétique mf.

diabolic adj diabolique; **~ally** adv diaboliquement.

diadem n diadème m.

diagnosis n (med) diagnostic m.

diagnostic adj diagnostique; * npl **~s** diagnostic m.

diagonal adj diagonal; **~ly** adv diagonalement; * n diagonale f.

diagram n diagramme m.

dial n cadran m.

dial code n code m.

dialect n dialecte m.

dialog(ue) n dialogue m.

dial tone n tonalité f.

diameter n diamètre m.

diametrical adj diamétral; **~ly** adv diamétralement.

diamond n diamant m.

diamond-cutter n tailleur de diamant m.

diamonds npl (cards) carreaux mpl.

diaper n couche f.

diaphragm n diaphragme m.

diarrhoea n diarrhée f.

diary n journal m.

dice npl dés mpl.

dictate vt dicter; * n ordre m.

dictation n dictée f.

dictatorial adj dictatorial.

dictatorship n dictature f.

diction n diction f.

dictionary n dictionnaire m.

didactic adj didactique.

die vi mourir; **to ~ away** s'affaiblir; **to ~ down** s'éteindre.

die n (sing de dice) dé m.

diehard n réactionnaire mf.

diesel n diesel m.

diet n diète f; régime m; * vi être au régime.

dietary adj diététique.

differ vi différer.

difference n différence f.

different adj différent; **~ly** adv différemment.

differentiate vt différencier.

difficult adj difficile.

difficulty n difficulté f.

diffidence n timidité f; manque d'assurance m.

diffident adj timide; mal assuré; ~**ly** adv avec timidité.

diffraction n diffraction f.

diffuse vt diffuser, répandre; * adj diffus.

diffusion n diffusion f.

dig vt creuser; * n coup m.

digest vt digérer.

digestible adj digestible.

digestion n digestion f.

digestive adj digestif.

digger n excavatrice f.

digit n chiffre m.

digital adj digital.

dignified adj digne.

dignitary n dignitaire m.

dignity n dignité f.

digress vi faire une digression.

digression n digression f.

dike n digue f.

dilapidated adj délabré.

dilapidation n délabrement m.

dilate vt dilater; * vi se dilater.

dilemma n dilemme m.

diligence n assiduité f.

diligent adj assidu; ~**ly** adv avec assiduité.

dilute vt diluer.

dim adj indistinct; faible; sombre; * vt affaiblir; troubler.

dime n pièce de dix cents f.

dimension n dimension f.

diminish vt, vi diminuer.

diminution n diminution f.

diminutive n diminutif m.

dimly adv indistinctement; faiblement.

dimmer n interrupteur d'intensité m.

dimple n fossette f.

din n vacarme m.

dine vi dîner.

diner n restaurant (économique) m.

dinghy n canot pneumatique m.

dingy adj sale; miteux.

dinner n dîner m.

dinner time n heure du dîner f.

dinosaur n dinosaure m.

dint n: by ~ of à force de.

diocese n diocèse m.

dip vt tremper.

diphtheria n diphtérie f.

diphthong n diphtongue f.

diploma n diplôme m.

diplomacy n diplomatie f.

diplomat n diplomate m.

diplomatic adj diplomatique.

dipsomania n dipsomanie f.

dipstick n (auto) jauge f.

dire adj atroce; affreux.

direct adj direct; * vt diriger.

direction n direction f; instruction f.

directly adv directement; immédiatement.

director n directeur m, -trice f.

directory n annuaire m.

dirt n saleté f.

dirtiness n saleté f.

dirty adj sale.

disability n incapacité f; infirmité f.

disabled adj infirme.

disabuse vt détromper.

disadvantage n désavantage m; * vt désavantager.

disadvantageous adj désavantageux.

disaffected adj mécontent.

disagree vi ne pas être d'accord.

disagreeable adj désagréable; ~**bly** adv désagréablement.

disagreement n désaccord m.

disallow vt rejeter.

disappear vi disparaître.

disappearance n disparition f.

disappoint vt décevoir.

disappointed adj déçu.

disappointing adj décevant.

disappointment n déception f.

disapproval n désapprobation f.

disapprove vt ne pas approuver.

disarm vt désarmer.

disarmament n désarmement m.

disarray n désordre m.

disaster n désastre m.

disastrous vt désastreux.

disband vt disperser.

disbelief n incrédulité f.

disbelieve vt ne pas croire.

disburse vt débourser.

discard vt jeter.

discern vt discerner, percevoir.

discernible adj perceptible.

discerning adj perspicace.

discernment n perspicacité f.

discharge vt décharger; régler (une dette); remplir; * n décharge f; règlement m.

disciple n disciple m.

discipline n discipline f; * vt discipliner.

disclaim vt nier.

disclaimer n dénégation f.

disclose vt révéler.

disclosure n révélation f.

disco n discothèque f.

discoloration n décoloration f.

discolour vt décolorer.

discomfort n incommodité f.

disconcert vt déconcerter.

disconnect vt débrancher.

disconsolate adj inconsolable; ~ly adv inconsolablement.

discontent n mécontentement m; * adj mécontent.

discontented adj mécontent.

discontinue vt interrompre.

discord n discorde f.

discordant adj discordant.

discount n escompte m; remise f; * vt escompter.

discourage vt décourager.

discouraged adj découragé.

discouragement n découragement m.

discouraging adj décourageant.

discourse n discours m.

discourteous adj discourtois; ~ly adv de manière discourtoise.

discourtesy n manque de courtoisie m.

discover vt découvrir.

discovery n découverte f.

discredit vt discréditer.

discreditable adj peu honorable.

discreet adj discret; ~ly adv discrètement.

discrepancy n contradiction f.

discretion n discrétion f.

discretionary adj discrétionnaire.

discriminate vt distinguer; discriminer.

discrimination n discrimination f.

discursive adj discursif.

discuss vt discuter.

discussion n discussion f.

disdain vt dédaigner; * n dédain, mépris m.

disdainful adj dédaigneux, méprisant; ~ly adv dédaigneusement, avec mépris.

disease n maladie f.

diseased adj malade.

disembark vt, vi débarquer.

disembarkation n (mil) débarquement m.

disenchant vt désenchanter.

disenchanted adj désenchanté.

disenchantment n désenchantement m.

disengage vt dégager.

disentangle vt démêler.

disfigure vt défigurer.

disgrace n honte f; scandale m; * vt déshonorer.

disgraceful adj honteux; scandaleux; ~ly adv honteusement.

disgruntled adj mécontent.

disguise vt déguiser; * n déguisement m.

disgust n dégoût m; * vt dégoûter.

disgusting adj dégoûtant.

dish n plat m; assiette f; * vt servir dans un plat; **to ~ up** servir.

dishcloth n torchon à vaisselle m.

dishearten vt démoraliser.

disheveled adj ébouriffé.

dishonest adj malhonnête; ~ly adv malhonnêtement.

dishonesty n malhonnêteté f.

dishonor n déshonneur m; * vt déshonorer.

dishonorable adj déshonorable; ~bly adv de manière déshonorante.

dishtowel n torchon à vaisselle m.

dishwarmer n chauffe-plats m.

dishwasher n lave-vaisselle m; plongeur m, -euse f.

disillusion vt désillusionner.

disillusioned adj désillusionné.

disincentive n élément dissuasif m.

disinclination n aversion f.

disinclined adj peu enclin.

disinfect vt désinfecter.

disinfectant n désinfectant m.

disinherit vt déshériter.

disintegrate vi se désintégrer.

disinterested adj désintéressé; ~ly adv de manière désintéressée.

disjointed adj déréglé; décousu.

disk n disque m; disquette f.

diskette n disque m, disquette f.

dislike n aversion f; * vt ne pas aimer.

dislocate vt disloquer.

dislocation n dislocation f.

dislodge vt déloger.

disloyal adj déloyal; ~ly adv déloyalement.

disloyalty n déloyauté f.

dismal adj triste, lugubre.

dismantle vt démonter.

dismay n consternation f.

dismember vt démembrer.

dismiss vt renvoyer; écarter.

dismissal n renvoi m; rejet m.

dismount vt désarçonner; * vi descendre.

disobedience n désobéissance f.

disobedient adj désobéissant.

disobey vt désobéir.

disorder n désordre m.

disorderly adj en désordre, confus.

disorganization n désorganisation f.

disorganized adj désorganisé.

disorientated adj désorienté.

disown vt renier.

disparage vt dénigrer.

disparaging adj désobligeant.

disparity n disparité f.

dispassionate adj impartial; calme.

dispatch vt envoyer; * n envoi m; dépêche f.

dispel vt dissiper.

dispensary n dispensaire m.

dispense vt dispenser; distribuer.

disperse vt disperser.

dispirited adj démoralisé.

displace vt déplacer.

display vt exposer; faire preuve de; * n exposition f; déploiement m.

displeased adj mécontent.

displeasure n mécontentement m.

disposable adj à jeter.

disposal n disposition f.

dispose vt disposer.

disposed adj disposé.

disposition n disposition f.

dispossess vt déposséder.

disproportionate adj disproportionné.

disprove vt réfuter.

dispute n dispute f; controverse f; * vt mettre en cause.

disqualify vt rendre incapable; disqualifier.

disquiet n inquiétude f.

disquieting adj inquiétant.

disquisition n étude f.

disregard vt ne pas tenir compte de; mépriser; * n dédain m.

disreputable adj de mauvaise réputation.

disrespect n irrévérence f.

disrespectful adj irrespectueux; ~ly adv irrespectueusement.

disrobe vt dévêtir.

disrupt vt interrompre.

disruption n interruption f.

dissatisfaction n mécontentement m.

dissatisfied adj mécontent.

dissect vt disséquer.

dissection n dissection f.

disseminate vt disséminer.

dissension n dissension f.

dissent vi être en dissension; * n dissension f.

dissenter n dissident m, -e f.

dissertation n thèse f.

dissident n dissident m, -e f.

dissimilar adj dissemblable.

dissimilarity n dissemblance f.

dissimulation n dissimulation f.

dissipate vt dissiper.

dissipation n dissipation f.

dissociate vt dissocier.

dissolute adj dissolu.

dissolution n dissolution f.

dissolve vt dissoudre; * vi se dissoudre.

dissonance n dissonance f.

dissuade vt dissuader.

distance n distance f; **at a ~** de loin; * vt distancer.

distant adj distant.

distaste n dégoût m.

distasteful adj désagréable.

distend vt distendre.

distil vt distiller.

distillation n distillation f.

distillery n distillerie f.

distinct adj distinct; ~ly adv distinctement.

distinction n distinction f.

distinctive adj distinctif.

distinctness n clarté f.

distinguish vt distinguer; discerner.

distort vt déformer.

distorted adj déformé.

distortion n distortion f.

distract vt distraire.

distracted adj distrait; ~ly adj distraitement.

distraction n distraction f; confusion f.

distraught adj fou.

distress n souffrance f; détresse f; * vt désoler; affliger.

distressing adj affligeant.

distribute vt distribuer, répartir.

distribution n distribution f.

distributor n distributeur m.

district n district m.

district attorney n procureur de la République m.

distrustful adj méfiant.

disturb vt déranger.

disturbance n dérangement m; trouble m.

disturbed adj troublé.

disturbing adj troublant.

disuse n désuétude f.

disused adj abandonné.

ditch n fossé m.

dither vi hésiter.

ditto adv idem.

ditty n chansonnette f.

diuretic n (med) diurétique.

dive vi plonger.

diver n plongeur m, -euse f.

diverge vi diverger.

divergence n divergence f.

divergent adj divergent.

diverse adj divers, différent; ~ly adv différemment.

diversion n diversion f.

diversity n diversité f.

divert vt dévier; divertir.

divest vt dénuder; dépouiller.

divide vt diviser; * vi se diviser.

dividend n dividende m.

dividers npl (math) compas à pointes sèches m.

divine adj divin.

divinity n divinité f.

diving n plongeon m.

diving board n plongeoir m.

divisible adj divisible.

division n (math) division f.

divisor n (math) diviseur m.

divorce n divorce m; * vi divorcer.

divorced adj divorcé.

divulge vt divulguer.

dizziness n vertige m.

dizzy adj pris de vertige.

DJ n disc-jockey, DJ m.

do vt faire.

docile adj docile.

dock n dock m; * vi entrer aux docks.

docker n docker m.

dockyard n (mar) chantier naval m.

doctor n docteur m.

doctrinal adj doctrinal.

doctrine n doctrine f.

document n document m.

documentary adj documentaire.

dodge vt esquiver.

doe n biche f; ~ **rabbit** lapine f.

dog n chien m.

dogged adj tenace; ~ly adv tenacement.

dog kennel n refuge pour chiens m.

dogmatic adj dogmatique; ~ly adv dogmatiquement.

doings npl faits mpl.

do-it-yourself n bricolage m.

doleful adj lugubre, triste.

doll n poupée f.

dollar n dollar m.

dolphin n dauphin m.

domain n domaine m.

dome n dôme m.

domestic adj domestique.

domesticate vt domestiquer.

domestication n domestication f.

domesticity n domesticité f.

domicile n domicile m.

dominant adj dominant.

dominate vi dominer.

domination n domination f.

domineer vi dominer.

domineering adj dominant.

dominion n domination f.

dominoes npl domino m.

donate vt donner, faire don de.

donation n donation f.

done p, adj fait; cuit.

donkey n âne m.

donor n donneur m; donateur m.

doodle vi gribouiller.

doom n sort m.

door n porte f.

doorbell n sonnette f.

door handle n poignée de porte f.

doorman n portier m.

doormat n paillasson m.

doorplate n plaque f.

doorstep n pas de porte m.

doorway n entrée f.

dormant adj latent; dormant.

dormer window n lucarne f.

dormitory n dortoir m.

dormouse n loir m.

dosage n dose f; dosage m.

dose n dose f; * vt doser; donner une dose à.

dossier n dossier m.

dot n point m.

dote vi adorer.

dotingly adv avec adoration.

double adj double; * vt doubler; * n double m.

double bed n lit de deux personnes m.

double-breasted adj croisé.

double chin n double menton m.

double-dealing n duplicité f.

double-edged adj à double tranchant.

double entry n (com) comptabilité en partie double f.

double-lock vt fermer à double tour.

double room n chambre pour deux f.

doubly adv doublement.

doubt n doute m; * vt douter de.

doubtful adj douteux.

doubtless adv indubitablement.

dough n pâte f.

douse vt éteindre.

dove n colombe f.

dovecot n colombier m.

dowdy adj mal habillé.

down n duvet m; * prep en bas; **to sit ~** s'asseoir; **upside ~** à l'envers.

downcast adj démoralisé; baissé.

downfall n ruine f.

downhearted adj découragé.

downhill adv en descendant, dans la descente.

down payment n acompte m.

downpour n grosse averse f.

downright adj manifeste.

downstairs adv en bas.

down-to-earth adj pratique; terre à terre.

downtown adv dans le centre, en ville.

downward(s) adv vers le bas.

dowry n dot f.

doze vi somnoler.

dozen n douzaine f.

dozy adj somnolent.

drab adj gris; morne.

draft n brouillon m; traite f.

drag vt tirer; * n drague f; ennui m.

dragnet n seine f; filet m.

dragon n dragon m.

dragonfly n libellule f.

drain vt drainer; vider; * n tuyau d'écoulement m.

drainage n drainage m.

drainboard n égouttoir m.

drainpipe n tuyau d'écoulement m.

drake n canard mâle m.

dram n petit verre m.

drama n drame m.

dramatic adj dramatique; ~ally adv dramatiquement.

dramatist n dramaturge mf.

dramatize vt dramatiser.

drape vt draper.

drapes npl tentures fpl.

drastic adj radical.

draught n courant d'air m.

draughts npl jeu de dames m.

draughty adj exposé aux courants d'air.

draw vt tirer; dessiner; **to ~ nigh** s'approcher.

drawback n désavantage, inconvénient m.

drawer n tiroir m.

drawing n dessin m.

drawing board n planche à dessin f.

drawing room n salon m.

drawl vi parler d'une voix traînante.

dread n terreur f; * vt redouter, craindre.

dreadful adj horrible; ~ly adv horriblement.

dream n rêve m; * vi, vt rêver.

dreary adj triste, morne.

dredge vt draguer.

dregs npl lie f.

drench vt tremper.

dress vt habiller; panser; * vi s'habiller; * n robe f.

dresser n buffet m.

dressing n pansement m; sauce f.

dressing gown n peignoir m.

dressing room n loge f; garderobe f.

dressing table n coiffeuse f.

dressmaker n couturier m, -ière f.

dressy adj élégant.

dried adj séché.

drift n amoncellement m; courant m; sens m; * vi aller à la dérive.

driftwood n bois flottant m.

drill n perceuse f; (mil) exercice m; * vt percer.

drink vt, vi boire; * n boisson f.

drinkable adj potable; buvable.

drinker n buveur m, -euse f.

drinking bout n beuverie f.

drinking water n eau potable f.

drip vi goutter; * n goutte f; goutte-à-goutte m.

dripping n graisse f.

drive vt conduire; pousser; * vi conduire; * n promenade en voiture f; allée, entrée f.

drivel n imbécilités fpl; * vi baver; dire des imbécilités.

driver n conducteur m, -trice f; chauffeur m.

driveway n allée, entrée f.

driving n conduite f.

driving instructor n moniteur (-trice) d'auto-école m(f).

driving licence n permis m de conduire.

driving school n auto-école f.

driving test n (examen du) permis de conduire m.

drizzle vi pleuvasser.

droll adj drôle.

drone n bourdon m.

droop vi tomber.

drop n goutte f; * vt laisser tomber; * vi tomber; **to ~ out** se retirer; abandonner.

drop-out n marginal m.

dropper n compte-gouttes m invar.

dross n scories fpl.

drought n sécheresse f.

drove n: **in ~s** en troupe.

drown vt noyer; * vi se noyer.

drowsiness n somnolence f.

drowsy adj somnolent.

drudgery n corvée f.

drug n drogue f; * vt droguer.

drug addict n drogué m, -e f.

druggist n pharmacien m, -ienne f.

drugstore n pharmacie f.

drum n tambour m; * vi jouer du tambour.

drum majorette n majorette f.

drummer n batteur m.

drumstick n baguette de tambour f.

drunk adj ivre.

drunkard n ivrogne mf.

drunken adj ivre.

drunkenness n ivresse f.

dry adj sec; * vt faire sécher; * vi sécher.

dry-cleaning n nettoyage a sec m.

dry-goods store n mercerie f.

dryness n sécheresse f.

dry rot n pourriture f.

dual adj double.

dual-purpose adj à double emploi.

dubbed adj doublé.

dubious adj douteux.

duck n canard m; * vt, vi plonger.

duckling n caneton m.

dud adj nul; faux.

due adj dû, f due; * adv exactement; * n droit m; chose due f.

duel n duel m.

duet n (mus) duo m.

dull adj terne; insipide; gris; * vt ternir; atténuer.

duly adv dûment; en temps voulu.

dumb adj muet; **~ly** adv sans dire un mot.

dumbbell n haltère m; abruti m.

dumbfounded adj interloqué.

dummy n mannequin m; prête-nom m.

dump n tas m; * vt jeter; laisser tomber.

dumping n (com) dumping m.

dumpling n boulette de pâte f.

dumpy adj boulot.

dunce n cancre m.

dune n dune f.

dung n fumier m.

dungarees npl salopette f.

dungeon n donjon m; cachot m.

dupe n dupe f; * vt duper.

duplex n duplex m.

duplicate n duplicata m; copie f; * vt dupliquer.

duplicity n duplicité f.
durability n durabilité f.
durable adj durable.
duration n durée f.
during prep pendant.
dusk n crépuscule m.
dust n poussière f; * vt épousseter.
duster n plumier m.
dusty adj poussiéreux.
dutch courage n courage puisé dans la boisson m.
duteous adj fidèle, loyal.
dutiful adj obéissant, soumis; **~ly** adv avec obéissance.
duty n devoir m; obligation f.
duty-free adj hors taxe.
dwarf n nain m, naine f; * vt rapetisser.

dwell vi habiter, vivre.
dwelling n habitation f; domicile m.
dwindle vi diminuer.
dye vt teindre; * n teinture f.
dyer n teinturier m.
dyeing n teinturerie f; teinture f.
dye-works npl teinturerie f.
dying p, adj mourant, agonisant; * n mort f.
dynamic adj dynamique.
dynamics n dynamique f.
dynamite n dynamite f.
dynamiter n dynamiteur m, -euse f.
dynamo n dynamo f.
dynasty n dynastie f.
dysentery n dysenterie f.
dyspepsia n (med) dyspepsie f.
dyspeptic adj dyspeptique.

E

each pn chacun; **~ other** les uns les autres.
eager adj enthousiaste; ardent; **~ly** adv avec enthousiasme; ardemment.
eagerness n enthousiasme m; ardeur f; désir m.
eagle n aigle m.
eagle-eyed adj aux yeux d'aigle.
eaglet n aiglon m.
ear n oreille f; ouïe f; **by ~** en improvisant.
earache n mal d'oreille m.
eardrum n tympan m.
early adj premier; adv tôt, de bonne heure.
earmark vt destiner.
earn vt gagner.
earnest adj sérieux; **~ly** adv sérieusement.

earnestness n sérieux m.
earnings npl revenus mpl.
earphones npl écouteurs mpl.
earring n boucle d'oreille f.
earth n terre f; * vt brancher à la terre.
earthen adj de terre.
earthenware n poterie f.
earthquake n tremblement de terre m.
earthworm n ver de terre m.
earthy adj pratique; truculent.
earwig n perce-oreille m.
ease n aise f; facilité f; **at ~** à l'aise; * vt apaiser; soulager.
easel n chevalet m.
easily adv facilement.
easiness n facilité f.
east n est m; orient m.

Easter n Pâques fpl.
Easter egg n œuf de Pâques m.
easterly adj d'est.
eastern adj de l'est, oriental.
eastward(s) adv vers l'est.
easy adj facile; commode; ~ **going** décontracté.
easy chair n fauteuil m.
eat vt, vi manger.
eatable adj comestible; mangeable; * **~s** npl vivres mpl.
eaves npl avant-toit m.
eau de Cologne n eau de Cologne f.
eavesdrop vt espionner; écouter discrètement.
ebb n reflux m; * vi refluer; décliner.
ebony n ébène f.
eccentric adj excentrique.
eccentricity n excentricité f.
ecclesiastic adj ecclésiastique.
echo n écho m; * vi résonner.
eclectic adj éclectique.
eclipse n éclipse f; * vt éclipser.
ecology n écologie f.
economic(al) adj économique; économe.
economics npl économie f.
economist n économiste mf.
economize vt économiser.
economy n économie f.
ecstasy n extase f.
ecstatic adj extatique; ~**ally** adv avec extase.
eczema n eczéma m.
eddy n tourbillon m; * vi tourbillonner.
edge n fil m; pointe f; bord m; acrimonie f; * vt border; affiler.
edgeways, edgewise adv de côté.
edging n bordure f.

edgy adj nerveux.
edible adj mangeable; comestible.
edict n édit m; décret m.
edification n édification f.
edifice n édifice m.
edify vt édifier.
edit vt diriger; rédiger; couper.
edition n édition f.
editor n directeur m, -trice f; rédacteur m, -trice f.
editorial adj rédactionnel; * n éditorial m.
educate vt éduquer; instruire.
education n éducation f; instruction f.
eel n anguille f.
eerie adj inquiétant; surnaturel.
efface vt effacer.
effect n effet m; réalité f; ~**s** npl biens mpl; * vt effectuer.
effective adj efficace; effectif; ~**ly** adv effectivement, en effet.
effectiveness n efficacité f.
effectual adj efficace; ~**ly** adv efficacement.
effeminacy n caractère efféminé m.
effeminate adj efféminé.
effervescence n effervescence f.
effete adj stérile; faible.
efficacy n efficacité f.
efficiency n efficacité f.
efficient adj efficace.
effigy n effigie f.
effort n effort m.
effortless adj sans effort.
effrontery n effronterie f.
effusive adj chaleureux; expansif.
egg n œuf m; * **to ~ on** vt encourager.
eggcup n coquetier m.

eggplant n aubergine f.
eggshell n coquille d'œuf f.
ego(t)ism n égoïsme m.
ego(t)ist n égoïste mf.
ego(t)istical adj égoïste.
eiderdown n édredon m.
eight adj, n huit m.
eighteen adj, n dix-huit m.
eighteenth adj, n dix-huitième mf.
eighth adj, n huitième mf.
eightieth adj, n quatre-vingtième mf.
eighty adj, n quatre-vingt.
either pn n'importe lequel, n'importe laquelle; * conj ou, soit.
ejaculate vi s'exclamer; éjaculer.
ejaculation n exclamation f; éjaculation f.
eject vt éjecter, expulser.
ejection n éjection, expulsion f.
ejector seat n siège éjectable m.
eke vt augmenter; prolonger.
elaborate vt élaborer; * adj élaboré; compliqué; ~ly adv avec soin.
elapse vi passer.
elastic adj élastique.
elasticity n élasticité f.
elated adj exultant.
elation n exultation f.
elbow n coude m; * vt pousser du coude.
elbow-room n espace m; (fig) liberté, latitude f.
elder n sureau m; * adj aîné.
elderly adj d'un âge avancé.
elders npl anciens mpl.
eldest adj aîné.
elect vt élire; choisir; * adj élu; choisi.
election n élection f; choix m.

electioneering n propagande électorale f.
elective adj facultatif.
elector n électeur m, -trice f.
electoral adj électoral.
electorate n électorat m.
electric(al) adj électrique.
electric blanket n couverture électrique f.
electric cooker n cuisinière électrique f.
electric fire n radiateur électrique m.
electrician n électricien m.
electricity n électricité f.
electrify vt électriser.
electron n électron m.
electronic adj électronique; ~s npl électronique f.
elegance n élégance f.
elegant adj élégant; ~ly adv élégamment.
elegy n élégie f.
element n élément m.
elemental, elementary adj élémentaire.
elephant n éléphant m.
elephantine adj immense; lourd.
elevate vt élever, hausser.
elevation n élévation f; hauteur f.
elevator n ascenseur m.
eleven adj, n onze m.
eleventh adj, n onzième mf.
elf n elfe m.
elicit vt tirer.
eligibility n éligibilité f.
eligible adj éligible.
eliminate vt éliminer, écarter.
elk n élan m.
elliptic(al) adj elliptique.
elm n orme m.

elocution n élocution f.

elocutionist n professeur d'élocution m.

elongate vt allonger.

elope vi s'échapper, s'enfuir.

elopement n fugue, évasion f.

eloquence n éloquence f.

eloquent adj éloquent; **~ly** adv éloquemment.

else pn autre.

elsewhere adv ailleurs.

elucidate vt élucider, expliquer.

elucidation n élucidation, explication f.

elude vt éluder; éviter.

elusive, elusory adj insaisissable.

emaciated adj émacié.

emanate (from) vi émaner (de).

emancipate vt émanciper; affranchir.

emancipation n émancipation f; affranchissement m.

embalm vt embaumer.

embankment n talus m; quai m.

embargo n embargo m.

embark vt embarquer.

embarkation n embarcation f.

embarrass vt embarrasser.

embarrassed adj embarrassé.

embarrassing adj embarrassant.

embarrassment n embarras m.

embassy n ambassade f.

embed vt enchâsser; intégrer.

embellish vt embellir, orner.

embellishment n ornement m.

embers npl braise f.

embezzle vt détourner.

embezzlement n détournement de fonds m.

embitter vt rendre amer.

emblem n emblème m.

emblematic(al) adj emblématique, symbolique.

embodiment n incorporation f; incarnation f.

embody vt incorporer; incarner.

embrace vt étreindre; comprendre; * n étreinte f.

embroider vt broder.

embroidery n broderie f.

embroil vt impliquer.

embryo n embryon m.

emendation n correction f.

emerald n émeraude f.

emerge vi émerger; apparaître.

emergency n urgence f.

emergency cord n sonnette d'alarme f.

emergency exit n sortie de secours f.

emergency landing n atterrissage forcé m.

emergency meeting n réunion extraordinaire f.

emery n émeri m.

emigrant n émigré m, -e f.

emigrate vi émigrer.

emigration n émigration f.

eminence n hauteur f; éminence, excellence f.

eminent adj élevé; éminent, distingué; **~ly** adv éminemment.

emission n émission f.

emit vt émettre.

emolument n émoluments mpl.

emotion n émotion f.

emotional adj émotionnel; ému.

emotive adj émotif.

emperor n empereur m.

emphasis n emphase f.

emphasize vt souligner, accentuer.

emphatic adj emphatique; **~ally** adv avec emphase.

empire n empire m.
employ vt employer.
employee n employé m, -e f.
employer n employeur m.
employment n emploi, travail m.
emporium n grand magasin m.
empress n impératrice f.
emptiness n vide m; futilité f.
empty adj vide; vain; * vt vider.
empty-handed adj les mains vides.
emulate vt imiter.
emulsion n émulsion f.
enable vt permettre.
enact vt promulguer; représenter.
enamel n émail m; * vt émailler.
enamor vt s'éprendre de.
encamp vi camper.
encampment n campement m.
encase vt entourer.
enchant vt enchanter.
enchanting adj enchanteur.
enchantment n enchantement m.
encircle vt encercler.
enclose vt entourer; inclure, joindre.
enclosure n clôture f; enceinte f.
encompass vt comprendre.
encore adv encore.
encounter n rencontre f; combat m; * vt rencontrer.
encourage vt encourager.
encouragement n encouragement m.
encroach vi empiéter (sur).
encroachment n empiètement m.
encrusted adj incrusté.
encumber vt embarrasser.
encumbrance n embarras m.
encyclical adj encyclique.
encyclopedia n encyclopédie f.

end n fin f; extrémité f; bout m; dessein m; **to the ~ that** afin que; **to no ~** en vain; **on ~** debout; * vt terminer, conclure; * vi terminer.
endanger vt mettre en danger.
endear vt faire aimer.
endearing adj sympathique.
endearment n expression de tendresse f.
endeavour vi s'efforcer, tenter; * n effort m.
endemic adj endémique.
ending n fin, conclusion f; dénouement m; terminaison f.
endive n (bot) endive f.
endless adj infini, perpétuel; **~ly** adv sans fin, perpétuellement.
endorse vt endosser; approuver.
endorsement n endos m; approbation f.
endow vt doter.
endowment n dotation f.
endurable adj supportable.
endurance n endurance f; patience f.
endure vt supporter; * vi durer.
endways, endwise adv debout.
enemy n ennemi mf.
energetic adj énergique, vigoureux.
energy n énergie, force f.
enervate vt affaiblir, ramollir.
enfeeble vt affaiblir.
enfold vt envelopper.
enforce vt mettre en vigueur.
enforced adj forcé.
enfranchise vt émanciper.
engage vt aborder; engager.
engaged adj fiancé; occupé.
engagement n engagement m; combat m; fiançailles fpl. **engagement ring** n bague de fiançailles f.

engaging *adj* attrayant.

engender *vt* engendrer; produire.

engine *n* moteur *m*; locomotive *f*.

engine driver *n* conducteur *m*.

engineer *n* ingénieur *m*; mécanicien *m*.

engineering *n* ingénierie *f*.

engrave *vt* graver.

engraving *n* gravure *f*.

engrossed *adj* absorbé.

engulf *vt* submerger.

enhance *vt* améliorer; réhausser.

enigma *n* énigme *f*.

enjoy *vt* aimer; avoir; **to ~ oneself** s'amuser.

enjoyable *adj* agréable; amusant.

enjoyment *n* plaisir *m*; jouissance *f*.

enlarge *vt* agrandir; étendre; dilater.

enlargement *n* agrandissement *m*; extension *f*; dilatation *f*.

enlighten *vt* éclairer.

enlightened *adj* éclairé.

Enlightenment *n*: **the ~** le Siècle des lumières *m*.

enlist *vt* recruter.

enlistment *n* recrutement *m*.

enliven *vt* animer; égayer.

enmity *n* inimitié *f*; haine *f*.

enormity *n* énormité *f*; atrocité *f*.

enormous *adj* énorme; **~ly** *adv* énormément.

enough *adv* suffisamment; assez; * *n* assez *m*.

enounce *vt* déclarer.

enquire *vt* = inquire.

enrage *vt* rendre furieux.

enrapture *vt* enchanter, enthousiasmer.

enrich *vt* enrichir; orner.

enrichment *n* enrichissement *m*.

enrol *vt* enrôler; inscrire.

enrolment *n* inscription *f*.

en route *adv* en route.

ensign *n* (*mil*) drapeau *m*; porte-étendard *m*; (*mar*) pavillon *m*.

enslave *vt* asservir.

ensue *vi* s'ensuivre.

ensure *vt* assurer.

entail *vt* impliquer, entraîner.

entangle *vt* emmêler, embrouiller.

entanglement *n* emmêlement *m*.

enter *vt* entrer dans; inscrire; **to ~ for** se présenter à; **to ~ into** commencer; faire partie de.

enterprise *n* entreprise *f*.

enterprising *adj* entreprenant.

entertain *vt* divertir; recevoir; avoir.

entertainer *n* artiste *mf*.

entertaining *adj* divertissant, amusant.

entertainment *n* divertissement, passe-temps *m*.

enthralled *adj* captivé.

enthralling *adj* captivant.

enthrone *vt* introniser.

enthusiasm *n* enthousiasme *m*.

enthusiast *n* enthousiaste *mf*.

enthusiastic *adj* enthousiaste.

entice *vt* tenter; séduire.

entire *adj* entier, complet; parfait; **~ly** *adv* entièrement.

entirety *n* intégralité *f*.

entitle *vt* intituler; conférer un droit à.

entitled *adj* intitulé; **to be ~ to** avoir le droit de.

entity *n* entité *f*.

entourage n entourage m.

entrails npl entrailles fpl.

entrance n entrée f; admission f.

entrance examination n examen d'entrée m.

entrance fee n droit d'inscription m.

entrance hall n vestibule m.

entrance ramp n bretelle d'accès f.

entrant n participant m, -e f; candidat m, -e f.

entrap vt piéger.

entreat vt implorer, supplier.

entreaty n supplication, prière f.

entrepreneur n entrepreneur m.

entrust vt confier.

entry n entrée f.

entry phone n interphone m.

entwine vt entrelacer.

enumerate vt énumérer.

enunciate vt énoncer.

enunciation n énonciation f.

envelop vt envelopper.

envelope n enveloppe f.

enviable adj enviable.

envious adj envieux; ~**ly** adv avec envie.

environment n environnement m.

environmental adj relatif à l'environnement.

environs npl environs mpl.

envisage vt envisager.

envoy n envoyé m, -e f.

envy n envie f; * vt envier.

ephemeral adj éphémère.

epic adj épique; * n récit épique m.

epidemic adj épidémique; * n épidémie f.

epilepsy n épilepsie f.

epileptic adj épileptique.

epilog(ue) n épilogue m.

Epiphany n Epiphanie f.

episcopacy n épiscopat m.

episcopal adj épiscopal.

episcopalian adj épiscopal m.

episode n épisode m.

epistle n épître f.

epistolary adj épistolaire.

epitaph n épithète f.

epitome n modèle m; résumé m.

epitomize vt incarner; résumer.

epoch n époque f.

equable adj uniforme; ~**bly** adv uniformément.

equal adj égal; semblable; * n égal m, -e f; * vt égaler.

equality n égalité f.

equalize vt égaliser.

equalizer n point égalisateur m.

equally adv également.

equanimity n équanimité f.

equate vt égaliser.

equation n équation f.

equator n équateur m.

equatorial adj équatorial.

equestrian adj équestre.

equilateral adj équilatéral.

equilibrium n équilibre m.

equinox n équinoxe m.

equip vt équiper.

equipment n équipement m.

equitable adj équitable, impartial; ~**bly** adv équitablement.

equity n équité, justice, impartialité f.

equivalent adj, n équivalent m.

equivocal adj équivoque, ambigu; ~**ly** adv d'une manière équivoque.

equivocate vt équivoquer, user d'équivoques.

equivocation n équivoques fpl.

era n ère f.

eradicate vt supprimer; extirper.

eradication n suppression f; extirpation f.

erase vt effacer; gommer.

eraser n gomme f.

erect vt ériger; élever; * adj droit, debout.

erection n érection f; structure f.

ermine n hermine f.

erode vt éroder; ronger.

erotic adj érotique.

err vi se tromper.

errand n message m; commission f.

errand boy n garçon de courses, messager m.

errata npl errata m.

erratic adj changeant; irrégulier.

erroneous adj erroné, faux; ~ly adv erronément, faussement.

error n erreur f.

erudite adj érudit.

erudition n érudition f.

erupt vi entrer en éruption; faire éruption.

eruption n éruption f.

escalate vi monter en flèche; s'intensifier.

escalation n montée en flèche f; intensification f.

escalator n escalier roulant m.

escapade n fredaine f.

escape vt éviter; échapper à; * vi s'évader, s'échapper; * n évasion, fuite f; **to make one's ~** prendre la fuite.

escapism n évasion de la réalité f.

eschew vt fuir; éviter.

escort n escorte f; * vt escorter.

esoteric adj ésotérique.

especial adj spécial; ~ly adv spécialement.

espionage n espionnage m.

esplanade n (mil) esplanade f.

espouse vt épouser.

essay n essai m.

essence n essence f.

essential n essentiel m; * adj essentiel, principal; ~ly adv essentiellement.

establish vt établir; fonder; démontrer.

establishment n établissement m; fondation f; institution f.

estate n état m; domaine m; biens mpl.

esteem vt estimer; apprécier; * n estime f; considération f.

esthetic adj esthétique; ~s npl esthétique f.

estimate vt estimer; évaluer.

estimation n estimation, évaluation f; opinion f.

estrange vt éloigner, séparer.

estranged adj séparé.

estrangement n séparation f; distance f.

estuary n estuaire m.

etch vt graver à l'eau forte.

etching n gravure à l'eau forte f.

eternal adj éternel, perpétuel; ~ly adv éternellement.

eternity n éternité f.

ether n éther m.

ethical adj éthique, moral; ~ly adv éthiquement.

ethics npl éthique f.

ethnic adj ethnique.

ethos n génie m.

etiquette n étiquette f.

etymological adj étymologique.

etymologist n étymologiste mf.

etymology n étymologie f.

Eucharist n Eucharistie f.

eulogy n éloge m.

eunuch n eunuque m.

euphemism n euphémisme m.

evacuate vt évacuer.

evacuation n évacuation f.

evade vt éviter; échapper à.

evaluate vt évaluer.

evangelic(al) adj évangélique.

evangelist n évangéliste m.

evaporate vt faire évaporer; * vi s'évaporer; se volatiliser.

evaporated milk n lait condensé m.

evaporation n évaporation f.

evasion n dérobade f.

evasive adj évasif; ~ly adv évasivement.

eve n veille f.

even adj égal; uni; pair; * adv même; encore; * vt égaliser; unir; * vi: to ~ out s'égaliser.

even-handed adj impartial, équitable.

evening n soir m, soirée f.

evening class n cours du soir m.

evening dress n robe du soir f; tenue de soirée f.

evenly adv également; uniment.

evenness n égalité f; uniformité f; régularité f; impartialité f.

event n événement m; épreuve f.

eventful adj mouvementé.

eventual adj final; ~ly adv finalement, en fin de comptes.

eventuality n éventualité f.

ever adv toujours; jamais; déjà; for

~ and ~ pour toujours; ~ since depuis.

evergreen adj à feuilles persistantes; * n arbre à feuilles persistantes m.

everlasting adj éternel.

evermore adv toujours.

every adj chacun, chacune; ~ where partout; ~ thing tout; ~ one, ~ body tout le monde.

evict vt expulser.

eviction n expulsion f.

evidence n évidence f; témoignage m; preuve f; * vt témoigner de.

evident adj évident; manifeste; ~ly adv manifestement, de toute évidence.

evil adj mauvais; malveillant; * n mal m.

evil-minded adj malintentionné.

evocative adj évocateur.

evoke vt évoquer.

evolution n évolution f.

evolve vt développer; * vi se développer, évoluer.

ewe n brebis f.

exacerbate vt exacerber.

exact adj exact; * vt exiger.

exacting adj exigeant.

exaction n exaction f; extorsion f.

exactly adv exactement.

exactness, exactitude n exactitude f.

exaggerate vt exagérer.

exaggeration n exagération f.

exalt vt exalter; élever.

exaltation n exaltation f; élévation f.

exalted adj exalté; élevé.

examination n examen m.

examine vt examiner.

examiner n examinateur m, -trice f.

example n exemple m.

exasperate vt exaspérer, irriter.

exasperation n exaspération, irritation f.

excavate vt excaver, creuser.

excavation n excavation f.

exceed vt excéder, dépasser.

exceedingly adv trop; extrêmement.

excel vt surpasser; vi exceller.

excellence n excellence f; supériorité f.

Excellency n Excellence (titre) f.

excellent adj excellent; ~ly adv excellemment, admirablement.

except vt excepter, exclure; ~(ing) prep excepté, à l'exception de.

exception n exception f.

exceptional adj exceptionnel.

excerpt n extrait m.

excess n excès m.

excessive adj excessif; ~ly adv excessivement.

exchange vt échanger; permuter; * n échange m; change m.

exchange rate n taux de change m.

excise n impôt m.

excitability n excitabilité f.

excitable adj excitable.

excite vt exciter; animer; enthousiasmer; stimuler.

excited adj animé, enthousiaste; excité.

excitement n animation f, enthousiasme m.

exciting adj passionnant; stimulant.

exclaim vi s'exclamer.

exclamation n exclamation f.

exclamation mark n point d'exclamation m.

exclamatory adj exclamatif.

exclude vt exclure.

exclusion n exclusion f; exception f.

exclusive adj exclusif; ~ly adv exclusivement.

excommunicate vt excommunier.

excommunication n excommunion f.

excrement n excrément m.

excruciating adj atroce, horrible.

exculpate vt disculper; justifier.

excursion n excursion f; digression f.

excusable adj excusable.

excuse vt excuser; pardonner; * n excuse f.

execute vt exécuter.

execution n exécution f.

executioner n bourreau m.

executive adj exécutif.

executor n exécuteur testamentaire m.

exemplary adj exemplaire.

exemplify vt exemplifier.

exempt adj exempt.

exemption n exemption f.

exercise n exercice m; * vi prendre de l'exercice; * vt exercer; montrer.

exercise book n cahier m.

exert vt employer, exercer; **to ~ oneself** s'efforcer.

exertion n effort m.

exhale vt exhaler; expirer.

exhaust n échappement m; * vt épuiser.

exhausted adj épuisé.

exhaustion n épuisement m.

exhaustive adj exhaustif, complet.

exhibit 333 **explore**

exhibit vt exhiber; montrer; * n (law) pièce à conviction f.

exhibition n exposition, présentation f.

exhilarating adj stimulant.

exhilaration n joie f; stimulation f.

exhort vt exhorter.

exhortation n exhortation f.

exhume vt exhumer, déterrer.

exile n exil m; * vt exiler, déporter.

exist vi exister.

existence n existence f.

existent adj existant.

existing adj actuel, présent.

exit n sortie f; * vi sortir.

exit ramp n bretelle d'accès f.

exodus n exode m.

exonerate vt disculper; décharger.

exoneration n disculpation f; décharge f.

exorbitant adj exorbitant, excessif.

exorcise vt exorciser.

exorcism n exorcisme m.

exotic adj exotique.

expand vt étendre; dilater.

expanse n étendue f.

expansion n expansion f.

expansive adj expansif.

expatriate vt expatrier.

expect vt attendre; espérer; penser.

expectance, expectancy n attente f; espoir m.

expectant adj d'attente.

expectant mother n femme enceinte f.

expectation n expectative f; attente f.

expediency n convenance f; opportunité f.

expedient adj opportun; * n expédient m; **~ly** adv de manière opportune.

expedite vt accélérer; expédier.

expedition n expédition f.

expeditious adj expéditif; **~ly** adv de manière expéditive.

expel vt expulser.

expend vt dépenser; utiliser.

expendable adj jetable; remplaçable.

expenditure n dépense f.

expense n dépense f; coût m.

expense account n frais mpl.

expensive adj cher; coûteux; **~ly** adv de manière coûteuse; à grands frais.

experience n expérience f; pratique f; * vt ressentir, éprouver; connaître.

experienced adj expérimenté.

experiment n expérience f; * vi expérimenter.

experimental adj expérimental; **~ly** adv expérimentalement.

expert adj expert.

expertise n habileté f.

expiration n expiration f; mort f.

expire vi expirer.

explain vt expliquer.

explanation n explication f.

explanatory adj explicatif.

expletive adj explétif.

explicable adj explicable.

explicit adj explicite; **~ly** adv explicitement.

explode vt faire exploser; vi exploser.

exploit vt exploiter; * n exploit m.

exploitation n exploitation f.

exploration n exploration f.

exploratory adj exploratoire.

explore vt explorer, examiner; sonder.

explorer *n* explorateur *m*, -trice *f*.

explosion *n* explosion *f*.

explosive *adj*, *n* explosif *m*.

exponent *n* (*math*) exposant *m*.

export *vt* exporter.

export, exportation *n* exportation *f*.

exporter *n* exportateur *m*, -trice *f*.

expose *vt* exposer; dévoiler.

exposed *adj* exposé.

exposition *n* exposition *f*; interprétation *f*.

expostulate *vi* débattre, discuter.

exposure *n* exposition *f*; temps de pose *m*; cliché *m*.

exposure meter *n* photomètre *m*.

expound *vt* interpréter.

express *vt* exprimer; * *adj* exprès; * *n* exprès *m*; (*rail*) rapide *m*.

expression *n* expression *f*; locution *f*.

expressionless *adj* inexpressif.

expressive *adj* expressif; **~ly** *adv* d'une manière expressive.

expressly *adv* expressément.

expressway *n* autoroute *f*.

expropriate *vt* exproprier.

expropriation *n* (*law*) expropriation *f*.

expulsion *n* expulsion *f*.

expurgate *vt* expurger.

exquisite *adj* exquis; **~ly** *adv* exquisément.

extant *adj* existant.

extempore *adv* à l'improviste.

extemporize *vi* improviser.

extend *vt* étendre; élargir; * *vi* s'étendre.

extension *n* extension *f*.

extensive *adj* étendu; important; **~ly** *adv* considérablement.

extent *n* extension *f*.

extenuate *vt* atténuer.

extenuating *adj* atténuant.

exterior *adj*, *n* extérieur *m*.

exterminate *vt* exterminer; supprimer.

extermination *n* extermination *f*; suppression *f*.

external *adj* externe; **~ly** *adv* extérieurement; **~s** *npl* extérieur *m*.

extinct *adj* disparu; éteint.

extinction *n* extinction *f*.

extinguish *vt* éteindre; supprimer.

extinguisher *n* extincteur *m*.

extirpate *vt* extirper.

extol *vt* louer, exalter.

extort *vt* extorquer; arracher.

extortion *n* extorsion *f*.

extortionate *adj* excessif.

extra *adv* particulièrement; *n* supplément *m*.

extract *vt* extraire; * *n* extrait *m*.

extraction *n* extraction *f*; origine *f*.

extracurricular *adj* périscolaire.

extradite *vt* extrader.

extradition *n* (*law*) extradition *f*.

extramarital *adj* extérieur au mariage.

extramural *adj* extra-muros.

extraneous *adj* superflu; sans rapport.

extraordinarily *adv* extraordinairement.

extraordinary *adj* extraordinaire.

extravagance *n* extravagance *f*; gaspillage *m*.

extravagant *adj* extravagant; exorbitant; gaspilleur; **~ly** *adv* de manière extravagante; en gaspillant.

extreme adj extrême; suprême; ultime; * n extrême m; ~**ly** adv extrêmement.

extremist adj, n extrémiste mf.

extremity n extrémité f.

extricate vt extirper, démêler.

extrinsic(al) adj extrinsèque.

extrovert adj, n extraverti m, -e f.

exuberance n exubérance f.

exuberant adj exubérant; ~**ly** adv avec exubérance.

exude vi exsuder.

exult vi exulter, triompher.

exultation n exultation f.

eye n œil m; * vt regarder, observer; lorgner.

eyeball n globe oculaire m.

eyebrow n sourcil m.

eyelash n cil m.

eyelid n paupière f.

eyesight n vue f.

eyesore n monstruosité f.

eyetooth n canine f.

eyewitness n témoin oculaire m.

eyrie n aire f.

F

fable n fable f; légende f.

fabric n tissu m.

fabricate vt fabriquer; inventer.

fabrication n fabrication f; invention f.

fabulous adj fabuleux; ~**ly** adv fabuleusement.

facade n façade f.

face n visage m, figure f; surface f; façade f; mine f; apparence f; * vt faire face à; affronter; **to ~ up to** faire face à.

face cream n crème pour le visage f.

face-lift n lifting m.

face powder n poudre de riz f.

facet n facette f.

facetious adj facétieux, plaisant, spirituel; ~**ly** adv facétieusement.

face value n valeur nominale f.

facial adj facial.

facile adj facile; superficiel.

facilitate vt faciliter.

facility n facilité f; équipement m, infrastructure f.

facing n revers m; * prep en face de.

facsimile n fac-similé m.

fact n fait m; réalité f; **in ~** en fait.

faction n faction f; dissension f.

factor n facteur m.

factory n usine f.

factual adj factuel, basé sur les faits.

faculty n faculté f; le corps enseignant m.

fad n engouement m.

fade vi se faner; perdre son éclat.

fail vt échouer à; omettre; manquer à ses engagements envers; * vi échouer; faiblir; manquer.

failing n défaut m.

failure n échec m; panne f; raté m; faillite f; manquement m.

faint vi s'évanouir, défaillir; * n évanouissement m; * adj faible; ~**ly** adv faiblement.

fainthearted adj timide, timoré, pusillanime.

faintness n faiblesse f; légèreté f.

fair adj beau; blond; clair; favorable; juste, équitable; considérable; passable; * adv loyalement; * n foire f.

fairly adv équitablement; absolument.

fairness n beauté f; justice f.

fair play n fair-play, franc-jeu m.

fairy n fée f.

fairy tale n conte de fées m.

faith n foi f; croyance f; fidélité f.

faithful adj fidèle, loyal; ~ly adv fidèlement.

faithfulness n fidélité, loyauté f.

fake n falsification f; imposteur m; * adj faux; * vt feindre; falsifier.

falcon n faucon m.

falconry n fauconnerie f.

fall vi tomber; s'effondrer; diminuer, baisser; **to ~ asleep** s'endormir; **to ~ back** reculer; **to ~ back on** avoir recours à; **to ~ behind** être à la traîne; **to ~ down** tomber; **to ~ for** se faire avoir; tomber amoureux de; **to ~ in** s'enfoncer; **to ~ short** échouer; **to ~ sick** tomber malade; **to ~ in love** tomber amoureux; **to ~ off** tomber; diminuer; **to ~ out** se produire; se quereller; **to ~ in** chute f; automne m.

fallacious adj fallacieux, trompeur; ~ly adv d'une manière fallacieuse.

fallacy n erreur f; sophisme m; tromperie f.

fallibility n faillibilité f.

fallible adj faillible.

fallout n retombées radioactives fpl.

fallout shelter n abri antiatomique m.

fallow adj en jachère; **~ deer** n daim m.

false adj faux; **~ly** adv faussement.

false alarm n fausse alerte f.

falsehood, falseness n mensonge m; fausseté f.

falsify vt falsifier.

falsity n fausseté f.

falter vi vaciller; faiblir.

faltering adj chancelant.

fame n réputation f; renommée f, notoriété f.

famed adj célèbre.

familiar adj familier; domestique; **~ly** adv familièrement.

familiarity n familiarité f.

familiarize vt familiariser.

family n famille f.

family business n affaire de famille f.

family doctor n médecin de famille m.

famine n famine f; disette f.

famished adj affamé.

famous adj célèbre, fameux; **~ly** adv fameusement.

fan n éventail m; ventilateur m; jeune admirateur m, -trice f; * vt éventer; attiser.

fanatic adj, n fanatique mf.

fanaticism n fanatisme m.

fan belt n courroie de ventilateur f.

fanciful adj fantasque, capricieux; **~ly** adv capricieusement.

fancy n fantaisie, imagination f; caprice m; * vt avoir envie de; s'imaginer.

fancy-goods npl nouveautés fpl.

fancy dress n travesti m, déguisement m.

fancydress ball n bal masqué m.

fanfare n (mus) fanfare f.

fang n croc m.

fantastic adj fantastique; excentrique; **~ally** adv fantastiquement.

fantasy n imagination f.

far adv loin; * adj lointain, éloigné; **~ and away** de très loin; **~ off** lointain.

faraway adj lointain.

farce n farce f.

farcical adj grotesque.

fare n prix (du voyage) m; tarif m; régime alimentaire m; voyageur m, -euse f; client m, -e f.

farewell n adieu m; **~!** excl adieu!

farm n ferme f, exploitation agricole f; * vt cultiver.

farmer n fermier m; agriculteur m.

farmhand n ouvrier agricole m.

farmhouse n maison de ferme f.

farming n agriculture f.

farmland n terres arables fpl.

farmyard n cour de ferme f.

far-reaching adj d'une grande portée.

fart n (sl) pet m; * vi péter.

farther adv plus loin; * adj plus éloigné.

farthest adv le plus lointain; le plus loin; au plus.

fascinate vt fasciner, captiver.

fascinating adj fascinant.

fascination n fascination f; charme m.

fascism n fascisme m.

fashion n manière, façon f; forme f; coutume f; mode f; style m; **people of ~** personnes élégantes fpl; * vt façonner, confectionner.

fashionable adj à la mode; chic;

the ~ world le beau monde; **~bly** adv à la mode.

fashion show n défilé de mode m.

fast vi jeûner; * n jeûne m; * adj rapide; ferme, stable; * adv rapidement; fermement; solidement.

fasten vt attacher; fixer; attribuer; * vi se fixer, s'attacher.

fastener, fastening n attache f; fermoir m.

fast food n restauration rapide f.

fastidious adj minutieux, méticuleux; **~ly** adv minutieusement.

fat adj gros, gras; * n graisse f.

fatal adj mortel; néfaste; **~ly** adv mortellement.

fatalism n fatalisme m.

fatalist n fataliste mf.

fatality n accident mortel m, fatalité f.

fate n destin, sort m.

fateful adj fatidique.

father n père m.

fatherhood n paternité f.

father-in-law n beau-père m.

fatherland n patrie f.

fatherly adj (adv) paternel(lement).

fathom n brasse (mesure) f; * vt sonder; pénétrer.

fatigue n fatigue f; * vt fatiguer, lasser.

fatten vt, vi engraisser.

fatty adj gras, graisseux.

fatuous adj imbécile, stupide, niais.

faucet n robinet m.

fault n défaut m, faute f; délit m; faille f.

faultfinder n chicaneur m, -euse f.

faultless adj irréprochable.

faulty adj défectueux.

fauna n faune f.

faux pas n impair m.

favor n faveur f; approbation f; avantage m; * vt favoriser, préférer.

favorable adj favorable, propice; **~bly** adv favorablement.

favored adj favorisé.

favorite n favori m; * adj favori.

favoritism n favoritisme m.

fawn n faon m; * vi flatter servilement.

fawningly adv d'une flatterie servile.

fax n télécopieur, fax m; télécopie f, fax m; * vt envoyer par fax, télécopier.

fear vt craindre; * n crainte f.

fearful adj effrayant; craintif, peureux; **~ly** adv terriblement; craintivement.

fearless adj intrépide, courageux; **~ly** adv courageusement.

fearlessness n intrépidité f.

feasibility n faisabilité f.

feasible adj faisable, réalisable.

feast n festin, banquet m; fête f; * vi banqueter.

feat n exploit m; prouesse f.

feather n plume f;.

feather bed n lit de plumes.

feature n caractéristique f; trait m; * vi figurer.

feature film n long métrage m.

February n février m.

federal adj fédéral.

federalist n fédéraliste mf.

federate vt fédérer; * vi se fédérer.

federation n fédération f.

fed-up adj: **to be** ~ en avoir marre.

fee n honoraires mpl; frais mpl.

feeble adj faible, frêle.

feebleness n faiblesse f.

feebly adv faiblement.

feed vt nourrir; alimenter; **to** ~ **on** se nourrir de; * vi manger; se nourrir; * n nourriture f; alimentation f.

feedback n réaction f.

feel vt sentir; toucher; croire; **to** ~ **around** tâtonner, fouiller; * n sensation f; toucher m.

feeler n antenne f; (fig) tentative f.

feeling n sensation f; sentiment m.

feelingly adv avec émotion.

feign vt inventer; feindre, simuler.

feline adj félin.

fellow n homme, type m; membre m.

fellow citizen n concitoyen m -enne f.

fellow countryman n compatriote m.

fellow feeling n sympathie f.

fellow men npl semblables mpl.

fellowship n camaraderie f; association f.

fellow student n copain (copine) de fac m(f).

fellow traveller n compagnon (compagne) de voyage m(f).

felon n criminel m, -elle f.

felony n crime m.

felt n feutre m.

felt-tip pen n feutre m.

female n femelle f; * adj de sexe féminin, femelle.

feminine adj féminin.

feminist n féministe mf.

fen n marais m.

fence n barrière f; clôture f; * vt
clôturer; * vi faire de l'escrime.

fencing n escrime f.

fender n pare-chocs m invar.

fennel n (bot) fenouil m.

ferment n agitation f; * vi fermenter.

fern n (bot) fougère f.

ferocious adj féroce; ~ly adv
férocement.

ferocity n férocité f.

ferret n furet m; * vt fureter; **to ~
out** découvrir, dénicher.

ferry n bac m; ferry m; * vt transporter.

fertile adj fertile, fécond.

fertility n fertilité, fécondité f.

fertilize vt fertiliser.

fertilizer n engrais m.

fervent adj fervent; ardent; ~ly adv
avec ferveur.

fervid adj ardent, véhément.

fervor n ferveur, ardeur f.

fester vi suppurer; s'envenimer.

festival n fête f; festival m.

festive adj de fête.

festivity n fête f, réjouissances fpl.

fetch vt aller chercher.

fetching adj charmant, séduisant.

fête n fête f.

fetid adj fétide, nauséabond.

fetus n fœtus m.

feud n fief m; rivalité, dissension f.

feudal adj féodal.

feudalism n féodalité f.

fever n fièvre f.

feverish adj fiévreux.

few adj peu; **a ~** quelques; **~ and
far between** rares.

fewer n moins (de) ; * adv moins.

fewest adj le moins (de).

fiancé n fiancé m.

fiancée n fiancée f.

fib n bobard m; * vi raconter des
bobards.

fibre n fibre f.

fibreglass n fibre de verre f.

fickle adj volage, inconstant.

fiction n fiction f; invention f.

fictional adj fictif.

fictitious adj fictif, imaginaire;
feint; ~ly adv fictivement.

fiddle n violon m; combine f; * vi
jouer du violon.

fiddler n violoniste mf.

fidelity n fidélité, loyauté f.

fidget vi s'agiter, s'impatienter.

fidgety adj agité, impatient.

field n champ m; étendue f; domaine m.

field day n (mil) jour de grandes
manœuvres m.

fieldmouse n mulot m.

fieldwork n recherches sur le terrain fpl.

fiend n démon m; mordu m.

fiendish adj diabolique.

fierce adj féroce, violent; acharné,
furieux; ~ly adv férocement

fierceness n férocité, fureur f.

fiery adj ardent; fougueux.

fifteen adj, n quinze m.

fifteenth adj, n quinzième mf.

fifth adj, n cinquième mf; ~ly adv
cinquièmement.

fiftieth adj, n cinquantième mf.

fifty adj, n cinquante m.

fig n figue f.

fight vt, vi se battre (contre); combattre; lutter ;* n bataille f; combat m; lutte f.

fighter n combattant m; lutteur m; chasseur m.

fighting n combat m.

fig-leaf n feuille de figuier f.

fig tree n figuier m.

figurative adj figuratif; **~ly** adv figurativement.

figure n figure f; forme, silhouette f; image f; chiffre m; * vi figurer; avoir du sens; **to ~ out** comprendre.

figurehead n figure de proue f.

filament n filament m; fibre f.

filch vt chiper.

filcher n voleur m, -euse f.

file n file f; liste f; (mil) colonne, rangée f; lime f; dossier m; fi- chier m; * vt enregistrer; limer; classer; déposer; * vi **to ~ in/out** entrer/sortir en file; **to ~ past** défiler devant.

filing cabinet n classeur (meuble) m.

fill vt remplir; **to ~ in** remplir; **to ~ up** remplir (jusqu'au bord).

fillet n filet m.

fillet steak n filet de bœuf m.

filling station n station-service f.

fillip n (fig) coup de fouet m.

filly n pouliche f.

film n pellicule f; film f; cellophane m; * vt filmer; * vi s'embuer.

film star n vedette de cinéma f.

filmstrip n film m.

filter n filtre m; * vt filtrer.

filter-tipped adj à bout filtre.

filth(iness) n immondice, ordure f; saleté, crasse f.

filthy adj crasseux, dégoûtant.

fin n nageoire f.

final adj dernier; définitif; **~ly** adv finalement.

finale n finale m.

finalist n finaliste mf.

finalize vt parachever, rendre définitif.

finance n finance f.

financial adj financier.

financier n financier m.

find vt trouver, découvrir; **to ~ out** découvrir; démasquer; **to ~ one's self** se retrouver; * vt trouvaille f.

findings npl résultats mpl, conclusions fpl; verdict m.

fine adj fin; pur; aigu; raffiné; beau, f belle; délicat; subtil; élégant; * n amende f; * vt infliger une amende à.

fine arts npl beaux arts mpl.

finely adv magnifiquement.

finery n parure f.

finesse n finesse, subtilité f.

finger n doigt m; * vt toucher, manier.

fingernail n ongle m.

fingerprint n empreinte digitale f.

fingertip n bout du doigt m.

finicky adj pointilleux, difficile.

finish vt finir, terminer, achever; **to ~ off** finir; **to ~ up** terminer; * vi: **to ~ up** se retrouver.

finishing line n ligne d'arrivée f.

finishing school n école privée (pour jeunes filles) f.

finite adj fini.

fir (tree) n sapin m

fire n feu m; incendie m; * vt mettre le feu à; incendier; tirer; * vi s'enflammer, faire feu.

fire alarm n alarme d'incendie f.

firearm n arme à feu f.

fireball n boule de feu f.

fire department n pompiers mpl.

fire engine n voiture de pompiers f.

fire escape n escalier de secours m.

fire extinguisher n extincteur m.

firefly n luciole f.

fireman n pompier m.

fireplace n cheminée f, foyer m.

fireproof adj ignifugé.

fireside n coin du feu m.

fire station n caserne de pompiers f.

firewater n eau de vie f.

firewood n bois de chauffage m.

fireworks npl feu d'artifice m.

firing n fusillade f.

firing squad n peloton d'exécution m.

firm adj ferme, solide; constant; * n (com) compagnie f; **~ly** adv fermement.

firmament n firmament m.

firmness n fermeté f; résolution f.

first adj premier; * adv premièrement; **at ~** d'abord; **~ly** adv en premier lieu.

first aid n premiers secours mpl.

first-aid kit n trousse de premiers secours f.

first-class adj de première classe, de première catégorie.

first-hand adj de première main.

First Lady n première dame, femme du président d'un pays f.

first name n prénom m.

first-rate adj de première qualité.

fiscal adj fiscal.

fish n poisson m; * vi pêcher.

fishbone n arête f.

fisherman n pêcheur m.

fish farm n entreprise de pisciculture f.

fishing n pêche f.

fishing line n ligne de pêche f.

fishing rod n canne à pêche f.

fishing tackle n attirail de pêche m.

fish market n marché au poisson m.

fishseller n poissonnier m, -ière f.

fishstore n poissonnerie f.

fishy adj (fig) suspect.

fissure n fissure, crevasse f.

fist n poing m.

fit n accès m, attaque f; crise f; * adj en forme; capable; adapté à, qui convient; * vt aller à; ajuster, adapter; **to ~ out** équiper; * vi (bien) aller; **to ~ in** s'accorder avec; être en harmonie avec.

fitment n meuble encastré m.

fitness n forme physique f; aptitudes fpl.

fitted carpet n moquette f.

fitted kitchen n cuisine encastrée f.

fitter n monteur m.

fitting adj qui convient, approprié, juste; * n accessoire m; **~s** pl installations fpl.

five adj, n cinq m.

five spot n (sl) billet de cinq dollars m.

fix n vt fixer, établir; **to ~ up** arranger.

fixation n obsession f.

fixed adj fixe.

fixings npl garniture f; accessoires mpl.

fixture n rencontre f.

fizz(le) vi pétiller.

fizzy adj gazeux.

flabbergasted adj abasourdi.

flabby adj mou, f molle, flasque.

flaccid adj flasque, mou, f molle.

flag n drapeau m; iris m; * vi s'affaiblir.

flagpole n mât aux drapeaux m.

flagrant adj flagrant.

flagship n vaisseau amiral m.

flagstop n arrêt facultatif m.

flair n flair m; talent m.

flak n tir antiaérien m; critiques fpl.

flake n flocon m; paillette f; * vi s'effriter, s'écailler.

flaky adj floconneux; friable.

flamboyant adj flamboyant; ostentatoire.

flame n flamme f; ardeur f.

flamingo n flamant m.

flammable adj inflammable.

flank n flanc m; (also mil); * vt flanquer.

flannel n flanelle f.

flap n battement m; rabat m; * vt, vi battre.

flare vi luire, briller; **to ~ up** s'embraser; se mettre en colère; éclater; * n flamme f.

flash n éclat m; éclair m; * vt faire briller; allumer.

flashbulb n ampoule de flash f.

flash cube n cube de flash m.

flashlight n fanal m.

flashy adj tape-à-l'œil, voyant.

flask n flasque f, flacon m.

flat adj plat; uniforme; insipide; * n plaine f, plat m; (mus) si bémol m; **~ly** adv horizontalement; platement; également; catégoriquement.

flatness n égalité f; monotonie f.

flatten vt aplanir; aplatir.

flatter vt flatter.

flattering adj flatteur.

flattery n flatterie f.

flatulence n (med) flatulence f.

flaunt vt étaler, afficher.

flavour n saveur f; * vt parfumer; assaisonner.

flavoured adj savoureux, parfumé.

flavourless adj insipide.

flaw n défaut m; imperfection f.

flawless adj parfait.

flax n lin m.

flea n puce f.

flea bite n piqûre de puce f.

fleck n petite tache f; particule f.

flee vi fuir de m; * vi s'enfuir; fuir.

fleece n toison f; * vt (sl) tondre.

fleet n flotte f; parc m.

fleeting adj fugace, fugitif.

flesh n chair f.

flesh wound n blessure superficielle f.

fleshy adj charnu.

flex n cordon m; * vt fléchir.

flexibility n flexibilité f.

flexible adj flexible, souple.

flick n petit coup m; * vt donner un petit coup à.

flicker vt vaciller; trembloter.

flier n aviateur m, -trice f.

flight n vol m; fuite f; volée f; (fig) envolée f.

flight attendant n steward m, hôtesse de l'air f.

flight deck n cabine de pilotage f.

flimsy adj léger; fragile.

flinch vi sourciller.

fling vt lancer, jeter.

flint n silex m.

flip vt lancer.

flippant *adj* désinvolte, cavalier.

flipper *n* nageoire *f*.

flirt *vi* flirter; * *n* charmeur *m*, -euse *f*.

flirtation *n* flirt *f*.

flit *vi* voler, voleter.

float *vt* faire flotter; lancer; * *vi* flotter; * *n* flotteur *m*; char (de carnaval) *m*; provision *f*.

flock *n* troupeau *m*; volée *f*; foule *f*; * *vi* affluer.

flog *vt* fustiger.

flogging *n* fustigation, flagellation *f*.

flood *n* inondation *f*; marée haute *f*; déluge *m*; * *vt* inonder.

flooding *n* inondation *f*.

floodlight *n* projecteur *m*.

floor *n* sol *m*; plancher *m*; étage *m*; * *vt* parqueter; déconcerter.

floorboard *n* planche *f*.

floor lamp *n* lampadaire *m*.

floor show *n* spectacle de cabaret *m*.

flop *n* four, fiasco *m*.

floppy *adj* lâche; * *n* disquette *f*.

flora *n* flore *f*.

floral *adj* floral.

florescence *n* floraison *f*.

florid *adj* fleuri.

florist *n* fleuriste *mf*.

florist's (shop) *n* boutique de fleuriste *f*.

flotilla *n* (*mar*) flotille *f*.

flounder *n* flet *m*; * *vi* patauger.

flour *n* farine *f*.

flourish *vi* fleurir; prospérer; * *n* fioriture *f*; (*mus*) fioriture *f*.

flourishing *adj* florissant.

flout *vt* mépriser, se moquer de.

flow *vi* couler; circuler; monter (marée); ondoyer; * *n* flux *m*; écoulement *m*; flot *m*.

flow chart *n* organigramme *m*.

flower *n* fleur *f*; * *vi* fleurir.

flowerbed *n* parterre de fleurs *m*.

flowerpot *n* pot de fleurs *m*.

flowery *adj* fleuri.

flower show *n* exposition de fleurs *f*.

fluctuate *vi* fluctuer.

fluctuation *n* fluctuation *f*.

fluency *n* aisance *f*.

fluent *adj* coulant; facile; **~ly** *adv* couramment.

fluff *n* peluche *f*; **~y** *adj* duveteux.

fluid *adj*, *n* fluide *m*.

fluidity *n* fluidité *f*.

fluke *n* (*sl*) veine *f*.

fluoride *n* fluorure *m*.

flurry *n* rafale *f*; agitation *f*.

flush *vt*: **to ~ out** nettoyer à grande eau; * *vi* rougir; * *n* rougeur *f*; éclat *m*.

flushed *adj* rouge.

fluster *vt* énerver.

flustered *adj* énervé.

flute *n* flûte *f*.

flutter *vi* voleter; s'agiter; * *n* agitation *f*; émoi *m*.

flux *n* flux *m*.

fly *vt* piloter; transporter par avion; * *vi* voler; fuir; **to ~ away/off** s'envoler; * *n* mouche *f*; braguette *f*.

flying *n* aviation *f*.

flying saucer *n* soucoupe volante *f*.

flypast *n* défilé aérien *m*.

flysheet *n* feuille volante *f*.

foal *n* poulain *m*.

foam *n* écume *f*; * *vi* écumer.

foam rubber *n* caoutchouc mousse *m*.

foamy *adj* écumeux.

focus *n* foyer *m*; centre *m*.

fodder *n* fourrage *m*.

foe n ennemi m, -e f, adversaire mf.

fog n brouillard m.

foggy adj brumeux.

fog light n feu de brouillard m.

foible n point faible m.

foil vt déjouer; * n papier d'aluminium m; fleuret m.

fold n pli m; parc à moutons m; * vt plier; **to ~ up** faire faillite; * vi: **to ~ up** plier, replier.

folder n chemise f; dépliant m.

folding adj pliant.

folding chair n chaise pliante f.

foliage n feuillage m.

folio n folio m.

folk n gens mpl.

folklore n folklore m.

folk song n chant folklorique m.

follow vt suivre; **to ~ up** suivre; exploiter; * vi suivre, s'ensuivre, résulter.

follower n serviteur m; disciple mf, partisan m, -e f; adhérent m, -e f; admirateur m, -trice f.

following adj suivant; * n partisans mpl.

folly n folie, extravagance f.

foment vt fomenter.

fond adj affectueux; **to be ~ of** aimer; **~ly** adv affectueusement.

fondle vt caresser.

fondness n prédilection f; affection f.

font n fonts baptismaux mpl.

food n nourriture f.

food mixer n mixer m.

food poisoning n intoxication alimentaire f.

food processor n robot m.

foodstuffs npl denrées alimentaires fpl.

fool n imbécile mf, idiot m, -e f; * vt duper.

foolhardy adj téméraire.

foolish adj idiot, insensé; **~ly** adv bêtement.

foolproof adj infaillible.

foolscap n papier ministre m.

foot n pied m; patte f; **on** or **by ~** à pied.

footage n métrage m.

football n football m; ballon de football m.

footballer n footballeur m, -euse f.

footbrake n frein à pied m.

footbridge n passerelle f.

foothills npl contreforts mpl.

foothold n prise (pour le pied) f.

footing n prise (pour le pied) f; statut m; situation f; plan m.

footlights npl feux de la rampe mpl.

footman n valet de pied m; soldat d'infanterie m.

footnote n note (de bas de page) f.

footpath n sentier m.

footprint n empreinte (de pas) f.

footsore adj aux pieds endoloris.

footstep n pas m.

footwear n chaussures fpl.

for prep pour; en raison de; pendant; * conj car; **as ~ me** quant à moi; **what ~?** pourquoi?; pourquoi faire?

forage n fourrage m; * vt fourrager; fouiller.

foray n incursion f.

forbid vt interdire, défendre; empêcher; **God ~!** pourvu que non!

forbidding adj menaçant; sévère.

force n force f; puissance, vigueur f; violence f; **~s** pl forces armées *fpl*; * *vt* forcer, obliger, contraindre; imposer.

forced *adj* forcé.

forced march *n* (*mil*) marche forcée *f*.

forceful *adj* énergique.

forceps *n* forceps *m*.

forcible *adj* énergique, vigoureux, puissant; **~bly** *adv* énergiquement, avec véhémence.

ford *n* gué *m*; * *vt* passer à gué.

fore *n*: **to the ~** en évidence.

forearm *n* avant-bras *m*.

foreboding *n* pressentiment *m*.

forecast *vt* prévoir; * *n* prévision *f*.

forecourt *n* avant-cour *f*.

forefather *n* aïeul, ancêtre *m*.

forefinger *n* index *m*.

forefront *n*: **in the ~ of** au premier plan de.

forego *vt* renoncer à, s'abstenir de.

foregone *adj* passé; anticipé.

foreground *n* premier plan *m*.

forehead *n* front *m*.

foreign *adj* étranger.

foreigner *n* étranger *m*, -ère *f*.

foreign exchange *n* devises *fpl*.

foreleg *n* patte de devant *f*.

foreman *n* contremaître *m*; (*law*) premier juré *m*.

foremost *adj* principal.

forenoon *n* matinée *f*.

forensic *adj* judiciaire.

forerunner *n* précurseur *m*; signe avant-coureur *m*.

foresee *vt* prévoir.

foreshadow *vt* présager.

foresight *n* prévoyance *f*; pre science *f*.

forest *n* forêt *f*.

forestall *vt* anticiper; prévenir.

forester *n* garde forestier *m*.

forestry *n* sylviculture *f*.

foretaste *n* avant-goût *m*.

foretell *vt* prédire.

forethought *n* prévoyance *f*; préméditation *f*.

forever *adv* toujours; un temps infini.

forewarn *vt* prévenir à l'avance.

foreword *n* préface *f*.

forfeit *n* amende *f*; confiscation *f*; * *vt* perdre.

forge *n* forge *f*; usine métallurgique *f*; * *vt* forger; contrefaire * *vi*: **to ~ ahead** aller de l'avant.

forger *n* faussaire *m*.

forgery *n* contrefaçon *f*.

forget *vt* oublier.

forgetful *adj* étourdi; négligent.

forgetfulness *n* étourderie *f*; négligence *f*.

forget-me-not *n* (*bot*) myosotis *m*.

forgive *vt* pardonner.

forgiveness *n* pardon *m*; indulgence *f*.

fork *n* fourchette *f*; fourche *f*; * *vi* bifurquer; **to ~ out** (*sl*) casquer.

forked *adj* fourchu.

fork-lift truck *n* chariot élévateur *m*.

forlorn *adj* malheureux, abandonné.

form *n* forme *f*; formule *f*; formulaire *m*; formalité *f*; moule *m*; * *vt* former.

formal *adj* formel; méthodique; cérémonieux; **~ly** *adv* formellement.

formality *n* formalité *f*; cérémonie *f*.

format *n* format *m*; * *vt* formater.

formation n formation f.

formative adj formateur m, -trice f.

former adj précédent, ancien; **~ly** adv autrefois, jadis.

formidable adj effrayant, terrible.

formula n formule f.

formulate vt formuler.

forsake vt abandonner, renoncer à.

fort n fort m.

forte n fort m.

forthcoming adj prochain; sociable.

forthright adj franc.

forthwith adv immédiatement, tout de suite.

fortieth adj, n quarantième mf.

fortification n fortification f.

fortify vt fortifier, renforcer.

fortitude n stoïcisme m; courage m.

fortnight n quinze jours mpl; deux semaines fpl; * adj **~ly** bimensuel; * adv **~ly** tous les quinze jours.

fortress n (mil) forteresse f.

fortuitous adj fortuit; imprévu; **~ly** adv fortuitement.

fortunate adj chanceux; **~ly** adv heureusement.

fortune n chance f, sort m; fortune f.

fortune-teller n diseuse de bonne aventure f.

forty adj, n quarante m.

forum n forum m, tribune f.

forward adj avancé; précoce; présomptueux; **~(s)** adv en avant, vers l'avant; * vt transmettre; promouvoir; expédier.

forwardness n précocité f; effronterie f.

fossil adj fossilisé; * n fossile m.

foster vt élever.

foster child n enfant adoptif m.

foster father n père adoptif m.

foster mother n mère adoptive f.

foul adj infect, ignoble; vil, déloyal; **~ copy** n copie illisible f; **~ly** adv salement; ignoblement; * vt polluer.

foul play n jeu déloyal m; meurtre m.

found vt fonder, créer; établir, édifier; fondre.

foundation n foundation f; fondement m.

founder n fondateur m, -trice f; fondeur m; * vi (mar) couler.

foundling n enfant trouvé(e) mf.

foundry n fonderie f.

fount, fountain n fontaine f.

fountainhead n source, origine f.

four adj, n quatre m.

fourfold adj quadruple.

four-poster (bed) n lit à baldaquin m.

foursome n groupe de quatre personnes m.

fourteen adj, n quatorze m.

fourteenth adj, n quatorzième mf.

fourth n quatrième mf; * n quart m; **~ly** adv quatrièmement.

fowl n volaille f.

fox n renard f; (fig) rusé m.

foyer n vestibule m.

fracas n rixe f.

fraction n fraction f.

fracture n fracture f; * vt fracturer.

fragile adj fragile; frêle.

fragility n fragilité f; faiblesse, délicatesse f.

fragment n fragment m.

fragmentary adj fragmentaire.

fragrance n parfum m.

fragrant *adj* parfumé, odorant; ~**ly** *adv* en exhalant un parfum.

frail *adj* frêle, fragile.

frailty *n* fragilité *f*; faiblesse *f*.

frame *n* charpente *f*; châssis *m*, armature *f*; cadre *m*; structure *f*; monture *f*; * *vt* encadrer; concevoir; construire; former.

frame of mind *n* état d'esprit *m*.

framework *n* charpente *f*; structure *f*, cadre *m*.

franchise *n* droit de vote *m*; franchise *f*.

frank *adj* franc, direct.

frankly *adv* franchement.

frankness *n* franchise *f*.

frantic *adj* frénétique, effréné.

fraternal *adj*, ~**ly** *adv* fraternel(lement).

fraternity *n* fraternité *f*.

fraternize *vi* fraterniser.

fratricide *n* fratricide *mf*.

fraud *n* fraude, tromperie *f*.

fraudulence *n* caractère frauduleux *m*.

fraudulent *adj* frauduleux; ~**ly** *adv* frauduleusement.

fraught *adj* plein, chargé.

fray *n* rixe, bagarre, querelle *f*.

freak *n* caprice *m*; phénomène *m*.

freckle *n* tache de rousseur *f*.

freckled *adj* couvert de taches de rousseur.

free *adj* libre; autonome; gratuit; dégagé; * *vt* affranchir; libérer; débarrasser.

freedom *n* liberté *f*.

freehold *n* propriété libre *f*.

free-for-all *n* mêlée générale *f*.

free gift *n* prime *f*.

free kick *n* coup franc *m*.

freelance *adj* indépendant; * *adv* en indépendant.

freely *adv* librement; franchement; libéralement.

freemason *n* franc-maçon *m*.

freemasonry *n* franc-maçonnerie *f*.

freepost *n* port payé *m*.

free-range *adj* de ferme.

freethinker *n* libre-penseur *m*, -euse *f*.

freethinking *n* libre pensée *f*.

free trade *n* libre échange *m*.

freeway *n* autoroute *f*.

freewheel *vi* rouler au point mort.

free will *n* libre arbitre *m*.

freeze *vi* geler; * *vt* congeler; geler.

freeze-dried *adj* lyophilisé.

freezer *n* congélateur *m*.

freezing *n* gelé.

freezing point *n* point de congélation *m*.

freight *n* cargaison *f*; fret *m*.

freighter *n* affréteur *m*.

freight train *n* train de marchandises *m*.

French bean *n* haricot vert *m*.

French fries *npl* frites *fpl*.

French window *n* porte-fenêtre *f*.

frenzied *adj* fou, frénétique.

frenzy *n* frénésie *f*; folie *f*.

frequency *n* fréquence *f*.

frequent *adj* fréquent; ~**ly** *adv* fréquemment; * *vt* fréquenter.

fresco *n* fresque *f*.

fresh *adj* frais; nouveau, récent; ~ **water** *n* eau douce *f*.

freshen *vt* rafraîchir; * *vi* se rafraîchir.

freshly *adv* nouvellement; récemment.

freshman n nouveau m, -elle f.

freshness n fraîcheur f.

freshwater adj d'eau douce.

fret vi s'agiter, se tracasser.

friar n moine m.

friction n friction f.

Friday n vendredi m; Good ~ Vendredi Saint m.

friend n ami m, -e f.

friendless adj sans amis.

friendliness n amitié, bienveillance f.

friendly adj amical.

friendship n amitié f.

frieze n frise f.

frigate n (mar) frégate f.

fright n peur, frayeur f.

frighten vt effrayer.

frightened adj effrayé, apeuré.

frightening adj effrayant.

frightful adj épouvantable, effroyable; ~ly adv affreusement, effroyablement.

frigid adj froid, glacé; frigide; ~ly adv froidement.

fringe n frange f.

fringe benefits npl avantages en nature mpl.

frisk vt fouiller.

frisky adj vif, fringant.

fritter vt: to ~ away gaspiller.

frivolity n frivolité f.

frivolous adj frivole, léger.

frizz(le) vt faire trop griller; friser.

frizzy adj frisé.

fro adv: to go to and ~ aller et venir.

frock n robe f.

frog n grenouille f.

frolic vi folâtrer, gambader.

frolicsome adj folâtre, gai.

from prep de; depuis; à partir de.

front n avant, devant m; façade f; front m; * adj de devant; premier.

frontal adj de front.

front door n porte d'entrée f.

frontier n frontière f.

front page n première page f.

front-wheel drive n (auto) traction avant f.

frost n gel m; gelée f; * vt geler.

frostbite n engelure f.

frostbitten adj gelé.

frosted adj gelé, givré.

frosty adj glacial; givré.

froth n écume f; * vi écumer.

frothy adj mousseux, écumeux.

frown vt froncer les sourcils; * n froncement de sourcils m.

frozen adj gelé.

frugal adj frugal; économique; simple; ~ly adv frugalement.

fruit n fruit m.

fruiterer n fruitier m, -ière f.

fruiterer's (shop) n fruiterie f.

fruitful adj fécond, fertile; fructueux, utile; ~ly adv fructueusement.

fruitfulness n fertilité f; caractère fructueux m.

fruition n réalisation f.

fruit juice n jus de fruit m.

fruitless adj stérile; infécond; ~ly adv vainement, inutilement.

fruit salad n salade de fruits f.

fruit tree n arbre fruitier m.

frustrate vt contrecarrer; annuler.

frustrated adj frustré.

frustration n frustration f.

fry vt frire.

frying pan n poêle f.

fuchsia n (bot) fuchsia m.

fudge n caramel m.

fuel n combustible, carburant m.

fuel tank n réservoir à carburant m.

fugitive adj, n fugitif m, -ive f.

fugue n (mus) fugue f.

fulcrum n pivot m.

fulfill vt accomplir; réaliser.

fulfillment n accomplissement m.

full adj plein, rempli; complet; * adv pleinement, entièrement.

full-blown adj complet.

full-fledged adj diplômé, qualifié.

full-length adj en pied; de long métrage.

full moon n pleine lune f.

fullness n plénitude f; abondance f.

full-scale adj grandeur nature ; total, complet.

full-time adj à plein temps.

fully adv pleinement, entièrement.

fulsome adj exagéré.

fumble vi manier gauchement; farfouiller.

fume vi exhaler des vapeurs; rager, fumer; * ~s npl exhalaisons f pl.

fumigate vt fumiger.

fun n amusement m; plaisir m; **to have ~** (bien) s'amuser.

function n fonction f.

functional adj fonctionnel.

fund n fonds m; * vt financer.

fundamental adj fondamental; **~ly** adv fondamentalement.

funeral service n office des morts m.

funeral n enterrement m.

funereal adj funèbre, lugubre.

fungus n champignon m; moisissure f.

funnel n entonnoir m; cheminée f.

funny adj amusant; curieux.

fur n fourrure f.

fur coat n manteau de fourrure m.

furious adj furieux; déchaîné; **~ly** adv furieusement.

furlong n mesure de longueur (220 yards = 201 mètres), furlong m.

furnace n fourneau m; chaudière f.

furnish vt meubler; fournir; pourvoir.

furnishings npl mobilier m.

furniture n meubles mpl.

furrow n sillon m; * vt sillonner; rider.

furry adj à poil.

further adj supplémentaire; plus lointain; * adv plus loin, plus avant; en outre; de plus; * vt faire avancer; favoriser; promouvoir.

further education n formation continue f.

furthermore adv de plus.

furthest adj le plus loin, le plus éloigné.

furtive adj furtif; secret; **~ly** adv furtivement.

fury n fureur f; furie f; colère f.

fuse vt fondre; faire sauter; * vi fondre, sauter; * n fusible m; amorce f.

fuse box n boîte à fusibles f.

fusion n fusion f.

fuss n tapage m; histoires fpl.

fussy adj tatillon, chipoteur.

futile adj futile, vain.

futility n futilité f.

future adj futur; * n futur m; avenir m.

fuzzy adj flou, confus; crépu.

G

gab n (fam) bavardage m.

gabble vi baragouiner; * n charabia m.

gable n pignon m.

gadget n gadget m.

gaffe n gaffe f.

gag n bâillon m; blague f; * vt bâillonner.

gaiety n gaieté f.

gaily adv gaiement.

gain n gain m; bénéfice m; * vt gagner; atteindre.

gait n démarche f; maintien m.

gala n gala m.

galaxy n galaxie f.

gale n grand vent m.

gall n bile f; fiel m.

gallant adj galant.

gall bladder n vésicule biliaire f.

gallery n galerie f.

galley n galère f; cuisine f.

gallon n gallon m (mesure).

gallop n galop m; * vi galoper.

gallows n potence f.

gallstone n calcul biliaire m.

galore adv en abondance.

galvanize vt galvaniser.

gambit n stratagème m.

gamble vi jouer; spéculer; * n risque m; pari m.

gambler n joueur m, -euse f.

gambling n jeu m.

game n jeu m; divertissement m; partie f; gibier m; * vi jouer.

gamekeeper n garde-chasse m.

gaming n jeu m.

gammon n jambon m.

gamut n (mus) gamme f.

gander n jars m.

gang n gang m, bande f.

gangrene n gangrène f.

gangster n gangster m.

gangway n passerelle f.

gap n trou m; vide m; intervalle, écart m.

gape vi être bouche bée; bâiller.

gaping adj béant.

garage n garage m.

garbage n ordures fpl.

garbage can n poubelle f.

garbage man n éboueur m.

garbled adj embrouillé; trompeur.

garden n jardin m.

garden hose n tuyau d'arrosage m.

gardener n jardinier m, -ière f.

gardening n jardinage m.

gargle vi se gargariser.

gargoyle n gargouille f.

garish adj tapageur.

garland n guirlande f.

garlic n ail m.

garment n vêtement m.

garnish vt garnir, décorer; * n garniture f.

garret n mansarde f.

garrison n (mil) garnison f; * vt (mil) mettre en garnison; protéger d'une garnison.

garrote vt étrangler.

garrulous adj locace, bavard.

garter n jarretelle f.

gas n gaz m; essence f.

gas burner n brûleur à gaz m.

gas cylinder n bouteille de gaz f.

gaseous *adj* gazeux.

gas fire *n* radiateur à gaz *m*.

gash *n* entaille *f*; fente *f*; * *vt* entailler.

gasket *n* joint d'étanchéité *m*.

gasp *vi* haleter; * *n* halètements *mpl*.

gas mask *n* masque à gaz *m*.

gas meter *n* compteur à gaz *m*.

gasoline *n* essence *f*.

gas pedal *n* accélérateur *m*.

gas ring *n* brûleur à gaz *m*.

gas station *n* poste d'essence *m*.

gassy *adj* gazeux.

gas tap *n* robinet de gaz *m*.

gastric *adj* gastrique.

gastronomic *adj* gastronomique.

gasworks *npl* usine de gaz *f*.

gate *n* porte *f*; portail *m*.

gateway *n* passage *m*.

gather *vt* rassembler; ramasser; comprendre; * *vi* se rassembler.

gathering *n* réunion *f*; récolte *f*.

gauche *adj* gauche.

gaudy *adj* criard.

gauge *n* calibre *m*; écartement *m*; * *vt* mesurer; calibrer.

gaunt *adj*, *n* maigre *mf*.

gauze *n* gaze *f*.

gay *adj* gai; vif; homosexuel.

gaze *vi* contempler, considérer; * *n* regard *m*.

gazelle *n* gazelle *f*.

gazette *n* gazette *f*.

gazetteer *n* répertoire géographique *m*.

gear *n* équipement *m*, matériel *m*; appareil *m*; affaires *fpl*; vitesse *f*.

gearbox *n* boîte de vitesses *f*.

gear shift *n* levier de vitesse *m*.

gear wheel *n* roue d'engrenage *f*.

gel *n* gel *m*.

gelatin(e) *n* gélatine *f*.

gelignite *n* gélignite *f*.

gem *n* pierre précieuse *f*; perle *f*.

Gemini *n* Gémeaux *mpl* (signe du zodiaque).

gender *n* genre *m*.

gene *n* gène *m*.

genealogical *adj* généalogique.

genealogy *n* généalogie *f*.

general *adj* général; commun, usuel; **in ~** en général; **~ly** *adv* généralement; * *n* général *m*; générale *f*.

general delivery *n* poste restante *f*.

general election *n* élections générales *fpl*.

generality *n* généralité; majeure partie *f*.

generalization *n* généralisation *f*.

generalize *vt* généraliser.

generate *vt* engendrer; produire; causer.

generation *n* génération *f*.

generator *n* générateur *m*.

generic *adj* générique.

generosity *n* générosité, libéralité *f*.

generous *adj* généreux.

genetics *npl* génétique *f*.

genial *adj* bienveillant; doux.

genitals *npl* organes génitaux *mpl*.

genitive *n* (*gr*) génitif *m*.

genius *n* génie *m*.

genteel *adj* élégant.

gentile *n* gentil *m*, -ille *f*.

gentle *adj* doux, *f* douce, modéré.

gentleman *n* gentleman *m*.

gentleness *n* douceur *f*.

gently *adv* doucement.

gentry *n* aristocratie *f*.

gents *n* toilettes pour hommes *fpl*.

genuflexion n génuflexion f.
genuine adj authentique; sincère; **~ly** adv authentiquement; sincèrement.
genus n genre m.
geographer n géographe mf.
geographical adj géographique.
geography n géographie f.
geological adj géologique.
geologist n géologue mf.
geology n géologie f.
geometric(al) adj géométrique.
geometry n géométrie f.
geranium n (bot) géranium m.
geriatric n malade gériatrique mf; * adj gériatrique.
germ n (bot) germe m.
germinate vi germer.
gesticulate vi gesticuler.
gesture n geste m.
get vt avoir; obtenir; atteindre; gagner; attraper; * vi devenir; aller; **to ~ the better** avoir l'avantage, surpasser.
geyser n geyser m; chauffe-eau m invar.
ghastly adj affreux; sinistre.
gherkin n cornichon m.
ghost n fantôme, spectre m.
ghostly adj spectral.
giant n géant m, -e f.
gibberish n charabia m; sornettes fpl.
gibe vi se moquer; * n moquerie f.
giblets npl abattis (de volaille) mpl.
giddiness n vertige m.
giddy adj vertigineux.
gift n cadeau m; don m; talent m.
gifted adj talentueux; doué.
gift voucher n bon-cadeau m.

gigantic adj gigantesque.
giggle vi rire bêtement.
gild vt dorer.
gilding, gilt n dorure f.
gill n quart de pinte m; **~s** pl branchies fpl.
gilt-edged adj de premier ordre.
gimmick n truc m.
gin n gin m.
ginger n gingembre m.
gingerbread n pain d'épice m.
ginger-haired adj roux, f rousse.
giraffe n girafe f.
girder n poutre f.
girdle n gaine f; ceinture f.
girl n fille f.
girlfriend n amie f; petite amie f.
girlish adj de fille.
giro n virement m.
girth n sangle f; circonférence f.
gist n essence f.
give vt donner; offrir; prononcer; faire; consacrer; **to ~ away** offrir; trahir; révéler; **to ~ back** rendre; **to ~ in** vi céder; vt remettre; **to ~ off** dégager; **to ~ out** distribuer; **to ~ up** vi abandonner; vt renoncer à.
gizzard n gésier m.
glacial adj glacial.
glacier n glacier m.
glad adj joyeux, content; **I am ~ to see that** je me réjouis de voir que; **~ly** adv avec joie, avec plaisir.
gladden vt réjouir.
gladiator n gladiateur m.
glamor n attrait m, séduction f.
glamorous adj attrayant, séduisant.
glance n regard m; * vi regarder; jeter un coup d'œil.
glancing adj oblique.

gland n glande f.

glare n éclat m; regard féroce m; * vi éblouir, briller; lancer des regards indignés.

glaring adj éclatant; évident; furieux.

glass n verre m; longue-vue f; miroir m; **~es** pl lunettes fpl; * adj de verre.

glassware n verrerie f.

glassy adj vitreux, cristallin.

glaze vt vitrer; vernisser.

glazier n vitrier m.

gleam n rayon m; * vi rayonner, briller.

gleaming adj brillant.

glean vt glaner.

glee n joie f; exultation f.

glen n vallée f.

glib adj facile; volubile; **~ly** adv facilement; volubilement.

glide vi glisser; planer.

gliding n vol plané m.

glimmer n lueur f; * vi luire.

glimpse n aperçu m; vision f; * vt entrevoir.

glint vi briller, scintiller.

glisten, glitter vi luire, briller.

gloat vi exulter.

global adj global; mondial.

globe n globe m; sphère f.

gloom, gloominess n obscurité f; mélancolie, tristesse f; **~ily** adv sombrement; tristement.

gloomy adj sombre, obscur; triste, mélancolique.

glorification n glorification f.

glorify vt glorifier, célébrer.

glorious adj glorieux, illustre; **~ly** adv glorieusement.

glory n gloire, célébrité f.

gloss n glose f; lustre m; * vt gloser, interpréter; lustrer; **to ~ over** passer sur.

glossary n glossaire m.

glossy adj lustré, brillant.

glove n gant m.

glove compartment n boîte à gants f.

glow vi rougeoyer; rayonner; * n rougeoiement m; éclat m; feu m.

glower vi lancer des regards méchants.

glue n colle f; * vt coller.

gluey adj gluant, visqueux.

glum adj abattu, triste.

glut n surabondance f.

glutinous adj glutineux.

glutton n glouton m, -onne f.

gluttony n gloutonnerie f.

glycerine n glycérine f.

gnarled adj noueux.

gnash vt: **to ~ one's teeth** grincer des dents.

gnat n moucheron m.

gnaw vt ronger.

gnome n gnome m.

go vi aller; s'en aller, partir; disparaître; se perdre; **to ~ ahead** continuer; **to ~ away** s'en aller; **to ~ back** repartir; **to ~ by** passer; **to ~ for** vt se lancer sur; aimer; **to ~ in** entrer; **to ~ off** s'en aller, partir; se passer; se gâter; **to ~ on** continuer; se passer; **to ~ out** sortir; s'éteindre; **to ~ up** monter.

goad n aiguillon m; * vt aiguillonner; stimuler.

go-ahead adj entreprenant; * n feu vert m.

goal n but, objectif m.

goalkeeper n gardien de but m.

goalpost n poteau de but m.

goatherd n chevrier m, -ière f.

gobble vt engloutir, avaler.

go-between n intermédiaire mf.

goblet n coupe f.

goblin n lutin m.

God n Dieu m.

godchild n filleul m, -e f.

goddaughter n filleule f.

goddess n déesse f.

godfather n parrain m.

godforsaken adj perdu.

godhead n divinité f.

godless adj impie, athée.

godlike adj divin.

godliness n piété, dévotion, sainteté f.

godly adj pieux, dévot, religieux; droit.

godmother n marraine f.

godsend n don du ciel m.

godson n filleul m.

goggle-eyed adj aux yeux exorbités de surprise.

goggles npl lunettes fpl; lunettes de plongée fpl.

going n départ m; sortie f; progrès m.

gold n or m.

golden adj doré; d'or; excellent; ~ **rule** n règle d'or f.

goldfish n poisson rouge m.

gold-plated adj plaqué or.

goldsmith n orfèvre m.

golf n golf m.

golf ball n balle de golf f.

golf club n club de golf m.

golf course n terrain de golf m.

golfer n golfeur m, -euse f.

gondolier n gondolier m.

gone adj parti; perdu; passé; fini; mort, disparu.

gong n gong m.

good adj bon; bienveillant; favorable; valable; * adv bien; * n bien m; avantage m; ~s pl biens mpl; marchandises fpl.

goodbye ! excl au revoir!

Good Friday n Vendredi Saint m.

goodies npl gourmandises fpl.

good-looking adj beau.

good nature n bon caractère m.

good-natured adj qui a bon caractère.

goodness n bonté f; qualité f.

goodwill n bienveillance f.

goose n oie f.

gooseberry n groseille à maquereau f.

goosebumps npl chair de poule f.

goose-step n pas de l'oie m.

gore n sang m; * vt blesser d'un coup de corne.

gorge n gorge f; * vt engloutir, avaler.

gorgeous adj merveilleux.

gorilla n gorille m.

gorse n ajonc m.

gory adj sanglant.

goshawk n autour m.

gospel n évangile m.

gossamer n gaze f; toile d'araignée f.

gossip n commérages, cancans mpl; * vi cancaner, faire des commérages.

gothic adj gothique.

gout n goutte f (maladie).

govern vt gouverner, diriger.

governess n gouvernante f.

government n gouvernement m; administration publique f.

governor n gouverneur m.

gown n toge f; robe f; robe de chambre f.

grab vt saisir.

grace n grâce f; faveur f; pardon m; grâces fpl; **to say** ~ dire le bénédicité; * vt orner; honorer.

graceful adj gracieux; **~ly** adv gracieusement.

gracious adj gracieux; favorable; **~ly** adv gracieusement.

gradation n gradation f.

grade n degré m; degré f; classe f.

grade crossing n passage à niveau m.

grade school n école primaire f.

gradient n (rail) rampe f.

gradual adj graduel; **~ly** adv graduellement.

graduate vi obtenir son diplôme.

graduation n remise des diplômes f.

graffiti n graffiti mpl.

graft n greffe f; * vt greffer.

grain n grain m; graine f; céréales fpl.

gram n gramme m.

grammar n grammaire f.

grammatical adj, **~ly** adv grammatical(ement).

granary n grenier m.

grand adj grandiose; magnifique.

grandchild n petit-fils m; petite-fille f; **grandchildren** pl petits-enfants m pl.

grandad n pépé m.

granddaughter n petite-fille f; **great-** ~ arrière-petite-fille f.

grandeur n grandeur f; pompe f.

grandfather n grand-père m; **great-** ~ arrière-grand-père m.

grandiose adj grandiose.

grandma n mémé f.

grandmother n grand-mère f; **great-** ~ arrière-grand-mère f.

grandparents npl grands-parents mpl.

grand piano n piano à queue m.

grandson n petit-fils m; **great-** ~ arrière-petit-fils m.

grandstand n tribune f.

granite n granit m.

granny n mémé f.

grant vt accorder; **to take for ~ed** considérer comme acquis; * n bourse f; allocation f.

granulate vt granuler.

granule n granule m.

grape n raisin m; **bunch of ~s** grappe de raisin f.

grapefruit n pamplemousse m.

graph n graphe, graphique m.

graphic(al) adj graphique; pittoresque; **~ally** adv graphiquement.

graphics n art graphique m; graphiques mpl.

grapnel n (mar) grappin m.

grasp vt saisir, empoigner; comprendre; * n poigne f; compréhension f; prise f.

grasping adj avide.

grass n herbe f.

grasshopper n sauterelle f.

grassland n prés mpl.

grass-roots adj populaire; de base.

grass snake n couleuvre f.

grassy adj herbeux.

grate n grille f; * vt râper; grincer (des dents); * vi grincer.

grateful adj reconnaissant; **~ly** adv avec reconnaissance.

gratefulness n gratitude, reconnaissance f.

gratification n satisfaction f.

gratify vt satisfaire; faire plaisir à.

gratifying adj réjouissant.

grating n grillage m; grincement m; * adj grinçant; énervant.

gratis adv gratis, gratuitement.

gratitude n gratitude, reconnaissance f.

gratuitous adj gratuit; volontaire; ~ly adv gratuitement.

gratuity n gratification f.

grave n tombe f; * adj grave, sérieux; ~ly adv gravement, sérieusement.

grave digger n fossoyeur m.

gravel n gravier m.

gravestone n pierre tombale f.

graveyard n cimetière m.

gravitate vi graviter.

gravitation n gravitation f.

gravity n gravité f.

gravy n jus de viande m; sauce f.

graze vt paître; effleurer; * vi paître.

grease n graisse f; * vt graisser.

greaseproof adj gras.

greasy adj gras.

great adj grand; important; fort; ~ly adv énormément.

greatcoat n pardessus m.

greatness n grandeur f; importance f; pouvoir m; noblesse f.

greedily adv avidement.

greediness, greed n avidité f; gloutonnerie f.

greedy adj avide; glouton.

Greek n grec (langue) m.

green adj vert; inexpérimenté; * n vert m; verdure f; ~s npl légumes verts mpl.

greenback n billet m.

green belt n zone verte f.

green card n carte verte f; permis de travail m.

greenery n verdure f.

greengrocer n marchand(e) de fruits et légumes m(f).

greenhouse n serre f.

greenish adj verdâtre.

greenness n verdure f; manque d'expérience m.

green room n foyer des artistes m.

greet vt saluer; accueillir.

greeting n salutation f; accueil m.

greeting(s) card n carte de vœux f.

grenade n (mil) grenade f.

grenadier n grenadier m.

grey adj gris; * n gris m.

grey-haired adj aux cheveux gris.

greyhound n lévrier m.

greyish adj grisâtre; grisonnant.

greyness n couleur grise f; grisaille f.

grid n grille f; réseau m.

gridiron n gril m; terrain de football américain m.

grief n chagrin m, douleur, peine f.

grievance n grief m; doléance f; différend m; injustice f; tort m.

grieve vt peiner, affliger; * vi se chagriner, s'affliger.

grievous adj douloureux; grave, atroce; ~ly adv douloureusement; cruellement.

griffin n griffon m.

grill n gril m; grillade f; * vt faire griller; interroger, cuisiner.

grille n grille f.

grim adj peu engageant; sinistre.

grimace n grimace f; moue f.

grime n saleté f.

grimy adj crasseux.

grin n grimace f; sourire m; * vi grimacer; sourire.

grind vt moudre; piler, broyer; affûter, aiguiser; * vi grincer.

grinder n moulin f; rémouleur m; molaire f.

grip n prise f; poignée f; valise f; * vt saisir, agripper.

gripping adj passionnant.

grisly adj horrible; sinistre.

gristle n tendons, nerfs mpl.

gristly adj tendineux.

grit n gravillon m; cran m.

groan vi gémir; grogner; * n gémissement m; grognement m.

grocer n épicier m, -ière f.

groceries npl épicerie f, provisions fpl.

grocer's (shop) n épicerie f.

groggy adj sonné, étourdi.

groin n aine f.

groom n palefrenier m; valet m; marié m; * vt panser; préparer.

groove n rainure f.

grope vt chercher à tâtons; * vi tâtonner.

gross adj gros, corpulent; épais; grossier; brut; ~ly adv énormément.

grotesque adj grotesque.

grotto n grotte f.

ground n terre f, sol m; terrain, territoire m; fondement m; raison fondamentale f; fond m; * vt retenir au sol; fonder; mettre une prise de terre f.

ground floor n rez-de-chaussée m.

grounding n connaissances de base fpl.

groundless adj sans fondement; ~ly adv sans fondement.

ground staff n personnel au sol m.

groundwork n travaux de préparation mpl.

group n groupe m; * vt regrouper.

grouse n grouse f, coq de bruyère m; * vi grogner.

grove n bosquet m.

grovel vi se traîner; ramper.

grow vt cultiver; faire pousser; * vi pousser; grandir; augmenter; ~ up grandir.

grower n cultivateur m, -trice f; producteur m, -trice f.

growing adj croissant; grandissant.

growl vi grogner; * n grognement m.

grown-up n adulte mf.

growth n croissance f; augmentation f; poussée f.

grub n asticot m.

grubby adj sale.

grudge n rancune f; * vt accorder à contrecœur; vi avoir de la rancune.

grudgingly adv à contrecœur.

grueling adj difficile, pénible.

gruesome adj horrible.

gruff adj brusque; ~ly adv brusquement.

gruffness n brusquerie f.

grumble vi grogner; grommeler.

grumpy adj ronchon, grincheux.

grunt vi grogner; * n grognement m.

G-string n cache-sexe m.

guarantee n garantie f; * vt garantir.

guard n garde f; garde m; * vt garder; défendre.

guarded adj prudent; surveillé.

guardroom n (*mil*) corps de garde m.

guardian n tuteur m, -trice f; gardien m, -ienne f.

guardianship n tutelle f.

guerrilla n guérillero m.

guerrilla warfare n guérilla f.

guess vt deviner; supposer; * vi deviner; * n conjecture f.

guesswork n conjectures fpl.

guest n invité, -ée f; client n, -e f.

guest room n chambre d'amis f.

guffaw n éclat de rire m.

guidance n guidage m; direction f.

guide vt guider, diriger; * n guide m.

guide dog n chien d'aveugle m.

guidelines npl directives fpl.

guidebook n guide m.

guild n association f; corporation f.

guile n astuce f.

guillotine n guillotine f; * vt guillotiner.

guilt n culpabilité f.

guiltless adj innocent.

guilty adj coupable.

guinea pig n cochon d'Inde, cobaye m.

guise n apparence f.

guitar n guitare f.

gulf n golfe m; abîme m.

gull n mouette f.

gullet n œsophage m.

gullibility n crédulité f.

gullible adj crédule.

gully n ravine f.

gulp n gorgée f; * vi, vt avaler.

gum n gomme f; gencive f; chewing-gum m; * vt coller.

gum tree n gommier m.

gun n pistolet m; fusil m.

gunboat n canonnière f.

gun carriage n affût de canon m.

gunfire n coups de feu mpl.

gunman n homme armé m.

gunmetal n bronze à canon m.

gunner n artilleur m.

gunnery n artillerie f.

gunpoint n: at ~ sous la menace d'une arme à feu.

gunpowder n poudre à canon f.

gunshot n coup de feu m.

gunsmith n armurier m.

gurgle vi gargouiller.

guru n gourou m.

gush vi jaillir; bouillonner; * n jaillissement m.

gushing adj jaillissant; très exubérant.

gusset n soufflet m.

gust n rafale f; bouffée f.

gusto n plaisir m, délectation f.

gusty adj venteux.

gut n intestin m; ~s npl cœur au ventre m; * vt vider.

gutter n gouttière f; caniveau m.

guttural adj guttural.

guy n mec, type m.

guzzle vt bouffer, engloutir; avaler.

gym(nasium) n gymnase m.

gymnast n gymnaste mf.

gymnastic adj gymnastique; ~s npl gymnastique f.

gynecologist n gynécologue mf.

gypsy n gitan m, -e f.

gyrate vi tourner.

H

haberdasher n mercier m, -ière f.

haberdashery n mercerie f.

habit n habitude f.

habitable adj habitable.

habitat n habitat m.

habitual adj habituel; **~ly** adv d'habitude, habituellement.

hack n coupure, entaille f; * vt entailler, couper.

hackneyed adj rebattu.

haddock n aiglefin m.

haemorrhage n hémorragie f.

haemorrhoids npl hémorroïdes fpl.

hag n sorcière f.

haggard adj décharné; blême; hagard.

haggle vi marchander.

hail n grêle f; * vt saluer; * vi grêler.

hailstone n grêlon m.

hair n cheveu m; poil m.

hairbrush n brosse à cheveux f.

haircut n coupe de cheveux f.

hairdresser n coiffeur m, -euse f.

hairdryer n séchoir à cheveux m.

hairless adj chauve; sans poils.

hairnet n filet à cheveux m.

hairpin n épingle à cheveux f.

hairpin bend n virage en épingle à cheveux m.

hair remover n crème dépilatoire f.

hairspray n laque à cheveux f.

hairstyle n coiffure f.

hairy adj chevelu; poilu.

hale adj vigoureux.

half n moitié f; * adj demi; * adv à moitié.

half-caste adj métis.

half-hearted adj peu enthousiaste.

half-hour n demi-heure f.

half-moon n demi-lune f.

half-price adj à moitié prix.

half-time n mi-temps f.

halfway adv à mi-chemin.

hall n vestibule m.

hallmark n marque f.

hallow vt consacrer, sanctifier.

hallucination n hallucination f.

halo n halo m.

halt vi s'arrêter; * n arrêt m; halte f.

halve vt couper en deux.

ham n jambon m.

hamburger n hamburger m.

hamlet n hameau m.

hammer n marteau m; * vt marteler.

hammock n hamac m.

hamper n panier m; * vt embarrasser, entraver.

hamstring vt couper les jarrets à.

hand n main f; ouvrier m, -ière f; aiguille f; **at ~** à portée de main; * vt donner, passer.

handbag n sac à main m.

handbell n sonnette f.

handbook n manuel m.

handbrake n frein à main m.

handcuff n menotte f.

handful n poignée f.

handicap n handicap m.

handicapped adj handicapé.

handicraft n artisanat m.

handiwork n travail manuel m.

handkerchief n mouchoir m.

handle n manche m; queue f; anse f; poignée f; * vt manier; traiter, prendre.

handlebars npl guidon m.

handling n maniement m; traitement m.

handrail n garde-fou m.

handshake n poignée de mains f.

handsome adj beau; **~ly** adv élégamment.

handwriting n écriture f.

handy adj pratique; adroit.

hang vt accrocher; pendre; * vi pendre, être accroché; être pendu.

hanger n cintre m.

hanger-on n parasite m.

hangings npl tapisserie f.

hangman n bourreau m.

hangover n gueule de bois f.

hang-up n complexe m.

hanker n avoir envie.

haphazard adj fortuit.

hapless adj malheureux.

happen vi se passer; **I ~ to have one** il se trouve que j'en ai un.

happening n événement m.

happily adv heureusement; gaiement.

happiness n bonheur m.

happy adj heureux.

harangue n harangue f; * vt haranguer.

harass vt harceler; tourmenter.

harbinger n précurseur m.

harbour n port m; * vt héberger; entretenir, nourrir.

hard adj dur; pénible; sévère, rigide; **~ of hearing** dur d'oreille; **~ by** tout près.

harden vt, vi durcir.

hard-headed adj réaliste.

hard-hearted adj au cœur dur, insensible.

hardiness n robustesse f.

hardly adv à peine; **~ ever** presque jamais.

hardness n dureté f; difficulté f; sévérité f.

hardship n épreuve(s) f(pl).

hard-up adj fauché, sans le sou.

hardware n matériel m; quincaillerie f.

hardwearing adj résistant.

hardy adj fort, robuste; résistant.

hare n lièvre m.

hare-brained adj écervelé.

hare-lipped adj qui a un bec de lièvre.

haricot n haricot blanc m.

harlequin n arlequin m.

harm n mal m; tort m; * vt faire du mal à; nuire à.

harmful adj nuisible.

harmless adj inoffensif.

harmonic adj harmonique.

harmonious adj harmonieux; **~ly** adv harmonieusement.

harmonize vt harmoniser.

harmony n harmonie f.

harness n harnais m; * vt harnacher.

harp n harpe f.

harpist n harpiste mf.

harpoon n harpon m.

harpsichord n clavecin m.

harrow n herse f; * vt dévaster.

harry vt harceler; dévaster.

harsh adj dur; austère; rude; **~ly** adv sévèrement; durement.

harshness n aspérité, dureté f; austérité f.

harvest n récolte f; moisson f; * vt récolter; moissonner.

harvester n moissonneur m, -euse f; moissonneuse f (machine).

hash n hachis m; gâchis m.

hassock n agenouilloir m.

haste n hâte f; **to be in ~** être pressé.

hasten vt accélérer, hâter; * vi se dépêcher.

hastily adv à la hâte, précipitamment.

hastiness n précipitation f.

hasty adj hâtif; irréfléchi.

hat n chapeau m.

hatbox n carton à chapeau m.

hatch vt couver; faire éclore; tramer; * n écoutille f.

hatchback n (auto) voiture à hayon arrière f.

hatchet n hachette f.

hatchway n (mar) écoutille f.

hate n haine f; * vt haïr, détester.

hateful adj odieux, détestable.

hatred n haine f.

hatter n chapelier m, -ière f.

haughtily adv hautainement.

haughtiness n orgueil m; hauteur f.

haughty adj hautain, orgueilleux.

haul vt tirer; * n prise f; butin m.

hauler n camionneur m.

haunch n hanche f.

haunt vt hanter; fréquenter; * n repaire m.

have vt avoir; posséder.

haven n refuge m.

haversack n sac à dos m.

havoc n ravages mpl.

hawk n faucon m; * vi chasser au faucon.

hawthorn n aubépine f.

hay n foin m.

hay fever n rhume des foins m.

hayloft n fenil m.

hayrick, haystack n meule de foin f.

hazard n risque, danger m; * vt risquer.

hazardous adj risqué, dangereux.

haze n brume f.

hazel n noisetier m; * adj noisette.

hazelnut n noisette f.

hazy adj brumeux.

he pn il.

head n tête f; chef m; esprit m; * vt conduire; **to ~ for** se diriger vers.

headache n mal de tête m.

headdress n coiffe f.

headland n promontoire m.

headlight n phare m.

headline n titre m.

headlong adv à toute allure.

headmaster n directeur m.

head office n siège social m.

headphones npl écouteurs mpl.

headquarters npl (mil) quartier général m; siège social m.

headroom n hauteur f.

headstrong adj têtu.

headwaiter n maître d'hôtel m.

headway n progrès m(pl).

heady adj capiteux.

heal vt, vi guérir.

health n santé f.

healthiness n bonne santé f.

healthy adj en bonne santé; sain.

heap n tas m; * vt entasser.

hear vt entendre; écouter; * vi entendre; avoir des nouvelles.

hearing n ouïe f.

hearing aid n audiophone m.

hearsay n rumeur f.

hearse n corbillard m.

heart n cœur m; **by** ~ par cœur; **with all my** ~ de tout cœur.

heart attack n crise cardiaque f.

heartbreaking adj à fendre le cœur.

heartburn n acidité f.

heart failure n arrêt cardiaque m.

heartfelt adj sincère.

hearth n foyer m.

heartily adv sincèrement, cordialement.

heartiness n cordialité, sincérité f.

heartless adj cruel; **~ly** adv cruellement.

hearty adj cordial.

heat n chaleur f; * vt chauffer.

heater n radiateur m.

heather n (bot) bruyère f.

heathen n païen m, païenne f; **~ish** adj sauvage, barbare.

heating n chauffage m.

heatwave n onde de chaleur f.

heave vt lever; tirer; * n effort m.

heaven n ciel m.

heavenly adj divin.

heavily adv lourdement.

heaviness n lourdeur f.

heavy adj lourd, pesant; considérable.

Hebrew n hébreu m (langue).

heckle vt interrompre.

hectic adj agité.

hedge n haie f; * vt entourer d'une haie.

hedgehog n hérisson m.

heed vt tenir compte de; * n soin m; attention f.

heedless adj inattentif, étourdi; **~ly** adv étourdiment.

heel n talon m; **to take to one's ~s** prendre ses jambes à son cou.

hefty adj fort; gros.

heifer n génisse f.

height n hauteur f; altitude f.

heighten vt rehausser; augmenter; intensifier.

heinous adj atroce.

heir n héritier m; ~ **apparent** héritier présomptif.

heiress n héritière f.

heirloom n héritage m.

helicopter n hélicoptère m.

hell n enfer m.

hellish adj infernal.

helm n (mar) barre f.

helmet n casque m.

help vt aider, secourir; **I cannot ~ it** je n'y peux rien; je ne peux pas m'en empêcher; * n aide f; secours m.

helper n aide mf.

helpful adj utile; qui rend service.

helping n portion f.

helpless adj impuissant; **~ly** adv désespérément; sans pouvoir rien faire.

helter-skelter adv n'importe comment, en désordre.

hem n ourlet m; * vt ourler.

he-man n dur, mâle m.

hemisphere n hémisphère m.

hemp n chanvre m.

hen n poule f.

henchman n acolyte m.

henceforth, **henceforward** adv dorénavant.

hen-house n poulailler m.

hepatitis n hépatite f.

her *pn* son, sa, ses; elle; la; lui.

herald *n* héraut *m*.

heraldry *n* héraldique *f*.

herb *n* herbe *f*; **~s** *pl* fines herbes *fpl*.

herbaceous *adj* herbacé.

herbalist *n* herboriste *mf*.

herbivorous *adj* herbivore.

herd *n* troupeau *m*.

here *adv* ici.

hereabout(s) *adv* dans les environs.

hereafter *adv* plus tard; claprès.

hereby *adv* par la présente.

hereditary *adj* héréditaire.

heredity *n* hérédité *f*.

heresy *n* hérésie *f*.

heretic *n*, *adj* hérétique *mf*.

herewith *adv* avec ceci.

heritage *n* patrimoine, héritage *m*.

hermetic *adj* hermétique; **~ly** *adv* hermétiquement.

hermit *n* ermite *m*.

hermitage *n* ermitage *m*.

hernia *n* hernie *f*.

hero *n* héros *m*.

heroic *adj* héroïque; **~ally** *adv* héroïquement.

heroine *n* héroïne *f*.

heroism *n* héroïsme *m*.

heron *n* héron *m*.

herring *n* hareng *m*.

hers *pn* le sien, la sienne, le(s) sien(ne)s, à elle.

herself *pn* elle-même.

hesitant *adj* hésitant.

hesitate *vi* hésiter.

hesitation *n* hésitation *f*.

heterogeneous *adj* hétérogène.

heterosexual *adj*, *n* hétérosexuel *m*, -elle *f*.

hew *vt* tailler; couper.

heyday *n* apogée *m*.

hi *excl* salut!

hiatus *n* (*gr*) hiatus *m*.

hibernate *vi* hiberner.

hiccup *n* hoquet *m*; * *vi* avoir le hoquet.

hickory *n* noyer d'Amérique *m*.

hide *vt* cacher; * *n* cuir *m*; peau *f*.

hideaway *n* cachette *f*.

hideous *adj* hideux; horrible; **~ly** *adv* horriblement.

hiding-place *n* cachette *f*.

hierarchy *n* hiérarchie *f*.

hieroglyphic *adj* hiéroglyphique; * *n* hiéroglyphe *m*.

hi-fi *n* hi-fi *f invar*.

higgledy-piggledy *adv* pêle-mêle.

high *adj* haut; élevé.

high altar *n* maître-autel *m*.

high chair *n* chaise haute *f*.

high-handed *adj* tyrannique.

highlands *npl* terres montagneuses *fpl*.

highlight *n* point fort *m*.

highly *adj* extrêmement, hautement.

highness *n* hauteur *f*; altesse *f*.

high school *n* lycée *m*.

high-strung *adj* nerveux, tendu.

high water *n* marée haute *f*.

highway *n* grande route *f*.

hike *vi* faire une randonnée.

hijack *vt* détourner.

hijacker *n* pirate de l'air *m*.

hilarious *adj* hilarant; hilare.

hill *n* colline *f*.

hillock *n* petite colline *f*.

hillside *n* coteau *m*.

hilly *adj* montagneux.

hilt *n* poignée *f*.

him pn lui; le.

himself pn lui-même; soi.

hind adj derrière; * n biche f.

hinder vt gêner, entraver.

hindrance n gêne f, obstacle m.

hindmost adj dernier.

hindquarter n arrière-train m.

hindsight n: **with** ~ rétrospectivement.

hinge n charnière f; gond m.

hint n allusion f; insinuation f; * vt insinuer; suggérer.

hip n hanche f.

hippopotamus n hippopotame m.

hire vt louer; * n location f.

his pn son, sa, ses; le sien, la sienne, le(s) sien(ne)s; à lui.

Hispanic adj hispanique.

hiss vt, vi siffler.

historian n historien m, -ienne f.

historic(al) adj historique; ~**ally** adv historiquement.

history n histoire f.

histrionic adj théâtral.

hit vt frapper; atteindre; heurter; * n coup m; succès m.

hitch vt accrocher; * n nœud m; anicroche f.

hitch-hike vi faire du stop.

hitherto adv jusqu'à présent, jusqu'ici.

hive n ruche f.

hoard n stock m; trésor caché m; * vt accumuler, amasser.

hoar-frost n givre m.

hoarse adj rauque; ~**ly** adv d'une voix rauque.

hoarseness n voix rauque f.

hoax n canular m; * vt faire un canular b.

hobble vi boitiller.

hobby n passe-temps m invar.

hobbyhorse n cheval de bataille m.

hobo n vagabond m.

hockey n hockey m.

hodge-podge n confusion f.

hoe n binette f; * vt biner.

hog n porc m.

hoist vt hisser; * n grue f.

hold vt tenir; détenir; contenir; **to** ~ **on to** se tenir à; * vi valoir; * n prise f; pouvoir m.

holder n détenteur m, -trice f; titulaire mf.

holding n possession f.

holdup n hold-up m; retard m.

hole n trou m.

holiday n jour de congé m; jour férié m; ~**s** pl vacances fpl.

holiness n sainteté f.

hollow adj creux; * n creux m; * vt creuser, vider.

holly n (bot) houx m.

hollyhock n rose trémière f.

holocaust n holocauste f.

holster n étui de révolver m.

holy adj saint; bénit; sacré.

holy water n eau bénite f.

holy week n semaine sainte f.

homage n hommage m.

home n maison f; patrie f; domicile m; ~**ly** adj simple.

home address n domicile m.

homeless adj sans abri.

homeliness n simplicité f.

homely adj simple.

home-made adj fait maison.

homeopathist n homéopathe mf.

homeopathy n homéopathie f.

homesick adj nostalgique, qui a le mal du pays.

homesickness n nostalgie f, mal du pays m.

hometown n ville natale f.

homeward adj vers chez soi; vers son pays.

homework n devoirs mpl.

homicidal adj homicide.

homicide n homicide m; homicide mf.

homogeneous adj homogène.

homosexual adj, n homosexuel m, -elle f.

honest adj honnête; **~ly** adv honnêtement.

honesty n honnêteté f.

honey n miel m.

honeycomb n rayon de miel m.

honeymoon n lune de miel f.

honeysuckle n (bot) chèvrefeuille m.

honor n honneur m; * vt honorer.

honorable adj honorable.

honorably adv honorablement.

honorary adj honoraire.

hood n capot m; capuche f.

hoodlum n truand m.

hoof n sabot m.

hook n crochet m; hameçon m; **by ~ or by crook** coûte que coûte; * vt accrocher.

hooked adj crochu m.

hooligan n vandale m.

hoop n cerceau m.

hooter n sirène f.

hop n (bot) houblon m; saut m; * vi sauter.

hope n espoir m, espérance f; * vi espérer.

hopeful adj plein d'espoir; prometteur; **~ly** adv avec espoir.

hopefulness n bon espoir m.

hopeless adj désespéré; **~ly** adv désespérément.

horde n horde f.

horizon n horizon m.

horizontal adj horizontal; **~ly** adv horizontalement.

hormone n hormone f.

horn n corne f.

horned adj à cornes.

hornet n frelon m.

horny adj calleux.

horoscope n horoscope m.

horrendous adj horrible.

horrible adj horrible.

horribly adv horriblement; énormément.

horrid adj horrible.

horrific adj horrible, affreux.

horrify vt horrifier.

horror n horreur f.

horror film n film d'horreur m.

hors d'œuvre n hors-d'œuvre m invar.

horse n cheval m.

horseback adv: **on ~** à cheval.

horse-breaker n dresseur (-euse) de chevaux m (f).

horse chesnut n marron d'Inde m.

horsefly n taon m.

horseman n cavalier m.

horsemanship n équitation f.

horsepower n cheval-vapeur m; puissance en chevaux f.

horse race n course de chevaux f.

horseradish n raifort m.

horseshoe n fer à cheval m.

horsewoman n cavalière f.

horticulture n horticulture f.

horticulturist n horticulteur m, -trice f.

hose-pipe n tuyau m.

hosiery n bonneterie f.

hospitable adj hospitalier.

hospitably adv avec hospitalité.

hospital n hôpital m.

hospitality n hospitalité f.

host n hôte m; hostie f.

hostage n otage m.

hostess n hôtesse f.

hostile adj hostile.

hostility n hostilité f.

hot adj chaud; épicé.

hotbed n foyer m.

hotdog n hot-dog m.

hotel n hôtel m.

hotelier n hôtelier m, -ière f.

hotheaded adj exalté.

hot-house n serre f.

hotline n téléphone rouge m.

hotplate n plaque chauffante f.

hotly adv violemment.

hound n chien de chasse m.

hour n heure f.

hour-glass n sablier m.

hourly adv toutes les heures.

house n maison f; maisonnée f; * vt loger.

houseboat n péniche f.

housebreaker n cambrioleur m.

housebreaking n cambriolage m.

household n famille f, ménage m.

householder n propriétaire mf; chef de famille m.

housekeeper n gouvernante f.

housekeeping n travaux ménagers mpl.

houseless adv sans abri.

house-warming party n pendaison de crémaillère f.

housewife n ménagère f.

housework n travaux ménagers mpl.

housing n logement m.

housing development n urbanisation f.

hovel n taudis m.

hover vi planer.

how adv comme; comment; ~ do you do! enchanté.

however adv de quelque manière que; cependant, néanmoins.

howl vi hurler; * n hurlement m.

hub n centre m; moyeu m.

hubbub n vacarme m.

hubcap n enjoliveur m.

hue n teinte f; nuance f.

huff n: in a ~ fâché.

hug vt étreindre; * n étreinte f.

huge adj énorme; ~ly adv énormément.

hulk n (mar) carcasse f; ponton m.

hull n (mar) coque f.

hum vi chantonner.

human adj humain.

humane adj humain; ~ly adv humainement.

humanist n humaniste mf.

humanitarian adj humanitaire.

humanity n humanité f.

humanize vt humaniser.

humanly adv humainement.

humble adj humble, modeste; * vt humilier.

humbleness n humilité f.

humbly adv humblement.

humbug n blagues fpl.

humdrum adj monotone.

humid adj humide.

humidity n humidité f.

humiliate vt humilier.

humiliation n humiliation f.

humility n humilité f.

humming-bird n colibri m.

humorist n humoriste mf.

humorous adj humoristique; **~ly** adv avec humour.

humour n sens de l'humour m, humour m; * vt complaire à.

hump n bosse f.

hunch n bosse f; **~backed** adj bossu.

hundred adj cent; * n centaine f.

hundredth adj centième.

hundredweight n quintal m.

hunger n faim f; * vi avoir faim.

hunger strike n grève de la faim f.

hungrily adv avidement.

hungry adj qui a faim, affamé.

hunt vt chasser; poursuivre; chercher; * vi chasser; * n chasse f.

hunter n chasseur m.

hunting n chasse f.

huntsman n chasseur m.

hurdle n haie f.

hurl vt lancer avec violence, jeter.

hurricane n ouragan m.

hurried adj fait à la hâte; précipité; **~ly** adv hâtivement; précipitamment.

hurry vt presser; * vi se presser, se dépêcher; * n hâte f.

hurt vt faire mal à; blesser; * n mal m.

hurtful adj blessant; **~ly** adv de manière blessante.

husband n mari m.

husbandry n agriculture f.

hush! chut!, silence!; * vt faire taire; * vi se taire.

husk n coque f.

huskiness n voix rauque f.

husky adj rauque.

hustings n plate-forme électorale f.

hustle vt pousser avec force, bousculer.

hut n cabane, hutte f.

hutch n clapier m.

hyacinth n jacinthe f.

hydrant n bouche d'incendie f.

hydraulic adj hydraulique; **~s** npl hydraulique f.

hydroelectric adj hydroélectrique.

hydrofoil n hydrofoil m.

hydrogen n hydrogène m.

hydrophobia n hydrophobie f.

hyena n hyène f.

hygiene n hygiène f.

hygienic adj hygiénique.

hymn n hymne m.

hyperbole n hyperbole f.

hypermarket n hypermarché m.

hyphen n (gr) trait d'union m.

hypochondria n hypocondrie f.

hypochondriac adj, n hypocondriaque mf.

hypocrisy n hypocrisie f.

hypocrite n hypocrite mf.

hypocritical adj hypocrite.

hypothesis n hypothèse f.

hypothetical adj, **~ly** adv hypothétique(ment).

hysterical adj hystérique.

hysterics npl hystérie f; crise de nerfs f.

I

I *pn* je, j'; moi

ice *n* glace *f*; * *vt* glacer; geler.

ice-ax *n* piolet *m*.

iceberg *n* iceberg *m*.

ice-bound *adj* fermé par les glaces.

icebox *n* glacière *f*.

ice cream *n* glace *f*.

ice rink *n* patinoire *f*.

ice skating *n* patinage sur glace *m*.

icicle *n* stalactite *f*.

iconoclast *n* iconoclaste *mf*.

icy *adj* glacé.

idea *n* idée *f*.

ideal *adj* idéal; **~ly** *adv* idéalement.

idealist *n* idéaliste *mf*.

identical *adj* identique.

identification *n* identification *f*.

identify *vt* identifier.

identity *n* identité *f*.

ideology *n* idéologie *f*.

idiom *n* expression idiomatique *f*.

idiomatic *adj* idiomatique.

idiosyncrasy *n* idiosyncrasie *f*.

idiot *n* imbécile *mf*.

idiotic *adj* idiot, bête.

idle *adj* désœuvré; au repos; inutile.

idleness *n* paresse *f*; oisiveté *f*.

idler *n* paresseux *m*, -euse *f*.

idly *adv* oisivement; paresseusement; vainement.

idol *n* idole *f*.

idolatry *n* idôlatrie *f*.

idolize *vt* idôlatrer.

idyllic *adj* idyllique.

i.e. *adv* c.-à-d., c'est-à-dire.

if *conj* si; **~ not** sinon.

igloo *n* igloo *m*.

ignite *vt* allumer, enflammer.

ignition *n* (*chem*) ignition *f*; allumage *m*.

ignition key *n* clé de contact *f*.

ignoble *adj* ignoble; bas.

ignominious *adj* ignominieux; **~ly** *adv* ignominieusement.

ignominy *n* ignominie, infamie *f*.

ignoramus *n* ignorant *m*, -e *f*.

ignorance *n* ignorance *f*.

ignorant *adj* ignorant; **~ly** *adv* par ignorance.

ignore *vt* ne pas tenir compte de.

ill *adj* malade; * *n* mal *m*; dommage *m*; * *adv* mal.

ill-advised *adj* malavisé.

illegal *adj* **~ly** *adv* illégal(ement).

illegality *n* illégalité *f*.

illegible *adj* illisible.

illegibly *adv* illisiblement.

illegitimacy *n* illégitimité *f*.

illegitimate *adj* illégitime; **~ly** *adv* illégitimement.

ill feeling *n* rancœur *f*.

illicit *adj* illicite.

illiterate *adj* analphabète, illettré.

illness *n* maladie *f*.

illogical *adj* illogique.

ill-timed *adj* inopportun.

ill-treat *vt* maltraiter.

illuminate *vt* illuminer.

illumination *n* illumination *f*.

illusion *n* illusion *f*.

illusory *adj* illusoire.

illustrate *vt* illustrer.

illustration 369 **imperfection**

illustration n illustration f.
illustrative adj qui illustre.
illustrious adj illustre.
ill-will n malveillance f.
image n image f.
imagery n images fpl.
imaginable adj imaginable.
imaginary adj imaginaire.
imagination n imagination f.
imaginative adj imaginatif.
imagine vt imaginer.
imbalance n déséquilibre m.
imbecile adj imbécile, idiot.
imbibe vt boire; imbiber; absorber.
imbue vt imprégner.
imitate vt imiter.
imitation n imitation f.
imitative adj imitatif.
immaculate adj immaculé.
immaterial adj insignifiant.
immature adj pas mûr.
immeasurable adj incommensurable.
immeasurably adv immensément.
immediate adj immédiat; **~ly** adv immédiatement.
immense adj immense; énorme; **~ly** adv immensément.
immensity n immensité f.
immerse vt immerger.
immersion n immersion f.
immigrant n immigrant m, -e f.
immigration n immigration f.
imminent adj imminent.
immobile adj immobile.
immobility n immobilité f.
immoderate adj immodéré, excessif; **~ly** adv immodérément.
immodest adj immodeste.
immoral adj immoral.

immorality n immoralité f.
immortal adj immortel.
immortality n immortalité f.
immortalize vt immortaliser.
immune adj immunisé.
immunity n immunité f.
immunize vt immuniser.
immutable adj immuable.
imp n lutin m.
impact n impact m.
impair vt diminuer; affaiblir.
impale vt empaler.
impalpable adj impalpable.
impart vt communiquer.
impartial adj **~ly** adv impartial(ement).
impartiality n impartialité f.
impassable adj impraticable; infranchissable.
impasse n impasse f.
impassive adj impassible.
impatience n impatience f.
impatient adj impatient; **~ly** adv impatiemment.
impeach vt accuser.
impeccable adj impeccable.
impecunious adj impécunieux.
impede vt empêcher; entraver.
impediment n obstacle m.
impel vt pousser.
impending adj imminent.
impenetrable adj impénétrable.
imperative adj impératif.
imperceptible adj imperceptible.
imperceptibly adv imperceptiblement.
imperfect adj, **~ly** imparfait(ement); * n (gr) imparfait m.
imperfection n imperfection f; défaut m.

imperial adj impérial.

imperialism n impérialisme m.

imperious adj impérieux; **~ly** adv impérieusement.

impermeable adj imperméable.

impersonal adj, **~ly** adv impersonel(lement).

impersonate vt se faire passer pour.

impertinence n impertinence f.

impertinent adj impertinent; **~ly** adv impertinemment.

imperturbable adj imperturbable.

impervious adj imperméable; indifférent.

impetuosity n impétuosité f.

impetuous adj impétueux; **~ly** adv impétueusement.

impetus n élan m.

impiety n impiété f.

impinge (on) vi affecter; empiéter (sur).

impious adj impie.

implacable adj implacable.

implacably adv implacablement.

implant vt implanter.

implement n outil m; ustensile m.

implicate vt impliquer.

implication n implication f.

implicit adj implicite; **~ly** adv implicitement.

implore vt supplier.

imply vt supposer.

impolite adj impoli.

impoliteness n impolitesse f.

impolitic adj imprudent; impolitique.

import vt importer; * n importation f.

importance n importance f.

important adj important.

importation n importation f.

importer n importateur m, -trice f.

importunate adj importun.

importune vt importuner.

importunity n importunité f.

impose vt imposer.

imposing adj imposant.

imposition n imposition f.

impossibility n impossibilité f.

impossible adj impossible.

impostor n imposteur m.

impotence n impotence f.

impotent adj impotent; **~ly** adv faiblement.

impound vt confisquer.

impoverish vt appauvrir.

impoverished adj appauvri.

impoverishment n appauvrissement m.

impracticability n impraticabilité f.

impracticable adj impraticable.

impractical adj peu pratique.

imprecation n imprécation, malédiction f.

imprecise adj imprécis.

impregnable adj inexpugnable.

impregnate vt imprégner; féconder.

impregnation n fécondation f; imprégnation f.

impress vt impressionner.

impression n impression f; édition f.

impressionable adj impressionnable.

impressive adj impressionnant.

imprint n empreinte f; * vt imprimer; marquer.

imprison vt emprisonner.

imprisonment n emprisonnement m.

improbability n improbabilité f.
improbable adj improbable.
impromptu adj impromptu.
improper adj indécent; déplacé; impropre; **~ly** adv indécemment; de manière déplacée; improprement.
impropriety n impropriété f; inconvenance f.
improve vt améliorer; * vi s'améliorer.
improvement n amélioration f.
improvident adj imprévoyant.
improvise vt improviser.
imprudence n imprudence f.
imprudent adj imprudent.
impudence n impudence f.
impudent adj impudent; **~ly** adv impudemment.
impugn vt attaquer.
impulse n impulsion f.
impulsive adj impulsif.
impunity n impunité f.
impure adj impur; **~ly** adv impurement.
impurity n impureté f.
in prep dans; en.
inability n incapacité f.
inaccessible adj inaccessible.
inaccuracy n inexactitude f.
inaccurate adj inexact.
inaction n inaction f.
inactive adj inactif.
inactivity n inactivité f.
inadequate adj inadéquat.
inadmissible adj inadmissible.
inadvertently adv par inadvertance.
inalienable adj inaliénable.
inane adj inepte.
inanimate adj inanimé.

inapplicable adj inapplicable.
inappropriate adj impropre.
inasmuch adv attendu que.
inattentive adj inattentif.
inaudible adj inaudible.
inaugural adj inaugural.
inaugurate vt inaugurer.
inauguration n inauguration f.
inauspicious adj peu propice.
in-between adj intermédiaire.
inborn, inbred adj inné.
incalculable adj incalculable.
incandescent adj incandescent.
incantation n incantation f.
incapable adj incapable.
incapacitate vt mettre dans l'incapacité.
incapacity n incapacité f.
incarcerate vt incarcérer.
incarnate adj incarné.
incarnation n incarnation f.
incautious adj imprudent; **~ly** adv imprudemment.
incendiary n bombe incendiaire f; incendiaire mf.
incense n encens m; * vt exaspérer.
incentive n stimulant m; prime, aide f.
inception n commencement m.
incessant adj incessant, continuel; **~ly** adv continuellement.
incest n inceste m.
incestuous adj incestueux.
inch n pouce m; **~ by ~** petit à petit.
incidence n fréquence f.
incident n incident m.
incidental adj fortuit; **~ly** adv incidemment.
incinerator n incinérateur m.

incipient *adj* naissant.

incise *vt* inciser.

incision *n* incision *f*.

incisive *adj* incisif.

incisor *n* incisive *f*.

incite *vt* inciter, encourager.

inclement *adj* inclément.

inclination *n* inclination, propension *f*.

incline *vt* incliner; * *vi* s'incliner.

include *vt* inclure, comprendre.

including *prep* inclus, y compris.

inclusion *n* inclusion *f*.

inclusive *adj* inclus; tout compris.

incognito *adv* incognito.

incoherence *n* incohérence *f*.

incoherent *adj* incohérent; ~ly *adv* d'une manière incohérente.

income *n* revenu *m*; recettes *fpl*.

income tax *n* impôt sur le revenu *m*.

incoming *adj* entrant; nouveau.

incomparable *adj* incomparable.

incomparably *adv* incomparablement.

incompatibility *n* incompatibilité *f*.

incompatible *adj* incompatible.

incompetence *n* incompétence *f*.

incompetent *adj* incompétent; ~ly *adv* de manière incompétente.

incomplete *adj* incomplet.

incomprehensibility *n* incompréhensibilité *f*.

incomprehensible *adj* incompréhensible.

inconceivable *adj* inconcevable.

inconclusive *adj* peu concluant; * *adv* d'une manière peu concluante.

incongruity *n* incongruité *f*.

incongruous *adj* incongru; ~ly *adv* incongrûment.

inconsequential *adj* inconséquent.

inconsiderate *adj* sans considération; inconsidéré; ~ly *adv* sans considération.

inconsistency *n* inconsistance *f*.

inconsistent *adj* inconsistant.

inconsolable *adj* inconsolable.

inconspicuous *adj* discret.

incontinence *n* incontinence *f*.

incontinent *adj* incontinent.

incontrovertible *adj* incontestable.

inconvenience *n* inconvénient, désagrément *m*; * *vt* incommoder.

inconvenient *adj* incommode; ~ly *adv* incommodément.

incorporate *vt* incorporer; * *vi* s'incorporer.

incorporated company *n* société constituée *f*.

incorporation *n* incorporation *f*.

incorrect *adj* incorrect, inexact; ~ly *adv* incorrectement.

incorrigible *adj* incorrigible.

incorruptibility *n* incorruptibilité *f*.

incorruptible *adj* incorruptible.

increase *vt*, *vi* augmenter; * *n* augmentation *f*.

increasing *adj* croissant; *adv* ~ly de plus en plus.

incredible *adj* incroyable.

incredulity *n* incrédulité *f*.

incredulous *adj* incrédule.

increment *n* augmentation *f*.

incriminate *vt* incriminer.

incrust *vt* incruster.

incubate *vi* couver.

incubator *n* couveuse *f*.

inculcate *vt* inculquer.

incumbent *adj* nécessaire; * *n* titulaire *mf*.

incur *vt* encourir.

incurability *n* incurabilité *f*.

incurable *adj* incurable.

incursion *n* incursion *f*.

indebted *adj* endetté; redevable.

indecency *n* indécence *f*.

indecent *adj* indécent; **~ly** *adv* indécemment.

indecision *n* indécision, irrésolution *f*.

indecisive *adj* indécis, irrésolu.

indecorous *adj* inconvenant.

indeed *adv* vraiment.

indefatigable *adj* infatigable.

indefinite *adj*, **~ly** *adv* indéfini(ment).

indelible *adj* indélébile.

indelicacy *n* indélicatesse *f*.

indelicate *adj* peu délicat.

indemnify *vt* indemniser.

indemnity *n* indemnité *f*.

indent *vt* bosseler; renfoncer.

independence *n* indépendance *f*.

independent *adj* indépendant; **~ly** *adv* indépendamment.

indescribable *adj* indescriptible.

indestructible *adj* indestructible.

indeterminate *adj* indéterminé.

index *n* indice *m*.

index card *n* fiche *f*.

indexed *adj* indexé.

index finger *n* index *m*.

indicate *vt* indiquer.

indication *n* indication *f*; indice *m*.

indicative *adj*, *n* (gr) indicatif *m*.

indicator *n* indicateur *m*.

indict *vt* accuser.

indictment *n* accusation *f*.

indifference *n* indifférence *f*.

indifferent *adj* indifférent; **~ly** *adv* indifféremment.

indigenous *adj* indigène.

indigent *adj* indigent.

indigestible *adj* indigeste.

indigestion *n* indigestion *f*.

indignant *adj* indigné.

indignation *n* indignation *f*.

indignity *n* indignité *f*.

indigo *n* indigo *m*.

indirect *adj* indirect; **~ly** *adv* indirectement.

indiscreet *adj* indiscret; **~ly** *adv* indiscrètement.

indiscretion *n* indiscrétion *f*.

indiscriminate *adj*, **~ly** *adv* sans discernement.

indispensable *adj* indispensable.

indisposed *adj* indisposé.

indisposition *n* indisposition *f*.

indisputable *adj* indiscutable.

indisputably *adv* indiscutablement.

indistinct *adj* indistinct, confus; **~ly** *adv* indistinctement.

indistinguishable *adj* indistinctible.

individual *adj*, **~ly** *adv* individuel(lement); * *n* individu *m*.

individuality *n* individualité *f*.

indivisible *adv*, **~bly** *adv* indivisible(ment).

indoctrinate *vt* endoctriner.

indoctrination *n* endoctrinement *m*.

indolence *n* indolence *f*.

indolent *adj* indolent; **~ly** *adv* indolemment.

indomitable *adj* indomptable.

indoors *adv* à l'intérieur.

indubitably *adv* indubitablement.

induce *vt* persuader; causer, provoquer.

inducement *n* encouragement *m*; incitation *f*.

induction *n* induction *f*.

indulge *vt* céder à; *vi* se permettre, se laisser aller.

indulgence *n* indulgence *f*.

indulgent *adj* indulgent; ~ly *adv* avec indulgence.

industrial *adj* industriel.

industrialist *n* industriel *m*.

industrialize *vt* industrialiser.

industrial park *n* zone industrielle *f*.

industrious *adj* travailleur.

industry *n* industrie *f*.

inebriated *vt* ivre.

inebriation *n* ivresse *f*.

inedible *adj* non comestible.

ineffable *adj* ineffable.

ineffective, ineffectual *adj* inefficace; ~ly *adv* inefficacement.

inefficiency *n* inefficacité *f*.

inefficient *adj* inefficace.

ineligible *adj* inéligible.

inept *adj* inepte; déplacé.

ineptitude *n* ineptie *f*; manque d'à-propos *m*.

inequality *n* inégalité *f*.

inert *adj* inerte.

inertia *n* inertie *f*.

inescapable *adj* inévitable.

inestimable *adj* inestimable.

inevitable *adj* inévitable.

inevitably *adv* inévitablement.

inexcusable *adj* inexcusable.

inexhaustible *adj* inépuisable.

inexorable *adj* inexorable.

inexpedient *adj* imprudent, inopportun.

inexpensive *adj* bon marché.

inexperience *n* inexpérience *f*.

inexperienced *adj* inexpérimenté.

inexpert *adj* inexpert.

inexplicable *adj* inexplicable.

inexpressible *adj* indicible; inexprimable.

inextricably *adv* inextricablement.

infallibility *n* infaillibilité *f*.

infallible *adj* infaillible.

infamous *adj* vil, infâme; ~ly *adv* vilement.

infamy *n* infamie *f*.

infancy *n* enfance *f*.

infant *n* bébé *m*; enfant *mf*.

infanticide *n* infanticide *mf*.

infantile *adj* infantile.

infantry *n* infanterie *f*.

infatuated *adj* fou.

infatuation *n* folie *f*; obsession *f*.

infect *vt* infecter.

infection *n* infection *f*.

infectious *adj* contagieux; infectieux.

infer *vt* inférer.

inference *n* inférence *f*.

inferior *adj* inférieur; * *n* subordonné *m*, -e *f*.

inferiority *n* infériorité *f*.

infernal *adj* infernal.

inferno *n* enfer *m*.

infest *vt* infester.

infidel *n* infidèle *mf*.

infidelity *n* infidélité *f*.

infiltrate *vi* s'infiltrer.

infinite *adj*, ~ly *adv* infini(ment).

infinitive *n* (*gr*) infinitif *m*.

infinity *n* infini *m*; infinité *f*.

infirm *adj* infirme.

infirmary *n* infirmerie *f*.

infirmity *n* infirmité *f*.

inflame *vt* enflammer; * *vi* s'enflammer.

inflammation *n* inflammation *f*.

inflammatory *adj* inflammatoire.

inflatable *adj* gonflable.

inflate *vt* gonfler.

inflation *n* inflation *f*.

inflection *n* inflexion *f*.

inflexibility *n* inflexibilité *f*.

inflexible *adj* inflexible.

inflexibly *adv* inflexiblement.

inflict *vt* infliger.

influence *n* influence *f*; * *vt* influencer.

influential *adj* influent.

influenza *n* grippe *f*.

influx *n* affluence *f*.

inform *vt* informer.

informal *adj* informel; simple; familier.

informality *n* simplicité *f*.

informant *n* informateur *m*, -trice *f*.

information *n* information *f*.

infraction *n* infraction *f*.

infra-red *adj* infrarouge.

infrastructure *n* infrastructure *f*.

infrequent *adj*, **~ly** *adv* rare(ment).

infringe *vt* enfreindre.

infringement *n* infraction *f*.

infuriate *vt* rendre furieux.

infuse *vt* infuser.

infusion *n* infusion *f*.

ingenious *adj* ingénieux; **~ly** *adv* ingénieusement.

ingenuity *n* ingéniosité *f*.

ingenuous *adj*, **~ly** *adv* ingénu(ment); sincère(ment).

inglorious *adj* honteux; **~ly** *adv* honteusement.

ingot *n* lingot *m*.

ingrained *adj* invétéré.

ingratiate *vi*: **~ with sb** chercher à entrer dans les bonnes grâces de qn.

ingratitude *n* ingratitude *f*.

ingredient *n* ingrédient *m*.

inhabit *vt*, *vi* habiter.

inhabitable *adj* habitable.

inhabitant *n* habitant *m*, -e *f*.

inhale *vt* inhaler.

inherent *adj* inhérent.

inherit *vt* hériter.

inheritance *n* héritage *m*.

inheritor *n* héritier *m*, -ière *f*.

inhibit *vt* inhiber.

inhibited *adj* inhibé.

inhibition *n* inhibition *f*.

inhospitable *adj* inhospitalier.

inhospitality *n* inhospitalité *f*.

inhuman *adj* inhumain; **~ly** *adv* inhumainement.

inhumanity *n* inhumanité, cruauté *f*.

inimical *adj* hostile, ennemi.

inimitable *adj* inimitable.

iniquitous *adj* inique, injuste.

iniquity *n* iniquité, injustice *f*.

initial *adj* initial; * *n* initiale *f*.

initially *adv* au début.

initiate *vt* commencer; initier.

initiation *n* début, commencement *m*; initiation *f*.

initiative *n* initiative *f*.

inject *vt* injecter.

injection *n* injection *f*.

injudicious *adj* peu judicieux.

injunction *n* injonction *f*; ordre *m*.

injure *vt* blesser.

injury n blessure f; tort m.

injury time n arrêts de jeu mpl.

injustice n injustice f.

ink n encre f.

inkling n soupçon m.

inkstand n encrier m.

inlaid adj incrusté.

inland adj intérieur; * adv vers l'intérieur, dans les terres.

in-laws npl belle-famille f.

inlay vt incruster.

inlet n entrée f; bras de mer m.

inmate n détenu m, -e f.

inmost adj le plus profond.

inn n auberge f; hôtel m.

innate adj inné.

inner adj intérieur.

innermost adj le plus profond.

inner tube n chambre à air f.

innkeeper n aubergiste mf, hôtelier m, -ière f.

innocence n innocence f.

innocent adj innocent; ~ly adv innocemment.

innocuous adj inoffensif; ~ly adv de manière inoffensive.

innovate vt innover.

innovation n innovation f.

innuendo n allusion f; insinuation f.

innumerable adj innombrable.

inoculate vt inoculer.

inoculation n inoculation f.

inoffensive adj inoffensif.

inopportune adj inopportun.

inordinately adv démesurément.

inorganic adj inorganique.

inpatient n patient(e) hospitalisé(e) m(f).

input n entrée f; consommation f.

inquest n enquête f.

inquire vt, vi demander; **to ~ about** s'informer de; **to ~ after** vt demander des nouvelles de; **to ~ into** vt faire des recherches sur; enquêter sur.

inquiry n demande de renseignements f; enquête f.

inquisition n investigation f.

inquisitive adj curieux.

inroad n incursion f.

insane adj fou, f folle.

insanity n folie f.

insatiable adj insatiable.

inscribe vt inscrire; dédier.

inscription n inscription f; dédicace f.

inscrutable adj impénétrable.

insect n insecte m.

insecticide n insecticide m.

insecure adj peu assuré.

insecurity n insécurité f.

insemination n insémination f.

insensible adj inconscient; insensible.

insensitive adj insensible.

inseparable adj inséparable.

insert vt introduire, insérer.

insertion n insertion f.

inshore adj côtier.

inside n intérieur m; * adv à l'intérieur.

inside out adv à l'envers; à fond.

insidious adj insidieux; ~ly insidieusement.

insight n perspicacité f.

insignia npl insignes mpl.

insignificant adj insignifiant.

insincere adj peu sincère.

insincerity n manque de sincérité m.

insinuate vt insinuer.

insinuation n insinuation f.

insipid adj insipide.

insist vi insister.

insistence n insistance f.

insistent adj insistant.

insole n semelle intérieure f.

insolence n insolence f.

insolent adj insolent; **~ly** adv insolemment.

insoluble adj insoluble.

insolvency n insolvabilité f.

insolvent adj insolvable.

insomnia n insomnie f.

insomuch conj à tel point.

inspect vt examiner, inspecter.

inspection n inspection f.

inspector n inspecteur m, -trice f.

inspiration n inspiration f.

inspire vt inspirer.

instability n instabilité f.

instal vt installer.

installation n installation f.

instalment n installation f; versement m.

instalment plan n plan de vente à tempérament m.

instance n exemple m; **for ~** par exemple.

instant adj instantané; **~ly** adv immédiatement; * n instant, moment m.

instantaneous adj, **~ly** adv instantané(ment).

instead (of) pr au lieu, à la place (de).

instep n cou-de-pied m.

instigate vt inciter; susciter.

instigation n incitation f.

instill vt instiller; inspirer.

instinct n instinct m.

instinctive adj instinctif; **~ly** adv instinctivement, d'instinct.

institute vt instituer; * n institut m.

institution n institution f.

instruct vt instruire.

instruction n instruction f.

instructive adj instructif.

instructor n professeur m; moniteur m, -trice f.

instrument n instrument m.

instrumental adj instrumental.

insubordinate adj insubordonné.

insubordination n insubordination f.

insufferable adj insupportable.

insufferably adv insupportablement.

insufficiency n insuffisance f.

insufficient adj insuffisant; **~ly** adv insuffisamment.

insular adj insulaire; borné.

insulate vt isoler; insonoriser.

insulating tape n ruban isolant m.

insulation n isolation f; insonorisation f.

insulin n insuline f.

insult vt insulter; * n insulte f.

insulting adj insultant.

insuperable adj insurmontable.

insurance n (com) assurance f.

insurance policy n police d'assurance f.

insure vt assurer.

insurgent n insurgé, rebelle m.

insurmountable adj insurmontable.

insurrection n insurrection f.

intact adj intact.

intake n admission f; consommation f.

integral adj intégrant; (chem) intégral; * n intégrale f.

integrate vt intégrer.

integration n intégration f.

integrity n intégrité f.

intellect n intellect m.

intellectual adj intellectuel.

intelligence n intelligence f.

intelligent adj intelligent.

intelligentsia n intelligentsia f.

intelligible adj intelligible.

intelligibly adv intelligiblement.

intemperate adj, **~ly** adv immodéré(ment).

intend vt avoir l'intention de.

intendant n intendant m, -e f.

intended adj voulu.

intense adj intense; **~ly** adv intensément.

intensify vt intensifier.

intensity n intensité f.

intensive adj intensif.

intensive care unit n service de soins intensifs m.

intent adj résolu; attentif; **~ly** adv attentivement; * n intention f, dessein m.

intention n intention f, dessein m.

intentional adj intentionnel; **~ly** adv à dessein, intentionnellement.

inter vt enterrer.

interaction n interaction f.

intercede vi intercéder.

intercept vt intercepter.

intercession n intercession f.

interchange n échange m.

intercom n interphone m.

intercourse n relations sexuelles fpl.

interest vt intéresser; * n intérêt m.

interesting adj intéressant.

interest rate n taux d'intérêt m.

interfere vi s'ingérer.

interference n ingérence f; interférence f.

interim adj intérimaire.

interior adj intérieur.

interior designer n décorateur (-trice) d'intérieur m(f).

interjection n (gr) interjection f.

interlock vi s'entremêler.

interlocutor n interlocuteur m, -trice f.

interloper n intrus m, -e f.

interlude n intermède m.

intermarriage n intermariage m.

intermediary n intermédiaire mf.

intermediate adj intermédiaire.

interment n enterrement m.

interminable adj interminable.

intermingle vt entremêler; * vi s'entremêler.

intermission n entracte m; interruption f.

intermittent adj intermittent.

intern n interne mf.

internal adj intérieur; interne; **~ly** adv intérieurement.

international adj international.

interplay n interaction f.

interpose vt interposer.

interpret vt interpréter.

interpretation n interprétation f.

interpreter n interprète mf.

interregnum n interrègne m.

interrelated adj en corrélation.

interrogate vt interroger.

interrogation n interrogatoire m.

interrogative adj interrogatif.

interrupt vt interrompre.

interruption n interruption f.
intersect vi se croiser.
intersection n croisement m.
intersperse vt parsemer.
intertwine vt entrelacer.
interval n intervalle m; mitemps f.
intervene vi intervenir.
intervention n intervention f.
interview n entrevue f; interview f;
* vt faire passer une entrevue à;
interviewer.
interviewer n interviewer m.
interweave vt entrelacer.
intestate adj intestat.
intestinal adj intestinal.
intestine n intestin m.
intimacy n intimité f.
intimate n intime mf; * adj, ~ly
adv intime(ment); * vt insinuer,
laisser entendre.
intimidate vt intimider.
into prep dans, en.
intolerable adj intolérable.
intolerably adv intolérablement.
intolerance n intolérance f.
intolerant adj intolérant.
intonation n intonation f.
intoxicate vt enivrer.
intoxication n ivresse f.
intractable adj intraitable.
intransitive adj (gr) intransitif.
intravenous adj intraveineux.
in-tray n courrier à l'arrivée m.
intrepid adj intrépide; ~ly adv
intrépidement.
intrepidity n intrépidité f.
intricacy n complexité f.
intricate adj complexe, compliqué; ~ly adv de manière compli-
quée.

intrigue n intrigue f; * vi intriguer.
intriguing adj intrigant.
intrinsic adj, ~ally adv intrin-
sèque(ment).
introduce vt introduire.
introduction n introduction f.
introductory adj d'introduction.
introspection n introspection f.
introvert n introverti m, -ie f.
intrude vi s'ingérer, s'immiscer.
intruder n intrus m, -e f.
intrusion n intrusion f.
intuition n intuition f.
intuitive adj intuitif.
inundate vt inonder.
inundation n inondation f.
inure vt accoutumer, habituer.
invade vt envahir.
invader n envahisseur m, -euse f.
invalid adj invalide; * n invalide
mf.
invalidate vt invalider, annuler.
invaluable adj inappréciable.
invariable adj invariable.
invariably adv invariablement.
invasion n invasion f.
invective n invective f.
inveigle vt persuader, entraîner.
invent vt inventer.
invention n invention f.
inventive adj inventif.
inventor n inventeur m, -trice f.
inventory n inventaire m.
inverse n inverse.
inversion n inversion f.
invert vt inverser.
invest vt investir.
investigate vt faire des recherches
sur; examiner.

investigation n investigation f; recherches fpl.

investigator n investigateur m, -trice f; chercheur m, -euse f.

investment n investissement m.

inveterate adj invétéré.

invidious adj odieux; désobligeant.

invigilate vt surveiller.

invigorating adj vivifiant.

invincible adj invincible.

invincibly adv invinciblement.

inviolable adj inviolable.

invisible adj invisible.

invisibly adv invisiblement.

invitation n invitation f.

invite vt inviter.

inviting adj attrayant, tentant.

invoice n (com) facture f.

invoke vt invoquer.

involuntarily adv involontairement.

involuntary adj involontaire.

involve vt impliquer, entraîner.

involved adj compliqué.

involvement n implication f; confusion f.

invulnerable adj invulnérable.

inward adj intérieur; intime; ~, ~s adv vers l'intérieur.

iodine n (chem) iode m.

I.O.U. (I owe you) n reçu m.

irascible adj irascible.

irate, ireful adj irrité.

iris n iris m.

irksome adj fastidieux, ennuyeux.

iron n fer m; * adj de fer; * vt repasser.

ironic adj, ~ly adv ironique(ment).

ironing n repassage m.

ironing board n table à repasser f.

iron ore n minerai de fer m.

ironwork n ferronnerie f; ~s pl ferronneries fpl.

irony n ironie f.

irradiate vt irradier.

irrational adj irrationnel.

irreconcilable adj irréconciliable; inconciliable.

irregular adj irrégulier; ~ly adv irrégulièrement.

irregularity n irrégularité f.

irrelevant adj hors de propos.

irreligious adj irréligieux.

irreparable adj irréparable.

irreplaceable adj irremplaçable.

irrepressible adj irrépressible.

irreproachable adj irréprochable.

irresistible adj irrésistible.

irresolute adj, ~ly adv irrésolu(ment).

irresponsible adj irresponsable.

irretrievably adv irréparablement.

irreverence n irrévérence f.

irreverent adj irrévérencieux; ~ly adv irrévérencieusement.

irrigate vt irriguer.

irrigation n irrigation f.

irritability n irritabilité f.

irritable adj irritable.

irritant n (med) irritant m.

irritate vt irriter.

irritating adj irritant.

irritation n irritation f.

Islam n Islam m.

island n île f.

islander n insulaire mf.

isle n île f.

isolate vt isoler.

isolation n isolement m.

issue n sujet m, question f; * vt publier; distribuer; fournir.

isthmus n isthme m.

it pn il, elle; le, la; cela, ça, ce, c'.

italic n italique m.

itch n démangeaison f; * vi avoir des démangeaisons.

item n article m.

itemize vt détailler.

itinerant adj ambulant, itinérant.

itinerary n itinéraire m.

its pn son, sa, ses.

itself pn lui-même, elle-même.

ivory n ivoire m.

ivy n lierre m.

J

jab vt planter, enfoncer.

jabber vi bafouiller.

jack n cric m; valet m.

jackal n chacal m.

jackboots npl bottes de militaire fpl.

jackdaw n choucas m.

jacket n veste f; couverture f.

jack-knife vi se mettre en travers.

jack plug n prise à fiche f.

jackpot n gros lot m.

jade n jade m.

jagged adj dentelé.

jaguar n jaguar m.

jail n prison f.

jailbird n prisonnier m, -ière f.

jailer n geôlier m, -ière f.

jam n confiture f; embouteillage m.

jangle vi cliqueter.

janitor n portier m.

January n janvier m.

jar vi se heurter; (mus) détonner; grincer; * n pot m.

jargon n jargon m.

jasmine n jasmin m.

jaundice n jaunisse f.

jaunt n promenade f.

jaunty adj enjoué.

javelin n javelot m.

jaw n mâchoire f.

jay n geai m.

jazz n jazz m.

jealous adj jaloux.

jealousy n jalousie f.

jeans npl jean m.

jeep n jeep f.

jeer vi se moquer, railler; * n raillerie, moquerie f.

jelly n gelée f.

jelly-fish n méduse f.

jeopardize vt risquer, mettre en péril.

jerk n secousse f; * vt donner une secousse à.

jerky adj saccadé.

jersey n jersey m.

jest n blague, plaisanterie f.

jester n bouffon m.

jestingly adv en plaisantant.

Jesuit n jésuite m.

Jesus n Jésus m.

jet n avion à réaction m; jet m; gicleur m.

jet engine n moteur à réaction m.

jettison vt se défaire de.

jetty n jetée f.

Jew n Juif m.

jewel n bijou m.

jeweller n bijoutier m, -ière f.

jewellery n bijoux mpl.

jewellery store n bijouterie f.

Jewess n Juive f.

jewish adj juif.

jib n (mar) foc m.

jibe n raillerie, moquerie f.

jig n gigue f.

jigsaw n puzzle m.

jilt vt laisser tomber.

jinx n porte-malheur m invar.

job n travail m.

jockey n jockey m.

jocular adj joyeux; facétieux.

jog vi faire du jogging.

jogging n jogging m.

join vt joindre, unir; **to ~ in** participer à; * vi se réunir; se joindre.

joiner n menuisier m.

joinery n menuiserie f.

joint n articulation f; * adj commun.

jointly adv conjointement.

joint-stock company n (com) société par actions f.

joke n blague, plaisanterie f; * vi blaguer, plaisanter.

joker n blagueur m, -euse f.

jollity n gaieté f.

jolly adj gai, joyeux.

jolt vt secouer; * n secousse f.

jostle vt bousculer.

journal n revue f.

journalism n journalisme m.

journalist n journaliste mf.

journey n voyage m; * vi voyager.

jovial adj jovial, gai; **~ly** adv jovialement.

joy n joie f.

joyful, joyous adj joyeux, gai; **~ly** adv joyeusement.

joystick n manche à balai m.

jubilant adj joyeux.

jubilation n jubilation f.

jubilee n jubilé m.

Judaism n judaïsme m.

judge n juge m; * vt juger.

judgment n jugement m.

judicial adj, **~ly** adv judiciaire(ment).

judiciary n pouvoir judiciaire m.

judicious adj judicieux.

judo n judo m.

jug n cruche f.

juggle vi jongler.

juggler n jongleur m, -euse f.

juice n jus m; suc m.

juicy adj juteux.

jukebox n juke-box m.

July n juillet m.

jumble vt mélanger; * n mélange m; fouillis m.

jump vi sauter; * n saut m.

jumper n pull m; sauteur m, -euse f.

jumpy adj nerveux.

juncture n conjoncture f.

June n juin m.

jungle n jungle f.

junior adj plus jeune.

juniper n (bot) genièvre m.

junk n cochonnerie f; bric-à-brac m invar.

junta n junte f.

jurisdiction n juridiction f.

jurisprudence n jurisprudence f.

jurist n juriste mf.

juror, juryman n juré m.

jury n jury m.

just adj juste; * adv justement, exactement; **~ as** juste quand; **~ now** tout de suite.

justice n justice f.
justifiably adv légitimement.
justification n justification f.
justify vt justifier.
justly adv justement.

justness n justesse f.
jut vi; **to ~ out** faire saillie, dépasser.
jute n jute m.
juvenile adj juvénile; pour enfants.
juxtaposition n juxtaposition f.

K

kaleidoscope n kaléidoscope m.
kangaroo n kangourou m.
karate n karaté m.
kebab n brochette f.
keel n (mar) quille f.
keen adj aiguisé; vif; enthousiaste.
keenness n enthousiasme m.
keep vt garder, conserver; tenir.
keeper n gardien m, -ienne f.
keepsake n souvenir m.
keg n baril m.
kennel n niche f.
kernel n amande f; noyau m.
kerosene n kérosène m.
ketchup n ketchup m.
kettle n bouilloire f.
kettle-drum n timbale f.
key n clé, clef f; (mus) ton m; touche f.
keyboard n clavier m.
keyhole n trou de la serrure m.
keynote n (mus) tonique f.
key ring n porte-clefs m invar.
keystone n clef de voûte f.
khaki n kaki m.
kick vi (vt) donner un coup de pied (à); n coup de pied m; plaisir m.
kid n gamin m, -e f.
kidnap vt kidnapper.
kidnapper n kidnappeur m, -euse f.
kidnapping n kidnapping m.
kidney n rein m; rognon m.

killer n assassin m.
killing n assassinat m.
kiln n four m.
kilo n kilo m.
kilobyte n kilo-octet m.
kilogram n kilogramme m.
kilometre n kilomètre m.
kilt n kilt m.
kin n parents mpl; **next of ~** parent proche m.
kind adj gentil; * n genre m, sorte f.
kindergarten n jardin d'enfants m.
kind-hearted adj bon.
kindle vt allumer; * vi s'allumer.
kindliness n gentillesse, bonté f.
kindly adj bon, bienveillant.
kindness n bonté f.
kindred adj apparenté.
kinetic adj cinétique.
king n roi m.
kingdom n royaume m.
kingfisher n martin-pêcheur m.
kiosk n kiosque m.
kiss n baiser m; * vt embrasser.
kissing n baisers mpl.
kit n équipement m.
kitchen n cuisine f.
kitchen garden n potager m.
kite n cerf-volant m.
kitten n chaton m.
knack n don, chic m.
knapsack n sac à dos m.

knave n fripouille f; (cards) valet m.

knead vt pétrir.

knee n genou m.

knee-deep adj jusqu'aux genoux.

kneel vi s'agenouiller.

knell n glas m.

knife n couteau m.

knight n chevalier m.

knit vt, vi tricoter; **to ~ the brows** froncer les sourcils.

knitter n tricoteur m, -euse f.

knitting pin n aiguille à tricoter f.

knitwear n tricots mpl.

knob n bouton m; nœud m (du bois).

knock vt, vi cogner, frapper; **to ~ down** abattre; * n coup m.

knocker n heurtoir m.

knock-kneed adj aux genoux cagneux.

knock-out n knock-out m.

knoll n butte f.

knot n nœud m; * vt nouer.

knotty adj emmêlé; épineux.

know vt, vi savoir; connaître.

know-all n je-sais-tout m.

know-how n savoir-faire m.

knowing adj entendu; ~ly adv en connaissance de cause.

knowledge n connaissances fpl.

knowledgeable adj bien informé.

knuckle n articulation f.

L

label n étiquette f.

laboratory n laboratoire m.

labour n travail m; **to be in ~** être en train d'accoucher; * vi travailler.

labourer n ouvrier m.

laborious adj laborieux; pénible; ~ly adv laborieusement.

labour union n syndicat m.

labyrinth n labyrinthe m.

lace n lacet m; dentelle f; * vt lacer.

lacerate vt lacérer.

lack vt manquer de; * vi manquer; * n manque m.

lackadaisical adj sans soin.

lackey n laquais m.

laconic adj laconique.

lacquer n laque f.

lad n garçon m.

ladder n échelle f.

ladle n louche f.

ladleful n louchée f.

lady n dame f.

ladybird n coccinelle f.

ladykiller n bourreau des cœurs m.

ladylike adj distingué.

ladyship n madame f.

lag vi se laisser distancer.

lager n bière blonde f.

lagoon n lagune f.

laidback adj décontracté.

lair n repaire m.

laity n laïcité f.

lake n lac m.

lamb n agneau m; * vi agneler.

lambswool n laine d'agneau f.

lame adj boiteux.

lament vt se lamenter sur; * vi se lamenter; * n lamentation f.

lamentable adj lamentable, déplorable.

lamentation n lamentation f.

laminated adj laminé.

lamp n lampe f.

lampoon n satire f.

lampshade n abat-jour m invar.

lance n lance f; bistouri m; * vt inciser.

lancet n bistouri m.

land n pays m; terre f; * vt débarquer; * vi atterrir, débarquer.

land forces npl armée de terre f.

landholder n propriétaire terrien m.

landing n atterrissage m.

landing strip n piste d'atterrissage f.

landlady n propriétaire f.

landlord n propriétaire m.

landlubber n marin d'eau douce m.

landmark n point de repère m.

landowner n propriétaire terrien m.

landscape n paysage m.

landslide n glissement de terrain m.

lane n allée, ruelle f; file f.

language n langue f; langage m.

languid adj languissant; ~ly adv languissamment.

languish vi languir.

lank adj raide, plat.

lanky adj grand et maigre.

lantern n lanterne f.

lap n genoux mpl; * vt laper.

lapdog n chien d'appartement m.

lapel n revers m.

lapse n laps m; défaillance f; * vi expirer, se périmer; se relâcher.

larceny n vol m.

larch n mélèze m.

lard n saindoux m.

larder n garde-manger m invar.

large adj grand; at ~ en liberté; ~ly adv en grande partie.

large-scale adj à grande échelle.

largesse n largesse f.

lark n alouette f.

larva n larve f.

laryngitis n laryngite f.

larynx n larynx m.

lascivious adj lascif; ~ly adv lascivement.

laser n laser m.

lash n coup de fouet m; * vt fouetter; attacher.

lasso n lasso m.

last adj dernier; at ~ enfin; ~ly adv finalement; * n dernier m, dernière f; forme f (de cordonnier); * vi durer.

last-ditch adj ultime.

lasting adj, ~ly adv durable(ment).

last-minute adj de dernière minute.

latch n loquet m.

latch-key n clef de porte d'entrée f.

late adj en retard; défunt; (rail) the train is ten minutes ~ le train a dix minutes de retard; * adv tard; ~ly adv récemment.

latecomer n retardataire mf.

latent adj latent.

lateral adj, ~ly adv latérale(ment).

lathe n tour m.

lather n mousse f.

latitude n latitude f.

latrine n latrine f.

latter adj dernier; ~ly adv récemment.

lattice n treillis m.

laudable adj louable.

laudably adv louablement.

laugh vi rire; to ~ at vt rire de, se moquer de; * n rire m.

laughable adj risible; dérisoire.

laughing stock n risée f.

laughter n rires mpl.

launch vt lancer; * vi se lancer; * n (mar) vedette f.

launching n lancement m.

launching pad n rampe de lancement f.

launder vt laver.

laundrette, laundromat n laverie automatique f.

laundry n lessive f.

laurel n laurier m.

lava n lave f.

lavatory n toilettes fpl.

lavender n (bot) lavande f.

lavish adj prodigue; ~ly adv avec prodigalité; * vt prodiguer.

law n loi f; droit m.

law-abiding adj respectueux de la loi.

law and order n ordre public m.

law court n tribunal m.

lawful adj légal; légitime; ~ly adv légalement.

lawless adj anarchique.

lawlessness n anarchie f.

lawmaker n législateur m, -trice f.

lawn n pelouse f, gazon m.

lawnmower n tondeuse à gazon f.

law school n faculté de droit f.

law suit n procès m.

lawyer n avocat m; notaire m.

lax adj relâché.

laxative n laxatif m.

laxity vt relâchement m; flou m.

lay vt placer; mettre; pondre; **to claim** réclamer; prétendre (à); * vi pondre.

layabout n paresseux m, -euse f.

layer n couche f.

layette n layette f.

layman n laïc m.

layout n disposition f; présentation f.

laze vi paresser.

lazily adv paresseusement.

laziness n paresse f.

lazy adj paresseux.

lead n plomb m; * vt, vi conduire, mener.

leader n chef m.

leadership n direction f.

leading adj principal; premier; ~ **article** n article de fond m.

leaf n feuille f.

leaflet n feuillet m; prospectus m.

leafy adj feuillu.

league n ligue f; lieue f.

leak n fuite f; * vi (mar) faire eau.

leaky adj qui fuit.

lean vt appuyer; * vi s'appuyer; * adj maigre.

leap vi sauter; * n saut m.

leapfrog n saute-mouton m.

leap year n année bisextile f.

learn vt, vi apprendre.

learned adj instruit.

learner n élève mf; débutant m, -e f.

learning n érudition f.

lease n bail m; * vt louer.

leasehold n bail m.

leash n laisse f.

least adj moindre; **at ~** au moins; **not in the ~** pas du tout.

leather n cuir m.

leathery adj qui a l'aspect du cuir.

leave n permission f; congé m; **to take ~** prendre congé; * vt laisser.

leaven n levain m; * vt faire lever.

leavings npl restes mpl.

lecherous adj lascif.

lecture n conférence f; * vi faire une conférence.

lecturer n conférencier m, -ière f.

ledge n rebord m.

ledger n (com) grand livre m.

lee n (mar) côté sous le vent m.

leech n sangsue f.

leek n (bot) poireau m.

leer vt regarder d'un œil lascif.

lees npl lie f.

leeward adj (mar) sous le vent.

leeway n liberté d'action f.

left adj gauche; **on the ~** à gauche.

left-handed adj gaucher.

left-luggage office n consigne f.

leftovers npl restes mpl.

leg n jambe f; patte f.

legacy n héritage, legs m.

legal adj légal, légitime; **~ly** adv légalement.

legal holiday n jour férié m.

legality n légalité, légitimité f.

legalize vt légaliser.

legal tender n monnaie légale f.

legate n légat m.

legatee n légataire mf.

legation n légation f.

legend n légende f.

legendary adj légendaire.

legible adj lisible.

legibly adv lisiblement.

legion n légion f.

legislate vi, vt légiférer.

legislation n législation f.

legislative adj législatif.

legislator n législateur m, -trice f.

legislature n corps législatif m.

legitimacy n légitimité f.

legitimate adj légitime; **~ly** adv légitimement; * vt légitimer.

leisure n loisir m; **~ly** adj tranquille; **at ~** au calme.

lemon n citron m.

lemonade n limonade f.

lemon tea n thé au citron m.

lemon tree n citronnier m.

lend vt prêter.

length n longueur f; durée f; **at ~** longuement; enfin.

lengthen vt allonger; * vi s'allonger.

lengthways, lengthwise adv dans le sens de la longueur.

lengthy adj long.

lenient adj indulgent.

lens n lentille f.

Lent n Carême m.

lentil n lentille f.

Leo n Lion m (signe du zodiaque).

leopard n léopard m.

leotard n justaucorps m.

leper n lépreux m, -euse f.

leprosy n lèpre f.

lesbian n lesbienne f.

less adj moins; * adv moins.

lessen vt, vi diminuer.

lesser adj moindre.

lesson n leçon f.

lest conj de crainte que.

let vt laisser, permettre; louer.

lethal adj mortel.

lethargic adj léthargique.

lethargy n léthargie f.

letter n lettre f.

letter bomb n lettre piégée f.

letter box boite aux lettres f.

lettering n inscription f.

letter of credit n lettre de crédit f.

lettuce n salade f.

leukaemia n leucémie f.

level adj plat, égal; à niveau; * n niveau m; * vt niveler.

level-headed adj sensé.

lever n levier m.

leverage n effet de levier m; prise f.

levity n légèreté f.

levy n levée f; prélèvement m; * vt prélever.

lewd adj obscène.

lexicon n lexique m.

liability n responsabilité f.

liable adj sujet (à); responsable.

liaise vi effectuer une liaison.

liaison n liaison f.

liar n menteur m, -euse f.

libel n diffamation f; * vt diffamer.

libellous adj diffamatoire.

liberal adj libéral; généreux; ~ly adv libéralement.

liberality n libéralité, générosité f.

liberate vt libérer.

liberation n libération f.

libertine n libertin m, -ine f.

liberty n liberté f.

Libra n Balance f (signe du zodiaque).

librarian n bibliothécaire mf.

library n bibliothèque f.

libretto n livret m.

licence n licence f; permis m; permission f.

licentious adj licencieux.

lichen n (bot) lichen m.

lick vt lécher.

lid n couvercle m.

lie n mensonge m; * vi mentir; être allongé.

lieu n: in ~ of au lieu de.

lieutenant n lieutenant m.

life n vie f; **for ~** pour toute la vie.

life belt n gilet de sauvetage m.

lifeboat n canot de sauvetage m.

life-guard n maître nageur m; garde du corps m.

life jacket n gilet de sauvetage m.

lifeless adj mort; sans vie.

lifelike adj naturel.

lifeline n bouée de sauvetage f.

life sentence n condamnation à perpétuité f.

life-sized adj grandeur nature.

lifespan n durée de vie f.

lifestyle n style de vie m.

life-support system n système de respiration artificielle m.

lifetime n vie f.

lift n lever.

ligament n ligament m.

light n lumière f; * adj léger; clair; * vt allumer; éclairer.

light bulb n ampoule f.

lighten vi s'éclaircir; * vt éclairer; éclaircir; alléger.

lighter n briquet m.

light-headed adj étourdi.

lighthearted adj joyeux.

lighthouse n (mar) phare m.

lighting n éclairage m.

lightly adv légèrement.

lightning n éclair m.

lightning rod n paratonnerre m.

light pen n crayon optique m.

lightweight adj léger.

light year n année-lumière f.

ligneous adj ligneux.

like adj pareil; * adv comme; * vt, vi aimer.

likeable adj sympathique.

likelihood n probabilité f.

likely adj probable, vraisemblable.

liken vt comparer.

likeness n ressemblance f.

likewise adv pareillement.

liking n goût m.

lilac n lilas m.

lily n lis m; ~ **of the valley** muguet m.

limb n membre m.

limber adj flexible, souple.

lime n chaux f; lime f; ~ **tree** tilleul m.

limestone n pierre à chaux f.

limit n limite f; * vt limiter.

limitation n limitation f; restriction f.

limitless adj illimité.

limo(usine) n limousine f.

limp vi boiter; * n boitement m; * adj mou.

limpet n patelle f.

limpid adj limpide.

line n ligne f; ride f; * vt rayer; rider.

lineage n lignage m.

linear adj linéaire.

lined adj rayé; ridé.

linen n lin m.

liner n transatlantique m.

linesman n juge de ligne m.

linger vi traîner.

lingerie n lingerie f.

lingering adj long.

linguist n linguiste mf.

linguistic adj linguistique.

linguistics n linguistique f.

liniment n liniment m.

lining n doublure f.

link n chaînon m; * vt relier.

linnet n linotte f.

linoleum n linoléum m.

linseed n graine de lin f.

lint n peluche f.

lintel n linteau m.

lion n lion m.

lioness n lionne f.

lip n lèvre f; bord m.

lip-read vi lire sur les lèvres.

lip salve n pommade pour les lèvres f.

lipstick n rouge à lèvres m.

liqueur n liqueur f.

liquid adj liquide; * n liquide m.

liquidate vt liquider.

liquidation n liquidation f.

liquidize vt liquéfier.

liquor n spiritueux m.

liquorice n réglisse m/f.

liquor store n magasin de vins et spiritueux m.

lisp vi zézayer; * n zézaiement m.

list n liste f; * vt faire une liste de.

listen vi écouter.

listless adj indifférent.

litany n litanie f.

literal adj ~ly adv littéral(ement).

literary adj littéraire.

literate adj cultivé.

literature n littérature f.

lithe adj agile.

lithograph n lithographie f.

lithography n lithographie f.

litigation n litige m.

litigious adj litigieux.

litre n litre m.

litter n litière f; ordures fpl; * vt recouvrir.

little adj petit; ~ **by** ~ petit à petit; * n peu m.

liturgy n liturgie f.
live vi vivre; habiter; **to ~ on** vt se nourrir de; **to ~ up to** vt faire honneur à; * adj vivant.
livelihood n moyens de subsistance mpl.
liveliness n vivacité f.
lively adj vif.
liven up vt animer.
liver n foie m.
livery n livrée f.
livestock n bétail m.
livid adj livide; furieux.
living n vie f; * adj vivant.
living room n salle de séjour f.
lizard n lézard m.
load vt charger; * n charge f.
loaded adj chargé.
loaf n pain m.
loafer n paresseux m, -euse f.
loam n terreau m.
loan n prêt m.
loathe vt détester.
loathing n aversion f.
loathsome adj dégoûtant.
lobby n vestibule m.
lobe n lobe m.
lobster n langouste f.
local adj local.
local anaesthetic n anesthésique local m.
local government n administration municipale, administration locale f.
locality n localité f.
localize vt localiser.
locally adv localement.
locate vt localiser.
location n situation f.
loch n loch m.

lock n serrure f; * vt fermer à clé.
locker n casier m.
locket n médaillon m.
lockout n grève patronale f.
locksmith n serrurier m.
lock-up n cellule f.
locomotive n locomotive f.
locust n sauterelle f.
lodge n loge du gardien f; * vi se loger.
lodger n locataire mf.
loft n grenier m.
lofty adj haut.
log n bûche f.
logbook n (mar) journal de bord m.
logic n logique f.
logical adj logique.
logo n logo m.
loin n rein m.
loiter vi s'attarder.
loll vi se prélasser.
lollipop n sucette f.
lonely, lonesome adj seul, solitaire.
loneliness n solitude f.
long adj long, f longue; * vi désirer.
long-distance n: ~ **call** appel interurbain m.
longevity n longévité f.
long-haired adj aux cheveux longs.
longing n désir m.
longitude n longitude f.
longitudinal adj longitudinal.
long jump n saut en longueur m.
long-playing record n trentetrois tours m.
long-range adj à longue portée.
long-term adj à long terme.

long wave n grandes ondes fpl.

long-winded adj prolixe.

look vi regarder; sembler; **to ~ after** vt s'occuper de; garder; **to ~ for** vt chercher; **to ~ forward to** vt attendre avec impatience; **to ~ out for** vt guetter; * n aspect m; regard m.

looking glass n miroir m.

look-out n (mil) sentinelle f; vigie f.

loom n métier à tisser m; * vi menacer.

loop n boucle f.

loophole n échappatoire f.

loose adj lâché; desserré; ~ly adv approximativement; ~, **loosen** vt lâcher; desserrer.

loot vt piller; * n butin m.

lop vt élaguer.

lop-sided adj de travers; déséquilibré.

loquacious adj loquace.

loquacity n loquacité f.

lord n seigneur m.

lore n savoir m.

lose vt, vi perdre.

loss n perte f; **to be at a ~** ne pas savoir que faire.

lost and found n objets trouvés mpl.

lot n sort f; lot m; **a ~** beaucoup.

lotion n lotion f.

lottery n loterie f.

loud adj fort, bruyant; ~ly adv bruyamment; haut.

loudspeaker n haut-parleur m.

lounge n salon m.

louse n (pl lice) pou m.

lousy adj minable.

lout n vaurien m.

lovable adj sympathique.

love n amour m; **to fall in ~** tomber amoureux; * vt aimer.

love letter n lettre d'amour f.

love life n vie sentimentale f.

loveliness n beauté f.

lovely adj beau.

lover n amant m.

love-sick adj fou amoureux.

loving adj affectueux.

low adj bas; * vi meugler.

low-cut adj décolleté.

lower adj plus bas; * vt baisser.

lowest adj le plus bas.

lowland n plaine f.

lowliness n humilité f.

lowly adj humble.

low-water n basse mer f.

loyal adj loyal, fidèle; ~ly adv loyalement.

loyalty n loyauté f; fidélité f.

lozenge n pastille f.

lubricant n lubrifiant m.

lubricate vt lubrifier.

lucid adj lucide.

luck n chance f.

luckily adv heureusement, par chance.

luckless adj malchanceux.

lucky adj chanceux, qui a de la chance.

lucrative adj lucratif.

ludicrous adj absurde.

lug vt traîner.

luggage n bagages mpl.

lugubrious adj lugubre, triste.

lukewarm adj tiède.

lull vt bercer; * n répit m.

lullaby n berceuse f.

lumbago n lumbago m.

lumberjack n bûcheron m.
lumber room n débarras m.
luminous adj lumineux.
lump n bosse f; grosseur f; morceau m; * vt réunir.
lump sum n somme globale f.
lunacy n folie f.
lunar adj lunaire.
lunatic adj fou, f folle.
lunch, luncheon n déjeuner m.
lungs npl poumons mpl.
lurch n embardée f.
lure n leurre m; attrait m; * vt séduire, attirer.
lurid adj blême; horrible.
lurk vi se cacher.
luscious adj délicieux.
lush adj luxuriant.
lust n luxure f; sensualité f; désir m; * vi désirer; **to ~ after** vt convoiter.
luster n lustre m.

lustful adj luxurieux, voluptueux; **~ly** adv luxurieusement.
lusty adj fort, vigoureux.
lute n luth m.
Lutheran n luthérien m, -ienne f.
luxuriance n exubérance, luxuriance f.
luxuriant adj exubérant, luxuriant.
luxuriate vi pousser de manière exubérante.
luxurious adj luxueux; **~ly** adv luxueusement.
luxury n luxe m.
lying n mensonges mpl.
lymph n lymphe f.
lynch vt lyncher.
lynx n linx m.
lyrical adj lyrique.
lyrics npl paroles fpl.

M

macaroni n macaronis mpl.
macaroon n macaron m.
mace n massue f; macis m.
macerate vt macérer.
machination n machination f.
machine n machine f.
machine gun n mitrailleuse f.
machinery n machinerie f; mécanisme m.
mackerel n maquereau m.
mad adj fou, f folle; furieux; insensé.
madam n madame f.
madden vt rendre fou; rendre furieux.
madder n (bot) garance f.

madhouse n asile de fous m.
madly adv à la folie; comme un fou.
madman n fou m.
madness n folie f.
magazine n magazine m, revue f; magasin m.
maggot n asticot m.
magic n magie f; * adj, **~ally** adv magique(ment).
magician n magicien m, -ienne f.
magisterial adj, **~ly** adv magistral(ement).
magistracy n magistrature f.
magistrate n magistrat m.

magnanimity n magnanimité f.

magnanimous adj, **~ly** adv magnanime(ment).

magnet n aimant m.

magnetic adj magnétique.

magnetism n magnétisme m.

magnificence n magnificence f.

magnificent adj, **~ly** adv magnifique(ment).

magnify vt grossir; exagérer.

magnifying glass n loupe f.

magnitude n magnitude f.

magpie n pie f.

mahogany n acajou m.

maid n bonne f.

maiden n jeune fille f.

maiden name n nom de jeune fille m.

mail n courrier m.

mailbox n boîte aux lettres f.

mail coach n malle-poste f.

mailing list n liste de publipostage f.

mail-order n vente par correspondance f.

mail train n (rail) train-poste m.

maim vt mutiler.

main adj principal; essentiel; **in the ~** en général.

mainland n continent m.

main line n (rail) grande ligne f.

mainly adv principalement, essentiellement.

main street n rue principale f.

maintain vt maintenir; soutenir.

maintenance n entretien m.

maize n maïs m.

majestic adj majestueux; **~ally** adv majestueusement.

majesty n majesté f.

major adj majeur; * n (mil) commandant m.

majority n majorité f.

make vt faire; **to ~ for** se diriger vers; **to ~ up** inventer; **to ~ up for** compenser; * n marque f.

make-believe n invention f.

makeshift adj improvisé, de fortune.

make-up n maquillage m.

make-up remover n démaquillant m.

malady n maladie f.

malaise n malaise m.

malaria n malaria f.

malcontent adj, n mécontent m, -e f.

male adj mâle; masculin; * n mâle m.

malevolence n malveillance f.

malevolent adj malveillant; **~ly** adv avec malveillance.

malfunction n mauvais fonctionnement m.

malice n malice f.

malicious adj méchant; **~ly** adv méchamment.

malign adj nocif; * vt calomnier.

malignant adj méchant; **~ly** adv méchamment.

mall n centre commercial m.

malleable adj malléable.

mallet n maillet m.

mallows n (bot) mauve f.

malnutrition n malnutrition f.

malpractice n négligence f.

malt n malt m.

maltreat vt maltraiter.

mammal n mammifère m.

mammoth adj gigantesque.

man n homme m; * vt (mar) équiper en personnel.

manacle n entrave f; ~**s** pl menottes fpl.

manage vt diriger; réussir; * vi réussir.

manageable adj maniable.

management n direction f.

manager n directeur m.

manageress n directrice f.

managerial adj directorial.

managing director n directeur général m.

mandarin n mandarine f; mandarin m.

mandate n mandat m.

mandatory n obligatoire.

mane n crinière f.

manfully adv vaillamment.

manger n mangeoire f.

mangle n essoreuse f; * vt mutiler.

mangy adj miteux.

manhandle vt maltraiter; manutentionner.

manhood n âge d'homme m; virilité f.

man-hour n heure-homme f.

mania n manie f.

maniac n maniaque mf.

manic adj maniaque.

manicure n manucure f.

manifest adj manifeste; * vt manifester.

manifestation n manifestation f.

manifesto n manifeste m.

manipulate vt manipuler.

manipulation n manipulation f.

mankind n humanité f.

manlike adj viril; d'homme.

manliness n virilité f; courage m.

manly adj viril.

man-made n artificiel.

manner n manière f; attitude f; ~**s** pl manières fpl.

manoeuvre n manœuvre f.

manpower n main-d'œuvre f.

mansion n château m.

manslaughter n homicide involontaire m.

mantelpiece n manteau de cheminée m.

manual adj, n manuel m.

manufacture n fabrication f; * vt fabriquer.

manufacturer n fabricant m.

manure n fumier m; engrais m; purin m; * vt bonifier.

manuscript n manuscrit m.

many adj beaucoup de; ~ **a time** de nombreuses fois; **how** ~? combien?; **as** ~ **as** autant que.

map n carte f; plan m; * vt dessiner un plan de; **to** ~ **out** programmer.

maple n érable m.

mar vt gâter, gâcher.

marathon n marathon m.

marauder n maraudeur m, -euse f.

marble n marbre m; * adj marbré.

March n mars m.

march n marche f; * vi marcher.

marchpast n défilé m.

mare n jument f.

margarine n margarine f.

margin n marge f; bord m.

marginal adj marginal.

marigold n (bot) calendula f, souci m.

marijuana n marijuana f.

marinate vt mariner.

marine adj marin; * n soldat de marine m.

mariner n marin m.

marital adj matrimonial.

maritime adj maritime.

marjoram n marjolaine f.

mark n marque f; signe m; * vt marquer.

marker n marque f; marqueur m.

market n marché m.

marketable adj vendable.

marketing n marketing m.

marketplace n marché m.

market research n étude de marché f.

market value n valeur sur le marché f.

marksman n tireur d'élite m.

marmalade n confiture d'oranges f.

maroon adj marron.

marquee n tente f.

marriage n mariage m.

marriageable adj mariable.

marriage certificate n acte de mariage m.

married adj marié; conjugal.

marrow n moelle f.

marry vi se marier.

marsh n marécage m.

marshal n maréchal m.

marshy adj marécageux.

marten n martre f.

martial adj martial; ~ **law** n loi martiale f.

martyr n martyr m, -e f.

martyrdom n martyre m.

marvel n merveille f; * vi s'émerveiller.

marvellous adj merveilleux; **~ly** adv merveilleusement.

marzipan n massepain m, pâte d'amandes f.

mascara n mascara m.

masculine adj masculin, viril.

mash n bouillie, purée f.

mask n masque m; * vt masquer.

masochist n masochiste mf.

mason n maçon m.

masonry n maçonnerie f.

masquerade n mascarade f.

mass n masse f; messe f; multitude f.

massacre n massacre m; * vt massacrer.

massage n massage m.

masseur n masseur m.

masseuse n masseuse f.

massive adj énorme.

mass media npl média mpl.

mast n mât m.

master n maître m; * vt maîtriser.

masterly adj magistral.

mastermind vt diriger.

masterpiece n chef-d'œuvre m.

mastery n maîtrise f.

masticate vt mastiquer.

mastiff n mastiff m.

mat n tapis m.

match n allumette f; match m; * vt égaler; * vi bien aller ensemble.

matchbox n boîte d'allumettes f.

matchless adj incomparable, sans pareil.

matchmaker n marieur m, -euse f.

mate n camarade mf; * vt accoupler.

material adj, **~ly** adv matériel(lement).

materialism n matérialisme m.

maternal adj maternel.

maternity dress n robe de grossesse f.

maternity hospital n maternité f.

math n maths fpl.

mathematical adj, **~ly** adv mathématique(ment).

mathematician n mathématicien m, -ienne f.

mathematics npl mathématiques fpl.

matinee n matinée f.

mating n accouplement m.

matins npl matines fpl.

matriculate vt immatriculer.

matriculation n immatriculation f.

matrimonial adj matrimonial.

mat(t) adj mat.

matted adj emmêlé.

matter n matière, substance f; sujet m; affaire f; **what is the ~?** que se passe-t-il? **a ~ of fact** un fait; * vi importer.

mattress n matelas m.

mature adj mûr; * vi mûrir.

maturity n maturité f.

maul vt meurtrir.

mausoleum n mausolée m.

mauve adj mauve.

maxim n maxime f.

maximum n maximum m.

may v aux pouvoir; **~ be** peutêtre.

May n mai m.

Mayday n le Premier Mai m.

mayonnaise n mayonnaise f.

mayor n maire m.

mayoress n mairesse f.

maze n labyrinthe m.

me pn moi; me.

meadow n prairie f, pré m.

meagre adj pauvre.

meagreness n pauvreté f.

meal n repas m; farine f.

mealtime n heure du repas f.

mean adj avare, mesquin; moyen; **in the ~time, ~while** pendant ce temps-là; **~s** npl moyens mpl; * vt, vi signifier.

meander vi serpenter.

meaning n sens m, signification f.

meaningful adj significatif.

meaningless adj vide de sens.

meanness n avarice, mesquinerie f.

meantime, meanwhile adv pendant ce temps-là.

measles npl rougeole f.

measure n mesure f; * vt mesurer.

measurement n mesure f.

meat n viande f.

meatball n boulette de viande f.

meaty adj riche.

mechanic n mécanicien m.

mechanical adj, **~ly** adv mécanique(ment).

mechanics npl mécanique f.

mechanism n mécanisme m.

medal n médaille f.

medallion n médaillon m.

medallist n médaillé m, -e f.

meddle vi se mêler des affaires des autres.

meddler n fouineur m, -euse f, indiscret m, -ète f.

media npl média mpl.

median n médiane f.

mediate vi agir en tant que médiateur.

mediation n médiation f.

mediator n médiateur m, -trice f.

medical *adj* médical.

medicate *vt* traiter.

medicated *adj* médical.

medicinal *adj* médicinal.

medicine *n* médecine *f*; médicament *m*.

medieval *adj* médiéval.

mediocre *adj* médiocre.

mediocrity *n* médiocrité *f*.

meditate *vi* méditer.

meditation *n* méditation *f*.

meditative *adj* méditatif.

Mediterranean *adj* méditerranéen.

medium *n* milieu *m*; médium *m*; * *adj* moyen.

medium wave *n* ondes moyennes *fpl*.

medley *n* mélange *m*.

meek *adj* doux; ~ly *adv* doucement.

meekness *n* douceur *f*.

meet *vt* rencontrer; **to ~ with** retrouver; * *vi* se rencontrer; se retrouver.

meeting *n* réunion *f*; congrès *m*.

megaphone *n* mégaphone *m*.

melancholy *n* mélancolie *f*; * *adj* mélancolique.

mellow *adj* mûr; doux; * *vi* mûrir.

mellowness *n* maturité *f*.

melodious *adj* mélodieux; ~ly *adv* mélodieusement.

melody *n* mélodie *f*.

melon *n* melon *m*.

melt *vt* faire fondre; * *vi* fondre.

melting point *n* point de fusion *m*.

member *n* membre *m*.

membership *n* nombre de membres *m*.

membrane *n* membrane *f*.

memento *n* mémento *m*.

memo *n* note de service *f*.

memoir *n* mémoire *m*.

memorable *adj* mémorable.

memorandum *n* mémorandum *m*; note de service *f*.

memorial *n* monument commémoratif, mémorial *m*.

memorize *vt* mémoriser.

memory *n* mémoire *f*; souvenir *m*.

menace *n* menace *f*; * *vt* menacer.

menacing *adj* menaçant.

menagerie *n* ménagerie *f*.

mend *vt* réparer; raccommoder.

mending *n* réparation *f*; raccommodage *m*.

menial *adj* vil.

meningitis *n* méningite *f*.

menopause *n* ménopause *f*.

menstruation *n* menstruation *f*.

mental *adj* mental.

mentality *n* mentalité *f*.

mentally *adv* mentalement.

mention *n* mention *f*; * *vt* mentionner.

mentor *n* mentor *m*.

menu *n* menu *m*.

mercantile *adj* commercial.

mercenary *adj*, *n* mercenaire *m*.

merchandise *n* marchandise *f*.

merchant *n* négociant *m*, -e *f*.

merchantman *n* navire marchand *m*.

merchant marine *n* marine marchande *f*.

merciful *adj* miséricordieux.

merciless *adj*, ~ly *adv* impitoyable(ment).

mercury *n* mercure *m*.

mercy *n* pitié *f*.

mere *adj*, ~ly *adv* simple(ment).

merge vt, vi fusionner.

merger n fusion f.

meridian n méridien m.

meringue n meringue f.

merit n mérite m; * vt mériter.

meritorious adj méritoire.

mermaid n sirène f.

merrily adv joyeusement.

merriment n divertissement m; réjouissance f.

merry adj joyeux.

merry-go-round n manège m.

mesh n maille f.

mesmerize vt hypnotiser.

mess n désordre m; confusion f; (mil) mess m; **to ~ up** vt mettre en désordre.

message n message m.

messenger n messager m, -ère f.

metabolism n métabolisme m.

metal n métal m.

metallic adj métallique.

metallurgy n métallurgie f.

metamorphosis n métamorphose f.

metaphor n métaphore f.

metaphoric(al) adj métaphorique.

metaphysical adj métaphysique.

metaphysics npl métaphysique f.

mete (out) vt distribuer.

meteor n météore m.

meteorological adj météorologique.

meteorology n météorologie f.

meter n compteur m; mètre m.

method n méthode f.

methodical adj, **~ly** adv méthodique(ment).

Methodist n méthodiste mf.

metric adj métrique.

metropolis n métropole f.

metropolitan adj métropolitain.

mettle n courage m.

mettlesome adj courageux.

mew vi miauler.

mezzanine n mezzanine f.

microbe n microbe m.

microphone n microphone m.

microchip n microprocesseur m, puce f.

microscope n microscope m.

microscopic adj microscopique.

microwave n four à microondes m.

mid adj demi; mi-.

midday n midi m.

middle adj moyen; du milieu; * n milieu m.

middle name n deuxième prénom m.

middleweight n poids moyen m.

middling adj moyen, passable.

midge n moucheron m.

midget n nain m, -e f.

midnight n minuit m.

midriff n diaphragme m; estomac m.

midst n milieu m.

midsummer n milieu de l'été m.

midway adv à mi-chemin.

midwife n sage-femme f.

midwifery n obstétrique f.

might n force f.

mighty adj fort, puissant.

migraine n migraine f.

migrate vi émigrer.

migration n émigration f.

migratory adj migratoire.

mike n micro m.

mild adj doux; modéré **~ly** adv doucement.

mildew n moisissure f; mildiou m.

mildness n douceur f.

mile n mille m.

mileage n kilométrage m.

milieu n milieu m.

militant adj militant.

military adj militaire.

militate vi militer.

militia n milice f.

milk n lait m; * vt traire; exploiter.

milkshake n milk-shake m.

milky adj laiteux; **M~ Way** n Voie lactée f.

mill n moulin m; * vt moudre.

millennium n millénaire m.

miller n meunier m.

millet n (bot) millet m.

milligram n milligramme m.

milliliter n millilitre m.

millimeter n millimètre m.

milliner n chapelier m, -ière f.

millinery n chapellerie f.

million n million m.

millionaire n millionaire mf.

millionth adj, n millionième m.

millstone n meule f.

mime n mime m.

mimic vt mimer.

mimicry n mimique f.

mince vt hacher.

mind n esprit m; * vt prendre soin de; * vi: **do you ~?** est-ce que cela vous dérange?

minded adj disposé.

mindful adj conscient; attentif.

mindless adj insouciant.

mine pn le mien, la mienne, les miens, les miennes; à moi; * n mine f; * vi exploiter la mine.

minefield n champ de mines m.

miner n mineur m.

mineral adj, n minéral m.

mineralogy n minéralogie f.

mineral water n eau minérale f.

minesweeper n dragueur de mines m.

mingle vt mêler.

miniature n miniature f.

minimal adj minime.

minimize vt minimiser.

minimum n minimum m.

mining n exploitation minière f.

minion n larbin m; favorit(te) m(f).

minister n ministre m; * vt servir.

ministerial adj ministériel.

ministry n ministère m.

mink n vison m.

minnow n vairon m.

minor adj mineur m, -e f.

minority n minorité f.

minstrel n ménestrel m.

mint n (bot) menthe f; hôtel de la Monnaie m; * vt frapper.

minus adv moins.

minute adj minuscule; **~ly** adv minutieusement.

minute n minute f.

miracle n miracle m.

miraculous adj miraculeux.

mirage n mirage m.

mire n bourbe f.

mirky adj trouble; ténébreux.

mirror n miroir m.

mirth n allégresse f.

mirthful adj joyeux.

misadventure n mésaventure f.

misanthropist n misanthrope mf.

misapply vt mal appliquer.

misapprehension n méprise f.

misbehave vi se conduire mal.

misbehaviour n mauvaise conduite f.

miscalculate vt mal calculer.

miscarriage n fausse couche f.

miscarry vi faire une fausse couche; échouer.

miscellaneous adj divers, varié.

miscellany n mélange, assortiment m.

mischief n mal, tort m.

mischievous adj mauvais; espiègle.

misconception n méprise f.

misconduct n mauvaise conduite f.

misconstrue vt mal interpréter.

miscount vt mal compter.

miscreant n scélérat m.

misdeed n méfait m.

misdemeanour n délit m.

misdirect vt mal diriger.

miser n avare mf.

miserable adj malheureux.

miserly adj mesquin, avare.

misery n malheur m; misère f.

misfit n inadapté m, -e f.

misfortune n infortune f.

misgiving n doute m.

misgovern vt mal gouverner.

misguided adj malencontreux; malavisé.

mishandle vt mal traiter; mal s'y prendre avec.

mishap n mésaventure f.

misinform vt mal renseigner.

misinterpret vt mal interpréter.

misjudge vt méjuger.

mislay vt égarer.

mislead vt induire en erreur.

mismanage vt mal administrer.

mismanagement n mauvaise administration f.

misnomer n nom inapproprié m.

misogynist n misogyne mf.

misplace vt égarer.

misprint vt mal imprimer; * n coquille f.

misrepresent vt mal représenter.

Miss n Mlle, Mademoiselle f.

miss vt rater; s'ennuyer de.

missal n missel m.

misshape n déformation f.

missile n missile m.

missing adj perdu; absent.

mission n mission f.

missionary n missionnaire mf.

misspent adj gaspillé.

mist n brouillard m.

mistake vt confondre; * vi se tromper; **to be mistaken** se tromper; * n méprise f; erreur f.

Mister n Monsieur m.

mistletoe n (bot) gui m.

mistress n maîtresse f.

mistrust vt se méfier de; * n méfiance f.

mistrustful adj méfiant.

misty adj brumeux.

misunderstand vt mal comprendre.

misunderstanding n malentendu m.

misuse vt faire un mauvais usage de; abuser de.

miter n mitre f.

mitigate vt atténuer.

mitigation n atténuation f.

mittens npl moufles fpl.

mix vt mélanger.

mixed adj mélangé; mixte.

mixed-up adj confus.

mixer n mixeur m.

mixture n mélange m.

mix-up n confusion f.

moan n gémissement m; * vi gémir; se plaindre.

moat n fossé m.

mob n foule f; masse f.

mobile adj mobile.

mobile home n caravane f.

mobility n mobilité f.

mobilize vt (mil) mobiliser.

moccasin n mocassin m.

mock vt se moquer de.

mockery n moquerie f.

mode n mode m.

model n modèle m; * vt modeler.

moderate adj, ~ly adv modéré(ment); * vt modérer.

moderation n modération f.

modern adj moderne.

modernize vt moderniser.

modest adj, ~ly adv modeste(ment).

modesty n modestie f.

modicum n minimum m.

modification n modification f.

modify vt modifier.

modulate vt moduler.

modulation n (mus) modulation f.

module n module m.

mogul n magnat m.

mohair n mohair m.

moist adj humide.

moisten vt humidifier.

moisture n humidité f.

molar n molaire f.

molasses npl mélasse f.

mole n taupe f.

molecule n molécule f.

molehill n taupinière f.

molest vt importuner.

mollify vt apaiser.

mollusk n mollusque m.

mollycoddle vt dorloter.

molten adj fondu.

mom n maman f.

moment n moment m.

momentarily adv momentanément.

momentary adj momentané.

momentous adj capital.

momentum n vitesse f; élan m.

mommy n maman f.

monarch n monarque m.

monarchy n monarchie f.

monastery n monastère m.

monastic adj monastique.

Monday n lundi m.

monetary adj monétaire.

money n argent m; pièce de monnaie f.

money order n mandat m.

mongol n (med) mongolien m, -ienne f.

mongrel adj, n bâtard m, -e f.

monitor n moniteur m, -trice f.

monk n moine m.

monkey n singe m.

monochrome adj monochrome.

monocle n monocle m.

monologue n monologue m.

monopolize vt monopoliser.

monopoly n monopole m.

monosyllable n monosyllabe f.

monotonous adj monotone.

monotony n monotonie f.

monsoon n mousson f.

monster n monstre m.

monstrosity n monstruosité f.

monstrous adj monstrueux; ~ly adv monstrueusement.

montage n montage m.

month n mois m.

monthly adj mensuel; adv mensuellement.

monument n monument m.

monumental adj monumental.

moo vi meugler.

mood n humeur f.

moodiness n mauvaise humeur f.

moody adj de mauvaise humeur; lunatique.

moon n lune f.

moonbeams npl rayons de lune mpl.

moonlight n clair de lune m.

moor n lande f; * vt (mar) amarrer.

moorland n lande f.

moose n élan m.

mop n lavette f; * vt frotter.

mope vi être triste.

moped n vélomoteur m.

moral adj, ~ly adv moral(ement); ~s npl moralité f.

morale n moral m.

moralist n moraliste mf.

morality n moralité f.

moralize vt, vi moraliser.

morass n marais m.

morbid adj morbide.

more adj, adv plus; **never** ~ plus jamais; **once** ~ encore une fois; ~ **and** ~ de plus en plus; **so much the** ~ d'autant plus.

moreover adv de plus, en outre.

morgue n morgue f.

morning n matin m; **good** ~ bonjour.

moron n imbécile mf.

morose adj morose.

morphine n morphine f.

morse n morse m.

morsel n bouchée f; morceau m.

mortal adj, ~ly adv mortel(lement); * n mortel m, -elle f.

mortality n mortalité f.

mortar n mortier m.

mortgage n hypothèque f; * vt hypothéquer.

mortgage company n banque de prêts hypothécaires f.

mortgager n débiteur (-trice) hypothécaire m(f).

mortification n mortification f.

mortify vt mortifier.

mortuary n morgue f.

mosaic n mosaïque f.

mosque n mosquée f.

mosquito n moustique m.

moss n (bot) mousse f.

mossy adj moussu.

most adj, pn la plupart de; * adv extrêmement; **at** ~ au maximum; ~ly adv surtout, essentiellement.

motel n motel m.

moth n papillon de nuit m.

mothball n boule de naphtaline f.

mother n mère f.

motherhood n maternité f.

mother-in-law n belle-mère f.

motherless adj sans mère.

motherly adj maternel.

mother-of-pearl n nacre f.

mother-to-be n future maman f.

mother tongue n langue maternelle f.

motif n motif m.

motion n mouvement m.

motionless adj immobile.

motion picture n film m.

motivated adj motivé.

motive n motif m.

motley adj bigarré.

motor n moteur m.

motorbike n moto f.

motorboat n canot à moteur m.

motorcycle n motocyclette f.

motor vehicle n automobile f.

mottled adj bigarré.

motto n devise f.

mould n moule m; * vt mouler.

moulder vi s'effriter.

mouldy adj moisi.

moult vi muer.

mound n monticule m.

mount n mont m; * vt gravir.

mountain n montagne f.

mountaineer n alpiniste mf.

mountaineering n alpinisme m.

mountainous adj montagneux.

mourn vt pleurer.

mourner n personne en deuil f.

mournful adj, ~ly adv triste(ment).

mourning n deuil m.

mouse n (pl mice) souris f.

mousse n mousse f.

moustache n moustache f.

mouth n bouche f; embouchure f.

mouthful n bouchée f.

mouth organ n harmonica m.

mouthpiece n bec m; microphone m.

mouthwash n eau dentifrice f.

mouthwatering adj appétissant.

movable adj mobile.

move vt déplacer; toucher, émouvoir; * vi bouger; * n mouvement m.

movement n mouvement m.

movie n film m.

movie camera n caméra f.

moving adj touchant, émouvant.

mow vt tondre.

mower n tondeuse f.

Mrs n Mme, Madame f.

much adj, pn beaucoup; adv beaucoup, très.

muck n saleté f.

mucous adj muqueux.

mucus n mucus m.

mud n boue f.

muddle vt confondre; embrouiller; * n confusion f; désordre m.

muddy adj boueux.

mudguard n garde-boue m invar.

muffle vt assourdir.

mug n tasse f.

muggy adj lourd.

mulberry n mûre f; ~ tree mûrier m.

mule n mulet m; mule f.

mull vt méditer.

multifarious adj divers.

multiple adj multiple.

multiplication n multiplication f; ~ table table de multiplication f.

multiply vt multiplier.

multitude n multitude f.

mumble vt, vi grommeler.

mummy n momie f.

mumps npl oreillons mpl.

munch vt mâcher.

mundane adj banal.

municipal adj municipal.

municipality n municipalité f.

munificence n munificence f.

munitions npl munitions fpl.

mural n mural m.

murder n assassinat, meurtre m; homicide volontaire m; * vt assassiner.

murderer n assassin, meurtrier m.

murderess n meurtrière f.

murderous adj meurtrier.
murky adj obscur.
murmur n murmure m; * vt, vi murmurer.
muscle n muscle m.
muscular adj musculaire.
muse vi méditer, rêver.
museum n musée m.
mushroom n (bot) champignon m.
music n musique f.
musical adj musical; mélodieux.
musician n musicien m, -ienne f.
musk n musc m.
muslin n mousseline f.
mussel n moule f.
must v aux devoir.
mustard n moutarde f.
muster vt rassembler.
musty adj moisi.
mute adj muet, silencieux.
muted adj sourd.
mutilate vt mutiler.
mutilation n mutilation f.

mutiny n mutinerie f; vi se mutiner, se révolter.
mutter vt, vi grommeler, marmonner; * n grommellement m.
mutton n mouton m.
mutual adj, ~ly adv mutuel(lement), réciproque(ment).
muzzle n muselière f; museau m; * vt museler.
my pn mon, ma, mes.
myriad n myriade f.
myrrh n myrrhe f.
myrtle n myrte m.
myself pn moi-même.
mysterious adj mystérieux; ~ly adv mystérieusement.
mystery n mystère m.
mystic(al) adj mystique.
mystify vt mystifier; laisser perplexe.
mystique n mystique f.
myth n mythe m.
mythology n mythologie f.

N

nab vt attraper.
nag n bourrin m; * vt harceler.
nagging adj persistant; * npl harcèlement m.
nail n ongle m; clou m; * vt clouer.
nailbrush n brosse à ongles f.
nailfile n lime à ongles f.
nail polish n vernis à ongles m.
nail scissors npl ciseaux à ongles mpl.
naïve adj naïf.
naked adj nu; dénudé; pur, simple.
name n nom m; réputation f; * vt nommer; mentionner.

nameless adj anonyme.
namely adv à savoir.
namesake n homonyme m.
nanny n nourrice f.
nap n sieste f, somme m.
napalm n napalm m.
nape n nuque f.
napkin n serviette f.
narcissus n (bot) narcisse m.
narcotic adj, n narcotique m.
narrate vt narrer, raconter.
narrative adj narratif; * n narration f.

narrow adj, **~ly** adv étroit(ement); * vt resserrer; limiter.

narrow-minded adj à l'esprit étroit.

nasal adj nasal.

nasty adj méchant; mauvais; sale.

natal adj natal.

nation n nation f.

national adj, **~ly** adv national(ement).

nationalism n nationalisme m.

nationalist adj, n nationaliste mf.

nationality n nationalité f.

nationalize vt nationaliser.

nationwide adj au niveau national.

native adj natal; * n autochtone mf.

native language n langue maternelle f.

Nativity n Nativité f.

natural adj, **~ly** adv naturel(lement).

natural gas n gaz naturel m.

naturalist n naturaliste m.

naturalize vt naturaliser.

nature n nature f; sorte f.

naught n zéro m.

naughty adj méchant.

nausea n nausée, envie de vomir f.

nauseate vt donner des nausées à.

nauseous adj écœurant.

nautic(al), naval adj nautique.

nave n nef (d'église) f.

navel n nombril m.

navigate vi naviguer.

navigation n navigation f.

navy n marine f.

Nazi n Nazi m, -e f.

near prep près de; * adv près; à côté; * adj proche.

nearby adj proche.

nearly adv presque.

near-sighted adj myope.

neat adj soigné; net, propre; **~ly** adv proprement; élégamment.

nebulous adj nébuleux.

necessarily adv nécessairement.

necessary adj nécessaire.

necessitate vt nécessiter.

necessity n nécessité f.

neck n cou m; * vi se bécoter.

necklace n collier m.

necktie n cravate f.

nectar n nectar m.

née adj: **~** Brown née Brown.

need n besoin m; pauvreté f; * vt avoir besoin de, nécessiter.

needle n aiguille f.

needless adj superflu, inutile.

needlework n couture f.

needy adj nécessiteux, pauvre.

negation n négation f.

negative adj négatif; **~ly** adv négativement; * n négative f; négation f; négatif m.

neglect vt négliger; * n négligence f.

negligee n négligé, déshabillé m.

negligence n négligence f; manque de soin m.

negligent adj négligent; **~ly** adv négligemment.

negligible adj négligeable.

negotiate vt, vi négocier.

negotiation n négociation f.

Negress n Noire f.

Negro adj noir; * n Noire m.

neigh vi hennir; * n hennissement m.

neighbour n voisin m, -e f; * vt être voisin de.

neighbourhood n voisinage m.

neighbouring adj voisin.

neighbourly adj sociable.

neither conj ni; * pn aucun, ni l'un ni l'autre.

neon n néon m.

neon light n lumière au néon f.

nephew n neveu m.

nepotism n népotisme m.

nerve n nerf m; courage m; toupet m.

nerve-racking adj exaspérant.

nervous adj nerveux.

nervous breakdown n dépression nerveuse f.

nest n nid m; nichée f.

nest egg n (fig) économies fpl.

nestle vi, vt se blottir.

net n filet m.

netball n netball m.

net curtain n voile m.

netting n filet m.

nettle n ortie f.

network n réseau f.

neurosis n névrose f.

neurotic adj, n névrosé m, -e f.

neuter adj (gr) neutre.

neutral adj neutre.

neutrality n neutralité f.

neutralize vt neutraliser.

neutron n neutron m.

neutron bomb n bombe à neutrons f.

never adv jamais; **~ mind** ça ne fait rien.

never-ending adj interminable.

nevertheless adv cependant, néanmoins.

new adj neuf; nouveau; dernier; **~ly** adv nouvellement.

newborn adj nouveau-né, f nouveau-née.

newcomer n nouveau venu m, nouvelle venue f.

new-fangled adj moderne.

news npl nouvelles, informations fpl.

news agency n agence de presse f.

newscaster n présentateur m, -trice f.

newsdealer n marchand(e) de journaux m(f).

news flash n flash d'information m.

newsletter n bulletin m.

newspaper n journal m.

newsreel n actualités fpl.

New Year n Nouvel An m; **~'s Day** n Jour du Nouvel An m; **~'s Eve** Saint-Sylvestre f.

next adj prochain; **the ~ day** le jour suivant; * adv ensuite, après.

nib n pointe f; plume f.

nibble vt mordiller.

nice adj gentil, f gentille; agréable; joli; **~ly** adv gentiment; bien.

nice-looking adj beau, f belle.

niche n niche f.

nick n entaille f; * vt (sl) faucher.

nickel n nickel m; pièce de cinq cents (U.S.) f.

nickname n surnom m; * vt surnommer.

nicotine n nicotine f.

niece n nièce f.

niggling adj insignifiant.

night n nuit f; **by ~** de nuit; **good ~** bonne nuit.

nightclub n boîte de nuit f.

nightfall n tombée de la nuit f.

nightingale n rossignol m.

nightly adv tous les soirs; toutes les nuits; * adj nocturne.

nightmare n cauchemar m.

night school n cours du soir mpl.

night shift n équipe de nuit f.

night time n nuit f.

nihilist n nihiliste mf.

nimble adj léger; agile, souple.

nine adj, n neuf m.

nineteen adj, n dix-neuf m.

nineteenth adj, n dix-neuvième mf.

ninetieth adj, n quatre-vingt-dixième mf.

ninety adj, n quatre-vingt-dix m.

ninth adj, n neuvième mf.

nip vt pincer; mordre.

nipple n mamelon m; tétine f.

nit n lente f.

nitrogen n nitrogène m.

no adv non; * adj aucun; pas de.

nobility n noblesse f.

noble adj noble; * n noble mf.

nobleman n noble m.

nobody pn personne.

nocturnal adj nocturne.

nod n signe de tête; * vi faire un signe de la tête; somnoler.

noise n bruit m.

noisily adv bruyamment.

noisiness n bruit, tapage m.

noisy adj bruyant.

nominal adj, ~ly adv nominal (ement).

nominate vt nommer.

nomination n nomination f.

nominative n (gr) nominatif m.

nominee n candidat m, -e f.

non-alcoholic adj non alcoolisé.

non-aligned adj non-aligné.

nonchalant adj nonchalant.

non-committal adj réservé.

nonconformist n non-conformiste mf.

nondescript adj quelconque.

none pn aucun; personne.

nonentity n nullité f.

nonetheless adv cependant.

nonexistent adj inexistant.

nonfiction n ouvrages non romanesques mpl.

nonplussed adj perplexe.

nonsense n absurdité f.

nonsensical adj absurde.

nonsmoker n non-fumeur m.

nonstick adj anti-adhérent.

nonstop adj direct; * adv sans s'arrêter.

noodles npl nouilles fpl.

noon n midi m.

noose n nœud coulant m.

nor conj ni.

normal adj normal.

north n nord m; * adj du nord.

North America n Amérique du Nord f.

northeast n nord-est m.

northerly, northern adj du nord.

North Pole n pôle Nord m.

northward(s) adv vers le nord.

northwest n nord-ouest m.

nose n nez m.

nosebleed n saignement de nez m.

nosedive n piqué m.

nostalgia n nostalgie f.

nostril n narine f.

not adv pas; non.

notable adj notable.

notably adv notamment.

notary n notaire m.

notch n cran m, dent f; * vt denteler.

note n note f; billet m; mot m; marque f; * vt noter, marquer; remarquer.

notebook n carnet m.

noted adj célèbre, connu.

notepad n bloc-notes m.

notepaper n papier à lettres m.

nothing n rien m; good for ~ bon à rien.

notice n notice f; avis m; * vt remarquer.

noticeable adj visible.

notification n notification f.

notify vt notifier.

notion n notion f; opinion f; idée f.

notoriety n notoriété f.

notorious adj notoire; ~ly adv notoirement.

notwithstanding conj quoique.

nougat n nougat m.

nought n zéro m.

noun n (gr) nom, substantif m.

nourish vt nourrir, alimenter.

nourishing adj nourrissant.

nourishment n nourriture f, aliments mpl.

novel n roman m.

novelist n romancier m, -ière f.

novelty n nouveauté f.

November n novembre m.

novice n novice mf.

now adv maintenant; ~ and then de temps en temps.

nowadays adv de nos jours, à l'heure actuelle.

nowhere adv nulle part.

noxious adj nocif.

nozzle n douille f.

nuance n nuance f.

nuclear adj nucléaire.

nucleus n noyau m.

nude adj nu.

nudge vt donner un coup de coude à.

nudist n nudiste mf.

nudity n nudité f.

nuisance n ennui m; gêne f.

nuke n (col) bombe atomique f; * vt atomiser.

null adj nul.

nullify vt annuler; invalider.

numb adj engourdi; * vt engourdir.

number n numéro, nombre m; quantité f; * vt numéroter; compter.

numberplate n plaque d'immatriculation f.

numbness n engourdissement m.

numeral n chiffre m.

numerical adj numérique.

numerous adj nombreux.

nun n religieuse f.

nunnery n couvent m.

nuptial adj nuptial; ~s npl noces fpl.

nurse n infirmière f; * vt soigner; ménager.

nursery n crèche f; chambre d'enfant f.

nursery rhyme n comptine f.

nursery school n (école) maternelle f.

nursing home n maison de repos f.

nurture vt élever.

nut n noix f.

nutcrackers npl casse-noix m invar.

nutmeg n noix de muscade f.

nutritious adj nutritif.

nut shell n coquille de noix f.

nylon n nylon m; * adj en nylon.

O

oak n chêne m.

oar n rame f.

oasis n oasis f.

oat n avoine f.

oath n serment m.

oatmeal n flocons d'avoine mpl.

oats npl avoine f.

obedience n obéissance f.

obedient adj obéissant; **~ly** adv avec obéissance.

obese adj obèse.

obesity n obésité f.

obey vt obéir à.

obituary n nécrologie f.

object n objet m; * vt objecter.

objection n objection f.

objectionable adj désagréable.

objective adj, n objectif m.

obligation n obligation f.

obligatory adj obligatoire.

oblige vt obliger; rendre service à.

obliging adj obligeant.

oblique adj oblique; indirect; **~ly** adv obliquement.

obliterate vt effacer.

oblivion n oubli m.

oblivious adj oublieux.

oblong adj oblong.

obnoxious adj odieux.

oboe n hautbois m.

obscene adj obscène.

obscenity n obscénité f.

obscure adj obscur; **~ly** adv obscurément; * vt obscurcir.

obscurity n obscurité f.

observance n observation f; observance f.

observant adj observateur; respectueux.

observation n observation f.

observatory n observatoire m.

observe vt observer.

observer n observateur m, -trice f.

observingly adv attentivement.

obsess vt obséder.

obsessive adj obsédant.

obsolete adj désuet.

obstacle n obstacle m.

obstinate adj obstiné; **~ly** adv obstinément.

obstruct vt obstruer; entraver.

obstruction n obstruction f; encombrement m.

obtain vt obtenir.

obtainable adj disponible.

obtrusive adj importun.

obtuse adj obtus.

obvious adj évident; **~ly** adv évidemment.

occasion n occasion f; * vt occasionner, causer.

occasional adj occasionnel; **~ly** adv occasionnellement.

occupant, occupier n occupant m, -e f; locataire mf.

occupation n occupation f; emploi m.

occupy vt occuper.

occur vi se produire, arriver.

occurrence n incident m.

ocean n océan m.

ocean-going adj de haute mer.

oceanic adj océanique.

ocher n ocre f.

octave n octave f.

October n octobre m.

octopus n poulpe m.

odd adj impair; étrange; quelconque; **~ly** adv étrangement.

oddity n singularité, particularité f.

odd jobs npl petits travaux mpl.

oddness n étrangeté f; singularité f.

odds npl chances fpl.

odious adj odieux.

odometer n compteur m invar.

odor n odeur f; parfum m.

odorous adj odorant.

of prep de; à.

off adj éteint; fermé; annulé; en congé; **~!** excl du vent!

offend vt offenser, blesser; choquer; * vi pécher.

offender n délinquant m, -e f.

offense n offense f; injure f.

offensive adj offensant; injurieux; **~ly** adv d'une manière offensante.

offer vt offrir; * n offre f.

offering n offrande f; offre f.

offhand adj désinvolte; * adv soudainement.

office n bureau m; poste m, fonctions fpl; service m.

office automation n bureautique f.

office building n immeuble de bureaux m.

office hours npl heures de bureau fpl.

officer n officier m; fonctionnaire mf.

office worker n employé(e) de bureau m(f).

official adj, **~ly** adv officiel(lement); * n employé m, -e f.

officiate vi officier.

officious adj officieux; **~ly** adv officieusement.

off-line adj, adv hors ligne.

off-peak adj de basse saison.

off-season adj, adv hors-saison.

offset vt compenser; décaler.

offshoot n ramification f.

offshore adj côtier.

offside adj hors jeu.

offspring n progéniture f; descendance f.

offstage adv en coulisses.

off-the-rack adj prêt-à-porter.

ogle vt lorgner.

oil n huile f; * vt huiler.

oilcan n burette d'huile f; bidon d'huile m.

oilfield n gisement pétrolifère m.

oil filter n filtre à huile m.

oil painting n peinture à l'huile f.

oil rig n derrick m.

oil tanker n pétrolier m.

oil well n puits pétrolifère m.

oily adj huileux; gras.

ointment n onguent m.

O.K., okay excl O.K., d'accord; * adj bien; * vt approuver.

old adj vieux, f vieille.

old age n vieillesse f.

old-fashioned adj démodé.

olive n olivier m; olive f.

olive oil n huile d'olive f.

omelet(te) n omelette f.

omen n augure, présage m.

ominous adj menaçant.

omission n omission f; négligence f.

omit vt omettre.

omnipotence n omnipotence f.

omnipotent adj omnipotent, tout-puissant.

on prep sur, dessus; en; pour; * adj allumé, branché; ouvert; de service.

once adv une fois; **at ~** tout de suite; **all at ~** tout d'un coup; **~ more** encore une fois.

oncoming adj qui arrive.

one adj un, une; **~ by ~** un par un.

one-day excursion n billet d'aller-retour valable une journée m.

one-man adj individuel.

onerous adj lourd; onéreux.

oneself pn soi-même.

one-sided adj partial.

one-to-one adj face à face.

ongoing adj continu; en cours.

onion n oignon m.

on-line adj, adv en ligne.

onlooker n spectateur m, -trice f.

only adj seul, unique; * adv seulement.

onset, onslaught n début m; attaque f.

onus n responsabilité f.

onward(s) adv en avant.

ooze vi suinter.

opaque adj opaque.

open adj ouvert; public; déclaré; sincère, franc; **~ly** adv ouvertement; * vt ouvrir; * vi s'ouvrir; commencer; **to ~ on to** donner lieu à; **to ~ up** vt ouvrir; vi s'ouvrir.

opening n ouverture f; (com) débouché m; inauguration f; commencement m.

open-minded adj aux idées larges.

openness n clarté f; franchise, sincérité f.

opera n opéra m.

opera house n théâtre de l'opéra m.

operate vi fonctionner; opérer.

operation n fonctionnement m; opération f.

operational adj opérationnel.

operative adj actif; en vigueur.

operator n opérateur m, -trice f; téléphoniste mf.

ophthalmic adj ophtalmique.

opine vt être d'avis (que).

opinion n opinion f; jugement m.

opinionated adj entêté.

opinion poll n sondage m.

opponent n opposant m, -e f; adversaire mf.

opportune adj opportun.

opportunist n opportuniste mf.

opportunity n occasion f.

oppose vt s'opposer à.

opposing adj opposé.

opposite adj opposé; contraire; * adv en face; prep en face de; * n contraire m.

opposition n opposition f; résistance f.

oppress vt opprimer.

oppression n oppression f.

oppressive adj oppressif.

oppressor n oppresseur m.

optic(al) adj optique; **~s** npl optique f.

optician n opticien m, -ienne f.

optimist n optimiste mf.

optimistic adj optimiste.

optimum adj optimum.

option n option f.

optional adj optionnel; facultatif.

opulent adj opulent.

or conj ou.

oracle n oracle m.

oral adj oral, verbal; **~ly** adv oralement.

orange n orange f.

orator n orateur m, -trice f.

orbit n orbite f.

orchard n verger m.

orchestra n orchestre m.

orchestral adj orchestral.

orchid n orchidée f.

ordain vt ordonner.

ordeal n épreuve f.

order n ordre m; commande f; mandat m; classe f; * vt ordonner; commander; mettre en ordre.

order form n bon de commande m.

orderly adj ordonné; réglé.

ordinarily adv ordinairement.

ordinary adj ordinaire.

ordination n ordination f.

ordnance n artillerie f.

ore n minerai m.

organ n organe m; orgue m.

organic(al) adj organique.

organism n organisme m.

organist n organiste mf.

organization n organisation f.

organize vt organiser.

orgasm n orgasme m.

orgy n orgie f.

oriental adj oriental.

orifice n orifice m.

origin n origine f.

original adj original; originel; **~ly** adv à l'origine; originalement.

originality n originalité f.

originate vi provenir (de); être originaire (de).

ornament n ornement m; * vt ornementer, décorer.

ornamental adj ornemental.

ornate adj ornementé.

orphan adj, n orphelin m, -e f.

orphanage n orphelinat m.

orthodox adj orthodoxe.

orthodoxy n orthodoxie f.

orthography n orthographe f.

orthopaedic adj orthopédique.

oscillate vi osciller.

osprey n balbuzard pêcheur m.

ostensibly adv selon les apparences.

ostentatious adj ostentatoire.

osteopath n ostéopathe m.

ostracize vt frapper d'ostracisme.

ostrich n autruche f.

other pn autre.

otherwise adv autrement.

otter n loutre f.

ouch excl aïe!

ought v aux devoir; falloir.

ounce n once f.

our pn notre, pl nos.

ours pn le nôtre, la nôtre, les nôtres; à nous.

ourselves pn pl nous-mêmes.

oust vt évincer; déposséder.

out adv dehors; éteint.

outback n intérieur m.

outboard adj: **~ motor** (moteur) hors-bord m.

outbreak n éruption f; explosion f.

outburst n explosion f.

outcast n paria m.

outcome n résultat m.

outcry n protestations fpl.

outdated adj démodé; périmé.

outdo vt surpasser.

outdoor adj de plein air, **~s** adv à l'extérieur.

outer adj extérieur.

outermost adj extrême; le plus à l'extérieur.

outer space n espace m.

outfit n tenue f; équipement m.

outfitter n confectionneur m, -euse f.

outgoing adj extroverti; sortant.

outgrow vt devenir plus grand que.

outhouse n dépendances fpl.

outing n excursion f.

outlandish adj bizarre.

outlaw n hors-la-loi m; * vt proscrire.

outlay n dépenses fpl, frais mpl.

outlet n sortie f; débouché m.

outline n contour m; grandes lignes fpl.

outlive vt survivre à.

outlook n perspective f.

outlying adj distant, éloigné.

outmoded adj démodé.

outnumber vt être plus nombreux que.

out-of-date adj périmé; démodé.

outpatient n patient(e) en consultation externe m(f).

outpost n avant-poste m.

output n rendement m, sortie f.

outrage n outrage m; * vt outrager.

outrageous adj outrageant; atroce; ~ly adv outrageusement; atrocement.

outright adv absolument, complètement; * adj absolu, complet.

outrun vt gagner de vitesse, distancer.

outset n commencement m.

outshine vt éclipser.

outside n surface f; extérieur m;

apparence f; * adv dehors; * prep en dehors de.

outsider n étranger m, -ère f.

outsize adj grande taille.

outskirts npl périphérie f, alentours mpl.

outspoken adj franc.

outstanding adj exceptionnel; en suspens.

outstretch vi s'étendre.

outstrip vt devancer; surpasser.

out-tray n courrier au départ m.

outward adj extérieur; vers l'extérieur; d'aller; ~ly adv à l'extérieur, extérieurement.

outweigh vt peser plus lourd que; l'emporter sur.

outwit vt être plus spirituel que.

oval n, adj ovale m.

ovary n ovaire m.

oven n four m.

ovenproof adj allant au four.

over prep sur, dessus; plus de; pendant; **all** ~ de tous côtés; * adj fini; en trop, en plus; ~ **again** à nouveau; ~ **and** ~ de nombreuses fois.

overall adj total; * adv dans l'ensemble; ~**s** npl salopette f.

overawe vt impressionner.

overbalance vi perdre l'équilibre.

overbearing adj despotique.

overboard adv (mar) par-dessus bord.

overbook vt surréserver.

overcast adj couvert.

overcharge vt surcharger; faire payer un prix excessif à.

overcoat n pardessus m.

overcome vt vaincre; surmonter.

overconfident adj trop confiant.

overcrowded adj bondé; surpeuplé.

overdo vi exagérer.

overdose n overdose f.

overdraft n découvert m.

overdrawn adj à découvert.

overdress vi s'habiller trop élégamment.

overdue adj en retard; arriéré.

overeat vi trop manger.

overestimate vt surestimer.

overflow vt déborder de; * vi déborder; * n inondation f; surplus m.

overgrown adj envahi.

overgrowth n végétation envahissante f.

overhang vt surplomber.

overhaul vt réviser; * n révision f.

overhead adv en l'air, au-dessus.

overhear vt entendre par hasard.

overjoyed adj fou de joie.

overkill n exagération f.

overland adj, adv par voie de terre.

overlap vi se chevaucher.

overleaf adv au dos.

overload vt surcharger.

overlook vt dominer; donner sur; oublier; laisser passer, tolérer; négliger.

overnight adv pendant la nuit; * adj de nuit.

overpass n pont surélevé m.

overpower vt dominer, écraser.

overpowering adj écrasant.

overrate vt surévaluer.

override vt outrepasser.

overriding adj prédominant.

overrule vt rejeter; annuler.

overrun vt envahir; infester; dépasser.

overseas adv à l'étranger; outremer; * adj étranger.

oversee vt inspecter, surveiller.

overseer n contremaître m.

overshadow vt éclipser.

overshoot vt dépasser.

oversight n oubli m; erreur f.

oversleep vi se réveiller en retard.

overspill n excédent de population m.

overstate vi exagérer.

overstep vt dépasser.

overt adj ouvert; public; ~ly adv ouvertement.

overtake vt doubler.

overthrow vt renverser; détruire; * n renversement m; ruine, déroute f.

overtime n heures supplémentaires fpl.

overtone n harmonique mf; note f.

overture n ouverture f.

overturn vt renverser.

overweight adj trop lourd.

overwhelm vt écraser; submerger.

overwhelming adj écrasant; irrésistible.

overwork vi se surmener, trop travailler.

owe vt devoir; être redevable de.

owing adj dû; ~ to en raison de.

owl n chouette f.

own adj propre; my ~ mon, ma, mes propre(s); * vt posséder; to ~ up vi confesser.

owner n propriétaire mf.

ownership n possession f.

ox n bœuf m; **~en** pl bœufs mpl.

oxidize vt oxyder.
oxygen n oxygène m.
oxygen mask n masque à oxygène m.

oxygen tent n tente à oxygène f.
oyster n huître f.
ozone n ozone m.

P

pa n papa m.
pace n pas m; allure f; * vt arpenter; * vi marcher.
pacemaker n meneur m, -euse f de train; (med) pacemaker m.
pacific(al) adj pacifique.
pacification n pacification f.
pacify vt pacifier.
pack n paquet m; jeu de cartes m; bande f; * vt empaqueter; remplier; * vi faire ses valises.
package n paquet m; accord m.
package tour n voyage organisé m.
packet n paquet m.
packing n emballage m.
pact n pacte m.
pad n bloc m; coussinet, tampon m; plateforme f; (sl) piaule f; * vt rembourrer.
padding n rembourrage m.
paddle vi ramer; * n pagaie f.
paddle steamer n vapeur à roues f.
paddock n paddock m.
paddy n rizière f.
pagan adj, n païen m, païenne f.
page n page f; page m.
pageant n grand spectacle m.
pageantry n pompe f.
pail n seau m.
pain n douleur f; mal m; peine f; * vt peiner.
pained adj peiné.
painful adj douloureux; pénible; **~ly**

adv douloureusement; péniblement; à grand-peine.
painkiller n analgésique m.
painless adj indolore; sans peine.
painstaking adj soigneux.
paint vt peindre.
paintbrush n pinceau m.
painter n peintre m.
painting n peinture f; tableau m.
paintwork n peinture f.
pair n paire f.
pajamas npl = **pyjamas**.
pal n copain n, copine f, pote m.
palatable adj savoureux.
palate n palais m.
palatial adj grandiose.
palaver n discussions fpl; situation embrouillée f.
pale adj pâle; clair.
palette n palette f.
paling n palissade f.
pall n nuage de fumée m; * vi perdre sa saveur.
pallet n palette f.
palliative adj, n palliatif m.
pallid adj pâle.
pallor n pâleur f.
palm n (bot) palme f, palmier m.
palmistry n chiromancie f.
Palm Sunday n Dimanche des Rameaux m.
palpable adj palpable; évident.
palpitation n palpitation f.

paltry adj dérisoire; mesquin.

pamper vt gâter, dorloter.

pamphlet n pamphlet m; brochure f.

pan n casserole f; poêle f.

panacea n panacée f.

panache n panache m.

pancake n crêpe f.

pandemonium n pandémonium m.

pane n vitre f.

panel n panneau m; comité m.

panelling n lambrissage m.

pang n angoisse f; tourment m.

panic adj, n (de) panique f.

panicky adj paniqué, affolé.

panic-stricken adj pris de panique.

pansy n (bot) pensée f.

pant vi haleter.

panther n panthère f.

panties npl (petite) culotte f.

pantihose n collant m.

pantry n placard m.

pants npl slip m; pantalon m.

papacy n papauté f.

papal adj papal.

paper n papier m; journal m; libellé d'examen; exposé m, étude f; ~s pl documents mpl; (com) fonds mpl; * adj en papier; * vt garnir de papier; tapisser.

paperback n livre de poche m.

paper bag n sac en papier m.

paper clip n trombone m.

paperweight n presse-papiers m.

paperwork n paperasserie f.

paprika n paprica m.

par n équivalence f; égalité f; pair m; **at ~** (com) au pair.

parable n parabole f.

parachute n parachute m; * vi sauter en parachute.

parade n parade f; (mil) défilé m; * vt faire défiler, faire parader; * vi défiler, parader; se pavaner.

paradise n paradis m.

paradox n paradoxe m.

paradoxical adj paradoxal.

paragon n modèle absolu m.

paragraph n paragraphe m.

parallel adj parallèle; * n parallèle f; * vt mettre en parallèle; comparer.

paralyse vt paralyser.

paralysis n paralysie f.

paralytic(al) adj paralytique.

paramedic n auxiliaire médical(e) m(f).

paramount adj suprême, supérieur.

paranoid adj paranoïaque.

paraphernalia n affaires fpl; attirail m.

parasite n parasite m.

parasol n parasol m.

paratrooper n parachutiste m.

parcel n paquet m; parcelle f; * vt empaqueter, emballer.

parch vt dessécher.

parched adj mort de soif.

parchment n parchemin m.

pardon n pardon m; * vt pardonner.

parent n père m; mère f; ~s parents mpl.

parentage n parenté f; origine f.

parental adj paternel.

parenthesis n parenthèse f.

parish n paroisse f; * adj paroissial.

parishioner n paroissien m, -ienne f.

parity n parité f.

park n parc m; * vt garer; vi se garer.

parking n stationnement m.

parking lot n parking m.

parking meter n parcomètre m.

parking ticket n amende pour stationnement interdit f.

parlance n langage m.

parliament n parlement m.

parliamentary adj parlementaire.

parlour n parloir m; salon m.

parody n parodie f; * vt parodier.

parole n: **on ~** sur parole.

parricide n parricide m; parricide mf.

parrot n perroquet m.

parry vt parer.

parsley n (bot) persil m.

parsnip n (bot) navet m.

part n partie f; part f; rôle (d'acteur) m; raie f; **~s** pl parties fpl; parages mpl; * vt séparer; diviser; * vi se séparer; se diviser; **to ~ with** vt céder; se défaire de; donner; **~ly** adv en partie.

partial adj partial; **~ly** adv avec partialité; partiellement.

participant n participant m, -e f.

participate vi participer (à).

participation n participation f.

participle n (gr) participe m.

particle n particule f.

particular adj particulier, singulier; **~ly** adv particulièrement; * n particulier m; particularité f.

parting n séparation f; raie (dans les cheveux) f.

partisan n partisan m, -e f.

partition n partition, séparation f; * vt diviser en plusieurs parties, partager.

partner n associé, -e f; cavalier m, -ière f.

partnership n association f; société f.

partridge n perdrix f.

party n parti m; fête f.

pass vt passer; dépasser; adopter; être admis à; * vi passer; * n permis m; passage m; **to ~ away** vi mourir; **to ~ by** vi passer; négliger, oublier; **to ~ on** vt transmettre; passer.

passable adj passable; praticable.

passage n passage m; traversée f; couloir m.

passbook n livret d'épargne m.

passenger n passager m, -ère f.

passer-by n passant m, -e f.

passing adj passager.

passion n passion f; amour m; emportement m.

passionate adj passionné; **~ly** adv passionnément; ardemment.

passive adj passif; **~ly** adv passivement.

passkey n passe-partout m invar.

Passover n Pâque f.

passport n passeport m.

passport control n contrôle des passeports m.

password n mot de passe m.

past adj passé; * n (gr) prétérit m; passé m; * prep au-delà de; après.

pasta n pâtes fpl.

paste n pâte f; colle f; * vt coller.

pasteurized adj pasteurisé.

pastime n passe-temps m invar; divertissement m.

pastor n pasteur m.

pastoral adj pastoral.

pastry n pâtisserie f.

pasture n pâture f.

pasty adj pâteux; pâle.

pat vt tapoter.

patch n pièce f; tache f; terrain m; * vt rapiécer; **to ~ up** réparer; faire la paix dans.

patchwork n patchwork m.

pâté n pâté m.

patent adj breveté; évident; * n brevet m; * vt faire breveter.

patentee n détenteur d'un brevet m.

patent leather n cuir verni m.

paternal adj paternel.

paternity n paternité f.

path n chemin, sentier m.

pathetic adj, **~ally** adv pathétique(ment); lamentable(ment).

pathological adj pathologique.

pathology n pathologie f.

pathos n pathétique m.

pathway n sentier m.

patience n patience f.

patient adj patient; **~ly** adv patiemment; * n patient m, -e f.

patio n patio m.

patriarch m patriarche m.

patriot n patriote mf.

patriotic adj patriotique.

patriotism n patriotisme m.

patrol n patrouille f; * vi patrouiller.

patrol car n voiture de patrouille f.

patrolman n agent de police m.

patron n protecteur m; client m, -e f.

patronage n patronage m; clientèle f.

patronize vt patronner, protéger.

patter n trottinement m; bavardage m; * vi trottiner.

pattern n motif m; modèle m.

paunch n panse f; ventre m.

pauper n pauvre mf.

pause n pause f; * vi faire une pause; hésiter.

pave vt paver; carreler.

pavement n trottoir m.

pavilion n pavillon m.

paving stone n pavé m.

paw n patte f; * vt tripoter.

pawn n pion m; gage m; * vt engager.

pawn broker n prêteur(-euse) sur gages m(f).

pawnshop n mont-de-piété m.

pay vt payer; **to ~ back** vt rembourser; **to ~ for** payer; **to ~ off** vt liquider; vi payer; rapporter; * n paie f; salaire m.

payable adj payable.

pay day n jour de paie m.

payee n porteur m.

pay envelope n enveloppe de paie f.

paymaster n caissier m.

payment n paiement m.

pay-phone n téléphone public m.

payroll n liste des employés f.

pea n pois m.

peace n paix f.

peaceful adj paisible; pacifique.

peach n pêche f.

peacock n paon m.

peak n pic m; maximum m.

peak hours, peak period n heures de pointe fpl.

peal n carillon m; grondement m.

peanut n cacahuète f.

pear n poire f.

pearl n perle f.

peasant n paysan m, -anne f.

peat n tourbe f.

pebble n caillou m; galet m.

peck n coup de bec m; * vt picoter.

pecking order n hiérarchie f.

peculiar adj étrange, singulier; ~ly adv étrangement.

peculiarity n particularité, singularité f.

pedal n pédale f; * vi pédaler.

pedant n pédant m, -e f.

pedantic adj pédant.

peddler n vendeur ambulant m.

pedestal n piédestal m.

pedestrian n piéton m, -onne f; * adj pédestre.

pediatrics n pédiatrie f.

pedigree n généalogie f; pedigree m; * adj de race.

peek vi regarder à la dérobée.

peel vt peler; éplucher; * vi peler; * n peau f; pelure f.

peer n pair m.

peerless adj incomparable.

peeved adj fâché.

peevish adj maussade, ronchon (fam).

peg n cheville f; piquet m; * vt cheviller.

pelican n pélican m.

pellet n boulette f.

pelt n fourrure f; * vt arroser; * vi pleuvoir à verse.

pen n stylo m; plume f; enclos m.

penal adj pénal.

penalty n peine f; sanction f; amende f.

penance n pénitence f.

pence n = pl of penny.

pencil n crayon m.

pencil case n trousse f.

pendant n pendentif m.

pending adj pendant.

pendulum n pendule m.

penetrate vt pénétrer dans.

penguin n pingouin m.

penicillin n pénicilline f.

peninsula n péninsule f.

penis n pénis m.

penitence n pénitence f.

penitent adj, n pénitent m, -e f.

penitentiary n pénitencier m.

penknife n canif m.

pennant n fanion m.

penniless adj sans le sou.

penny n penny m.

penpal n correspondant m, -e f.

pension n pension f; * vt pensionner.

pensive adj pensif; ~ly adv pensivement.

pentagon n: the P~ le Pentagone.

Pentecost n la Pentecôte f.

penthouse n appartement situé sur le toit d'un immeuble m.

pent-up adj reprimé, refoulé.

penultimate adj pénultième, avant-dernier.

penury n pénurie f.

people n peuple m; nation f; gens mpl; * vt peupler.

pep n énergie f; **to ~ up** vt animer.

pepper n poivre m; * vt poivrer.

peppermint n menthe poivrée f.

per prep par.

per annum adv par an.

per capita adj, adv par habitant.

perceive vt percevoir.

percentage n pourcentage m.

perception n perception f; notion f.

perch n perche f.

perchance adv par hasard.

percolate *vt* filtrer.

percolator *n* percolateur *m*.

percussion *n* percussion *f*.

perdition *n* perte, ruine *f*.

peremptory *adj* péremptoire; décisif.

perennial *adj* perpétuel.

perfect *adj* parfait; idéal; **~ly** *adv* parfaitement; * *vt* parfaire, perfectionner.

perfection *n* perfection *f*.

perforate *vt* perforer.

perforation *n* perforation *f*.

perform *vt* exécuter; effectuer; * *vi* donner une représentation, tenir un rôle.

performance *n* exécution *f*; accomplissement *m*; rendement *m*; représentation *f*.

performer *n* exécutant *m*, -e *f*; acteur *m*, -trice *f*.

perfume *n* parfum *m*; * *vt* parfumer.

perhaps *adv* peut-être.

peril *n* péril, danger *m*.

perilous *adj* dangereux; **~ly** *adv* dangereusement.

perimeter *n* périmètre *m*.

period *n* période *f*; époque *f*; règles *fpl*.

periodic(al) *adj* périodique; **~ally** *adv* périodiquement.

periodical *n* journal *m*.

peripheral *adj* périphérique; * *n* unité périphérique *f*.

perish *vi* périr.

perishable *adj* périssable.

perjure *vt* parjurer.

perjury *n* parjure *m*.

perk *n* extra, à-côté *m*.

perky *adj* animé, plein d'entrain.

perm *n* permanente *f*.

permanent *adj* permanent; **~ly** *adv* en permanence.

permeate *vt* pénétrer, traverser.

permissible *adj* permis.

permission *n* permission *f*.

permissive *adj* permissif.

permit *vt* permettre; * *n* permis *m*.

permutation *n* permutation *f*.

perpendicular *adj*, **~ly** *adv* perpendiculaire(ment); * *n* perpendiculaire *f*.

perpetrate *vt* perpétrer, commettre.

perpetual *adj* perpétuel; **~ly** *adv* perpétuellement.

perpetuate *vt* perpétuer, éterniser.

perplex *vt* confondre, laisser perplexe.

persecute *vt* persécuter; importuner.

persecution *n* persécution *f*.

perseverance *n* persévérance *f*.

persevere *vi* persévérer.

persist *vi* persister.

persistence *n* persistance *f*.

persistent *adj* persistant.

person *n* personne *f*.

personable *adj* attrayant.

personage *n* personnage *m*.

personal *adj*, **~ly** *adv* personnel(lement).

personal assistant *n* assistant *m*, -e *f*.

personal column *n* annonces personnelles *fpl*.

personal computer *n* ordinateur individuel *m*.

personality *n* personnalité *f*.

personification *n* personnification *f*.

personify *vt* personnifier.

personnel n personnel m.
perspective n perspective f.
perspiration n transpiration f.
perspire vi transpirer.
persuade vt persuader.
persuasion n persuasion f.
persuasive adj persuasif; **-ly** adv de manière persuasive.
pert adj plein d'entrain.
pertaining: ~ **to** prep relatif à.
pertinent adj pertinent; **-ly** adv de manière pertinente.
pertness n impertinence f; entrain m.
perturb vt perturber.
perusal n lecture f.
peruse vt lire; examiner attentivement.
pervade vt pénétrer, traverser.
perverse adj pervers, dépravé; **-ly** adv perversement.
pervert vt pervertir, corrompre.
pessimist n pessimiste mf.
pest n insecte nuisible m; casse-pieds (fam) mf invar.
pester vt importuner, fatiguer.
pestilence n peste f.
pet n animal domestique m; préféré m, -e f; * vt gâter; * vi se peloter (fam).
petal n (bot) pétale m.
petite adj menue.
petition n pétition f; * vt présenter une pétition à; supplier.
petrified adj pétrifié.
petroleum n pétrole m.
petticoat n jupon m.
pettiness n insignifiance f.
petty adj mesquin; insignifiant.
petty cash n argent destiné aux dépenses courantes m.

petty officer n second maître m.
petulant adj pétulant.
pew n banc m.
pewter n étain m.
phantom n fantôme m.
Pharisee n Pharisien m.
pharmaceutic(al) adj pharmaceutique.
pharmacist n pharmacien m, -ienne f.
pharmacy n pharmacie f.
phase n phase f.
pheasant n faisan m.
phenomenal adj phénoménal.
phenomenon n phénomène m.
phial n fiole f.
philanthropic adj philanthropique.
philanthropist n philanthrope mf.
philanthropy n philanthropie f.
philologist n philologue mf.
philology n philologie f.
philosopher n philosophe mf.
philosophic(al) adj, **-ally** adv philosophique(ment).
philosophize vi philosopher.
philosophy n philosophie f; **natural** ~ **sciences** naturelles fpl.
phlegm n flegme m.
phlegmatic(al) adj flegmatique.
phobia n phobie f.
phone n téléphone m; * vt téléphoner à; **to** ~ **back** vt, vi rappeler; **to** ~ **up** vt appeler au téléphone.
phone book n annuaire m.
phone box, phone booth n cabine téléphonique f.
phone call n coup de téléphone m.
phosphorus n phosphore m.
photocopier n photocopieuse f.
photocopy n photocopie f.

photograph n photo(graphie) f; * vt photographier.

photographer n photographe mf.

photographic adj photographique.

photography n photo(graphie) f.

phrase n phrase f; locution f; * vt exprimer.

phrase book n guide de conversation m.

physical adj, **~ly** adv physique(ment).

physical education n éducation physique f.

physician n médecin m.

physicist n physicien m, -ienne f.

physiological adj physiologique.

physiologist n physiologiste, physiologue mf.

physiology n physiologie f.

physiotherapy n physiothérapie f.

physique n physique m.

pianist n pianiste mf.

piano n piano m.

piccolo n piccolo m.

pick vt choisir; cueillir; gratter; to **~ on** vt s'en prendre à; to **~ out** vt choisir; to **~ up** vi s'améliorer; se remettre; * vt ramasser; décrocher; arrêter; acheter; * n pic m; choix m.

pickaxe n pic m.

picket n piquet m.

pickle n saumure f; * vt saumurer.

pickpocket n pickpocket m.

pickup n (auto) fourgonnette f.

picnic n pique-nique m.

pictorial adj pictural; illustré.

picture n image f; peinture f; photo f; * vt dépeindre; se figurer.

picture book n livre d'images m.

picturesque adj pittoresque.

pie n gâteau m; tarte f; pâté en croûte m.

piece n morceau m; pièce f; tranche f; * vt raccommoder.

piecemeal adv en morceaux; * adj partiel.

piecework n travail à la pièce m.

pier n jetée f.

pierce vt percer, transpercer.

piercing adj perçant.

piety n piété, dévotion f.

pig n cochon m.

pigeon n pigeon m.

pigeonhole n casier m.

piggy bank n tirelire f.

pigheaded adj têtu.

pigsty n porcherie f.

pigtail n natte f.

pike n brochet m; pique f.

pile n tas m; pile f; amas m; poil m; **~s** pl hémorroïdes fpl; * vt entasser, empiler.

pile-up n carambolage m.

pilfer vt chaparder.

pilgrim n pèlerin m.

pilgrimage n pèlerinage m.

pill n pilule f.

pillage vt piller, mettre à sac.

pillar n pilier m.

pillion n siège arrière m.

pillow n oreiller m.

pillow case n taie d'oreiller f.

pilot n pilote m; * vt piloter; (fig) mener.

pilot light n témoin m.

pimp n proxénète, maquereau (fam) m.

pimple n bouton m.

pin n épingle f; goupille f; **~s and needles** npl fourmis fpl; * vt épingler; goupiller.

pinafore n tablier m.

pinball n flipper m.

pincers n pinces, tenailles fpl.

pinch vt pincer; (sl) piquer, faucher; * vi serrer; * n pincement m; pincée f.

pincushion n pelote à épingles f.

pine n (bot) pin m; * vi languir.

pineapple n ananas m.

ping n tintement m.

pink n, adj rose m.

pinnacle n sommet m.

pinpoint vt préciser; souligner.

pint n pinte f.

pioneer n pionnier m.

pious adj pieux, dévot; **~ly** adv pieusement.

pip n pépin m.

pipe n tube, tuyau m; pipe f; **~s** tuyauterie f.

pipe cleaner n cure-pipe m.

pipe dream n rêve impossible m.

pipeline n canalisation f; oléoduc m; gazoduc m.

piper n joueur de cornemuse m.

piping adj bouillant; aigu, f aiguë.

pique n pique f; dépit m.

piracy n piraterie f.

pirate n pirate m.

pirouette n pirouette f; vi pirouetter.

Pisces n Poissons mpl (signe du zodiaque).

piss n (sl) pisse f; * vi pisser.

pistol n pistolet m.

piston n piston m.

pit n noyau m; mine f; fosse f.

pitch n lancement m; ton m; * vt lancer, jeter; * vi tomber; piquer du nez.

pitchblack adj noir comme dans un four.

pitcher n cruche f.

pitchfork n fourche f.

pitfall n piège m.

pithy adj moelleux.

pitiable adj pitoyable; déplorable.

pitiful adj pitoyable; lamentable; **~ly** adv pitoyablement.

pittance n salaire de misère m; pitance f.

pity n pitié f; * vt avoir pitié de.

pivot n pivot, axe m.

pizza n pizza f.

placard n affiche f.

placate vt apaiser.

place n endroit, lieu m; place f; * vt placer; mettre.

placid adj placide, calme; **~ly** adv placidement.

plagiarism n plagiat m.

plague n peste f; * vt tourmenter; infester.

plaice n carrelet m.

plaid n tartan m; plaid m.

plain adj uni; simple; clair, sincère; commun; évident; **~ly** adv simplement; clairement; * n plaine f.

plaintiff n (law) plaignant m, -e f.

plait n pli m; tresse f; * vt plier; tresser.

plan n plan m; projet m; * vt projeter.

plane n avion m; plan m; rabot m; * vt aplanir; raboter.

planet n planète f.

planetary *adj* planétaire.

plank *n* planche *f*.

planner *n* planificateur *m*, -trice *f*.

planning *n* planification *f*.

plant *n* plante *f*; usine *f*; machinerie *f*; * *vt* planter.

plantation *n* plantation *f*.

plaque *n* plaque *f*.

plaster *n* plâtre *m*; emplâtre *m*; * *vt* plâtrer; emplâtrer.

plastered *adj* (sl) bourré, soûl.

plasterer *n* plâtrier *m*.

plastic *adj* plastique.

plastic surgery *n* chirurgie esthétique *f*.

plate *n* assiette *f*; plaque *f*; lame *f*.

plateau *n* plateau *m*.

plate glass *n* vitre *f*.

platform *n* plateforme *f*.

platinum *n* platine *m*.

platitude *n* platitude *f*.

platoon *n* (mil) peloton *m*.

platter *n* écuelle *f*; plat *m*.

plaudit *n* applaudissement *m*.

plausible *adj* plausible.

play *n* jeu *m*; pièce de théâtre *f*; * *vt, vi* jouer; (also mus) **to ~ down** *vt* rabaisser; minimiser.

playboy *n* playboy *m*.

player *n* joueur *m*, -euse *f*; acteur *m*, -trice *f*.

playful *adj* enjoué, amusé; **~ly** *adv* d'une manière enjouée; pour s'amuser.

playmate *n* camarade de jeu *mf*.

playground *n* cour de récréation *f*; jardin d'enfants *m*.

playgroup *n* école maternelle *f*.

play-off *n* belle *f*.

playpen *n* parc pour enfant *m*.

plaything *n* jouet *m*.

playwright *n* dramaturge *mf*.

plea *n* appel *m*; excuse *f*, prétexte *m*.

plead *vt* plaider; prétexter.

pleasant *adj* agréable; plaisant; aimable; **~ly** *adv* agréablement.

please *vt* faire plaisir à.

pleased *adj* content.

pleasing *adj* agréable, plaisant.

pleasure *n* plaisir *m*; gré *m*, volonté *f*.

pleat *n* pli *m*.

pledge *n* promesse *f*; gage *m*; * *vt* engager; promettre.

plentiful *adj* copieux; abondant.

plenty *n* abondance *f*; **~ of** beaucoup de.

plethora *n* pléthore *f*.

pleurisy *n* pleurésie *f*.

pliable, pliant *adj* pliable, pliant; souple.

pliers *npl* tenailles *fpl*.

plight *n* épreuve *f*; situation difficile *f*.

plinth *n* plinthe *f*.

plod *vi* se traîner, avancer péniblement.

plot *n* petit morceau de terrain *m*; complot *m*; intrigue *f*; * *vt* tracer; comploter; conspirer.

plough *n* charrue *f*; * *vt* labourer; **to ~ back** *vt* réinvestir; **to ~ through** *vi* se faire un chemin; avancer péniblement.

ploy *n* truc *m*.

pluck *vt* tirer; arracher; déplumer; * *n* courage *m*.

plucky *adj* courageux.

plug n tampon m; bouchon m; bougie f; prise f; * vt boucher.

plum n prune f.

plumage n plumage m.

plumb n aplomb m; * adv d'aplomb; * vt plomber; sonder.

plumber n plombier m.

plume n plume f.

plump adj rondouillet, dodu.

plum tree n prunier m.

plunder vt mettre à sac, piller; * n pillage m; butin m.

plunge vi plonger; s'élancer.

plunger n piston m.

pluperfect n (gr) plus-que-parfait m.

plural adj, n pluriel m.

plurality n pluralité f.

plus n signe plus, m; * prep plus.

plush adj en peluche.

plutonium n plutonium m.

ply vt manier avec vigueur; * vi s'appliquer; (mar) faire la navette.

plywood n contreplaqué m.

pneumatic adj pneumatique.

pneumatic drill n marteau pneumatique m.

pneumonia n pneumonie f.

poach vt pocher; braconner; vi braconner.

poached adj poché.

poacher n braconnier m.

poaching n braconnage m.

pocket n poche f; * vt empocher.

pocketbook n sac à main m.

pocket money n argent de poche m.

pod n cosse f.

podgy adj boudiné.

poem n poème m.

poet n poète m.

poetess n poétesse f.

poetic adj poétique.

poetry n poésie f.

poignant adj poignant.

point n pointe f; point m; promontoire m; ~ of view n point de vue m; * vt pointer; tailler en pointe; indiquer.

point-blank adv à bout portant; directement.

pointed adj pointu; acéré; ~ly adv subtilement.

pointer n auguille f; pointer m.

pointless adj inutile.

poise n attitude f; équilibre m.

poison n poison m; * vt empoisonner.

poisoning n empoisonnement m.

poisonous adj vénéneux.

poker n tison m; poker m.

poker-faced adj au visage impassible.

poky adj exigu, f exiguë.

polar adj polaire.

pole n pôle m; mât m; perche f.

pole bean n haricot en rames m.

pole vault n saut à la perche m.

police n police f.

police car n voiture de police f.

policeman n agent de police m.

police state n état policier m.

police station n commissariat m.

policewoman n femme agent de police f.

policy n politique f; police d'assurance f.

polio n polio f.

polish vt polir; cirer; **to ~ off** vt parachever; expédier; * n poli m.

polished adj poli; ciré; élégant.

polite adj, **~ly** adv poli(ment), courtois(ement).

politeness n politesse, courtoisie f.

politic adj politique; rusé.

political adj politique.

politician n homme (femme) politique m(f).

politics npl politique f.

polka n polka f; **~ dot** n pois m.

poll n liste électorale f; vote m; sondage m.

pollen n (bot) pollen m.

pollute vt polluer; corrompre.

pollution n pollution, contamination f.

polo n polo m.

polyester n polyester m.

polyethylene n polyéthylène m.

polygamy n polygamie f.

polystyrene n polystyrène m.

polytechnic n école d'enseignement technique f.

pomegranate n grenade f.

pomp n pompe f; splendeur f.

pompom n pompon m.

pompous adj pompeux.

pond n mare f; étang m.

ponder vt considérer; réfléchir à.

ponderous adj lourd, pesant.

pontiff n pontife m.

pontoon n ponton m.

pony n poney m.

ponytail n queue de cheval f.

pool n flaque d'eau f; piscine f; * vt grouper.

poor adj pauvre; mauvais; **~ly** adv pauvrement; **the ~** n les pauvres mpl.

pop n pop m; papa m; boisson gazeuse f; éclatement m; * **to ~ in/off** vi entrer/sortir un instant.

pop concert n concert de musique pop m.

popcorn n popcorn m.

Pope n pape m.

poplar n peuplier m.

poppy n (bot) pavot m.

popsicle n esquimau m.

populace n populace f.

popular adj, **~ly** adv populaire(ment).

popularity n popularité f.

popularize vt populariser.

populate vi peupler.

population n population f.

populous adj populeux.

porcelain n porcelaine f.

porch n porche m.

porcupine n porc-épic m.

pore n pore m.

pork n porc m.

pornography n pornographie f.

porous adj poreux.

porpoise n marsouin m.

porridge n porridge m, flocons d'avoine mpl.

port n port m; (mar) sabord m; porto (vin) m.

portable adj portable, portatif.

portal n portail m.

porter n portier m; garçon m.

portfolio n serviette f; carton m; portefeuille m.

porthole n hublot m.

portico n portique m.

portion n portion, part f.

portly adj corpulent.

portrait n portrait m.

portray vt faire le portrait de; dépeindre.

pose n posture f; pose f; * vi, vt poser.

posh adj chic; bourgeois.

position n position f; situation f; * vt mettre en position.

positive adj positif; réel; favorable; ~ly adv positivement; assurément.

posse n peloton m.

possess vt posséder.

possession n possession f.

possessive adj possessif.

possibility n possibilité f.

possible adj possible; ~ly adv peut-être.

post n courrier m; poste f; emploi m; poste m; pieu m; * vt poster; fixer.

postage n port m.

postage stamp n timbre m.

postcard n carte postale f.

postdate vt postdater.

poster n poster m.

posterior n postérieur m.

posterity n postérité f.

postgraduate n licencié m, -e f.

posthumous adj posthume.

postman n facteur m.

postmark n cachet de la poste m.

postmaster n receveur des postes m.

post office n poste f, bureau de poste m.

postpone vt remettre; différer.

postscript n post-scriptum m.

posture n posture f.

postwar adj d'après-guerre.

posy n petit bouquet de fleurs m.

pot n pot m; marmite f; (sl) marijuana f; * vt empoter; mettre en pot.

potato n pomme de terre, patate (fam) f.

potato peeler n couteau éplucheur m.

potbellied adj ventru.

potent adj puissant.

potential adj potentiel.

pothole n trou m.

potion n potion f.

potted adj en pot.

potter n potier m.

pottery n poterie f.

potty adj insignifiant; (sl) fou, maboul.

pouch n sac m.

poultice n cataplasme m.

poultry n volaille f.

pound n livre f; livre sterling f; fourrière f; * vt concasser; * vi taper fort.

pour vt verser; servir; * vi couler; pleuvoir à verse.

pout vi faire la moue.

poverty n pauvreté f.

powder n poudre f; * vt saupoudrer.

powder compact n poudrier m.

powdered milk n lait en poudre m.

powder puff n houppette f.

powder room n toilettes fpl.

powdery adj poudreux.

power n pouvoir m; puissance f; empire m; autorité f; force f; * vt propulser.

powerful adj puissant; ~ly adv puissamment; avec force.

powerless adj impotent.

power station n centrale électrique f.

practicable adj praticable; faisable.

practical adj, **~ly** adv pratique(ment).

practicality n faisabilité f.

practical joke n farce f.

practice n pratique f; usage m; entraînement m; **~s** pl agissements mpl.

practise vt pratiquer, exercer; * vi s'exercer, s'entraîner.

practitioner n médecin m.

pragmatic adj pragmatique.

prairie n prairie f.

praise n éloge m; louange f; * vt louer.

praiseworthy adj digne d'éloges.

prance vi cabrioler.

prank n folie, extravagance f.

prattle vi jacasser; * n jacasserie f.

prawn n crevette f.

pray vi prier.

prayer n prière f.

prayer book n livre de messe m.

preach vt prêcher.

preacher n prédicateur m.

preamble n préambule m.

precarious adj précaire, incertain; **~ly** adv précairement.

precaution n précaution f.

precautionary adj préventif.

precede vt précéder.

precedence n précédence f.

precedent adj, n précédent m.

precinct n limite f; enceinte f; circonscription f.

precious adj précieux.

precipice n précipice m.

precipitate vt précipiter; * adj précipité m.

precise n précis, exact; **~ly** adv précisément, exactement.

precision n précision, exactitude f.

preclude vt prévenir, empêcher.

precocious adj précoce, prématuré.

preconceive vt préconcevoir.

preconception n préjugé m; idée préconçue f.

precondition n condition préalable f.

precursor n précurseur m.

predator n prédateur m.

predecessor n prédécesseur m.

predestination n prédestination f.

predicament n situation difficile f.

predict vt prédire.

predictable adj prévisible.

prediction n prédiction f.

predilection n prédilection f.

predominant adj prédominant.

predominate vt prédominer.

preen vt nettoyer (ses plumes).

prefab n maison préfabriquée f.

preface n préface f.

prefer vt préférer.

preferable adj préférable.

preferably adv de préférence.

preference n préférence f.

preferential adj préférentiel.

preferment n promotion f; préférence f.

prefix vt préfixer; * n (gr) préfixe m.

pregnancy n grossesse f.

pregnant adj enceinte.

prehistoric adj préhistorique.

prejudice n préjudice, tort m; préjugé m; * vt préjudicier à, faire du tort à.

prejudiced *adj* qui a des préjugés; partial.

prejudicial *adj* préjudiciable.

preliminary *adj* préliminaire.

prelude *n* prélude *m*.

premarital *adj* préconjugal.

premature *adj*, **~ly** *adv* prématuré(ment).

premeditation *n* préméditation *f*.

premier *n* premier ministre *m*.

première *n* première *f*.

premise *n* prémisse *f*.

premises *npl* locaux *mpl*.

premium *n* prix *m*; indemnité *f*; prime *f*.

premonition *n* pressentiment *m*, prémonition *f*.

preoccupied *adj* préoccupé; absorbé.

prepaid *adj* port payé.

preparation *n* préparation *f*.

preparatory *adj* préparatoire.

prepare *vt* préparer; * *vi* se préparer.

preponderance *n* prépondérance *f*.

preposition *n* préposition *f*.

preposterous *adj* ridicule, absurde.

prerequisite *n* condition requise *f*.

prerogative *n* prérogative *f*.

prescribe *vt* prescrire.

prescription *n* prescription *f*; ordonnance *f*.

presence *n* présence *f*.

present *n* cadeau *m*; * *adj* présent; actuel; **~ly** *adv* actuellement; * *vt* offrir, donner; présenter.

presentable *adj* présentable.

presentation *n* présentation *f*.

present-day *adj* actuel.

presenter *n* présentateur *m*, -trice *f*.

presentiment *n* pressentiment *m*, prémonition *f*.

preservation *n* préservation *f*.

preservative *n* préservatif *m*.

preserve *vt* préserver; conserver; faire des conserves de; * *n* conserve *f*; confiture *f*.

preside *vi* présider; diriger.

presidency *n* présidence *f*.

president *n* président *m*.

presidential *adj* présidentiel.

press *vt* appuyer sur; serrer; pressurer; * *vi* se presser; * *n* presse *f*; pressoir *m*; pression *f*.

press agency *n* agence de presse *f*.

press conference *n* conférence de presse *f*.

pressing *adj* pressant; urgent; **~ly** *adv* de manière pressante; d'urgence.

pressure *n* pression *f*.

pressure cooker *n* autocuiseur *m*.

pressure group *n* groupe de pression *m*.

pressurized *adj* pressurisé.

prestige *n* prestige *m*.

presumable *adj* vraisemblable.

presumably *adv* vraisemblablement.

presume *vt* présumer, supposer.

presumption *n* présomption *f*.

presumptuous *adj* présomptueux.

presuppose *vt* présupposer.

pretence *n* prétexte *m*; simulation *f*; prétention *f*.

pretend *vi* prétendre; faire semblant.

pretender *n* prétendant *m*.

pretension *n* prétention *f*.

pretentious *adj* prétentieux.

preterite *n* prétérit *f*.

pretext n prétexte m.

pretty adj joli, mignon; * adv assez; plutôt.

prevail vi prévaloir; prédominer.

prevailing adj prédominant.

prevalent adj prédominant.

prevent vt prévenir; empêcher; éviter.

prevention n prévention f.

preventive adj préventif.

preview n avant-première f.

previous adj précédent; antérieur; **~ly** adv auparavant.

prewar adj d'avant-guerre.

prey n proie f.

price n prix m.

priceless adj inappréciable.

price list n tarif m.

prick vt piquer; exciter; * n piqûre f; pointe f.

prickle n picotement m; épine f.

prickly adj épineux.

pride n orgueil m; vanité f; fierté f.

priest n prêtre m.

priestess n prêtresse f.

priesthood n sacerdoce m, prêtrise f.

priestly adj sacerdotal.

priggish adj affecté.

prim adj prude, affecté.

primacy n primauté f.

primarily adv principalement, surtout.

primary adj primaire; principal, premier.

primate n primate m.

prime n (fig) fleur f; commencement m; * adj premier; principal; excellent; * vt amorcer.

prime minister n premier ministre m.

primeval adj primitif.

priming n amorçage m.

primitive adj primitif; **~ly** adv primitivement.

primrose n (bot) primevère f.

prince n prince m.

princess n princesse f.

principal adj, **~ly** adv principal(ement); * n principal m.

principality n principauté f.

principle n principe m.

print vt imprimer; * n impression f; estampe f; caractères imprimés mpl; **out of ~** épuisé (livres).

printed matter n imprimés mpl.

printer n imprimeur m; imprimante f.

printing n impression f.

prior adj antérieur, précédent; * n prieur m.

priority n priorité f.

priory n prieuré m.

prism n prisme m.

prison n prison f.

prisoner n prisonnier m, -ière f.

pristine adj d'origine; intact.

privacy n intimité f.

private adj privé; secret; particulier; **~ soldier** n simple soldat m; **~ly** adv en privé.

private eye n détective privé m.

privet n troène m.

privilege n privilège m.

prize n prix m; * vt apprécier, évaluer; **to ~ open** ouvrir par la force, forcer.

prize-giving n distribution des prix f.

prizewinner n gagnant m, -e f.

pro prep pour.

probability n probabilité f; vraisemblance f.

probable *adj* probable, vraisemblable; **~bly** *adv* probablement.

probation *n* essai *m*; probation *f*.

probationary *adj* d'essai.

probe *n* sonde *f*; enquête *f*; * *vt* sonder; * *vi* faire des recherches.

problem *n* problème *m*.

problematical, **~ly** *adv* problématique(ment).

procedure *n* procédure *f*.

proceed *vi* procéder; provenir; poursuivre; **~s** *npl* produit *m*; montant *m*; **gross ~s** bénéfices bruts *mpl*; **net ~s** bénéfices nets *mpl*.

proceedings *n* procédure *f*; procédé *m*; procès *m*.

process *n* processus *m*; procédé *m*.

procession *n* procession *f*.

proclaim *vt* proclamer; promulguer.

proclamation *n* proclamation *f*; décret *m*.

procrastinate *vt* différer, retarder.

proctor *n* censeur *m*.

procure *vt* procurer.

procurement *n* obtention *f*.

prod *vt* pousser.

prodigal *adj* prodigue.

prodigious *adj* prodigieux; **~ly** *adv* prodigieusement.

prodigy *n* prodige *m*.

produce *vt* produire; créer; fabriquer; * *n* produit *m*.

produce dealer *n* revendeur *m*, -euse *f*.

producer *n* producteur *m*, -trice *f*.

product *n* produit *m*; œuvre *f*; fruit *m*.

production *n* production *f*; produit *m*.

production line *n* ligne de production *f*.

productive *adj* productif.

productivity *n* productivité *f*.

profane *vt* profaner.

profess *vt* professer; exercer; déclarer.

profession *n* profession *f*.

professional *adj* professionnel.

professor *n* professeur *m*.

proficiency *n* capacité *f*.

proficient *adj* compétent.

profile *n* profil *m*.

profit *n* bénéfice *m*, profit *m*; avantage *m*; * *vi* profiter (de).

profitability *n* rentabilité *f*.

profitable *adj* profitable, avantageux.

profiteering *n* exploitation *f*, mercantilisme *m*.

profound *adj*, **~ly** *adv* profond(ément).

profuse *adj* profus; prodigue; **~ly** *adv* à profusion.

program(me) *n* programme *m*.

programming *n* programmation *f*.

programmer *n* programmeur *m*, -euse *f*.

progress *n* progrès *m*; cours *m*; * *vi* progresser.

progression *n* progression *f*; avance *f*.

progressive *adj* progressif; **~ly** *adv* progressivement.

prohibit *vt* prohiber; défendre.

prohibition *n* prohibition *f*.

project *vt* projeter; * *n* projet *m*.

projectile *n* projectile *m*.

projection *n* projection *f*.

projector *n* projecteur *m*.

proletarian *adj* prolétaire.

proletariat n prolétariat m.

prolific adj prolifique, fécond.

prolix adj prolixe, diffus.

prolog n prologue m.

prolong vt prolonger.

prom n bal m; concert-promenade m.

promenade n promenade f.

prominence n proéminence f; éminence f.

prominent adj proéminent.

promiscuous adj immoral, débauché.

promise n promesse f; * vt promettre.

promising adj prometteur.

promontory n promontoire m.

promote vt promouvoir.

promoter n promoteur m.

promotion n promotion f.

prompt adj, ~ly adv promptement); * vt suggérer; inciter; souffler (au théâtre).

prompter n souffleur m, -euse f.

prone adj enclin (à).

prong n dent f.

pronoun n pronom m.

pronounce vt prononcer; déclarer.

pronounced adj marqué, prononcé.

pronouncement n déclaration f.

pronunciation n prononciation f.

proof n preuve f; * adj imperméable; résistant.

prop vt soutenir; * n appui, soutien m; tuteur m.

propaganda n propagande f.

propel vt propulser.

propeller n hélice f.

propensity n propension, tendance f.

proper adj propre; convenable;

exact; approprié; ~ly adv convenablement; correctement.

property n propriété f.

prophecy n prophétie f.

prophesy vt prophétiser, prédire.

prophet n prophète m.

prophetic adj prophétique.

proportion n proportion f; symétrie f.

proportional adj proportionnel.

proportionate adj proportionné.

proposal n proposition f; offre f.

propose vt proposer.

proposition n proposition f.

proprietor n propriétaire mf.

propriety n propriété f.

pro rata adv au prorata.

prosaic adj prosaïque.

prose n prose f.

prosecute vt poursuivre en justice.

prosecution n poursuites fpl; accusation f.

prosecutor n plaignant m, -e f.

prospect n perspective f; espoir m; * vt, vi prospecter.

prospecting n prospection f.

prospective adj probable; futur.

prospector n prospecteur m, -trice f.

prospectus n prospectus m.

prosper vi prospérer.

prosperity n prospérité f.

prosperous adj prospère.

prostitute n prostituée f.

prostitution n prostitution f.

prostrate adj prostré.

protagonist n protagoniste mf.

protect vt protéger; abriter.

protection n protection f.

protective adj protecteur.

protector n protecteur m, -trice f.
protégé n protégé m, -e f.
protein n protéine f.
protest vi protester; * n protestation f.
Protestant n protestant m, -e f.
protester n manifestant m, -e f; protestataire mf.
protocol n protocole m.
prototype n prototype m.
protracted adj prolongé.
protrude vi déborder, ressortir.
proud adj fier, orgueilleux; **~ly** adv fièrement.
prove vt prouver; justifier; * vi s'avérer; se révéler.
proverb n proverbe m.
proverbial adj, **~ly** adv proverbial(ement).
provide vt fournir; **to ~ for** pourvoir aux besoins de; prévoir.
provided conj: **~ that** pourvu que.
providence n providence f.
province n province f; compétence f.
provincial adj, n provincial m, -e f.
provision n provision f; disposition f.
provisional adj, **~ly** adv provisoire(ment).
proviso n stipulation f.
provocation n provocation f.
provocative adj provocateur.
provoke vt provoquer.
prow n (mar) proue f.
prowess n prouesse f.
prowl vi rôder.
prowler n rôdeur m, -euse f.
proximity n proximité f.

proxy n procuration f; délégué m, -e f.
prudence n prudence f.
prudent adj prudent, circonspect; **~ly** adv prudemment.
prudish adj prude.
prune vt tailler; * n pruneau m.
prussic acid n acide prussique m.
pry vi espionner; **to ~ open** vt forcer.
psalm n psaume m.
pseudonym n pseudonyme m.
psyche n psyché f.
psychiatric adj psychiatrique.
psychiatrist n psychiatre mf.
psychiatry n psychiatrie f.
psychic adj psychique.
psychoanalysis n psychanalyse f.
psychoanalyst n psychanaliste mf.
psychological adj psychologique.
psychologist n psychologue mf.
psychology n psychologie f.
puberty n puberté f.
public adj public; commun; **~ly** adv publiquement; * n public m.
public address system n sonorisation f.
publican n patron(ne) de pub m(f).
publication n publication f; édition f.
publicity n publicité f.
publicize vt faire de la publicité pour.
public opinion n opinion publique f.
public school n école privée f.
publish vt publier.
publisher n éditeur m, -trice f.
publishing n édition f.
pucker vt plisser.

pudding n pudding m; dessert m.

puddle n flaque d'eau f.

puerile adj puéril.

puff n souple m; bouffée f; * vt souffler; dégager; * vi souffler; bouffer.

puff pastry n pâte feuilletée f.

puffy adj bouffi, gonflé.

pull vt tirer; arracher; **to ~ down** faire descendre; abattre; **to ~ in** vi s'arrêter; entrer en gare; **to ~ off** enlever; **to ~ out** vi partir; vt arracher; **to ~ through** vi s'en sortir; se remettre; **to ~ up** vi s'arrêter; * vt arracher; arrêter; * n tirage m; secousse f.

pulley n poulie f.

pullover n pullover m.

pulp n pulpe f.

pulpit n chaire f.

pulsate vi battre.

pulse n pouls m; légumes mpl.

pulverize vt pulvériser.

pumice n pierre ponce f.

pummel vt battre.

pump n pompe f; * vt pomper; puiser.

pumpkin n citrouille f.

pun n jeu de mots m; * vi faire des jeux de mots.

punch n coup de poing m; poinçon m; punch m; * vt cogner; perforer; poinçonner.

punctual adj ponctuel, exact; **~ly** adv ponctuellement.

punctuate vt ponctuer.

punctuation n ponctuation f.

pundit n expert m.

pungent adj piquant, âcre; mordant.

punish vt punir.

punishment n châtiment m, punition f; peine f.

punk n punk mf; minable mf; **~ (music)** punk m.

punt n bateau plat m.

puny adj chétif, maigrelet.

pup n chiot m; * vi avoir des chiots, mettre bas.

pupil n élève mf; pupille mf.

puppet n marionnette f.

puppy n chiot m.

purchase vt acheter; * n achat m; acquisition f.

purchaser n acheteur m, -euse f.

pure adj pur; **~ly** adv purement.

purée n purée f.

purge vt purger.

purification n purification f.

purify vt purifier.

purist n puriste m.

puritan n puritain m, -e f.

purity n pureté f.

purl n maille à l'envers f.

purple adj, n pourpre, violet m.

purport vt: **to ~** prétendre.

purpose n intention f; but, dessein m; **to the ~** à propos; **to no ~** en vain; **on ~** exprès, à dessein.

purposeful adj résolu.

purr vi ronronner.

purse n sac à main m; portemonnaie m invar.

purser n commissaire m.

pursue vi poursuivre; suivre.

pursuit n poursuite f; occupation f.

purveyor n fournisseur m, -euse f.

push vt pousser; presser; **to ~ aside** écarter; **to ~ off** vi (sl) se casser; **to ~ on** vi continuer; * n poussée f; impulsion f; effort m; énergie f.

pusher n trafiquant de drogues m.

push-up n pompe f.

put vt mettre, poser; proposer; obliger; to ~ away ranger; to ~ down poser par terre; rabaisser; attribuer; to ~ forward avancer; to ~ off remettre; décourager; to ~ on mettre; allumer; prendre; affecter; to ~ out éteindre; faire sortir; déranger; to ~ up lever; augmenter; loger.

putrid adj putride.

putt n putt m;* vt, vi putter.

putty n mastic m.

puzzle n énigme f; casse-tête m invar.

puzzling adj étrange.

pyjamas npl pyjama m.

pylon n pylône m.

pyramid n pyramide f.

python n python m.

Q

quack vi cancaner; * n canard m; (sl) charlatan m.

quadrangle n quadrilatère m.

quadrant n quadrant m.

quadrilateral adj quadrilatéral.

quadruped n quadrupède m.

quadruple adj quadruple.

quadruplet n quadruplé m, -e f.

quagmire n marécage m.

quail n caille f.

quaint adj désuet; bizarre.

quake vi trembler.

Quaker n quaker m.

qualification n qualification f; diplôme m.

qualified adj qualifié; diplômé.

qualify vt qualifier; modérer; * vi se qualifier.

quality n qualité f.

qualm n scrupule m.

quandary n incertitude f, doute m.

quantitative adj quantitatif.

quantity n quantité f.

quarantine n quarantaine f.

quarrel n dispute, querelle f; * vi se disputer, se quereller.

quarrelsome adj querelleur.

quarry n carrière f.

quarter n quart m; a ~ of an hour un quart d'heure; * vt diviser en quatre.

quarterly adj trimestriel; * adv tous les trimestres.

quartermaster n (mil) intendant m.

quartet n (mus) quartette m; quatuor m.

quartz n (min) quartz m.

quash vt écraser; annuler.

quay n quai m.

queasy adj qui a des nausées; écœurant.

queen n reine f; femme f.

queer adj extrange; (sl) pédale f.

quell vt étouffer; apaiser.

quench vt assouvir; éteindre.

query n question f; * vt demander.

quest n recherche f.

question n question f; sujet m; doute m; * vt douter de; mettre en question; questionner.

questionable adj discutable; douteux.

questioner n interrogateur m.
question mark n point d'interrogation m.
questionnaire n questionnaire m.
quibble vi chicaner.
quick adj rapide; vif; prompt; **~ly** adv rapidement, vite.
quicken vt presser; accélérer; * vi s'accélérer.
quicksand n sables mouvants mpl.
quicksilver n mercure m.
quick-witted adj à l'esprit vif.
quiet adj calme; silencieux; **~ly** adv calmement.
quietness n calme m, tranquillité f; silence m.
quinine n quinine f.
quintet n (mus) quintette m.
quintuple adj quintuple.
quintuplet n quintuplé m, -e f.

quip n sarcasme m; * vt railler.
quirk n particularité f.
quit vt arrêter de; quitter; * vi abandonner; démissionner; * adj quitte.
quite adv assez; complètement, absolument.
quits adj quitte.
quiver vi trembler.
quixotic adj donquichottesque.
quiz n concours m; examen m; * vt interroger.
quizzical adj railleur.
quota n quota m.
quotation n citation f.
quotation marks npl guillemets mpl.
quote vt citer.
quotient n quotient m.

R

rabbi n rabbi, rabbin m.
rabbit n lapin m.
rabbit hutch n clapier m.
rabble n cohue f.
rabid adj forcené, enragé.
rabies n rage f.
race n course f; race f; * vt faire une course avec; * vi courir; faire une course; aller très vite; foncer.
racer n cheval de course m.
racial adj racial; **~ist** adj, n raciste mf.
raciness n vivacité f.
racing n courses fpl.
rack n casier m; étagère f; * vt soumettre au supplice du chevalet; tourmenter.

racket n vacarme m; raquette f.
rack-rent n loyer démesuré m.
racy adj piquant, plein de verve.
radiance n rayonnement m, éclat m.
radiant adj rayonnant, radieux.
radiate vt, vi rayonner, irradier.
radiation n irradiation f.
radiator n radiateur m.
radical adj, **~ly** adv radical(ement).
radicalism n radicalisme m.
radio n radio f.
radioactive adj radioactif.
radish n radis m.
radius n radius m.
raffle n tombola f; * vt mettre en tombola.
raft n radeau, train de flottage m.

rafter n chevron m.

rag n lambeau m, loque f.

ragamuffin n va-nu-pieds m invar; galopin m.

rage n rage f; fureur f; * vi être furieux; faire rage.

ragged adj déguenillé.

raging adj furieux, déchaîné, enragé.

ragman, ~ picker n chiffonnier m.

raid n raid m; * vt faire un raid sur.

raider n raider m.

rail n rambarde f, garde-fou m; (rail) rail, chemin de fer m; * vt entourer d'une barrière.

raillery n taquinerie f.

railroad, railway n chemin de fer m.

raiment n vêtements mpl.

rain n pluie f; * vi pleuvoir.

rainbow n arc-en-ciel m.

rainwater n eau de pluie f.

rainy adj pluvieux.

raise vt lever, soulever; ériger, édifier; élever.

raisin n raisin sec m.

rake n râteau m; libertin m; * vt ratisser.

rakish adj libertin, débauché.

rally vt (mil) rallier; * vi se rallier.

ram n bélier m; navire bélier m; * vt enfoncer.

ramble vi errer; faire une randonnée; * n excursion à pied, randonnée f.

rambler n excursionniste mf.

ramification n ramification f.

ramify vi se ramifier.

ramp n rampe f.

rampant adj exubérant.

rampart n terre-plein m; (mil) rempart m.

ramrod n baguette f; refouloir m.

ramshackle adj délabré.

ranch n ranch m.

rancid adj rance.

rancour n rancœur f.

random adj fortuit, fait au hasard; at ~ au hasard.

range vt ranger, classer; * vi s'étendre; * n rangée f; ordre m; portée f; chaîne f; champ de tir m; fourneau de cuisine m.

ranger n garde forestier m.

rank adj exubérant; fétide; flagrant; * n rang m, classe f, grade m.

rankle vi rester sur le cœur.

rankness n exubérance f; odeur rance f.

ransack vt saccager, piller.

ransom n rançon f.

rant vi déclamer.

rap vi donner un coup sec; * n petit coup sec m.

rapacious adj rapace; ~ly adv avec rapacité.

rapacity n rapacité f.

rape n viol m; rapt m; (bot) colza m; * vt violer.

rapid adj ~ly adv rapide(ment).

rapidity n rapidité f.

rapier n rapière f.

rapt adj extasié; absorbé.

rapture n ravissement m; extase f.

rapturous adj de ravissement.

rare adj ~ly adv rare(ment).

rarity n rareté f.

rascal n vaurien m.

rash adj imprudent, téméraire; ~ly adv sans réfléchir; * n vague f; éruption (cutanée) f.

rashness n imprudence f.
rasp n râpe f; * vt râper.
raspberry n framboise f; ~ **bush** framboisier m.
rat n rat m.
rate n taux, prix, cours m; classe f; vitesse f; * vt estimer, évaluer.
rather adv plutôt; quelque peu.
ratification n ratification f.
ratify vt ratifier.
rating n estimation f; classement m; indice m.
ratio n rapport m.
ration n ration f; (mil) vivres mpl.
rational adj rationnel; raisonnable; ~**ly** adv rationnellement.
rationality n rationalité f.
rattan n (bot) rotin m.
rattle vi s'entrechoquer; cliqueter * vt faire s'entrechoquer; * n fracas m; cliquetis m.
rattlesnake n serpent à sonnettes m.
ravage vt ravager, piller; dévaster; * n ravage m.
rave vi délirer.
raven n corbeau m.
ravenous adj ~**ly** adv vorace(ment).
ravine n ravin m.
ravish vt enchanter; ravir.
ravishing adj enchanteur.
raw adj cru; brut; novice.
rawboned adj décharné; maigre.
rawness n crudité f; inexpérience f.
ray n rayon m; (fish) raie f.
raze vt raser.
razor n rasoir m.
reach vt atteindre; arriver à; * vi s'étendre, porter; * n portée f.
react vi réagir.

reaction n réaction f.
read vt vi lire.
readable adj lisible.
reader n lecteur m -trice f.
readily adv volontiers; facilement.
readiness n bonne volonté f; empressement m.
reading n lecture f.
reading room n salle de lecture f.
readjust vt réajuster, réadapter.
ready adj prêt; enclin; disposé.
real adj réel, vrai; ~**ly** adv vraiment.
realisation n réalisation f.
realise vt se rendre compte de; réaliser.
reality n réalité f.
realm n royaume m.
ream n rame f de papier.
reap vt moissonner.
reaper n moissonneuse f (machine).
reappear vi réapparaître.
rear n arrière m; derrière m; * vt élever, dresser.
rearmament n réarmement m.
reason n raison f; cause f; * vt vi raisonner.
reasonable adj raisonnable.
reasonableness n bon sens m, sagesse f.
reasonably adv raisonnablement.
reasoning n raisonnement m.
reassure vt rassurer; (com) réassurer.
rebel n rebelle mf; * vi se rebeller.
rebellion n rébellion f.
rebellious adj rebelle.
rebound vi rebondir.
rebuff n rebuffade f; * vt repousser.
rebuild vt reconstruire.

rebuke vt réprimander; * n réprimande f.

rebut vt réfuter.

recalcitrant adj récalcitrant.

recall vt (se) rappeler; retirer; * n retrait m.

recant vt rétracter, désavouer.

recantation n rétractation f.

recapitulate vt récapituler.

recapitulation n récapitulation f.

recapture n reprise f.

recede vi reculer.

receipt n reçu m; réception f; ~s npl recettes fpl.

receivable adj recevable.

receive vt recevoir; accueillir.

recent adj récent, neuf; ~ly adv récemment.

receptacle n récipient m.

reception n réception f.

recess n (law) vacance f; renfoncement m; recoin m.

recession n recul m; (com) récession f.

recipe n recette f.

recipient n destinataire mf.

reciprocal adj ~ly adv réciproque(ment).

reciprocate vi rendre la pareille.

reciprocity n réciprocité f.

recital n récit m; récital m.

recite vt réciter; exposer, énumérer.

reckless adj téméraire; ~ly adv imprudemment.

reckon vt compter, calculer; * vi calculer.

reckoning n compte m; calcul m.

reclaim vt assainir; récupérer.

reclaimable adj remboursable; récupérable.

recline vt reposer; * vi être allongé.

recluse n reclus m -e f.

recognise vt reconnaître.

recognition n reconnaissance f.

recoil vi reculer.

recollect vt se rappeler, se souvenir de.

recollection n souvenir m.

recommence vt recommencer.

recommend vt recommander.

recommendation n recommandation f.

recompense n récompense f; * vt récompenser.

reconcilable adj conciliable.

reconcile vt réconcilier.

reconciliation n réconciliation f.

recondite adj abstrus, obscur.

reconnoitre vt (mil) reconnaître.

reconsider vt reconsidérer.

reconstruct vt reconstruire.

record vt enregistrer; consigner par écrit; * n rapport m, registre m; disque m; record m; ~s npl archives fpl.

recorder n magnétophone m, archiviste mf; (mus) flûte à bec f.

recount vt raconter.

recourse n recours m.

recover vt retrouver; reprendre; récupérer; * vi se remettre, se rétablir.

recoverable adj récupérable.

recovery n guérison f; reprise f.

recreation n détente f; récréation f.

recriminate vi récriminer.

recrimination n récrimination f.

recruit vt recruter; * n (mil) recrue f.

recruiting n recrutement m.

rectangle n rectangle m.

rectangular adj rectangulaire.

rectification n rectification f.
rectify vt rectifier.
rectilinear adj rectiligne.
rectitude n rectitude f.
rector n pasteur m.
recumbent adj couché, étendu.
recur vi se reproduire.
recurrence n répétition f.
recurrent adj répétitif.
red adj rouge; * n rouge m.
redden vt rougir.
reddish adj rougeâtre.
redeem vt racheter, rembourser.
redeemable adj rachetable.
Redeemer n Rédempteur m.
redemption n rachat m.
redeploy vt réaffecter.
redhanded adj: **to catch sb ~** prendre quelqu'un la main dans le sac.
redhot adj brûlant, ardent.
red-letter day n jour à marquer d'une pierre blanche f.
redness n rougeur, rousseur f.
redolent adj parfumé, odorant.
redouble vt vi redoubler.
redress vt réparer; corriger; redresser; * n réparation f, redressement m.
redskin n Peau-Rouge mf.
red tape n (fig) paperasserie f.
reduce vt réduire; diminuer; abaisser.
reducible adj réductible.
reduction n réduction f; baisse f.
redundancy n licenciement m.
redundant adj superflu; licencié.
reed n roseau m.
reedy adj couvert de roseaux.
reef n (mar) ris m; récif m.
reek n puanteur f; * vi empester; puer.

reel n bobine f; bande f; dévidoir m; * vi chanceler.
re-election n réélection f.
re-engage vt rengager.
re-enter vt rentrer.
re-establish vt rétablir; réhabiliter.
re-establishment n rétablissement m; restauration f.
refectory n réfectoire m.
refer vt soumettre, renvoyer; se référer à; * vi se référer.
referee n arbitre m.
reference n référence, allusion f.
refine vt raffiner, affiner.
refinement n raffinement m; raffinerie f; culture f.
refinery n raffinerie f.
refit vt réparer (also mar)
reflect vt réfléchir, refléter; * vi réfléchir.
reflection n réflexion, pensée f.
reflector n réflecteur m; cataphote m.
reflex adj réflexe.
reform vt réformer; * vi se réformer.
reform, reformation n réforme f.
reformer n réformateur m -trice f.
reformist n réformiste mf.
refract vt réfracter.
refraction n réfraction f.
refrain vi: **to ~ from sth** s'abstenir de qch.
refresh vt rafraîchir.
refreshment n rafraîchissement m.
refrigerator n glacière f; réfrigérateur m.
refuel vi se ravitailler (en carburant).
refuge n refuge, asile m.
refugee n réfugié m -e f.

refund vt rembourser; * n remboursement m.

refurbish vt rénover.

refusal n refus m.

refuse vt refuser; * n déchets mpl.

refute vt réfuter.

regain vt recouvrer, reprendre.

regal adj royal.

regale vt régaler.

regalia n insignes mpl.

regard vt considérer; * n considération f; respect m.

regarding pr en ce qui concerne.

regardless adv quand même, malgré tout.

regatta n régate f.

regency n régence f.

regenerate vt régénérer; * adj régénéré.

regeneration n régénération f.

regent n régent m.

regime n régime m.

regiment n régiment m.

region n région f.

register n registre m; * vt enregistrer; **~ed letter** n lettre recommandée f.

registrar n officier d'état civil m.

registration n enregistrement m.

registry n enregistrement m.

regressive adj régressif.

regret n regret m * vt regretter.

regretful adj plein de regrets.

regular adj régulier; ordinaire; **~ly** adv régulièrement; * n habitué m -e f.

regularity n régularité f.

regulate vt régler, réglementer.

regulation n règlement m; réglementation f.

regulator n régulateur m.

rehabilitate vt réhabiliter.

rehabilitation n réhabilitation f.

rehearsal n répétition f.

rehearse vt répéter; raconter.

reign n règne m; * vi régner.

reimburse vt rembourser.

reimbursement n remboursement m.

rein n rêne f; * vt ~ **in** (fig) contenir.

reindeer n renne m.

reinforce vt renforcer.

reinstate vt réintégrer.

reinsure vt (com) réassurer.

reissue n réédition f.

reiterate vt réitérer.

reiteration n réitération, répétition f.

reject vt rejeter.

rejection n refus, rejet m.

rejoice vt réjouir; * vi se réjouir.

rejoicing n réjouissance f.

relapse vi retomber; * n rechute f.

relate vt relater; rapprocher; * vi se rapporter.

related adj apparenté.

relation n rapport m; parent m.

relationship n lien de parenté m; relation f; rapport m.

relative adj relatif; **~ly** adv relativement; * n parent m -e f.

relax vt relâcher; détendre; * vi se relâcher; se détendre.

relaxation n relâchement m; détente f.

relay n relais m; * vt retransmettre.

release vt libérer, relâcher; * n libération f; décharge f.

relegate vt reléguer.

relegation n relégation f.

relent vi s'adoucir.

relentless adj implacable.

relevant adj pertinent.

reliable adj fiable, digne de confiance.

reliance n confiance f.

relic n relique f.

relief n soulagement m; secours m.

relieve vt soulager, alléger; secourir.

religion n religion f.

religious adj religieux; **~ly** adv religieusement.

relinquish vt abandonner, renoncer à.

relish n saveur f; goût m; attrait m; * vt savourer, se délecter de.

reluctance n répugnance f.

reluctant adj peu disposé.

rely vi compter sur, avoir confiance en.

remain vi rester, demeurer.

remainder n reste, restant m.

remains npl restes, vestiges mpl; dépouille f.

remand vt: **to ~ in custody** mettre en détention préventive.

remark n remarque, observation f; * vt (faire) remarquer, (faire) observer.

remarkable adj remarquable, notable.

remarkably adv remarquablement.

remarry vi se remarier.

remedial adj de rattrapage.

remedy n remède, recours m; * vt remédier à.

remember vt se souvenir de; se rappeler.

remembrance n mémoire f; souvenir m.

remind vt rappeler.

reminiscence n réminiscence f.

remiss adj négligent.

remission n rémission f.

remit vt remettre, pardonner; * vi diminuer.

remittance n remise f.

remnant n reste, restant m.

remodel vt remodeler.

remonstrate vi protester.

remorse n remords m.

remorseless adj implacable.

remote adj lointain, éloigné; **~ly** adv au loin, de loin.

remoteness n éloignement m; isolement m.

removable adj amovible.

removal n suppression f; déménagement m.

remove vt enlever; * vi déménager.

remunerate vt rémunérer.

remuneration n rémunération f.

render vt rendre, remettre; traduire; (law) rendre.

rendezvous n rendez-vous m; point de ralliement m.

renegade n renégat m -e f.

renew vt renouveler.

renewal n renouvellement m.

rennet n présure f.

renounce vt renoncer à.

renovate vt rénover.

renovation n rénovation f.

renown n renommée f; célébrité f.

renowned adj célèbre, renommé.

rent n loyer m; location f; * vt louer.

rental n loyer m.

renunciation n renonciation f.

reopen vt rouvrir.

reorganisation n réorganisation f.

reorganise vt réorganiser.

repair vt réparer; * n réparation f.

repairable adj réparable.

reparation n réparation f.

repartee n répartie, réplique f.

repatriate vt rapatrier.

repay vt rembourser; rendre, récompenser.

repayment n remboursement m.

repeal vt abroger, annuler; * n abrogation, annulation f.

repeat vt répéter.

repeatedly adv à plusieurs reprises.

repeater n montre à répétition f.

repel vt repousser, rebuter.

repent vi se repentir.

repentance n repentir m.

repentant adj repentant.

repertory n répertoire m.

repetition n répétition f, réitération f.

replace vt replacer; remplacer.

replant vt replanter.

replenish vt remplir de nouveau.

replete adj rempli, rassasié.

reply n réponse f; * vi répondre.

report vt rapporter, relater; rendre compte de; * n rapport m; compte rendu m; rumeur f.

reporter n journaliste mf.

repose vi (se) reposer; * n repos m.

repository n dépôt m.

repossess vt reprendre possession de.

reprehend vt condamner.

reprehensible adj répréhensible.

represent vt représenter.

representation n représentation f.

representative adj représentatif; * n représentant(e) m(f).

repress vt réprimer, contenir.

repression n répression f.

repressive adj répressif.

reprieve vt accorder un sursis ou un répit à; * n sursis m.

reprimand vt réprimander, blâmer; * n blâme m; réprimande f.

reprint vt réimprimer.

reprisal n représailles fpl.

reproach n reproche, opprobre m; * vt reprocher.

reproachful adj réprobateur; ~ly adv d'un air de reproche.

reproduce vt reproduire.

reproduction n reproduction f.

reptile n reptile m.

republic n république f.

republican adj n républicain m -e f.

republicanism n républicanisme m.

repudiate vt renier.

repugnance n répugnance f, dégoût m.

repugnant adj répugnant; ~ly adv avec répugnance.

repulse vt repousser, rejeter; * n rebuffade f; refus m.

repulsion n répulsion f.

repulsive adj répulsif.

reputable adj honorable.

reputation n réputation f.

repute n renom m.

request n demande, requête f; * vt demander.

require vt demander, nécessiter.

requirement n besoin m; exigence f.

requisite adj nécessaire, indispensable; * n objet(s) nécessaire(s) m(pl).

requisition n demande; (mil) réquisition f.

requite vt rembourser.

rescind vt annuler, abroger.

rescue vt sauver, secourir; * n secours m, délivrance f.

research vt faire des/de la recherche(s); * n recherche(s) f(pl).

resemblance n ressemblance f.

resemble vt ressembler à.

resent vt être contrarié/irrité par.

resentful adj plein de ressentiment; amer; ~ly adv avec ressentiment.

resentment n ressentiment m.

reservation n réserve f; réservation f.

reserve vt réserver; * n réserve f.

reservedly adv avec réserve.

reservoir n réservoir m.

reside vi résider.

residence n résidence f; séjour m.

resident adj résidant; * n résident m -e f.

residuary adj restant; ~ legatee n (law) légataire universel m.

residue n reste, résidu m.

residuum n (chem) résidu m.

resign vt démissionner de, renoncer à, céder; se résigner à; * vi démissionner.

resignation n démission f.

resin n résine f.

resinous adj résineux.

resist vt résister, s'opposer.

resistance n résistance f.

resolute adj ~ly adv résolu(ment).

resolution n résolution f.

resolve vt résoudre; * vi (se) résoudre, (se) décider.

resonance n résonance f.

resonant adj résonant.

resort vi recourir; * n lieu de vacances m; recours m.

resound vi résonner.

resource n ressource(s) f(pl); expédient m.

respect n respect m; égard m; rapport m; ~s pl respects mpl; * vt respecter.

respectability n respectabilité f.

respectable adj respectable; considérable; ~bly adv convenablement.

respectful adj respectueux; ~ly adv respectueusement.

respecting prep en ce qui concerne.

respective adj respectif; ~ly adv respectivement.

respirator n respirateur m.

respiratory adj respiratoire.

respite n répit m; (law) sursis m; * vt repousser, différer.

resplendence n resplendissement m, splendeur f.

resplendent adj resplendissant.

respond vi répondre; réagir.

respondent n (law) défendeur m -deresse f.

response n réponse, réaction f.

responsibility n responsabilité f.

responsible adj responsable.

responsive adj sensible à, réceptif.

rest n repos m; (mus) pause f; reste, restant m; * vt faire/or laisser reposer; appuyer; * vi se reposer, reposer.

resting place n lieu de repos m.

restitution n restitution f.

restive adj rétif, récalcitrant; agité.

restless adj agité; instable.

restoration n restauration f.

restorative adj fortifiant.

restore vt restituer, restaurer.

restrain vt retenir, contenir.

restraint n contrainte, entrave f.

restrict vt restreindre, limiter.

restriction n restriction f.

restrictive adj restrictif.

rest room n (US) toilettes fpl.

result vi résulter; * n résultat m.

resume vt reprendre.

resurrection n résurrection f.

resuscitate vt réanimer.

retail vt vendre au détail, détailler; * n vente au détail f.

retain vt retenir, conserver.

retainer n serviteur m; ~s pl arrhes fpl; suite f.

retake vt reprendre.

retaliate vi se venger.

retaliation n représailles fpl.

retardation n retard m.

retarded adj qui retient bien.

retch vi avoir des haut-le-cœur.

retention n rétention f.

retentive adj qui retient bien.

reticence n réticence f.

reticule n réticule m.

retina n rétine f.

retire vt mettre à la retraite; * vi se retirer; prendre sa retraite.

retired adj retraité, à la retraite.

retirement n isolement m; retraite f.

retort vt rétorquer; * n réplique f.

retouch vt retoucher.

retrace vt retracer.

retract vt rétracter; retirer.

retrain vt recycler.

retraining n recyclage m.

retreat n repli m; * vi se retirer.

retribution n châtiment m; récompense f.

retrievable adj récupérable; réparable.

retrieve vt récupérer, recouvrer.

retriever n chien d'arrêt m.

retrograde adj rétrograde.

retrospect, retrospection n regard rétrospectif m.

retrospective adj rétrospectif.

return vt rendre; restituer; renvoyer; * n retour m; renvoi m; récompense f; revenu m; remboursement m.

reunion n réunion f.

reunite vt réunir; * vi se réunir.

reveal vt révéler.

revel vi faire la fête.

revelation n révélation f.

reveller n fêtard m.

revelry n fête f.

revenge vt venger; * n vengeance f.

revengeful adj vindicatif.

revenue n revenu m; rente f.

reverberate vt réverbérer; * vi résonner, retentir; se réverbérer.

reverberation n répercussion f; réverbération f.

revere vt révérer, vénérer.

reverence n vénération f; * vt révérer.

reverend adj révérend; vénérable; * n curé m.

reverent, reverential adj révérenciel, respectueux.

reversal n renversement m; annulation f.

reverse vt renverser; annuler; * vi

faire marche arrière; * n inverse m; contraire m; revers m.

reversible adj révocable; réversible.

reversion n retour m; réversion f.

revert vi revenir; retourner.

review vt revoir; (mil) passer en revue; * n revue f; examen m.

reviewer n critique m.

revile vt vilipender.

revise vt réviser; mettre à jour.

reviser n réviseur m.

revision n révision f.

revisit vt retourner voir.

revival n reprise f; renouveau m.

revive vt ranimer; raviver; * vi reprendre connaissance; reprendre.

revocation n révocation f.

revoke vt révoquer, annuler.

revolt vi se révolter; * n révolte f.

revolting adj exécrable.

revolution n révolution f.

revolutionary adj n révolutionnaire mf.

revolve vt (re)tourner; * vi tourner.

revolving adj tournant.

revue n revue f.

revulsion n écœurement m.

reward n récompense f; * vt récompenser.

rhapsody n r(h)apsodie f.

rhetoric n rhétorique f.

rhetorical adj rhétorique.

rheumatic adj rhumatisant.

rheumatism n rhumatisme m.

rhinoceros n rhinocéros m.

rhombus n rhombe m.

rhomboid n rhomboïd m.

rhubarb n rhubarbe f.

rhyme n rime f; vers mpl; * vi rimer.

rhythm n rythme m.

rhythmical adj rythmique.

rib n côte f.

ribald adj paillard.

ribbon n ruban m; lambeaux mpl.

rice n riz m.

rich adj riche; somptueux; abondant; ~ly adv richement.

riches npl richesse f.

richness n richesse f; abondance f.

rickets n rachitisme m.

rickety adj rachitique.

rid vt débarrasser; se débarrasser de.

riddance n: good ~! bon débarras!

riddle n énigme f; crible m; * vt cribler.

ride vi monter à cheval; aller en voiture; * n promenade à cheval ou en voiture f.

rider n cavalier m -ière f.

ridge n arête, crête f; chaîne f; * vt rider, strier.

ridicule n ridicule m; raillerie f; * vt ridiculiser.

ridiculous adj ~ly adv ridicule(ment).

riding n équitation f; monte f.

riding habit n tenue d'amazone f.

riding school n manège m.

rife adj répandu, abondant.

riffraff n racaille f.

rifle vt dévaliser, piller; strier, rayer; * n fusil m.

rifleman n fusilier m.

rig vt équiper; truquer; (mar) gréer; * n gréement m; plateforme de forage f.

rigging n (mar) gréement m.

right adj droit, bien; juste; équitable; ~! bien!, bon!; ~ly adv bien; correctement; à juste titre; * n justice f; raison f; droit m; droite f; * vt redresser.

righteous adj droit, vertueux; ~ly adv vertueusement.

righteousness n droiture f; vertu f.

rigid adj rigide; sévère, strict; ~ly adv rigidement.

rigidity n rigidité f; sévérité f.

rigmarole n galimatias m.

rigorous adj rigoureux; ~ly adv rigoureusement.

rigour n rigueur f; sévérité f.

rim n bord m, monture f.

rind n peau, écorce f.

ring n anneau, cercle, rond m; bague f; tintement m de cloche; * vt sonner; * vi sonner, retentir; ~ **the bell** sonner.

ringer n carillonneur m.

ringleader n meneur m.

ringlet n anglaise f.

ringworm n (med) teigne f.

rink n (also **ice** ~) patinoire f.

rinse vt rincer.

riot n émeute f; * vi se livrer à une émeute.

rioter n émeutier m, -ière f.

riotous adj séditieux; dissolu; ~ly adv de façon tapageuse.

rip vt déchirer, fendre.

ripe adj mûr.

ripen vt vi mûrir.

ripeness n maturité f.

rip-off n (sl): **it's a** ~! c'est du vol!

ripple n rider f; * vi se rider; * n ondulation f, ride f.

rise vi se lever; naître; se soulever; monter; provenir de; s'élever;

croître; ressusciter; * n hausse f; augmentation f; montée f; lever m; source f.

rising n insurrection f; levée, clôture f.

risk n risque, danger m; * vt risquer.

risky adj risqué.

rissole n rissole f.

rite n rite m.

ritual adj n rituel m.

rival adj rival; * n rival m -e f; * vt rivaliser avec, concurrencer.

rivalry n rivalité f.

river n rivière f.

rivet n rivet m; * vt riveter, river.

rivulet n petit ruisseau m.

roach n blatte f.

road n route f.

roadsign n panneau de signalisation m.

roadstead n (mar) rade f.

roadworks npl travaux routiers mpl.

roam vt parcourir; errer dans; * vi errer.

roan adj rouan.

roar vi hurler, rugir; mugir; * n hurlement m; rugissement m, mugissement m; grondement m.

roast vt rôtir; griller.

roast beef n rôti de bœuf m.

rob vt voler.

robber n voleur m -euse f.

robbery n vol m.

robe n robe (de cérémonie) f; peignoir m de bain; * vt revêtir d'une robe de cérémonie.

robin (redbreast) n rouge-gorge m.

robust adj robuste.

robustness n robustesse f.

rock n roche f; rocher m; roc m; * vt bercer; balancer; ébranler; * vi (se) balancer.

rock and roll n rock (and roll) m.

rock crystal n cristal de roche m.

rocket n fusée f.

rocking chair n fauteuil à bascule m.

rock salt n sel gemme m.

rocky adj rocheux.

rod n baguette, tringle, canne f.

rodent n rongeur m.

roe n chevreuil m; œufs mpl de poisson.

roebuck n chevreuil (mâle) m.

rogation n rogations fpl.

rogue n coquin, polisson m; gredin m.

roguish adj coquin.

roll vt rouler; étendre; enrouler; * vi (se) rouler; * n roulement m; rouleau m; liste f; catalogue m; liasse f; petit pain m.

roller n rouleau, cylindre m.

roller skates npl patins à roulettes mpl.

rolling pin n rouleau à pâtisserie m.

Roman Catholic adj n catholique mf.

romance n romance f; roman m; conte m; fable f.

romantic adj romantique.

romp vi jouer bruyamment.

roof n toit m; voûte f; * vt couvrir.

roofing n toiture f.

rook n freux m; tour f (aux échecs).

room n pièce, salle f; place f, espace m; chambre f.

roominess n grande envergure f.

rooming house n pension f.

roomy adj spacieux.

roost n perchoir m; * vi se percher.

root n racine f; origine f; * vt vi ~ out extirper; dénicher.

rooted adj enraciné; ancré.

rope n corde f; cordage m; * vi attacher.

ropemaker n cordier m.

rosary n rosaire m.

rose n rose f.

rosebed n massif de roses m.

rosebud n bouton de rose m.

rosebush n rosier m.

rosemary n (bot) romarin m.

rosette n rosette f.

rose wine n (vin) rosé m.

rosewood n bois de rose m.

rosiness n couleur rosée f.

rosy adj rosé.

rot vi pourrir; * n pourriture f.

rotate vt faire tourner; * vi tourner.

rotation n rotation f.

rote n: by ~ par cœur.

rotten adj pourri; corrompu.

rottenness n pourriture f.

rotund adj rond, replet, arrondi.

rouble n rouble m.

rouge n rouge (à joues) m.

rough adj accidenté, inégal, rugueux; rude, brutal, brusque; houleux; ~ly adv rudement.

roughcast n crépi m.

roughen vt rendre rugueux.

roughness n rugosité f; rudesse, brusquerie f; agitation f.

round adj rond, circulaire; rondelet; franc; * n cercle m; rond m; tour m; tournée f; partie f; ronde f; canon m; série f; * adv autour de; environ; ~ly adv rondement; franchement; * vt contourner; arrondir.

roundabout adj détourné, indirect; * n rond-point m.

roundness n rondeur f.

rouse vt réveiller; exciter.

rout n déroute, débâcle f; * vt mettre en déroute.

route n itinéraire m; route f.

routine adj habituel; * n routine f; numéro m.

rove vi vagabonder, errer.

rover n vagabond m -e f; pirate m.

row n querelle f; vacarme m.

row n rangée, file f; * vt (mar) ramer.

rowdy n hooligan, voyou m.

rower n rameur m -euse f.

royal adj royal; princier; ~ly adv royalement.

royalist n royaliste mf.

royalty n royauté f; droits d'auteur mpl; royalties fpl; redevance f; membres de la famille royale mpl.

rub vt frotter; irriter; * n frottement m; (fig) ennui m; difficulté f.

rubber n caoutchouc m, gomme f; préservatif m.

rubber n caoutchouc m, gomme f; préservatif m.

rubber-band n élastique m.

rubbish n détritus m; ordures fpl; bêtises fpl; décombres mpl.

rubric n rubrique f.

ruby n rubis m.

rucksack n sac à dos m.

rudder n gouvernail m.

ruddiness n teint vif m, rougeur f.

ruddy adj coloré, rouge.

rude adj impoli, rude, brusque; grossier; primitif; ~ly adv impoliment, grossièrement.

rudeness n impolitesse f; rudesse, insolence f.

rudiment n rudiments mpl.

rue vt regretter amèrement; * n (bot) rue f.

rueful adj triste.

ruffian n voyou m, brute f; * adj brutal.

ruffle vt ébouriffer, déranger; rider.

rug n tapis m, carpette f.

rugby n rugby m.

rugged adj accidenté, déchiqueté; rude; robuste.

ruin n ruine f; perte f; ruines fpl; * vt ruiner; détruire.

ruinous adj ruineux.

rule n règle f; règlement m; pouvoir m; domination f; * vt gouverner, dominer; décider, régler, diriger.

ruler n dirigeant m, -e f; règle f.

rum n rhum m.

rumble vi gronder, tonner.

ruminate vt ruminer.

rummage vi fouiller.

rumour n rumeur f; * vt faire courir le bruit.

rump n croupe f.

run vt diriger; organiser; faire couler; passer; **to ~ the risk** courir le risque; * vi courir; fuir, se sauver; filer; fonctionner; aller; couler; concourir; * n course, compétition f; parcours m; cours m; série f; mode f; ruée f.

runaway n fugitif m, -ive f, fuyard m.

rung n barreau, échelon m.

runner n coureur m; concurrent m, -e f; messager m.

running n course f; direction f.

runway n piste de décollage f.

rupture n rupture f; hernie f; * vt rompre; * vi se rompre.

rural adj rural, champêtre.

ruse n ruse f, stratagème m.

rush n jonc m; ruée f; hâte f; * vt pousser vivement; * vi se précipiter, s'élancer.

rusk n biscotte f.

russet adj roux.

rust n rouille f; * vi se rouiller.

rustic adj rustique; * n paysan, rustaud m.

rustiness n rouille f.

rustle vi bruire; * vt faire bruire; froisser.

rustling n vol de bétail m; bruissement m.

rusty adj rouillé; roux.

rut n rut m; ornière f.

ruthless adj cruel, impitoyable; **~ly** adv sans pitié.

rye n (bot) seigle m.

S

Sabbath n sabbat m; dimanche m.

saber n sabre m.

sable n zibeline f.

sabotage n sabotage m.

saccharin n saccharine f.

sachet n sachet m.

sack n sac m; * vt mettre à sac; renvoyer.

sacrament n sacrement m; Eucharistie f.

sacramental adj sacramentel.

sacred adj saint, sacré; inviolable.

sacredness n (caractère) sacré m.

sacrifice n sacrifice m; * vt sacrifier.

sacrificial adj sacrificiel.

sacrilege n sacrilège m.

sacrilegious adj sacrilège.

sad adj triste, déprimé; attristant; regrettable; **~ly** adv tristement.

sadden vt attrister.

saddle n selle f; col m; * vt seller.

saddlebag n sacoche de selle f.

saddler n sellier m.

sadness n tristesse f.

safari n safari m.

safe adj sûr; en sécurité; hors de danger; sans danger; **~ly** adv sans accident; **~ and sound** sain et sauf; * n coffre-fort m.

safe-conduct n sauf-conduit m.

safeguard n sauvegarde f; * vt sauvegarder, protéger.

safety n sécurité f; sûreté f.

safety belt n ceinture de sécurité f.

safety pin n épingle de nourrice f.

saffron n safran m.

sage n (bot) sauge f; sage m; * adj sage; **~ly** adv avec sagesse.

Sagittarius n Sagittaire m (signe du zodiaque).

sago n (bot) sagou m.

sail n voile f; * vt piloter; * vi aller à la voile, naviguer.

sailing n navigation f.

sailor n marin m.

saint n saint m, -e f.

sainted, saintly adj saint.

sake n bien m, égard m; **for God's ~** pour l'amour de Dieu.

salad n salade f.
salad bowl n saladier m.
salad dressing n vinaigrette f.
salad oil n huile de table f.
salamander n salamandre f.
salary n salaire m.
sale n vente f; solde m.
saleable adj vendable.
salesman n vendeur m.
saleswoman n vendeuse f.
salient adj saillant.
saline adj salin.
saliva n salive f.
sallow adj jaunâtre, cireux.
sally n (mil) sortie, saillie f; * vi saillir.
salmon n saumon m.
salmon trout n truite saumonée f.
saloon n bar m.
salt n sel m; * vt saler.
salt cellar n salière f.
saltness n salinité f.
saltpetre n salpêtre m.
saltworks npl salin m.
salubrious adj salubre, sain.
salubrity n salubrité f.
salutary adj salutaire.
salutation n salutation(s) f(pl).
salute vt saluer; * n salut m.
salvage n (mar) droit de sauvetage m.
salvation n salut m.
salve n baume, onguent m.
salver n plateau m.
salvo n salve f; réserve f.
same adj même, identique.
sameness n identité f.
sample n échantillon m; prélèvement m; * vt goûter.
sampler n échantillonneur m, -euse f; modèle m.

sanatorium n sanatorium m.
sanctify vt sanctifier.
sanctimonious adj cagot.
sanction n sanction f; * vt sanctionner.
sanctity n sainteté f.
sanctuary n sanctuaire m; asile m.
sand n sable m; * vt sabler.
sandal n sandale f.
sandbag n (mil) sac de terre m.
sandpit n carrière de sable f.
sandstone n grès m.
sandwich n sandwich m.
sandy adj sablonneux, sableux.
sane adj sain.
sanguinary adj sanguinaire, sanglant.
sanguine adj sanguin.
sanitary towel n serviette hygiénique f.
sanity n santé mentale, raison f.
sap n sève f; * vt miner.
sapient adj sage, prudent.
sapling n jeune arbre m.
sapphire n saphir m.
sarcasm n sarcasme m.
sarcastic adj sarcastique, caustique; ~ally adv d'une manière sarcastique.
sarcophagus n sarcophage m.
sardine n sardine f.
sash n écharpe f; ceinture f.
sash window n fenêtre à guillotine f.
sassy adj insolent.
Satan n Satan m.
satanic(al) adj satanique.
satchel n cartable m.
satellite n satellite m.
satiate, sate vt rassasier, assouvir.

satin n satin m; * adj en ou de satin.

satire n satire f.

satiric(al) adj satirique; **~ly** adv d'une manière satirique.

satirist n écrivain satirique m.

satirize vt faire la satire de.

satisfaction n satisfaction f.

satisfactorily adv d'une manière satisfaisante.

satisfactory adj satisfaisant.

satisfy vt satisfaire; convaincre.

saturate vt saturer.

Saturday n samedi m.

saturnine adj saturnien, sombre.

satyr n satyre m.

sauce n sauce f; assaisonnement m; * vt assaisonner.

saucepan n casserole f.

saucer n soucoupe f.

saucily adv avec impertinence.

sauciness n impertinence, insolence f.

saucy adj impertinent.

saunter vi flâner, se balader.

sausage n saucisse f.

savage adj sauvage, barbare; **~ly** adv sauvagement; * n sauvage mf.

savageness n sauvagerie f; barbarie f.

savagery n sauvagerie, barbarie f.

savannah n savane f.

save vt sauver; économiser; épargner; éviter; conserver; * adv sauf, à l'exception de; * n (sport) arrêt m.

saveloy n cervelas m.

saver n libérateur m, -trice f; épargnant m, -e f.

saving adj économique, économe;

* prep sauf, à l'exception de; *n sauvetage m; **~s** pl économies fpl, épargne f.

savings account n compte d'épargne m.

savings and loan association n organisme de crédit immobilier m.

savings bank n caisse d'épargne f.

Saviour n Sauveur m.

savour n saveur f; goût m; * vt déguster, savourer.

savouriness n goût m; saveur f.

savoury adj savoureux.

saw n scie f; * vt scier.

sawdust n sciure f.

sawfish n poisson scie m.

sawmill n scierie f.

sawyer n scieur m.

saxophone n saxophone m.

say vt dire.

saying n dicton, proverbe m.

scab n gale f; croûte f.

scabbard n gaine f; fourreau m.

scabby adj galeux.

scaffold n échafaud m; échafaudage m.

scaffolding n échafaudage m.

scald vt échauder; * n brûlure f.

scale n balance f; échelle f; gamme f; écaille f; * vt escalader; écailler.

scallion n échalote f.

scallop n feston m; * vt festonner.

scalp n cuir chevelu m; * vt scalper.

scamp n coquin m.

scamper vi galoper.

scampi npl langoustines fpl.

scan vt scruter; explorer; scander.

scandal n scandale m; infamie f.

scandalize vt scandaliser.

scandalous adj scandaleux; **~ly** adv scandaleusement.

scant, scanty adj rare, insuffisant.

scantily adv pauvrement, insuffisamment.

scantiness n insuffisance, pauvreté f.

scapegoat n bouc émissaire m.

scar n cicatrice f; * vt marquer d'une cicatrice.

scarce adj rare; **~ly** adv à peine.

scarcity n rareté f; pénurie f.

scare vt effrayer; * n peur; panique f.

scarecrow n épouvantail m.

scarf n écharpe f.

scarlatina n scarlatine f.

scarlet n écarlate f; * adj écarlate.

scarp n escarpement m.

scat interj (sl) ouste!

scatter vt éparpiller; disperser.

scavenger n charognard m; éboueur m.

scenario n scénario m; (also fig).

scene n scène f; lieu m; spectacle m, vue f.

scenery n vue f; décor (de théâtre) m.

scenic adj scénique.

scent n parfum m, odeur f; odorat m; piste f; * vt parfumer.

scent bottle n flacon à parfum m.

scentless adj sans odeur; inodore.

sceptic n sceptique mf.

sceptic(al) adj sceptique.

scepticism n scepticisme m.

sceptre n sceptre m.

schedule n horaire m; programme m; liste f.

m; système m; machination f; * vt machiner; * vi intriguer.

schemer n conspirateur m, -trice f, intrigant m, -e f.

schism n schisme m.

schismatic n schismatique mf.

scholar n élève mf, érudit m, -e f.

scholarship n savoir m, science f; bourse (d'études) f.

scholastic adj scolaire.

school n école f; * vt instruire.

schoolboy n écolier, élève m.

schoolgirl n écolière, élève f.

schooling n instruction, éducation f.

schoolmaster n instituteur, maître (d'école) m.

schoolmistress n institutrice, maîtresse (d'école) f.

schoolteacher n instituteur/trice mf; professeur mf.

schooner n (mart) goélette f.

sciatic n sciatique f.

sciatica n sciatique f.

science n science f.

scientific adj, **~ally** adv scientifique(ment).

scientist n scientifique mf.

scimitar n cimeterre m.

scintillate vi scintiller, étinceler.

scintillating adj brillant, scintillant.

scission n scission, division f.

scissors npl ciseaux mpl.

scoff vi se moquer.

scold vt réprimander; * vi grogner.

scoop n louche f; pelle f; exclusivité f; * vt évider; écoper.

scooter n scooter m; trottinette f.

scope n portée, envergure, étendue f; zone de compétence f; liberté d'action f.

scorch vt brûler; roussir, griller; * vi se brûler, roussir.

score n score m; marque f; entaille, rayure f; titre, égard m; compte m; (mus) partition f; vingtaine f; * vt marquer; souligner; * vi marquer un/des point(s).

scoreboard n tableau (d'affichage) m.

scorn vt mépriser; dédaigner; * n dédain, mépris m.

scornful adj dédaigneux; ~ly adv avec mépris.

Scorpio n Scorpion m (signe du zodiaque).

scorpion n scorpion m.

scotch vt mettre fin à.

Scotch n whisky m.

Scotch tape n scotch m.

scoundrel n vaurien m.

scour vt récurer, frotter; nettoyer; * vi battre la campagne.

scourge n fouet m; châtiment m; * vt fouetter; châtier.

scout n (mil) éclaireur m, -euse f; guetteur m; reconnaissance f; * vi aller en reconnaissance.

scowl vi se renfrogner; * n mine renfrognée f.

scragginess n décharnement m, maigreur extrême f, rugosité f.

scraggy adj rugueux; famélique.

scramble vi avancer à quatre pattes; grimper; se battre, se disputer; * n bousculade, ruée f; ascension f.

scrap n bout m; restes mpl; petit morceau m; bagarre f; ferraille f.

scrape vt, vi racler, gratter; * vt érafler; * n embarras m, ennui m.

scraper n racloir m.

scratch vt griffer, égratigner; gratter, griffonner; * n égratignure f.

scrawl vt, vi gribouiller; * n griffonnage m.

scream, **screech** vi hurler, pousser des cris; * n cri perçant, hurlement m.

screen n écran m; paravent m; rideau m; écran de cheminée; * vt abriter, cacher; projeter; passer au crible, sélectionner.

screenplay n scénario m.

screw n vis f; * vt visser; extorquer, soutirer.

screwdriver n tournevis m.

scribble vt gribouiller; * n gribouillage m.

scribe n scribe m.

scrimmage n mêlée f.

script n scénario m; script m.

scriptural adj biblique.

Scripture n Écriture sainte f.

scroll n rouleau (de papier ou parchemin) m.

scrub vt nettoyer à la brosse, récurer; annuler; * n broussailles fpl.

scruffy adj mal soigné.

scruple n scrupule m.

scrupulous adj scrupuleux; ~ly adv scrupuleusement.

scrutinize vt étudier minutieusement, examiner.

scrutiny n examen minutieux m.

scuffle n échauffourée, rixe f; * vi se bagarrer.

scull n aviron m.

scullery n arrière-cuisine f.

sculptor n sculpteur m, -trice f.

sculpture n sculpture f; * vt sculpter.

scum n écume f; crasse f; rebut m.

scurrilous adj injurieux; vil, ignoble; **~ly** adv injurieusement.

scurvy n scorbut m; * adj vil, mesquin.

scuttle n corbeille f; * vi courir précipitamment.

scythe n faux f.

sea n mer f; * adj marin; **heavy ~** mer houleuse f.

sea breeze n brise de mer f.

seacoast n côte f.

sea fight n combat naval m.

seafood n fruits de mer mpl.

sea front n bord de mer m.

seagreen adj vert glauque.

seagull n mouette f.

sea horse n hippocampe m.

seal n sceau m; phoque m; * vt sceller.

sealing wax n cire à cacheter f.

seam n couture f; * vt faire une couture.

seaman n marin m.

seamanship n habileté à naviguer f.

seamstress n couturière f.

seamy adj sordide.

sea plane n hydravion m.

seaport n port de mer m.

sear vt cautériser.

search vt fouiller; inspecter; examiner; scruter, sonder; * n fouille f; recherche f; perquisition f.

searchlight n projecteur m.

seashore n rivage m, bord de mer m.

seasick adj sujet au mal de mer.

seasickness n mal de mer m.

seaside n bord de mer m.

season n saison f; moment opportun m; assaisonnement m; * vt assaisonner; dessécher.

seasonable adj opportun, à propos.

seasonably adv de façon opportune, à propos.

seasoning n assaisonnement m.

season ticket n carte d'abonnement f.

seat n siège m; place f; derrière m; fond m; * vt (faire) asseoir; placer.

seat belt n ceinture de sécurité f.

seaward adj du large; **~s** adv vers le large.

seaweed n algue f.

seaworthy adj en état de naviguer.

secede vi faire sécession, se séparer.

secession n sécession f; séparation f.

seclude vt éloigner, isoler.

seclusion n solitude f; isolement m.

second adj, **~(ly)** adv deuxième(ment); * n second m; seconde f; (mus) seconde f; * vt aider; seconder.

secondary adj secondaire.

secondary school n collège d'enseignement secondaire m.

secondhand n article d'occasion m.

secrecy n secret m; discrétion f.

secret adj, n secret m; **~ly** adv secrètement.

secretary n secrétaire mf.

secrete vt cacher; (med) sécréter.

secretion n sécrétion f.

secretive adj secret, dissimulé.

sect n secte f.

sectarian n sectaire mf.

section n section f.

sector n secteur m.

secular adj séculaire.

secularize vt séculariser.

secure adj sûr; en sûreté **~ly** adv en sécurité; * vt mettre en sûreté; assurer.

security n sécurité f; sûreté f; protection f; caution f.

sedan n chaise à porteurs f.

sedate adj, **~ly** adv calme(ment), posé(ment).

sedateness n calme m.

sedative n sédatif m.

sedentary adj sédentaire.

sedge n (bot) carex m.

sediment n sédiment m; lie f; dépôt m.

sedition n sédition f.

seditious adj séditieux.

seduce vt séduire; corrompre.

seducer n séducteur m, -trice f.

seduction n séduction f.

seductive adj séduisant.

sedulous adj assidu; **~ly** adv assidûment.

see vt voir, remarquer, découvrir; connaître; juger; comprendre; * vi voir; comprendre; **~!** regarde!; tu vois!

seed n graine, semence f; * vi monter en graine.

seedling n semis m.

seedsman n grainetier m.

seed time n (époque des) semailles f(pl).

seedy adj minable.

seeing conj: ~ vu que.

seek vt chercher; demander.

seem vi paraître, sembler.

seeming n apparence f; **~ly** adv apparemment.

seemliness n bienséance f.

seemly adj convenable, bienséant.

seer n prophète m.

seesaw n bascule f; * vi osciller.

seethe vi bouillir, bouillonner.

segment n segment m.

seize vt saisir, attraper; opérer la saisie de.

seizure n capture f; saisie f.

seldom adv rarement, peu souvent.

select vt sélectionner, choisir; * adj choisi, sélectionné.

selection n sélection f.

self n soi-même; **the ~** le moi; * pref auto-.

self-command n maîtrise de soi f.

self-conceit n vanité f.

self-confident adj sûr de soi.

self-defence n autodéfense f.

self-denial n abnégation de soi f.

self-employed adj indépendant.

self-evident adj évident, qui va de soi.

self-governing adj autonome.

self-interest n intérêt personnel m.

selfish adj, **~ly** adv égoïste(ment).

selfishness n égoïsme m.

self-pity n apitoiement sur soi-même m.

self-portrait n autoportrait m.

self-possession n sang-froid m, assurance f.

self-reliant adj indépendant.

self-respect n respect de soi m.

selfsame adj exactement le même, identique.

self-satisfied *adj* suffisant.

self-seeking *adj* égoïste.

self-service *adj* libre-service.

self-styled *adj* soi-disant.

self-sufficient *adj* autosuffisant.

self-taught *adj* autodidacte.

self-willed *adj* obstiné, volontaire.

sell *vt* vendre; attraper; * *vi* se vendre.

seller *n* vendeur *m*, -euse *f*.

selling-off *n* liquidation *f*.

semblance *n* semblant *m*, apparence *f*.

semen *n* sperme *m*.

semester *n* semestre *m*.

semicircle *n* demi-cercle *m*.

semicircular *adj* semi-circulaire.

semicolon *n* point-virgule *m*.

semiconductor *n* semi-conducteur *n*.

seminary *n* séminaire *m*.

semitone *n* (*mus*) demi-ton *m*.

senate *n* sénat *m*.

senator *n* sénateur *m*, -trice *f*.

senatorial *adj* sénatorial.

send *vt* envoyer, expédier, adresser; émettre; pousser.

sender *n* expéditeur *m*, -trice *f*.

senile *adj* sénile.

senility *n* sénilité *f*.

senior *n* aîné *m*, -e *f*; * *adj* aîné; supérieur.

seniority *n* ancienneté *f*.

senna *n* (*bot*) séné *m*.

sensation *n* sensation *f*.

sense *n* sens *m*; sensation *f*; raison *f*; bon sens *m*; sentiment *m*.

senseless *adj* insensé; sans connaissance; ~ly *adv* stupidement.

senselessness *n* manque de bon sens *m*; absurdité *f*.

sensibility *n* sensibilité *f*.

sensible *adj* sensé, raisonnable; sensible.

sensibly *adj* raisonnablement.

sensitive *adj* sensible.

sensual, sensuous *adj*, ~ly *adv* sensuel(lement).

sensuality *n* sensualité *f*.

sentence *n* phrase *f*; condamnation *f*; * *vt* condamner, prononcer une sentence contre.

sententious *adj* sentencieux; ~ly *adv* sentencieusement.

sentient *adj* sensible.

sentiment *n* sentiment *m*; opinion *f*.

sentimental *adj* sentimental.

sentinel, sentry *n* sentinelle *f*.

sentry box *n* guérite *f*.

separable *adj* séparable.

separate *vt* séparer; * *vi* se séparer; * *adj* séparé; distinct; ~ly *adv* séparément.

separation *n* séparation *f*.

September *n* septembre *m*.

septennial *adj* septennal.

septuagenarian *n* septuagénaire *m*.

sepulchre *n* sépulcre *m*.

sequel *n* conséquence *f*; suite *f*.

sequence *n* ordre *m*, série *f*.

sequester, sequestrate *vt* séquestrer.

sequestration *n* séquestration *f*.

seraglio *n* sérail *m*.

seraph *n* séraphin *m*.

serenade *n* sérénade *f*; * *vt* jouer une sérénade pour.

serene *adj* serein, ~ly *adv* sereinement.

serenity *n* sérénité *f*.

serf *n* serf *m*, serve *f*.

serge n serge f.

sergeant n sergent m; caporalchef m; brigadier m.

serial adj de/en série; * n feuilleton m; téléroman m.

series n série f.

serious adj sérieux, grave; **~ly** adv sérieusement.

sermon n sermon m.

serous adj séreux.

serpent n serpent m.

serpentine adj sinueux; * n (chem) serpentine f.

serrated adj en dents de scie.

serum n sérum m.

servant n domestique mf.

servant-girl n servante, bonne f.

serve vt servir; desservir; faire; accomplir; * vi servir; être utile; **to ~ a warrant** remettre un mandat.

service n service m; office m; entretien m; * vt entretenir; réviser.

service station n station-service f.

serviceable adj utilisable; pratique.

servile adj servile.

servitude n servitude f, esclavage m.

session n séance, session f; réunion f.

set vt mettre, poser, placer; fixer, déterminer; * vi se coucher (soleil); se figer; se mettre; * n jeu m; service m; ensemble m; (cine) plateau m; set m; groupe m, bande f; * adj fixe, figé; prêt; déterminé.

settee n canapé m.

setter n setter m.

setting n disposition f; cadre m;

monture f; **~ of the sun** coucher du soleil m.

settle vt poser, installer, arranger; régler; calmer; * vi se poser; s'installer; se calmer.

settlement n règlement m; établissement m; accord m; résolution f; colonie f; colonisation f.

settler n colon m, colonisateur m, -trice f.

set-to n lutte f; combat m.

seven adj, n sept m.

seventeen adj, n dix-sept m.

seventeenth adj, n dix-septième mf.

seventh adj, n septième mf.

seventieth adj, n soixante-dixième mf.

seventy adj, n soixante-dix m.

sever vt séparer.

several adj, pn plusieurs.

severance n séparation f.

severe adj sévère, rigoureux, austère, dur; **~ly** adv sévèrement.

severity n sévérité f.

sew vt, vi coudre.

sewer n égout m.

sewerage n (système d') égouts mpl; eaux d'égout fpl.

sex n sexe m.

sewing machine n machine à coudre f.

sexist adj, n sexiste mf.

sextant n sextant m.

sexton n sacristain m.

sexual adj sexuel.

sexy adj sexy.

shabbily adv petitement, mesquinement.

shabbiness n aspect décrépit ou miteux.

shabby adj miteux.

shackle vt enchaîner; ~s npl chaînes fpl.

shade n ombre, obscurité f; nuance f; abat-jour m; * vt ombrager; abriter; atténuer.

shadiness n ombre f; ombrage m.

shadow n ombre f.

shadowy adj ombragé; sombre; indistinct.

shady adj ombreux, ombragé; sombre.

shaft n flèche f; fût m; puits m; (tech) arbre m; rayon m.

shag n tabac m; cormoran huppé m.

shaggy adj hirsute.

shake vt secouer; agiter; * vi trembler; chanceler; to ~ hands se serrer la main; * n secousse f; tremblement m.

shaking adj tremblant.

shaky adj tremblant.

shallow adj peu profond, superficiel; futile.

shallowness n manque de profondeur m; futilité f.

sham vt feindre; * n imitation f; imposture f; * adj feint, simulé.

shambles npl désordre m.

shame n honte f; * vt faire honte à, déshonorer.

shamefaced adj honteux, confus.

shameful adj honteux; scandaleux; ~ly adv honteusement.

shameless adj, ~ly adv effronté(ment).

shamelessness n effronterie, impudeur f.

shammy n chamois m.

shampoo vt faire un shampooing à; * n shampooing m.

shamrock n trèfle m.

shank n jambe f; hampe f; tuyau (de pipe) m; canon m.

shanty n baraque f.

shanty town n bidonville m.

shape n former; façonner; modeler; * vi prendre forme; * n forme, figure f; modèle m.

shapeless adj informe.

shapely adj bien proportionné.

share n part, portion f; (com) action f; soc (de charrue) m; * vt partager; répartir; * vi partager.

sharer n participant m.

shark n requin m.

sharp adj aigu, acéré, malin; fin; pénétrant; âpre, mordant, cinglant; perçant; vif, violent ; * n (mus) dièse m; * adv pile .

sharpen vt aiguiser, affûter.

sharply adv brusquement; sévèrement; vivement; nettement.

sharpness n tranchant m; finesse, acuité f; aigreur f.

shatter vt fracasser, détruire; * vi se fracasser.

shave vt raser, raboter; * vi se raser; n rasoir électrique m.

shaver n rasoir électrique m.

shaving n rasage m.

shaving brush n blaireau m.

shaving cream n crème à raser f.

shawl n châle m.

she pn elle.

sheaf n gerbe f; liasse f.

shear vt tondre; ~s npl cisailles fpl.

sheath n fourreau m.

shed vt verser, répandre; perdre; * n hangar m; cabane f.

sheen n lustre m.

sheep n mouton m.

sheepfold n parc à moutons m.

sheepish adj penaud; timide.

sheepishness n timidité f, air penaud m.

sheep-run n pâturage pour moutons m.

sheepskin n peau de mouton f.

sheer adj pur, absolu, véritable; abrupt; * adv abruptement.

sheet n drap m; plaque f; feuille (de papier) f; (mar) écoute f.

sheet anchor n ancre de veille f.

sheeting n toile pour draps f.

sheet iron n tôle f.

sheet lightning n éclairs en nappes mpl.

shelf n étagère f; (mar) écueil m; saillie f; **on the ~** au rancart.

shell n coquille f; carcasse f, écorce f; obus m; * vt écosser, décortiquer; bombarder; * vi se décortiquer.

shellfish npl invar crustacé m; fruits de mer mpl.

shelter n abri m; asile, refuge m; * vt abriter; protéger; * vi s'abriter.

shelve vt mettre au rancart.

shelving n rayonnage m.

shepherd n berger m.

shepherdess n bergère f.

sherbet n sorbet m.

sheriff n shérif m.

sherry n xérès m.

shield n bouclier m; écran protecteur m; * vt protéger.

shift vi changer; se déplacer; * vt

changer, bouger; transférer; * n changement m; roulement m.

shinbone n tibia m.

shine vi briller, reluire, illuminer; * vt cirer; * n éclat m.

shingle n galets mpl; **~s** pl (med) zona m.

shining adj resplendissant; * n éclat m.

shiny adj brillant, reluisant.

ship n bateau m; navire m; bâtiment m; * vt embarquer; transporter.

shipbuilding n construction navale f.

shipmate n (mar) camarade de bord m.

shipment n cargaison f.

shipowner n armateur m.

shipwreck n naufrage m.

shirt n chemise f.

shit excl (sl) merde!

shiver vi frissonner.

shoal n banc m.

shock n choc m; décharge f; coup m; * vt bouleverser; choquer.

shock absorber n amortisseur m.

shoddy adj de mauvaise qualité.

shoe n chaussure f; fer (à cheval) m; * vt chausser; ferrer (un cheval).

shoeblack n cireur de chaussures m.

shoehorn n chausse-pied m.

shoelace n lacet de chaussure m.

shoemaker n cordonnier m.

shoestring n lacet de chaussure m.

shoot vt tirer, lancer, décocher; * vi pousser, bourgeonner; passer en flèche; s'élancer; * n pousse f.

shooter n tireur m, -euse f.

shooting n fusillade f; tir m.

shop n magasin m; atelier m.

shopfront n devanture f.

shoplifter n voleur(-euse) à l'étalage m(f).

shopper n acheteur m, -euse f.

shopping n courses fpl.

shopping centre n centre commercial m.

shore n rivage, bord m, côte f.

short adj court, bref, succinct, concis; **~ly** adv brièvement; rapidement.

shortcoming n insuffisance f; défaut m.

shorten vt raccourcir; abréger.

shortness n petitesse f, brièveté f.

short-sighted adj myope.

short-sightedness n myopie f.

shortwave n ondes courtes fpl.

shot n coup m; décharge f; plomb m; tentative f; prise f.

shotgun n fusil de chasse m.

shoulder n épaule f; accotement m; * vt charger sur son épaule.

shout vi crier; * vt crier; * n cri m, acclamation f.

shouting n cris mpl.

shove vt vi pousser; * n poussée f.

shovel n pelle f; * vt pelleter.

show vt montrer; faire voir, présenter; prouver; expliquer; * vi se voir; * n exposition f; spectacle m; manifestation f; salon m.

show business n monde du spectacle m.

shower n averse f; douche f; (fig) torrent m; * vi pleuvoir.

showery adj pluvieux.

showroom n salle d'exposition f.

showy adj voyant, ostentatoire.

shred n lambeau m, parcelle f; * vt mettre en lambeaux.

shrew n mégère f; musaraigne f.

shrewd adj astucieux; perspicace; **~ly** adv astucieusement.

shrewdness n astuce f.

shriek vt, vi hurler; * n hurlement m.

shrill adj aigu, strident.

shrillness n ton aigu m.

shrimp n crevette f; nabot m, -e f, avorton m.

shrine n lieu saint m.

shrink vi rétrécir; se réduire, rapetisser.

shrivel vi se ratatiner, se flétrir; * vt ratatiner.

shroud n voile m; linceul m; * vt envelopper, voiler; ensevelir.

Shrove Tuesday n Mardi gras m.

shrub n arbuste m.

shrubbery n massif d'arbustes m.

shrug n hausser les épaules; * n haussement d'épaules m.

shudder vi frissonner; * n frisson m.

shuffle vt mélanger; battre.

shun vt fuir, éviter.

shunt n (rail) aiguiller.

shut vt fermer; vi (se) fermer.

shutter n volet m.

shuttle n navette f.

shuttlecock n volant m.

shy adj timide; réservé; embarrassé, gauche; **~ly** adv timidement.

shyness n timidité f.

sibling n enfants de mêmes parents mpl.

sibyl n sibylle f.

sick adj malade; écœuré.

sicken vt rendre malade; * vi tomber malade.

sickle n faucille f.

sick leave n congé de maladie m.

sickliness n état maladif m.

sickly adj maladif.

sickness n maladie f.

sick pay n indemnité de maladie f.

side n côté m; flanc m; camp m; parti m; * adj latéral; secondaire; * vi se ranger du côté de.

sideboard n buffet m.

sidelight n veilleuse f.

sidelong adj oblique.

sideways adv de côté, obliquement.

siding n (rail) voie de garage f.

sidle vi avancer de côté; avancer furtivement.

siege n (mil) siège m.

sieve n tamis m; crible m; passoire f; * vt tamiser.

sift vt tamiser; passer au crible; dégager.

sigh vi soupirer, gémir; * n soupir m.

sight n vue f; mire f; spectacle m.

sightless adj aveugle.

sightly adj agréable à regarder; séduisant.

sightseeing n tourisme m.

sign n signe m, indication f; panneau m; geste m; trace f; * vt signer.

signal n signal m; * adj insigne, remarquable.

signalize vt signaler.

signal lamp n (rail) lampe de signalisation f.

signalman n (rail) aiguilleur m.

signature n signature f.

signet n sceau m.

significance n importance f.

significant adj considérable.

signify vt signifier.

signpost n poteau indicateur m.

silence n silence m; * vt imposer le silence à.

silent adj silencieux; ~ly adv silencieusement.

silex n silex m.

silicon chip n puce de silicium f.

silk n soie f.

silken adj soyeux; satiné.

silkiness n soyeux m.

silkworm n ver à soie m.

silky adj soyeux; satiné.

sill n rebord m; seuil m.

silliness n stupidité, bêtise, niaiserie f.

silly adj bête, stupide.

silver n argent m; * adj en argent.

silversmith n orfèvre m.

silvery adj argenté.

similar adj semblable; similaire; ~ly adv de la même façon.

similarity n ressemblance f.

simile n comparaison f.

simmer vi cuire à feux doux, mijoter.

simony n simonie f.

simper vi minauder; * n sourire affecté m.

simple adj simple; naïf.

simpleton n nigaud m, -e f.

simplicity n simplicité f; naïveté f.

simplification n simplification f.

simplify vt simplifier.

simply adv simplement; seulement.

simulate vt simuler, feindre.

simulation n simulation f.

simultaneous *adj* simultané.

sin *n* péché *m*; * *vi* pécher.

since *adv* depuis; * *prep* depuis; * *conj* depuis que; puisque.

sincere *adj*, **~ly** *adv* sincère(ment); yours **~ly** veuillez agréer, Monsieur/Madame, l'expression de mes salutations distinguées.

sincerity *n* sincérité *f*.

sinecure *n* sinécure *f*.

sinew *n* tendon *m*; nerf *m*.

sinewy *adj* nerveux; tendineux.

sinful *adj* coupable, honteux; **~ly** *adv* honteusement.

sinfulness *n* corruption *f*, péché *m*.

sing *vi*, *vt* chanter; (*poet*) *vt* célébrer.

singe *vt* roussir.

singer *n* chanteur *m*, -euse *f*.

singing *n* chant *m*.

single *adj* seul, unique, simple; célibataire; * *n* aller simple *m*; 45 tours *m*; * *vt* distinguer; séparer.

singly *adv* séparément.

singular *adj* singulier, rare; * *n* singulier *m*; **~ly** *adv* singulièrement.

singularity *n* singularité *f*.

sinister *adj* sinistre; de mauvais augure, funeste.

sink *vi* couler; sombrer; s'affaisser; tomber très bas, baisser; * *vt* couler, faire sombrer; ruiner; * *n* évier *m*.

sinking fund *n* fonds d'amortissement *m*.

sinner *n* pécheur *m*; pécheresse *f*.

sinuosity *n* sinuosité *f*.

sinuous *adj* sinueux.

sinus *n* sinus *m*.

sip *vt* boire à petites gorgées; * *n* petite gorgée *f*.

siphon *n* siphon *m*.

sir *n* monsieur *m*.

sire *n* étalon *m*.

siren *n* sirène *f*.

sirloin *n* aloyau (de bœuf) *m*.

sister *n* sœur *f*.

sister-in-law *n* belle-sœur *f*.

sisterhood *n* solidarité féminine *f*.

sisterly *adj* de sœur.

sit *vi* s'asseoir; se trouver; * *vt* se présenter à.

site *n* emplacement *m*; site *m*.

sit-in *n* sit-in *m*, manifestation avec occupation de lieux publics *f*.

sitting *n* séance, réunion *f*; position assise *f*.

sitting room *n* salle de séjour *f*.

situated *adj* situé.

situation *n* situation *f*.

six *adj*, *n* six *m*.

sixteen *adj*, *n* seize *m*.

sixteenth *adj*, *n* seizième *mf*.

sixth *adj*, *n* sixième *mf*.

sixtieth *adj*, *n* soixantième *mf*.

sixty *adj*, *n* soixante *m*.

size *n* taille, grandeur *f*; volume *m*; dimension *f*; ampleur *f*; étendue *f*.

sizeable *adj* assez grand.

skate *n* patin *m*; * *vi* patiner.

skateboard *n* planche à roulettes *f*, skateboard *m*.

skating *n* patinage *m*.

skating rink *n* patinoire *f*.

skein *n* écheveau *m*.

skeleton *n* squelette *m*.

skeleton key *n* passe-(partout) *m*.

sketch *n* croquis *m*; esquisse *f*; * *vt* esquisser, faire un croquis de.

skewer n broche f; brochette f; * vt embrocher.

ski n ski m; * vi skier.

ski boot n chaussure de ski f.

skid n dérapage m; * vi déraper.

skier n skieur m, -euse f.

skiing n ski m.

skill n habileté, adresse, dextérité f.

skilled adj adroit; qualifié.

skilful adj, **~ly** adv adroit(ement), habile(ment).

skilfulness n habileté f.

skim vt écrémer; effleurer.

skimmed milk n lait écrémé m.

skimmer n écumoire f.

skin n peau f; * vt écorcher.

skin diving n plongée sous-marine f.

skinned adj dépouillé.

skinny adj maigre, efflanqué.

skip vi sautiller, gambader; * vt sauter, passer; * n saut, bond m; benne f.

ski pants npl fuseau (de ski) m.

skipper n capitaine m.

skirmish n escarmouche f; * vi s'engager dans une escarmouche.

skirt n jupe f; bordure f; * vt contourner.

skit n parodie, satire f.

skittish adj espiègle, fantasque; coquet; inconstant; **~ly** adv d'une manière espiègle.

skittle n quille f.

skulk vi se cacher, rôder furtivement.

skull n crâne m.

skullcap n calotte f.

sky n ciel m.

skylight n lucarne f.

skyrocket n fusée f.

skyscraper n gratte-ciel m invar.

slab n dalle f.

slack adj lâche, mou, indolent, négligent.

slack(en) vt relâcher; ralentir; diminuer; * vi se relâcher, ralentir.

slackness n manque d'énergie, ralentissement m; laisser-aller m.

slag n scories fpl.

slam vt claquer violemment; * vi se refermer en claquant.

slander vt calomnier, dire du mal de; * n calomnie f.

slanderer n calomniateur m, -trice f.

slanderous adj calomnieux; **~ly** adv calomnieusement.

slang n argot m.

slant vi pencher; être incliné; * n inclinaison f; point de vue m.

slanting adj en pente, incliné.

slap n claque f; (on the face) gifle f; * adv en plein; * vt donner une claque à, gifler.

slash vt entailler; * n entaille f.

slate n ardoise f.

slater n ardoisier m.

slating n recouvrement en ardoises m.

slaughter n carnage, massacre m; * vt abattre; massacrer.

slaughterer n tueur, meurtrier m.

slaughterhouse n abattoir m.

slave n esclave mf; * vi travailler comme un nègre.

slaver n bave f; * vi baver.

slavery n esclavage m.

slavish adj servile, d'esclave; **~ly** adv servilement.

slavishness n servilité f.

slay vt tuer.

slayer n tueur m, -euse f.

sleazy adj louche, sordide.

sledge, sleigh n traîneau m.

sledgehammer n marteau de forgeron m.

sleek adj lisse et brillant, luisant.

sleep vi dormir; * n sommeil m.

sleeper n dormeur m, -euse f.

sleepily adv d'un air endormi.

sleepiness n envie de dormir f.

sleeping bag n sac de couchage m.

sleeping pill n somnifère m.

sleepless adj sans sommeil.

sleepwalking n somnambulisme m.

sleepy adj qui a envie de dormir; endormi.

sleet n neige fondue f.

sleeve n manche f.

sleight n: ~ of hand tour de passe-passe m.

slender adj svelte, mince, élancé; faible; **~ly** adv faiblement.

slenderness n sveltesse f, minceur f; faiblesse f.

slice n tranche f; spatule f; * vt couper (en tranches).

slide vi glisser; faire des glissades; * n glissade f; coulisse f; diapositive f; toboggan m.

sliding adj glissant; coulissant.

slight adj léger, mince, petit; * n affront m; * vt manquer d'égards pour.

slightly adv légèrement.

slightness n fragilité f; insignifiance f.

slim adj mince; * vi maigrir.

slime n vase f; dépôt visqueux m.

sliminess n viscosité f.

slimming n amaigrissement m.

slimy adj visqueux, gluant.

sling n fronde f; écharpe f; * vt lancer.

slink vi s'en aller furtivement; s'éclipser.

slip vi (se) glisser, se faufiler; * vt glisser; * n glissade f; faux-pas m; oubli m; fiche f.

slipper n pantoufle f.

slippery adj glissant.

slipshod adj négligé.

slipway n cale f.

slit vt fendre, inciser; * n fente, incision f.

slobber n bave f.

sloe n prunelle f.

slogan n slogan m.

sloop n (mar) sloop m.

slop n fange f; bouillon m; **~s** pl eaux sales fpl.

slope n inclinaison f; pente f; déclivité f; versant m; * vt incliner.

sloping adj en pente; incliné.

sloppy adj négligé; peu soigné.

sloth n paresse f.

slouch vi manquer de tenue; se tenir d'une façon négligée.

slovenliness n négligence f; manque de soin m.

slovenly adj négligé, sale, débraillé.

slow adj lent; lourd; ennuyeux; **~ly** adv lentement.

slowness n lenteur f, lourdeur f, manque d'intérêt m.

slow worm n orvet m.

slug n lingot m; limace f; jeton m; coup m.

sluggish adj paresseux; léthargique; **~ly** adv paresseusement.

sluggishness n paresse, mollesse f.

sluice n écluse f; * vt lâcher les vannes.

slum n taudis m; quartier pauvre m.

slumber vi dormir paisiblement; * n sommeil paisible m.

slump n récession f.

slur vt dénigrer; calomnier; mal articuler; * n calomnie f.

slush n neige fondante f.

slut n traînée f.

sly adj rusé; **~ly** adv de façon rusée.

slyness n ruse, finesse f.

smack n léger goût m; claque f; gros baiser retentissant m; * vi sentir; embrasser bruyamment; * vt donner une claque à.

small adj petit, menu.

smallish adj assez petit.

smallness n petitesse f.

smallpox n variole f.

smalltalk n conversation f.

smart adj élégant; rapide; astucieux; vif; * vi brûler.

smartly adv astucieusement, vivement; avec élégance; habilement.

smartness n astuce, vivacité, finesse f.

smash vt casser, briser; détruire; * vi se briser (en mille morceaux), se fracasser; * n fracas m; coup violent m.

smattering n connaissances superficielles fpl.

smear n (med) frottis m; * vt enduire; salir.

smell vt, vi sentir; * n odorat m; odeur f; mauvaise odeur f.

smelly adj malodorant.

smelt n éperlan m; * vt fondre.

smelter n fondeur m.

smile vi sourire; * n sourire m.

smirk vi sourire d'un air affecté.

smite vt frapper.

smith n forgeron m.

smithy n forge f.

smock n blouse f.

smoke n fumée f; vapeur f; * vt, vi fumer.

smokeless adj sans fumée.

smoker n fumeur m, -euse f.

smoke shop n bureau de tabac m.

smoking : 'no ~' "interdiction de fumer".

smoky adj enfumé; qui fume.

smooth adj lisse, uni, égal; doucereux, mielleux; * vt lisser; aplanir; adoucir.

smoothly adv facilement; doucement.

smoothness n douceur f; aspect lisse m; air doucereux m.

smother vt étouffer; réprimer.

smoulder vi couver.

smudge vt salir; * n tache f.

smug adj suffisant.

smuggle vt passer en contrebande.

smuggler n contrebandier m, -ière f.

smuggling n contrebande f.

smut n saleté f; trace de suie f.

smuttiness n suie f; obscénité f.

smutty adj noirci; obscène.

snack n collation f.

snack bar n snack-bar m.

snag n obstacle m.

snail n escargot m.

snake n serpent m.

snaky adj sinueux.

snap vt casser net; * vi se casser

net; claquer; mordre; parler sèchement; **to ~ one's fingers** faire claquer ses doigts; * *n* claquement *m*; photographie *f*.

snapdragon *n* (*bot*) gueule-deloup *f*.

snap fastener *n* bouton-pression *m*.

snare *n* piège *m*; collet *m*.

snarl *vi* gronder férocement.

snatch *vt* saisir; s'emparer de; * *n* geste vif *m*; vol *m*; fragment *m*.

sneak *vi* se glisser furtivement; * *n* faux-jeton *m*.

sneakers *npl* chaussures de basket *fpl*.

sneer *vi* parler d'un ton méprisant; ricaner.

sneeringly *adv* d'un ton méprisant.

sneeze *vi* éternuer.

sniff *vt* renifler; * *vi* renifler.

snigger *vi* rire sous cape.

snip *vt* donner de petits coups de ciseaux dans; * *n* petit coup de ciseaux *m*; petit bout *m*.

snipe *n* bécassine *f*.

sniper *n* franc-tireur *m*.

snivel *n* pleurnicherie *f*; * *vi* pleurnicher.

sniveller *n* pleurnicheur *m*, -euse *f*.

snob *n* snob *mf*.

snobbish *adj* snob.

snooze *n* petit somme *m*; * *vi* faire un somme.

snore *vi* ronfler.

snorkel *n* tube respiratoire *m*.

snort *vi* renifler fortement.

snout *n* museau *m*; groin *m*.

snow *n* neige *f*; * *vi* neiger.

snowball *n* boule de neige *f*.

snowdrop *n* (*bot*) perce-neige *m invar*.

snowman *n* bonhomme de neige *m*.

snowplough *n* chasse-neige *m invar*.

snowy *adj* neigeux; enneigé.

snub *vt* repousser, rejeter.

snub-nosed *adj* au nez retroussé.

snuff *n* tabac à priser *m*.

snuffbox *n* tabatière *f*.

snuffle *vi* parler d'une voix nasillarde, nasiller.

snug *adj* confortable, douillet; bien abrité.

so *adv* si, tellement, aussi; ainsi.

soak *vt* tremper; * *vt* faire tremper.

soap *n* savon *m*; * *vt* savonner.

soap bubble *n* bulle de savon *f*.

soap opera *n* feuilleton à l'eau de rose *m*.

soap powder *n* lessive *f*.

soapsuds *n* mousse de savon *f*.

soapy *adj* savonneux.

soar *vi* monter en flèche.

sob *n* sanglot *m*; * *vi* sangloter.

sober *adj* sobre; sérieux; **~ly** *adv* sobrement; sérieusement.

sobriety *n* sobriété *f*; sérieux, calme *m*.

soccer *n* football *m*.

sociability *n* sociabilité *f*.

sociable *adj* sociable, liant.

sociably *adv* sociablement.

social *adj* social, sociable; **~ly** *adv* socialement.

socialism *n* socialisme *m*.

socialist *n* socialiste *mf*.

social work *n* assistance sociale *f*.

social worker *n* assistant(e) social(e) *m(f)*.

society n société f; compagnie f.

sociologist n sociologue mf.

sociology n sociologie f.

sock n chaussette f.

socket n prise de courant f.

sod n gazon m.

soda n soude f; eau de Seltz f, soda m.

sofa n sofa m.

soft adj doux, moelleux; aimable, gentil; ~**ly** adv doucement; tendrement .

soften vt (r)amollir, adoucir; atténuer.

soft-hearted adj compatissant.

softness n douceur, mollesse f.

soft-spoken adj à la voix douce.

software n logiciel m.

soil vt salir, souiller; * n salissure, souillure f; sol m; terre f.

sojourn vi séjourner; * n séjour m.

solace vt consoler, soulager; * n consolation f.

solar adj solaire.

solder vt souder; * n soudure f.

soldier n soldat m.

soldierly adj militaire.

sole n plante du pied f; semelle (de chaussure) f; sole f; * adj seul, unique.

solecism n (gr) solécisme m.

solemn adj, ~**ly** adv solennel(lement).

solemnity n solennité f.

solemnize vt solenniser.

solicit vt solliciter; quémander.

solicitation n sollicitation f.

solicitor n notaire m.

solicitous adj plein de sollicitude; ~**ly** adv avec sollicitude.

solicitude n sollicitude f.

solid adj solide, compact; * n solide m; ~**ly** adv solidement.

solidify vt solidifier.

solidity n solidité f.

soliloquy n soliloque m.

solitaire n solitaire m.

solitary adj solitaire, retiré; * n anachorète m.

solitude n solitude f.

solo n (mus) solo m.

solstice n solstice m.

soluble adj soluble.

solution n solution f.

solve vt résoudre.

solvency n solvabilité f.

solvent adj solvable; n (chem) solvant m.

some adj du, de la, de l', des; quelques; quelconque; certain(e)s; quelque.

somebody pn quelqu'un.

somehow adv d'une façon ou d'une autre.

someplace adv quelque part.

something pn quelque chose.

sometime adv au cours de, un jour ou l'autre.

sometimes adv quelquefois, parfois.

somewhat adv quelque peu.

somewhere adv quelque part.

somnambulism n somnambulisme m.

somnambulist n somnambule mf.

somnolence n somnolence f.

somnolent adj somnolent.

son n fils m.

sonata n (mus) sonate f.

song n chanson f.

son-in-law n gendre m.

sonnet n sonnet m.

sonorous adj sonore.

soon adv bientôt; **as ~ as** dès que.

sooner adv plus tôt; plutôt.

soot n suie f.

soothe vt calmer, apaiser; flatter.

soothsayer n devin m.

sop n pain trempé m.

sophism n sophisme m.

sophist n sophiste mf.

sophistical adj sophistiqué.

sophisticate vt falsifier; sophistiquer.

sophisticated adj sophistiqué.

sophistry n sophistique f.

sophomore n étudiant(e) de seconde année m(f).

soporific adj soporifique.

sorcerer n sorcier m.

sorceress n sorcière f.

sorcery n sorcellerie f.

sordid adj sordide, sale; avide.

sordidness n aspect sordide m, saleté f.

sore n plaie, blessure f; * adj douloureux, sensible; contrarié; **~ly** adv gravement.

sorrel n (bot) oseille f; * adj alezanroux.

sorrow n peine f; chagrin m; * vi se lamenter.

sorrowful adj triste, affligé; **~ly** adv tristement.

sorry adj désolé, navré; déplorable; **I am ~** je suis désolé.

sort n sorte f; genre m; espèce f; race f; manière f; * vt classer; trier.

soul n âme f; essence f; personne f.

sound adj sain; solide; valide; **~ly** adv sainement, solidement; * n son m; bruit m; * vt sonner (de); * vi sonner, retentir; ressembler; sembler.

sounding board n table d'harmonie f; abat-voix m.

sound effects npl bruitage m.

soundings npl (mar) sondages mpl; (mar) fonds mpl.

soundness n santé f; solidité f.

soundtrack n bande sonore f.

soup n soupe f.

sour adj aigre, acide; acerbe; revêche; **~ly** adv aigrement; * vt aigrir, faire tourner; * vi s'aigrir; tourner.

source n source f; origine f.

sourness n acidité, aigreur f; acrimonie f.

souse n (sl) soûlard m, -e f; * vt mariner; faire tremper.

souvenir n souvenir m.

south n sud m; * adj sud, du sud, au sud; * adv au sud; vers le sud.

southerly, southern adj du sud, sud, méridional.

southward(s) adv vers le sud.

southwester n (mar) vent du sud-ouest m; suroît m.

sovereign adj, n souverain m, -e f.

sovereignty n souveraineté f.

sow n truie f.

sow vt semer; disperser.

sowing time n époque des semailles f.

soy n soja m.

space n espace m; intervalle m; * vt espacer.

spacecraft n vaisseau spatial m.

spaceman/woman n astronaute mf.

spacious adj spacieux, ample; **~ly** adv spacieusement.

spaciousness n dimensions spacieuses fpl, espace m.

spade n bêche f; pique m.

spaghetti n spaghetti mpl.

span n envergure f; * vt enjamber; embrasser.

spangle n paillette f; * vt orner de paillettes.

spaniel n épagneul m.

Spanish adj espagnol; * n espagnol m; Espagnol m, -e f.

spar n (mar) espar m; * vi s'entraîner.

spare vt, vi épargner; ménager; éviter; se passer de; * adj de trop; de réserve.

sparing adj limité, modéré, économe; **~ly** adv frugalement, avec modération.

spark n étincelle f.

sparkle n scintillement m, étincelle f; * vi étinceler; briller.

spark plug n bougie f.

sparrow n moineau m.

sparrowhawk n épervier m.

sparse adj clairsemé, épars; **~ly** adv faiblement.

spasm n spasme m.

spasmodic adj spasmodique.

spatter vt éclabousser; * vi gicler.

spatula n spatule f.

spawn n frai m; * vt pondre; engendrer.

spawning n frai m.

speak vt parler; dire; * vi parler, s'entretenir; prendre la parole.

speaker n haut-parleur m; interlocuteur m, -trice f; orateur m.

spear n lance f; harpon m; * vt transpercer d'un coup de lance.

special adj spécial, particulier; **~ly** adv spécialement.

speciality n spécialité f.

species n espèce f.

specific adj spécifique; * n remède spécifique m.

specifically adv spécifiquement; explicitement.

specification n spécification f.

specify vt spécifier.

specimen n spécimen m; exemple m.

specious adj spécieux.

speck(le) n grain, tache f; * vt tacheter, moucheter.

spectacle n spectacle m.

spectator n spectateur m, -trice f.

spectral adj spectral; **~ analysis** n analyse spectrale f.

spectre n spectre m.

speculate vi spéculer; méditer.

speculation n spéculation f; conjecture f; méditation f.

speculative adj spéculatif, méditatif.

speculum n spéculum m.

speech n parole f; discours m; langage m; élocution f.

speechify vi discourir.

speechless adj muet.

speed n vitesse f; rapidité f; * vt presser; accélérer; * vi se presser.

speedboat n vedette f.

speedily adv rapidement, vite.

speediness n rapidité, promptitude, célérité f.

speed limit n limitation de vitesse f.

speedometer n compteur de vitesse m.

speedway n piste de course f.

speedy adj rapide, prompt.

spell n charme, sortilège m; période f; * vt écrire; épeler; ensorceler, envoûter; * s'écrire; s'épeler.

spelling n orthographe f.

spend vt dépenser; passer; épuiser; gaspiller.

spendthrift n dépenser m, -ière f.

spent adj épuisé.

sperm n sperme m.

spermaceti n spermaceti m.

spew vi (sl) vomir.

sphere n sphère f.

spherical adj sphérique; ~ly adv de forme sphérique.

spice n épice f; * vt épicer.

spick-and-span adj impeccable; tiré à quatre épingles.

spicy adj épicé.

spider n araignée f.

spigot n clef de robinet f.

spike n pointe f; clou m; * vt clouter.

spill vt renverser, répandre; * vi se répandre.

spin vt filer; inventer, fabriquer; faire tourner; * vi tourner; * n tournoiement m; tour (en voiture) m.

spinach n épinard m.

spinal adj spinal.

spindle n fuseau m; broche f.

spine n colonne vertébrale, épine dorsale f.

spinet n (mus) épinette f.

spinner n fileur m; fileuse f.

spinning wheel n rouet m.

spin-off n sous-produit m.

spinster n célibataire f.

spiral adj, ~ly adv en spirale.

spire n flèche f; aiguille f; tige f.

spirit n esprit m; âme f; caractère m; disposition f; courage m; humeur f; * vt encourager; animer; **to ~ away** faire disparaître comme par enchantement.

spirited adj vif, fougueux; ~ly adv fougueusement.

spirit lamp n lampe à alcool f.

spiritless adj sans entrain, abattu.

spiritual adj, ~ly adv spirituel(lement).

spiritualist n spiritualiste mf.

spirituality n spiritualité f.

spit n crachat m; salive f; * vt, vi cracher; crépiter.

spite n dépit m, rancune f; **in ~ of** en dépit de, malgré; * vt vexer.

spiteful adj rancunier, malveillant; ~ly adv par méchanceté, par rancune.

spitefulness n méchanceté f; rancune f.

spittle n salive f; crachat m.

splash vt éclabousser, faire gicler; * vi barboter; * n éclaboussure f; tache f.

spleen n rate f; spleen m.

splendid adj splendide, magnifique; ~ly adv splendidement.

splendour n splendeur f; magnificence f.

splice vt (mar) épisser, abouter.

splint n éclisse f.

splinter n éclat m; esquille f; écharde f; * vt (vi) (se) fendre en éclats.

split n fente f; rupture f; * vt fendre, diviser; * vi se fendre.

spoil vt abîmer; gâter; gâcher.

spoiled adj abîmé; gâté.

spoke n rayon (de roue) m.

spokesman n porte-parole m invar.

spokeswoman n porte-parole f invar.

sponge n éponge f; * vt éponger; * vi être un parasite.

sponger n parasite m.

sponginess n spongiosité f.

spongy adj spongieux.

sponsor n caution m; parrain m; marraine f.

sponsorship n parrainage m.

spontaneity n spontanéité f.

spontaneous adj, **~ly** adv spontané(ment).

spool n bobine f; rouleau m.

spoon n cuiller f.

spoonful n cuillerée f.

sporadic(al) adj sporadique.

sport n sport m; jeu m; divertissement, amusement m.

sport jacket n veste sport f.

sports car n voiture de sport f.

sportsman n sportif m.

sportswear n vêtements de sport mpl.

sportswoman n sportive f.

spot n tache f; point m; endroit m; pois m; * vt apercevoir; tacher.

spotless adj impeccable, immaculé.

spotlight n feu de projecteur m.

spotted, spotty adj tacheté; à pois.

spouse n époux m; épouse f.

spout vi jaillir; gicler; déblatérer; * vt faire jaillir; * n bec m; gargouille f; jet m.

sprain adj foulé; * n entorse f.

sprat n sprat m.

sprawl vi s'étaler.

spray n spray m; pulvérisation f; embruns mpl.

spread vt étendre, étaler; répandre, propager; * vi s'étendre, se répandre; * n propagation, diffusion f.

spree n fête f.

sprig n brin m.

sprightliness n vivacité f, entrain m.

sprightly adj alerte, vif, fringant.

spring vi bondir; sauter; provenir; découler; émaner, naître; * n printemps m; élasticité f; ressort m; saut m; source f.

springiness n élasticité f.

springtime n printemps m.

springwater n eau de source f.

springy adj élastique.

sprinkle vt arroser.

sprinkling n arrosage m.

sprout n pousse f, germe m; **~s** npl choux de Bruxelles mpl; * vi germer.

spruce adj net, impeccable; **~ly** adv tiré à quatre épingles; * vt se mettre sur son trente-et-un.

spruceness n élégance f.

spur n éperon m; ergot (coq) m; stimulant m; * vt éperonner; stimuler.

spurious adj faux, feint; falsifié, de contrefaçon; bâtard.

spurn vt repousser avec mépris.

sputter vi postillonner; bredouiller; bafouiller.

spy n espion m, -onne f; * vt apercevoir; espionner; vi espionner.

squabble *vi* se disputer, se quereller; * *n* querelle, dispute *f*.

squad *n* escouade *f*; brigade *f*; équipe *f*.

squadron *n* (mil) escadron *m*.

squalid *adj* misérable, sordide.

squall *n* rafale *f*; bourrasque *f*; * *vi* piailler.

squally *adj* qui souffle en rafales.

squalor *n* saleté *f*; misère *f*.

squander *vt* gaspiller, dilapider.

square *adj* carré; catégorique; honnête; * *n* carré *m*; place *f*; équerre *f*; * *vt* cadrer; mettre en ordre, régler; * *vi* cadrer.

squareness *n* forme carrée *f*.

squash *vt* écraser; * *n* squash *m*.

squat *vi* s'accroupir; * *adj* accroupi; trapu, courtaud.

squatter *n* squatter *m*.

squaw *n* squaw, femme peau-rouge *f*.

squeak *vi* grincer, crier; * *n* cri, couinement *m*.

squeal *vi* pousser un cri aigu, couiner.

squeamish *adj* exigeant; délicat.

squeeze *vt* presser, tordre; comprimer; * *n* pression *f*; serrement de main *m*; cohue *f*.

squid *n* calmar *m*.

squint *adj* atteint de strabisme; * *vi* loucher; * *n* strabisme *m*.

squirrel *n* écureuil *m*.

squirt *vt* faire gicler; * *n* giclée *f*; jet *m*; seringue *f*.

stab *vt* poignarder; * *n* coup de couteau *m*.

stability *n* stabilité, solidité *f*.

stable *n* écurie *f*; * *vt* mettre à l'écurie; * *adj* stable.

stack *n* pile *f*; * *vt* empiler.

staff *n* personnel *m*; bâton *m*; soutien *m*.

stag *n* cerf *m*.

stage *n* étape *f*; scène *f*; échafaudage *m*; théâtre *m*; stade *m*; estrade *f*.

stagger *vi* vaciller, tituber; hésiter; * *vt* stupéfier; échelonner.

stagnation *n* stagnation *f*.

stagnant *adj* stagnant.

stagnate *vi* stagner.

staid *adj* posé, sérieux.

stain *vt* tacher; ternir; * *n* tache *f*.

stainless *adj* sans tache; immaculé.

stair *n* marche *f*; ~s *pl* escalier *m*.

staircase *n* escalier *m*.

stake *n* pieu *m*; enjeu *m*; * *vt* marquer; délimiter.

stale *adj* rassis, rance.

staleness *n* manque de fraîcheur *m*; rance *m*.

stalk *vi* avancer d'un air majestueux; * *n* tige, queue *f*, trognon *m*.

stall *n* stalle *f*; stand, étalage *m*; (fauteuil d') orchestre *m*; emplacement *m*; * *vt* caler; * *vi* caler; atermoyer.

stallion *n* étalon *m*.

stalwart *n* partisan fidèle *m*.

stamen *n* étamine *f*.

stamina *n* résistance *f*.

stammer *vi* bégayer; * *n* bégaiement *m*.

stamp *vt* trépigner; timbrer, affranchir; tamponner; * *vi* trépigner; * *n* timbre *m*; cachet *m*; tampon *m*; empreinte *f*; estampille *f*.

stampede *n* débandade *f*.

stand vi être debout, se tenir; se maintenir; résister; être situé, se trouver; rester, durer; s'arrêter, faire halte; * vt poser; résister; soutenir, supporter; * n position, prise de position f; pied, support m; étalage m; état m; tribune f; stand m.

standard n étendard m; modèle m; étalon m; norme f; * adj normal.

standing adj permanent, fixe, établi; en pied; * n durée f; importance f; rang m.

standstill n arrêt m; immobilisation f.

staple n agrafe f; * adj principal, de base; * vt agrafer.

star n étoile f; astérisque m.

starboard n tribord m.

starch n amidon m; * vt amidonner.

stare vi: to ~ at regarder fixement; * n regard fixe m.

stark adj raide, rigide; pur; * adv complètement.

starling n étourneau m.

starry adj étoilé.

start vi commencer, débuter; sursauter, tressaillir; démarrer, se mettre en route; * vt commencer; amorcer; lancer; mettre en marche; * n début m; ouverture f; sursaut m; départ m; avance f.

starter n starter, démarreur m.

starting point n point de départ m.

startle vt faire sursauter.

startling adj surprenant, alarmant.

starvation n inanition, faim f.

starve vi mourir de faim.

state n état m; condition f; pompe f, apparat m; **the S~s** les Etats-Unis mpl; * vt déclarer; exposer.

stateliness n majesté, grandeur f.

stately adj majestueux, imposant.

statement n déclaration, affirmation f.

statesman n homme d'Etat m.

statesmanship n qualité d'homme politique f.

static adj statique; * n parasites mpl.

station n station f; place, position f; condition f, rang m; situation f; condition f; (rail) gare f; * vt placer.

stationary adj stationnaire, immobile.

stationer n papetier m, -ière f.

stationery n papeterie f.

station wagon n break m.

statistical adj statistique.

statistics npl statistiques fpl.

statuary n statuaire f.

statue n statue f.

stature n stature, taille f.

statute n statut m; loi f.

stay n séjour m; **~s** npl corset m; * vi rester, demeurer; tenir; loger; **to ~ in** rester à la maison; **to ~ on** rester encore quelque temps; **to ~ up** ne pas se coucher.

stead n place f, lieu m.

steadfast adj ferme, résolu, inébranlable; **~ly** adv fermement, résolument.

steadily adv fermement; régulièrement.

steadiness n fermeté, stabilité f.

steady adj stable, solide; * vt affermir.

steak n biftek m; steak m.

steal vt, vi voler.

stealth n vol m; **by ~** à la dérobée.

stealthily adv furtivement.

stealthy adj furtif.

steam n vapeur f; buée f; * vt cuire à la vapeur; * vi fumer.

steam engine n locomotive à vapeur f.

steamer, steamboat n (bateau à) vapeur, paquebot m.

steel n acier m; * adj d'acier.

steelyard n balance romaine f.

steep adj abrupt; excessif; * vt tremper.

steeple n clocher m; flèche f.

steeplechase n steeple (course) m.

steepness n raideur f; escarpement m.

steer n bouvillon m; * vt conduire; diriger; gouverner; * vi tenir le gouvernail.

steering n direction f.

steering wheel n volant m.

stellar adj stellaire.

stem n tige f, tronc m; souche f; pied m; tuyau m; * vt endiguer.

stench n odeur fétide f.

stencil n stencil m.

stenographer n sténographe mf.

stenography n sténographie f.

step n pas m, marche f; trace f; * vi faire un pas; marcher.

stepbrother n demi-frère m.

stepdaughter n belle-fille f.

stepfather n beau-père m.

stepmother n belle-mère f.

stepping stone n pierre de gué f.

stepsister n demi-sœur f.

stepson n beau-fils m.

stereo n stéréo f.

stereotype n stéréotype m; * vt stéréotyper.

sterile adj stérile.

sterility n stérilité f.

sterling adj de bon aloi, vrai, véritable; * n livres sterling fpl.

stern adj sévère, rigide, strict; * n (mar) poupe f; **~ly** adv sévèrement.

stethoscope n (med) stéthoscope m.

stevedore n (mar) docker m.

stew vt faire cuire à l'étouffée; * n ragoût m.

steward n intendant m; (mar) steward m.

stewardess n hôtesse de l'air f.

stewardship n intendance f.

stick n bâton m; canne f; baguette f; * vt coller; piquer; planter; supporter; * vi tenir; se planter; rester fidèle.

stickiness n viscosité f.

stick-up n braquage, hold-up m.

sticky adj collant, poisseux.

stiff adj raide, rigide; inflexible; dur; entêté; **~ly** adv raidement; obstinément.

stiffen vt raidir, renforcer; * vi se raidir.

stiff neck n torticolis m.

stiffness n raideur, rigidité f; opiniâtreté f.

stifle vt étouffer.

stifling adj suffocant.

stigma n stigmate m.

stigmatize vt stigmatiser.

stile n tourniquet m.

stiletto n stylet m; talon aiguille m.

still vt calmer, apaiser; faire taire; * adj silencieux, calme; * n alam- bic m; * adv encore; toujours; quand même, tout de même.

stillborn adj mort-né.

stillness n calme m, tranquillité f.

stilts npl échasses fpl.

stimulant n stimulant m.

stimulate vt stimuler.

stimulation n stimulant m; stimulation f.

stimulus n stimulus m.

sting vt piquer; * vi brûler; * n dard m; piqûre f; aiguillon m.

stingily adv avec avarice.

stinginess n mesquinerie, avarice f.

stingy adj mesquin, avare, pingre.

stink vi puer; * n puanteur f.

stint n tâche assignée f.

stipulate vt stipuler.

stipulation n stipulation f.

stir vt remuer; agiter; exciter; * vi remuer, bouger; * n agitation f; émoi m.

stirrup n étrier m.

stitch vt coudre; * n point m; point de suture m.

stoat n hermine f.

stock n réserve f; provision f; bouillon m; souche f; lignée f; capital m; fonds mpl; ~s pl valeurs mobilières fpl; * vt approvisionner, stocker.

stockade n prison militaire f.

stockbroker n agent de change m.

stock exchange n Bourse f.

stockholder n actionnaire mf.

stocking n bas m.

stock market n Bourse f.

stoic n stoïque mf.

stoical adj, ~ly adv stoïque(ment).

stoicism n stoïcisme m.

stole n étole f.

stomach n estomac m; ventre m; * vt digérer; endurer.

stone n pierre f; caillou m; noyau m; * adj de pierre; * vt lancer des pierres sur; dénoyauter; empierrer.

stone deaf adj sourd comme un pot.

stoning n empierrement m.

stony adj pierreux, rocailleux; dur.

stool n tabouret m; rebord, appui m.

stoop vi se baisser, se pencher; * n inclination en avant f.

stop vt arrêter, interrompre; boucher; * vi s'arrêter, cesser; * n arrêt m; halte f; pause f; point m.

stopover n escale; étape f.

stoppage, stopping n obstruction f; engorgement m; (rail) suppression f.

stopwatch n chronomètre m.

storage n emmagasinage m; entreposage m.

store n provision f; réserve f; entrepôt m, magasin m; * vt mettre en réserve, accumuler, emmagasiner.

storekeeper n marchand m, -e f.

stork n cigogne f.

storm n tempête f, orage m; assaut m; * vt prendre d'assaut; * vi faire rage.

stormily adv violemment.

stormy adj orageux; houleux.

story n histoire f; récit m; étage m.

stout adj corpulent, robuste, vigoureux; solide; **~ly** adv solidement; vaillamment; résolument.

stoutness n vigueur f; puissance f; corpulence f.

stove n poêle m; cuisinière f.

stow vt ranger, mettre en place; (mar) arrimer.

straggle vi être disséminé.

straggler n traînard m, -e f.

straight adj droit; direct; franc; * adv droit; directement.

straightaway adv immédiatement, tout de suite.

straighten vt redresser.

straightforward adj honnête; franc; direct.

straightforwardness n honnêteté f.

strain vt tendre; fouler; forcer; mettre à l'épreuve; * vi peiner; * n tension f; effort m; entorse f; contrainte f; lignée f; accent m; ton m.

strainer n passoire f.

strait n détroit m; embarras m; situation critique f.

strait-jacket n camisole de force f.

strand n brin m; rivage m, rive f.

strange adj inconnu; étrange; **~ly** adv étrangement, curieusement.

strangeness n étrangeté f; nouveauté f.

stranger n inconnu(e) m(f), étranger m, -ère f.

strangle vt étrangler.

strangulation n strangulation f.

strap n lanière, sangle f; courroie f; * vt attacher avec une courroie.

strapping adj robuste, charpenté.

stratagem n stratagème m.

strategic adj stratégique m.

strategy n stratégie f.

stratum n strate f.

straw n paille f.

strawberry n fraise f.

stray vi s'égarer; vagabonder; * adj perdu; errant.

streak n raie, bande f; filet m; * vt strier.

stream n ruisseau m, rivière f; torrent m; * vi ruisseler.

streamer n serpentin m.

street n rue f.

streetcar n tramway m.

strength n force, puissance f; vigueur f; robustesse f.

strengthen vt fortifier; confirmer, renforcer.

strenuous adj ardu; vigoureux.

stress n pression f; stress m; tension f; contrainte f; importance f; accent m; * vt souligner; accentuer.

stretch vt étendre, étirer; élargir; forcer; * vi s'étendre, s'étirer; * n extension f; étendue f; période f.

stretcher n brancard m.

strew vt éparpiller; semer.

strict adj strict, sévère; exact, rigoureux, précis; **~ly** adv strictement, sévèrement.

strictness n sévérité f; rigueur f.

stride n grand pas m; * vi marcher à grandes enjambées.

strife n conflit m, lutte f.

strike vt frapper; heurter; attaquer; rayer; * vi frapper; se mettre en grève; sonner; * n coup m; grève f; découverte f.

striker n gréviste mf.

striking adj frappant; saisissant; **~ly** adv remarquablement.

string n ficelle f; corde f; cordon m; rang m; fibre f; * vt munir d'une corde; enfiler; suspendre.

stringent adj rigoureux.

stringy adj filandreux.

strip vt déshabiller, dévêtir; * vi se déshabiller; * n bande f; langue f; bandelette f.

stripe n raie, rayure f; coup de fouet m; * vt rayer.

strive vi s'efforcer; s'évertuer; lutter, se battre.

stroke n coup m; trait m; course f; caresse f; apoplexie f; * vt caresser.

stroll n petit tour; * vi flâner.

strong adj fort, vigoureux, robuste; puissant; intense; **~ly** adv fortement, énergiquement.

strongbox n coffre-fort m.

stronghold n forteresse f.

strophe n strophe f.

structure n structure f; construction f.

struggle vi lutter; se battre; se démener; * n lutte f.

strum vt (mus) tapoter de.

strut vi se pavaner; * n démarche affectée f.

stub n souche f; bout m; talon m.

stubble n chaume m; barbe de plusieurs jours f.

stubborn adj entêté, obstiné; **~ly** adv obstinément.

stubbornness n entêtement m, obstination f.

stucco n stuc m.

stud n clou m; crampon m; écurie f.

student n, adj étudiant m, -e f.

stud horse n étalon m.

studio n studio, atelier m.

studio apartment n studio m.

studious adj studieux; sérieux; **~ly** adv studieusement, sérieusement.

study n étude f; études fpl; méditation f; * vt étudier; observer; * vi étudier; faire des études.

stuff n matière f; matériaux mpl; étoffe f; * vt (rem)bourrer, remplir; empailler.

stuffing n rembourrage m.

stuffy adj mal aéré; collet monté.

stumble vi trébucher; * n faux pas, trébuchement m.

stumbling block n hésitation f; pierre d'achoppement f.

stump n souche f; moignon m; bout m.

stun vt étourdir; stupéfier.

stunner n personne ou chose extraordinaire f.

stunt n cascade f; coup de publicité m; * vt empêcher de croître.

stuntman n cascadeur m.

stupefy vt hébéter; stupéfier.

stupendous adj prodigieux, remarquable.

stupid adj, **~ly** adv stupide(ment).

stupidity n stupidité f.

stupor n stupeur f.

sturdily adv fortement.

sturdiness n force, robustesse f; résolution f.

sturdy adj vigoureux, robuste, fort; hardi, résolu.

sturgeon n esturgeon m.

stutter vi bégayer.

sty n porcherie f; taudis m.

stye n orgelet m.

style n style m; mode f; * vt appeler, dénommer; créer, dessiner.

stylish adj élégant, qui a du chic.

suave adj suave.

subdivide vt subdiviser.

subdivision n subdivision f.

subdue vt subjuguer, assujettir; contenir, réfréner; adoucir.

subject adj soumis; sujet à; * n sujet m; thème m; * vt soumettre; exposer.

subjection n sujétion f.

subjugate vt subjuguer, assujettir.

subjugation n subjugation f.

subjunctive n subjonctif m.

sublet vt sous-louer.

sublimate vt sublimer.

sublime adj sublime, suprême; ~ly adv sublimement; * n sublime m.

sublimity n sublimité f.

submachine gun n mitraillette f.

submarine adj, n sous-marin m.

submerge vt submerger.

submersion n submersion f.

submission n soumission f.

submissive adj soumis, docile; ~ly adv avec soumission.

submissiveness n docilité f; soumission f.

submit vt soumettre; * vi se soumettre.

subordinate adj subalterne, inférieur; * vt subordonner.

subordination n subordination f.

subpoena n citation f; * vt citer.

subscribe vi souscrire; * vt apposer; signer.

subscriber n souscripteur m, -trice f.

subscription n souscription f.

subsequent adj, ~ly adv ultérieur(ement).

subservient adj subordonné; utile.

subside vi s'affaisser, baisser.

subsidence n affaissement m.

subsidiary adj subsidiaire.

subsidize vt subventionner, fournir des subsides à.

subsidy n subvention f; subside m.

subsist vi subsister; exister.

subsistence n existence f; subsistance f.

substance n substance f; fond m; essentiel m.

substantial adj considérable; réel, substantiel; solide; ~ly adv considérablement.

substantiate vt justifier.

substantive n substantif m.

substitute vt substituer; * n remplaçant m, -e f.

substitution n substitution f.

substratum n substrat m.

subterfuge n subterfuge m; fauxfuyant m.

subterranean adj souterrain.

subtitle n sous-titre m.

subtle adj subtile.

subtlety n subtilité f.

subtly adv subtilement.

subtract vt (math) soustraire.

suburb n banlieue f.

suburban adj de banlieue.

subversion n subversion f.

subversive adj subversif.

subvert vt subvertir, renverser.

subway n métro m.

succeed vi réussir; succéder; avoir du succès; * vt succéder à, suivre.

success n succès m.

successful adj couronné de succès, qui réussit; **~ly** adv avec succès.

succession n succession f.

successive adj successif; **~ly** adv successivement.

successor n successeur m.

succinct adj succinct, concis; **~ly** adv succinctement.

succulent adj succulent.

succumb vi succomber.

such adj tel, pareil; **~ as** tel que.

suck vt, vi sucer; vi téter.

suckle vt allaiter.

suckling n nourrisson m.

suction n (med) succion f.

sudden adj, **~ly** adv soudain(ement), subit(ement).

suddenness n soudaineté f.

suds npl mousse de savon f.

sue vt poursuivre en justice; supplier.

suede n daim m.

suet n graisse de rognon f.

suffer vt souffrir, subir; tolérer, endurer; * vi souffrir.

suffering n souffrance f; douleur f.

suffice vi suffire, être suffisant.

sufficiency n quantité suffisante; aisance f.

sufficient adj suffisant; **~ly** adv suffisamment.

suffocate vt, vi étouffer.

suffocation n suffocation f.

suffrage n suffrage, vote m.

suffuse vt baigner, se répandre sur.

sugar n sucre m; * vt sucrer.

sugar beet n betterave à sucre f.

sugar cane n canne à sucre f.

sugar loaf n pain de sucre m.

sugar plum n bonbon m.

sugary adj sucré.

suggest vt suggérer.

suggestion n suggestion f.

suicidal adj suicidaire.

suicide n suicide m; suicidé m, -e f.

suit n procès m; pétition f; costume m; tailleur m; requête f; * vt convenir à; aller à; arranger, adapter.

suitable adj qui convient, approprié.

suitably adv convenablement.

suitcase n valise f.

suite n suite f; escorte f; mobilier m; cortège m.

suitor n plaideur m; prétendant m.

sulkiness n bouderie f.

sulky adj boudeur, maussade.

sullen adj maussade; sombre; **~ly** adv d'un air maussade; de mauvaise grâce.

sullenness n maussaderie f; silence m.

sulphur n soufre m.

sulphurous adj sulphureux.

sultan n sultan m.

sultana n sultane f; raisin sec m.

sultry adj étouffant; chaud.

sum n somme f; total m; **to ~ up** vt résumer; récapituler; * vi résumer.

summarily adv sommairement.

summary adj, n résumé m.

summer n été m.

summerhouse n gloriette f, pavillon de jardin m.

summit n sommet m; cime f.

summon vt convoquer, citer à comparaître; sommer; (mil) sommer de se rendre.

summons n convocation f; sommation f.

sumptuous adj somptueux; **~ly** adv somptueusement.

sun n soleil m.

sunbathe vi prendre un bain de soleil, se faire bronzer.

sunburnt adj bronzé, hâlé.

Sunday n dimanche m.

sundial n cadran solaire m.

sundry adj divers, différent.

sunflower n tournesol m.

sunglasses npl lunettes de soleil fpl.

sunless adj sans soleil.

sunlight n lumière du soleil f.

sunny adj ensoleillé; radieux.

sunrise n lever du soleil m.

sun roof n toit ouvrant m.

sunset n coucher du soleil m.

sunshade n parasol m.

sunshine n (lumière du) soleil m; ensoleillement m.

sunstroke n insolation f.

suntan n bronzage m.

suntan oil n huile solaire f.

super adj (fam) sensationnel.

superannuated adj en retraite.

superannuation n retraite, pension de retraite f.

superb adj, **~ly** adv superbe(ment).

supercargo n (mar) subrécargue m.

supercilious adj hautain, dédaigneux; **~ly** adv avec dédain.

superficial adj, **~ly** adv superficiel(lement).

superfluity n surabondance, superfluité f.

superfluous adj superflu.

superhuman adj surhumain.

superintendent n directeur m, -trice f.

superior adj, n supérieur m, -e f.

superiority n supériorité f.

superlative adj, n superlatif m; **~ly** adv extrêmement, au suprême degré.

supermarket n supermarché m.

supernatural n surnaturel.

supernumerary adj surnuméraire.

superpower n superpuissance f.

supersede vt remplacer; supplanter.

supersonic adj supersonique.

superstition n superstition f.

superstitious adj superstitieux; **~ly** adv superstitieusement.

superstructure n superstructure f.

supertanker n gros pétrolier, supertanker m.

supervene vi survenir.

supervise vt surveiller, superviser.

supervision n surveillance f.

supervisor n surveillant m, -e f.

supine adj couché, étendu sur le dos; indolent.

supper n dîner m.

supplant vt supplanter.

supple adj souple, flexible; obséquieux.

supplement n supplément m.

supplementary adj supplémentaire.

suppleness n souplesse f.

suppli(c)ant n suppliant m, -e f.

supplicate vt supplier.

supplication n supplique, supplication f.

supplier n fournisseur m.

supply *vt* fournir, approvisionner; suppléer à, remédier à; * *n* approvisionnement *m*; provision *f*.

support *vt* soutenir; supporter, appuyer; * *n* appui *m*.

supportable *adj* supportable.

supporter *n* partisan *m*; supporter *m*, adepte *mf*.

suppose *vt*, *vi* supposer.

supposition *n* supposition *f*.

suppress *vt* supprimer.

suppression *n* suppression *f*.

supremacy *n* suprématie *f*.

supreme *adj*, **~ly** *adv* suprême(ment).

surcharge *vt* surcharger; * *n* surtaxe *f*.

sure *adj* sûr, certain; infaillible; **to be ~** certainement; **~ly** *adv* sûrement, certainement, sans doute.

sureness *n* certitude, sûreté *f*.

surety *n* certitude *f*; caution *f*.

surf *n* (*mar*) ressac *m*.

surface *n* surface *f*; * *vt* revêtir; * *vi* remonter à la surface.

surfboard *n* planche (de surf) *f*.

surfeit *n* excès *m*.

surge *n* vague, montée *f*; * *vi* déferler.

surgeon *n* chirurgien *m*.

surgery *n* chirurgie *m*.

surgical *adj* chirurgical.

surliness *n* air revêche, bourru *m*.

surly *adj* revêche, bourru.

surmise *vt* conjecturer; * *n* conjecture *f*.

surmount *vt* surmonter.

surmountable *adj* surmontable.

surname *n* nom de famille *m*.

surpass *vt* surpasser, dépasser.

surpassing *adj* sans pareil, incomparable.

surplice *n* surplis *m*.

surplus *n* excédent *m*; surplus *m*; * *adj* en surplus.

surprise *vt* surprendre; * *n* surprise *f*.

surprising *adj* surprenant.

surrender *vt* rendre; céder; * *vi* se rendre; * *n* reddition *f*.

surreptitious *adj*, **~ly** *adv* subreptice(ment).

surrogate *vt* remplacer; * *n* substitut *m*.

surrogate mother *n* mèreporteuse *f*.

surround *vt* entourer, cerner, encercler.

survey *vt* examiner, inspecter; faire le relevé de; * *n* enquête *f*; relevé (des plans) *m*.

survive *vi* survivre; * *vt* survivre à.

survivor *n* survivant *m*, -e *f*.

susceptibility *n* sensibilité *f*.

susceptible *adj* sensible.

suspect *vt* soupçonner; * *n* suspect *m*, -e *f*.

suspend *vt* suspendre.

suspense *n* incertitude *f*; suspense *m*.

suspension *n* suspension *f*.

suspension bridge *n* pont suspendu *m*.

suspicion *n* soupçon *m*.

suspicious *adj* soupçonneux; **~ly** *adv* soupçonneusement.

suspiciousness *n* caractère soupçonneux *m*.

sustain *vt* soutenir, supporter, maintenir; subir.

sustenance *n* (moyens de) subsistance *f*.

suture n suture f.

swab n tampon m; prélèvement m.

swaddle vt emmailloter.

swaddling-clothes npl langes mpl.

swagger vi plastronner.

swallow n hirondelle f; * vt avaler.

swamp n marais m.

swampy adj marécageux.

swan n cygne m.

swap vt échanger; * n échange m.

swarm n essaim m; grouillement m; nuée f; * vi fourmiller; grouiller de monde; pulluler.

swarthy adj basané.

swarthiness n teint basané m.

swashbuckling adj fanfaron.

swath n andain m.

swathe vt emmailloter; * n bande f.

sway vt balancer; * vi se balancer, osciller; * n balancement m; emprise, domination, puissance f.

swear vt jurer; faire prêter serment; * vi jurer.

sweat n sueur f; * vi suer, transpirer.

sweater, sweatshirt n pullover m.

sweep vt balayer; ramoner; * vi s'étendre; avancer rapidement, majestueusement; * n coup de balai m; grand geste m; champ m.

sweeping adj rapide; ~s pl balayures fpl.

sweepstake n sweepstake m.

sweet adj sucré, doux, agréable; suave; gentil; mélodieux; adorable; * adv doux; sucré; * n bonbon m.

sweetbread n ris de veau m.

sweeten vt sucrer; adoucir; assainir; purifier.

sweetener n édulcorant m.

sweetheart n petit(e) ami(e) m(f); chéri m, -e f.

sweetmeats npl sucreries fpl.

sweetness n goût sucré m, douceur f.

swell vi gonfler; enfler; augmenter; * vt gonfler, enfler, grossir; * n houle f; * adj (fam) génial, épatant.

swelling n gonflement m; boursouflure, tuméfaction f.

swelter vi étouffer de chaleur.

swerve vi faire un écart; * vt dévier.

swift adj rapide, prompt, vif; * n martinet m.

swiftly adv rapidement.

swiftness n rapidité, promptitude f.

swill vt boire avidement; * n pâtée f.

swim vi nager; * vt traverser à la nage; * n baignade f.

swimming n natation f; vertige m.

swimming pool n piscine f.

swimsuit n maillot de bain m.

swindle vt escroquer.

swindler n escroc m.

swine n pourceau, porc m.

swing vi se balancer, osciller; virer; * vt balancer; faire tourner; influencer; * n balancement m; rythme m.

swinging adj (fam) rythmé.

swinging door n porte battante f.

swirl n tourbillon m.

switch n baguette f; interrupteur m;

(rail) aiguille f; * vt changer de; **to ~ off** éteindre; **to ~ on** allumer.

switchboard n standard (téléphonique) m.

swivel vt faire pivoter.

swoon vi s'évanouir; * n évanouissement m, défaillance f.

swoop vi se fondre sur; * n descente en piqué f; descente, rafle f; **in one ~** d'un seul coup.

sword n épée f.

swordfish n espadon m.

swordsman n tireur d'épée m.

sycamore n sycomore m.

sycophant n sycophante mf.

syllabic adj syllabique.

syllable n syllabe f.

syllabus n programme d'un cours m.

syllogism n syllogisme m.

sylph n sylphe m; sylphide f.

symbol n symbole m.

symbolic(al) adj symbolique.

symbolize vt symboliser.

symmetrical adj, **~ly** adv symétrique(ment).

symmetry n symétrie f.

sympathetic adj compatissant; **~ally** adv avec compassion.

sympathize vi compatir.

sympathy n compassion f.

symphony n symphonie f.

symposium n symposium m.

symptom n symptôme m.

synagogue n synagogue f.

synchronism n synchronisme m.

syndicate n syndicat m.

syndrome n syndrome m.

synod n synode m.

synonym n synonyme m.

synonymous adj synonyme; **~ly** adv de façon synonyme.

synopsis n synopsis f; résumé m.

synoptical adj synoptique.

syntax n syntaxe f.

synthesis n synthèse f.

syringe n seringue f; * vt seringuer.

system n système m.

systematic adj, **~ally** adv systématique(ment).

systems analyst n analyste de systèmes mf.

T

tab n patte f; étiquette f.

tabernacle n tabernacle m.

table n table f; * vt mettre en forme de tableau; ajourner; **~ d'hôte** repas à prix fixe m.

tablecloth n nappe f.

tablespoon n grande cuiller f.

tablet n tablette f; comprimé m.

table tennis n ping-pong m.

taboo adj, n tabou m; * vt proscrire.

tabular adj tabulaire.

tacit adj, **~ly** adv tacite(ment).

taciturn adj taciturne.

tack n broquette f; bord m; * vt clouer; * vi tirer des bordées.

tackle n attirail, équipement, matériel m; plaquage m; (mar) appareil de levage m, apparaux mpl.

tact n tact m.

tactician n tacticien m.

tactics npl tactique f.

tadpole n têtard m.

taffeta n taffetas m.

tag n ferret m; * vt ferrer.

tail n queue f; basque f; * vt suivre, filer.

tailgate n hayon arrière m.

tailor n tailleur m.

tailoring n métier de tailleur m.

tailor-made adj fait sur mesure.

tailwind n vent arrière m.

taint n infecter, polluer; vicier; * n tache, souillure f.

tainted adj infecté; souillé.

take vt prendre, saisir; apporter, emporter; conduire; enlever, retirer; passer; * to ~ away vt enlever; emporter; to ~ back vt reprendre; raccompagner; to ~ down vt descendre; prendre (notes); to ~ in vt saisir, comprendre; recevoir; to ~ off vt décoller; vt enlever; imi- ter; to ~ on vt accepter; engager; s'attaquer à; to ~ out vt sortir; enlever; to ~ to vt se prendre d'amitié pour; to ~ up vt monter; occuper; se mettre à; * n prise f.

takeoff n décollage m.

takeover n prise de possession f.

takings npl recette f.

talc n talc m.

talent n talent m; don m.

talented adj talentueux.

talisman n talisman m.

talk vi parler, bavarder; causer; * n conversation f; discussion f; entretien m.

talkative adj loquace.

talk show n débat télévisé m.

tall adj grand, élevé; incroyable.

tally vi correspondre.

talon n serre f.

tambourine n tambourin m.

tame adj apprivoisé, domestiqué; ~ly adv docilement; fadement; * vt apprivoiser, domestiquer.

tameness n nature apprivoisée f; soumission f.

tamper vi toucher à.

tampon n tampon m.

tan vt, vi bronzer; * n bronzage m.

tang n saveur forte f.

tangent n tangente f.

tangerine n mandarine f.

tangible adj tangible.

tangle vt enchevêtrer, embrouiller.

tank n réservoir m; citerne f.

tanker n pétrolier m; camionciterne m.

tanned adj bronzé.

tantalizing adj tentant.

tantamount adj équivalent (à).

tantrum n accès de colère m.

tap vt taper doucement; exploiter; inciser; * n petite tape f; robinet m.

tape n ruban m; * vt enregistrer.

tape measure n mètre à ruban m.

taper n cierge m.

tape recorder n magnétophone m.

tapestry n tapisserie f.

tar n goudron m.

target n cible f.

tariff n tarif m.

tarmac n piste f.

tarnish vt ternir.

tarpaulin n bâche (goudronnée) f.

tarragon n (bot) estragon m.

tart adj acidulé, âpre; * n tarte, tartelette f.

tartan *n* tartan *m*.

tartar *n* tartre *m*.

task *n* tâche *f*.

tassel *n* gland *m*.

taste *n* goût *m*; saveur *f*; pincée *f*; penchant *m*; * *vt* sentir le goût de; goûter à; déguster; savourer; * *vi* avoir du goût.

tasteful *adj* de bon goût; ~**ly** avec goût.

tasteless *adj* insipide, sans goût.

tasty *adj* savoureux.

tattoo *n* tatouage *m*; * *vt* tatouer.

taunt *vt* railler; accabler de sarcasmes; * *n* raillerie *f*, sarcasme *m*.

Taurus *n* Taureau *m* (signe du zodiaque).

taut *adj* tendu.

tautological *adj* tautologique.

tautology *n* tautologie *f*.

tawdry *adj* tapageur, voyant, clinquant.

tax *n* impôt *m*; contribution *f*; * *vt* imposer; mettre à l'épreuve.

taxable *adj* imposable.

taxation *n* imposition *f*.

tax collector *n* percepteur *m*.

tax-free *adj* exonéré d'impôts.

taxi *n* taxi *m*; * *vi* rouler sur la piste.

taxi driver *n* chauffeur de taxi *m*.

taxi stand *n* station de taxis *f*.

tax payer *n* contribuable *mf*.

tax relief *n* dégrèvement fiscal *m*.

tax return *n* déclaration d'impôts *f*.

tea *n* thé *m*.

teach *vt* enseigner, apprendre; * *vi* enseigner.

teacher *n* professeur *m*; instituteur *m*, -trice *f*.

teaching *n* enseignement *m*.

teacup *n* tasse à thé *f*.

teak *n* teck *m*.

team *n* équipe *f*.

teamster *n* routier *m*.

teamwork *n* travail d'équipe *m*.

teapot *n* théière *f*.

tear *vt* déchirer; **to ~ up** mettre en morceaux.

tear *n* larme *f*.

tearful *adj* larmoyant; ~**ly** *adv* en pleurant.

tear gas *n* gaz lacrymogène *m*.

tease *vt* taquiner.

tea-service, tea-set *n* service à thé *m*.

teaspoon *n* petite cuiller *f*.

teat *n* tétine *f*, mamelon *m*.

technical *adj* technique.

technicality *n* technicité *f*.

technician *n* technicien *m*, -ienne *f*.

technique *n* technique *f*.

technological *adj* technologique.

technology *n* technologie *f*.

teddy (bear) *n* ours en peluche *m*.

tedious *adj* ennuyeux, fastidieux; ~**ly** *adv* fastidieusement.

tedium *n* ennui, manque d'intérêt *m*.

tee *n* tee *m*.

teem *vi* grouiller (de).

teenage *adj* adolescent; ~**r** *n* adolescent(e) *m(f)*.

teens *npl* adolescence (de 13 à 20 ans) *f*.

tee-shirt *n* T-shirt *m*.

teeth *npl* de tooth.

teethe *vi* faire ses premières dents.

teetotal *adj* antialcoolique, qui ne boit jamais d'alcool.

teetotaller *n* personne qui ne boit jamais d'alcool *f*.

telegram n télégramme m.

telegraph n télégraphe m.

telegraphic adj télégraphique.

telegraphy n télégraphie f.

telepathy n télépathie f.

telephone n téléphone m.

telephone booth n cabine téléphonique f.

telephone call n appel téléphonique m.

telephone directory n annuaire m.

telephone number n numéro de téléphone m.

telescope n télescope m.

telescopic adj télescopique.

televise vt téléviser.

television n télévision f.

television set n téléviseur, poste de télévision m.

telex n télex m; vt envoyer par télex.

tell vt dire; raconter.

teller n caissier m, -ière f.

telling adj révélateur.

telltale adj dénonciateur.

temper vt tempérer, modérer; * n colère f.

temperament n tempérament m.

temperance n tempérance, modération f.

temperate adj tempéré, modéré, mesuré.

temperature n température f.

tempest n tempête f.

tempestuous adj de tempête.

template n gabarit m.

temple n temple m; tempe f.

temporarily adv temporairement.

temporary adj temporaire.

tempt vt tenter.

temptation n tentation f.

tempting adj tentant.

ten adj, n dix m.

tenable adj défendable.

tenacious adj tenance, ~ly adv avec ténacité.

tenacity n ténacité f.

tenancy n location f.

tenant n locataire mf.

tend vt garder, surveiller; * vi avoir tendance (à).

tendency n tendance f.

tender adj tendre, délicat; sensible; ~ly adv tendrement; * n offre f; * vt offrir.

tenderness n tendresse f.

tendon n tendon m.

tenement n appartement m.

tenet n doctrine f; principe m.

tennis n tennis m.

tennis court n court ou terrain de tennis m.

tennis player n joueur(-euse) de tennis m(f).

tennis racket n raquette de tennis f.

tennis shoes npl chaussures de tennis fpl.

tenor n (mus) ténor m; sens m; substance f.

tense adj tendu; * n (gr) temps m.

tension n tension f.

tent n tente f.

tentacle n tentacule m.

tentative adj timide, hésitant; ~ly adv à titre d'essai.

tenth adj, n dixième mf.

tenuous adj ténu.

tenure n titularisation f.

tepid adj tiède.

term n terme m; trimestre m; mot

m; condition, clause *f*; * *vt* appeler, nommer.

terminal *adj* terminal; * *n* aérogare *f*; terminal *m*.

terminate *vt* terminer.

termination *n* fin, conclusion *f*.

terminus *n* terminus *m*.

terrace *n* terrace *f*.

terrain *n* terrain *m*.

terrestrial *adj* terrestre.

terrible *adj* terrible.

terribly *adv* terriblement.

terrier *n* terrier *m*.

terrific *adj* terrifiant; fantastique.

terrify *vt* terrifier, épouvanter.

territorial *adj* territorial.

territory *n* territoire *m*.

terror *n* terreur *f*.

terrorism *n* terrorisme *m*.

terrorist *n* terroriste *mf*.

terrorize *vt* terroriser.

terse *adj* concis, net.

test *n* essai *m*; épreuve *f*; * *vt* essayer; examiner.

testament *n* testament *m*.

tester *n* contrôleur *m*, -euse *f*.

testicles *npl* testicules *mpl*.

testify *vt* témoigner, déclarer sous serment.

testimonial *n* certificat *m*.

testimony *n* témoignage *m*.

test pilot *n* pilote d'essai *m*.

test tube *n* éprouvette *f*.

testy *adj* irritable.

tetanus *n* tétanos *m*.

tether *vt* attacher.

text *n* texte *m*.

textbook *n* manuel *m*.

textiles *npl* textiles *mpl*.

textual *adj* textuel.

texture *n* texture *f*; tissu *m*.

than *adv* que; de.

thank *vt* remercier, dire merci à.

thankful *adj* reconnaissant; ~ly *adv* avec reconnaissance.

thankfulness *n* reconnaissance *f*.

thankless *adj* ingrat.

thanks *npl* remerciement(s) *m(pl)*.

thanksgiving *n* action de grâce *f*.

that *pn* cela, ça, ce; qui, que; celui-là; * *conj* que; afin que; **so ~** pour que.

thatch *n* chaume *m*; * *vt* couvrir de chaume.

thaw *n* dégel *m*; * *vi* fondre, dégeler.

the *art* le, la, l', les.

theatre *n* théâtre *m*.

theatre-goer *n* habitué(e) du théâtre *m(f)*.

theatrical *adj* théâtral.

theft *n* vol *m*.

their *pn* leur(s); ~s le leur; la leur; les leurs; à elles; à eux.

them *pn* les; leur.

theme *n* thème *m*.

themselves *pn pl* eux-mêmes *mpl*, elles-mêmes *fpl*; se.

then *adv* alors, à cette époque-là; ensuite; en ce cas; * *conj* donc; en ce cas; * *adj* d'alors; **now and ~** de temps en temps.

theologic(al) *adj* théologique.

theologian *n* théologien *m*, -ne *f*.

theology *n* théologie *f*.

theorem *n* théorème *m*.

theoretic(al) *adj*, ~ly *adv* théorique(ment).

theorist *n* théoricien *m*, -ne *f*.

theorize *vt* théoriser.

theory n théorie f.

therapeutics n thérapeutique f.

therapist n thérapeute mf.

therapy n thérapie f.

there adv y, là.

thereabout(s) adv par là, près de là.

thereafter adv par la suite; après.

thereby adv de cette façon.

therefore adv donc, par conséquent.

thermal adj thermal.

thermal printer n imprimante thermique f.

thermometer n thermomètre m.

thermostat n thermostat m.

thesaurus n trésor m; dictionnaire de synonymes m.

these pn pl ceux-ci, celles-ci.

thesis n thèse f.

they pn pl ils, elles.

thick adj épais, gros; dense; obtus.

thicken vi (s')épaissir, grossir.

thicket n fourré m.

thickness n épaisseur f.

thickset adj trapu; râblé.

thick-skinned adj à la peau épaisse.

thief n voleur m, -euse f.

thigh n cuisse f.

thimble n dé (à coudre) m.

thin adj mince, fin, maigre; clair; * vt amincir; délayer; éclaircir.

thing n chose f; objet m; truc m.

think vi penser, réfléchir, imaginer; * vt penser, croire, juger; **to ~ over** vt réfléchir à; **to ~ up** vt imaginer.

thinker n penseur m, -euse f.

thinking n pensée f; réflexion f; opinion f.

third adj troisième; * n troisième mf; tiers m; **~ly** adv troisièmement.

third rate adj médiocre, de mauvaise qualité.

thirst n soif f.

thirsty adj assoiffé.

thirteen adj, n treize m.

thirteenth adj, n treizième mf.

thirtieth adj, n trentième mf.

thirty adj, n trente m.

this adj ce, cet, cette, ces; * pn ceci, ce.

thistle n chardon m.

thorn n épine f; aubépine f.

thorny adj épineux.

thorough prep à travers, par; * adj consciencieux, approfondi; **~ly** adv minutieusement, à fond.

thoroughbred adj pur-sang, de race.

thoroughfare n rue, artère f.

those pn pl ceux-là, celles-là; * adj ces, ces...là.

though conj bien que, malgré le fait que; * adv pourtant.

thought n pensée, réflexion f; opinion f; intention f.

thoughtful adj pensif.

thoughtless adj étourdi; irréfléchi; **~ly** adv étourdiment, à la légère.

thousand adj, n mille m.

thousandth adj, n millième mf.

thrash vt battre; rouer de coups.

thread n fil m; filetage m; * vt enfiler.

threadbare adj râpé, élimé.

threat n menace f.

threaten vt menacer.

three adj, n trois m.

three-dimensional adj à trois dimensions, tridimensionnel.

three-ply adj à trois fils ou épaisseurs.

threshold n seuil m.

thrifty adj économe.

thrill vt faire frissonner; * n frisson m.

thriller n film ou roman à suspense m.

thrive vi prospérer; bien se développer.

throat n gorge f.

throb vi palpiter; vibrer; lanciner.

throne n trône m.

throng n foule f; * vi affluer.

throttle n accélérateur m; * vt étrangler.

through prep à travers; pendant; par, grâce à; * adj direct; * adv complètement.

throughout prep partout dans; * adv partout.

throw vt jeter, lancer, projeter; * n jet m; lancement m; **to ~ away** vt jeter; **to ~ off** vt rejeter; **to ~ out** vt jeter dehors; **to ~ up** vt, vi vomir.

throwaway adj à jeter.

thru = through.

thrush n grive f.

thrust vt pousser violemment; enfoncer; * n poussée f.

thud n bruit sourd m.

thug n voyou m.

thumb n pouce m.

thumbtack n punaise f.

thump n coup de poing m; * vi frapper, cogner; * vt cogner à.

thunder n tonnerre m; * vi tonner.

thunderbolt n coup de foudre m.

thunderclap n coup de tonnerre m.

thunderstorm n orage m.

thundery adj orageux.

Thursday n jeudi m.

thus adv ainsi, de cette manière.

thwart vt contrecarrer.

thyme n (bot) thym m.

thyroid n thyroïde f.

tiara n tiare f.

tic n tic m.

tick n tic-tac m; instant m; * vt cocher; **to ~ over** vi tourner au ralenti; aller doucement.

ticket n billet, ticket m; étiquette f; carte f.

ticket collector n (rail) contrôleur m, -euse f.

ticket office n guichet m.

tickle vt chatouiller.

ticklish adj chatouilleux.

tidal adj (mar) de la marée.

tidal wave n raz-de-marée m.

tide n époque f; marée f.

tidy adj rangé, en ordre; ordonné; soigné.

tie vt attacher, nouer; * vi se nouer; **to ~ up** vt ficeler; attacher; amarrer; conclure; * n attache f; lacet m; égalité f.

tier n gradin m; étage m.

tiger n tigre m.

tight adj raide, tendu; serré; hermétique; * adv très fort.

tighten vt (re)serrer, tendre.

tightfisted adj avare.

tightly adv très fort.

tightrope n corde raide f.

tigress n tigresse f.

tile n tuile f; carreau m; * vt couvrir de tuiles.

tiled adj en tuiles, carrelé.

till n caisse f; * vt labourer, cultiver.

tiller n barre du gouvernail f.

tilt vt pencher; * vi s'incliner.

timber n bois de construction m; arbres mpl.

time n temps m; période f; heure f; moment m; (mus) mesure f; **in** ~ à temps; **from** ~ **to** ~ de temps en temps; * vt fixer; chronométrer.

time bomb n bombe à retardement f.

time lag n décalage m.

timeless adj éternel.

timely adj opportun.

time off n temps libre m.

timer n sablier m; minuteur m.

time scale n durée f.

time zone n fuseau horaire m.

timid adj timide, timoré; ~ly adv timidement.

timidity n timidité f.

timing n chronométrage m.

tin n étain m; boîte (de conserve) f.

tinfoil n papier d'aluminium m.

tinge n teinte f.

tingle vi picoter; vibrer, frissonner.

tingling n picotement m; frisson m.

tinker n rétameur f; romanichel m, -elle f.

tinkle vi tinter.

tinplate n fer-blanc m.

tinsel n guirlande f.

tint n teinte f; * vt teinter.

tinted adj teinté; fumé.

tiny adj minuscule, tout petit.

tip n pointe f, bout m; pourboire m; conseil, tuyau m; * vt donner un pourboire à; pencher; effleurer.

tip-off n avertissement m.

tipsy adj gai, éméché.

tiptop adj excellent, de premier ordre.

tirade n diatribe f.

tire n pneu m; * vt fatiguer; * vi se fatiguer; se lasser.

tireless adj infatigable.

tiresome adj ennuyeux, fatigant.

tiring adj fatigant.

tissue n tissu m; mouchoir en papier m.

tissue paper n papier de soie m.

titbit n friandise f; bon morceau m.

titillate vt titiller.

title n titre m.

title deed n titre de propriété m.

title page n page de titre f.

titter vi rire sottement; * n petit rire sot m.

titular adj titulaire.

to prep à; vers; en; chez; moins; de.

toad n crapaud m.

toadstool n (bot) champignon vénéneux m.

toast vt (faire) griller; porter un toast à la santé de; * n toast m.

toaster n grille-pain m invar.

tobacco n tabac m.

tobacconist n marchand(e) de tabac m(f).

tobacco pouch n blague à tabac f.

tobacco shop n bureau de tabac m.

toboggan n toboggan m.

today adv aujourd'hui.

toddler n enfant qui commence à marcher m.

toddy n grog m.

toe n orteil m; pointe f.

together adv ensemble; en même temps.

toil vi travailler dur, peiner; se donner du mal; * n dur travail m; labeur m; peine f.

toilet n toilette f; toilettes fpl; * adj de toilette.

toilet bag n trousse de toilette f.

toilet bowl n cuvette des toilettes f.

toilet paper n papier hygiénique m.

toiletries npl articles de toilette mpl.

token n signe m; marque f; souvenir m; bon m; jeton m.

tolerable adj tolérable; passable.

tolerance n tolérance f.

tolerant adj tolérant.

tolerate vt tolérer.

toll n péage m; nombre de victimes m; * vi sonner.

tomato n tomate f.

tomb n tombeau m; tombe f.

tomboy n garçon manqué m.

tombstone n pierre tombale f.

tomcat n matou m.

tomorrow adv, n demain m.

ton n tonne f.

tone n ton m; tonalité f; * vi s'harmoniser; **to ~ down** vt adoucir.

tone-deaf adj qui n'a pas de l'oreille.

tongs npl pinces fpl.

tongue n langue f.

tongue-tied adj muet.

tongue-twister n phrase difficile à prononcer f.

tonic n (med) tonique m.

tonight adv, n ce soir (m).

tonnage n tonnage m.

tonsil n amygdale f.

tonsure n tonsure f.

too adv aussi; trop.

tool n outil m; ustensile m.

tool box n caisse à outils f.

toot vi klaxonner.

tooth n dent f.

toothache n rage de dents f.

toothbrush n brosse à dents f.

toothless adj édenté.

toothpaste n dentifrice m.

toothpick n cure-dent m.

top n sommet m, cime f; haut m; tête f; dessus m; couvercle m; étage supérieur m; * adj du haut; premier; * vt dépasser; être au sommet de; **to ~ off** couronner.

topaz n topaze f.

top floor n dernier étage m.

top-heavy adj instable, déséquilibré.

topic n sujet m; **~al** adj d'actualité.

topless adj torse nu, aux seins nus.

top-level adj au plus haut niveau.

topmost adj le plus haut.

topographic(al) adj topographique.

topography n topographie f.

topple vt renverser; * vi basculer.

top-secret adj ultra-secret.

topsy-turvy adv sens dessus dessous.

torch n torche f.

torment vt tourmenter; * n tourment m.

tornado n tornade f.

torrent n torrent m.

torrid adj torride.

tortoise n tortue f.

tortoiseshell adj en écaille de tortue.

tortuous adj tortueux, sinueux.

torture n torture f; * vt torturer.

toss vt lancer, jeter; agiter, secouer.

total adj total, global; ~ly adv totalement.

totalitarian adj totalitaire.

totality n totalité f.

totter vi chanceler.

touch vt toucher; to ~ on ; to ~ up retoucher; * n toucher m; contact m; touche f.

touch-and-go adj incertain, précaire.

touchdown n atterrissage m; but m.

touched adj touché; timbré.

touching adj touchant, attendrissant.

touchstone n pierre de touche f.

touchwood n amadou m.

touchy adj susceptible.

tough adj dur; pénible; résistant; fort; * n dure m.

toughen vt durcir.

toupee n postiche m.

tour n voyage m; visite f; * vt visiter.

touring n voyages touristiques mpl.

tourism n tourisme m.

tourist n touriste mf.

tourist office n office de tourisme m.

tournament n tournoi m.

tow n remorquage m; * vt remorquer.

toward(s) prep vers, dans la direction de; envers, à l'égard de.

towel n serviette f.

towelling n tissu éponge m.

towel rack n porte-serviette m invar.

tower n tour f.

towering adj imposant.

town n ville f.

town clerk n secrétaire de mairie mf.

town hall n mairie f.

towrope n câble de remorquage m.

toy n jouet m.

toyshop n magasin de jouets m.

trace n trace, piste f; * vt tracer, esquisser; retrouver.

track n trace f; empreinte f; chemin m; voie f; piste f; * vt suivre à la trace.

tracksuit n survêtement m.

tract n étendue, région f; période f; brochure f.

traction n traction f.

trade n commerce m, affaires fpl; échange m; métier m; * vi faire le commerce (de); commercer.

trade fair n foire commerciale f.

trademark n marque de fabrique f.

trade name n raison commerciale f.

trader n négociant m, -e f.

tradesman n fournisseur, commerçant m.

trade(s) union n syndicat m.

trade unionist n syndicaliste mf.

trading n commerce m; * adj commercial.

tradition n tradition f

traditional adj traditionnel.

traffic n circulation f; négoce m; * vi faire le commerce (de).

traffic circle n rond-point m.

traffic jam n embouteillage m.

trafficker n trafiquant m, -e f.

traffic lights npl feux de signalisation mpl.

tragedy n tragédie f.

tragic adj, ~ally adv tragique(ment).

tragicomedy n tragi-comédie f.

trail vt suivre la piste de; traîner; vi traîner; * n traînée f; trace f; queue f.

trailer n remorque f; caravane f; bande-annonce f.

train vt entraîner; former; * n train m; traîne f; file f.

trained adj qualifié; diplômé.

trainee n stagiaire mf.

trainer n entraîneur m.

training n formation f; entraînement m.

trait n trait m.

traitor n traître m.

tramp n clochard m, -e f; (sl) putain f; * vi marcher d'un pas lourd; * vt piétiner.

trample vt piétiner.

trampoline n trampoline m.

trance n transe f; extase f.

tranquil adj tranquille.

tranquillize vt tranquilliser.

tranquillizer n tranquillisant m.

transact vt traiter.

transaction n transaction f; opération f.

transatlantic adj transatlantique.

transcend vt transcender, dépasser; surpasser.

transcription n transcription f; copie f.

transfer vt transférer, déplacer; * n transfert m; mutation f; décalcomanie f.

transform vt transformer.

transformation n transformation f.

transfusion n transfusion f.

transient adj transitoire, passager.

transit n transit m.

transition n transition f; passage m.

transitional adj de transition.

transitive adj transitif.

translate vt traduire.

translation n traduction f.

translator n traducteur m, -trice f.

transmission n transmission f.

transmit vt transmettre.

transmitter n transmetteur m; émetteur m.

transparency n transparence f.

transparent adj transparent.

transpire vi transpirer; arriver.

transplant vt transplanter; * n transplantation f.

transport vt transporter; * n transport m.

transportation n moyen de transport m.

trap n piège m; * vt prendre au piège; bloquer.

trap door n trappe f.

trapeze n trapèze m.

trappings npl ornements mpl.

trash n camelote f; inepties fpl.

trash can n poubelle f.

trashy adj sans valeur, de mauvaise qualité.

travel vi voyager; * vt parcourir; * n voyage m.

travel agency n agence de voyages f.

travel agent n agent de voyages m.

traveller n voyageur m, -euse f.

traveller's cheque n chèque de voyage m.

travelling n voyages mpl.

travel sickness n mal de mer/de l'air m.

travesty n parodie f.

trawler n chalutier m.

tray n plateau m; tiroir m.

treacherous adj traître, perfide.

treachery n traîtrise f.

tread vi marcher ; écraser ; * n pas m ; bruit de pas m ; bande de roulement f.

treason n trahison f ; **high ~** haute trahison f.

treasure n trésor m ; * vt conserver précieusement.

treasurer n trésorier m, -ière f.

treat vt traiter ; offrir ; * n cadeau m ; plaisir m.

treatise n traité m.

treatment n traitement m.

treaty n traité m.

treble adj triple ; * vt, vi tripler ; * n (mus) soprano m.

treble clef n clef de sol f.

tree n arbre m.

trek n randonnée f ; étape f.

trellis n treillis m.

tremble vi trembler.

trembling n tremblement m ; frisson m.

tremendous adj terrible ; énorme ; formidable.

tremor n tremblement m.

trench n fossé m ; (mil) tranchée f.

trend n tendance f ; direction f ; mode f.

trendy adj dernier cri.

trepidation n vive inquiétude f.

trespass vt transgresser, violer.

tress n boucle de cheveu f, tresse f.

trestle n tréteau, chevalet m.

trial n procès m ; épreuve f ; essai m ; peine f.

triangle n triangle m.

triangular adj triangulaire.

tribal adj tribal.

tribe n tribu f.

tribulation n tribulation f.

tribunal n tribunal m.

tributary adj, n tributaire m.

tribute n tribut m.

trice n instant m.

trick n ruse, astuce f, tour m ; blague f ; pli m ; * vt attraper.

trickery n supercherie f.

trickle vi couler goutte à goutte ; * n filet m.

tricky adj délicat ; difficile.

tricycle n tricycle m.

trifle n bagatelle, vétille f ; * vi jouer ; badiner.

trifling adj futile, insignifiant.

trigger n détente f ; **to ~ off** vi déclencher.

trigonometry n trigonométrie f.

trill n trille f ; * vi triller.

trim adj net, soigné ; bien tenu ; en parfait état ; * vt arranger ; tailler ; orner.

trimmings npl ornements mpl.

Trinity n Trinité f.

trinket n bibelot m, babiole f ; colifichet m.

trio n (mus) trio m.

trip vt faire trébucher ; * vi trébucher ; faire un faux pas ; **to ~ up** vi trébucher ; vt faire trébucher ; * n faux pas m ; voyage m.

tripe n tripes fpl ; bêtises fpl.

triple adj triple ; * vt, vi tripler.

triplets npl triplés mpl.

triplicate n copie en trois exemplaires f.

tripod n trépied m.

trite adj banal ; usé.

triumph n triomphe m ; * vi triompher.

triumphal adj triomphal.

triumphant adj triomphant; victorieux; **~ly** adv triomphalement.

trivia npl futilités fpl.

trivial adj insignifiant, sans importance; **~ly** adv banalement.

triviality n banalité f.

trolley n chariot m.

trombone n trombone m.

troop n bande f; **~s** npl troupes fpl.

trooper n soldat de cavalerie m.

trophy n trophée m.

tropical adj tropical.

trot n trot m; * vi trotter.

trouble vt affliger; tourmenter; * n problème m; ennui m; difficulté f; affliction, peine f.

troubled adj inquiet; agité.

troublemaker n agitateur m, -trice f.

troubleshooter n médiateur m.

troublesome adj pénible.

trough n abreuvoir m; auge f.

troupe n troupe f.

trousers npl pantalon m.

trout n truite f.

trowel n truelle f.

truce n trêve f.

truck n camion m; wagon m.

truck driver n routier m.

truck farm n jardin maraîcher m.

truculent adj brutal, agressif.

trudge vi marcher lourdement.

true adj vrai, véritable; sincère; exact.

truelove n bien-aimé m, -e f.

truffle n truffe f.

truly adv vraiment; sincèrement.

trump n atout m.

trumpet n trompette f.

trunk n malle f, coffre m; trompe f.

truss n botte f; * vt botteler; trousser.

trust n confiance f; trust m; fidéicommis m; * vt avoir confiance; confier à.

trusted adj de confiance.

trustee n fidéicommissaire m, curateur m, -trice f.

trustful adj confiant.

trustily adv fidèlement.

trusting adj confiant.

trustworthy adj digne de confiance.

trusty adj fidèle, loyal; sûr.

truth n vérité f; **in ~** en vérité.

truthful adj véridique; qui dit la vérité.

truthfulness n véracité f.

try vt essayer, tâcher, chercher à; expérimenter; mettre à l'épreuve; tenter; juger; * vi essayer; **to ~ on** vt essayer; **to ~ out** vt essayer; * n tentative f; essai m.

trying adj pénible; fatigant.

tub n cuve f, bac m; baignoire f.

tuba n tuba m.

tube n tube m; métro m.

tuberculosis n tuberculose f.

tubing n tuyaux mpl.

tuck n pli m; * vt mettre.

tucker vt fatiguer.

Tuesday n mardi m.

tuft n touffe f; houppe f.

tug vt remorquer; * n remorqueur m.

tuition n cours, enseignement m.

tulip n tulipe f.

tumble vi tomber, faire une chute; se jeter; * vt renverser; culbuter; * n chute f; culbute f.

tumbledown adj délabré.

tumbler n verre m.

tummy n ventre m.

tumour n tumeur f.

tumultuous adj tumultueux.

tuna n thon m.

tune n air m; accord m; harmonie f; * vt accorder; syntoniser.

tuneful adj mélodieux, harmonieux.

tuner n syntoniseur m.

tunic n tunique f.

tuning fork n (mus) diapason m.

tunnel n tunnel m; * vt creuser un tunnel dans.

turban n turban m.

turbine n turbine f.

turbulence n turbulence, agitation f.

turbulent adj turbulent, agité.

tureen n soupière f.

turf n gazon m; * vt gazonner.

turgid adj turgide.

turkey n dinde f.

turmoil n agitation f; trouble m.

turn vi (se) tourner; devenir; changer; se retourner; se changer, se transformer; tourner; **to ~ back** revenir; **to ~ around** se retourner; **to ~ in** aller se coucher; **to ~ off** vi tourner; vt éteindre; fermer; **to ~ on** vt allumer; ouvrir; **to ~ out** s'avérer; **to ~ over** vi se retourner; vt tourner; **to ~ up** vi arriver; se présenter; vt monter; * n tour m; tournure f; virage m; tendance f.

turncoat n renégat m.

turning n embranchement m.

turnip n navet m.

turn-off n sortie (d'autoroute) f; embranchement m.

turnout n production f.

turnover n chiffre d'affaires m.

turnpike n autoroute à péage f.

turnstile n tourniquet m.

turntable n platine f.

turpentine n (essence de) térében-thine f.

turquoise n turquoise f.

turret n tourelle f.

turtle n tortue marine f.

turtledove n tourterelle f.

tusk n défense f.

tussle n lutte f.

tutor n professeur particulier m; directeur d'études m; * vt enseigner, donner des cours particuliers à.

tuxedo n smoking m.

twang n bruit sec m; ton nasillard m.

tweezers npl pince à épiler f.

twelfth adj n douzième mf.

twelve adj, n douze m.

twentieth adj, n vingtième mf.

twenty adj, n vingt m.

twice adv deux fois.

twig n brindille f; * vi comprendre.

twilight n crépuscule m.

twin n jumeau m, -elle f.

twine vi s'enrouler; serpenter; * n ficelle f.

twinge vt élancer; * n élancement m; remords m.

twinkle vi scintiller; clignoter.

twirl vi faire tournoyer; * vi tournoyer; * n tournoiement m.

twist vt tordre, tortiller; entortiller; * vi serpenter; * n torsion f; tournant m; rouleau m.

twit n (sl) crétin m, -e f.

twitch vi avoir un mouvement nerveux; * n tic m.

twitter vi gazouiller; * n gazouillis m.
two adj, n deux m.
two-door adj à deux portes.
two-faced adj hypocrite.
twofold adj double; * adv au double.
two-seater n voiture/avion à deux places f/m.
twosome n paire f; couple m.
tycoon n magnat m.
type n type m; caractère m; exemple m; * vi taper à la machine.

typecast adj enfermé dans un rôle.
typeface n œil de caractère m.
typescript n texte dactylographié m.
typewriter n machine à écrire f.
typewritten adj dactylographié.
typical adj typique.
tyrannical adj tyrannique.
tyranny n tyrannie f.
tyrant n tyran m.

U

ubiquitous adj doué d'ubiquité.
udder n pis m.
ugh excl pouah!, berk!
ugliness n laideur f.
ugly adj laid; inquiétant.
ulcer n ulcère m.
ulterior adj ultérieur.
ultimate adj final; ~ly adv finalement; à la fin.
ultimatum n ultimatum m.
ultramarine n, adj outremer m.
ultrasound n ultrason m.
umbilical cord n cordon ombilical m.
umbrella n parapluie m.
umpire n arbitre m.
umpteen adj un très grand nombre de, beaucoup de.
unable adj incapable.
unaccompanied adj non accompagné, seul.
unaccomplished adj inaccompli, inachevé.
unaccountable adj inexplicable.
unaccountably adv inexplicablement.
unaccustomed adj inaccoutumé, inhabituel.

unacknowledged adj non reconnu; (resté) sans réponse.
unacquainted adj qui ignore, qui n'a pas connaissance de.
unadorned adj sans ornement.
unadulterated adj pur; sans mélange.
unaffected adj sincère; non affecté.
unaided adj sans aide.
unaltered adj inchangé.
unambitious adj sans ambition.
unanimity n unanimité f.
unanimous adj, ~ly adv unanime(ment).
unanswerable adj incontestable.
unanswered adj sans réponse.
unapproachable adj inaccessible.
unarmed adj non armé, désarmé.
unassuming adj sans prétention, modeste.
unattached adj indépendant; libre.
unattainable adj inaccessible.
unattended adj sans surveillance.
unauthorized adj sans autorisation.
unavoidable adj inévitable.
unavoidably adv inévitablement.

unaware *adj* ignorant; inconscient.

unawares *adv* à l'improviste; par mégarde.

unbalanced *adj* déséquilibré; non soldé.

unbearable *adj* insupportable.

unbecoming *adj* malséant, déplacé.

unbelievable *adj* incroyable.

unbend *vi* se détendre; * *vt* redresser.

unbiased *adj* impartial.

unblemished *adj* sans tache, sans défaut.

unborn *adj* à naître, pas encore né.

unbreakable *adj* incassable.

unbroken *adj* non brisé; intact; ininterrompu; indompté .

unbutton *vt* déboutonner.

uncalled-for *adj* injustifié.

uncanny *adj* mystérieux.

unceasing *adj* incessant, continu.

unceremonious *adj* brusque.

uncertain *adj* incertain, douteux.

uncertainty *n* incertitude *f.*

unchangeable *adj* immuable.

unchanged *adj* inchangé.

unchanging *adj* invariable, immuable.

uncharitable *adj* peu charitable.

unchecked *adj* non maîtrisé.

unchristian *adj* peu chrétien.

uncivil *adj* impoli, grossier.

uncivilized *adj* barbare, non civilisé.

uncle *n* oncle *m.*

uncomfortable *adj* inconfortable; incommode; désagréable.

uncomfortably *adv* inconfortablement; mal; désagréablement.

uncommon *adj* rare, extraordinaire.

uncompromising *adj* intransigeant.

unconcerned *adj* indifférent.

unconditional *adj* inconditionnel, absolu.

unconfined *adj* illimité, sans bornes.

unconfirmed *adj* non confirmé.

unconnected *adj* sans rapport.

unconquerable *adj* invincible, insurmontable.

unconscious *adj* inconscient; **~ly** *adv* inconsciemment, sans s'en rendre compte.

unconstrained *adj* non contraint, libre.

uncontrollable *adj* irrésistible; qui ne peut être maîtrisé.

unconventional *adj* peu conventionnel.

unconvincing *adj* peu convaincant.

uncork *vt* déboucher.

uncorrected *adj* non corrigé.

uncouth *adj* grossier.

uncover *vt* découvrir.

uncultivated *adj* inculte.

uncut *adj* non taillé, intégral.

undamaged *adj* non endommagé, indemne.

undaunted *adj* intrépide.

undecided *adj* indécis.

undefiled *adj* pur, immaculé.

undeniable *adj* indéniable, incontestable; **~bly** *adv* incontestablement.

under *prep* sous; dessous; moins de; selon; * *adv* au-dessous, en-dessous.

under-age *adj* mineur.

undercharge *vt* ne pas faire payer assez.

underclothing n sous-vêtements mpl.

undercoat n première couche f.

undercover adj secret, clandestin.

undercurrent n courant sous-marin m.

undercut vt vendre moins cher que.

underdeveloped adj sous-développé, insuffisamment développé.

underdog n opprimé m, -e f.

underdone adj pas assez cuit.

underestimate vt sous-estimer.

undergo vt subir; supporter.

undergraduate n étudiant(e) en licence m(f).

underground n mouvement clandestin m.

undergrowth n broussailles fpl, sous-bois m.

underhand adv en cachette; * adj secret, clandestin.

underlie vi être à la base de.

underline vt souligner.

undermine vt saper.

underneath adv (en) dessous; * prep sous, au-dessous de.

underpaid adj sous-payé.

underprivileged adj défavorisé.

underrate vt sous-estimer.

undersecretary n sous-secrétaire mf.

undershirt n maillot de corps m.

undershorts npl caleçon m.

underside n dessous m.

understand vt comprendre.

understandable adj compréhensible.

understanding n compréhension f; intelligence f; entendement m; accord m; * adj compréhensif.

understatement n affirmation en dessous de la vérité f.

undertake vt entreprendre.

undertaking n entreprise f; engagement m.

undervalue vt sous-estimer.

underwater adj sous-marin; * adv sous l'eau.

underwear n sous-vêtements mpl, dessous mpl.

underworld n pègre f.

underwrite vt souscrire à; assurer contre.

underwriter n assureur m.

undeserved adj immérité; ~ly adv à tort, indûment.

undeserving adj peu méritant.

undesirable adj peu souhaitable.

undetermined adj indéterminé; indécis.

undigested adj non digéré.

undiminished adj non diminué.

undisciplined adj indiscipliné.

undisguised adj non déguisé.

undismayed adj non découragé.

undisputed adj incontesté.

undisturbed adj non dérangé, paisible.

undivided adj indivisé, entier.

undo vt défaire; détruire.

undoing n ruine f.

undoubted adj, ~ly adv indubitable(ment).

undress vi se déshabiller.

undue adj excessif; injuste.

undulating adj ondulant.

unduly adv trop, excessivement.

undying adj éternel.

unearth vt déterrer.

unearthly adj surnaturel.

uneasy adj inquiet; troublé, gêné.

uneducated adj sans instruction.

unemployed adj au chômage.

unemployment n chômage m.

unending adj interminable.

unenlightened adj peu éclairé.

unenviable adj peu enviable.

unequal adj, ~ly adv inégal(ement).

unequaled adj inégalé.

unerring adj, ~ly adv infaillible(ment).

uneven adj inégal; impair; ~ly adv inégalement.

unexpected adj inattendu; inopiné; ~ly adv de manière inattendue; inopinément.

unexplored adj inexploré.

unfailing adj infaillible, certain.

unfair adj injuste; inéquitable; ~ly adv injustement.

unfaithful adj infidèle.

unfaithfulness n infidélité f.

unfaltering adj ferme, assuré.

unfamiliar adj peu familier, peu connu.

unfashionable adj démodé; ~bly adv sans se préoccuper de la mode.

unfasten vt détacher, défaire.

unfathomable adj insondable, impénétrable.

unfavourable adj défavorable.

unfeeling adj insensible, impitoyable.

unfinished adj inachevé, incomplet.

unfit adj inapte; impropre.

unfold vt déplier; révéler; * vi s'ouvrir.

unforeseen adj imprévu.

unforgettable adj inoubliable.

unforgivable adj impardonnable.

unforgiving adj implacable.

unfortunate adj malheureux, malchanceux; ~ly adv malheureusement, par malheur.

unfounded adj sans fondement.

unfriendly adj inamical.

unfruitful adj stérile; infructueux.

unfurnished adj non meublé.

ungainly adj gauche.

ungentlemanly adj peu galant.

ungovernable adj ingouvernable, irrépressible.

ungrateful adj ingrat; peu reconnaissant; ~ly adv avec ingratitude.

ungrounded adj infondé.

unhappily adv malheureusemnt.

unhappiness n tristesse f.

unhappy adj malheureux.

unharmed adj indemne, sain et sauf.

unhealthy adj malsain; maladif.

unheard-of adj inédit, sans précédent.

unheeding adj insouciant; distrait.

unhook vt décrocher; dégrafer.

unhoped(-for) adj inespéré.

unhurt adj indemne.

unicorn n licorne f.

uniform adj uniforme; ~ly adv uniformément; * n uniforme m.

uniformity adj uniformité f.

unify vt unifier.

unimaginable adj inimaginable.

unimpaired adj non diminué, intact.

unimportant adj sans importance.

uninformed *adj* mal informé.

uninhabitable *adj* inhabitable.

uninhabited *adj* inhabité, désert.

uninjured *adj* indemne, sain et sauf.

unintelligible *adj* inintelligible.

unintelligibly *adj* inintelligible-ment.

unintentional *adj* involontaire.

uninterested *adj* indifférent.

uninteresting *adj* inintéressant.

uninterrupted *adj* ininterrompu, continu.

uninvited *adj* sans être invité.

union *n* union *f*; syndicat *m*.

unionist *n* syndicaliste *mf*.

unique *adj* unique, exceptionnel.

unison *n* unisson *m*.

unit *n* unité *f*.

unitarian *n* unitarien *m*, -ienne *f*.

unite *vt* unir; * *vi* s'unir.

unitedly *adv* conjointement, ensemble.

United States (of America) *npl* Etats-Unis *mpl*.

unity *n* unité, harmonie *f*, accord *m*.

universal *adj* , ~ly *adv* univer-sel(lement).

universe *n* univers *m*.

university *n* université *f*.

unjust *adj*, ~ly *adv* injuste(ment).

unkempt *adj* négligé; débraillé.

unkind *adj* peu aimable; méchant.

unknowingly *adv* inconsciem-ment.

unknown *adj* inconnu.

unlawful *adj* illégal, illicite; ~ly *adv* illégalement.

unlawfulness *n* illégalité *f*.

unleash *vt* lâcher, déchaîner.

unless *conj* à moins que/de, sauf.

unlicensed *adj* illicite.

unlike, unlikely *adj* différent, dis-semblable; improbable; invrai-semblable; ~ly *adv* impro-bablement.

unlikelihood *n* improbabilité *f*.

unlimited *adj* illimité.

unlisted *adj* ne figurant pas sur une liste/sur l'annuaire.

unload *vt* décharger.

unlock *vt* ouvrir, déverrouiller.

unluckily *adv* malheureusement.

unlucky *adj* malchanceux.

unmanageable *adj* difficile, peu maniable, impossible.

unmannered *adj* mal élevé, im-poli.

unmannerly *adj* mal élevé, impoli.

unmarried *adj* célibataire, qui n'est pas marié.

unmask *vt* démasquer.

unmentionable *adj* qu'il ne faut pas mentionner.

unmerited *adj* immérité.

unmindful *adj* oublieux, indiffé-rent.

unmistakable *adj* indubitable; ~ly *adv* sans aucun doute.

unmitigated *adj* absolu.

unmoved *adj* insensible, impassi-ble.

unnatural *adj* non naturel; pervers; affecté.

unnecessary *adj* inutile, superflu.

unneighbourly *adj* peu aimable avec ses voisins, peu sociable.

unnoticed *adj* inaperçu.

unnumbered *adj* innombrable.

unobserved *adj* inaperçu.

unobtainable *adj* impossible à obtenir; introuvable.

unobtrusive *adj* discret.

unoccupied *adj* inoccupé.

unoffending *adj* inoffensif, innocent.

unofficial *adj* non officiel.

unorthodox *adj* hétérodoxe; peu orthodoxe.

unpack *vt* défaire; déballer.

unpaid *adj* non payé.

unpalatable *adj* désagréable au goût.

unparalleled *adj* incomparable; sans pareil.

unpleasant *adj*, **~ly** *adv* désagréable(ment).

unpleasantness *n* caractère désagréable *m*.

unplug *vt* débrancher.

unpolished *adj* non ciré; fruste, rude.

unpopular *adj* impopulaire.

unpractised *adj* inexpérimenté, inexercé.

unprecedented *adj* sans précédent.

unpredictable *adj* imprévisible.

unprejudiced *adj* impartial.

unprepared *adj* qui n'est pas préparé.

unprofitable *adj* inutile; peu rentable.

unprotected *adj* sans protection; exposé.

unpublished *adj* inédit.

unpunished *adj* impuni.

unqualified *adj* non qualifié; sans réserve.

unquestionable *adj* incontestable,

indiscutable; **~ly** *adv* indiscutablement, sans conteste.

unquestioned *adj* incontesté, indiscuté.

unravel *vt* débrouiller.

unread *adj* qui n'a pas été lu; inculte.

unreal *adj* irréel.

unrealistic *adj* irréaliste.

unreasonable *adv* déraisonnable.

unreasonably *adj* déraisonnablement.

unregarded *adj* négligé; dont on ne fait pas de cas.

unrelated *adj* sans rapport; sans lien de parenté.

unrelenting *adj* implacable.

unreliable *adj* peu fiable.

unremitting *adj* inlassable, constant.

unrepentant *adj* impénitent.

unreserved *adj* sans réserve; franc; **~ly** *adv* sans réserve.

unrest *n* agitation *f*; troubles *mpl*.

unrestrained *adj* non contenu; non réprimé.

unripe *adj* vert, pas mûr.

unrivalled *adj* sans égal, sans pareil.

unroll *vt* dérouler.

unruliness *n* indiscipline *f*; turbulence *f*.

unruly *adj* indiscipliné.

unsafe *adj* dangereux, peu sûr.

unsatisfactory *adj* peu satisfaisant.

unsavoury *adj* désagréable, insipide.

unscathed *adj* indemne.

unscrew *vt* dévisser.

unscrupulous *adj* sans scrupules.

unseasonable *adj* hors de saison, inopportun.

unseemly *adj* inconvenant.

unseen *adj* invisible; inaperçu.

unselfish *adj* généreux.

unsettle *vt* perturber.

unsettled *adj* perturbé; instable; variable.

unshaken *adj* inébranlable, ferme.

unshaven *adj* non rasé.

unsightly *adj* disgracieux, laid.

unskilled *adj* inexpérimenté.

unskilful *adj* maladroit, malhabile.

unsociable *adj* insociable, sauvage.

unspeakable *adj* ineffable, indicible.

unstable *adj* instable.

unsteadily *adv* d'un pas chancelant; d'une manière mal assurée.

unsteady *adj* instable.

unstudied *adj* naturel; spontané.

unsuccessful *adj* infructueux, vain; **~ly** *adv* sans succès.

unsuitable *adj* peu approprié; inopportun.

unsure *adj* peu sûr.

unsympathetic *adj* peu compatissant.

untamed *adj* sauvage.

untapped *adj* non exploité.

untenable *adj* insoutenable.

unthinkable *adj* inconcevable.

unthinking *adj* irréfléchi, étourdi.

untidiness *n* désordre *m*.

untidy *adj* en désordre; peu soigné.

untie *vt* dénouer, défaire.

until *prep* jusqu'à; * *conj* jusqu'à ce que.

untimely *adj* intempestif.

untiring *adj* infatigable.

untold *adj* jamais révélé; indicible; incalculable.

untouched *adj* intact.

untoward *adj* fâcheux; indiscipliné.

untried *adj* qui n'a pas été essayé *ou* mis à l'épreuve.

untroubled *adj* tranquille, paisible.

untrue *adj* faux.

untrustworthy *adj* indigne de confiance.

untruth *n* mensonge *m*, fausseté *f*.

unused *adj* neuf, inutilisé.

unusual *adj* habituel, exceptionnel; **~ly** *adv* exceptionnellement, rarement.

unveil *vt* dévoiler.

unwavering *adj* inébranlable.

unwelcome *adj* importun.

unwell *adj* indisposé, souffrant.

unwieldy *adj* peu maniable.

unwilling *adj* peu disposé; **~ly** *adv* de mauvaise grâce.

unwillingness *n* mauvaise grâce, mauvaise volonté *f*.

unwind *vt* dérouler; * *vi* se détendre.

unwise *adj* imprudent.

unwitting *adj* involontaire.

unworkable *adj* impraticable.

unworthy *adj* indigne.

unwrap *vt* défaire.

unwritten *adj* non écrit.

up *adv* en haut, en l'air; levé; * *prep* au haut de; vers.

upbringing *n* éducation *f*.

update *vt* mettre à jour.

upheaval *n* bouleversement *m*.

uphill *adj* difficile, pénible; * *adv* en montant.

uphold *vt* soutenir.

upholstery n tapisserie f.

upkeep n entretien m.

uplift vt élever.

upon prep sur.

upper adj supérieur; (plus) élevé.

upper-class adj aristocratique.

upper-hand n (fig) dessus m.

uppermost adj le plus haut, le plus élevé; **to be ~** prédominer.

upright adj droit, vertical; droit, honnête.

uprising n soulèvement m.

uproar n tumulte m, vacarme m.

uproot vt déraciner.

upset vt renverser; déranger, bouleverser; * n désordre m; bouleversement m; * adj vexé; bouleversé.

upshot n résultat m; aboutissement m; conclusion f.

upside-down adv sens dessus dessous.

upstairs adv en haut (d'un escalier).

upstart n parvenu m, -e f.

uptight adj très tendu.

up-to-date adj à jour.

upturn n amélioration f.

upward adj ascendant; **~s** adv vers le haut; en montant.

urban adj urbain.

urbane adj courtois.

urchin n oursin m.

urge vt pousser; * n impulsion f; désir ardent m.

urgency n urgence f.

urgent adj urgent.

urinal n urinoir m.

urinate vi uriner.

urine n urine f.

urn n urne f.

us pn nous.

usage n traitement m; usage m.

use n usage m; utilisation f, emploi m; * vt se servir de, utiliser.

used adj usagé.

useful adj, **~ly** adv utile(ment).

usefulness n utilité f.

useless adj, **~ly** adv inutile(ment).

uselessness n inutilité f.

user-friendly adj facile à utiliser.

usher n huissier m; placeur m.

usherette n ouvreuse f.

usual adj habituel, courant; **~ly** adv habituellement.

usurer n usurier m, -ière f.

usurp vt usurper.

usury n usure f.

utensil n ustensile m.

uterus n utérus m.

utility n utilité f.

utilize vt utiliser.

utmost adj extrême, le plus grand; dernier.

utter adj complet; absolu; total; * vt prononcer; proférer; émettre.

utterance n expression f.

utterly adv complètement, tout à fait.

V

vacancy n chambre libre f.

vacant adj vacant; inoccupé; libre.

vacant lot n terrain vague m.

vacate vt quitter; démissionner.

vacation n vacances fpl.

vacationer n vacancier m, -ière f.

vaccinate vt vacciner.

vaccination n vaccination f.

vaccine n vaccin m.

vacuous adj vide.

vacuum n vide m.

vacuum bottle n thermos m.

vagina n vagin m.

vagrant n vagabond m, -e f.

vague adj, **~ly** adv vague(ment).

vain adj vain, inutile; vaniteux.

valet n valet de chambre m.

valiant adj courageux, brave.

valid adj valide, valable.

valley n vallée f.

valour n courage m, bravoure f.

valuable adj précieux, de valeur; **~s** npl objets de valeur mpl.

valuation n évaluation, estimation f.

value n valeur f; * vt évaluer; tenir à, apprécier.

valued adj précieux, estimé.

valve n soupape f.

vampire n vampire m.

van n camionnette f.

vandal n vandale mf.

vandalism n vandalisme m.

vandalize vt saccager.

vanguard n avant-garde f.

vanilla n vanille f.

vanish vi disparaître, se dissiper.

vanity n vanité f.

vanity case n vanity-case m.

vanquish vt vaincre.

vantage point n position avantageuse f.

vapour n vapeur f.

variable adj variable; changeant.

variance n désaccord, différend m.

variation n variation f.

varicose vein n varice f.

varied adj varié.

variety n variété f.

variety show n spectacle de variétés m.

various adj divers, différent.

varnish n vernis m; * vt vernir.

vary vt, vi varier; vi changer.

vase n vase m.

vast adj vaste; immense.

vat n cuve f.

vault n voûte f; cave f, caveau m; saut m; * vi sauter.

veal n veau m.

veer vi (mar) virer.

vegetable adj végétal; * n végétal m; **~s** pl légumes mpl.

vegetable garden n (jardin) potager m.

vegetarian n végétarien m, -ienne f.

vegetate vi végéter.

vegetation n végétation f.

vehemence n véhémence, fougue f.

vehement adj véhément, violent; **~ly** adv avec véhémence.

vehicle n véhicule m.

veil n voile m; * vt voiler, dissimuler.

vein n veine f; nervure f; disposition f.

velocity n vitesse f.

velvet n velours m.

vending machine n distributeur automatic m.

vendor n vendeur m.

veneer n placage m; vernis m.

venerable adj vénérable.

venerate vt vénérer.

veneration n vénération f.

venereal adj vénérien.

vengeance n vengeance f.

venial adj véniel.

venison n venaison f.

venom n venin m.

venomous adj vénéneux; **~ly** adv avec animosité.

vent n orifice m; conduit m; * vt décharger.

ventilate vt aérer.

ventilation n ventilation, aération f.

ventilator n ventilateur m.

ventriloquist n ventriloque mf.

venture n entreprise f; vi s'aventurer; * vt risquer, hasarder.

venue n lieu de réunion m.

veranda(h) n véranda f.

verb n (gr) verbe m.

verbal adj verbal, oral; **~ly** adv verbalement.

verbatim adv textuellement, mot pour mot.

verbose adj verbeux.

verdant adj verdoyant.

verdict n (law) verdict m; jugement m.

verification n vérification f.

verify vt vérifier.

veritable adj véritable.

vermin n vermine f.

vermouth n vermout(h) m.

versatile adj doué de talents multiples; versatile.

verse n vers m; verset m.

versed adj versé.

version n version f.

versus prep contre.

vertebra n vertèbre f.

vertebral, vertebrate adj vertébral.

vertex n sommet m.

vertical adj, **~ly** adv vertical(ement).

vertigo n vertige m.

verve n verve f.

very adj vrai, véritable; exactement, même; * adv très, fort, bien.

vessel n récipient m; vase m; navire m.

vest n gilet m.

vestibule n vestibule m.

vestige n vestige m.

vestment n vêtement de cérémonie m; chasuble f.

vestry n sacristie f.

veteran adj, n vétéran m.

veterinarian n vétérinaire mf.

veterinary adj vétérinaire.

veto n véto m; * vt opposer son véto à.

vex vt contrarier.

vexed adj contrarié.

via prep via, par.

viaduct n viaduc m.

vial n fiole, ampoule f.

vibrate vi vibrer.

vibration n vibration f.

vicarious adj par personne interposée.

vice n vice m; défaut m; étau m.

vice-chairman n vice-président m.

vice versa adv vice versa.

vicinity n voisinage m, proximité f.

vicious adj méchant; **~ly** adv méchamment.

victim n victime f.

victimize vt prendre pour victime.

victor n vainqueur m.

victorious adj victorieux.

victory n victoire f.

video n vidéo f; vidéocassette f; magnétoscope m.

video tape n bande vidéo f.

viewer n téléspectateur m, -trice f.

vie vi rivaliser.

view n vue f; perspective f; opinion f; panorama m; * vt voir; examiner.

viewfinder n viseur m.

viewpoint n point de vue m.

vigil n veille f; vigile f.

vigilance n vigilance f.

vigilant adj vigilant, attentif.

vigor n vigueur f; énergie f.

vigorous adj vigoureux; ~ly adv vigoureusement.

vile adj vil, infâme; exécrable.

vilify vt diffamer.

villa n pavillon m; maison de campagne f.

village n village m.

villager n villageois m, -e f.

villain n scélérat m.

vindicate vt venger, défendre.

vindication n défense f; justification f.

vindictive adj vindicatif.

vine n vigne f.

vinegar n vinaigre m.

vineyard n vignoble m.

vintage n vendange(s) f(pl).

vinyl n vinyle m.

viola n (mus) viole f.

violate vt violer.

violation n violation f.

violence n violence f.

violent adj violent; ~ly adv violemment.

violet n (bot) violette f.

violin n (mus) violon m.

violinist n violiniste mf.

violoncello n (mus) violoncelle m.

viper n vipère f.

virgin n, adj vierge f.

virginity n virginité f.

Virgo n Vierge f (signe du zodiaque).

virile adj viril.

virility n virilité f.

virtual adj, ~ly adv de fait, pratiquement.

virtue n vertu f.

virtuous adj virtueux.

virulent adj virulent.

virus n virus m.

visa n visa m.

vis-a-vis prep vis-à-vis.

viscous adj visqueux, gluant.

visibility n visibilité f.

visible adj visible.

visibly adv visiblement.

vision n vision f; vue f.

visit vt visiter; * n visite f.

visitation n visite f.

visiting hours npl heures de visite fpl.

visitor n visiteur m, -euse f; touriste mf.

visor n visière f.

vista n vue, perspective f.

visual adj visuel.

visual aid n support visuel m.

visualize vt s'imaginer.

vital adj vital; essentiel; indispensable; ~ly adv vitalement; ~s npl organes vitaux mpl.

vitality n vitalité f.

vital statistics npl statistiques démographiques fpl.

vitamin n vitamine f.

vitiate vt vicier.

vivacious adj vif.

vivid adj vif; vivant; frappant; **~ly** adv de façon éclatante; de façon frappante.

vivisection n vivisection f.

vocabulary n vocabulaire m.

vocal adj oral.

vocation n vocation f; profession f, métier m; **~al** adj professionnel.

vocative n vocatif m.

vociferous adj bruyant.

vodka n vodka f.

vogue n vogue f; mode f.

voice n voix f; * vt exprimer.

void adj vide; * n vide m.

volatile adj volatile; versatile.

volcanic adj volcanique.

volcano n volcan m.

volition n volonté f.

volley n volée f; salve f; grêle f.

volleyball n volley-ball m.

volt n volt m.

voltage n voltage m.

voluble adj volubile, loquace.

volume n volume m.

voluntarily adv volontairement.

voluntary adj volontaire.

volunteer n volontaire mf; * vi se porter volontaire .

voluptuous adj voluptueux.

vomit vt, vi vomir; * n vomissement m.

voracious adj **~ly** adv vorace(ment).

vortex n tourbillon m.

vote n vote, suffrage m; voix f; * vt voter.

voter n électeur m, -trice f.

voting n vote m.

voucher n bon m.

vow n vœu m; * vt jurer.

vowel n voyelle f.

voyage n voyage par mer m; traversée f.

vulgar adj vulgaire; grossier.

vulgarity n grossièreté f; vulgarité f.

vulnerable adj vulnérable.

vulture n vautour m.

W

wad n tampon m; bouchon m.

waddle vi se dandiner.

wade vi patauger.

wading pool n petit bassin (pour enfants) m.

wafer n gaufrette f; plaque f.

waffle n gaufre f.

waft vt porter, apporter; * vi flotter.

wag vi, vt remuer.

wage n salaire m.

wage earner n salarié m, -e f.

wager n pari m; * vt parier.

wages npl salaire m.

waggle vt remuer.

waggon n chariot m; (rail) wagon m.

wail n gémissement m, plainte f; * vi gémir.

waist n taille f.

waistline n taille f.

wait vi attendre; * n attente f; arrêt m.

waiter n serveur m.

waiting list n liste d'attente f.

waiting room n salle d'attente f.

waive vt renoncer à.

wake vi se réveiller; * vt réveiller; * n veillée f; (mar) sillage m.

waken vt réveiller; * vi se réveiller.

walk vi marcher, aller à pied; * vt parcourir; * n promenade f; marche f.

walker n marcheur m, -euse f.

walkie-talkie n talkie-walkie m.

walking n marche à pied f.

walking stick n canne f.

walkout n grève f.

walkover n (sl) victoire facile f, gâteau m.

walkway n passage pour piétons m.

wall n mur m; muraille f; paroi f.

walled adj muré.

wallet n portefeuille m.

wallflower n (bot) giroflée f.

wallow vi se vautrer.

wallpaper n papier peint m.

walnut n noix f; noyer m.

walrus n morse m.

waltz n valse f.

wan adj pâle.

wand n baguette (magique) f.

wander vi errer; aller sans but.

wane vi décroître.

want vt vouloir; demander; * vi manquer; * n besoin m; manque m.

wanting adj manquant, qui manque, qui fait défaut.

wanton adj lascif; capricieux.

war n guerre f.

ward n salle f; pupille mf.

wardrobe n garde-robe f, penderie f.

warehouse n entrepôt m.

warfare n guerre f.

warhead n ogive f.

warily adv avec circonspection.

wariness n circonspection, prudence f.

warm adj chaud; chaleureux; * vt réchauffer; **to ~ up** vi se réchauffer; s'échauffer; s'animer; vt réchauffer.

warm-hearted adj affectueux.

warmly adv chaudement, chaleureusement.

warmth n chaleur f.

warn vt prévenir; avertir.

warning n avertissement m.

warning light n voyant lumineux m.

warp vi se voiler; * vt voiler; fausser.

warrant n garantie f; mandat m.

warranty n garantie f.

warren n terrier m.

warrior n guerrier m, -ière f.

warship n navire de guerre m.

wart n verrue f.

wary adj prudent, circonspect.

wash vt laver; * vi se laver; * n lavage m; lessive f.

washable adj lavable.

washbowl n lavabo m.

washcloth n gant de toilette m.

washer n rondelle f.

washing n linge à laver m; lessive f.

washing machine n machine à laver f.

washing-up n vaisselle f.

wash-out n (sl) fiasco m.

washroom n toilettes fpl.

wasp n abeille f.

wastage n spillage m; perte f.

waste vt gaspiller; dévaster, saccager; perdre; * vi se perdre; * n gaspillage m; détérioration f; terre inculte f; déchets mpl.

wasteful adj gaspilleur; prodigue; **~ly** adv avec prodigalité.

waste paper n vieux papiers mpl.

waste pipe n tuyau d'échappement m.

watch n montre f; surveillance f; garde f; * vt regarder; observer; surveiller; faire attention à; * vi regarder; monter la garde.

watchdog n chien de garde m.

watchful adj vigilant; **~ly** adv avec vigilance.

watchmaker n horloger m.

watchman n veilleur de nuit m; gardien m.

watchtower n tour de guet f.

watchword n mot de passe m; mot d'ordre m.

water n eau f; * vt arroser, mouiller; * vi pleurer, larmoyer.

water closet n W.C. mpl.

watercolour n aquarelle f.

waterfall n cascade f.

water heater n chauffe-eau m invar.

watering-can n arrosoir m.

water level n niveau de l'eau m.

waterlily n nénuphar m.

water line n ligne de flottaison f.

waterlogged adj imprégné d'eau.

water main n conduite principale d'eau f.

watermark n filigrane m.

water melon n pastèque f.

watershed n moment critique m.

watertight adj étanche.

waterworks npl usine hydraulique f.

watery adj aqueux; détrempé; délavé.

watt n watt m.

wave n vague f; lame f; onde f; * vi faire signe de la main; onduler; * vt agiter.

wavelength n longueur d'ondes f.

waver vi vaciller, osciller.

wavering adj hésitant.

wavy adj ondulé.

wax n cire f; * vt cirer; * vi croître.

wax paper n papier paraffiné m.

waxworks n musée de cire m.

way n chemin m; voie f; route f; manière f; direction f; **to give ~** céder.

waylay vt attirer dans une embuscade.

wayward adj capricieux.

we pn nous.

weak adj , **~ly** adv faible(ment).

weaken vt affaiblir.

weakling n personne faible f.

weakness n faiblesse f; point faible m.

wealth n richesse f; abondance f.

wealthy adj riche.

wean vt sevrer.

weapon n arme f.

wear vt porter; user; * vi s'user; **to ~ away** user; vi s'user; **to ~ down** user; **to ~ off** vi s'effacer; **to ~ out** vi s'user; s'épuiser; vt user; * n usage m; usure f.

weariness n lassitude f; fatigue f; ennui m.

wearisome adj fatigant.

weary adj las, fatigué; ennuyeux.

weasel n belette f.

weather n temps m; * vt surmonter.

weather-beaten adj ayant souffert des intempéries.

weather cock n girouette f.

weather forecast n prévisions météorologiques fpl.

weave vt tisser; entrelacer.

weaving n tissage m.

web n tissu m; toile f; palmure f.

wed vt épouser; * vi se marier.

wedding n mariage m; noces fpl.

wedding day n jour du mariage m.

wedding dress n robe de mariée f.

wedding present n cadeau de mariage m.

wedding ring n alliance f.

wedge n cale f; * vt caler; enfoncer.

wedlock n mariage m.

Wednesday n mercredi m.

wee adj petit.

weed n mauvaise herbe f; * vt désherber.

weedkiller n désherbant m.

weedy adj envahi par les mauvaises herbes.

week n semaine f; **tomorrow ~** demain en huit; **yesterday ~** il y a eu une semaine hier.

weekday n jour de semaine, jour ouvrable m.

weekend n week-end m, fin de semaine f.

weekly adj de la semaine, hebdomadaire; * adv chaque semaine, par semaine.

weep vt, vi pleurer.

weeping willow n saule pleureur m.

weigh vt, vi peser.

weight n poids m.

weightily adv pesament.

weightlifter n haltérophile m.

weighty adj lourd; important.

welcome adj opportun; ~! bienvenue !; * n accueil m; * vt accueillir.

weld vt souder; * n soudure f.

welfare n bien-être m; assistance sociale f.

welfare state n Etat-providence m.

well n source f; fontaine f; puits m; * adj bien, bon; * adv bien; **as ~ as** aussi bien que, en plus de, comme.

well-behaved adj bien élevé.

well-being n bien-être m.

well-bred adj bien élevé.

well-built adj bien bâti, solide.

well-deserved adj bien mérité.

well-dressed adj bien habillé.

well-known adj connu, célèbre.

well-mannered adj poli, bien élevé.

well-meaning adj bien intentionné.

well-off adj aisé, dans l'aisance.

well-to-do adj aisé, riche.

well-wisher n admirateur m, -trice f.

wench n jeune fille, jeune femme f.

west n ouest, Occident m; * adj ouest, de/à l'ouest; * adv vers/à l'ouest.

westerly, western adj (d')ouest.

westward adv vers l'ouest.

wet adj mouillé, humide; * n humidité f; * vt mouiller.

wet-nurse n nourrice f.

wet suit n combinaison de plongée f.

whack vt donner un grand coup à; * n grand coup m.

whale n baleine f.

wharf n quai m.

what pn ce que qui, (qu'est-ce) que, quoi; que, qui; ce qui, ce que; quel(le), que; * adj quel(s), quelle(s); * excl quoi! comment!

whatever pn quoi que; tout; n'importe quoi.

wheat n blé m.

wheedle vt cajoler, câliner.

wheel n roue f; volant m; gouvernail m; * vt tourner; pousser, rouler; * vi tourner en rond, tournoyer.

wheelbarrow n brouette f.

wheelchair n fauteuil roulant m.

wheel clamp n sabot m.

wheeze vi respirer bruyamment.

when adv, conj quand.

whenever adv quand; chaque fois que.

where adv où; * conj où; any~ n'importe où; every~ partout.

whereabout(s) adv où.

whereas conj tandis que; attendu que.

whereby pn par lequel (laquelle), au moyen duquel (de laquelle).

wherever adv où que.

whereupon conj sur quoi; après quoi.

wherewithal npl ressources fpl.

whet vt aiguiser.

whether conj si.

which pn lequel, laquelle; celui/celle(s)/ceux que, celui/celle(s)/ceux qui; ce qui, ce que; quoi, ce dont * adj quel(s), quelle(s).

whiff n bouffée, odeur f.

while n moment m; a ~ quelque temps; * conj pendant que; alors que; quoique.

whim n caprice m.

whimper vi gémir, pleurnicher.

whimsical adj capricieux, fantasque.

whine vi gémir, se plaindre; * n gémissement m, plainte f.

whinny vi hennir.

whip n fouet m; cravache f; * vt fouetter; battre.

whipped cream n crème fouettée f.

whirl n tourbillon m; tournoyer; aller à toute allure; * vt faire tourbillonner, faire tournoyer.

whirlpool n tourbillon m.

whirlwind n tornade f.

whisky n whisky m.

whisper vi chuchoter; murmurer.

whispering n chuchotement m; murmure m.

whistle vi siffler; * n sifflement m.

white adj blanc; pâle; * n blanc m; blanc d'œuf m.

white elephant n objet superflu m.

white-hot adj chauffé à blanc.

white lie n petit mensonge, mensonge innocent m.

whiten vt, vi blanchir.

whiteness n blancheur f; pâleur f.

whitewash n blanc de chaux m; * vt blanchir à la chaux; disculper.

whiting n merlan m.

whitish adj blanchâtre.

who pn qui.

whoever pn quiconque, qui que ce soit, quel(le) que soit.

whole adj tout, entier; intact, complet; sain; * n tout m; ensemble m.

wholehearted adj sincère.

wholemeal adj complet.

wholesale n vente en gros f.

wholesome adj sain, salubre.

wholewheat adj complet.

wholly adv complètement.

whom pn qui; que.

whooping cough n coqueluche f.

whore n putain f.

why n pourquoi m; * conj pourquoi; * excl eh bien!; tiens!

wick n mèche f.

wicked adj méchant, mauvais; **~ly** adv méchamment.

wickedness n méchanceté, perversité f.

wicker n osier m; * adj en osier.

wide adj large, ample; grand; **~ly** adv partout; **far** and **~** de tous côtés.

wide-awake adj bien réveillé.

widen vt élargir, agrandir.

widespread adj très répandu.

widow n veuve f.

widower n veuf m.

width n largeur f.

wield vt manier, brandir.

wife n femme f; épouse f.

wig n perruque f.

wiggle vt agiter; * vi s'agiter.

wild adj sauvage, féroce; désert; fou; furieux.

wilderness n étendue déserte f.

wild life n faune f.

wildly adv violemment; furieusement; follement.

wilful adj délibéré, entêté.

wilfulness n obstination f.

wiliness n ruse, astuce f.

will n volonté f; testament m; * vt vouloir.

willing adj prêt, disposé; **~ly** adv volontiers, de bon cœur.

willingness n bonne volonté f, empressement m.

willow n saule m.

willpower n volonté f.

wilt vi se fâner.

wily adj astucieux.

win vt gagner, conquérir; remporter.

wince vi tressaillir.

winch n treuil m.

wind n vent m; souffle m; gaz mpl.

wind vt enrouler; envelopper; donner un tour de; * vi serpenter.

windfall n fruit abattu par le vent m.

winding adj tortueux.

windmill n moulin à vent m.

window n fenêtre f.

window box n jardinière f.

window cleaner n laveur(-euse) de carreaux m(f).

window ledge n rebord de fenêtre m.

window pane n carreau m.

window sill n rebord de fenêtre m.

windpipe n trachée f.

windscreen n pare-brise m invar.

windscreen washer n lave-glace m invar.

windscreen wiper n essuie-glace m invar.

windy adj venteux.

wine n vin m.

wine cellar n cave (à vin) f.

wine glass n verre à vin m.

wine list n carte des vins f.

wine merchant n négociant en vins m.

wine-tasting n dégustation de vins f.

wing n aile f.

winged adj ailé.

winger n ailier m.

wink vi faire un clin d'œil; * n clin d'œil m; clignement m.

winner n gagnant m, -e f; vainqueur m.

winning post n poteau d'arrivée m.

winter n hiver m; * vi hiverner.

winter sports npl sports d'hiver mpl.

wintry adj d'hiver, hivernal.

wipe vt essuyer; effacer.

wire n fil m; télégramme m; * vt installer des fils électriques à; télégraphier.

wiring n installation électrique f.

wiry adj effilé et nerveux.

wisdom n sagesse, prudence f.

wisdom teeth npl dents de sagesse fpl.

wise adj sage, avisé, judicieux, prudent.

wisecrack n bon mot m, plaisanterie f.

wish vt souhaiter, désirer; * n souhait, désir m.

wishful adj désireux.

wisp n brin m; mince volute f.

wistful adj nostalgique, rêveur.

wit n esprit m, intelligence f.

witch n sorcière f.

witchcraft n sorcellerie f.

with prep avec; à; de; contre.

withdraw vt retirer; rappeler; annuler; * vi se retirer.

withdrawal n retrait m.

withdrawn adj réservé.

wither vi se flétrir, se faner.

withhold vt détenir, retenir, empêcher.

within prep à l'intérieur de; * adv dedans; à l'intérieur.

without prep sans.

withstand vt résister à.

witless adj sot, stupide.

witness n témoin m; témoignage m; * vt être témoin de; attester.

witness stand n barre des témoins f.

witticism n mot d'esprit m.

wittily adv spirituellement.

wittingly adv sciemment, à dessein.

witty adj spirituel, plein d'esprit.

wizard n sorcier, magicien m.

wobble vi trembler.

woe n malheur m; affliction f.

woeful adj triste, malheureux; ~ly adv tristement.

wolf n loup m; she ~ louve f.

woman n femme f.

womanish adj de femme.

womanly adj féminin, de femme.

womb n utérus m.

women's lib n mouvement de libération de la femme m.

wonder n merveille f; miracle m; émerveillement m; * vi s'émerveiller.

wonderful adj merveilleux; ~ly adv merveilleusement.

wondrous adj merveilleux.

won't abrev de will not.

wont n coutume f.

woo vt faire la cour à.

wood n bois m.

wood alcohol n alcool méthylique m.

wood carving n sculpture sur bois f.

woodcut n gravure sur bois f.

woodcutter n graveur sur bois m; bûcheron m.

wooded adj boisé.

wooden adj de bois, en bois.

woodland n région boisée f.

woodlouse n cloporte m.

woodman n forestier m; gardeforestier m.

woodpecker n pic m.

woodwind n bois mpl.

woodwork n menuiserie f.

woodworm n ver du bois m.

wool n laine f.

woollen adj de laine.

woollens npl lainages mpl.

woolly adj laineux, de laine.

word n mot m; parole f; * vt exprimer; rédiger.

wordiness n verbosité f.

wording n rédaction f.

word processing n traitement de texte m.

word processor n machine à traitement de texte f.

wordy adj verbeux.

work vi travailler; opérer; fonctionner; fermenter; * vt (faire) travailler, faire fonctionner; façonner; * to ~ out vi marcher; * vt résoudre; * n travail m; œuvre f; ouvrage m; emploi m.

workable adj exploitable.

workaholic n drogué du travail m.

worker n travailleur m, -euse f; ouvrier m, -ère f.

workforce n main-d'œuvre f.

working-class adj ouvrier.

workman n ouvrier, artisan m.

workmanship n exécution f; qualité du travail f.

workmate n camarade de travail mf.

workshop n atelier m.

world n monde m; * adj du monde; mondial.

worldliness n mondanité f; attachement aux choses matérielles m.

worldly adj mondain; terrestre.

worldwide adj mondial.

worm n ver m; filet m.

worn-out adj épuisé; usé.

worried adj inquiet.

worry vt inquiéter; n souci m.

worrying adj inquiétant.

worse adj, adv pire; * n le pire.

worship n culte m; adoration f; your ~ Monsieur le Maire, Monsieur le Juge; * vt adorer, vénérer.

worst adj le pire; * adv le plus mal; * n le pire m.

worth n valeur f, prix m; mérite m.

worthily adv dignement, à juste titre.

worthless adj sans valeur; inutile.

worthwhile adj qui vaut la peine; louable.

worthy adj digne; louable.

would-be adj soi-disant.

wound n blessure f; * vt blesser.

wrangle vi se disputer; * n dispute f.

wrap vt envelopper.

wrath n colère f.

wreath n couronne, guirlande f.

wreck n naufrage m; ruines fpl; destruction f; épave f; * vt causer le naufrage de; démolir.

wreckage n naufrage m; épave f; débris mpl.

wren n roitelet m.

wrench vt tordre; forcer; tourner violemment; * n clé f; torsion violente f.

wrest vt arracher.

wrestle vi lutter.

wrestling n lutte f.

wretched adj malheureux, misérable.

wriggle vi remuer, se tortiller.

wring vt tordre; essorer; arracher.

wrinkle n ride f; * vt rider; * vi se rider.

wrist n poignet m.

wristband n manchette de chemise f.

wristwatch n montre-bracelet f.

writ n écriture f; assignation f; acte judiciaire m.

write vt écrire; composer; **to ~ down** consigner par écrit; **to ~ off** annuler; réduire; **to ~ up** rédiger.

write-off n perte f.

writer n écrivain m; auteur m.

writhe vi se tordre.

writing n écriture f; œuvres fpl; écrit m.

writing desk n bureau m.

writing paper n papier à lettres m.

wrong n mal m; injustice f; tort m; injure f; * adj mauvais; mal; injuste; inopportun; faux, erroné; * adv mal, inexactement; * vt faire du tort à, léser.

wrongful adj injuste.

wrongly adv injustement.

wry adj ironique.

XYZ

xenon n xénon m.

xenophobe n xénophobe mf.

xenophobia n xénophobie f.

xenophobic adj xénophobique.

Xmas abbr Noël m.

X-ray n rayon X m.

xylophone n xylophone m.

yacht n yacht m.

yachting n navigation de plaisance f.

Yankee n yankee m.

yard n yard (0,914 m) m; cour f.

yardstick n critère d'évaluation m.

yarn n longue histoire f; fil m.

yawn vi bâiller; * n bâillement m.

yawning adj béant.

yeah adv oui, ouais (fam).

year n année f.

yearbook n annuaire m.

yearling n animal âgé d'un an m.

yearly adj, adv annuel(lement).

yearn vi languir.

yearning n désir ardent m.

yeast n levure f.

yell vi hurler; * n hurlement m.

yellow adj, n jaune m.

yellowish adj jaunâtre.

yelp vi japper, glapir; * n jappement m.

yes adv, n oui m.

yesterday adv, n hier (m).

yet conj pourtant; cependant; * adv encore.

yew n if m.

yield vt donner, produire; rapporter; * vi se rendre; céder; * n production f; récolte f; rendement m.

yoga n yoga m.

yog(h)urt n yaourt m.

yoke n joug m.

yolk n jaune d'œuf m.

yonder adv là-bas.

you pn vous; tu; te; toi.

young adj jeune; **~er** adj plus jeune.

youngster n jeune m.

your(s) pn ton, ta, tes; votre, vos; le tien, la tienne, les tiens, les tiennes; le/la vôtre, les vôtres;

sincerely ~s je vous prie d'agréer, Monsieur/Madame, l'expression de mes sentiments les meilleurs.

yourself *pn* toi-même; vous-même(s).

youth *n* jeunesse, adolescence *f*; jeune homme *m*.

youthful *adj* jeune.

youthfulness *n* jeunesse *f*.

yuppie (*adj*) *n* (de) jeune cadre dynamique *m*.

zany *adj* farfelu.

zap *vt* flinguer.

zeal *n* zèle *m*; ardeur *f*.

zealous *adj* zélé.

zebra *n* zèbre *m*.

zenith *n* zénith *m*.

zero *n* zéro *m*.

zest *n* enthousiasme *m*.

zigzag *n* zigzag *m*.

zinc *n* zinc *m*.

zip, zipper *n* fermeture éclair *f*.

zip code *n* code postal *m*.

zodiac *n* zodiaque *m*.

zone *n* zone *f*; secteur *m*.

zoo *n* zoo *m*.

zoological *adj* zoologique.

zoologist *n* zoologiste *mf*.

zoology *n* zoologie *f*.

zoom *vi* vrombir.

zoom lens *n* zoom *m*.

Verbs

Verbes Irréguliers en Anglais

	Prétérit	Participe du passé		Prétérit	Participe du passé
arise	arose	arisen	deal	dealt	dealt
awake	awoke	awaked, awoken	dig	dug	dug
			do [he/she/it does]	did	done
be [I am, you/we/they are, he/she/it is, gérondif being]			draw	drew	drawn
	was, were	been	dream	dreamed, dreamt	dreamed, dreamt
bear	bore	borne	drink	drank	drunk
beat	beat	beaten	drive	drove	driven
become	became	become	dwell	dwelt, dwelled	dwelt, dwelled
begin	began	begun			
behold	beheld	beheld	eat	ate	eaten
bend	bent	bent	fall	fell	fallen
beseech	besought, beseeched	besought, beseeched	feed	fed	fed
beset	beset	beset	feel	felt	felt
bet	bet, betted	bet, betted	mistake	mistook	mistaken
bid	bade, bid	bade, bid, bidden	fight	fought	fought
			find	found	found
bite	bit	bitten	flee	fled	fled
bleed	bled	bled	fling	flung	flung
bless	blessed	blessed, blest	fly [he/she/it flies]		
				flew	flown
blow	blew	blown	forbid	forbade	forbidden
break	broke	broken	forecast	forecast	forecast
breed	bred	bred	forget	forgot	forgotten
bring	brought	brought	forgive	forgave	forgiven
build	built	built	forsake	forsook	forsaken
burn	burnt, burned	burnt, burned	foresee	foresaw	foreseen
burst	burst	burst	freeze	froze	frozen
buy	bought	bought	get	got	got, gotten
can	could	(been able)	give	gave	given
cast	cast	cast	go [he/she/it goes]	went	gone
catch	caught	caught	grind	ground	ground
choose	chose	chosen	grow	grew	grown
cling	clung	clung	hang	hung, hanged	hung, hanged
come	came	come	have [I/you/we/they have, he/she/it has, gérondif having]		
cost	cost	cost		had	had
creep	crept	crept			
cut	cut	cut			

	Prétérit	Participe du passé		Prétérit	Participe du passé
hear	heard	heard	saw	sawed	sawn
hide	hid	hidden	say	said	said
hit	hit	hit	see	saw	seen
hold	held	held	seek	sought	sought
hurt	hurt	hurt	sell	sold	sold
keep	kept	kept	send	sent	sent
kneel	knelt, kneeled	knelt, kneeled	set	set	set
			sew	sewed	sewn
know	knew	known	shake	shook	shaken
lay	laid	laid	shall	should	–
lead	led	led	shear	sheared	sheared, shorn
lean	leant, leaned	leant, leaned	shed	shed	shed
leap	leapt, leaped	leapt, leaped	shine	shone	shone
			shoot	shot	shot
learn	learnt, learned	learnt, learned	show	showd	shown, showed
leave	left	left	shrink	shrank	shrunk
lend	lent	lent	shut	shut	shut
let	let	let	sing	sang	sung
lie [gérondif lying]	lay	lain	sink	sank	sunk
			sit	sat	sat
light	lighted, lit	lighted, lit	slay	slew	slain
			sleep	slept	slept
lose	lost	lost	slide	slid	slid
make	made	made	sling	slung	slung
may	might	–	smell	smelt, smelled	smelt, smelled
mean	meant	meant			
meet	met	met	sow	sowed	sown
mow	mowed	mowed, mown	speak	spoke	spoken
must	(had to)	(had to)	speed	sped, speeded	sped, speeded
overcome	overcame	overcome			
pay	paid	paid	spell	spelt, spelled	spelt, spelled
put	put	put	spend	spent	spent
quit	quitted	quitted	spill	spilt, spilled	spilt, spilled
read	read	read	spin	spun	spun
rid	rid	rid	spit	spat	spat
ride	rode	ridden	split	split	split
ring	rang	rung	spoil	spoilt	spoilt
rise	rose	risen			
run	ran	run			

	Prétérit	Participe du passé		Prétérit	Participe du passé
spread	spread	spread	think	thought	thought
spring	sprang	sprung	throw	threw	thrown
stand	stood	stood	thrust	thrust	thrust
steal	stole	stolen	tread	trod	trodden
stick	stuck	stuck	understand	understood	understood
sting	stung	stung	upset	upset	upset
stink	stank	stunk	wake	woke	woken
stride	strode	stridden	wear	wore	worn
strike	struck	struck	weave	wove,	wove,
strive	strove	striven			weaved	weaved
swear	swore	sworn	wed	wed,	wed,
sweep	swept	swept			wedded	wedded
swell	swelled	swelled, swollen	weep	wept	wept
			win	won	won
swim	swam	swum	wind	wound	wound
swing	swung	swung	withdraw	withdrew	withdrawn
take	took	taken	withhold	withheld	withheld
teach	taught	taught	withstand	withstood	withstood
tear	tore	torn	wring	wrung	wrung
tell	told	told	write	wrote	written

French Verbs

Regular

infinitive	donner	finir	vendre
	to give	*to finish*	*to sell*
gerund	donnant	finissant	vendant
past participle	donné	fini	vendu
present	je donne	je finis	je vends
	tu donnes	tu finis	tu vends
	il donne	il finit	il vend
	nous donnons	nous finissons	nous vendons
	vous donnez	vous finissez	vous vendez
	ils donnent	ils finissent	ils vendent
imperfect	donnais	finissais	vendais
	donnais	finissais	vendais
	donnait	finissait	vendait
	donnions	finissions	vendions
	donniez	finissiez	vendiez
	donnaient	finissaient	vendaient
future	donnerai	finirai	vendrai
	donneras	finiras	vendras
	donnera	finira	vendra
	donnerons	finirons	vendrons
	donnerez	finirez	vendrez
	donneront	finiront	vendront
conditional	donnerais	finirais	vendrais
	donnerais	finirais	vendrais
	donnerait	finirait	vendrait
	donnerions	finirions	vendrions
	donneriez	finiriez	vendriez
	donneraint	finiraient	vendraient
past historic	donnai	finis	vendis
	donnas	finis	vendis
	donna	finit	vendit
	donnâmes	finîmes	vendîmes
	donnâtes	finîtes	vendîtes
	donnèrent	finirent	vendirent
present subjunctive	donne	finisse	vende

donnes	finisses	vendes
donne	finisse	vende
donnions	finissions	vendions
donniez	finissiez	vendiez
donnent	finissent	vendent

imperfect subjunctive

donnasse	finisse	vendisse
donnasses	finisses	vendisses
donnât	finît	vendît
donnassions	finissions	vendissions
donnassiez	finissiez	vendissiez
donnassent	finissent	vendissent

Auxiliary verbs

Infinitive

être	avoir		
to be	*to have*	serez	aurez
present participle		seront	auront
étant	ayant	*conditional*	
past participle		serais	aurais
été	eu	serais	aurais
present		serait	aurait
je suis	j'ai	serions	aurions
tu es	tu as	seriez	auriez
il est	il a	seraient	auraient
nous sommes	nous avons	*past historic*	
vous êtes	vous avez	fus	eus
ils sont	ils ont	fus	eus
imperfect		fut	eut
étais	avais	fûmes	eûmes
étais	avais	fûtes	eûtes
était	avait	furent	eurent
étions	avions	*present subjunctive*	
étiez	aviez	sois	aie
étaient	avaient	sois	aies
future		soit	ait
serai	aurai	soyons	ayons
seras	auras	soyez	ayez
sera	aura	soient	aient
serons	aurons		

imperfect subjunctive

fusse	eusse	fussions	eussions
fusses	eusses	fussiez	eussiez
fût	eût	fussent	eussent

Irregular Verbs

acheter	**acquérir**	**aller**	**appeler**
to buy	*to acquire*	*to go*	*to call*
present			
achète	acquiers	vais	appelle
achètes	acquiers	vas	appelles
achète	acquiert	va	appelle
achetons	acquérons	allons	appelons
achetez	acquérez	allez	appelez
achètent	acquièrent	vont	appellent
imperfect			
achetais	acquérais	allais	apellais
achetais	acquérais	allais	apellais
achetait	acquérait	allait	apellait
achetions	acquérions	allions	apelions
achetiez	acquériez	alliez	apelliez
achetaient	acquérient	allaient	apellaient
future			
achèterai	acquerrai	irai	appellerai
achèteras	acquerras	iras	appelleras
achètera	acquerra	ira	appellera
achèterons	acquerrons	irons	appellerons
achèterez	acquerrez	irez	appellerez
achèteront	acquerront	iront	appelleront
conditional			
achèterais	acquerrais	irais	appellerais
achèterais	acquerrais	irais	appellerais
achèterait	acquerrait	iriat	appellerait
achèterions	acquerrions	irions	appellerions
achèteriez	acquerriez	iriez	appelleriez
achèterient	acquerrient	iraient	appelleriont
past historic			
achetai	acquis	allai	appelai
achetas	acquis	allas	appelas

acheta	acquit	alla	appela
achetâmes	acquîmes	allâmes	appelâmes
achetâtes	acquîtes	allâtes	appelâtes
achetèrent	acquirent	allèrent	appelèrent

present subjunctive

achète	acquière	aille	appelle
achètes	acquières	ailles	appelles
achète	acquière	aille	appelle
achetions	acquiérions	aillions	appelions
achetiez	acquiériez	ailliez	appeliez
achètent	acquièrent	aillent	appellent

imperfect subjunctive

achetasse	acquisse	allasse	appelasse
achetasses	acquisses	allasses	appelasses
achetât	acquî	allât	appelât
achetassions	acquissions	allassions	appelassions
achetassiez	acquissiez	allassiez	appelassiez
achetassent	acquissent	allassent	appelassent

appuyer	**s'asseoir**	**battre**	**boire**
to lean	*to sit down*	*to hit*	*to drink*
present			
appuie	m'assieds	bats	bois
appuies	t'assieds	bats	bois
appuie	s'assied	bat	boit
appuyons	nous asseyons	battons	buvons
appuyez	vous asseyez	battez	buvez
appuient	s'asseyent	battent	boivent
imperfect			
appuyais	m'asseyais	battais	buvais
appuyais	t'asseyais	battais	buvais
appuyait	s'asseyait	battait	buvait
appuyions	nous asseyion	battions	buvions
appuyiez	vous asseyiez	battiez	buviez
appuyaient	s'asseyaient	battaient	buvaient
future			
appuierai	m'assiérai	battrai	boirai
appuieras	t'assiéras	battras	boiras
appuiera	s'assiéra	battra	boira

appuierons	nous assiérons	battrons	boirons
appuierez	vous assiérez	battrez	boirez
appuieront	s'assiéront	battront	boiront

conditional

appuierais	m'assiérais	battrais	boirais
appuierais	t'assiérais	battrais	boirais
appuierait	s'assiérait	battrait	boirait
appuierions	nous assiérions	battrions	boirions
appuieriez	vous assiériez	battriez	boiriez
appuieraient	s'assiéraient	battraient	boiraient

past historic

appuyai	m'assis	battis	bus
appuyas	t'assis	battis	bus
appuya	s'assit	battit	but
appuyâmes	nous assîmes	battîmes	bûmes
appuyâtes	vous assîtes	battîtes	bûtes
appuyèrent	s'assirent	battirent	burent

present subjunctive

appuie	m'asseye	batte	boive
appuies	t'asseyes	battes	boives
appuie	s'asseye	batte	boive
appuyions	nous asseyions	battions	buvions
appuyiez	vous asseyiez	battiez	buviez
appuient	s'asseyent	battent	boivent

imperfect subjunctive

appuyasse	m'assisse	battisse	busse
appuyasses	t'assisses	battisses	busses
appuyât	s'assît	battît	bût
appuyassions	nous assissions	battissions	bussions
appuyassiez	vous assissiez	battissiez	bussiez
appuyassent	s'assissent	battissent	bussent

| **commencer** | **conduire** | **connaître** | **courir** |
| *to begin* | *to drive* | *to know* | *to run* |

present

commence	conduis	connais	cours
commences	conduis	connais	cours
commence	conduit	connaît	court
commençons	conduisons	connaissons	courons
commencez	conduisez	connaissez	courez

commencent	conduisent	connaissent	courent
imperfect			
commençais	conduisais	connaissais	courais
commençais	conduisais	connaissais	courais
commençait	conduisait	connaissait	courait
commencions	conduisions	connaissions	courions
commenciez	conduisiez	connaissiez	couriez
commençaient	conduisaient	connaissaient	couraient
future			
commencerai	conduirai	connaîtrai	courrai
commenceras	conduiras	connaîtras	courras
commencera	conduira	connaîtra	courra
commencerons	conduirons	connaîtrons	courrons
commencerez	conduirez	connaîtrez	courrez
commenceront	conduiront	connaîtront	courront
conditional			
commencerais	conduirais	connaîtrais	courrais
commencerais	conduirais	connaîtrais	courrais
commencerait	conduirait	connaîtrait	courrait
commencerions	conduirions	connaîtrions	courrions
commenceriez	conduiriez	connaîtriez	courriez
commenceraient	conduiraient	connaîtraient	courraient
past historic			
commençai	conduisis	connus	courus
commenças	conduisis	connus	courus
commença	conduisit	connut	courut
commençâmes	conduisîmes	connûmes	courûmes
commençâtes	conduisîtes	connûtes	courûtes
commencèrent	conduisirent	connurent	coururent
present subjunctive			
commence	conduise	connaisse	coure
commences	conduises	connaisses	coures
commence	conduise	connaisse	coure
commencions	conduisions	connaissions	courions
commenciez	conduisiez	connaissiez	couriez
commence	conduisent	connaissent	courent
imperfect subjunctive			
commençasse	conduisisse	connusse	courusse
commençasses	conduisisses	connusses	courusses
commençât	conduisît	connût	courût

commençassions	conduisissions	connussions	courussions
commençassiez	conduisissiez	connussiez	courussiez
commençassent	conduisissent	connussent	courussent

| **couvrir** | **craindre** | **croire** | **devoir** |
| to cover | to fear | to believe | to owe, have to |

present

couvre	crains	crois	dois
couvres	crains	crois	dois
couvre	craint	croit	doit
couvrons	craignons	croyons	devons
couvrez	craignez	croyez	devez
couvrent	craignent	croient	doivent

imperfect

couvrais	craignais	croyais	devais
couvrais	craignais	croyais	devais
couvrait	craignait	croyait	devait
couvrions	craignions	croyions	devions
couvriez	craigniez	croyiez	deviez
couvraient	craignient	croyaient	devaient

future

couvrirai	craindrai	croirai	devrai
couvriras	craindras	croiras	devras
couvrira	craindra	croira	devra
couvrirons	craindrons	croirons	devrons
courirez	craindrez	croirez	devrez
couvriront	craindront	croiront	devront

conditional

couvrirais	craindrais	croirais	devrais
couvrirais	craindrais	croirais	devrais
couvrirait	craindrait	croirait	devrait
couvririons	craindrions	croirions	devrions
couvririez	craindriez	croiriez	devriez
couvriront	craindraient	croiraient	devraient

past historic

couvris	craignis	crus	dus
couvris	craignis	crus	dus
couvrit	craignit	crut	dut
couvrîmes	craignîmes	crûmes	dûmes
couvrîtes	craignîtes	crûtes	dûtes

couvrirent	craignirent	crurent	durent

present subjunctive

couvre	craigne	croie	doive
couvres	craignes	croies	doives
couvre	craigne	croie	doive
couvrions	craignions	croyions	devions
couvriez	craigniez	croyiez	deviez
couvrent	craignent	croient	doivent

imperfect subjunctive

couvrisse	craignisse	crusse	dusse
couvrisses	craignisses	crusses	dusses
couvrît	craignît	crût	dût
couvrissions	craignissions	crussions	dussions
couvrissiez	craignissiez	crussiez	dussiez
couvrissent	craignissent	crussent	dussent

dire	**écrire**	**envoyer**	**faire**
to say	*to write*	*to send*	*to do; to make*

present

dis	écris	envoie	fais
dis	écris	envoies	fais
dit	écrit	envoie	fait
disons	écrivons	envoyons	faisons
dites	écrivez	envoyez	faites
disent	écrivent	envoient	font

imperfect

disais	écrivais	envoyais	faisais
disais	écrivais	envoyais	faisais
disait	écrivait	envoyait	faisait
disions	écrivions	envoyions	faisions
disiez	écriviez	envoyiez	faisiez
disaient	écrivaient	envoyaient	faisaient

future

dirai	écrirai	enverrai	ferai
diras	écriras	enverras	feras
dira	écrira	enverra	fera
dirons	écrirons	enverrons	ferons
direz	écrirez	enverrez	ferez
diront	écriraient	enverront	feront

conditional

dirais	écrirais	enverrais	ferais
dirais	écrirais	enverrais	ferais
dirait	écrirait	enverrait	ferait
dirions	écririons	enverrions	ferions
diriez	écririez	enverriez	feriez
diraient	écriraient	enverraient	feraient

past historic

dis	écrivis	envoyai	fis
dis	écrivis	envoyas	fis
dit	écrivit	envoya	fit
dîmes	écrivîmes	envoyâmes	fîmes
dîtes	écrivîtes	envoyâtes	fîtes
dirent	écrivirent	envoyèrent	firent

present subjunctive

dise	écrive	envoie	fasse
dises	écrives	envoies	fasses
dise	écrive	envoie	fasse
disions	écrivions	envoyions	fassions
disiez	écriviez	envoyiez	fassiez
disent	écrivent	envoient	fassent

imperfect subjunctive

disse	écrivisse	envoyasse	fisse
disses	écrivisses	envoyasses	fisses
dit	écrivît	envoyât	fit
dissions	écrivissions	envoyassions	fissions
dissiez	écrivissiez	envoyassiez	fissiez
dissent	écrivissent	envoyassent	fissent

fuir	**haïr**	**jeter**	**lire**
to flee	*to hate*	*to throw*	*to read*

present

fuis	hais	jette	lis
fuis	hais	jettes	lis
fuit	hait	jette	lit
fuyons	haïssons	jetons	lisons
fuyez	haïssez	jetez	lisez
fuient	haïssent	jettent	lisent

imperfect

| fuyais | haïssais | jetais | lisais |
| fuyais | haïssais | jetais | lisais |

fuyait	haïssait	jetait	lisait
fuyions	haïssions	jetions	lisions
fuyiez	haïssiez	jetiez	lisiez
fuyaient	haïssaient	jetaient	lisaient

future

fuirai	haïrai	jetterai	lirai
fuiras	haïras	jetteras	liras
fuira	haïra	jettera	lira
fuirons	haïrons	jetterons	lirons
fuirez	haïrez	jetterez	lirez
fuiront	haïront	jetteront	liront

conditional

fuirais	haïrais	jetterais	lirais
fuirais	haïrais	jetterais	lirais
fuirait	haïrait	jetterait	lirait
fuirions	haïrions	jetterions	lirions
fuiriez	haïriez	jetteriez	liriez
fuiraient	haïraient	jetteraient	liraient

past historic

fuis	haïs	jetai	lus
fuis	haïs	jetas	lus
fuit	haït	jeta	lut
fuîmes	haïmes	jetâmes	lûmes
fuîtes	haïtes	jetâtes	lûte
fuirent	haïrent	jetèrent	lurent

present subjunctive

fuie	haïsse	jette	lise
fuies	haïsses	jettes	lises
fuie	haïsse	jette	lise
fuyions	haïssions	jetions	lisions
fuyiez	haïssiez	jetiez	lisiez
fuient	haïssent	jettent	lisent

imperfect subjunctive

fuisse	haïsse	jetasse	lusse
fuisses	haïsses	jetasses	lusses
fuît	haït	jetât	lût
fuissions	haïssions	jetassions	lussions
fuissiez	haïssiez	jetassiez	lussiez
fuissent	haïssent	jetassent	lussent

manger	mettre	mourir	mouvoir
to eat	*to put*	*to die*	*to drive, to move*
present			
mange	mets	meurs	meus
manges	mets	meurs	meus
mange	met	meurt	meut
mangeons	mettons	mourons	mouvons
mangez	mettez	mourez	mouvez
mangent	mettent	meurent	meuvent
imperfect			
mangeais	mettais	mourais	mouvais
mangeais	mettais	mourais	mouvais
mangeait	mettait	mourait	mouvait
mangions	mettions	mourions	mouvions
mangiez	mettiez	mouriez	mouviez
mangeaient	mettaient	mouraient	mouvaient
future			
mangerai	mettrai	mourrai	mouvrai
mangeras	mettras	mourras	mouvras
mangera	mettra	mourra	mouvra
mangerons	mettrons	mourrons	mouvrons
mangerez	mettrez	mourrez	mouvrez
mangeront	mettront	mourront	mouvront
conditional			
mangerais	mettrais	mourrais	mouvrais
mangerais	mettrais	mourrais	mouvrais
mangerait	mettrait	mourrait	mouvrait
mangerions	mettrions	mourrions	mouvrions
mangeriez	mettriez	mourriez	mouvriez
mangeraient	mettraient	mourraient	mouvraient
past historic			
mangeai	mis	mourus	mus
mangeas	mis	mourus	mus
mangea	mit	mourut	mut
mangeâmes	mîmes	mourûmes	mûmes
mangeâtes	mîtes	mourûtes	mûtes
mangèrent	mirent	moururent	murent
present subjunctive			
mange	mette	meure	meuve
manges	mettes	meures	meuves

mange	mette	meure	meuve
mangions	mettions	mourions	mouvions
mangiez	mettiez	mouriez	mouviez
mangent	mettent	meurent	meuvent

imperfect subjunctive

mangeasse	misse	mourusse	musse
mangeasses	misses	mourusses	musses
mangeât	mît	mourût	mût
mangeassions	missions	mourussions	mussions
mangeassiez	missiez	mourussiez	mussiez
mangeassent	missent	mourussent	mussent

naître	**partir**	**plaire**	**pouvoir**
to be born	*to leave*	*to please*	*to be able;can*

present

nais	pars	plais	peux
nais	pars	plais	peux
naît	part	plaît	peut
naissons	partons	plaison	pouvons
naissez	partez	plaisez	pouvez
naissent	partent	plaisent	peuvent

imperfect

naissais	partais	plaisais	pouvais
naissais	partais	plaisais	pouvais
naissait	partait	plaisait	pouvait
naissions	partions	plaisions	pouvions
naissiez	partiez	plaisiez	pouviez
naissaient	partaient	plaisaient	pouvaient

future

naîtrai	partirai	plairai	pourrai
naîtras	partiras	plairas	pourras
naîtra	partira	plaira	pourra
naîtrons	partirons	plairons	pourrons
naîtrez	partirez	plairez	pourrez
naîtront	partiront	plairont	pourront

conditional

naîtrais	partirais	plairais	pourrais
naîtrais	partirais	plairais	pourrais
naîtrait	partirait	plairait	pourrait
naîtrions	partirions	plairions	pourrions

| naîtriez | partiriez | plairiez | pourriez |
| naîtraient | partiraient | plairaient | pourraient |

past historic

naquis	partis	plus	pus
naquis	partis	plus	pus
naquit	partit	plut	put
naquîmes	partîmes	plûmes	pûmes
naquîtes	partîtes	plûtes	pûtes
naquirent	partirent	plurent	purent

present subjunctive

naisse	parte	plaise	puisse
naisses	partes	plaises	puisses
naisse	parte	plaise	puisse
naissions	partions	plaisions	puissions
naissiez	partiez	plaisiez	puissiez
naissent	partent	plaisent	puissent

imperfect subjunctive

naquisse	partisse	plusse	pusse
naquisses	partisses	plusses	pusses
naquît	partît	plût	pût
naquissions	partissions	plussions	pussions
naquissiez	partissiez	plussiez	pussiez
naquissent	partissent	plussent	pussent

| **préférer** | **prendre** | **recevoir** | **rire** |
| *to prefer* | *to take* | *to receive* | *to laugh* |

present

préfère	prends	reçois	ris
préfères	prends	reçois	ris
préfère	prend	reçoit	rit
préférons	prenons	recevons	rions
préférez	prenez	recevez	riez
préfèrent	prennent	reçoivent	rient

imperfect

préférais	prenais	recevais	riais
préférais	prenais	recevais	riais
préférait	prenait	recevait	riait
préférions	prenions	recevions	riions
préfériez	preniez	receviez	riiez
préféraient	prenaient	recevaient	riaient

future

préférerai	prendrai	recevrai	rirai
préféreras	prendras	recevras	riras
préférera	prendra	recevra	rira
préférerons	prendrons	recevrons	rirons
préférerez	prendrez	recevrez	rirez
préféreront	prendront	recevront	riront

conditional

préférerais	prendrais	recevrais	rirais
préférerais	prendrais	recevrais	rirais
préférerait	prendrait	recevrait	rirait
préférerions	prendrions	recevrions	ririons
préféreriez	prendriez	recevriez	ririez
préféreraient	prendraient	recevraient	riraient

past historic

préférai	pris	reçus	ris
préféras	pris	reçus	ris
préféra	prit	reçut	rit
préférâmes	prîmes	reçûmes	rîmes
préférâtes	prîtes	reçûtes	rîtes
préférèrent	prirent	reçurent	rirent

present subjunctive

préfère	prenne	reçoive	rie
préfères	prennes	reçoives	ries
préfère	prenne	reçoive	rie
préférions	prenions	recevions	riions
préfériez	preniez	receviez	riiez
préfèrent	prennent	reçoivent	rient

imperfect subjunctive

préférasse	prisse	reçusse	risse
préférasses	prisses	reçusses	risses
préférât	prît	reçût	rît
préférassions	prissions	reçussions	rissions
préférassiez	prissiez	reçussiez	rissiez
préférassent	prissent	reçussent	rissent

savoir	suffire	suivre	tenir
to know	*to be enough*	*to follow*	*to hold*
present			
sais	suffis	suis	tiens
sais	suffis	suis	tiens
sait	suffit	suit	tient
savons	suffisons	suivons	tenons
savez	suffisez	suivez	tenez
savent	suffisent	suivent	tiennent
imperfect			
savais	suffisais	suivais	tenais
savais	suffisais	suivais	tenais
savait	suffisait	suivait	tenait
savions	suffisions	suivions	tenions
saviez	suffisiez	suiviez	teniez
savaient	suffisiaent	suivaient	tenaient
future			
saurai	suffirai	suivrai	tiendrai
sauras	suffiras	suivras	tiendras
saura	suffira	suivra	tiendra
saurons	suffirons	suivrons	tiendrons
saurez	suffirez	suivrez	tiendrez
sauront	suffiront	suivront	tiendront
conditional			
saurais	suffirais	suivrais	tiendrais
saurais	suffirais	suivrais	tiendrais
saurait	suffirait	suivrait	tiendrait
saurions	suffirions	suivrions	tiendrions
sauriez	suffiriez	suiviez	tiendriez
sauraient	suffiraient	suivraient	tiendraient
past historic			
sus	suffis	suivis	tins
sus	suffis	suivis	tins
sut	suffit	suivit	tint
sûmes	suffîmes	suivîmes	tînmes
sûtes	suffîtes	suivîtes	tîntes
surent	suffirent	suivirent	tinrent
present subjunctive			
sache	suffise	suivre	tienne
saches	suffises	suivres	tiennes

sache	suffise	suive	tienne
sachions	suffisions	suivions	tenions
sachiez	suffisiez	suiviez	teniez
sachent	suffisent	suivent	tiennent

imperfect subjunctive

susse	suffisse	suivisse	tinsse
susses	suffisses	suivisses	tinsses
sût	suffît	suivît	tînt
sussions	suffissions	suivissions	tinssions
sussiez	suffissiez	suivissiez	tinssiez
sussent	suffissent	suivissent	tinssent

| **valoir** | **venir** | **vivre** | **voir** |
| *to be worth* | *to come* | *to live* | *to see* |

present

vaux	viens	vis	vois
vaux	viens	vis	vois
vaut	vient	vit	voit
valons	venons	vivons	voyons
valez	venez	vivez	voyez
valent	viennent	vivent	voient

imperfect

valais	venais	vivais	voyais
valais	venais	vivais	voyais
valait	venait	vivait	voyait
valions	venions	vivions	voyions
valiez	veniez	viviez	voyiez
valaient	venaient	vivaient	voyaient

future

vaudrai	viendrai	vivrai	verrai
vaudras	viendras	vivras	verras
vaudra	viendra	vivra	verra
vaudrons	viendrons	vivrons	verrons
vaudrez	viendrez	vivrez	verrez
vaudront	viendront	vivront	verront

conditional

vaudrais	viendrais	vivrais	verrais
vaudrais	viendrais	vivrais	verrais
vaudrait	viendrait	vivrait	verrait
vaudrions	viendrions	vivrions	verrions
vaudriez	viendriez	vivriez	verriez

vaudraient	viendraient	vivraient	verraient
past historic			
valus	vins	vécus	vis
valus	vins	vécus	vis
valut	vint	vécut	vit
valûmes	vînmes	vécûmes	vîmes
valûtes	vîntes	vécûtes	vîtes
valurent	vinrent	vécurent	virent
present subjunctive			
vaille	vienne	vive	voie
vailles	viennes	vives	voies
vaille	vienne	vive	voie
valions	venions	vivions	voyions
vailiez	veniez	viviez	voyiez
vaillent	viennent	vivent	voient
imperfect subjunctive			
valusse	vinsse	vécusse	visse
valusses	vinsses	vécusses	visses
valût	vînt	vécût	vît
valussions	vinssions	vécussions	vissions
valussiez	vinssiez	vécussiez	vissiez
valussent	vinssent	vécussent	vissent